Branch Lines of Strathearn

A view of Lochearnhead shortly after it opened, showing the island platform, the extensive use of concrete for the platform edges and the station building. The signal box of standard Caledonian Railway design appears far larger than necessary for such a small station, and indeed it had a relatively short life, closing as early as 1921 after only sixteen years in use. What may appear to be a wooden foot crossing just behind the train is in fact the boxing protecting the signal rods and cranks where they run under the rails and the platform to the base of the signal box.

Courtesy of Perth Museum & Art Gallery, Perth & Kinross Council

Branch Lines of Strathearn
Tourists, Tatties and Trains

John Young

Lightmoor Press & the Caledonian Railway Association

Ex-Caledonian Railway Pickersgill 4-4-0 No. 14459 draws into the branch line platform at Gleneagles with a Down train one late afternoon during early LM&SR days. This view shows the profusion of signals at the south end of the station, with even the main line signals still retaining their lower quadrant arms at this stage. The telegraph pole route runs along to the south side the main line, while on the extreme right the terminal pole for the overhead power lines can just be seen above the trees. This electricity supply for Gleneagles Hotel ran along the north side of the line from an electricity sub-station next to Bridge of Allan station to Gleneagles station, then by underground cable to the hotel.

Author's collection

Contents

Foreword 6
Acknowledgements 6
Introduction 7

Chapter 1   Railways Reach Crieff 9
Chapter 2   The Extension to Upper Strathearn 33
Chapter 3   Gleneagles to Crieff – The Line Described 55
Chapter 4   Almond Valley Jct to Crieff – The Line Described 73
Chapter 5   Crieff to Balquhidder – The Line Described 95
Chapter 6   The Golden Age of the Caledonian Railway 115
Chapter 7   Gleneagles Hotel 155
Chapter 8   The Challenging Years Under the LM&SR 179
Chapter 9   Safety and Signalling 211
Chapter 10   British Railways and the Struggle for Survival 247

Appendices
  1 Chronology of Main Events 281
  2 Station Codes 282
  3 Telegraph Message Circuits 283
  4 LM&SR Country Lorry Services 284
  5 Whistles for Engines 285
  6 Routes Over Which Engines May Run 286
  7 Caledonian and L&NWR Souvenir Time Table & Guide 1912 287
  8 The Methven Railway Song 288
  9 The Crieff & Methven Junction Railway Song 289

Bibliography 291
Index 293
Biography of the Author 296

Published by LIGHTMOOR PRESS in conjunction with the CALEDONIAN RAILWAY ASSOCIATION
© John Young, Lightmoor Press and the Caledonian Railway Association 2014
Designed by Nigel Nicholson

British Library Cataloguing-in-Publication Data. A catalogue record for this book is available from the British Library
ISBN 9781 899889 88 4
All rights reserved. No part of this publication may be reproduced, stored in a retrieval system or transmitted in any form or by any means,
electronic, mechanical, photocopying, recording or otherwise, without the written permission of the publisher

LIGHTMOOR PRESS
Unit 144B, Lydney Trading Estate, Harbour Road, Lydney, Gloucestershire GL15 5EJ
www.lightmoor.co.uk
Lightmoor Press is an imprint of Black Dwarf Lightmoor Publications Ltd
Printed by Berforts Information Press, Eynsham, Oxford

Foreword

This book brings together my original work written in 1963, augmented by much additional material gathered over the past fifty years, with the extensive research largely undertaken locally by David Ferguson and the late Lindsay Horne. I am particularly indebted to them for so generously putting their material at my disposal, and to David Ferguson for his unstinting support including his corrections and comments on the drafts. It is a matter of great regret that Lindsay Horne did not live to see this project brought to fruition.

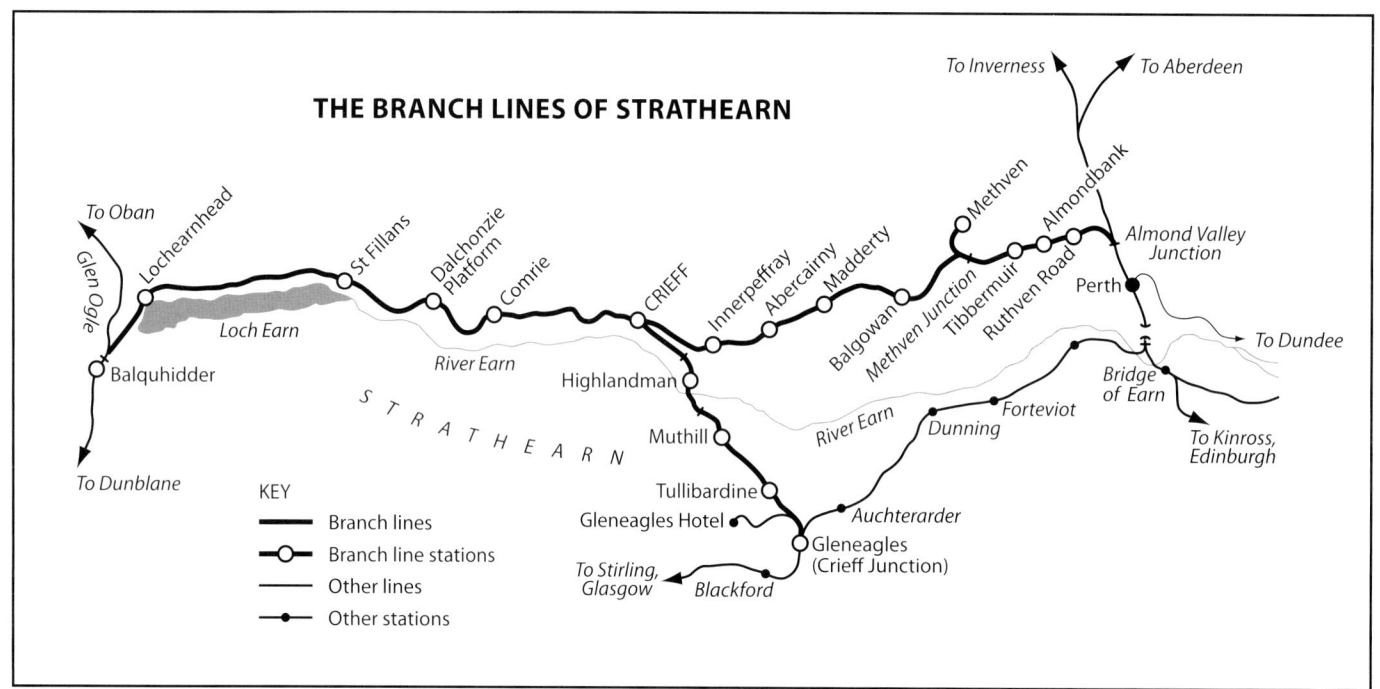

Acknowledgements

Writing this history could not have been completed without the help, advice and assistance of many individuals and organisation, foremost among them being David Ferguson and the late Lindsay Horne whose substantial contributions have already been mentioned.

I am most grateful to the Caledonian Railway Association, particularly Jim MacIntosh, the Chairman, for agreeing to be joint publishers of this book and making the CRA photographic archive available, and to Neil Parkhouse of Black Dwarf Lightmoor for taking on this project. My thanks in particular to Nigel Nicholson for his patience and perseverance in turning the original material into the book it is now.

Thanks are due to the National Railway Museum, the Scottish Records Office, Stephen Connelly and his staff at The AK Bell Library in Perth, Paul Adair of Perth Museums and Art Galleries, Kim Downie of the University Library at Aberdeen, Margaret Ellis and Kate Newton of the Gleneagles Hotel and the staff of Diageo corporate archives, and on behalf of David Ferguson, the staff of Crieff Library and also Alan Simpson for his research at the SRO. I would also like to acknowledge the help of Barry Hoper of 'Transport Treasury', Hugh Davies of 'Photos of the Fifties' and Jim Page of the Angus Railway Group for their help in sourcing images, and to Dr RM Casserley and John Morten for permission to use their fathers' photographs. I am particularly grateful to John Alsop for permission to use some of the many images from his collection.

My thanks also to all the members of the Caledonian Railway Association who responded so generously to my request for information and who have helped in various ways, most notably David Gallagher for re-working the signalling diagrams, Donald Peddie for restoration of images, and to John Paton, Roger Pidgeon and David Stirling for sourcing additional images and material.

I am also most grateful to Bernard Byrom for allowing me to draw on his earlier book on *The Railways of Upper Strathearn*, to Dr Jim Grant for the use of images of Gleneagles Hotel, and to my late father for the many original documents from his legal firm and his early photography from Caledonian Railway days.

In respect of my original research during the 1960s, I must thank the staff of the British Railways Divisional Engineer's Office in Perth for permission to copy or trace the original plans, subsequently destroyed, for all the stations along the line, and to the *Perthshire Advertiser* for access to their original archives in St. John's Square, Perth. Also to the staff of the local stations, notably, Inspector Walter Kennedy, Foreman Bob Campbell and Miss Martha Soutar of Gleneagles station. I am also indebted to numerous individuals who provided photographs and information in those early days, including OS Nock, WAC (Bill) Smith, Alan Dunbar, John Hulme, George Robin, GM Ure, David Stewart, C Lawson Kerr, Pryd Jones, Forbes Alexander, Ed Nicoll, W Ross Young of Perth, Kerr Edgar, Bob Maguire, and Alexander Reid of Methven.

Finally, my thanks to my wife Sue for her encouragement and forbearance and for bringing her English degree into play in proof reading and correcting the entire work.

If I have inadvertently omitted any individual or organisation from this lengthy list dating back over fifty years, I apologise.

Introduction

Half a century has now passed since the last passenger train left Crieff and the station was locked up for the final time. As the headline in the local paper put it *'After 108 years, Crieff is off the railway map'*. Three years later the surviving goods service ceased, bringing to an end over a century of local railways in Strathearn.

This year sees three significant anniversaries for the local railways in Strathearn. It marks the fiftieth anniversary of the closure of the Gleneagles to Crieff and Comrie line to passengers on 6th July 1964, the centenary of work starting on Gleneagles Hotel in the spring of 1914, and the ninetieth anniversary of the opening of the hotel on 5th June 1924.

This book tells of the development of the branch lines in Strathearn, sometimes a tortuous and protracted process, which itself was spread over a period of more than half a century, and traces their history from the opening of the first line, the Crieff Junction Railway, to the final closure of the last line to Crieff in 1967. It includes a detailed description of these lines and its stations, for in the fifty years since their closure much of this has disappeared without trace, and few people under the age of sixty will have any first hand recollection of this once extensive network.

With the possible exception of the Lochearnhead, St. Fillans and Comrie Railway, all the branch lines of Strathearn were the result of local enterprise, although all subsequently fell on hard times and were absorbed by larger companies, eventually becoming part of the Caledonian Railway. It is perhaps significant that the last line to be built, the speculative and largely unprofitable Lochearnhead, St. Fillans and Comrie Railway, was the first to close in 1951 after only forty-six years of operation, and that among the others, the last to lose its passenger service was the Gleneagles to Crieff line, the original Crieff Junction Railway.

Research on this book began over fifty years ago, and much of the original material gathered then and subsequently is no longer available. In addition to material obtained from British Railways, the County Archives in Perth, the Scottish Record Office in Edinburgh and the National Railway Museum at York, I have made extensive use of first hand material from local sources, including my father's former legal practice, Young & Kennaway WS of Auchterarder. I have refrained from making over much use of the more academic sources such as company minute books, but rather have focussed on the history of the branch lines of Strathearn as local railways, the important part they played in the development of the district, the communities they served, and their place in those communities. In this respect it is as much a social history as a history of the railways themselves.

In doing so, extensive use has been made of contemporary newspaper reports, particularly from the *Strathearn Herald, Crieff Journal, Perthshire Advertiser & Journal* and other local newspapers. Coverage, particularly in the early days of the exciting development of railways was comprehensive. The language used may sometimes seem quaint today, but it has an immediacy which brings history to life and conveys the views and norms of that time.

The locomotives and rolling stock used on these lines was essentially similar to those seen elsewhere on the Caledonian, LM&SR and British Railways systems, with the possible exception of the steam railcar used for a time on the Methven branch, and the railbus used on the Gleneagles to Comrie line in the final years. Those seeking detailed information on these generic aspects of railways will be able to find them in the more general histories of the railways concerned. One aspect of local railway history, however, which is often overlooked, is the signalling, which was specific to the individual station layouts, and a separate chapter has been included to cover this particular aspect of railway operations in Strathearn.

Finally, no history of the railways of Strathearn would be complete without a description of the construction and operation of the illustrious and world renowned Gleneagles Hotel and its golf courses. It is now over thirty years since it passed out of public ownership, and there are many who are unaware of its origins as a prestige railway hotel and some of the unique aspects of its operation.

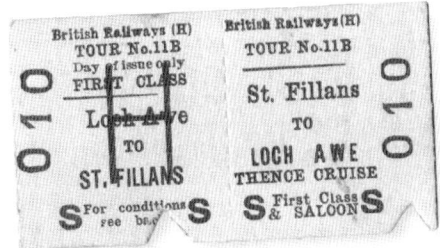

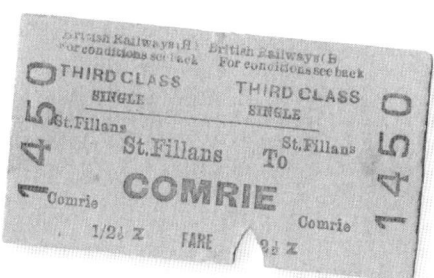

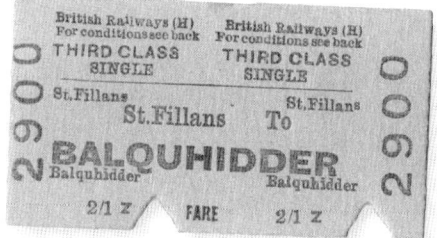

A selection of tickets from St. Fillans. Both the Third Class Singles, to Balquhidder in one direction and to Comrie in the other, are British Railways specimens from the four-year period between nationalisation and closure in 1951 – there would seem to have sufficient traffic for new tickets to be printed once the LM&SR stock was exhausted. The First Class Tour ticket for Tour 11B is also a BR ticket, showing that these excursions continued to be run in the post-war years, although the low serial number indicates that there was little demand for First Class tickets on this tour.
Author's collection

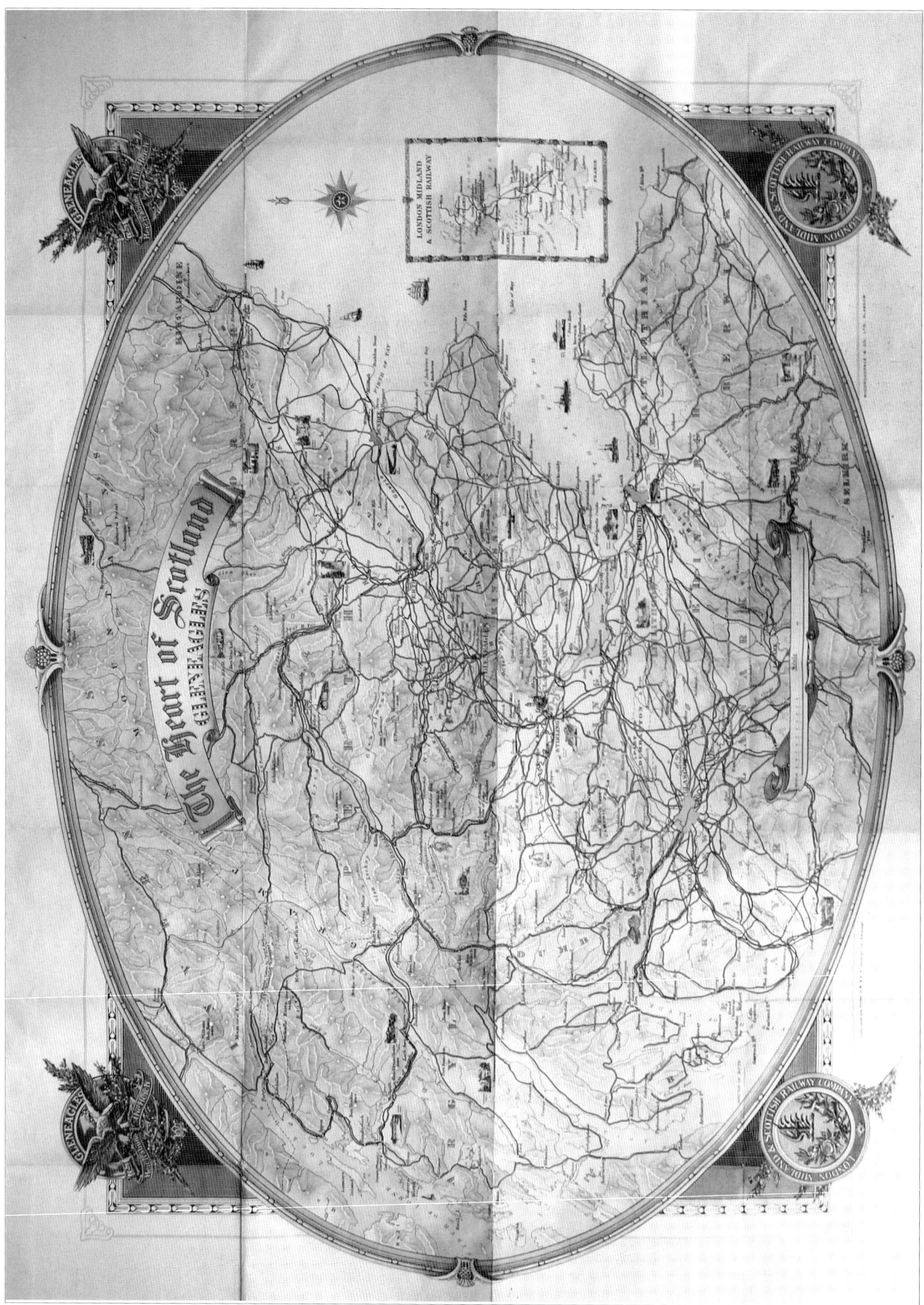

'The Gleneagles Map' was produced in 1924 for both the home and overseas market. Case bound on linen, it opens to some 3½ feet square depicting the central region of Scotland with Gleneagles at its centre. A magnificent map made to impress the visitor, it was embellished with the crests of Gleneagles Hotel and the London Midland & Scottish Railway Company. *Author's collection*

Chapter 1

Railways Reach Crieff

The Crieff Junction Railway

The origins of the branch lines of Strathearn can be traced back to events over a decade before the first railway reached Crieff, when in 1841 the first survey was carried out for the Scottish Central Railway line from Stirling to Perth. Two alternative routes were proposed, one via Auchterarder and Dunning, approaching Perth from the south, and the other via Crieff and the Pow Burn valley, entering Perth from the north.

However, owing to the prevailing economic depression, no further progress was made with these proposals until 1844.

In that year the Scottish Central Railway considered the two options for the main line from Stirling to Perth. Both were feasible: the northern route via Crieff was easily graded and avoided the obstacle of Moncrieffe Hill which blocked the way to Perth from the south, whilst borings taken through Moncrieffe Hill indicated that there would be little difficulty in driving a tunnel through. The decision was taken to opt for the southern route. A further factor in favour of the southern approach was that it avoided the need for northbound trains entering Perth from the north and then having to reverse out again; southbound trains from the north would similarly have had to reverse at Perth.

It was considered, however, that a branch line to Crieff could be built at the same time as the main line. In the event, therefore, the 1841 survey for the stretch of line from Auchterarder to Crieff was not nugatory work, being used as the basis for the proposed branch line to Crieff.

The Scottish Central did not have things all their own way. In the mid-1840s the railway mania was in full swing, with numerous competing projects being promoted by rival companies in attempts to expand their own operations, while at the same time denying this to other companies. The complex machinations of the Scottish Central Railway and its rivals are comprehensively explained in Peter Marshall's excellent history of that company. Suffice to say that the Scottish Central favoured a branch line from Auchterarder to Crieff via Muthill – backing being sought at a Board meeting on 24th September 1845 – and opposed any attempts to reach Crieff by the Pow Burn valley which had originally been surveyed and considered as part of the main line.

Thus the Crieff line was one of the four branch lines proposed in the Scottish Central Railway Bill of 1846 (the others being one to Denny, one south of Alloa Ferry, and another to Perth Harbour). All four received the Royal Assent in July 1846, whereas a Bill to promote the rival Perth & Crieff Railway failed.

Royal Assent for the Scottish Central Railway's Stirling to Perth route having been granted in July of the previous year, 1845, work on the main line proceeded steadily, although the original target date for opening this section of 1st July 1847 proved to be optimistic. James Tasker, who had been appointed Resident Engineer of the Scottish Central, was also instructed to make an early start on the Crieff line. However, although that line was reported to have been staked out by February 1847, the focus of the Scottish Central's efforts was the main line from Stirling to Perth and little more was done on the branch line. The Scottish Central line finally opened on 22nd March 1848, nearly a year later than planned, but by that stage financial constraints had resulted in the postponement of any further construction of the Crieff branch. In the meantime, the Scottish Central had bought stock in the Dunblane, Doune & Callander Railway to forestall other companies making inroads into their territory and having the potential to become competition from the start.

The impecunious position of the Scottish Central did not deter those who were keen to see the railway extended to Crieff. The Scottish Central had allowed the powers granted under their 1845 Act to lapse, but the good folk of Crieff were determined not to be left behind in this age of railway expansion and a separate company was created for the purpose. The Crieff Junction Railway – which included prominent supporters such as the Marquis of Breadalbane

Figure 1.1
The Scottish Central Railway Act, authorising the construction of a branch line to Crieff from the Scottish Central line near Blackford, which received the Royal Assent on 16th July 1845. The Scottish Central did not fulfil its promise to build this line, and the powers granted under this Act subsequently lapsed. It was left to local businessmen and others to remedy this deficiency by creating their own company, the Crieff Junction Railway, which they duly did in 1853.

Author's collection

LEFT: Plate 1.1
William Young Esq of Belvidere, Auchterarder, one of the promoters of the Crieff Junction Railway listed in the Prospectus published in *The Times*. The author's great-great-grandfather, he was one of only four shareholders in Auchterarder who also invested in the Scottish Central Railway. A prominent local lawyer, his grandson, Major TE Young, was later involved with the opening of Gleneagles Hotel. He was also the Commissioner of the Common Muir, the area next to the Crieff Junction Railway which was frequently set on fire by steam engines during the early years of that line.
Author's collection

RIGHT: Figure 1.2
The Prospectus for the Crieff Junction Railway published in *The Times* on 14th October 1852. Membership of the Provisional Committee included several gentlemen who would subsequently play a significant part in developing the railways of Strathearn, including Sir David Dundas of Dunira, Mr DR Williamson of Lawers and Alexander Menteith of Broich, who would become the first Chairman of the Crieff Junction Railway. The only member from Auchterarder was William Young.
Author's collection

and Viscount Strathallan, in addition to prominent Crieff businessmen – published its prospectus in, among other papers, *The Times* of 14th October 1852. One of the Provisional Committee was William Young of Belvidere, Auchterarder, not only a prominent local solicitor, but also the author's great-great-grandfather.

The Times of that date reflected the continuing expansion of railways at the time, for in addition to that for the Crieff Junction Railway, this issue also carried prospectuses for the Hampstead & City Junction Railway, the Great Northern, Doncaster, Wakefield, Leeds & Bradford Railway and even the Royal Swedish Railway Company.

As with many such proposals at that time, the promoters of the Crieff Junction extolled the advantages of the area, the traffic which could be generated, and the lucrative returns to be made by shareholders. Crieff was recommended for its fine southern exposure and the '*remarkable salubrity of its climate*'. The district was described as '*eminently agricultural and fertile, exporting large surpluses of grain, potatoes, and cattle*', for which agricultural economy supplies of lime, coal, and manure were required. There was also timber, several '*inexhaustible*' quarries, fifty mills for the manufacture of wool and flax, oil and saw mills, tanning works and other industries. Added to these were eight distilleries producing some 141,000 gallons of spirit per annum, four breweries and fourteen malt works. Based on the traffic to and from the district currently carried over the Scottish Central, it was estimated that the goods traffic alone would generate £5,360 per annum.

The importance of Crieff in particular was stressed. It was calculated that during a six-week period in August/September of 1844, some 3,000 cattle, 29,659 sheep and 88 ponies passed along Amulree Road, whilst the three local distilleries produced 52,500 gallons of whisky.

The capital sought was £45,000 in £10 shares. Based on the anticipated income, less running costs, these would yield 6%, which, with the anticipated increase in revenue, would rise to 9%. The Scottish Central declined to invest in shares but, by way of their contribution, did agree to run the line at cost.

The inaugural meeting of the shareholders of the Crieff Junction Railway was held at Crieff on 13th October 1853, the Chairman of Directors being Sir David Dundas of Dunira, one of the members of the original Provisional Committee. In his report he stated:

'*It was a matter of much congratulation that the measures of this important undertaking were so far advanced, and a prospect so near of the fertile resources of this part of the country being laid open by means of a railway, which more than once had been attempted, but owing to one fatality or another had hitherto been denied. After the efforts stated in the report had failed to induce the promoters of the Scottish Central Company, at the starting of their line, to carry it within a few miles of the town of Crieff, an independent company was formed for making a line direct from Perth to Crieff, with a branch to join the Scottish Central near Auchterarder, but this measure was defeated by Parliament on the grounds that the Central Co had a right to the traffic of the district, and were ready to make a branch similar to that now about to be constructed. On the faith of this being done, the Central Co had obtained an Act to enable them to make their branch; but in place of following it out they allowed the prescribed period to expire and the powers to lapse. The accommodation of the district being thus deferred, influential meetings were held at Crieff in the summer of 1852, and a Committee was formed for the purpose of taking the necessary steps towards reviving the matter of a branch from Crieff to join the Scottish Central. This Committee put themselves in communication with Mr Bouch, Civil Engineer, a gentleman well known for his ability and skill in the construction of railways, who made a survey of the line and furnished an estimate of its cost. The Estimate, exclusive of land claims, engineering and Parliamentary expenses, was £32,630; and inclusive of every charge was £45,000. With the view of ascertaining the probable percentage which the undertaking would yield to those disposed to embark upon its construction, returns were procured from the books of the Scottish Central Co of the traffic entering upon that line and brought along that line in to the district. Further, the existing traffic in the district was carefully ascertained by competent persons during the summer of 1852, the remit of all which was to satisfy the Committee that the undertaking would yield a handsome return to the shareholders. Being thus assured, the Committee entered into communication with the principal landowners on the line, all of whom were found to be favourable to the introduction of the Railway, and to give the land required on reasonable terms. The steps necessary for procuring an Act were taken, but the promoters were threatened on the part of two road trustees on the grounds that the line would interfere with their interest in the revenue of the roads, upon the faith of which they had contracted obligations, and expended large sums of money. Ultimately however, those trustees accepted the terms and arrangements offered at the outset, and withdrew their opposition. The Bill afterwards passed both Houses of Parliament, and became law on 15th August last. Aware that the Crieff Junction would be the most important feeder of their line, the Scottish Central Co were desirous to aid in the advancement of the undertaking, though not to the extent which some expected. They had agreed to work the Crieff Junction at cost price, to supply the necessary plant, and to allow the Crieff Co, for the first 10 years after it being opened, a third of the free revenue of additional traffic brought upon the Central line by means of the Crieff Junction. With regards to construction of the line, the Directors had been in communication with contractors of undoubted responsibility, who had offered to do the work within the engineers estimate, and to have the line opened for the public in the course of next summer. This matter would be dealt with by the Directors who would this day be appointed. In resigning their trust into the hands of the Shareholders, the Chairman said that the Directors now retiring had to express their unabated confidence in the undertaking, that it would prove highly remunerative to the Shareholders, and be a great public benefit to the rich, populous and fertile district of Strathearn.'*

This report succinctly summarised the frustrations felt by the local people over the failure of the Scottish Central Railway Company to carry out their intention to build a branch line to Crieff, and the enthusiasm and zeal of the Provisional Committee in pressing ahead with all the necessary planning and preparations. It also makes mention for the first time of the Engineer appointed, Mr (later Sir) Thomas Bouch, who will be forever associated with the collapse of the first Tay Bridge (although more recent technical analysis of the disaster has sought to largely exonerate him). However, at that time Bouch was an established engineer with a solid reputation for building railways, albeit for doing it cheaply, which may have been a factor in his appointment, and hinted at the thrifty nature of the Crieff Junction Railway Board which will be noted elsewhere.

Planning and preparations continued the following year, and by the spring of 1855 the Board were able to report that they had awarded the contract for construction to Mr James Gowan at the Engineer's estimate of £33,000, the line to be ready to open by 1st September 1855.

All the extensive landowners concerned had readily given their permission and submitted to arbitration by a Mr Horne of Edinburgh, although some tenants on one of the estates *'imbued by an obstructive and litigious spirit'* had delayed proceedings by refusing entry to their land, resulting in the Crieff Junction Railway Company having to resort to legal action. Despite this, construction of the line was now well advanced and it was anticipated that it would be ready for opening on time. Designs for station buildings and level crossing lodges (at Strageath, Pittentian and Pittenzie) had been received and it was reported that *'construction will be proceeded with on the most economical principles'*.

Despite the initial optimism, however, matters did not all go according to plan, and the line was not ready for opening on the due date. Far from it, in fact, for at the Half Yearly meeting in October that year it was reported that the line had not opened as forecast the previous month, mainly due to difficulties which had been experienced by the contractor. This was largely due to an interdict by a local landowner to withdraw all his men from work for a considerable time, and also because of the number and cost of sidings required at Crieff Junction. Mr Bouch had, however, assured the Directors that *'without doubt the railway will be in full operation in the course of the ensuing month'* (this would have been in November 1855). This optimism was misplaced, for as late as the end of January the following year the line was reported to be *'in a dormant state owing to some dispute between the Directors and the Contractors'*. A meeting of the shareholders put pressure on the Board to resolve the apparent impasse and a month later the Directors were able to report that *'the misunderstanding between them and the contractors has been remedied'*. The weather that winter also gave rise to problems, and as late as 21st February it was stated that only a few weeks' good weather would be needed to allow the rails to be lifted and adjusted.

Plate 1.2
The '0' mile post plate for the Crieff Junction Railway was not actually on a post, but was bolted to the north side of the bridge spanning the main line at the west end of Crieff Junction station where the tracks to the Crieff branch diverged. Unlike the standard Caledonian Railway mile plates which were of cast iron, this was made of ¾ inch thick sheet steel with the figure '0', also fashioned from steel, riveted to the front. As a result it is surprisingly heavy, weighing over 20 lbs compared with the usual 13 lbs! *Author*

In the event the line was ready by the beginning of March and was opened with due ceremony on the 12th March 1856. The 9.00am express from Perth to Crieff Junction brought guests for the inaugural train, which left Crieff Junction for Crieff at 9.30am, hauled by what the local paper termed *'two massive engines'* decorated with flags. The formal opening ceremony was held at Crieff terminus at 12 noon in the presence of the Directors and shareholders. The special, complete with a brass band in an open truck, then travelled over the line to Crieff Junction before returning to Crieff where the proceedings concluded with a public dinner at the Drummond Arms Hotel. Some eighty gentlemen attended the dinner, with the usual glowing speeches and toasts. Even the townsfolk of Crieff entered into the spirit of the occasion, using tar barrels and other combustibles for a bonfire in James Square in the centre of the town, just outside the hotel.

Two days later, on 14th March, the line opened for goods traffic, but the commencement of passenger traffic had to wait until after the formal Board of Trade (BoT) inspection the following day. This was duly carried out by Colonel Wynne Royal Engineers, the BoT Inspector. He expressed himself well satisfied with what he described as *'the most complete line he had ever surveyed'*. He considered *'the Crieff Railway was in every sense a sound and excellent one,*

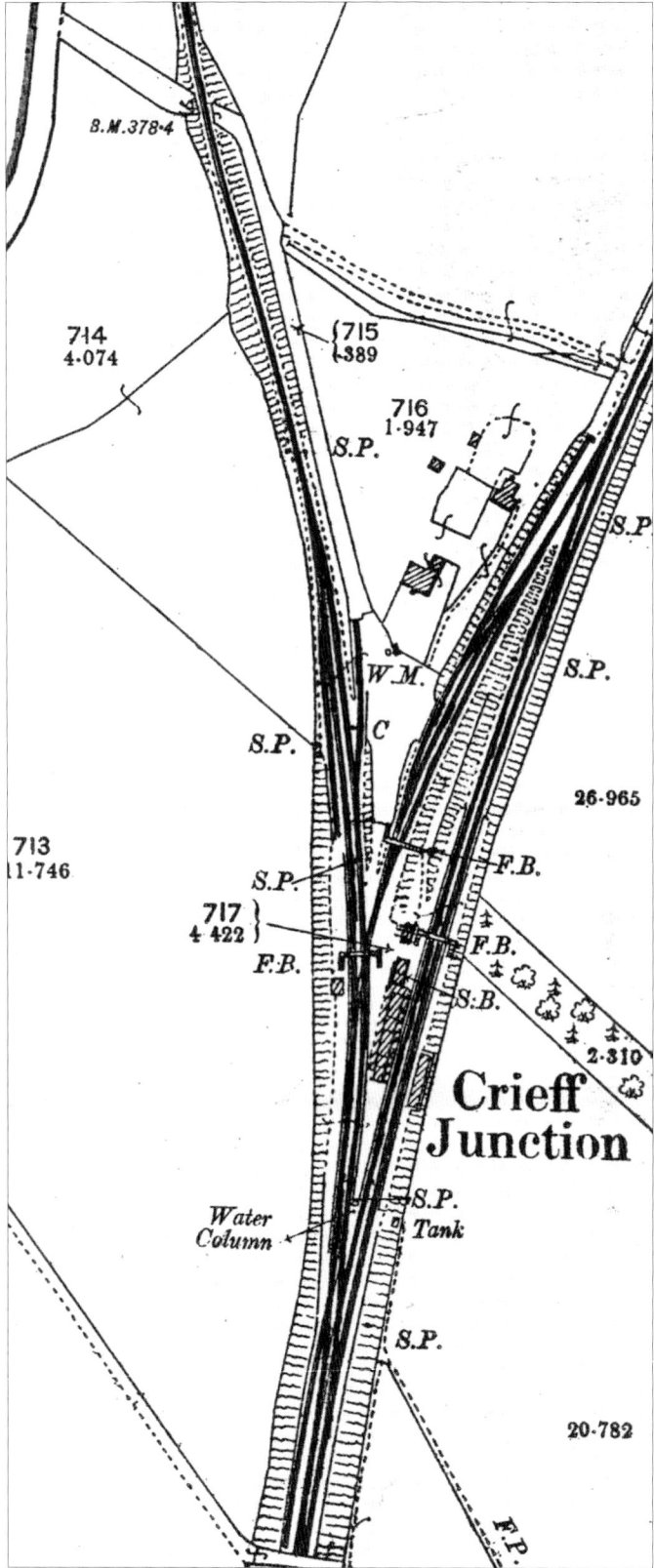

Figure 1.3
A ground plan of the original Crieff Junction station showing the layout of tracks, signals and other buildings. The three separate footbridges are clearly marked. What is evident is the limited amount of sidings despite the fact that additional sidings were built when it was opened. When the station was rebuilt in 1919, the alignment of the original branch line was used for the two long carriage sidings to be seen in the layout of Gleneagles. Scale 1:2,500. *Author's collection*

Plate 1.3
A Caledonian Railway hand lamp stamped 'CRIEFF JUNCTION Nº7'. Although dating from the later Caledonian Railway period, this is one of the few relics bearing the name of the original junction station which was renamed Gleneagles in 1912. It was standard practice for hand lamps issued to staff at particular stations to bear labels such as this identifying the station to which they belonged. This rare survivor was unearthed in the 1970s – fully sixty years after the name Crieff Junction disappeared. *Author*

Plate 1.4
An early postcard of Crieff Junction, taken from the west end showing the Crieff branch line platforms curving away to the left and the main line to Perth on the right. This was probably taken around 1900, in Caledonian days. Note the three separate footbridges over the branch line, main line and goods yard, and the profusion of enamel advertising signs. The station was renamed Gleneagles in 1912 but, having a rather untidy and unprepossessing layout, it was not judged suitable for the planned luxury hotel at Gleneagles and was completely rebuilt in 1919.
Author's collection

bridges, with one exception of substantial mason work'. The bridge concerned was probably the original wooden viaduct over the River Earn near Highlandman, but even this substantial timber structure was deemed satisfactory. Consisting of nine spans of about 30 feet, it lasted for nearly thirty years until replaced by an iron structure in 1885. Earlier doubts about the gradients were discounted and Colonel Wynne passed the line as fit for traffic. Thus the first passenger train ran on 16th March.

The opening of the railway to passenger traffic was marked with a holiday in Crieff, and the Crieff Junction Railway allowed passengers to travel free of charge that day. Many locals took advantage of this offer and it was said that some occupied the same seat all day, presumably riding back and forth several times to experience this new form of transport.

At its opening, the line had only two intermediate stations, at Muthill and Highlandman. However, by November 1856 plans were announced for a further station at Tullibardine. This was the result of an agreement between the Crieff Junction Railway Company and Viscount Strathallan, one of the principal supporters of the line, which recorded that:

'the erection on the line of the said railway of a siding for Mineral & Agricultural purposes on that part of my land of Tullibardine after disposed would be of great public utility and promote the common good of the country.'

The land was gifted free of charge with the proviso that if it ever ceased to be used as a railway, then it should revert to Strathallan Estate, this right being exercised 108 years later, after the line closed in 1964.

Tullibardine station opened for goods traffic in January 1857 and to passenger traffic, on request, on 1st March 1857, although passenger trains were not booked to stop at Tullibardine until 2nd May. Originally classed as a 'Public Delivery Siding', the station had only the most basic facilities, the station house not being added until the summer of 1860.

Plate 1.5
One of the substantial masonry bridges erected by the Crieff Junction Railway which were favourably commented upon by Colonel Wynne, the Board of Trade Inspector. This bridge simply connected two parts of a field at Easthill Farm near Auchterarder, where the line ran through the farmland. No trace remains of this bridge, which was demolished following closure in 1964 and the land returned to agriculture. The area is therefore once again a single field as it was prior to the construction of the railway in 1856, with little to show there ever was a railway here.
Author

Plate 1.6
This view of the deep cutting at Machany shortly after the track was lifted in 1964 shows the rugged nature of the engineering task on this section of the line about a mile south of Muthill station. The line had to be dug or blasted through solid rock, making it one of the most difficult sections in the construction of the Crieff Junction Railway. The bridge was another example of the substantial masonry structures referred to by Colonel Wynne, surviving to this day although much of the cutting had been used for landfill.
Author

The initial passenger train service was a modest four trains each way per day, the journey taking a leisurely 40 minutes to cover the 9 miles from the junction to Crieff, representing an average speed of around 20 mph depending on time spent at intermediate stations. The timetable for April 1856 was:

Crieff Junction	9.10am	11.15am	4.50pm	6.40pm
Muthill	9.32am	11.37am	5.12pm	7. 2pm
Highlandman	9.44am	11.49am	5.24pm	7.14pm
Crieff	9.50am	11.55am	5.30pm	7.20pm
Crieff	7. 6am	10.22am	4. 5pm	5.56pm
Highlandman	7.12pm	10.28am	4.11pm	6. 2pm
Muthill	7.24pm	10.50am	4.23pm	6.14pm
Crieff Junction	7.46pm	11.12am	4.45pm	6.36pm

These early trains were described as being hauled by a small single coupled engine with small box-like carriages painted green. There were no luggage vans in those days, with luggage simply being tied to the roof of the carriages and protected from the weather by a waterproof covering. It was later recounted that on one occasion no fewer than 180 boxes of game were piled on the top of one carriage.

The benefits of the new railway were soon being felt. By the end of the first month it was reported that passenger traffic was increasing daily, while goods traffic was '*immense*'. The example quoted was the arrival at Crieff of a train loaded with 30 tons of coal – all being sold within 2 hours. Imports of coal, lime and guano (bird droppings used as fertiliser) far exceeded expectations, while exports of wood, potatoes, grain and manufactured goods were also healthy. In particular, the availability of coal at moderate rates had a considerable impact on the local economy, supplanting wood, from the Ferntower and Ochtertyre estates, and peat as the primary source of fuel.

At the Half Yearly meeting on 1st May 1856 the figures for the first three weeks of operation showed that the line had carried 1,999½ passengers (children being counted as a half) and 1,561 tons of goods generating a gross revenue of £600 per month. The forecast that the line would yield very satisfactory dividends was greeted with cheers.

Over the following months traffic levels continued to increase with 3,284 passengers carried in April, the first full month of operation, and 4,348½ in May. Goods traffic increased commensurately, and it is worth noting that the revenue generated by goods traffic was roughly twice that for passenger traffic. It was evident that the economic wellbeing of the company was due largely to the goods traffic, as had originally been forecast, a point which seems to elude some present-day railway preservationists attempting to revive some long-closed rural railway.

That said, however, the passenger traffic was far from unimportant, and with the coming of the summer season the potential for tourist travel came into its own. One of the first of what would be many special excursion trains travelled to Crieff in May 1856: in honour of the Queen's Birthday, 600 inhabitants of Auchterarder, under the organisation of the 'Total Abstainers Society', made a trip to Crieff in a train of fourteen carriages, complete with music and banners. Arriving at 10.00am, they visited Ochtertyre before leaving again at 6.00pm. Throughout that first summer Messrs Henderson of Glasgow organised what would become a regular series of excursions to Crieff. On 4th July, 500 excursionists from Greenock visited Stirling, Crieff and Perth. The train divided at Crieff Junction and for those visiting Crieff, stage coaches took them from the station to Drummond Castle. Some passengers took advantage of the facility to stay until Monday for a small supplement.

A similar excursion was run later in July for visitors from Glasgow, Edinburgh and Arbroath with provision being made for seven-day tickets to enable those who wished to sample the delights of the local district. August was another busy month, with three large excursions including two more from the Total Abstainers. The first of these, on 15th August, carried fifty excursionists from Dunblane, Doune and Braco, who, complete with flute band, walked from Crieff station to Drummond Castle. A few days later a similar excursion from Dunfermline brought another 500 visitors to Crieff, and later in the month an excursion from Paisley enabled 300 people to visit Drummond Castle and Ochtertyre.

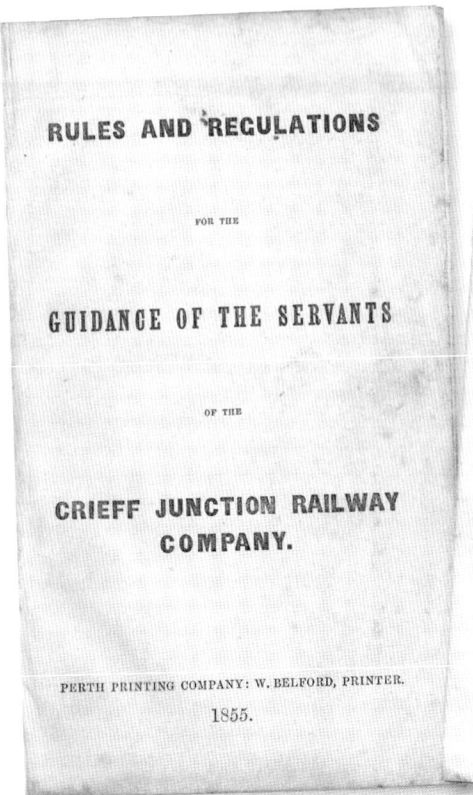

Figures 1.4 and 1.5
The Crieff Junction Railway issued its own Rule Book, as was the custom for independent railways. Measuring 4 inches by 7½ inches and bound in maroon leather, it ran to 89 pages. Published in 1855, there would only have been a small number of copies, the company having fewer than forty employees. The copy in the author's collection was acquired in 2013, nearly 150 years after the Crieff Junction Railway ceased to exist.

The title page of the Crieff Junction Railway Rule Book is over the signature of the then Secretary, John Ironside, who was soon to be replaced by Mr Veitch. Ironside, a local Crieff solicitor, later become the Secretary of the Crieff & Methven Junction Railway. This Rule Book became redundant when the Scottish Central Railway took over the line in August 1864. *Author's collection*

MONTHLY ACCOUNT MUST BE PAID BEFORE THE 15th OF THE MONTH FOLLOWING DATE.

Mr Findlay — Crieff Junction STATION, 19th May 1865

To THE CRIEFF JUNCTION RAILWAY COMPANY, Dr.

Date.	To or From.	Place.	Goods.	Weight.	Tolls.	Charges.	Total.
May 5	Crieff	Crieff Junct Slabs	1		2/3		- 2 3
" 12		"	1 Pcl				. . 3
							£ - 2 6

Paid Brothe Co

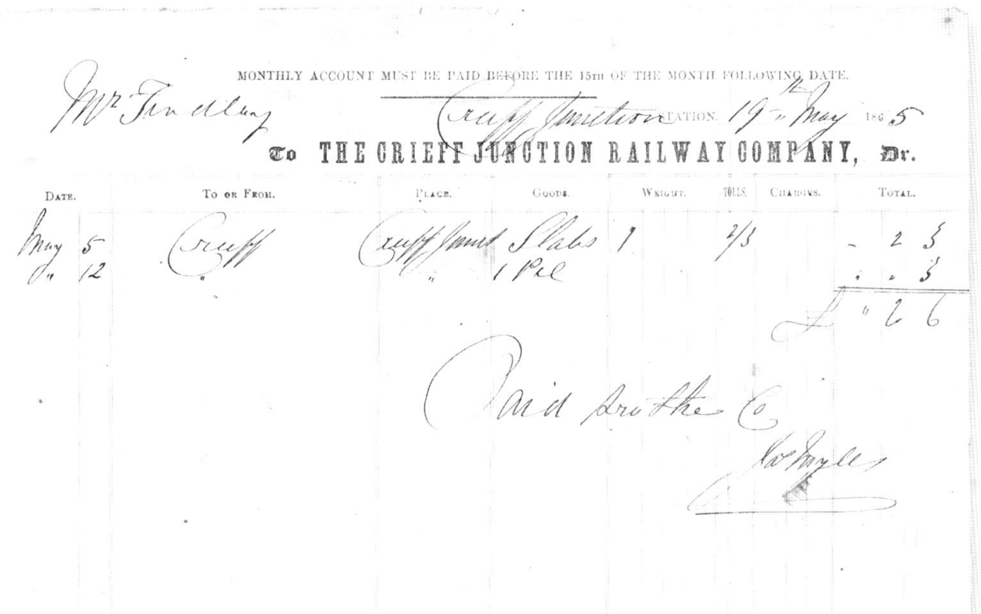

Figure 1.6
A Crieff Junction Railway Monthly Account for May 1865 for a Mr Findlay of Auchterarder. Mr Findlay was the Governor of the Poorhouse mentioned in Figure 1.7. It is worth noting that the Crieff Junction Railway having been absorbed by the Scottish Central Railway in August 1864, the station was still using Crieff Junction stationery nearly a year later. Some other examples have the title amended, but it would seem that economy was being exercised by the staff until supplies of the old stationery ran out.
Author's collection

Invoice, No.

To the Governor Poor House — Crieff Junct STATION, 11th Feby 1864

To the CRIEFF JUNCTION RAILWAY COMPANY,
FOR TOLLS, &c.

To or From.	Goods.	Tons.	Cwt.	Qrs.	Lbs.	Tolls.	Amount.	Paid on.	Total.
Edinr 4th Jany R.M.R.R.	1 P.P						7/8		- . 8

Received Payment, pro the Company,

NOTICE.—The Directors require the Tolls to be paid on delivery. The Porter or Carter is not to make any charge for delivery; it is therefore requested that nothing more be paid than what is stated in this Bill. For conditions of Tollage by this Company, see the back hereof.

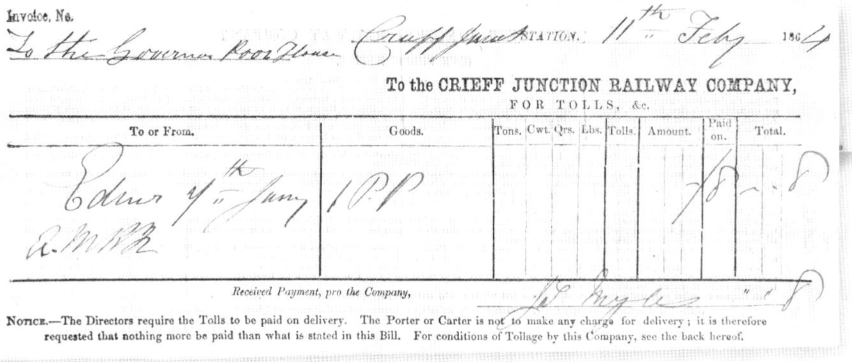

Figure 1.7
A Crieff Junction Railway Invoice issued on 11th February 1864 to the '*Governor of the Poorhouse*', more correctly named the 'Upper Strathearn Combination Poorhouse' which was situated only half a mile east of Crieff Junction station. Traffic for the Poorhouse was handled at the junction rather than Auchterarder station because it was much closer. For the most part Crieff Junction was a transfer point, so ephemera from this station is particularly rare. ***Author's collection***

The initial success of the Crieff Junction Railway buoyed the optimism of those advocating further expansion of railways in the district. As early as August 1856 *The Perthshire Advertiser* carried an article urging the extension of the line to Comrie, observing that half the traffic from Crieff originated in Comrie or west of Crieff. As described on page 21, moves were already afoot to promote a line from Perth to Methven. *The Perthshire Advertiser* of 1st September 1856 published a thought-provoking letter from local doctor Dr William Dean Fairless, pointing out that '*one railway begets another*'. He observed on the marked success of the Crieff Junction Railway and the fact that an Act for the Perth Almond Valley & Methven Railway was being obtained. He noted that there were also proposals for a line from Perth to Comrie, and suggested that the Crieff & Comrie and Crieff & Methven railways should coalesce under the title of the Perth & Western Railway. This far-sighted suggestion would eventually become a reality, but not until 1893 and under the Caledonian Railway Company.

All was not plain sailing for the fledgling Crieff Junction Railway Company. At the Half Yearly meeting in October 1856 the Directors warned that '*working expenses had been heavier for the bygone 6 months than may be expected for the future*'. This was largely due to '*ascertaining the wants of the district*' and '*adapting working to progressive development of traffic*'. The Directors were already looking for economies such as '*combining offices in the management*'. However, Net Revenue for the half year being £860 5s 1½d they felt able to declare a dividend of 5%, commenting that '*this was the first line in Scotland, which at the commencement, had yielded such a percentage*'.

One welcome improvement in the early days was the erection in December 1856 of '*a pretty and useful wooden bridge*' across the main line at Crieff Junction to allow passengers to cross the running lines safely. However, the local paper expressed the wish, which was to become a recurring theme in the years to come, for a suitable waiting room, the present one being '*devoid of comfort*'. That apart, the enthusiasm for the new enterprise was reflected in a report in *The Crieff Herald* in November 1856 which stated grandly that '*the public can now with confidence entrust their transit to the safekeeping of the officials of the A1 line*'.

The following first winter, of 1856/7, would seem to have been a lean time for the company, for at the Half Yearly meeting at the end of April 1857 the Board reported that the results for the previous six-month period had been disappointing and it was decided to declare no dividend. The poor results were partly due to a drop in passenger traffic during the winter months, but also to the '*excessive severity of the working expenses of the Scottish Central Railway*', a first hint of the discord between the two companies. Despite this downbeat report, a glowing speech at the dinner held to celebrate the first anniversary of the opening of the line declared that trade in Crieff had improved, that house properties in Crieff were greatly enhanced in value, and that '*traffic had exceeded the most flattering estimates*'. Mention was also made of the improvements in the Traffic Department of the Scottish Central following the appointment of Mr Butter Malcolm (who was also the General Manager of the Crieff Junction Railway Company) as their Superintendent, describing him as a gentleman of '*unrivalled personal energy and sagacity*'.

The optimism of the Directors was not shared by all. In December 1856 *The Crieff Herald* published a letter from 'Gang Forward' who complained that the journey from Crieff to Perth took six hours – or half a day – and that *'had driven some people to take to the road rather than encounter the discomfort of the wooden box while suffering their banishment at the lonely junction'*, this being a reference to the rather spartan facilities at Crieff Junction. In February, the same paper commented that *'passengers landed at the junction shivering from head to foot remain in the intensely cold atmosphere without coal or candle'*. Muthill station was no better, it was said, there being neither fire nor fireplace for passengers. The inadequacy of the accommodation was to become a recurring theme, but there were also complaints about the cost of fares and rates for coal.

The fortunes of the Crieff Junction Company recovered in the spring of 1857, although not to the same levels as the first year. Excursion traffic continued to develop, with the largest train yet bringing some 800 visitors from the Falkirk Iron Works, complete with brass band, to Crieff in mid July. The party got off at Muthill, walked the 3½ miles to Drummond Castle and then on to Crieff, another 3 miles, for the journey home.

This excursion traffic was not all one way, for the company also ran their own excursions from Crieff to places such as Edinburgh, Glasgow, Stirling and Perth. Typical of these was the excursion on 3rd October 1857, which conveyed 400 passengers to Glasgow and Edinburgh; leaving Crieff at 6.30am, three quarters of the passengers travelled to Edinburgh, with the remainder choosing Glasgow.

The development of the housing market in Crieff referred to earlier was something which the Crieff Junction was keen to encourage, and in July 1857 they announced the introduction of Contract tickets for owners of newly built houses. These Free Building tickets, colloquially referred to as 'Villa' tickets, would be available for each house built within a radius of one mile of Crieff, or within half a mile of Highlandman, and were for three, four or five years from the date of the foundations being laid; on a graduated scale according to the value of the house built (with the 2012 equivalent values), their availability of was:

– Houses valued up to £500 (£47,800) 3 years
– Houses valued at £600 (£57,476) 4 years
– Houses valued over £700 (£67,032) 5 years

In the event, the scheme for these tickets was terminated in November 1859, only a little over two years later.

Another development announced later that year, in October, which

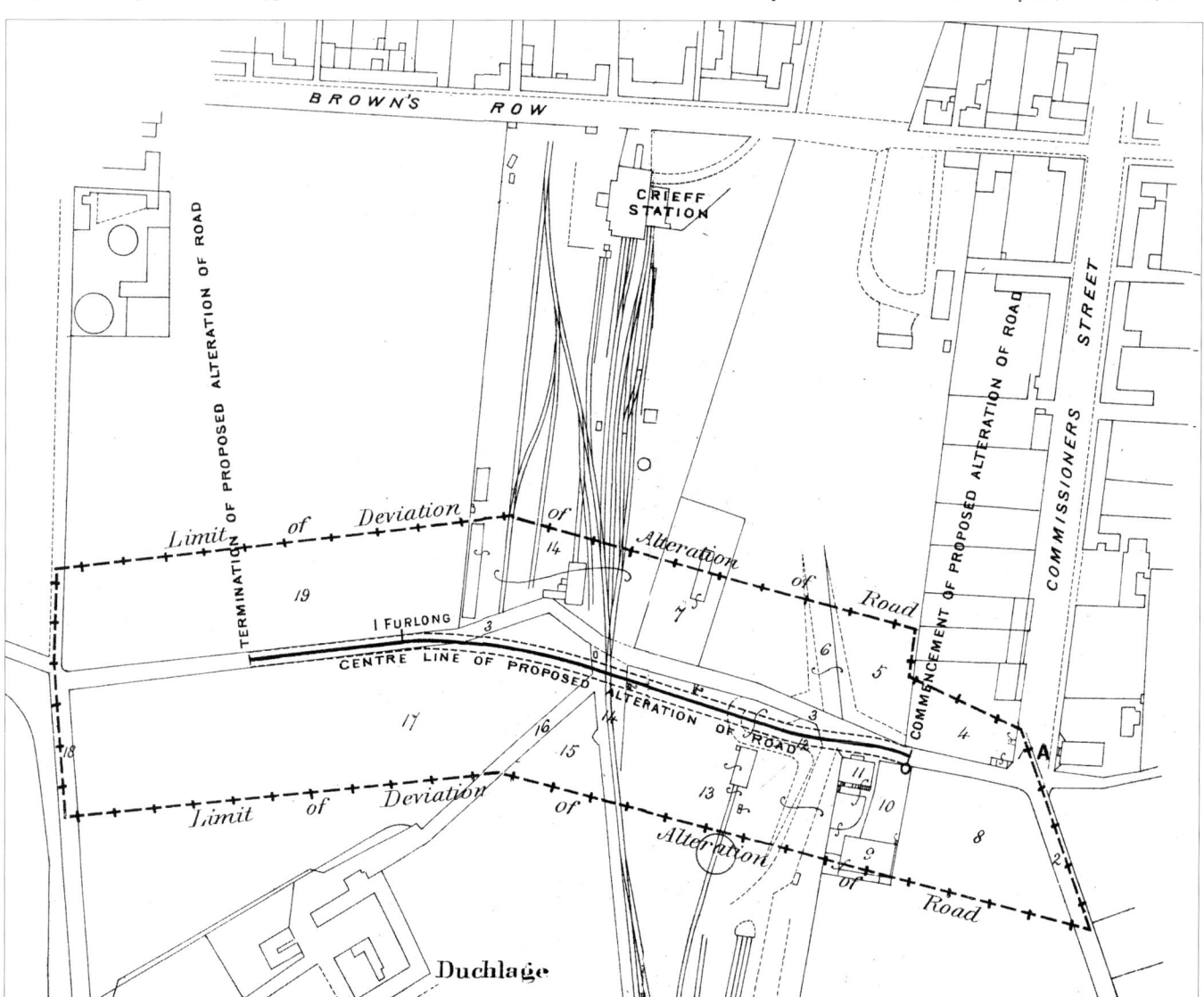

Figure 1.8
A plan of the original terminus station at Crieff. This plan dates from the Caledonian Railway Act 1865 which included proposals for a bridge to carry Duchlage Road over the railway, thus replacing the level crossing which presented increasing operational problems once the line to Perth was open. The original Crieff Junction Railway terminus is centre top while the engine shed is centre left near Duchlage Road. The later Crieff & Methven Junction engine shed, turntable and goods yard would be bottom right, below Duchlage Road.
Author's collection

the Crieff Junction sought to capitalise on, was the construction of a prestige educational establishment to be called Morrison's Academy, on the site of the Old Market Park in Crieff. Originally the preferred location was to have been Muthill, the benefactor's home village, but probably because of the distance, over 2 miles, between the village and Muthill station, it was decided to locate the school in Crieff. The survey for the Academy was not carried out until May 1879, but when construction began that September, the Directors reported that it was anticipated that large quantities of material would be required and that the *'Crieff Junction Railway should permanently benefit from this Educational Institution'*. As a further incentive, when the Academy opened on 1st October 1880, the railway offered Season tickets to pupils of Morrison's Academy at *'moderate rates'*.

The return of the excursion traffic that summer of 1857 brought a commensurate increase in revenue. Figures for the months of August were well up on the previous year, being:

- Number of Passengers carried   4,544
- Passenger Revenue   £214
- Goods Revenue   £228
- Total Revenue   £442

Despite these encouraging figures, the company was evidently feeling the pinch financially and rumours circulated that the Crieff Junction Railway was planning to work the line with their own locomotives and carriages rather than those of the Scottish Central, this being seen as a cheaper and more advantageous arrangement than the present system.

Meanwhile, the effects of other railway developments outside the district were being felt. By January 1858, construction of the Callander & Oban Railway was well advanced, with the opening of the line planned for May that year. There were calls for the Crieff Junction to put on an extra Up train at 6.30pm to cater for tourists from Lochearnhead (Balquhidder) travelling by stage coach. In fact the stage coach 'Benvorlich' had run as a connecting coach since the opening of the line throughout the summer seasons of 1856 and 1857.

Less welcome from the point of view of the Crieff Junction was the opening of the Perth Almond Valley & Methven Railway on 1st January 1858, as described later in this chapter. The utility of this alternative route to Perth soon became evident, with tentative proposals to link the line with Crieff. By June that year proposals were made for a coach service between Crieff and Methven to connect with the trains to the latter, although this service did not start running until the following May. When it did, the Crieff Junction responded to this competition by reducing their fares between Crieff and Perth.

The beneficial effect of the railway on the local economy was further evident from a report published by the Crieff Savings Bank in March 1858, which observed that prior to the arrival of the railway, trade had deserted the town with *'all spirit of enterprise sinking'*, but that since the line opened there had been a dramatic turnaround in its fortunes. This was reflected in the figures for savings at the bank which rose from £4,019 in 1850 to £7,335 in 1857, an increase of some 82%, or almost 12% per annum, an impressive growth rate.

Despite this apparent prosperity, the Crieff Junction continued to seek economies and at the end of March announced that Mr Veitch, the Company Secretary would henceforth combine that office with that of Accountant and Superintendent of the Crieff Terminus, thus dispensing with the post of stationmaster at Crieff. This caused some outcry locally for there had been three changes of stationmaster within the past five months. In October 1857, Mr William Roberts, the first and much respected stationmaster was replaced by Mr Chambers, who in turn was succeeded by Mr McGregor, only for him to lose his post under the reorganisation to Mr Veitch.

The departure of Mr William Roberts, who had done so much for the company in its early days, evidently left a sour taste. At a public dinner held in his honour on 3rd April 1858 it was said:

'We all regretted the causes, which combined, placed Mr Roberts in such a position as left him no other alternative consistent with his manly dignity than to resign the situation he had so well and cordially filled.'

It was notable that none of the Directors attended this event. The exact circumstances surrounding his precipitate departure are unclear. There was a suggestion that he had been wrongly suspected of embezzlement, or it may be that the unfortunate Mr Roberts, aware of the impending loss of his post under the reorganisation, had decided to jump before he was pushed. Whatever the reason, it was a sad end to his time at Crieff; but a man of his capabilities was not idle long, for shortly after this he was appointed stationmaster at Elgin on the newly opened line between Inverness and Keith, part of the Inverness & Aberdeen Junction Railway. Here his career flourished and he gained steady promotion on the Highland Railway, eventually becoming Superintendent of the Line of that company. His son, also called William, followed him into railway service, rising to become the Resident Engineer of the Highland Railway.

That such economies were necessary were reflected in the Half Yearly report for April 1859 when it was stated that the net results for the previous year were largely unchanged as the decrease in revenue had been matched by a corresponding reduction in expenditure. The poor results were largely attributed to the almost total absence of potato traffic resulting from the poor harvest in 1858, and the dividend to shareholders was reduced accordingly from 4% to 3%. Yet again discord emerged between the Crieff Junction and the Scottish Central, with the former seeking a reduction in the mileage rate for the Scottish Central Railway locomotive. The Scottish Central responded that their charges were restricted to prime costs with no profit margin, so were unwilling to budge. Unhappy with this, the Crieff Junction decided to review the matter at the break point in the Working Agreement due in two years time.

The company's fortunes continued to decline in early 1859, with a slight decrease in traffic revenue of £27 0s 0d over the past six months. Most of this was again attributed to the poor potato harvest the preceding year, for only 400 tons of potatoes had been carried that year from the 1858 harvest, while in 1858 some 1,000 tons were carried from the 1857 harvest.

Passenger traffic however continued to be healthy, bolstered by the usual programme of excursions during the summer months. At the end of July the largest excursion yet run carried 1,500 employees of the Edinburgh & Glasgow Railway, including a *'goodly proportion of the fairer sex'*, in an impressive train reported to consist of forty-four carriages! They were accompanied by the Glasgow Blind Institution Band, who, when the train left Crieff at 7.00pm that evening, played the train off to a rendition of 'Will Ye No Come Back Again'.

These excursions were notable events in the town – not only because of the trade which they generated, but also, with the novelty of the railway, as a public spectacle. Crowds would turn out to greet the arrival of the visitors and again to witness their departure. The numbers involved were often large, as can be seen from contemporary accounts, and improvisation was sometimes necessary to meet the demand for coaching stock. One such party from Dundee, a combination of employees from the Dundee, Perth & Aberdeen Junction Railway together with 400 from Messrs Malcolm Ogilvie of Dundee, accompanied by two bands, required three engines and twenty-nine carriages. A scarcity of rolling stock necessitated the use of two open carriages and, it being a rainy day, according to a newspaper report, onlookers were amazed to see *'a truck load of umbrellas come whirling along the line and a reflective mind was apt to suppose there might be refined cattle underneath!'*

Unfortunately not all the visitors were well behaved, and the same account noted that *'when the time drew near when they had to return home, the town presented an animated appearance as the drunks, male and female, began to exit the inns'*. Nor was this an

Plate 1.7
An official Caledonian Railway postcard of Crieff, termed the 'Montpelier of Scotland' by the Caledonian. Crieff was a popular holiday and tourist destination which was exploited to the full by the railways. The Crieff Junction Railway lost no time in promoting it as such, and excursion traffic during the summer months was a regular feature of their operation from the outset. *Author's collection*

isolated incident, for only a week earlier following an excursion of 400 employees from Lilybank Foundry in Dundee it was reported that *'We were sorry to see so many of the excursionists getting drunk instead of visiting Drummond Castle'*. However, after yet another excursion from Dundee only a month later, the same paper recorded that *'The Crieff publicans averred that "the trip wasna muckle good" (to them) – so we suppose the visitors were orderly and well behaved'*. There was no pleasing everybody! Those visiting Crieff were not the only ones to earn the opprobrium of the paper, however, for when the last excursion of the season from Crieff to Edinburgh and Glasgow at the end of October returned home it noted with regret that they were *'sorry to learn that a number of the excursionists had been paying too much attention to John Barleycorn'*!

Another altogether happier event that summer, and one which reflected the rural nature of the line, was the series of celebrations which heralded the birth of a son to the General Manager, Mr Butter Malcolm at the end of June. Crieff station and the trains were decorated with flags, a bonfire was built next to the station on part of the Meadows and a *feu de joie* of muskets fired.

Also notable was a special train on 7th August 1860 to take the Crieff Rifle Corps to the Royal Review in Edinburgh. This was the first recorded use of the railway for military purposes, something which would become common place, particularly during the two world wars in the following century.

Fortunately for the Crieff Junction Railway, the potato harvest in 1860 was much better than previous years, and in December it was reported that in the preceding six weeks between 8,000 and 9,000 Perth 'bolls' of potatoes had been sent by rail to southern markets. As a result, 1861 marked a resurgence in the company's fortunes, and at the Half Yearly meeting in April it was announced that they could afford to pay a dividend of 5½%, although in the eventuality the Directors erred on the side of caution, recommending that it remain at 4%.

Another cause for celebration arose in January 1861 with the marriage of Miss Ellen Menteath, daughter of the Chairman, Mr Alexander Menteath of Broich and Duchally. The groom and party arrived at Crieff by a special train, the engine and saloon decorated with flags and evergreens and, to cap it all, fifty detonators – the so-called *'Crieff Junction Artillery'* – were set off between the train passing Broich Estate and the terminus. The Chairman generously

Plate 1.8
Another Caledonian Railway official postcard. Drummond Castle and its gardens were a renowned tourist attraction, featuring regularly in excursions run to Crieff. Coaches took tourists from Crieff to the castle, which is actually nearer Muthill village than Crieff, but the numbers on the excursions were often so large that it was common practice for them to walk there and back, often with a band. *Author's collection*

Plate 1.9
A further Caledonian Railway official postcard. The large estate of Ochtertyre was just to the west of Crieff and was often visited by passengers arriving at Crieff on excursions. It was owned at the time by Sir Patrick Murray who later became one of the directors of the Crieff & Methven Junction Railway. *Author's collection*

sent a £5 donation to the Secretary for distribution among the staff.

Matters continued to improve during the spring and summer, and by the time of the sixteenth Half Yearly meeting on 26th September 1861, the Board were able to report that the balance of the Revenue Account had risen to £1,035 5s 3½d, an increase of £175 11s 9d over the previous year, while they had £284 2s 9½d in the Reserve Fund. On the basis of these figure they were able to recommend a dividend of 5%.

The summer season saw the return of excursion trains, one such being a group of 100 boys and trustees from Stuarts Free School in Perth who, accompanied by a flute band, visited Drummond Castle before returning for dinner at the Drummond Arms Hotel. Again, not all excursions were for visitors to Crieff. An excursion was run from Crieff on 24th June 1861 for those who wished to travel to Stirling to witness the laying of the foundation stone of the Wallace Monument. Return fares were 5/6d for First Class and 2/9d for Third.

Traffic levels were maintained throughout the winter period, and at the Half Yearly meeting in April 1862 the Board were able to report another increase in revenue of £265 6s 4d. However, they also noted that there had been a corresponding increase in expenditure of £110 18s 0d, due largely to the repainting of exposed timbers, station houses, waiting rooms, platforms, and, rather strangely, stone bridges. The dividend remained unaltered at 5%.

The level of traffic remained satisfactory throughout 1862, despite the general depression in trade then affecting the country. In June an interesting article in the *Strathearn Herald* on the timber trade in the district noted that nearly two thirds of the goods traffic carried on the line since its opening had been timber in the form of pit props, railway sleepers and raw timber. The other main commodity dispatched was potatoes which were, and still are, a major crop in the area. This, however, was very much seasonal traffic during the autumn months, with traffic levels also being largely dependent on the yield, as recounted earlier.

One unwise economy measure the company made in June was to dispense with the night-watchman at Crieff station who had been employed to guard not only the premises, but also the goods in transit. This change did not go un-noticed by the local 'ne'er do wells', who soon returned to their old ways; the local paper reported a case of the Police finding an Irishman by the name of Flynn *'standing by a sack which appeared to be full of something'*. Indeed it was – full of coal which he was stealing! Flynn was promptly arrested and sent to Perth for trial.

A more amusing incident occurred at the beginning of August when a young lady passenger at Crieff travelling Third Class attempted to board the train. Unfortunately she could not get in through the carriage door due to:

> *'the extraordinary size and strength of her crinoline. She was about to enter the more commodious 1st Class carriage when she was told by the ungallant Guard there that she must pay the 1st Class fare.'*

Perhaps the guard should have paid more heed to Rule 10 of the Crieff Junction Railway Rule Book which stated that *'Any act of rudeness or incivility to passengers will be severely dealt with'*. The newspaper concluded, equally ungallantly *'Ladies take warning'*!

The usual programme of excursions ran during the summer, one such being on 26th July to Muthill by the Band of Hope members, where 500 passengers visited Culdees Castle, a short walk from the station, on the banks of Machany Water. The Crieff Junction also laid on an excursion earlier in the month in connection with the Volunteer Review on the Inches at Perth, and for once demonstrated rare generosity in charging only a single fare for the return journey. Over 300 passengers took advantage of this magnanimous offer.

That autumn rumours surfaced, not for the first time, that the Scottish Central Railway wanted to take over the Crieff Junction. It was even suggested that if they did so they would cut off Tullibardine and make a new line to a station at Townhead in Auchterarder. These rumours were robustly denied by the Scottish Central as being *'without foundation'*. At about the same time, and proving that railway mania was still rampant, some influential inhabitants of Aberfeldy, Grandtully and Kenmore even floated the idea of a railway direct from Aberfeldy to Crieff by way of Amulree and then through the Sma' Glen. The local paper rightly poured scorn on this somewhat hare-brained idea, pointing out the heavy engineering which would be involved, possibly including a 20 mile long tunnel. Not surprisingly, nothing further was ever heard of this scheme.

That same month, the *Strathearn Herald*, a constant critic of the railway, wrote a stinging article on the company:

> *'It is nothing new to write upon the subject of accommodation (at Crieff Junction) for ever since the Crieff Railway was made a railway and the Crieff Junction Railway Directors sat for the first time to conduct the rather crooked business of this rather crooked line, it has been no great blessing upon the community ... the actions of the company are the most Jewish we know.'*

Such blunt and anti-Semitic wording would not be tolerated today but was of its time. The paper went on to specify that *'the traveller going to Perth on the 10.4am train has to wait somewhere around 1½ to 2 hours in that Siberian like locality of Crieff Junction'*.

The Half Yearly meeting in April 1863 revealed that the traffic levels had been maintained during the previous six months, yielding a net revenue of £1,637 10s 6d, a modest increase of £34 6s 3d over the previous half year. In recommending a dividend of 5%, the Board recorded that *'there were grounds for congratulation that despite the great depression in trade, unpropitious weather and reduced through fares, no department of the Crieff Junction had been materially affected'*.

Despite these reassuring noises, rumours again surfaced, this time in *The Scotsman*, that the line was to be leased to the Scottish Central, or even to the rival Scottish North Eastern Railway. It was said that the Scottish Central would only offer 5% whereas the Crieff Junction wanted 6%. All this speculation resulted in the Secretary of the Crieff Junction Railway, Mr Veitch, writing in the strongest possible terms to *The Scotsman*:

'But I beg to state that neither have the Crieff Junction Directors offered to lease the Crieff Railway to the Scottish Central, nor have they any contemplation to make offers to any of the company's you name. I now contradict the whole statement made in your newspaper yesterday.'

The *Strathearn Herald* continued to pillory the company, and in August published a letter from 'Amicus', a Glasgow visitor who wrote: *'It is a standing disgrace. To take one hour to travel 9 miles is absurd. The same journey to Greenloaning might be accomplished by a good horse with sprung cart'*. He complained that *'you are detained a whole hour at the junction'* and concluded tellingly: *'But I rather think the greater consideration is to get 5% for the Shareholders by any means – never mind the accommodation or welfare of the public'*.

The paper continued its crusade when on 3rd October it devoted an entire editorial to the perceived shortcomings of the company. Complaining about the *'Siberian climate of the Junction'*, it commented that passengers *'were trapped in to paying 2nd Class fares for what ought to have been Parliamentary tickets'* and that *'in general railway engines try to avoid hills. The Crieff Junction Railway sought them out'*. Concluding rather extravagantly that: *'in consequence, the Crieff Junction is the worst planned and worst constructed in the wide world'*, before forecasting ominously that *'there would not be a better choice for a railway than that which is proposed from Crieff to Methven'*.

An interesting proposal emerged in November 1867 when the *Edinburgh Gazette* carried details of a proposed railway to be called the Glendevon & Crieff Junction Railway. This proposal outlined plans for a connecting line between the Devon Valley Railway just east of Crook of Devon, running through the delightfully named Yetts O'Muchart and Glendevon to a point on the Scottish Central Railway just south of Kincardine Viaduct. It also proposed a connection from 10 chains east of Crieff Junction to a point on the Crieff Junction Railway near the Auchterarder Road level crossing.

The Devon Valley Railway would later become part of the North British Railway, and this line would have provided an alternative and more direct link to the Fife coalfields and beyond. This would have been unwelcome news for the Scottish Central Railway and, not surprisingly, nothing further was heard of this proposal. However, as will be mentioned later, the Scottish Central Railway did formulate its own plan for a spur line from the main line to the Crieff branch, but this too came to nought.

By the end of February the following year (1864) the *Strathearn Herald* reported that *'The Crieff Junction have literally thrown themselves at the feet of the Scottish Central supplicating them to renew their offer which a few months ago they disdainfully rejected'*, before adding with a degree of ill-concealed satisfaction and not a little modesty: *'That we have been instrumental in the death of the line we do not deny, for we have done the state a good service'*.

In March the promoters of the Crieff & Methven Junction Railway met with the Crieff Junction officials to seek an arrangement over a joint terminus at Crieff and the use of the present line from Highlandman station to Crieff, but no agreement was reached. Later that same month the Crieff Junction again objected to the Crieff & Methven Junction Bill at its third reading. That summer the threat of real competition came a step nearer when on 14th July the Crieff & Methven Junction Railway Act received the Royal Assent. Linked with the existing Perth Almond Valley & Methven Railway this would provide a direct line between Crieff and Perth. The days of the Crieff Junction Railway enjoying a monopoly of railway traffic to Crieff were numbered, and the Board knew it.

Unsurprisingly, the Half Yearly meeting at the end of the month was attended solely by the Directors and Officials. The Chairman attempted to put a positive gloss on it by stating that *'He had never seen so sparse a meeting of the Company, but he held that the Shareholders by their absence showed that they had full confidence in their Directors'*. The end was not far away and at an Extraordinary Meeting approval was given for the Crieff Junction to be transferred to the Scottish Central.

The *Strathearn Herald* sought to have the last word, stating that *'The Crieff Junction ceases to act for good or evil of the community'*. A sad epitaph for the short life of this little company which had started with such lofty ideals and fired the public enthusiasm but which ended in such ignominious circumstances.

The Scottish Central Railway finally took over the running of the Crieff Junction Railway from 1st August 1864, a little over six years after the line opened. Having operated the line since its inception, many things did not change – so, for example, the summer programme of excursions continued uninterrupted. Later that month another large excursion from Dundee brought over 1,000 passengers and two instrumental bands to Crieff, where they visited the ever popular Drummond Castle. At the end of August a special was also laid on from Crieff to Perth for the unveiling of the Albert statue, carrying some 200 passengers.

The preparations to install the 'Electric Telegraph' from Crieff Junction to Crieff were a welcome development the following month. Surveys were carried out and sites for posts were marked. Telegraph communication was then still in its infancy, and its arrival in Crieff was eagerly awaited, not least by the *Strathearn Herald* which stated:

'In a short time, therefore, we may expect that the commercial community and others will have all the advantages of telegraphic communications with the principal cities and towns of the empire, and that we will be now on equality with our most favoured contemporaries in supplying the latest news.'

In the event, the Electric Telegraph did not reach Crieff until the summer of 1866, nearly two years later, and then along the line of the Crieff & Methven Junction Railway from Perth. Only after this was established did the Caledonian Railway Company finally complete the telegraph line between Crieff Junction and Crieff.

A report on the arrangements agreed between the Scottish Central Railway and the Crieff Junction Railway for the former to take over the latter was prepared by the Directors of the Scottish Central Railway in preparation for the Special Meeting to be held after that company's Half Yearly meeting at the end of October 1864. This covered:

1. Undertaking of the Crieff Junction Co to be transferred to the Central Co as of 1st August 1864.

2. Transfer to be burdened with the debts due by the Crieff Junction Co on Capital Account.
3. Crieff Junction Co to relieve the Central Co of liabilities on Revenue Account prior to 31st July 1864.
4. The Central Co to allocate to shareholders in the Crieff Junction Co an amount of Ordinary Stock in the Central Co equal to the amount paid up by such shareholders respectively.
5. An Act of Parliament to be applied for to sanction the acquisition of the undertaking of the Crieff Junction Co on the terms stated.
6. Till the Act is obtained, the Crieff Junction Co to administer their affairs under the control of the Central Co who shall manage the Crieff Junction line, receive the revenue thereof, and pay working expenses, interest on debt, and a dividend to Crieff Junction shareholders at the rate of 5½%.
7. Arbitration.

This report was considered by the Special Meeting and the resolution to amalgamate the two companies was approved. In answer to a question from the floor, it was stated that the debt of the Crieff Junction Railway to be inherited by the Scottish Central Railway was £1,419 7s 7d. Hardly was the ink dry on this agreement approved by the meeting, however, than the first reports surfaced of an agreement by which the Caledonian Railway Company was to take over the Scottish Central Railway.

In the interim, the Scottish Central Railway continued with its own plans for developing the Crieff branch line as part of its system. One significant proposal was the construction of a spur from the main line just north of Crieff Junction to connect with the Crieff branch line just north of Auchterarder, thus permitting through running between Crieff and Perth without the necessity to reverse trains at Crieff Junction. This short stretch of line was surveyed and plans for it were included in the Scottish Central Railway Bill for 1865 which was approved by Parliament in February that year. The line was never constructed, however, and following the opening of the Crieff & Methven Junction Railway in 1866 which provided a direct route between Crieff and Perth, the need for it became redundant. The powers to construct the line were inherited by the Caledonian Railway when they took over the Scottish Central Railway and were finally abandoned by the Caledonian Act 1869.

In other aspects, the Scottish Central Railway carried on the work of the Crieff Junction Railway – for example, in offering season tickets for children attending Morrison's Academy in Crieff. Third Class fares (available for Second Class when there were no Third Class carriages in the train) for the autumn term were:

– Blackford	60s
– Crieff Junction	50s
– Tullibardine	45s
– Muthill	37s 6d
– Highlandman	25s

Although the Scottish Central Railway was now essentially in charge, the Crieff Junction Railway continued to exist as a company until the Scottish Central Railway 1865 Bill received the Royal Assent. Thus the penultimate meeting of the Crieff Junction Railway was held at the end of March. Despite the debt inherited by the Scottish Central Railway, the Directors, optimistic as ever, reported that they hoped that:

'The funds in hand will prove adequate to the extinction of all existing liabilities, and leave, perhaps, a balance at the disposal of the shareholders at their next Half Yearly meeting which it is expected and trusted will be the final and dissolution meeting of the Crieff Junction Railway.'

The final meeting of the company was held at the beginning of October 1865, when it was declared that the final balance sheet showed a credit of £398; after discussion of the fact that 'no allowance had hitherto been made to the Directors of the Company for their services', it was resolved that:

'The free balance remaining after the discharge of the Revenue obligations of the Company, and after payment of 5½% Dividend for the past half year, be allotted and paid over to the 5 Directors of the Company in consideration and requital of their official services as Directors.'

On that happy note, 'The usual vote of thanks terminated the proceedings' and, in this case, the short life of the Crieff Junction Railway Company.

Whilst the life of the Crieff Junction Railway was drawing to a close, however, the development of railways to Crieff continued. A special train was run to Crieff conveying Colonel Salkeld, Chairman of the Caledonian Railway, the Chairman of the Scottish North Eastern Railway, and Mr Buchanan, Engineer of the Crieff & Methven Junction Railway. A site meeting was held to consider a new joint station at Crieff in the meadows to the north of the existing terminus, and a proposed bridge to carry Duchlage Road over the railway, thereby dispensing with the existing level crossing. The results of this visit will be covered in more detail in the later account of the Crieff & Methven Junction Railway.

The involvement of the Caledonian Railway Company reflected the fact that the Scottish Central Railway had itself been taken over by the former on 1st August 1865. The *Strathearn Herald*, always well disposed towards the Scottish Central Railway, viewed this development with some scepticism, stating: *'We have long known that the CR is not the best run railway in the world, and in view of the new arrangement, we may yet come to rue the day the CR and Scottish Central Railway amalgamated'*. This amalgamation was the first in a series of takeovers which would eventually see the Caledonian Railway Company control the entire network of branch lines in Strathearn.

PERTH ALMOND VALLEY & METHVEN RAILWAY

Early in 1856, even while work on the Crieff Junction Railway was being completed, a group of local businessmen from Perth were contemplating the idea of constructing a line from Perth to the village of Methven, about 6 miles west of the city.

No doubt inspired by the early success of their Crieff counterparts, this group, headed by the Earl of Mansfield, wasted no time and made rapid progress. By summer, a Bill had been pushed through Parliament, with the result that the Perth Almond Valley & Methven Railway Company was incorporated by Act of Parliament on 29th July 1856. The Act, apart from the usual powers of construction and so forth, also included an agreement with the Scottish Midland Junction Railway Company which permitted the Perth Almond Valley & Methven Railway's trains to run over Scottish Midland Junction metals for the last 1½ miles to Perth. By coincidence, an Act was also approved on the same day authorising the amalgamation of the Scottish Midland Junction Railway with the Scottish North Eastern Railway, which latter concern undertook the original agreement.

The Perth Almond Valley & Methven Railway Bill outlined the proposal for a short branch line of 5¾ miles from a junction on the Scottish Midland Junction Railway to Methven. The capital cost was to be £25,000, of which £7,000 was to be contributed by the Scottish Midland Junction Railway, who also undertook to work the line with their plant. No particular engineering difficulties were anticipated, there being no tunnels, only moderate gradients, the maximum being 1 in 80, and favourable curves, the tightest being 17½ chains. The Bill was to have been opposed by the Scottish Central Railway, but on the day they were not represented and the Bill was passed unopposed.

The company lost little time in making a start on construction, and three weeks later the Engineer for the line, Mr Thomas Mitchell, placed an advertisement in the *Perthshire Advertiser* for 600 tons of rails (to be 65lb per yard) and 130 tons of cast iron chairs, to be delivered to Perth by 10th February 1857. The sleepers for the line were sourced locally, being acquired from a large stockpile already lying at Crieff station. By the end of December, a contract was let to Messrs Kerr & Crighton of Bankfoot for construction of the line at a cost of £2,000 per mile.

The first turf was cut on 3rd February 1857, without, it would seem, any great ceremony, and work proceeded rapidly. As was anticipated, the works were of a light nature, except for a cutting at Lochty just east of Almondbank station, there being few earthworks or bridges by virtue of the comparatively flat nature of the country through which the line ran. While work was in progress, a further advertisement was placed on 11th June inviting tenders for the construction of a station house and goods shed at the Methven terminus.

869

ANNO DECIMO NONO & VICESIMO

VICTORIÆ REGINÆ.

Cap. cxxxvi.

An Act for making a Railway from the *Scottish Midland Junction* Railway near the *Dunkeld Road Bridge* to *Methven* in the County of *Perth*. [29th *July* 1856.]

WHEREAS the making of a Railway from the *Scottish Midland Junction* Railway, from a Point near to the Bridge over the *Dunkeld* Turnpike Road in the *East Church* Parish of *Perth* to a Point at or near to the Village of *Methven* in the Parish of *Methven* in the County of *Perth*, would be of local and public Advantage: And whereas the Persons herein-after named, together with others, are willing at their own Expense to carry such Undertaking into execution: And whereas it is expedient that the Company to be incorporated for that Purpose and the *Scottish Midland Junction* Railway Company should be enabled to enter into Arrangements for the working and Use of the said Railway; but these Objects cannot be effected without the Authority of Parliament: May it therefore please Your Majesty that it may be enacted; and be it enacted by the Queen's most Excellent Majesty, by and with the Advice and Consent of the Lords Spiritual and Temporal, and Commons, in this present Parliament assembled, and by the Authority of the same, as follows:

I. In citing this Act for any Purpose whatever it shall be sufficient to use the Expression "The *Perth, Almond Valley, and Methven* Railway Act, 1856." Short Title.

[*Local.*] 23 *P* II. "The

Figure 1.9
The Perth Almond Valley & Methven Railway Act which received the Royal Assent on 29th July 1856. The preamble refers to the Scottish Midland Junction Railway, as it was at that time, although by the time the line to Methven opened it had been absorbed by the Scottish North Eastern Railway. The Act did, however, make provision for the impending amalgamation of the Scottish Midland Junction Railway with the Aberdeen Railway to form the Scottish North Eastern Railway, such that all the powers and provisions contained in the Act applying to the former would pass to the latter if and when the Bill proposing the amalgamation passed into law. ***Author's collection***

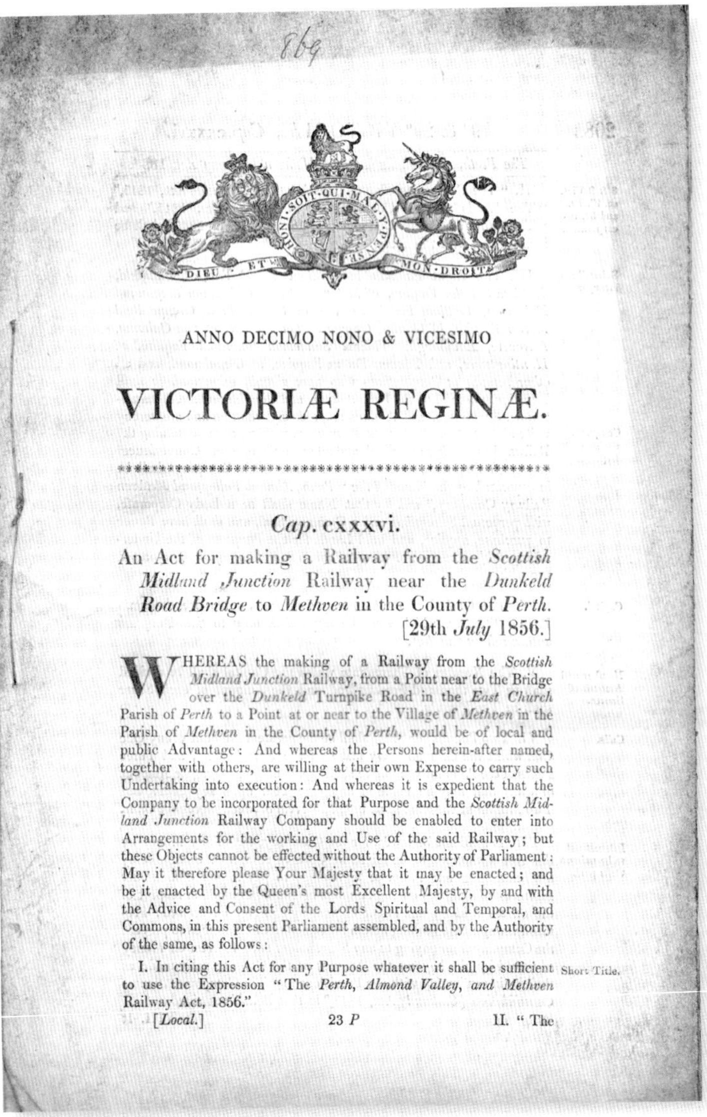

By August the work on the line was well advanced and it was forecast that it would be open for Christmas. The line was finished in October, only eight months after work had started, and the completed line was then inspected by Captain Tyler Royal Engineers, on behalf of the Board of Trade. It soon became evident, however, that in their eagerness to complete the line, the contractors had allowed standards to slip, and Captain Tyler found it far from satisfactory. He reported that only four sleepers had been laid per 16-foot length of rail whereas five were required, and he found three of the smaller bridges to be unsafe. In some places he noted that the ballast was only two or three inches deep beneath the track, as opposed to the 12 to 14 inches required, and in one place the sleepers were laid directly onto the clay bed of a cutting. He also recommended that a turntable be installed at Methven and that more signals be erected for the protection of level crossings.

These shortcomings were not sufficient to prevent the line opening for goods traffic, however, and on 22nd October a notice was published by Mr Thomas Johnson, the General Manager, who was then based at the General Station in Perth, to the effect that the line would be open for such traffic from Monday, 2nd November 1857.

Most, but not all, of Captain Tyler's recommendations had been carried out by the time he came for a second visit on 19th December 1857. As a result, the opening of the line was again delayed and the date for opening was finally fixed for 1st January 1858. Again this would seem to have occurred without any great ceremony, perhaps because the date had been several times delayed.

The line diverged from the Scottish North Eastern Railway's Aberdeen line about a mile and half north of Perth, it then followed a westerly route, passing south of Almondbank, and, about a mile past Tibbermore, turned northwards to Methven. There was only one intermediate station – at Almondbank – although there were also two halts – at Ruthven Road and Tibbermuir level crossings – where trains stopped by request. Tickets from these halts were issued by the guard and, as the regulations stipulated, no change was given. The line was operated initially on the 'One Engine in Steam' principle as described in Chapter 9.

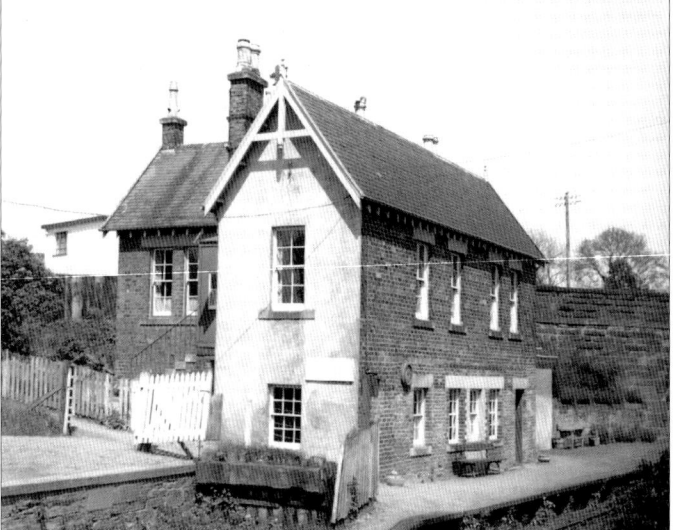

Plate 1.10
At the only intermediate station on the Perth Almond Valley & Methven Railway, Almondbank, the station house was a one off. The long narrow design was probably a matter of necessity given the limitations of the available land between the Perth to Crieff road and the platform. This house, slightly altered, survives today as a private residence. ***Author***

CHAPTER 1: RAILWAYS REACH CRIEFF

Plate 1.11
The passenger terminus station of the Perth Almond Valley & Methven Railway at Methven was the rather unprepossessing structure seen here. The line continued some way beyond this to the goods station, but passenger accommodation was fairly basic, with no awning over the platform. It survived for many years after the line closed to passengers in 1937, being used, as seen here, as the goods office. Interestingly, the building still retained its enamel Caledonian Railway trespass sign, seen here in 1961, nearly forty years after that railway was absorbed by the LM&SR. *Norris Forrest/transporttreasury.co.uk*

Initially the railway only provided a basic service of just two trains each way per day, but by May this had been increased to three, and during the summer months of August and September a further evening train was added. The journey time was 30 minutes from Perth to Methven and between 30 and 35 minutes from Methven to Perth, depending on other main line traffic at the junction:

Timetable for February 1858

Perth	8.30am	3.45pm
Almondbank	8.45am	4.00pm
Methven	9.00am	4.15pm
Methven	10.15am	5.00pm
Almondbank	10.30am	5.15pm
Perth	10.45am	5.30pm

Timetable for May 1858

Perth	8.30am	3.45pm	6.45pm
Almondbank	8.45am	4.05pm	7.05pm
Methven	9.00am	4.15pm	7.20pm
Methven	10.15am	12.00pm	5.00pm
Almondbank	10.30am	12.15pm	5.15pm
Perth	10.45am	12.35pm	5.30pm

Timetable for August 1858

Perth	8.30am	3.45pm	6.45pm	8.20pm
Almondbank	8.45am	4.05pm	7.05pm	8.35pm
Methven	9.00am	4.15pm	7.20pm	8.50pm
Methven	10.15am	12.00pm	5.00pm	9.00pm
Almondbank	10.30am	12.15pm	5.15pm	9.15pm
Perth	10.45am	12.35pm	5.30pm	9.30pm

The first Half Yearly meeting of the Perth Almond Valley & Methven Railway was held on 12th March 1858 in the Secretary's Office at 68, St. John Street, Perth, with Lord Mansfield in the chair. It was recorded that expenditure to date had been £19,723 16s 2d. The total cost of the line was under £4,000 per mile, which was claimed to be considerably less than any other line, and half the cost of many single lines.

The potential for Methven to act as a railhead for traffic between Perth and Crieff was soon appreciated, and the first proposals to run a coach between Crieff and Methven to connect with trains to and from Perth were raised at the beginning of July. The coach service, providing two journeys each way per day, started running the following year, in May 1859. The total journey time was some 2¼ hours and avoided the long wait at Crieff Junction, which had been the cause of regular complaints by patrons of the Crieff Junction Railway.

As a tourist destination, Methven could never match Crieff, which attracted excursion trains from Perth and beyond, but the company did run excursions for the benefit of the local population. The first of these, on 1st August 1858, conveyed a number of passengers, including workers from Tulloch and Ruthvenfield, to Dunkeld, rounding off the day at Birnam Hotel gardens where they were entertained by the Rifle Band.

The second Half Yearly meeting was held on 29th September 1858, being chaired by Mr Thomson of Balgowan in the absence of Lord Mansfield. The accounts showed that expenditure up to 31st July was £24,566 8s 9d, which included £1,839 being the cost of a locomotive and a number of goods wagons. These had been purchased to reduce the charges due to the Scottish North Eastern Railway. Mr Mitchell commented favourably that:

> '*The little injury being done in consequence of the lightness of the tank engine lately purchased and for some time in use, and which is admirably adapted for this railway, the uphold should be at a very low rate. This engine performs the whole work of the line in a very satisfactory manner.*'

He also reported that the goods sheds at Almondbank and Methven, an engine shed at Methven and a house for the crossing keeper at Ruthvenfield had been erected, and that a similar house for the pointsman at the junction with the Scottish North Eastern Railway was under construction. A siding and loading bank had also been laid at Huntingtower to cater for traffic from the bleach fields, which were a feature of the local bleaching and dyeing industry.

The first winter of 1858/9 was evidently a quiet one for the railway, and the Half Yearly meeting held on 25th March 1859 was equally quiet, being described as *'sparsely attended'*. There was little more the local paper could say for, as was reported, the meeting was held in private, as all previous meetings had been, with the press being expressly excluded. However, it was understood that traffic levels were increasing satisfactorily, although no dividend was declared.

In May the coach service between Crieff and Methven started running, which no doubt contributed to a continued increase in passenger traffic, and in July a large excursion travelled over the line. This was an interesting example of Victorian philanthropy, for 300 passengers from a works in Dundee arrived at Almondbank by train to *'spend the day at the country residence of their kind and generous master, Edward Caird Esq, Cromwell Park'*. Having been met at the station, the whole party, led by Mr Caird and his family, and accompanied by two bands and a number of flags, made their way to Cromwell Park to the cheers of onlookers. The trippers then visited the pleasure gardens at Lynedoch before having tea at Cromwell Park and departing by the special excursion train at 5.30pm.

The fortunes of the railway evidently continued to improve during the summer months, for the following Half Yearly meeting at the beginning of October was decidedly more upbeat. It was reported that the total expenditure in the Capital Account now stood at £29,715 8s 6½d, which was in excess of the original anticipated cost of £25,000, although it was pointed out that the bulk of this overspend was accounted for by the unplanned expenditure of £2,859 16s 9d on the locomotive and rolling stock. It was anticipated that this expenditure would be *'beneficial and economical'* for the company due to the savings in running costs. A comparison of traffic revenues for 1859 with those for the previous year showed an encouraging increase:

Passengers, Horses, Carriages, Dogs	£119 4s 8d
Goods and Minerals	£41 8s 1d
Livestock and Parcels	£7 14s 8d
Total increase for 1859 over 1858	£168 7s 5d

It was hoped that the Directors would soon be able to declare a dividend.

The end of the year brought a change in management of the railway as a consequence of the appointment of the current Manager and Secretary, Thomas Johnston, who was also the Scottish North Eastern Railway representative at Perth, to the post of General Manager of the Forth & Clyde Railway. He was replaced by Mr Henderson, the Scottish North Eastern Railway Manager at Montrose who was moved to Perth as their representative, and thus also became Manager and Secretary of the Perth Almond Valley & Methven Railway.

The next Half Yearly meeting in April 1860 was an interesting affair in that it had to be held at Glasgow Road station in Perth. This station had been built by the Scottish North Eastern Railway, due to a dispute with the Scottish Central Railway preventing the use of Perth General station except on payment of higher rates. The poor little Perth Almond Valley & Methven Railway was caught in the middle of this dispute in which it had no part, but being operated by the Scottish North Eastern Railway it was logical that the meeting be held at their new, and hopefully temporary, station. Despite a further increase in traffic revenue of £124 18s 7d over the previous year, the Board reported an excess of expenditure over income of £377 2s 11d,

indicating a continued rise in running costs. In fact revenue had risen progressively each half year:

– 31st July 1858	£649 12s 4d
– 31st January 1859	£781 18s 2d
– 31st July 1859	£817 19s 9d
– 31st January 1860	£906 16s 9d

One source of expenditure which was seemingly producing these pressures on the company's finances was the charges due to the Scottish North Eastern Railway for the use of their rolling stock and, when required, locomotives. The Board stated that they were contemplating purchasing one Composite and two Third Class carriages to reduce reliance on the Scottish North Eastern Railway. Their experience would seem to have been somewhat similar to the Crieff Junction Railway who had suffered from similar problems with the costs of their agreement with the Scottish Central Railway.

An interesting reference to the line was made in a notice in the *Perthshire Courier* of 18th April 1860, when a field on the Markfield Farm was advertised to let, stating that it was about one mile from Almond Bank station and half a mile from Gloagburn Siding on the Methven Railway. The name 'Almond Bank' was sometimes used for that station, but from the early days the railway always referred to it as 'Almondbank'. Similarly, 'Gloagburn Siding' was a title never used, despite being just north of the farm of that name, the halt being titled 'Tibbermuir Siding', later 'Tibbermuir Halt'. Again this name is sometimes referred to as 'Tibbermore', the name of the adjacent village, whereas the actual name 'Tibbermuir' was taken from the nearby Battle of Tibbermuir fought in 1644.

A less welcome mention in the local press came in the form of a letter from an aggrieved passenger who had travelled up from England to visit relatives in Almondbank. Unfamiliar with Perth station, he had followed the signs for the 'Methven and Almondbank Railway' with a finger board pointing to a row of about eight carriages with an engine at the front. He took his seat in the train and waited for it to leave. Hearing the engine start off he was alarmed to see that the carriage he was in was not moving, and looked up to see the engine departing with the first two carriages, leaving him stranded in one of the remaining six! To add insult to injury, the booking office clerk refused a refund, telling him that *'We never give back money'*. The unfortunate traveller had some caustic comments to make about the management or lack thereof of the Almond Valley Railway.

The Half Yearly meeting in October was held as usual in Perth General station, the disagreement between the Scottish North Eastern Railway and Scottish Central Railway presumably having been resolved. The Directors reported that the total expenditure in the Capital Account had now risen to £30,899 1s 3½d, an increase of a further £1,091 15s 5d, but there had been an increase in the Revenue Account of £286 8s 5½d and savings had been made on carriage workings. The Directors also held that they needed to purchase another locomotive as, although the existing engine was adequate, it often needed maintenance or repairs. They were looking for a second-hand engine at a cost of between £600 and £800 for use in emergencies. This measure was approved and an advertisement placed the following month.

In January 1861, to mark the third anniversary of the opening of the line, the employees of the railway, together with their wives and sweethearts, attended a festival held in the parish school room at Methven. Seventy people attended the event chaired by Mr Henderson, the Manager. Toasts given included *'Success to the railway'* and the evening concluded with a ball which went on until 3.30am when a special train conveyed the Perth guests home. The evening was judged to be such a success that it was proposed to repeat the event the following year.

During the winter of 1860/61, the company's financial situation improved considerably. Revenue increased by a further £314 14s 5d, not only balancing the deficit from the previous six months, but also offsetting the cost of the second-hand locomotive, and even producing a modest surplus of £55 12s 9½d. The extensive repairs to the original tank engine had resulted in a 100% increase in expenditure, so the company had proceeded to purchase a second-hand locomotive for only £400. This turnaround in the company's fortunes was maintained over the summer months; at the following meeting in October the Board were able to report a further increase in revenue of £203 17s 3d and for the first time were able to declare a dividend. Set at a modest 2%, it was stated that they hoped to raise it to 3%. Progress was indeed sustained through the winter of 1861/2 and at the meeting in March 1862 they were able to declare a dividend of 2½%. This was despite the general depression and the poor potato harvest in the autumn of 1861, which was down by 50%.

However 1862 was not a good year for the Perth Almond Valley & Methven Railway, as a combination of the continued depression in trade and a decrease in agricultural products, mainly potatoes, upon which the line depended heavily, led to a decline in traffic over the summer. Traffic revenue over the six months was down £107 5s 9½d compared with the previous year, but despite this, the Directors felt able to recommend a dividend of 2%. The continuing financial pressures on this small line were evidently a cause for concern and the future of the company was in some doubt.

On 27th December 1862 the *Perthshire Courier* reported that the Perth Almond Valley & Methven Railway was to be sold to the Scottish North Eastern Railway, although this would not take effect until an Act of Parliament had been obtained, which would probably not be before 1864. Unlike the rumours which had surrounded the Crieff Junction Railway, this story was not refuted and the following month the paper reaffirmed the report, adding that the Scottish North Eastern Railway would operate and manage the line until then.

That there was some substance to these reports was reflected in the fact that a Special General Meeting was called in March 1863, a few days prior to the scheduled Half Yearly meeting, to consider options for the way ahead. A proposal was considered whereby the Perth Almond Valley & Methven Railway would be leased in perpetuity to the Scottish North Eastern Railway. The latter would pay all the obligations of the Perth Almond Valley & Methven Railway and would pay 4% for each £100 of Stock.

The report by the Board at the Half Yearly meeting which followed made gloomy reading. It stated that there had been a falling off of traffic for some time, that the effect on a small line such as theirs was more severe. To underline this, it reported that the fall in potato traffic, an important source of revenue, had been as much as two thirds of the traffic carried in previous years. The Directors, however, struck a more positive note in support of the proposed amalgamation, stating that *'There was no reason why shareholders should fear as to the ultimate results of the line, for although they were not sufficient to pay 2½% yet, in future the Scottish North Eastern Railway would pay 4%.'*

Interestingly, while the meeting was mainly concerned with the demise of one small railway, concerns were raised regarding reports of yet another new railway, namely a proposed line to Crieff. This had been mooted some years previously, but was evidently now being considered more seriously. The concern expressed at the meeting that *'Methven would become a mere siding ... and in that case Methven would be much damaged'* was prophetic, and would become a reality in the next few years. At this juncture, however, it was stated that the meeting were unaware of any plans formed, nor of any schemes, and the subject was dropped.

Following adoption of the proposals which had been discussed at the Special General Meeting, the Scottish North Eastern Railway took over the running of the line and matters evidently began to improve. Revenue began to rise again and at the autumn meeting a dividend of 4% was declared, as had been forecast.

In August of 1863, officials of the Scottish North Eastern Railway travelled over the line judging entries for the Best Kept Station prizes. At that time there were only the two stations, Almondbank and Methven, and sadly history does not record who won that year, but the Best Kept Station competition was perpetuated by the Caledonian, which was to take over the Scottish North Eastern Railway only two years later, and of course by the London Midland & Scottish Railway (LM&SR), and even British Railways. In the years to come, local stations were to feature regularly in the list of prize winners. Another notable event that summer was the arrival of Volunteer battalions by special trains from Dundee and Perth to participate in a rifle match at Almond Valley.

A more light-hearted incident, redolent of life on a small rural branch line, occurred in May when a Mr Robert McLean of Perth was found guilty of the theft of four hares from Mr Colin Drummond while on the Methven Railway. History does not record exactly what happened, but suffice it to say that McLean, who absconded, was arrested and, having previous convictions for theft, was sentenced

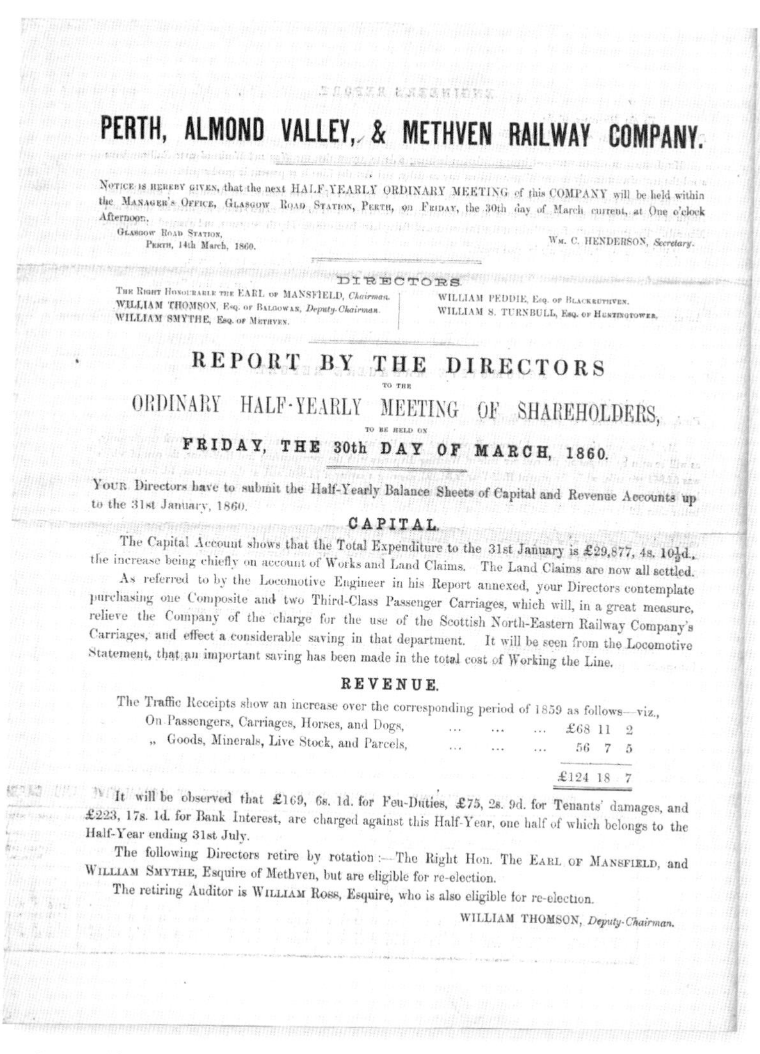

PERTH, ALMOND VALLEY, & METHVEN RAILWAY COMPANY.

NOTICE IS HEREBY GIVEN, that the next HALF-YEARLY ORDINARY MEETING of this COMPANY will be held within the MANAGER'S OFFICE, GLASGOW ROAD STATION, PERTH, on FRIDAY, the 30th day of March current, at One o'clock Afternoon.

GLASGOW ROAD STATION,
PERTH, 14th March, 1860.

WM. C. HENDERSON, *Secretary.*

DIRECTORS.

THE RIGHT HONOURABLE THE EARL OF MANSFIELD, *Chairman.*
WILLIAM THOMSON, ESQ. OF BALGOWAN, *Deputy-Chairman.*
WILLIAM SMYTHE, ESQ. OF METHVEN.
WILLIAM PEDDIE, ESQ. OF BLACKRUTHVEN.
WILLIAM S. TURNBULL, ESQ. OF HUNTINGTOWER.

REPORT BY THE DIRECTORS

TO THE

ORDINARY HALF-YEARLY MEETING OF SHAREHOLDERS,

TO BE HELD ON

FRIDAY, THE 30th DAY OF MARCH, 1860.

YOUR Directors have to submit the Half-Yearly Balance Sheets of Capital and Revenue Accounts up to the 31st January, 1860.

CAPITAL.

The Capital Account shows that the Total Expenditure to the 31st January is £29,877, 4s. 10½d., the increase being chiefly on account of Works and Land Claims. The Land Claims are now all settled.

As referred to by the Locomotive Engineer in his Report annexed, your Directors contemplate purchasing one Composite and two Third-Class Passenger Carriages, which will, in a great measure, relieve the Company of the charge for the use of the Scottish North-Eastern Railway Company's Carriages, and effect a considerable saving in that department. It will be seen from the Locomotive Statement, that an important saving has been made in the total cost of Working the Line.

REVENUE.

The Traffic Receipts show an increase over the corresponding period of 1859 as follows—viz.,

On Passengers, Carriages, Horses, and Dogs, ...	£68	11	2
„ Goods, Minerals, Live Stock, and Parcels, ...	56	7	5
	£124	18	7

It will be observed that £169, 6s. 1d. for Feu-Duties, £75, 2s. 9d. for Tenants' damages, and £223, 17s. 1d. for Bank Interest, are charged against this Half-Year, one half of which belongs to the Half-Year ending 31st July.

The following Directors retire by rotation:—The Right Hon. The EARL OF MANSFIELD, and WILLIAM SMYTHE, Esquire of Methven, but are eligible for re-election.

The retiring Auditor is WILLIAM ROSS, Esquire, who is also eligible for re-election.

WILLIAM THOMSON, *Deputy-Chairman.*

Figure 1.10
The Perth Almond Valley & Methven Railway Half Yearly report by the Directors for the meeting on 30th March 1860. The only known surviving piece of ephemera from this little company. This included a statement by the SNER engineer, Mr Willett, that the Pow Burn having been diverted at Almondbank, additional sidings had been laid. Mr Yarrow, the SNER Locomotive Manager reported favourably on the reduction in running costs but recommended that if the PAV&MR were to purchase their own carriages this would be more economical. *Courtesy Ian Dinmore*

to sixty days imprisonment. Quite apart from poaching, legitimate hunting was also quite common in such rural areas, and it is worth noting that the Scottish North Eastern Railway timetable poster of the period included a warning that passengers were forbidden from boarding the company's trains with loaded firearms.

The final year of the Perth Almond Valley & Methven Railway, 1864, saw the line continue to prosper under the Scottish North Eastern Railway. The Half Yearly meeting in March was a formality, with the declaration of a 4% dividend and notification that the Scottish North Eastern Railway was in the process of promoting a Bill in Parliament before the amalgamation. It was noted that the Parliamentary Committee report stipulated that '*The Bill does not authorise construction of any new work*', thus preventing it being used as a pretext for any expansion westwards. It was also noteworthy that the meeting was again chaired by Mr W Thompson of Balgowan, not only because Lord Mansfield had effectively stepped back from that role following the takeover by the Scottish North Eastern Railway, but also as Mr Thompson was a leading light in the nascent Crieff & Methven Junction Railway.

The true nature of the Scottish North Eastern Railway's intentions was reflected in statements made at the Special General Meeting of that company held in Aberdeen to consider the takeover of the Perth Almond Valley & Methven Railway, when it was reported that traffic on the line was quite up to expectations and steadily increasing but, more importantly, that '*When the Crieff and Methven line opened, they would have large addition to the traffic*'. A week later, on 27th May 1864, the Perth Almond Valley & Methven Railway also held a Special General Meeting, the last recorded, to consider '*The Bill now before Parliament*'. It was concluded that the Bill was in accordance with the agreement with the Scottish North Eastern Railway and it was duly approved. This final meeting of the company was again chaired by Mr Thompson. Barely a month later, on 23rd June 1864, the Bill received the Royal Assent and the Perth Almond Valley & Methven Railway ceased to exist.

Thus, another small railway, embarked upon with such enthusiasm and the high hopes of its promoters, had fallen victim to the harsh economic realities of the times and had been absorbed by one of the larger companies. However, the line would continue to play its part in the development of railways in Strathearn, and it would outlast not only the Scottish North Eastern Railway, but also the Caledonian, which was to take that company over only a few short years later.

CRIEFF & METHVEN JUNCTION RAILWAY

The idea of a railway between Crieff and Perth by way of the Pow Burn valley first arose long before any of the railways of Strathearn came into being, when in 1821 no less a person than Robert Stephenson surveyed a route from Aberdeen to Crieff. Stephenson tended to favour lines with easy gradients and avoided major earthworks as far as possible. His route followed a line not dissimilar to the Strathmore line through Angus which was eventually built, but his main line then headed along the Pow Burn valley to Crieff, with a short branch to Perth. Nothing ever came of this project, but, as already mentioned, the Crieff to Perth route was also surveyed in 1844 as one of the two possible routes for the Scottish Central Railway from Stirling to Perth. In the event, this part of the route was not chosen and, as part of the 1845 Act, the Scottish Central Railway undertook to construct a branch line to Crieff. This they never did, but what they did do was to successfully oppose a Bill for the Crieff and Perth Direct Railway which would have provided unwelcome competition for their own Crieff branch.

The Scottish Central Railway having failed to fulfil its promise to build a branch line to Crieff, and having allowed the powers vested in the 1845 Act to lapse, a separate company was established in 1853 and the line opened in 1856. A contemporary account of the Crieff & Methven Junction Railway commented that '*The success of that line, from the first, exceeded the expectations of its promoters and sufficiently proved the importance of the district as a source of railway traffic*'. It being stated:

'*But there were more important motives which exercised their influence on public opinion. The town of Crieff, even at this time (1863) had become a favourite place of summer resort; and it lay in the centre of a wide agricultural district. The Scottish North Eastern Railway Company had already formed a branch line to Methven. The space intervening between Crieff and the west most point of that line consisted of fertile land, 10½ miles in length. To construct a line along this vale and effect a junction with the Methven branch near Methven seemed the necessary complement of a proper railway system. And the Scottish North Eastern Railway Coy had promised to grant running powers over their branch to Perth, in which city important railway systems converged.*'

The so-called 'railway mania' was still rife. In May 1856 it was reported that the Caledonian Railway proposed a railway from Callander to Methven, a distance of 33 miles, by way of Glen Artney, Comrie and Crieff, but nothing further was heard of the idea. In September that year Messrs Blyth of Edinburgh actually made a survey of a line from the Crieff Junction Railway to the Methven line; however by December it was reported that this scheme had also fallen through, stating that '*The recent state of the money markets have deterred lenders*'.

The desirability of a line completing the link from Crieff to Perth had been raised by various individuals on a number of occasions, added to which was the discontent expressed over the time and inconvenience involved in a rail journey from Crieff to Perth via Crieff Junction. The introduction of a coach between Crieff and Methven in 1859 to connect with trains to Perth further illustrated the potential value of a direct railway link along the Pow Burn valley. In commenting on this proposed coach service from Crieff to Methven, *The Perthshire Advertiser* reported that:

'*It is only a question of time when the Methven Railway be extended to Crieff, and we have no doubt the experiment of trying a new coach to Methven will be advantageous to the shareholders of that line, and will teach the Directors of the Crieff Junction Railway a salutary lesson.*'

The contemporary account of the Crieff & Methven Junction Railway went on to say:

'*In these circumstances it is not a matter of wonder that the expediency of constructing a railway became a favourite topic of conversation. A meeting of those friendly to the scheme was convened, and held within the Drummond Arms Hotel, Crieff, on 14th May 1863. It was attended by many landowners, merchants, farmers and others. A railway was resolved upon, and means taken to elect a committee to further that end.*'

J Maxtone Graham Esq. of Cultoquhey, and DR Williamson Esq. of Lawers, took a leading part in the proceedings. A provisional committee was soon formed, consisting of fourteen landowners, with power to add to their number. This power was wisely exercised and the committee enlarged to thirty-four members, representing all classes interested. Sir David Dundas of Dunira was appointed Chairman, and Mr Maxtone Graham Vice-Chairman. It was significant that two of the principal promoters of the line were DR Williamson Esq. of Lawers, which was an estate between Crieff and Comrie, and Sir David Dundas whose large estate lay between Comrie and St. Fillans. Williamson would later go on to become Chairman of the Crieff & Comrie Railway and a Director of the Lochearnhead,

St. Fillans & Comrie Railway, while Sir David Dundas became Chairman of the Crieff Junction Railway.

The Provisional Committee then set about the necessary preparatory work. All the landowners along the line gave their assent to the proposed railway and agreed to take a feu-duty for the land required, to be referred to an '*eminent land valuator*'. Some interesting conditions were subsequently attached to the agreements by certain individuals (for an example, see page 32). A meeting was held at Methven in November 1861 for those in favour of a railway to Crieff, with Mr Anderson Henry of Woodend near Madderty in the chair. Those proposing the line estimated it would cost less than £50,000 to build and, following completion of a survey later that month, it was considered that '*The expense will be trifling compared with the other railways*'. The 10-mile line would be 7 miles shorter than the existing Crieff to Perth route by way of Crieff Junction. Mr Thomas Bouch, who had been the engineer for the Crieff Junction Railway, was appointed Engineer for the line, and John Ironside and Alexander Graham, solicitors, were made Joint Secretaries. Ironside had been the original Secretary of the Crieff Junction Railway (see Figure 1.7).

In publishing their Prospectus, the Directors, in consequence of the North British Railway Bill for a line between Edinburgh and Perth via Queensferry, declared that the object of the Crieff & Methven was to:

'*More fully develop the agricultural, commercial and manufacturing resources of Upper Strathearn and to open up a less expensive, more direct and expeditious communication with City of Perth, with the lime and coal fields of Fife, and the Northern and Southern markets.*'

The engineer estimated the cost of the undertaking at £50,000. Share Capital was to be raised by 5,000 shares of £10 each, but by October 1863 scarcely one half of the shares had been taken up. As a result, the Chairman travelled to Aberdeen for a meeting with the Directors of the Scottish North Eastern Railway '*to know whether they were disposed to assist. That Company willingly agreed to contribute one half of the amount and to become joint promoters of the Bill in Parliament*'. When the Committee met in December, it was reported that £7,400 had been subscribed by supporters in the district and that it was anticipated that the full amount of £50,000 would be raised by the end of the year. It was hoped that the railway would be open by Whitsuntide 1865.

The Crieff & Methven Junction Railway Bill was read in Parliament for the first and second times in February 1864, and the following month it was reported that the project received favourable comment in the Half Yearly meeting of the Scottish North Eastern Railway. At the third reading of the Bill in April, the report presented to the Committee commented that the existing Crieff Junction Railway '*did not meet the needs of the locality*' but that three-quarters of the proprietors along the whole length of the new proposed line were in favour. In terms of traffic: drainage materials, lime and manure were in demand, but that cartage was expensive, that large quantities of potatoes were grown locally and that large numbers of Highland cattle and sheep were sent to the district annually to graze. It was also said that locals were burning peat and wood because coal had become too expensive. Interestingly, it also reported that Mr McArthur, stationmaster at Methven supported the line.

The Committee endorsed the preamble to the report, but required that the new company use the existing Crieff Junction Railway terminus at Crieff and that the line be doubled over the last 9 furlongs into Crieff for the use of both companies. This would have required a junction near Highlandman. The two companies, however, were unable to reach an agreement on this, the result being two parallel lines running into Crieff, two separate stations, two goods depots, and two engine sheds. The planned station was to have been just to the north of the existing Crieff Junction Railway terminus but was never built. Consequently, when the line opened both railways had to share the original station. The anomaly of the parallel tracks into Crieff survived until 1964, each with its own level crossings and signalling, while the number of engine sheds continued to grow until at its peak Crieff had no less than three separate engine sheds, as is described in more detail in Chapter 6.

By September 1864, it was reported that the Engineer had measured the line and was seeking estimates from contractors. Work was expected to begin in the near future and it was anticipated that the first turf would be cut in a week or two. This, as was often the case, proved to be optimistic and it was not until a meeting on 21st February 1865 at the Drummond Arms Hotel that contracts were let. Mr John Granger of Perth was appointed prime contractor, and

Figure 1.11
The Crieff & Methven Junction Railway Act which received the Royal Assent on 14th July 1864. This Act made provision for two railways, the line from the Perth Almond Valley & Methven Railway to Crieff which was built and also a short spur from the proposed Crieff & Methven line to the Methven branch line. This connection, which would have allowed direct running from Crieff to Methven without the need to reverse direction at Methven Junction, was never built and the powers allowed to lapse. This Act also preserved the provisions of the previous Perth Almond Valley & Methven and Scottish North Eastern Railway Acts relating to that line. *Author's collection*

Perth and Crieff Trains.

	STATIONS	DOWN TRAINS					STATIONS	UP TRAINS			
Miles		1 1, 3 P. Class. a.m.	2 Mixed. 1, 3 P. Class. p.m.	3 1, 3 P. Class. p.m.	4 1, 3 P. Class. p.m.	Miles		1 1, 3 P. Class. a.m.	2 1, 3 P. Class. a.m.	3 Mixed. 1, 3 P. Class. p.m.	4 1, 3 P. Class. p.m.
	Dundee (Cal.) dep.	8 0	....	3 3	6 15		Crieff .... dep.	8 20	11 15	3 0	6 0
	Perth "	9 50	12 55	4 25	7 30	2	Innerpeffray "	8 25	11 20	3 8	6 5
4	Almond Bank "	10 2	1 15	4 37	7 42	4	Abercairney "	8 30	11 25	3 16	6 10
6¼	Methven Junc. "	10 7	1 25	4 42	7 47	6¼	Madderty "	8 37	11 32	3 25	6 17
8	Methven {ar.	10 27	....	5 2	8 7	8½	Balgowan "	8 42	11 37	3 35	6 22
	{dep.	9 52	....	4 27	7 22	11¼	Methven Jun. "	8 48	11 43	3 44	6 28
9	Balgowan "	10 13	1 35	4 48	7 53	12¼	Methven {ar.	9 18	12 3	....	6 48
11¼	Madderty "	10 19	1 44	4 54	7 59		{dep.	8 33	11 32	....	6 13
13¼	Abercairney "	10 25	1 53	5 0	8 5	13¼	Almond Bank "	8 53	11 48	4 0	6 33
15¼	Innerpeffray "	10 30	2 0	5 5	8 10	17¼	Perth "	9 5	12 0p	4 15	6 45
17¼	Crieff ar.	10 35	....	5 10	8 15		Dundee (Cal.) ar.	10 10	1 15	....	8 20

Ruthven Road and Tibbermuir Crossings.

Nos. 1 and 2 Down and Nos. 2 and 3 Up Trains will not stop at Ruthven Road nor Tibbermuir Crossings, except on Saturdays, when No. 3 Up Train will stop at Ruthven Road

Passengers by Nos. 3 and 4 Down Trains wishing to be set down at these places, will require to inform the Guard at Perth. Nos. 1, and 4 Up Trains will stop when signalled by the Gatekeepers to do so. The Guard will issue Tickets, but will not provide change.

☞ Only one Engine in steam, or two or more Engines coupled together, shall, under any circumstances, be on the Perth and Crieff Section at one and the same time, between Crieff Junction and Crieff, until further notice, without a special order from the Manager. The attention of the Station Masters at Perth and Crieff is very specially drawn to this Rule.

Figure 1.12
The Scottish North Eastern Railway Working Time Table for the Perth to Crieff line in 1866. Although Ruthven Road and Tibbermuir were not shown in the timetable, instructions regarding passengers joining or leaving trains at these halts were included. Note that passenger trains by then had only First and Third Class, but as the letter 'P' indicated, were all Parliamentary trains. The instructions also indicate that at this date the line was worked under 'One Engine in Steam' regulations. Such an arrangement for the Methven branch is not mentioned as at this time trains on that short section were still horse drawn.
Courtesy David Ferguson

was to supply all the materials other than rails, chairs, fishplates &c. Contracts for these were awarded to:

- Darlington Iron Co   Rails, fishplates, nuts & bolts
- J Whitelaw Dunfermline Foundry   Chairs
- Bass & Sons. Workington   Spikes

The first turf was cut on 23rd March 1865, the event being fully covered in the local press. It was reported that *'the ceremony of the cutting of the first sod promised to be one of the most spectacular events Crieff had seen for a number of years'*. A special ceremonial wheelbarrow and spade were made by Messrs Martins, cabinet makers, who proudly displayed the finished articles in their King Street premises. The date was fixed for 23rd March 1865. Stands were erected on the site of the ceremony and seats had to be booked in advance. The ceremony began with a procession which started off from the High Street at 12.45pm, consisting of the Directors, Burgh Councillors, office bearers, other important townsfolk and local dignitaries. The actual cutting of the first sod was performed by Mrs Maxtone Graham of Cultoquhey, wife of one of the Directors. A crowd of over 5,000 people watched, while music was provided by a band of the 8th Perthshire Rifles (Volunteers). An official reception was held afterwards in the Drummond Arms Hotel.

The handsome wheelbarrow and spade were afterwards presented to Mrs Maxtone Graham. Both bore commemorative silver plaques, engraved as follows:

'Presented by Sir David Dundas, Baronet of Dunira, Chairman; Sir Patrick Murray, Baronet of Ochtertyre; Charles H Drummond Moray Esq. of Abercairny; James Graham of Cultoquhey, Deputy Chairman; John Stirling Esq. of Kippendavie; J Anderson Henry Esq. of Woodend; William Lawson Esq. of Aberdeen; the first Directors of the Crieff & Methven Junction Railway – to Mrs Maxton Graham of Cultoquhey and Redgorton in grateful acknowledgement of her services in cutting the first turf of the railway at Crieff upon the 23rd day of March 1865.'

Work commenced immediately and progressed fairly rapidly owing to the comparative lack of major earthworks or engineering construction needed to negotiate such an easy route. At the beginning of April it was reported that materials were being delivered to site, and that masons, carpenters and excavators were working alongside each other. By mid-May it was reported that, after eight weeks of excellent weather, work had proceeded uninterrupted. The 'Abbey Cut' near Madderty, the heaviest engineering, was progressing steadily and it was commented that *'the band of veteran navvies under the skilful and energetic direction of Mr Donald Cameron were making good progress'*.

A noteworthy comment in the *Strathearn Herald* at the time recorded that:

'The inhabitants of Madderty have much reason to congratulate themselves in being as fortunate in having such a fine body of men located among them. The great majority of workmen regularly attend church every Sunday. Many of the men have become teetotallers.'

The inhabitants of Methven, it would seem, were not so lucky, for a few weeks later another newspaper report stated: *'Last Saturday was pay day at Methven. A number of them paraded drunkenly through the village. Three were arrested. Two were sentenced to 10 days imprisonment, another 30 days'*, adding that *'Apparently no alternative of payment is given to any navvy'*.

Meanwhile, the inaugural Half Yearly meeting of the company was held at the Drummond Arms Hotel in Crieff at the end of August 1865, when Sir David Dundas was elected Chairman. Following the meeting, Mr Bouch, the Engineer, accompanied by several *'landed proprietors'* inspected the line with a view to making final adjustments. Work continued steadily throughout the summer of 1865, and by the end of October the account of the railway recorded that:

'Much progress had been made. The bridges and culverts throughout the line were all but completed. The permanent way had been laid to the extent of 8¼ miles or thereby. The permanent fencing was still further advanced. At the time it was expected that the whole works would be completed by the following March.'

In July, estimates were prepared for the several stations which it was proposed to be built. The names used were those of the locality

Plate 1.12
The major engineering feat on the Crieff & Methven Junction Railway was a long cutting just west of Madderty station. Referred to as the 'Abbey Cut' in contemporary accounts, it was so called because it was just to the south of Inchaaffray Abbey. Seen here shortly after the track was lifted, the amount of earthwork involved in its construction by hand in 1865 is evident. *Author*

in which they were sited, but in most cases were not the names chosen when the stations eventually opened. These were, as was often the case, the name of a local village, not always in close proximity to the station – as was the case of Muthill on the Crieff Junction Railway, mentioned earlier. The stations were to be at:

– Peathills   Station named Innerpeffray
– Cowdens   Station named Abercairny
– Abbey bridge   Station named Madderty
– Balgowan   Station of that name.

At this stage it was still planned to build a new station at Crieff to serve the Crieff Junction Railway, the Crieff & Methven Junction Railway and, when built, the Crieff & Comrie Railway. The existing passenger terminus was to be converted into a goods station.

The first Ordinary Meeting of the company was held on 26th November 1865, again at the Drummond Arms Hotel. At this meeting it was reported that work was well in hand and it was planned to advertise shortly for some of the additional work to be carried out. Significantly, it was also agreed to take £5,000 of shares in the Crieff & Comrie Railway. This was in response to a circular inviting subscriptions towards that undertaking which had been sent out the previous year when interest in the line had been revived under the leadership of Colonel Williamson, as he was now called. There were also developments elsewhere in Strathearn. The Caledonian Railway and Scottish Central Railway Amalgamation Act, then in the process of going through Parliament, made provision for running powers over a number of lines including both the Perth Almond Valley & Methven Railway and the Crieff & Methven Junction Railway. All was not straightforward, however, for later in the month the *Perthshire Courier* reported that the Crieff & Comrie Railway had rejected an offer of £25,000 from the Scottish North Eastern Railway and the Crieff & Methven Junction Railway, but had accepted a similar offer from the Scottish Central Railway who were to work the line.

This rivalry between the Scottish North Eastern Railway and the Scottish Central Railway, soon to be part of the Caledonian, was reflected in a report on a meeting of the Crieff Town Council in January 1866. While the benefits to Crieff of the railways was acknowledged, comments were passed on the *'grabbing attitude'* of the Crieff Junction Railway and unhappiness over the expense of

Plate 1.13
The substantial masonry bridge at the west end of Madderty station – whose platforms are just visible in the background – was referred to in contemporary accounts as 'Abbey Bridge'. Built on a skew to accommodate the line of the road, it was specifically commented upon in the report by Captain Tyler, the Board of Trade Inspector. This view was taken in May 1968, shortly after the track had been lifted. *Author*

Plate 1.14
Three of the principal intermediate stations on the Crieff & Methven Junction Railway had substantial stone houses of similar villa design, the one exception being Balgowan which had a gatehouse for the nearby level crossing. This station at Innerpeffray shows how the passenger waiting shelter was incorporated into the design. It is a testament to their quality that all three of these houses have survived as private residence. *Author*

travel on the Caledonian. It was felt that as the Caledonian already had access to Crieff through the Crieff Junction Railway, steps should be taken to prevent the Crieff & Methven Junction Railway falling into the hands of the Caledonian. Rather, it was preferable to support the claims of the North British Railway (NBR) so as to encourage competition. It was decided that a committee be appointed to look into it, but sadly no record exists of their deliberations or the outcome.

That same month, January 1866, it was also reported that work on the line was progressing rapidly and that all the permanent way, with the exception of a short distance at Crieff, had been laid. This last section had been delayed due to a dispute over the price of land at the terminus which had to be settled by arbitration. It was also reported that *'in order to open the line in the specified time'*, the Crieff & Methven Junction Railway had foregone its stated intention of a separate terminus at Crieff and had made an agreement with the Crieff Junction Railway for both companies to run into the one existing terminus which was to be enlarged. This change of heart did not go down well with the *Strathearn Herald* which commented that *'It is now evident that there is to be no separate station at Crieff ... This is a bad sign ... We still hope for competition, but doubt it will now happen'*. Later that month it was reported that poles and wires for the long-awaited electric telegraph were expected to be completed in a few days.

At the beginning of 1866 it was reported that the embankment for the Abbey bridge across the railway near Madderty was nearly finished. The bridge was designed by the architect for the line, Mr James Kennedy. Architecture was evidently not his only talent as the

Plate 1.15
Nearly all stations had clocks which were visible from the platform, and many were dual, having an inside face visible in the booking office. The three Crieff & Methven Junction Railway stone station buildings had clocks neatly incorporated in the stonework above the mullioned window at the front. This one at Abercairny indicates that they were supplied by a local clockmaker, in this case JB Macowan of High Street, Crieff. *Author*

Plate 1.16
A view of the two parallel lines running into Crieff from the east, the line from Crieff Junction on the left and that from Perth on the right. This arrangement was the result of a failure between the Crieff Junction and Crieff & Methven Junction railways to agree on sharing a double line from the point at which the two routes converged. The result was this overgenerous track layout which survived for the next 100 years. *Author's collection*

report also records that he sang *'many fine songs at the evening entertainment for the navvies'*. Some 100 men and 30 horses were employed on the site at Madderty, and it was reported that rails were being laid and that ballasting would start shortly.

By the beginning of March 1866 work was sufficiently advanced for the Directors to travel over the line on a special engine from Crieff to carry out an inspection. A working agreement was entered into with the Scottish North Eastern Railway whereby that company would work the Crieff & Methven line. This was a logical arrangement, as the Scottish North Eastern Railway had by then been working the Perth Almond Valley & Methven Railway for nearly two years. However, the future of the Scottish North Eastern Railway itself was by now in the balance; the Caledonian, having absorbed the Scottish Central Railway the previous year, clearly had its sights set on this railway also. In March various petitions were raised in Crieff and Comrie in favour of the amalgamation of the Scottish North Eastern Railway with the Caledonian. This was supported by, among others, the tradesmen of Crieff representing two-thirds of the goods traffic carried over the Crieff Junction line. That said, this was not a universal view, and it was reported that a counter petition was being organised.

At their Half Yearly meeting in April 1865, the Board were able to report that although the line had not been ready to open in March as had been hoped, due to the previous three months of severe weather, it was now complete and the Board of Trade had been informed that it was ready for inspection. Preparations were in hand to open the line at the beginning of May.

Captain Yolland Royal Engineers, the Board of Trade Inspector, arrived in Crieff on 11th May and, accompanied by the Directors and others, set off from Crieff at 10am to inspect the line. He was satisfied with what he saw and pronounced the line fit to carry passenger traffic. The first message to be passed along the newly installed electric telegraph conveyed the news that the Board of Trade had passed the line. It was subsequently announced that the line would open on the Queen's Birthday, 21st May 1866.

Plate 1.17
At some time after the Caledonian Railway absorbed the Scottish North Eastern Railway, and with it the line from Almond Valley Junction to Crieff, they installed specially cast milepost plates along the route. This was most unusual for a country branch line, and only three other lines on the whole Caledonian system had such plates, the most notable being the main line from Carlisle to Aberdeen. These plates bore an abbreviated title of 'ALMOND JUNCTION' as shown here. There were only seventeen such plates, this one was originally located between Innerpeffray and Crieff. *Author*

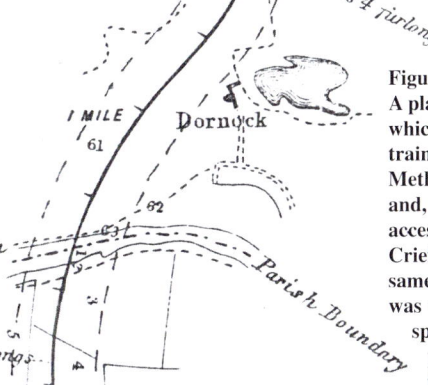

Figure 1.13
A plan showing the proposed spur at Highlandman which was never built. This would have allowed trains to travel between Crieff Junction and the Methven line without the need to reverse at Crieff, and, more importantly, it would have provided access for trains of both the Crieff Junction and Crieff & Methven Junction railways to run over the same line to Crieff. However, the southern junction was well south of Highlandman station and both spurs would have required level crossings – the plan would probably therefore have required three signal boxes, so it would have been both expensive in terms of capital expenditure and running costs. *Courtesy David Ferguson*

The line opened with due ceremony that day, a public holiday having been declared in Crieff. The inaugural train left Crieff at 11am (some sources say 11.30am), the locomotive being decked with flags and evergreens for the occasion. Over 1,000 people travelled to Perth in three special trains and a good number of folk took the opportunity to visit Crieff. The day's festivities culminated in a dinner for 100 guests at the County Hall in Perth, where one of the customary toasts was *'Success to our railway'*.

The opening of the line allowed through running of trains between Crieff and Perth, which had long been an aspiration of the townsfolk of Crieff. Sadly for the inhabitants of Methven, the fear that the short line from Methven Junction would become a siding soon became a reality. A few days after the opening of the Crieff & Methven Junction Railway, rumours surfaced of plans to replace the *'iron horse with a live horse'* on the Methven line. This indeed turned out to be the case, for a few weeks later, the local paper recorded complaints by Methven passengers that the line was being worked by a horse. To add insult to injury, there were no platforms at Methven Junction at that time and passengers changing trains had to negotiate a 6-foot drop from the carriages to ground level with the aid of ladders. One could be forgiven for considering that the opening of the new line represented a step backwards for the unfortunate Methven passengers.

One individual who managed to successfully extricate himself from the situation was the Methven stationmaster, Mr McArthur, who had supported the Crieff & Methven Junction Railway Bill when it went before Parliament. He was duly rewarded by being appointed the first stationmaster for the Crieff & Methven Junction Railway in the newly enlarged station at Crieff. He was evidently well regarded by the people of Methven, for he was presented by them with a gold watch on his departure. He did not linger long at Crieff, however, for barely three months after arriving there he was appointed stationmaster of Wishaw in Lanarkshire, the Caledonian Railway having by then taken over the Scottish North Eastern Railway on 1st August 1866. It would seem McArthur was an ambitious railwayman with an eye for the main chance, but sadly his tenure at Wishaw was short lived and his promising railway career cut short, for it was subsequently reported that he died at Methven on 30th October 1869, barely three years later.

The initial passenger service amounted to four trains each way per day, the journey taking 50 minutes, a vast improvement on the journey time via Crieff Junction, which still took anything between one hour 20 minutes and two hours. Good use was made of the new service and in the ten weeks from opening to 31st July 1866, the proportion of receipts due to the Crieff & Methven Junction Railway was given as £231 3s 11d, almost all of this being attributed to passenger traffic as the goods services started later. That said, goods traffic also built up encouragingly, with Madderty, which served a large and productive agricultural area, being the most lucrative station on the line. Unsurprisingly, potatoes were one of the predominant commodities being shipped out, as many as seven trucks being recorded in one day in May. Madderty also had the distinction of being a passing station and hence being the only intermediate station on the new line equipped with the electric telegraph.

The introduction of passenger services meant that Mr Drummond Moray of Abercairny was now entitled to exercise the arrangement referred to previously, and which was recorded in the contemporary account of the line as *'A curious obligation'*. It was minuted that:

'The Directors gave Mr Drummond Moray of Abercairny, who held 500 shares of the Company, the privilege of stopping certain trains for his accommodation at Abercairny Station. They resolved and agreed to stop Crieff & Methven trains, not being express trains or trains of other Companies running on the line, for first-class passengers on the laird giving notice to the guard of the train at a station which the train stops previous to it reaching Abercairny, and for first-class passengers leaving Abercairny by giving notice at the station two hours previous to the passing of the train.'

This obligation was to exist in perpetuity. It is not clear how often, if at all, this right was exercised, nor whether it survived the takeover by the Caledonian, but it is an interesting relic of its time.

It is noteworthy that it was the goods traffic which began to grow most rapidly, for nearly a century later it was the goods traffic which sustained the line for a good sixteen years after it had closed to passengers in 1951 – this was the last section of the branch lines in Strathearn when it finally closed in 1967. Large quantities of potatoes were being sent out of the Strath and it was reported that the number of goods trains seemed inadequate for the purpose. Indeed, there were complaints that the passenger trains were being interrupted by the goods traffic. On one occasion it was reported that one night a passenger train was kept waiting for one and half hours to allow a goods train to pass.

The amalgamation of the Scottish North Eastern Railway with the Caledonian on 1st August 1866 meant that the latter now operated both of the companies with lines running to Crieff, giving them the option as to how to route traffic. This monopoly was not viewed favourably by the *Strathearn Herald*, a constant advocate of the benefits of healthy competition, which complained that *'since the Caledonian Railway took over both lines to Crieff, the public have been shabbily treated compared to times of management with the Scottish Central Railway'*, adding somewhat prophetically that *'the day may not be far off when the Government will have to manage the railways'*. Nearly eighty-two years later this far-sighted prediction became reality with the nationalisation of the railways on 1st January 1948.

The Half Yearly meeting of the company was held, for what turned out to be the final time, at the Drummond Arms Hotel at the end of October, when it was confirmed that the Caledonian had worked the line since the 1st August amalgamation with the Scottish North Eastern Railway, and now owned 50% of the stock. It was reported that the Capital Account showed an excess of expenditure over income of £5,250 15s 6d, with some costs yet to be settled. It was considered, somewhat optimistically, that although the cost exceeded the original estimate, the cost per mile was still moderate. The Directors, however, recommended that the Crieff & Methven Junction should amalgamate with the Caledonian. Subsequently the remainder of the meetings were held in Glasgow, initially in April 1867 at the Queens Hotel, and thereafter at the Caledonian Railway Company offices.

This was the beginning of the end for the Crieff & Methven Junction Railway, as a contemporary account recalled:

'The shareholders of the Company gradually lost confidence in the ultimate success of the undertaking, and began to sell. By the next October (1868), the Board of Directors was entirely different from those originally appointed by the Act of Parliament of the Company.'

At their meeting in February 1869, the shareholders approved a Bill for the amalgamation of the company with the Caledonian. This was subsequently included as one of the measures in the Caledonian Railway (Abandonment &c) Act 1869 which received the Royal Assent on 26th July and authorised the amalgamation of the Crieff & Methven Junction Railway with the Caledonian.

Thus, by 1869 the Caledonian Railway had absorbed all three of the small railways in Strathearn and secured the dominant position it was to hold for over half a century, including the extension of the network of branch lines through Upper Strathearn described in the next chapter.

Chapter 2
The Extension to Upper Strathearn

The Crieff & Comrie Railway

With the opening of the Crieff Junction Railway on 14th March 1856, Crieff was connected to the railway network, not only in Scotland, but the whole of Great Britain. The benefits of this railway connection soon became evident and, as already referred to in Chapter 1, there were soon calls for the railway to be carried through to Comrie. However, as we shall see, the achievement of this goal was to be a long and, at times, tortuous process, and was not finally brought to fruition until 1st June 1893, over thirty-seven years later.

In 1856, the so-called 'railway mania' was still in full swing, with myriad different railways being proposed, some practical but many more speculative or just downright fanciful. Most of the latter never progressed beyond the initial stages of proposal, planning and sometimes surveying. The first mention of a railway to, or rather through, Comrie was reported on 22nd May 1856, only two months after the opening of the Crieff Junction line. This was for a railway linking Callander with Methven, running for 33 miles through Glen Artney, Comrie, and Crieff. Nothing further was heard of this proposal, but only a week later the local press reported an account of another route being surveyed; this was to run from Crieff to Comrie and then on to Lochearnhead, across the Braes of Balquhidder, down Loch Laichney to Callander. The first part of this line would have followed the course of the line finally opened in 1905 to link Crieff with Lochearnhead, while the second section would form part of the Callander & Oban Railway.

A more substantive proposal for a line to Comrie stemmed from a long letter published in the *Perthshire Advertiser* on 24th April 1856. This referred to the benefits of the newly opened Crieff Junction Railway and urged the extension of the line to Comrie. The writer referred to problems developers had had with constructing turnpike roads in the district, particularly that from Comrie up Glen Lednock to Loch Tay. Apparently only 6 miles of road were completed before work stopped as *'the originators fell short of the needful'*, or in other words, ran out of money! The writer went on to say that work on the road was about to restart, and emphasised the extension of the railway to complement it, going on to stress that *'if only the money hoarders could summon courage enough to embark on this venture'*.

The first evidence of any substantive work to build a railway was the account in the *Perthshire Advertiser* of 21st August 1856 of a public meeting held in Comrie. Mr Peter Drummond of Drumearn was in the chair, and a local banker, Mr Peter MacFarlane, addressed the meeting on the practicality of making a railway to Comrie. Mr Brown Chartered Engineer of Perth, who together with Mr Gowans had recently examined the ground, considered that *'it would be practicable to make a railway to Comrie'*. It was estimated that the sum required would be £30,000 (about £1.5 million in 2014) and that the line could be worked for some £1,500 per month, yielding an expected dividend of 5%. The proposed line would be an extension of the existing Crieff Junction Railway with the aim of developing the traffic of Upper Strathearn; it was reckoned that half the existing traffic carried on the Crieff Junction Railway originated from Comrie. It was agreed that a Committee be appointed to negotiate with landowners, and to see what arrangement the Scottish Central Railway and Crieff Junction Railway could offer.

The proposed line would be some 6 miles long, crossing the River Turret about half a mile west of Crieff and then running along the northern bank of the River Earn. It would pass to the north of Baird's Monument and then through the Carse of Strowan to terminate at the east end of the village.

By the end of October it was reported that Messrs Stewart & Wood, in the service of Mr Brown CE of Perth, had completed a survey of the line. This appears to have been the only activity undertaken subsequent to the August meeting, and nothing further was heard of this matter for several years. This was to become a characteristic of the Crieff & Comrie Railway project – short bursts of activity and enthusiasm followed by prolonged periods of inactivity when nothing appeared to be happening. It is little wonder that it took nearly forty years to get the railway to Comrie.

Another four years were to elapse before the proposal for a railway resurfaced, in the form of a letter to the Editor of the *Strathearn Herald*. The writer again raised the idea for a railway, and outlined the benefits of such a line to the area. This was followed up by an article in the paper on 22nd December 1860 promoting the idea of a railway from Crieff to Comrie, observing that *'It has been a long time coming'*. It seems, however, that this evoked little response, for about three months later, on 16th March 1861, the same paper published another article lamenting *'What has become of the Comrie railway? Has the idea evaporated in a newspaper paragraph?'* More pointedly, it also posed the question *'If it (Comrie) cannot support a regular stage, how can it take a hand in a railway?'* This hinted not so much at the lack of support, as to the reluctance of the locals to invest in an enterprise with only marginal prospects of success.

In the event, nothing much happened for another year when a meeting was held in mid-October 1862 at the Royal Hotel in Comrie to discuss the project. A number of gentlemen, under the chairmanship of Mr Pagan of Innergeldie, met to discuss the project. All were of the opinion that the line to Comrie was highly desirable and arrangements were made to call a public meeting on 25th October.

This meeting was chaired by Mr James Drummond, who had chaired the first such meeting over six years earlier. In addition to Mr Pagan, it was attended by a number of prominent local businessmen, including Messrs McIntyre, Swan, McDonald, Stalker and Stewart, together with Mr Ballantyne and Mr Brough, local bankers. Another member was the aptly named Mr Comrie who would later become a director of the Crieff & Comrie Railway Company. It was again considered that the line could be completed for £30,000 with every prospect of yielding a 5% dividend.

However, whereas the original route had been planned to run along the northern bank of the River Earn, which it would then cross at Strowan and terminate at Dalginross, south of Comrie, a new route was proposed. This would run along by McEwan's woollen mills, pass by Baird's Monument and run into Comrie along the north bank of the River Earn to terminate close to Mitchell's Mill. A resolution was agreed:

'That from the great want of Coal, Lime, and tiles, and the increasing demand of residences in the district, as well as the carrying of wood, potatoes and other farm produce, and passengers, to the town of Comrie, and the district around it, is in much need of railway accommodation, and for want of it will make no progress, and assume that importance, to which the locality entitles it.

That from previous survey calculations, it is certain that the line will be finished for £30,000, which shall be raised in £10 shares, and from the traffic there is every prospect of the line paying at least 5%.

That it is in the interest of every proprietor and tenant in the district to do everything in their power to promote the undertaking by taking shares and otherwise, and that subscriptions be raised for preliminary expenses.'

A large Committee was appointed to have the line again surveyed, and to make all the necessary arrangements to get a Bill before the next session of Parliament. A subscription sheet was opened to provide for preliminary expenses and a considerable sum of money subscribed. This revived interest in the line was reflected in the local press which reported that *'The prospect of a railway to Crieff is being pursued with vigour'*, whilst asserting that all the principal local landowners had been found to be *'highly favourable'* to the project. Those named were Lord Willoughby d'Eresby, Lord Abercrombie, Sir Patrick Keith Murray, Mr Graham Stirling of Strowan, and Mr Williamson of Lawers. In the case of Lord Willoughby, however, this would seem to have been premature, for barely a week later his Lordship wrote to the newspaper informing them that he was not in favour of the proposal, stating that he had informed the promoters that the project did not meet with his approval and that he considered that *'It would be injurious to the interests of the town of Crieff'*.

In the meantime, Mr Bouch had arrived in Comrie at the beginning of November 1862 to carry out the preliminary survey of the line. By the middle of the month it was reported that he and his two assistants had nearly completed the survey, but then bad weather intervened, a snowstorm bringing the survey to a halt. The result of this delay was that it was then almost too late for the necessary papers to be lodged for a Bill to be brought before the next session of Parliament as had been planned

Despite this, Bouch pressed ahead, and on 20th November the *Perthshire Advertiser* reported that the survey had been completed. The route selected was the original one, that is the Crieff terminus in Henderson's Meadow, from where the line was to run through the Town Meadow, over the River Turret, past Baird's Monument and follow the north bank of the River Earn to a field at the east end of Comrie. This meant the railway would not have to cross either the Rivers Earn or Lednock, resulting in a saving of some £1,200.

At the same time it was reported that the Provisional Committee were to meet the local landowners to settle boundaries and any other difficulties. It was reported that nearly £6,000 of shares had been taken up in Comrie and the neighbourhood, although this represented only a fifth of the capital required. In the event, the various delays meant that it became too late to lodge the Bill before Parliament. Once again, the Crieff & Comrie railway project went quiet.

Four months elapsed before anything further was heard, when on 11th April 1863 an intriguing report appeared in the *Strathearn Herald* to the effect that *'a nurseryman in Crieff was making preparations to supply trees to make sleepers for the Comrie railway'*. Given the proximity to 1st April, it was difficult to tell if this was a serious proposal, but given the protracted nature of the project, one could be forgiven for thinking that the nurseryman was actually planning to plant the trees!

The coming of spring 1863 saw further attempts to revive interest in the line. The *Strathearn Herald* ran an editorial lamenting the fact that *'preparations for a line to Comrie seem to have ceased'*. It went on to assert that:

'Comrie is nothing as to what it will be as an inland resort for summer visitors, and that the railway could create, as railways have done in other places, a flourishing traffic, and in a few years give a handsome return to shareholders.'

At about the same time, the *Perthshire Courier* observed that *'The scheme had been abandoned for some time, but now is to be taken up with vigour'*. However, it also raised, once again, the proposal for a direct line from Comrie to Methven, a distance of only (sic) 17 miles, asserting that the whole route along the banks of the Earn and the Pow did not present *'a single engineering difficulty'*.

On 2nd May 1863 the *Strathearn Herald* ran another editorial, attempting to revive interest in the project and stressing that *'The Comrie people must agitate for it'*. Nothing appears to have come of this, but a month later it was rumoured that the Scottish North Eastern Railway, which had absorbed the Perth Almond Valley & Methven Railway the previous December, was considering extending their line to Comrie. This would have revived the earlier proposal for a direct line from Comrie to Methven, but again, nothing further was heard of this proposal.

In September, a meeting was held to discuss the proposed Crieff & Methven Junction Railway and it was reckoned that *'on completion of that line, one for Comrie would follow immediately'*. The *Strathearn Herald* reported that an important move had already been made on this, and that Mr Williamson *'with his usual energy, had thrown himself into the movement, and has the other day issued a circular which speaks for itself'*:

*'Lawers House
21st September 1863*

Sir – you are probably aware that an effort is being made at present to form a railway between Crieff and Comrie, in order to develop more fully the resources of the district, and to promote the welfare and comfort of the inhabitants. It is of the utmost importance to the gentlemen who are promoting the scheme to know what local support they are to meet with. The capital required will be about £30,000 divided into 3000 shares of £10 each. Will you be kind enough to inform me how many shares you would be disposed to take in the event of the railway going on. The favour of the answer within the week of this date is requested.

*I am &c
David Williamson'*

The article went on to encourage the inhabitants of the Strath, particularly those about Comrie, to respond positively to this appeal and to take up as many shares as possible, quoting the old adage *'God helps them that help themselves'*. The Committee met again at the Royal Hotel at the end of the month, with Mr Drummond in the chair. The Secretaries submitted correspondence from gentlemen of the district and the plans submitted by Mr Bouch were approved. The Committee, recognising Mr Williamson's commitment and energy, and, most importantly, his local connections, also agreed to ask him to call on the noblemen and gentlemen of the district to join the Provisional Committee, or otherwise to assist the Committee.

By mid-October it was reported that £22,000 of shares had been subscribed, and it was anticipated that the balance would be easily raised. The following week the *Strathearn Herald* commented confidently that *'If the landed proprietors of Comrie had the energy of Mr Williamson of Lawers, the railway would soon be a great fact'*. Unfortunately even this burst of activity would seem to have been short lived, for on 5th December 1863 the *Strathearn Herald* reported that the promoters of the line had abandoned the scheme meantime, but added that if the Crieff & Methven Junction Railway went ahead it would be revived.

In the event, that is what happened. A month after the Crieff & Methven Junction Railway Act received the Royal Assent on 14th July 1864, a lengthy article appeared in the *Strathearn Herald* detailing the full Provisional Committee and publishing the first prospectus for the Crieff & Comrie Railway Company. Mr Williamson had evidently been busy, for the Committee now numbered thirty-seven members, with Sir Patrick Murray of Ochtertyre as Chairman, and himself as Vice-Chairman. Interestingly, one of the other members was Rev William Ogilvie, the Rector of the recently established Morrison's Academy.

The Prospectus, as most did, promoted the scheme in glowing terms, emphasising the value of the railway connection between the district and major cities and areas such as the Fife coalfields. It stressed the value of agriculture and other resources of the locality, particularly timber, and waxed lyrical about the unrivalled beauty of the scenery and the tourist potential. Significantly, the estimated cost had risen to £36,000, a 20% increase on that of only a year previously.

A public meeting was held in the Town Hall at Crieff on 1st September 1864 to report on the progress being made. It was announced somewhat optimistically that nearly all the share capital of £36,000 had been raised. It was also decided to appoint Mr Bouch as the Engineer. Meanwhile there had been some hard bargaining going on behind the scenes between the company and the Scottish Central and Scottish North Eastern railways, both of which were in keen competition to secure running powers over the line. The Scottish North Eastern Railway had already announced in the previous November that it would purchase 1,000 £10 shares. Eventually a compromise solution was arrived at: the Scottish North Eastern Railway were granted running powers over the line and the use of its stations and facilities, while the Scottish Central Railway agreed to work the line and to subscribe £20,000 towards the required capital. This amount had been agreed previously and formed the major part of the total £36,000.

The first Half Yearly meeting of the new company was held in December 1865. Despite the progress made, the Directors were evidently still having to work hard to promote the line, for on 27th January the *Strathearn Herald* commented that:

'Great exertions are being made by the promoters of this undertaking to get the line set agoing in March. The Directors and several others have doubled their original subscriptions and many shares have been taken in Comrie and neighbourhood in the last few days. Now is the time for those who wish to further the interest of the district to do so. It is regretted that some of the landowners in the district are doing very little if anything – the very men most interested.'

While these efforts were ongoing, the rivalry between the Caledonian Railway, which had taken over the Scottish Central Railway on 1st August 1865, and the Scottish North Eastern Railway rumbled on. On 3rd April, the *Strathearn Herald* reported that a petition had been raised by the inhabitants of Comrie in favour of the proposed amalgamation of the Caledonian Railway with the Scottish North Eastern Railway. It was also reported that a counter-petition had been raised, which was said to have 2,000 signatures, but, significantly, the petition in favour had been signed by the majority of the principal traders involved in railway traffic.

The second Half Yearly meeting of the company was held in the Drummond Arms Hotel on 25th April. Most of the business was routine, but the Directors were able to report that as a result of active canvassing in the district, sufficient stocks had been taken up to ensure the line being proceeded with.

With the amalgamation of the Caledonian Railway and the Scottish North Eastern Railway now becoming a reality (it took place on 1st August 1866), it was reported on 2nd June that the Directors of the Crieff & Comrie Railway had met with the Caledonian Railway in Glasgow. It was understood that at this meeting agreement was reached to proceed with preliminary arrangements for starting with the line as soon as the crops were off the ground.

At the Half Yearly meeting on 3rd November the Directors reported that they were prepared to take active measure for construction of the line immediately after the growing crops were cleared, so that by the same time next year the railway would be nearly ready for opening. A fortnight later it was reported that Mr Bouch had been engaged for its construction and had been instructed by the Directors to prepare advertisements for tenders. On 1st December 1866 the *Strathearn Herald* reported that:

'There was now no difficulty as to proceeding with the construction of the Crieff & Comrie Railway. Any problems now lie with local officials, and we trust that they will use their best efforts to proceed without delay.'

On 22nd December, the paper reported that the signing of papers by shareholders was now complete and that working plans were expected to be ready about February or March, such that in early spring *'active measures will be taken to carry out the undertaking'*. Somewhat more ominously however, the report went on to state that:

'In regard to this subject, we are officially authorised to give an emphatic contradiction to a statement in a contemporary, that there is not the least prospect when railway communication will be extended to Comrie.'

Nonetheless, work on the project proceeded, and on 12th January 1867 it was reported that Mr Buchanan, Engineer of the Crieff & Methven Junction Railway, had made a start on the Crieff & Comrie Railway. He was currently staking out the line and it was anticipated that navvies would start construction in a little over two months' time. It was expected that a ceremony for cutting the first sod would take place at Comrie soon and that the whole works would be completed by early in 1868. It also mentioned, perhaps optimistically, that this would only leave a 14-mile gap from the Callander & Oban Railway at Glen Ogle, then in the course of construction.

Despite this apparently promising start, the rumours which had been so emphatically denied the previous December now turned out to be all too well founded, for on 20th April, it was reported that:

'It appears that construction of this line has been abandoned meantime and will not proceed for some time to come. The Caledonian Railway were promoters of the line to the extent of half the capital (£20,000). It is said that the delay has resulted from the small number of shares subscribed in the district.'

The Caledonian Railway, having absorbed the Scottish Central Railway on 1st August 1865, had inherited the commitment by the latter to fund the Crieff & Comrie Railway to the extent of £20,000, and had only recently taken over the Crieff & Methven Junction Railway together with its debts, as mentioned in the previous chapter. Against the countrywide depression in the railway industry, the Caledonian were unwilling to proceed with another project, particularly one which appeared to lack wholehearted support locally.

Evidence that the Crieff & Comrie project was once again in the doldrums was reflected in the *Strathearn Herald* of 15th June which reported that during the sale of meadow grass at Crieff, mention was made of several trial pits which had been opened up by the Crieff & Comrie Railway workers some months previously. It was said that at the west end there was a pit full of water about 5 feet deep, unprotected by any fence. It was pointed out that it was the duty of the Police Commissioners, or failing that the Directors of the Crieff & Comrie Railway Company, to have it filled up. The newspaper felt that the latter would be the appropriate course *'for the Comrie railway scheme at present has gone to sleep'*.

At the Half Yearly meeting held at the Queens Hotel in Glasgow in May, it was reported that Mr Bouch had nearly completed the plans and specifications of works, but that as £10,000 of capital was still unsubscribed, it was felt expedient to obtain sanction from the

Caledonian Railway for work to proceed, as financial assistance from the Caledonian to meet the expenses of the undertaking was essential. A deputation of Crieff & Comrie Railway Directors had held a meeting with the Caledonian Railway Board who had explained, as already mentioned, that because of the depressed state of the railway industry they could not contribute the balance of the capital unsubscribed for. In the light of this, they could not recommend that the undertaking went ahead.

Over the next two years the Half Yearly meetings continued to be held in the offices of the Caledonian Railway, but little other than routine business was done, the project being effectively dead in the water. Then, on 31st October 1868, an Extraordinary Meeting was held with the Directors of the Caledonian Railway at which it was agreed to apply to the Board of Trade to abandon the scheme.

Subsequently, on the 11th May 1869 it was reported that the Board of Trade has issued a warrant for the abandonment of the Crieff & Comrie Railway on the grounds that the required capital had not been subscribed. Parliamentary and other expenses of £642 had been incurred, while the liabilities of the company were £1,887, meaning that £2,550 had been spent. However, as no notices had been served on landowners, no contract for the construction had yet been let, and there was no opposition to the warrant, it was granted. A final Half Yearly meeting was held on 26th April to wind up the Crieff & Comrie Railway Company, and it would be another twenty years before the scheme was resurrected.

Although the Crieff & Comrie Railway remained in abeyance, the district continued to be served by the horse-drawn coaches operated by the Caledonian Railway and others. Coaches between Crieff and Comrie were generally timed to connect with trains arriving at and departing from Crieff. On 17th May 1871, for example, a new coach was introduced on Monday mornings, leaving Comrie at 6.35am to arrive at Crieff at 7.35am. This connected with both the 7.45am to Perth along the Methven line and the 8.5am to Crieff Junction with connections to Edinburgh and Glasgow.

The Caledonian Railway continued to develop and promote the tourist potential of the area. At the end of the 1872 programme it was reported that they were going to erect additional stables and a coach house near the original Crieff Junction Railway engine shed at Crieff. In 1873 it was even reported that many prospective visitors could not reach the Lochearnhead games because of the inadequate capacity of the Caledonian Railway coaches. In 1874 the *Strathearn Herald* reported that the Caledonian Railway was going to put a steamer on Loch Earn. The paper enthused that:

'No greater attraction could be added to the already popular tour, supplying, as it would do, to the inland tourist in one day a trip by rail, coach, and steam boat, through scenery the most romantic and grand that Perthshire can boast of.'

During all this time, however, Colonel Williamson had not given

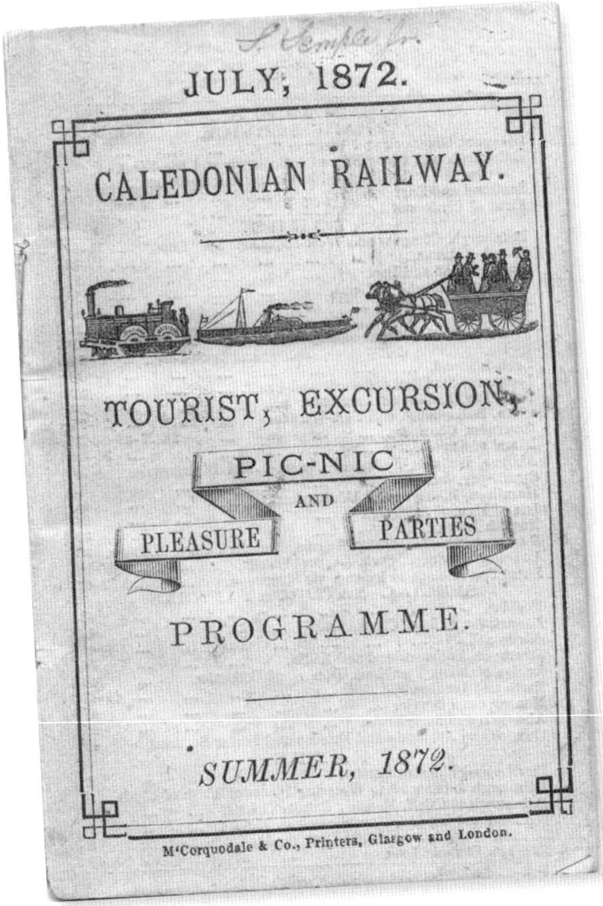

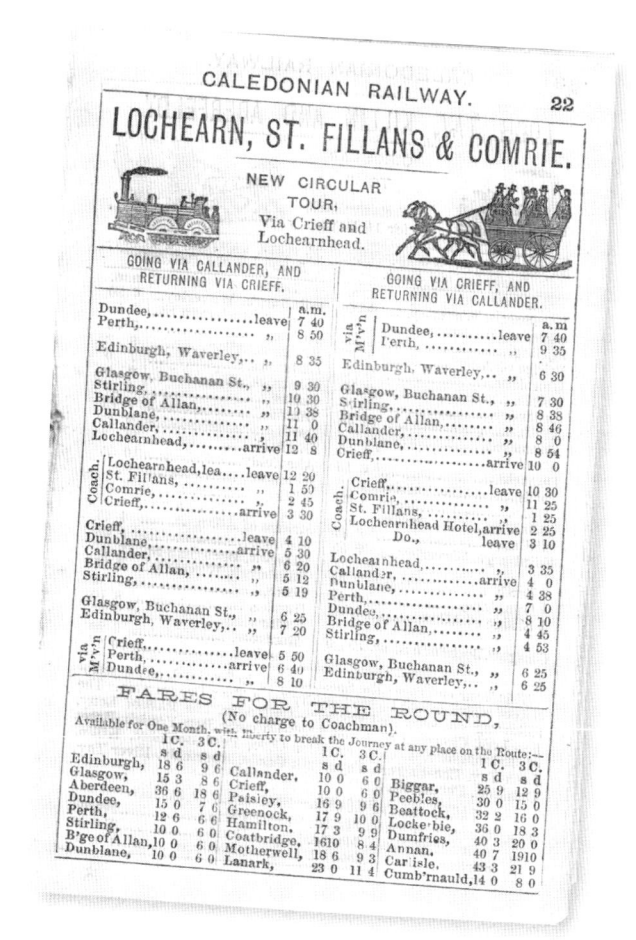

Figures 2.1 and 2.2
The Caledonian Railway Tourist, Excursion, Pic-nic and Pleasure Parties Programme for 1872. This little pocket booklet, measuring only 4 inches by 5 inches, ran to 49 pages and listed all the various excursions being run by the Caledonian Railway that season. Pre-eminent among them was the new circular tour.

Page 22 of the programme, *right*, gives details of the new circular tour of Lochearn, St. Fillans and Comrie, via Lochearnhead and Crieff. This circular tour continued in this form until the opening of the Crieff & Comrie Railway in 1893, when it was altered and the coaches ran between Comrie and Lochearnhead. Similarly, from 1901 the coaches ran between St. Fillans and Lochearnhead, and from 1905 the entire tour could be accomplished by rail.
Author's collection

ABOVE: Plate 2.1
One of the Caledonian Railway coaches which plied between Comrie, St. Fillans and Lochearnhead and which were used for the Circular Tour when it was introduced in 1872. The two-horse coaches could accommodate up to ten passengers, while the four-horse coaches, as shown here, could carry up to fifteen passengers, depending on the amount of luggage to be carried.
Courtesy Bernard Byrom

BELOW: Plate 2.2
Two of the Caledonian Railway's four-horse coaches seen outside the Royal Hotel in Comrie. This scene was probably taken prior to the opening of the railway, for after that time the coaches operated to and from Comrie station. Both coaches would appear to be well patronised.
Courtesy Bernard Byrom

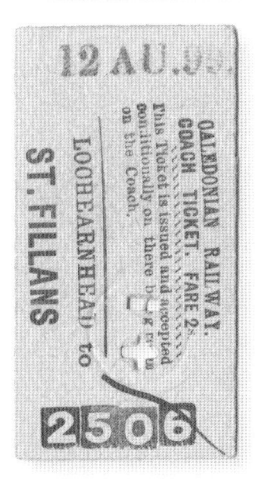

ABOVE RIGHT: Figure 2.3
Two rare examples of Caledonian Railway coach tickets issued from Lochearnhead to St. Fillans, one on 11th August 1898 and the other almost exactly a year later on 12th August 1899 – the 'Glorious Twelfth' – the start of the grouse season. It will be noted that these tickets were issued conditionally on there being space available on the coach, which was not always the case.
Author's collection

up on his ambition and in 1880, ten years after the Crieff & Comrie Railway Act was abandoned, he made another attempt to resurrect the railway scheme. In October that year it was reported that an engineer had been surveying the line of the railway between '*Crieff and Lochearnhead*'. It was stressed that the engineer was not employed by the railway, but by private parties, in this case presumably Colonel Williamson.

It was a full year before a meeting took place between Mr Stair, the Engineer, and Colonel Williamson, together with Colonel Colquhoun and Mr Miller. Following the meeting they went over part of the ground surveyed to look at certain alterations to the proposed route. At the end of October it was reported that a meeting of the Committee of the proposed Crieff & Lochearnhead Railway was held with Colonel Williamson in the chair. He outlined the Engineer's findings, particularly regarding the stretch of line at Baird's Monument which could be tunnelled or cut, the latter being cheaper. By taking the railway along the north side of the glen it was felt that they would remove Mr Stirling of Strowan's objections. Colonel Williamson also agreed to the station being sited in Laggan Park to the east of Comrie if Sir Sydney Dundas's Trustees continued their objections to it being at the back of the village as originally proposed.

He circulated potential shareholders with a detailed case for building the line, outlining the economic benefits and forecasting a dividend of between 5% and 6%. Unfortunately, only a few weeks later it was reported that this time a number of landowners along the proposed course of the line objected, and the project foundered. Interestingly, all the reports on this particular episode refer to the 'Crieff & Lochearnhead Railway' when in reality the intention at this stage was still limited to the Crieff to Comrie section.

It was another six years before a further attempt was made to build the railway. In January 1888 yet another public meeting was held, this time in the Mission Room at Comrie. A large group of the local landowners, local businessmen and others were present, and although Colonel Williamson was unable to attend he tendered his apologies and expressed his support for the project and his willingness to subscribe a substantial number of shares.

The meeting agreed to enter into discussions with the Caledonian Railway who held the key to the viability of the whole scheme. A deputation led by Captain Dundas of Dalchonzie subsequently met with the Chairman of the Caledonian Railway, but the latter was still unwilling to commit the Caledonian to invest in this new scheme unless it could be demonstrated how much support there was and how much capital could be raise locally.

A second public meeting was called at which the delegation reported this lack of success. After some debate, it was decided that a letter should be sent to the Caledonian Railway inviting them to subscribe between £20,000 and £25,000 to the project if the public raised a further £10,000 and the landowners sold their land at favourable terms. Captain Dundas duly wrote to the Caledonian Railway but received a disappointing reply from their Company Secretary to the effect that their Board were not prepared to agree the proposal to contribute to the capital – but if the promoters were to build the line at their own cost, the Caledonian would be prepared to work it for them.

The ball was now firmly back in the court of the local promoters of the line, and it must have been clear to them that unless and until they could garner sufficient support locally, particularly financial, they would not gain the support of the Caledonian. This Colonel Williamson set out to do, and the following year, 1889, a further and ultimately successful proposal was launched. The *Strathearn Herald* reported encouragingly that:

'The good people of Comrie, who in the year 1856 rejoiced over the first proposal of a railway extension to their village, having grown grey since that time and hope deferred, might well have made the heart sick of the whole affair; yet it must be confessed that they have manfully persevered amidst many failures during the past 33 years to attain their objective.'

This time the Committee did their homework more thoroughly. Shares were priced at a more affordable £1 each (with a minimum of ten shares) and the district was well canvassed. The principal promoters led by example, with Colonel Williamson subscribing 5,000 shares, Mr Gilchrist 1,000 shares, and both Mr McNaughton and Mr Drummond 500 shares apiece. In May 1889 the Directors of the Caledonian Railway agreed to work the new line if it were ever built, but still declined to provide any financial assistance. They underlined their position by refusing to meet a delegation of promoters to even discuss such support.

Faced with such intransigence, the proposers decided that they had little option but to proceed in their own, and this they duly did. In the interim they appointed as their Engineer Mr John Young CE of Perth (the author's namesake but no relation). John Young's name will feature later in this book (Chapter 7), for one of his apprentices had been a young man called Donald Matheson, later Chief Engineer and then General Manager of the Caledonian Railway, and whose vision led to the creation of the Gleneagles Hotel project.

The new Prospectus gave a brief history of the previous attempts to create a railway, stating that:

'So long ago as 1864, the advantages and commercial importance of connecting these two well-known towns in the great agricultural and tourist districts of Upper Strathearn were so obvious that an independent Railway company was formed.'

It then outlined the 1865 Act whereby the Scottish Central Railway was authorised to subscribe £20,000 and to work the railway in perpetuity. However, it then somewhat disingenuously went on to ascribe the failure of that scheme to problems with the Crieff & Methven Junction Railway which it erroneously stated was worked by the Scottish Central Railway. In fact the Crieff & Methven Junction Railway was worked by the Scottish Central's

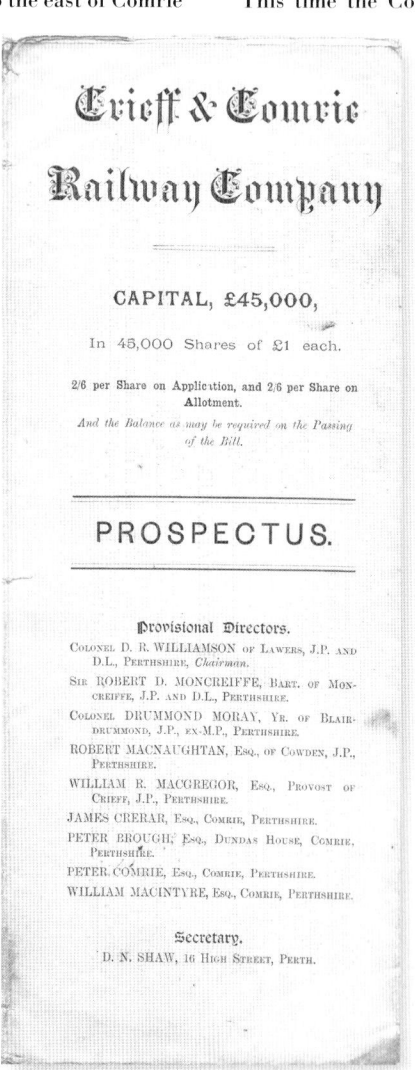

Figure 2.4
The Prospectus for the second Crieff & Comrie Railway Company, published on 10th August 1889. All the Provisional Directors were local Perthshire gentlemen. Shares were priced at £1 each, rather than the £10 which had proved a disincentive to investors in the original 1864 Prospectus.

Author's collection

CHAPTER 2: THE EXTENSION TO UPPER STRATHEARN

rival, the Scottish North Eastern Railway, and it was only when the latter was amalgamated with the Caledonian Railway in 1866 that problems arose, for through that amalgamation the Caledonian inherited the debts of the Crieff & Methven Junction Railway.

The Prospectus then went on to describe the district to be opened up, stating that:

'Comrie is a place of considerable size, and has largely increased in recent years. It possesses very great attractions to tourists, and is the centre of a wide agricultural and sporting district. It also contains extensive hotel and villa accommodation, and offers unusually good facilities for meeting the increased demand for house accommodation which would inevitably follow the opening of railway communication with the East and South.'

This emphasis on tourist and passenger traffic is also reflected in the Summary of Probable Traffic. First of these categories were tourists – not only travelling through the district, but also those on the ever popular 'Circular Tour' already mentioned. Second was regular passenger traffic between Crieff and Comrie, and only third was the goods traffic in terms of minerals, agricultural products and timber. The fourth source of traffic was wool exported from the district, and goods imported, whilst the fifth category was the traffic to and from St. Fillans which would pass over the line.

The Estimated Revenue was summarised as:

Passengers and Mails	£1,600	
Parcels, Carriages, Horses & Dogs	£250	
Livestock	£350	
Goods and Minerals	£1,400	
Total		£3,600
Working Expenses	£1,800	
Interest at say 4%	£1,500	
Total		£3,300
Apparent Surplus		£300

The use of the wording *'Apparent Surplus'* as it appeared in the Prospectus is an interesting piece of what might now be called 'weasel wording', reflecting as it did the preamble which stated that:

'From personal knowledge and reliable information obtained from resident proprietors, agriculturalists, merchants and others, the Directors believe that the following statement may be confidently accepted as a moderate estimate of the revenue to be expected.'

The promoters later issued a promotional sheet headed 'Extracts from the Press', which included a number of favourable reviews of the project. Not unnaturally, the *Strathearn Herald*, a constant supporter, recorded on 18th May 1889:

'The promoters of this latest attempt to obtain a railway to Comrie have wisely started it on a very popular basis, by making the shares so reasonable an amount that almost every working man can embark in the scheme, and we have no doubt that if it can be as economically carried out as is proposed in the prospectus, the promoters will get all that is proposed them as a return for their money. We do not at present go into figures, but it may be interesting to intending shareholders to know that one landed proprietor on the line of the railway is to give his land for free, and most, if not all, of the others are agreeable to give theirs at very reasonable rates. It may also be important to state that several gentlemen have signified their intention to becoming large shareholders to the amount, we understand, of about an eighth of the whole capital required. Comrie has

been too long isolated from railway communication, and from its growing importance as a summer resort, and situated as it is amongst some of the finest Scottish scenery, it would undoubtedly attract more traffic, and become in consequence a feeder to the Caledonian Railway system. Of course to make it perfect in this respect, the line would require to be carried all the way to Lochearnhead, and this, we doubt not, will be done ere long. In the meantime, money is required to make it a success, and at the price the shares are offered, the people of Comrie and surrounding district ought at once to show an example in this respect and their confidence in the scheme by going in largely for the stock. If they do so, the outside public will not be slow to follow so good an example by those who know the capabilities of the district.'

Similar, more encouraging reports were quoted from the *Dundee Courier and Argus* of 30th May, the *Perthshire Courier & Journal* of 19th June, the *Crieff Journal* of 21st June and the *Dundee Advertiser* of 8th August. Support even came from such unlikely sources as the *Rod & Gun*, while on 22nd July *The Whitehall Review* made favourable mention of the Crieff & Comrie. One article on 'Railway Enterprise in Scotland', concluding prophetically that:

'Scottish enterprise is eminently cautious, and in pursuing the judicious course of developing the resources of their own country, instead of trusting to uncertain investments abroad,

Figure 2.5
The promotional sheet issued by the Crieff & Comrie Railway Company containing a summary of selected statements which had appeared in the press. Not unnaturally, it was highly selective, including only those reports which portrayed the project in a positive light. Some extracts of this are recounted here.
Author's collection

they are exhibiting their natural characteristics in its most commendable form.'

One newspaper not included in this summary of adulation was the *Perthshire Advertiser*, and for good reason, for their assessment on 22nd May 1889 was far more pragmatic, and, as it turned out, pretty near the mark. Their report stated that:

'On paper this is a very satisfactory balance sheet; whether it will be realised in the event of the construction of the line is quite another matter. If it should the new railway will be quite unique in its earnings. A revenue of £1,500 from passengers means a traffic of this kind of a most abnormally thriving kind – something like the conveyance of forty or fifty thousand passengers. How £1,500 is to be raised from the conveyance of goods and minerals is another mystery. The Callander & Oban Railway, which is twelve times the length of the proposed new line, passes through a district not unlike that of Crieff, and possess the decided advantage of being a through line, only expects to earn something like £100 per mile in this kind of traffic. Yet the new Crieff line is expected to earn two and a half times as much, or £250 per mile. The total earnings of the Callander and Oban line amount to something like £320 per mile; but the Crieff line is expected to earn for all kinds of traffic £600 per mile. We do not believe that it will; and we think that the promoters would have been nearer the mark had they put down the expected earnings of the proposed line at £2,000, or £2,500 at the very outside. This balance would give a dividend of 2% upon the share capital, and if the shareholders get this, which is extremely doubtful, they would be very lucky.'

The promoters had a fair degree of success in canvassing for support; although not everyone they approached was willing or able to subscribe, they gained sufficient support to proceed with submitting a Bill to Parliament the following year. This Bill for the new Crieff & Comrie Railway Company came before a Select Committee in the spring of 1890. There were a number of objections to be overcome, principally those of Mr Graham Stirling of Strowan, and these are dealt with in some detail in *The Railways of Upper Strathearn* by Bernard Byrom. Suffice it to say, these were eventually resolved and the Bill went on to receive the Royal Assent on 25th July 1890.

News that the Bill had passed through Parliament was telegraphed to Comrie on 25th April, resulting in much rejoicing, with a bonfire being lit in celebration. However, the strong objections raised by Mr Stirling were not so easily forgiven and on 1st May the *Strathearn Herald* report on events mentioned that:

'On Friday, the inhabitants of Comrie rejoiced. As they had good reason to do, over their victory; but there was one regrettable incident in their joy, and that was, some of the more baser sort amongst them were so far left to themselves as to burn the effigy of Mr Graham Stirling of Strowan.'

The paper quite reasonably pointed out that he was only doing that to which he was entitled.

The creation of the Crieff & Comrie Railway had been a protracted

Summary of the creation of the Crieff & Comrie Railway

May 1856	First suggestion to extend the Crieff Junction Railway to Comrie.
Aug 1856	First public meeting in Comrie.
Oct 1856	Initial survey completed.
Dec 1860	Letter to *Strathearn Herald* promoting line.
Mar 1861	Article in *Strathearn Herald* asking what had become of the idea.
Oct 1862	Meeting held in Comrie. Committee appointed.
Oct 1862	Mr Bouch surveys the line.
Sep 1863	Circular published by Mr Williamson.
Jul 1864	Public meeting at Crieff. First Prospectus published.
Jan 1867	Reports that work would soon start.
Jun 1867	*Strathearn Herald* reported that *'project had gone to sleep'*.
Dec 1868	Caledonian Railway decline to subscribe balance of capital.
May 1869	Crieff & Comrie Railway formally abandoned.
Oct 1880	Proposed line surveyed by Mr Stair.
Oct 1881	Meeting with Mr Stair chaired by Colonel Williamson.
Nov 1881	Project abandoned due to objections and lack of support.
Jan 1888	Public meeting held in Comrie.
Aug 1889	Prospectus for new Crieff & Comrie Railway published.
Apr 1890	Crieff & Comrie Railway Act passed.

ABOVE: Figure 2.6

RIGHT: Figure 2.7
The Crieff & Comrie Railway Act 1890 which finally resulted in the line being built thirty-seven years after it was first suggested. This was the second Crieff & Comrie Railway Act, the previous one having been passed in 1864, was subsequently abandoned in 1869 before the line was built. *Author's collection*

CHAPTER 2: THE EXTENSION TO UPPER STRATHEARN

and convoluted process with a number of false starts. Figure 2.6 gives a brief summary tracing its progress.

After all the false starts of the past thirty-four years, work on the Crieff & Comrie Railway could now begin in earnest. In the ensuing months, Mr John Young prepared all the necessary plans and specifications and invited tenders for the various contracts. In January 1891 the main contract for construction was awarded to Messrs G McKay of Broughty Ferry at a cost of £22,000. Other contracts were:

- Steel rails   Cammel & Son, Sheffield
- Cast iron chairs   McFarlane Strong & Co, Glasgow
- Steel fishplates   Hurst & Co, Glasgow
- Chairs, spikes, bolts PW McLennan, Glasgow
- Sleepers   Bruce & Co, Glasgow
- Oak keys   P Sinclair & Co, Perth

The following month, February 1891, the winter weather notwithstanding, the cutting of the first turf was set, possibly ill-advisedly, for Friday 13th. The ceremony was carried out by Mrs Selina Williamson, wife of Colonel Williamson, in Laggan Park at 1.0pm. The event, which was witnessed by a large crowd, was preceded by an elaborate procession which included officials, civic dignitaries, bands, and even six navvies in working dress with wheelbarrows. Crieff Town Council were there in force together with Crieff Fire Brigade. The ceremony was followed by a lunch in the Public Hall, with fireworks and a bonfire at Lawers that evening.

Work on the line now started in earnest, with up to 200 navvies being employed at any one time. The line was due to be completed by 13th July 1892, but it was hoped that this could be achieved by 1st July. In the event both dates proved highly optimistic. Much of the construction work was relatively light and there was only one large bridge, that over the River Turret, but there were two sections of significant engineering, these being the tunnels under Burrell Street in Crieff and Strowan, together with their approach cuttings.

Originally it had been intended to make just a cutting through Drummwhandie Brae with a bridge at Burrell Street, but this plan was subsequently amended to include a short tunnel through the deepest part of the Brae, a change which was agreed by the Board of Trade.

Although work proceeded steadily, it was already apparent that costs were climbing and that further funds would be needed. In October 1891 Colonel Williamson had another meeting with Mr Bolton, Chairman of the Caledonian Railway, to seek a subscription towards the Crieff & Comrie Railway, but once again this was declined. In June 1892, he made yet another appeal to the Caledonian, for around £9,000 to enable the line to be completed, but this too was refused.

Not all the navvies employed on the Crieff & Comrie Railway were as diligent and well behaved as the majority of those who had worked on the Crieff & Methven Junction Railway several decades earlier, and sadly there were a number of accidents and fatalities as recounted in Chapter 9.

One incident, recorded in May 1892, makes interesting reading, for it was reported that '*a number of poachers and other idle waifs*' had been killing kelts and trout in the River Earn using dynamite, supposedly acquired from the huts of the contractors on the Crieff & Comrie Railway. Whether any navvies colluded in this enterprise is not known, but it would not have been surprising.

The first consignment of rails were delivered to Crieff in January 1892, where they were tested and ready for laying; but, despite this, the rate of progress was such that it soon became evident that the line would not be ready for July 1892. In February it was reported that great progress had been made in excavating the East Meadow in Crieff, the site of the new station, and by April it was reported that work was in hand creating the cutting from the Burrell Street tunnel up to the bridge under King Street. However, the tunnel through Monument Hill at Strowan had not been pierced until 23rd March 1892 – Colonel Williamson lit the fuse to blast the final gap and, having done so, walked through it himself. A month later, on

LEFT: Plate 2.3
The ceremony of cutting the first turf for the Crieff & Comrie Railway, about to be performed by the Hon Mrs Williamson, wife of the Chairman of the Crieff & Comrie Railway Company, in Laggan Park at Comrie on Friday, 13th February 1891. Despite the time of year, a large crowd turned out and the area was suitably decorated for the occasion.
Courtesy Bernard Byrom

RIGHT: Plate 2.4
The handsome ceremonial spade and wheelbarrow used by Mrs Williamson to perform the ceremony of cutting the first turf. The blade of the spade was ornately engraved sterling silver while the shaft was made of black ebony. The wheelbarrow, made by Stewart & Macfarlane, joiners, of Perth was made of polished mahogany. *Courtesy Bernard Byrom*

30th April, it was reported that the tunnel had now been cleared and the excavations from there through to Crieff had been roughly completed. The same report included a description of the erection of the large girders for the Duchlage Road bridge at the east end of the new station. This spectacle was watched by a large crowd of onlookers and was evidently done at night to avoid disrupting trains, for the work was carried out under artificial illumination using a novel illuminant called, appropriately enough, 'Sunlight'.

The provision of this bridge was necessary to carry the Duchlage Road over not only the original Crieff Junction Railway line, but also the Up and Down lines leading to the new station. Duchlage Road was diverted to the east of its original alignment (as shown in Figures 1.9 and 5.2), with substantial earth embankments leading up to each end of the bridge. The Crieff Junction and Crieff & Methven Junction lines were slewed to create a connection with the new station, falling slightly from the former Crieff & Methven Junction Railway sidings to the station. At the west end of the station, the Crieff & Comrie Railway was carried under the bridge at King Street (formerly known as Brown's Row), some 15 feet below street level, through a cutting in the West Meadow, varying in depth from 15 feet at King Street to 21 feet at the Burrell Street tunnel.

The plans for the new station at Crieff were prepared by Mr James Law, assistant to Mr Barr, the Caledonian Railway District Engineer at Perth, with the contractors being Messrs Kinnear Moodie & Co of Edinburgh.

The station was a grand affair, with two main platforms some 700 feet long, of which 300 feet was covered by a veranda or canopy. The station buildings extended 180 feet along the centre part of each platform, while the platforms were 20 feet wide opposite the offices and 15 feet wide at the ends. A zinc-covered footbridge, 52 feet long, spanned the three tracks.

The main booking hall and stationmaster's office were on the Up platform, or north side, while there were waiting rooms on both platforms. The Down platform housed the ticket collector's office, guard's room, and a lamp room capable of holding 150 oil lamps. There was also a boiler house for foot-warming pans capable of storing seventy-five pans. In addition to the approach carriageways from King Street to both Up and Down sides, a footpath was also created from Duchlage Road to the Up platform. It was reported on 20th May 1892 that Colonel Williamson, leading from the front as ever, rode over the bridge in King Street to formally declare it open!

The Half Yearly meeting on 31st August 1892 was, however, a less happy affair. Other than the Directors and officials, only a handful of shareholders attended. Colonel Williamson berated the contractors, McKay & Son, over the fact that under the terms of their contract the line should have been ready for opening five weeks ago, but was now well behind schedule. But the most pressing issue was the need for more capital to complete the line. Thus far £30,211 had been expended and a further £17,053 was yet to be spent, amounting to a total of £47,264. The Directors were willing to contribute a further £1,000, but this would still leave £8,000 to be found by the shareholders.

By December, the buildings at Comrie station were nearly finished and the engine shed at Comrie was completed. Sadly, the engine shed did not last long, being blown down in a gale less than a year later in November 1893, only a few months after the line opened. There is no record of the shed being rebuilt, so presumably it was found feasible to operate the line using locomotives based at Crieff.

At the following Half Yearly meeting, on 28th February 1893, the Engineer reported that about 5½ miles of the line was now completed, with 3½ miles of track completed and another mile laid and ready for ballasting. Comrie station was ready for painting and various station facilities were being completed. Unfortunately costs were still rising; by 31st January 1893 the line had cost £42,052, and this was to rise further to £48,749 by 31st July. Set against this the share issue had thus far only raised £36,713, leaving a considerable

Plate 2.5
The first train to arrive at Comrie station early on the morning of 1st June 1893. The impressive eight-coach train was hauled by Caledonian Railway 2-4-0 No. 467, designed by Benjamin Conner and built by Dübs & Co in 1875. Seen here standing at what was then the only platform, later the Down platform, the photographer is standing on the site of the Up platform which was created in 1901 when the line was extended through to St. Fillans. The siding was used to allow engines to run around their trains for the journey back to Crieff. *Courtesy Bernard Byrom*

gap. To bridge this, the Directors were compelled to guarantee an overdraft with their bankers, the Clydesdale Bank, and to arrange for the contractor to accept Lloyds bonds in part payment for the money due.

Despite these problems, work on the line was nearing completion and on 17th May the *Strathearn Herald* carried an account of the first run by the contractor's locomotive from Crieff to Comrie. The engine was decorated with flags and evergreens, and, of course, Colonel Williamson was on the footplate. Word had got round, such that there was a large crowd there to greet the arrival of this first train. Speeches were made, and three cheers given for the contractors, before the engine steamed back to Crieff. A few days later, an engineer's special carried officials of the Caledonian Railway over the line to conduct a detailed inspection of the railway and its engineering works in preparation for the Board of Trade inspection.

The formal Board of Trade inspection was carried out by Major General Hutchinson on 29th May 1893. He arrived by special train at Crieff at 9.0am, where he was met by Colonel Williamson and officials of both the Crieff & Comrie Railway and the Caledonian Railway. After first inspecting the signalling and the new station at Crieff, Major General Hutchinson boarded his special train and travelled over the line to Comrie. He made detailed inspections of the various bridges and tunnels along the line and at Strowan tunnel, near Baird's Monument, the train stopped so that he could get down and inspect the tunnel and cutting, this being the heaviest engineering on the line.

A charming story relating to this stop was the fact that the first members of the public to travel over the line were in fact a group of children from nearby Monzievaird School who, while the General was inspecting the tunnel, came down to see the 'Caley' 'Jumbo' which was hauling the special train. An official invited them onto the train, which then proceeded to Comrie. He then wrote a note explaining their absence and sent them home. Sadly history does not record what their teacher said when they returned from their great adventure!

On arrival at Comrie the General first inspected the signalling and station layout, and then expressed himself satisfied and declared the line ready for traffic. Following this he attended a lunch in his honour at the Commercial Hotel before departing back to Crieff.

The formalities having been completed, the line was formally opened two days later on 1st June 1893. The inaugural train left Crieff at 6.30am, the journey time to Comrie being 16 minutes, the speed not being excessive due to the curves on the line – in particular that through Strowan Tunnel which had a speed restriction of 12 mph. Although an air of celebration prevailed in Comrie, with many houses and public buildings being decorated with bunting and banners, and a public holiday having been declared, only a few people turned up to see the first train arrive, probably on account of the early hour.

Uncharacteristically, Colonel Williamson did not put in an appearance until around midday, by which time the village was thronged with sightseers, who had come from Crieff, and locals who had come for a trip on the railway. Even the coachman of the rival Crieff & Comrie stagecoach travelled on the 1.40pm train to Crieff.

The untiring efforts of the one man who had done so much over many years to bring the railway to Comrie, Colonel Williamson, were rightly recognised with a banquet held in his honour at the Public Hall on 20th September 1893. Some £200 was raised by public donations and the Colonel was presented with three large ornate silver plated bowls, while the Hon Mrs Williamson received a solid silver tea set of Indian design in recognition of the great interest she had also taken in the railway, and her support for her husband.

The day was another one of celebration for the village, with the streets once again being decorated. The Colonel and his wife were driven from their home at Lawers to the hall in an open carriage, being cheered on their way by an enthusiastic crowd. The usual speeches were made, toasts proposed and drunk, and generally the day was one for rejoicing, for after thirty-seven years, Comrie finally had its railway.

All was not well, however, for a disagreement between the Colonel and Mr Shaw, the Company Secretary, had led to the latter's dismissal, leaving him a bitter man. This was in sad contrast to the mood earlier that summer when a meeting of the shareholders in the Crieff & Comrie Railway from the west of Scotland was held in Glasgow, for the purpose of making a presentation to Mr Shaw. The presentation took the form of a testimonial in recognition of his many valuable services in the successful promotion and carrying through of the railway.

In addition to the unhappy departure of Mr Shaw, Mr McKay, the contractor, was suing the company for unpaid bills. Both these disputes were to rumble on for several years, with the contractor pursuing his case through the courts. Both were to play a part in the demise of the Crieff & Comrie Railway Company only five years later.

While all this was going on in the background, the Caledonian Railway got on with the task of operating the railway under the terms of the agreement incorporated in the Act of Parliament. The initial passenger service provided six trains each way per day between Crieff and Comrie originating over the Crieff Junction line, and a further train over the Crieff to Perth line.

In addition to this there was an early morning goods train which ran as required, daily except Fridays, departing from Crieff at 8.40am to arrive at Comrie at 9.00am. On Mondays this returned to Crieff as a cattle train at 9.15am, Comrie having to telegraph Crieff the previous Saturday if this was required. There was also a regular goods train in the afternoon, departing Crieff at 2.40pm to arrive at Comrie at 3.00pm, where it was allowed 40 minutes for shunting before departing again 3.40pm. This train ran through to Perth along the Methven line, calling at all stations other than Tibbermuir and Huntingtower sidings.

Passenger numbers continued to climb in the first few years as one might expect, but peaked in 1896 before starting a gradual decline. This was mirrored elsewhere on local lines, but came at an inopportune time for the fledgling Crieff & Comrie Railway which was still struggling financially. The figures for the first six years of operation speak for themselves:

Year	Annual Passenger Traffic Figures Booked	Arrived	Annual Receipts Coaching	Goods	Total
1893*	15,896	15,543	£1,417	£813	£2,229
1894	23,800	19,714	£2,098	£2,653	£4,751
1895	26,053	20,282	£2,217	£3,838	£6,055
1896	27,409	19,840	£2,285	£3,300	£5,585
1897	26,304	18,577	£2,397	£2,511	£4,908
1898	25,124	18,081	£2,821	£2,126	£4,447

* This was only a part year from 1st June.

The Half Yearly meeting in April 1894 was a sorry affair. Mr Shaw, who had been dismissed earlier in the month, led what could best be described as a revolt among some shareholders, and a heated debate over the finances of the company ensued. Despite this, the accounts were adopted and the Board re-elected. The following Half Yearly meeting, in October 1894, was less contentious, and the Chairman reported that the railway was in a prosperous state and that they were able to declare a dividend of 1½%. This dividend was maintained at the next Half Yearly meeting, in April 1895, when the Chairman again painted a rosy image of the railways finances, whilst omitting to mention the not insignificant outstanding claim of the contractor for £11,500.

LEFT: Figure 2.8
A rare copy of the first Half Yearly report issued by the Crieff & Comrie Railway Company on 31st July 1893, just two months after the line opened for traffic. The traffic and revenue figures were provisional only at this time, and the statement by the Engineer Mr John Young that the line was in good working condition and repair would seem superfluous given that it had only been open for two months, but this reflected the standard form of wording used in such reports. This was not only the first, but also the penultimate report produced by Mr Shaw, who was dismissed in May the following year.
Author's collection

ABOVE: Figure 2.9
An equally rare Shareholder's Dividend Statement for the Half Year ending 31st July 1896. The dividend rate payable was just 1½%, nowhere near the 5% which had been promised and forecast when the line was promoted. 1896 was the year in which the railway's finances peaked, and the dividend never rose above 1½%. Less than two years later the company was taken over by the Caledonian Railway. It can be seen that this certificate was issued by Thomas Dempster, who took over as Company Secretary from the unfortunate Mr Shaw.
Author's collection

The gradual increase in traffic, and consequently the company's finances, continued through 1895 and into 1896. However, it is interesting to note that whereas the Chairman reported at the Half Yearly meeting in October 1896 that revenue had increased slightly, the Caledonian Railway accounts for that period show that it actually fell in 1896. As the October meeting reported on figures for the six-month period ending on 31st July, one can surmise that the decline began during the ensuing five months.

By early 1897, the rot had set in and the company's prospects continued to decline. The Half Yearly meeting in October 1897 was a subdued occasion. The only attendees were Colonel Williamson, four fellow Directors and four shareholders. The Chairman acknowledged for the first time that the railway's financial position was not as healthy as in previous years, but the Directors still declared a 1½% dividend. This public meeting lasted only five minutes, after which the Directors met privately. The purpose of this second meeting was to discuss selling the company to the Caledonian Railway. The writing was on the wall for the Crieff & Comrie Railway.

Negotiations were entered into with the Caledonian, and on 9th February 1898 a Special Meeting of the Crieff & Comrie Railway shareholders was held. The Caledonian Railway – which already controlled the other three railway companies in Strathearn, and which had recently invested heavily in the Lochearnhead, St. Fillans & Comrie Railway which would complete the link-up with the Callander & Oban Railway – was prepared to be generous to secure this link to complete their east–west network and, equally importantly, to keep their rival, the North British Railway, at bay. The Caledonian therefore agreed to repay shareholders in full, and to assume responsibility for the company's outstanding liabilities. Thus, on 1st August 1898, the Caledonian absorbed the Crieff & Comrie Railway, and yet another of Strathearn's local railways fell victim to the harsh realities of railway economics.

LOCHEARNHEAD, ST. FILLANS & COMRIE RAILWAY

The last of the branch lines of Strathearn to be constructed, the Lochearnhead, St. Fillans & Comrie Railway, presented the greatest engineering challenges, and, at 15 miles, was also the longest. It passed through some of the most sparsely populated areas of the Strath, with only two villages of any significance, at St. Fillans and Lochearnhead. The real attraction of such a line, however, was that it would close the gap between Comrie and the Callander & Oban line at Lochearnhead, a long-held ambition of the Caledonian Railway.

By 1896, when the scheme was proposed, the Caledonian Railway was both the pre-eminent and the wealthiest railway company in Scotland. In 1865 it had amalgamated with the Scottish Central Railway, gaining control of the main line from Stirling to Perth, which ran along the southern side of Strathearn. It had then absorbed the Crieff Junction Railway as part of the Scottish Central Railway, and both the Perth Almond Valley & Methven and the Crieff & Methven

Junction railways through amalgamation with the Scottish North Eastern Railway, thus controlling the lines which ran along the eastern and northern sides of the Strath. It operated the Crieff & Comrie Railway in the east and the Callander & Oban Railway to the west, so it was hardly surprising therefore that the Caledonian not only encouraged the scheme, but also agreed to subscribe £82,500, over half the necessary capital of £162,000.

As early as December 1896, three of the promoters of the railway met with Mr Hogg, the Engineer of the Crieff & Comrie Railway to discuss plans for this new route. Subsequently, the promoters of the railway prepared a Bill which was presented to the 1897 session of Parliament. Unlike the earlier branch lines, this one did not have quite the same widespread local support. There were a number of objections to the Bill from, among others, a group of Comrie residents, Lady Helen McGregor of McGregor of Edinchip near Balquhidder, and the tenants of Edinchip Estate. The residents of Comrie were most concerned about the blocking up of various streets, damage to allotments and loss of amenity from the railway passing through Comrie on a high embankment and crossing three roads on substantial bridges.

Lady McGregor was even more upset by the proposals, for the Callander & Oban Railway already ran through her estate, passing close to the north of her house. The proposed new line would pass in front of her house and join the Callander & Oban line at Lochearnhead (renamed Balquhidder). Thus as she pointed out:

'the mansion house would be encompassed by two lines of railway. The result would be utterly to destroy the privacy and amenity of the house and grounds and seriously to depreciate their value', adding that 'the works proposed would also cut off the magnificent view of Loch Earn'.

She suggested that a shorter and easier route would be along the south side of Loch Earn, but her most telling comment was:

'None of the promoters of the railway have any interest in the district through which the proposed railway would pass and most of them are not even connected with the County of Perth, and they are, as your petitioner believes, promoting the railway not from any desire to serve the public in the best possible manner, but entirely from pecuniary motives.'

Her Ladyship was supported in her objections by seventeen of her crofters and tenants of Edinchip Estate, who also lodged a petition against the Bill, mainly on the grounds that the proposed line would cut through or destroy various crofts and holdings, leaving no access to some parts. It has to be said, however, that much of their petition reads very like that of her Ladyship, and Paragraph 9 was almost word for word the paragraph quoted above.

The inhabitants of Lochearnhead were not alone in their discontent, for many of the villagers of St. Fillans were equally unhappy. At a meeting of 'feuers' and others, held in late 1896, it was stated that 'This would practically ruin St Fillans as a summer residence'. Crofters were also concerned about the danger of fire to thatched cottages from sparks from engines. However, it was suspicion over the financial motives of the promoters, which, as with Lady McGregor, lay at the heart of their concerns. A poem reflecting this was even dedicated to the promoters:

"'Lives there a man with a soul so dead?"
St Fillan to promoters said,
Promoters answered back with glee:
"Not troubled much with soul are we,
But love to think of £ s d."
The saint concludes,
"Promote indeed! Promotion high,
Full six feet nearer to the sky.
A hen pen collar strong and good
Will end your mean promoting mood.
Strathearn will pay the £ s d."'

Two other petitions were lodged, one on behalf of the North British Railway and, more unusually, one from the Caledonian and Callander & Oban railways. Both of these objected to the proposed running powers to be granted under the Bill. In the case of the North British Railway, this related to running powers into Perth General Station, of which it was a joint owner with the Caledonian and Highland railways. The Caledonian objected to all the running powers proposed: over the Callander & Oban Railway all the way through to Oban, over the Crieff & Comrie Railway, and over the Crieff to Perth line including the General station. It seems strange that the promoters had not thought to resolve these issues with their Caledonian Railway backers when they drafted the Bill, but in the event all the running powers listed at Paragraph 54 of the draft Bill were deleted when the amended Bill went before Parliament.

These objections were considered by the Parliamentary Select Committee, which had been specifically tasked, among other matters, to investigate the impact on the scenery caused by the construction

Figure 2.10
The Lochearnhead, St. Fillans & Comrie Railway Act 1897. It is worth noting that the railway used this title and not the Comrie, St. Fillans and Lochearnhead Railway which would have been the logical way round as a follow-on from the Crieff & Comrie Railway. This erroneous form of wording is sometimes used by historians who could be forgiven for being confused by it! The Act reflects the Bill in the amended form which was submitted to Parliament after changes to accommodate some of the objections raised to the original Bill. *Author's collection*

of the railway. This was the first case in the United Kingdom where such environmental factors were taken into account and thus an important milestone in this area, whereas nowadays it is standard practice for such an assessment to be made in all such construction projects.

The petitions regarding the route through Comrie and Edinchip were not supported, however, and the report from the Committee dated 19th March 1897 contained only a couple of paragraphs relating to financial matters, beyond which it was stated that: *'There were no other circumstances of which in the opinion of the Committee, it is desirable that the House be informed'.*

It was not surprising that later in the year Colonel Williamson himself travelled to London to be on hand when the Bill went to Parliament for final approval. The Bill having passed without difficulty, he immediately telegraphed the good news to Comrie, and this evidently spread round the district. It was reported that flags were hoisted at Lochearnhead Post Office and the hotel, and a bonfire lit at St. Fillans where dancing went on into the night. The Bill subsequently received the Royal Assent on 9th August 1897.

The estimated cost of building the line reflected both its length and the more difficult nature of some of the terrain to be traversed. The estimate prepared by Crouch & Hogg, Engineers of Glasgow dated 29th December 1896 was as follows:

Cuttings – Rock	93,241 cu yds	£16,317
Cuttings – Soft Soil	189,034 cu yds	£11,814
Cuttings – Roads	13,696 cu yds	£1,027
Embankments	424,876 cu yds	£9,660
Bridges – Public Roads (10)		£7,500
Accommodation Bridges		£13,500
River and Stream Bridges		£6,500
Viaducts		£13,500
Culverts and Drains		£7,500
Metalling of Roads		£1,200
Retaining Walls		£1,000
Permanent Way (15m 1f 2 chs)		£33,330
Permanent Way – Sidings and Junctions		£3,000
Stations		£5,000
Total Construction Costs		£132,849
Contingencies		£13,301
Land and Buildings (121 acres)		£13,850
Total		£160,000

IN PARLIAMENT.
SESSION 1897.

LOCHEARNHEAD, ST. FILLANS AND COMRIE RAILWAY.

ESTIMATE OF EXPENSE.

Length of Line: Miles 15, f. 1, chs. 2 — Single line.

Earthworks:	Cubic yds.	Price per yd. s. d.	Amount £ s. d.	£ s. d.
Cuttings—Rock	93,241	3 6	16,317 3 6	
Soft Soil	189,034	1 3	11,814 12 6	
Roads	13,696	1 6	1,027 4 0	
TOTAL	295,971	—	29,159 0 0	29,159 0 0

		£ s. d.
Embankments, including Roads	424,786 cubic yards	9,660 0 0
Bridges—Public Roads	Number, 10	7,500 0 0
Accommodation Bridges and Works		13,500 0 0
River and Stream Bridges		6,500 0 0
Viaducts		15,500 0 0
Culverts and Drains		7,500 0 0
Metallings of Roads		1,200 0 0
Retaining Walls		1,000 0 0
Permanent Way, including Fencing: Miles 15, F. 1, Chs. 2	at Cost per mile £2,200 0 0	33,330 0 0
Permanent Way for Sidings, and Cost of Junctions		3,000 0 0
Stations		5,000 0 0
	£	132,849 0 0
Contingencies	10 per cent.	13,301 0 0
	£	146,150 0 0
Land and Buildings: A. 121, R. 0, P. 0		13,850 0 0
	TOTAL £	160,000 0 0

CROUCH & HOGG,
Engineers.

Glasgow, 29th December, 1896.

Figure 2.11
The Estimate of Expense for the Lochearnhead, St. Fillans & Comrie Railway drawn up by Crouch & Hogg, the Engineers in December 1896 as one of the supporting documents for the Bill. The figures give an idea of the impressive amount of work required for this stretch of line, particularly the volume of rock to be removed and the viaducts at Comrie, Glenogle and Edinchip. ***Author's collection***

The authorised capital of the company was £165,000, comprising 16,500 shares of £10 each. The Caledonian Railway's contribution was made on the condition that it had the option, within five years of opening, of taking over the whole undertaking. The Board of Directors reflected the amount of outside capital invested, and to some extent bore out Lady McGregor's observations, the only local representative being the redoubtable Colonel Williamson of Lawers. The full Board were:

- Colonel Home-Drummond (Chairman), Convenor of Perthshire County Council
- Mr JA Dewar, Lord Provost of Perth
- Mr JM Fraser of Rosemount, Perth
- Mr JB Nicholson, a Director of the Caledonian Railway and of the Town & County Bank
- Colonel DR Williamson of Lawers

The line was to be constructed in two sections, Comrie to St. Fillans, and St. Fillans to Balquhidder. There was little interest in the contract for the first section of the line, with only one tender being received, from John Paton CE of Glasgow. This was accepted in May 1899 and, on the 12th June 1899, the first turf was cut by Colonel Williamson in Laggan Park at Comrie, although it was a very low-key affair compared with previous occasions, there being little ceremony.

Work on construction began the following month, with around 400 navvies and thirty horses being employed on various stretches of the line. Groundwork started in Laggan Park and at Mill of Ross, and later that month a start was made on both the bridge over the River Lednock and the larger structure over the River Earn.

The navvies employed on this railway would appear to have been less well behaved than their church-going predecessors on the Crieff & Methven Railway, or even those employed on building the Crieff & Comrie Railway, for there were numerous reports in the local press over the following years of some of their number getting into trouble. Given the number of navvies needed and the relatively remote location, this is perhaps hardly surprising. Drink would appear to have been the main problem; with little else to do, a lot of time was spent in the local hostelries. One newspaper reported that:

'The sight of these men wandering aimlessly about the village after working hours is inexpressively sad. The disgraceful state of the streets crowded with drunken men is not to be wondered at when one knows that the poor fellows have only the public houses to fall back upon for rest and relaxation.'

CHAPTER 2: THE EXTENSION TO UPPER STRATHEARN

Plate 2.6
The small contractor's locomotive used for the construction of the Lochearnhead, St. Fillans & Comrie Railway. This locomotive would have been used to move materials around the site as work progressed, but various photographs prove that despite its limited endurance, it did manage to traverse the full length of the line. Seen here at St. Fillans, it was a primitive engine, which by today's standards looks somewhat hazardous with a basic brake system and rudimentary controls, to say nothing of the lack of crew comfort!
Author's collection

The same report recommended the establishment of a reading room; once again Colonel Williamson took the initiative, and in September 1899 a reading room sponsored by him was opened in Comrie. This no doubt helped ease the situation, but adverse reports of navvies' behaviour continued to appear in the press. In April 1900, the *Strathearn Herald* published a whole article entitled 'Notes from Comrie – Navvies and drink', and four months later a visitor to Comrie wrote to complain that his coach had passed by '*six navvies who were dead drunk*' lying by the side of the road.

Despite these problems with the navvies during their free time, there would appear to have been no complaints about their work and steady progress was made. By November 1899, the bridge carrying the road over the railway at Comrie station was almost complete and the stone piers of the bridge over the River Lednock were ready for the steelwork. The embankment behind the village and the viaduct leading to the bridges over Dundas Street and the River Earn were almost complete. About a mile and a half of the line to the west of the river Earn was also well advanced.

By the spring of 1900 the bridge over the River Lednock was complete; in characteristic style, Colonel Williamson opened it on the 18th April by driving the contractors 'pug' locomotive over it. Work was also put in hand to convert Comrie station from a terminus into a passing station, with a second platform on the Up side and a signal box. Later in the summer the focus of effort moved to St. Fillans, with the plant and equipment, together with the navvy's camp, being moved further up the line.

A notable feature of the Lochearnhead, St. Fillans & Comrie Railway was the extensive use of mass concrete for viaducts, bridges and bridge abutments. This relatively innovative method had been used on the West Highland Railway extension between Fort William and Mallaig, most famously on the 'horse shoe' viaduct at Glenfinnan. Not to be outdone by its rival, the Caledonian made much of the concrete structures on the Lochearnhead, St. Fillans & Comrie Railway, as is reflected in the staged publicity photographs taken when the line was inspected.

Work pressed ahead during the summer, the most difficult section being the rock cutting through Dunira Wood, and by the end of June the contractor's locomotive was able to work the full length of the line between Comrie and St. Fillans. However, it took a further two months' work before the line was ready for the Board of Trade Inspection. On 6th September 1901, Colonel Donop, the Board of Trade Inspector, carried out a thorough inspection of the line and passed it fit for traffic. Six days later, the Caledonian Railway ran a special train from Glasgow to St. Fillans, conveying Directors and officials. The two-coach train was hauled by the most famous Caledonian locomotive of them all, the 4-2-2 'Single' No. 123, which had participated in the 'Railway Race to the North' in 1888.

The first section of the line opened to passenger traffic on 1st October 1901, with an initial service of three trains each way per day. St. Fillans served as the temporary terminus of the line while work carried on towards Lochearnhead; in addition to the two platforms, there was a third through line behind the Up platform which allowed engines to run round the trains. There was no turntable at St. Fillans, so engines arriving chimney first from Comrie had to return tender first. That there was considerable enthusiasm initially in St. Fillans is reflected in the fact that in the first three months of operation, 8,854 tickets were sold, the equivalent of over 35,000 tickets annually. This figure dropped to just over 26,000 the following year, and from 1904

Plate 2.7
A view of the Down platform and building at St. Fillans station looking east shortly after it was built. The Up platform has yet to be surfaced and a contractor's crane is still at work on the head-shunt at the far end of the goods loop, site of the tragic accident involving a cattle train mentioned in Chapter 9. The bulk of Littleport Hill in the background gives an impression of the rugged beauty of the scenery of the district.
St. Rollox collection at NRM

Plate 2.8
Caledonian Railway 4-2-2 'Single' No. 123 with an inspection officer's train poses on the newly completed viaduct at Comrie. The carriages are standing on the iron span across the River Earn, with the six-arch viaduct and road-bridge in the background. The village of Comrie is off to the right of the church in this view. This official photograph portrays well the mass concrete construction of which the Caledonian Railway were so proud.
St. Rollox collection at NRM

CHAPTER 2: THE EXTENSION TO UPPER STRATHEARN

xxii.

CALEDONIAN RAILWAY.

The attention of the Public is respectfully directed to the new and improved

SERVICE OF EXPRESS TRAINS

BETWEEN

Glasgow Edinburgh
(BUCHANAN STREET) (PRINCES STREET)

AND

CALLANDER, CRIEFF, COMRIE, AND ST. FILLANS;

AND ALSO BETWEEN

Glasgow Edinburgh
(CENTRAL) (PRINCES STREET)

AND

PEEBLES, MOFFAT,

And STATIONS in the UPPER WARD of LANARKSHIRE.

For full particulars see the respective Tables herein.

R. MILLAR,
GLASGOW, 1902. General Manager.

LEFT: Figure 2.12
Page xxii of the Caledonian Railway Company Time Tables for July, August and September 1902 announcing, among other improvements, the new through services from Glasgow and Edinburgh to St. Fillans. The actual timetable for the service over the Crieff Junction to St. Fillans line was on pages 78 and 79 which are reproduced at Figures 2.13 and 2.14. Elsewhere in this timetable details were given of season ticket rates from Edinburgh, Glasgow, Perth and Dundee to stations on the line. *Author's collection*

BELOW: Figure 2.13
The July to September 1902 timetable for Down trains on the newly opened section between Comrie and St. Fillans. The initial service to St. Fillans was six trains per day, with the 10.10am, 12.00 noon and 4.5pm from Glasgow (Buchanan Street) and the 9.40am train from Edinburgh (Princes Street) conveying through carriages. Only two trains per day terminated at Comrie, the remainder all ran through to St. Fillans. *Author's collection*

BOTTOM: Figure 2.14
The July to September 1902 timetable for Up trains from St. Fillans on the newly opened section. The 8.0am train conveyed through carriages for both Edinburgh (Princes Street) and Glasgow (Buchanan Street), while the 3.00pm had through carriages for Edinburgh, and there were through carriages for Glasgow on the 11.15am, 3.0pm, and 6.20pm departures. At this stage, no mention is made of Dalchonzie Platform, which did not finally open until 15th July 1903. *Author's collection*

CRIEFF, COMRIE, and

To ST. FILLANS, Via Crieff Junction.	a.m.	a.m.		a.m.	noon.	Ex. Sats. p.m.	Sats. only. p.m.	Sats. only. p.m.			p.m.	p.m.	p.m.	p.m.	
GLASGOW (Buch. St.) leave	4f20	7 15	......	10 10	12 0	12 35	1 30	......	......	......	4 5	4 45	8 0		
EDIN- {Princes St. ,,	4 · 0	6 40	......	9 40	1120a	1 35	1 35	......	......	......	3 35	4 25	7 25		NOTES.
BURGH {Waverley ,,	......	6 33	......	......	11 12	1132a	1132a	......	......	......	3 30	4 9	6 40		
PERTH ,,	......	8 20	......	10 20	......	1 50p	1 50p	2 50	......	......	5 5	......	5 5		A Calls at Highlandman at 5.39 p.m. on Saturdays only.
	a.m.	a.m.			p.m.	p.m.	p.m.				p.m.	p.m.	p.m.	p.m.	
CRIEFF JUNCTION leave	6 8	9 7	......	11 30	1 30	3 12	3 12	......	......	......	5 26	6 14	9 30		f Starts from Central Station, Glasgow.
Tullibardine ,,	......	9 14	......	11 36	......	3 18	3 18	......	......	......	......	6 20	9 36		
Muthill ,,	6 20	9 20	......	11 42	1 42	3 24	3 24	......	......	......	5 35	6 26	9 42		
Highlandman ,,	......	9 28	......	11 48	......	3 30	3 30	......	......	......	A	6 32	9 48		
CRIEFF {arrive	6 29	9 33	......	11 53	1 50	3 35	3 35	3 30	......	5 35	5 42	6 37	9 53		
{leave	6 33	9 55	......	11 55	1 55	3 37	......	3 40	4 5	5 45	6 60	......			
COMRIE {arrive	6 48	10 10	......	12 10	2 10	3 52	......	3 55	4 20	6 0	7 5	......			
{leave	6 56	10 13	......	12 12	2 18	......	......	4 3	......	6 1	......	......			
ST. FILLANS arrive	7 8	10 25	......	12 25	2 30	......	......	4 15	......	6 12	......	......			

ST. FILLANS BRANCH.

From ST. FILLANS, Via Crieff Junction.	a.m.	a.m.	a.m.	a.m.	p.m.	p.m.	p.m.	p.m.	p.m.	p.m.	Sats. only. p.m.	
ST. FILLANS leave	......	8 0	......	11 15	1 25	3 0	......	6 20	......	......	7 5	NOTES.
COMRIE {arrive	......	8 12	......	11 27	1 37	3 12	......	6 32	......	......	7 17	
{leave	7 5	8 20	......	11 35	1 40	3 15	4 40	6 33	......	......	7 18	c Arrives at 8.55 p.m. on Saturdays.
CRIEFF {arrive	7 20	8 35	......	11 50	1 55	3 30	4 55	6 48	......	......	7 33	
{leave	7 23	8 45	10 40	11 54	2 0	3 35	4 57	6 50	......	7 15	7 36	
Highlandman ,,	7 27	8 49	......	10 44	......	2 4	......	......	......	7 19	......	
Muthill ,,	7 32	8 55	......	10 49	12 1	2 10	......	5 6	......	7 25	......	
Tullibardine ,,	7 37	9 0	......	10 55	......	2 17	......	5 12	......	7 31	......	
CRIEFF JUNCTION arrive	7 42	9 6	......	11 1	12 10	2 22	3 51	5 18	7 6	7 37	......	
PERTH arrive	8 40	......	......	11 46	......	3 20	......	6 10	7 45	......	8 20	
EDINBURGH {Princes St.,	10 30	......	10 40	......	1 5p	2 24	4 35	5 35	7 59	9 25	9 35	
{Waverley ,,	9 43	......	......	......	1 8	2 20	4 37	......	8 1	9 22	......	
GLASGOW (Buch. St.) ,,	9 15	......	10 25	......	1 10	1 45	4 30	5 15	8 0	9 c0	9 25	

ABOVE: **Plate 2.9**
Caledonian Railway 4-2-2 'Single' No. 123 with an inspection officer's train poses on the newly completed viaduct at Dundurn between Comrie and St. Fillans. This official photograph also portrays the mass concrete construction which, as new, stands out starkly against the surrounding woodland. The size of some of the trees which were a source of the extensive timber traffic from the district are well illustrated here. *St. Rollox collection at NRM*

Plate 2.10
A view looking down on St. Fillans station not long after it opened. At this stage it was serving as the temporary terminus for the line; an unidentified 4-4-0 has just brought a Down train into the station and is about to run round the carriages for the return trip. The necessity of the loop line behind the Up platform is well demonstrated here, both platform being occupied. The contractor's small works locomotive can be seen in the head-shunt on the left. *Author's collection*

onwards averaged only about 10,000 per annum, roughly half the number of passengers arriving.

Although the line to St. Fillans opened on 1st October 1901, the intermediate halt at Dalchonzie did not open until several years later. In July 1902 complaints appeared in the *Strathearn Herald* that although a passenger platform had been erected at Dalchonzie Siding, it was not being used. Nearly a year later, in May 1903, there was a further complaint that it was still not open, and it eventually opened on 15th July 1903. Even then it was only a simple platform and there were further complaints about the lack of any form of shelter. As late as March 1904 a letter was sent to Mr Miller, General Manager of the Caledonian Railway, who responded that he would have the matter considered, and eventually a basic shelter was provided.

However, while the line to St. Fillans was being completed and then opened, the Lochearnhead, St. Fillans & Comrie Railway was in real financial difficulty.

As early as the previous March, the Directors had recognised that they had insufficient funds to complete the line and approached the Caledonian Railway to take over the undertaking. At this stage the Caledonian was unwilling to do so, but when it became apparent that investors were unwilling to further invest in the company, the situation became critical. The Caledonian had already subscribed 50% of the capital (£82,500) and they were faced with the choice of abandoning the line or taking over the construction of the remaining 9½ miles. They chose the latter, and on 7th May 1901 signed an agreement with the Lochearnhead, St. Fillans & Comrie Railway to take over the bankrupt company with effect from 1st August 1902.

Thus, before the construction of the final section of line from St. Fillans to Lochearnhead was even completed, the Caledonian owned and operated all of the branch lines in Strathearn. All save the last had started out as local initiatives, largely locally funded and in some

Plate 2.11
The tunnel just west of St. Fillans where the line cut through the ridge which ran down from Monadh a Phuirt Mhoir towards Loch Earn. The only tunnel on this stretch of line, it was cut through solid rock and had substantial abutments of a similar mass concrete design to that used for the viaducts and bridges. *Author's collection*

Plate 2.12
The viaduct over the stream at the foot of Glen Tarken, just west St. Fillans, was one example of the use of mass concrete used on this section of line. It also gives an impression of the way in which the line clung to the hillside as it made its way along the northern side of Loch Earn. *Author's collection*

Plate 2.13
The newly completed station at Lochearnhead which replaced the original, which was then renamed Balquhidder. This view from the Callander & Oban line, on the slopes above the station, looking east shows the impressive viaduct across the mouth of Glen Ogle, and the scar caused by the earthworks along the northern shore of the Loch Earn. The renowned Lochearnhead Hotel is just visible behind the station.

University of Aberdeen GW Wilson collection

CHAPTER 2: THE EXTENSION TO UPPER STRATHEARN

Right: Plate 2.14
The sign which adorned the site office of the Engineers for the Lochearnhead, St. Fillans & Comrie Railway. This would likely have been moved as the site office location shifted progressively up the line. It appears to have been the last such sign used as it lists W Ross Rae as Resident Engineer, he having succeeded the late John Paton following the latter's untimely death in February 1902.
Author

Plate 2.15
Another view of the recently completed Lochearnhead station, taken from the overbridge at the west end of the station, looking east. The small locomotive in the foreground is another of the contractor's locomotives, a Barclay 0-4-0T. This was a conventional saddle tank engine, unlike the earlier contractor's locomotive at Plate 2.6.
University of Aberdeen GW Wilson collection

cases independently operated; but, within a few years, all had fallen on hard times and had been taken over by larger companies, all of which were subsequently amalgamated with the Caledonian. For the next quarter of a century, the Caledonian Railway reigned supreme.

In the meantime, Caledonian financing allowed work to continue on the second contract, starting in June 1901. However, six months later, the death of Mr John Paton from a chill, at the age of only forty years of age, brought work to a standstill. This sudden stoppage of work in the middle of winter had dramatic consequences for the navvies, for without work they did not receive any pay. Many drifted away in search of other work, but a hard frost right across Scotland had brought other work to a stop, so there was no work elsewhere either. The navvies started to return to St. Fillans, but many were said to be *'utterly destitute'* and a soup kitchen and other amenities were set up locally to aid them.

A new contractor, Mr W Ross Rae, was appointed as a matter of some urgency and work soon restarted. Later that summer, work continued on both the heavy earthworks – where the line ran along the north side of Loch Earn, and onto the massive viaducts at Glen Ogle and Edinchip. By the spring of 1904 the line was completed as far as Lochearnhead, and on 27th May it was inspected by a representative of the Board of Trade. On 16th June, a special train, again hauled by Caledonian Railway No. 123, carrying Caledonian Railway officials and members of the press, completed a round trip of the line. The line to Lochearnhead was opened to passenger traffic on 1st July and to goods traffic a week later on 8th July.

Lochearnhead was to serve as the temporary terminus for the next ten months while the final section to Balquhidder was completed, rather as St. Fillans had done the previous three years. This may in part explain the generous track layout at Lochearnhead, including a passing loop and substantial signal box. It was significant that neither of these lasted long, both being abolished only seventeen years later, in 1921. The line was finally fully opened through to Balquhidder on 1st May 1905.

A contemporary report portrayed the opening of the final section with the brave words: *'the last length of the iron road connecting the East and West coasts of Scotland will soon be laid'*. However, although the line was regularly used for the through routing of excursion and livestock traffic, it was never to become the vital east–west link its promoters had hoped for, and was only ever regarded as a country branch line. Nonetheless, with its opening, the network of branch lines in Strathearn was now complete.

ABOVE: Plate 2.16
A further view of Lochearnhead station shortly after completion, looking west from the goods yard. At least five contractor's hand trolleys can be seen stacked against the bank in the foreground, while the change in gradient as the line started the climb up to Balquhidder is well illustrated here. The structure to the left of the station building is the roof covering the steps down to the access subway, a similar one being provided at Balquhidder. *Author's collection*

RIGHT: Plate 2.17
An impressive view of the massive Edinchip viaduct, another prime example of the use of mass concrete, and another reason for the relatively high cost of the line. The short steel span was removed following demolition of the line in the 1950s, but a lighter span has been reinstated and the viaduct now forms a part of the Sustrans cycle network. *Author's collection*

BELOW: Plate 2.18
Balquhidder station shortly after completion of the rebuilding of the original Callander & Oban Railway station. Taken from the south, it shows the Up and Down main lines to the left, and the Comrie branch line platform and run-around loop to the right. Balquhidder West signal box and the engine shed can be seen in the background, while a navvy's wheelbarrow in the foreground indicates that work has not quite been finished.
Author's collection

Chapter 3
Gleneagles to Crieff – The Line Described

Gleneagles station, the erstwhile junction of the Strathearn lines with the former Caledonian Railway's main line from Carlisle to Perth, lies some 17¾ miles north-east of Stirling, and about 2 miles to the west of the town of Auchterarder. The station itself is situated in the very shadow of the Ochils, just to the south, and at the head of a small glen down which the burn of Ruthven Water flows before joining the River Earn some 7 miles to the north-east. Immediately to the north of an extensive cutting, in places over 100 feet deep, through which the main line enters the glen, the present-day station of Gleneagles occupies the site of the original Crieff Junction.

This earlier station was built to provide exchange facilities and a connection between the Scottish Central Railway, as it then was, and the Crieff Junction Railway, when the latter opened its branch in 1856; there had been no station at this site prior to that date. As described in Chapter 1, Crieff Junction station had three low platforms, with a wooden footbridge across the main lines, another across the branch line tracks, and a third to connect the platforms with the forecourt and access road. Accommodation comprised a heterogeneous collection of rather cramped buildings and outhouses, all wooden in construction. For the better part of sixty years this isolated junction continued to serve as the gateway to the expanding network of branch lines in Strathearn, unaware of the greatness which was to be thrust upon it. It was in the Edwardian era, preceding the First World War, that the well-established custom of the wealthy and titled classes seeking relaxation in spas and country hotels reached its height. The Caledonian Railway, led by its then general manager, Donald Matheson, ever mindful of the lucrative nature of these forms of traffic, resolved to build such a hotel resort which could be exclusively served by rail. As will be described in more detail in Chapter 7, the site chosen was on the White Muir, near the hamlet of Muirton to the west of Auchterarder. The hotel was only part of a grandiose plan, so characteristic of the almost regal Caledonian, which included not only three golf courses and other amenities, but also the complete rebuilding of Crieff Junction station.

The name of the existing station was changed to Gleneagles on 1st October 1912 as a precursor to the development of the hotel and golf courses of that name. Construction work began on the hotel in April 1914, but was halted in December that year by the onset of the First World War. Work on the golf courses and reconstruction of the station continued, however, and the new Gleneagles station was opened for traffic on 1st October 1918, just before the end of the war. Work was not finally finished until the following year, and a granite plaque set into the wall of the stationmaster's office on the island platform declares that it was *'built in 1919, the year of the peace after the Great War'*, thus reflecting the sentiment at the time that the war had been *'the war to end all wars'*. A similar plaque is set into the stone cairn on the King's course at the hotel, while a third one was built into the southern abutment of the bridge, now demolished, which carried the branch line over the main Sterling to Perth road.

The new station, built in the massive style so typical of the Caledonian, reflects the grandeur and extravagance of the hotel it was built to serve. Designed by the Caledonian's favourite architect, John Miller, it has often been acclaimed as possibly the finest example of Caledonian architecture, which reached its prime just

Plate 3.1
Gleneagles station from the south. The main line to Perth curves away to the right while the double junction for the Crieff branch line goes off to the left. The large enamel sign on the left read 'ALIGHT HERE FOR GLENEAGLES HOTEL AND GOLF COURSES'. The large water tank which supplied the station and locomotive water cranes is at the top of the slope to the right, but is hidden by trees in this shot taken in 1963. *Author*

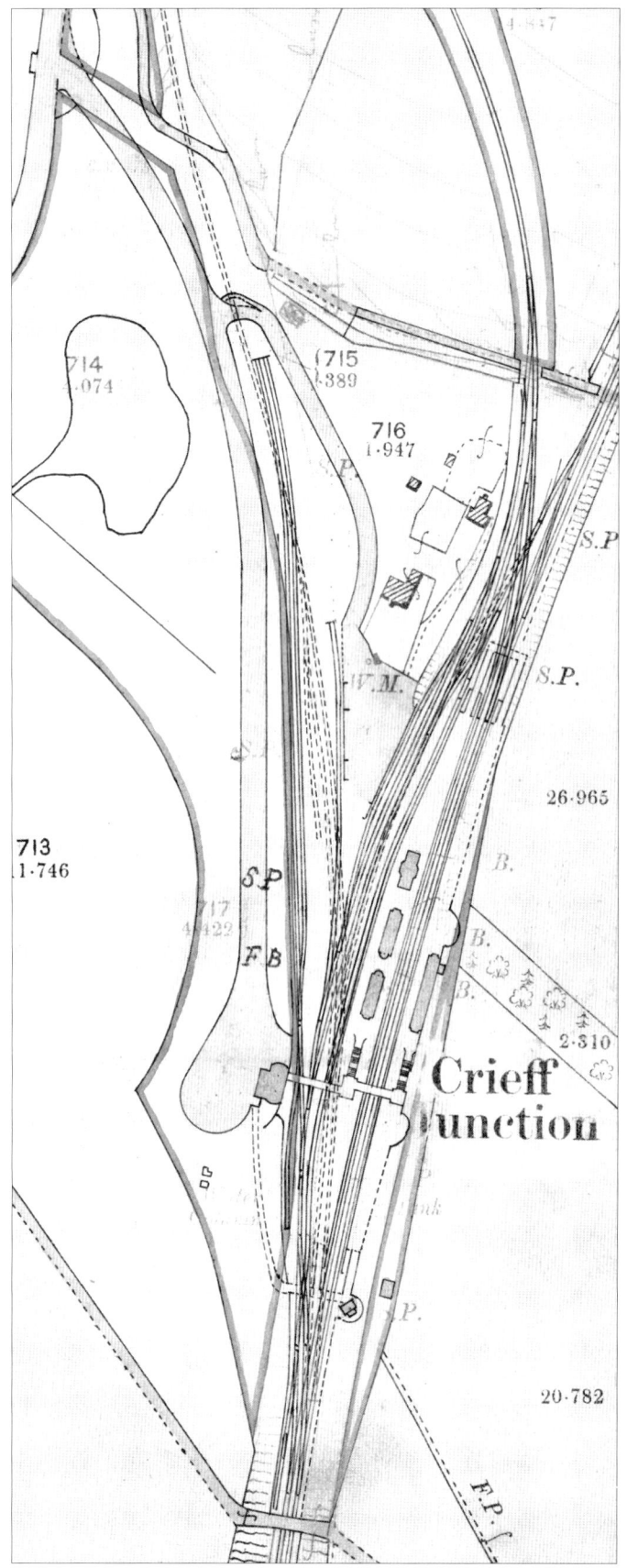

prior to the Grouping in 1923 (others being Stirling, Doune, and the now defunct Eglinton Street station just outside Glasgow). The entrance to the station and the approach road were completely remodelled as part of the Gleneagles scheme. The old muddy roadway, which had passed under a low bridge to reach the old station, was replaced by a splendid driveway leading up to the new station. Substantial stone walls with pillars flanked the entrance off the main Stirling to Perth road (later the A9). These would later be mirrored on the opposite side of the road by the entrance to the tree-lined avenue leading up to the hotel. This latter entrance has been blocked off in recent years, although the truncated avenue beyond remains. The approach road to the station climbed gently to a large circulating area outside the booking office.

This building, which was of pleasing design with crow stepped gables and canopy around the front, housed not only the booking office but also the parcels office. In addition there was

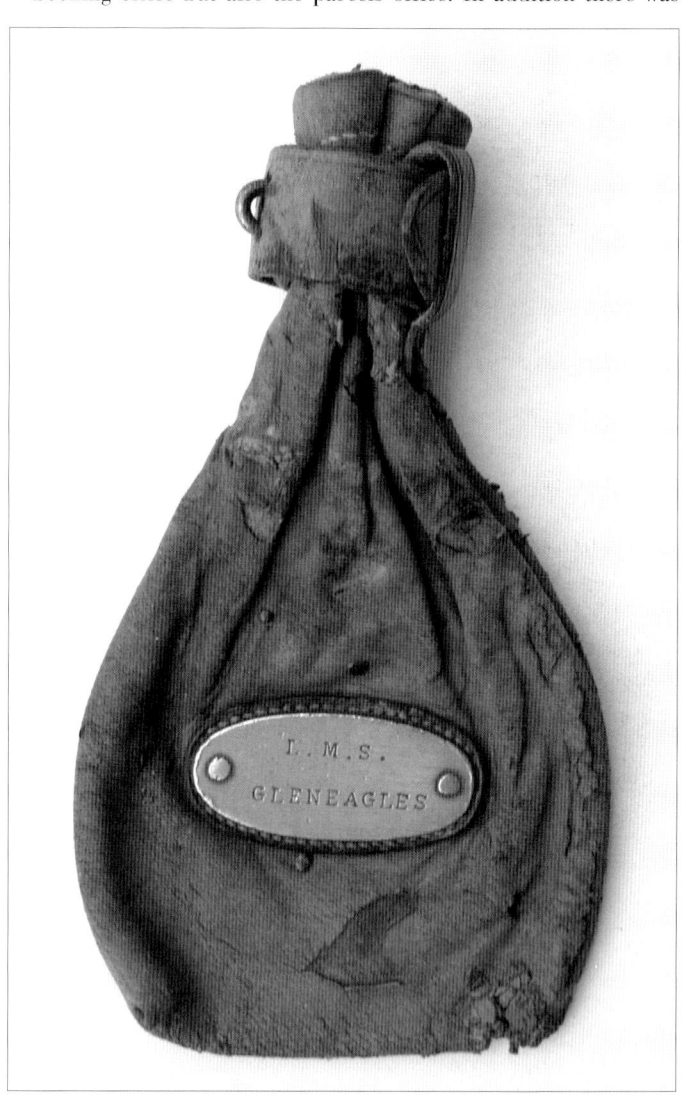

ABOVE: Plate 3.2
An LM&SR leather cash bag for Gleneagles station dating from the 1923–48 period. These padlocked bags were used to dispatch the day's takings either to the bank or to a travelling cash box on a specified train. This well-worn example has clearly seen considerable use.
Author

ABOVE LEFT: Figure 3.1
Map of Gleneagles station as rebuilt. The Ordnance Survey map is incorrect in still showing it as Crieff Junction, as the name changed seven years before it was rebuilt. This image from the official Caledonian Railway Engineer's map shows not only the new layout, but the former Crieff Junction alignment in dotted lines. It can be seen that the two long sidings follow the approximate line of the former branch line. The changes to the station approach road are also evident.
Author's collection

CHAPTER 3: GLENEAGLES TO CRIEFF – THE LINE DESCRIBED

a weighbridge and a public telephone kiosk. The initials 'CR' were proudly displayed on the front gable. Access to the platforms was by the connecting footbridge which spanned the goods yard and the branch line platform. Luggage and parcels traffic however had to be taken by barrow or trolley down a ramp from the back of the parcels office to track level at the west end of the platforms, where timber crossings provided access to the platforms.

The three new platforms served the Up Main, Down Main and Branch respectively. The Up platform boasted three waiting rooms of its own, while the island platform had three more, together with newspaper and fruit stalls, and the station offices. The platforms were covered by canopies which ran the length of the buildings and were connected by a massive iron footbridge which linked with the footbridge from the booking office situated at the top of an embankment to the north of the station. The signal box was a single-story stone building sited on the Down end of the island platform; with windows running the full length of all four sides for good sighting, it housed a fairly large frame of some 68 levers. All the buildings were of solid proportions in stone, and the whole was given a most pleasing effect by well laid out flower beds and shrubberies. Hanging flower baskets adorned the canopies and at the top of each set of stairs there were sets of shelves with colourful displays of potted plants.

In addition to the branch line platform, which also served as a refuge loop for the main line, there were three other running loops to the north of the station to facilitate shunting. The goods yard included two long sidings along the alignment of what had been the original branch line, another long siding used primarily for mineral traffic, two shorter sidings for goods traffic, and a larger loading dock with a scotch derrick and livestock pens. The two long sidings were often used for storing spare coaching stock, wagons for use on the hotel branch line and goods stock awaiting repair.

Plate 3.3
The station forecourt at Gleneagles. The building was of crow stepped design similar to Stirling station, with the initials 'CR' set in a stone block in each gable as can be seen here. To the left of the parked car was a luggage and parcels weighbridge, while the entrance to the booking office can be seen behind the car. The large turning circle was used by the Gleneagles Hotel bus and luggage lorry, and in later years also provided a limited amount of parking. *Author*

Plate 3.4
A view of the station footbridge taken from the forecourt. An ornamental flower bed and shrubs were laid out to add to the attractive entrance to the station. The footbridges were never covered in, but glazed shelters were provided at the head of each set of stairs which were themselves covered. In the days when the station was fully staffed, each of the covered areas at the top of the stairs had fitted shelves with colourful floral displays. *CRA collection*

SIDE ELEVATION

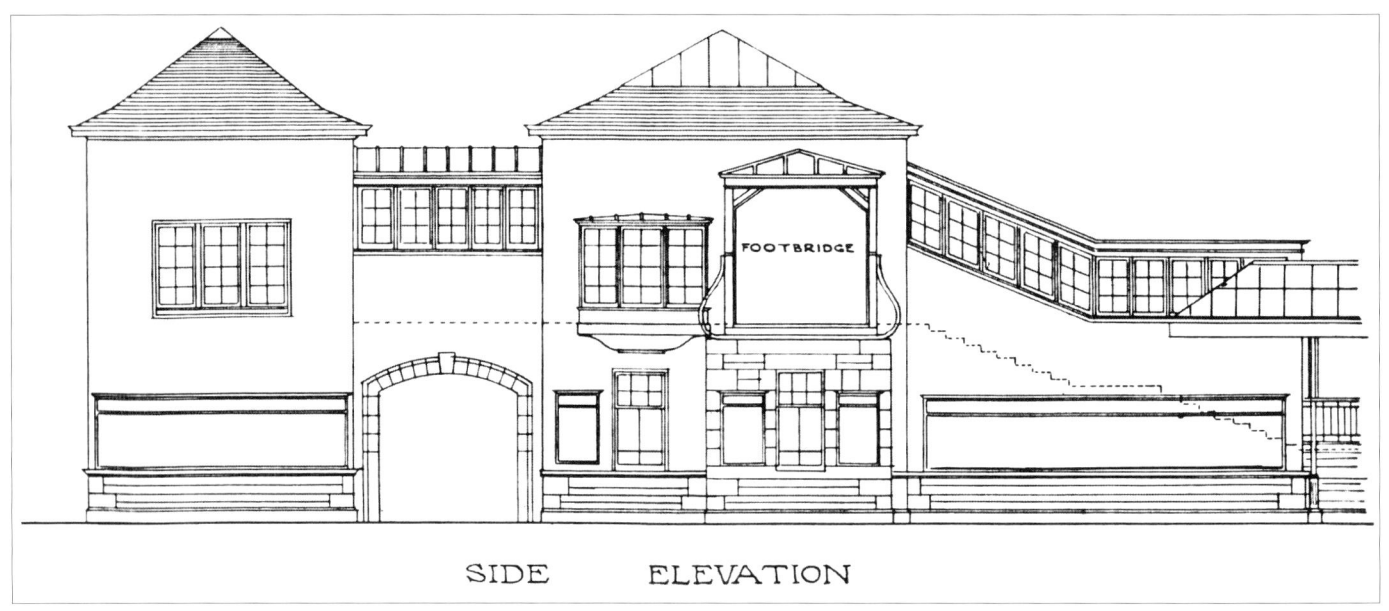

Figure 3.2
A Caledonian Railway drawing showing the luggage hoists which were planned for Gleneagles but never built. There were to be two hoists, one on the Up platform and one, as shown here, on the island platform. The towers housing the hoists were to match the original footbridge towers and would be linked to them by short bridges. These hoists would have avoided the necessity for luggage and parcels to be taken by barrow down the ramp from the booking office and across the main running lines. Since the barrow crossings over the running lines were abolished in the 1960s, passengers using the Up platform have had to carry luggage across the footbridge.
Author's collection

In the area between the goods yard and the branch line was the stationmaster's house and a pair of stone built cottages, occupied by members of staff. The whole goods yard was signalled with CR Stevens pattern lattice signals with lower quadrant arms, as described in Chapter 9. In the 'vee' between the branch line and the main running lines was a large area of spoil from the deep cutting which had been dug to the west of the station. Known as the 'dump' or 'coup', two sidings were laid here in the post-war era and it was used by engineer's trains and as a storage area. For a period a large amount of track assembled for the construction of the new marshalling yard at Perth in the 1950s was stored here.

Gleneagles was provided with a large water tank sited at the top of the embankment at the south end of the Up platform. This supplied water columns at the south end of the goods yard and at the north end of the Branch platform. These were primarily for replenishing engines on the branch line, and no water columns were provided on the main line platforms. This water supply also served the station and the staff cottages.

About 150 yards north of the station on the main line was a set of GPO (General Post Office) mail apparatus. The receiving net on the north side of the line was used to catch mail bags from the Down postal train, while the two pick up standards on the south side were used for mail being picked up by the Up postal train. A walking route was provided along each side of the main line from the station, so

Plate 3.5
A closer view of the west end of Gleneagles station in LM&SR days. The running in board carries the full title 'GLENEAGLES FOR AUCHTERARDER WEST AND JUNCTION FOR CRIEFF, COMRIE AND ST. FILLANS'. The station looks immaculate as it used to be, with platform edges neatly painted and well-tended flower beds. The floral displays at the heads of the stairs can just be discerned. The areas beneath the stairs were used to store barrows, ladders and cleaning and gardening materials. The strange angled pole visible between the flower beds is in fact a length of bullhead rail fashioned into a lamp standard. A Tilley lamp was winched into position on a wire. Being sited at a considerable height, it illuminated a wider area of platform than could be achieved with a conventional lamp post.
CRA collection

Plate 3.6
The stationmasters office at the bottom of the staircase leading to Platforms 1 and 2 on the island platform. This view is almost identical to that of the building at the foot of the stairs at Doune station depicted in a Caledonian Railway official postcard (ALSOP CR-055). The space above the bay window originally housed a clock, while the granite foundation stone inscribed 'BUILT IN 1919 THE YEAR OF THE PEACE AFTER THE GREAT WAR' is similar to those on the bridge which carried the Crieff branch line over the A9 road and on the cairn on the King's course at Gleneagles Hotel. Note the profusion of hanging baskets, while ex-CR 0-6-0 57252 can just be seen on the far left, shunting in the goods yard. *Author*

Plate 3.7
A close view of the Up platform and buildings. The doors to the store room under the stairs are open in this shot taken in 1963. The flower beds are still well maintained, although the ornate Caledonian Railway seat visible in Plate 3.5 has been replaced with a plain two-plank bench. This photograph gives a good view of the extensive overhead pole route which ran along the Up side of the line, and the braced double-pole system favoured by the Caledonian Railway. *Author*

BRANCH LINES OF STRATHEARN

LEFT: Figure 3.3
One of the original Caledonian Railway transfer labels for platform lamp glasses. These labels were soaked off the backing paper and applied to the inside of the front glass on platform lamps. Measuring 8 inches by 3 inches with rounded ends, they had white lettering on a dark blue ground. This label was part of a stock of transfers which were never used, but survived until acquired by the author in the 1960s, nearly forty years after the Caledonian Railway became part of the LM&SR. *Author's collection*

ABOVE: Plate 3.8
The Down platform taken from the north end of the station. This view taken in 1959 shows the signal box and the island platform buildings. These housed not only waiting rooms and toilets, but also three small shops at each end of the buildings. By this date only the John Menzies bookstall in the centre building survived. The station platforms are still well maintained, although the gardens were beginning to suffer. This photograph gives a good impression of the all-round view which could be had from the signal box which was glazed on all four sides, while the railbus can just be seen in the background setting off for Crieff. *Author's collection*

Plate 3.9
The island platform at Gleneagles, with the Branch platform (Platform 1) in the foreground and the connection with the Down main line in the background. Two of the kiosks were opposite each other at the ends of the island platform buildings, and although the book stall is closed, the posters are clearly visible. Three of the Caledonian Railway seats can be seen, together with one of the three drinking fountains provided at Gleneagles. *Author*

CHAPTER 3: GLENEAGLES TO CRIEFF – THE LINE DESCRIBED

the postman would usually park at the station and walk from there. This apparatus was removed following the cessation of postal trains in the 1970s.

Beyond the station the branch line curved north to cross the main Stirling to Perth road on a plate girder bridge, then swung sharply north-east towards Auchterarder and began to climb steeply at 1 in 51¾ past Greenwells Farm towards the outskirts of the town. This bridge replaced the original level crossing which had existed since the line opened in 1856, but which by the early 20th century had become a bone of contention due to delays caused to the increasing volume of road traffic. Even this new bridge was not wholly satisfactory as the relative levels of the railway and the road meant that the bridge had a clearance of only 15 feet, resulting in vehicles with high loads, often large ships boilers en route from Clydebank to Dundee, having to make a detour from Loaninghead via the Muirton to reach Auchterarder.

ABOVE: Plate 3.10
Gleneagles goods yard from the footbridge, showing the two long sidings to the left, the main sidings with loading banks and the scotch derrick, and the three running loops alongside the branch line platform. Although the carriage sidings on the left appear to be full of empty bogie wagons, probably belonging to the Engineering Department, the rest of the goods yard is depressingly empty, with only one wagon in revenue earning service being in evidence. *Author*

BELOW: Plate 3.11
A view of Gleneagles station from the east showing a similar large enamel board for Gleneagles Hotel to that in Plate 3.1. This shot gives a good view of the track layout at the north end of the station. As can be seen, although the main line signals had been converted to upper quadrant, the branch line signals remained lower quadrant right up to closure of the line in 1964. The extensive overhead pole route on the Up side is again visible on the left of this photograph. *Author*

ABOVE: Plate 3.12
A panoramic view looking north from the end of the Up platform as BR 4-6-2 No. 72007 draws into the station, while the railbus from Crieff approaches on the branch line. The pair of cottages on the left which provided staff accommodation have since been demolished. In the background of this view are the sidings on what was called 'The Dump', also known colloquially as 'The Coup'. This was the large area created by the huge amount of spoil removed from the deep cutting to the south of Gleneagles when the Scottish Central Railway main line was built in 1844. The sidings were used by the Engineer's Department, and in the 1960s a large quantity of track panels were stored here in preparation for the new marshalling yard at Perth.
CC Thornburn

RIGHT: Figure 3.4
The Caledonian Railway Gradient Diagram for the Gleneagles to Crieff section. The datum point (zero miles) from which it was measured was just north of the overbridge at the south end of the station. The mention of 'points to main line' refers to the connection at the north end of Gleneagles station. In addition to the intermediate stations, this diagram also shows the Gleneagles Hotel branch line and the viaduct over the River Earn. *Author's collection*

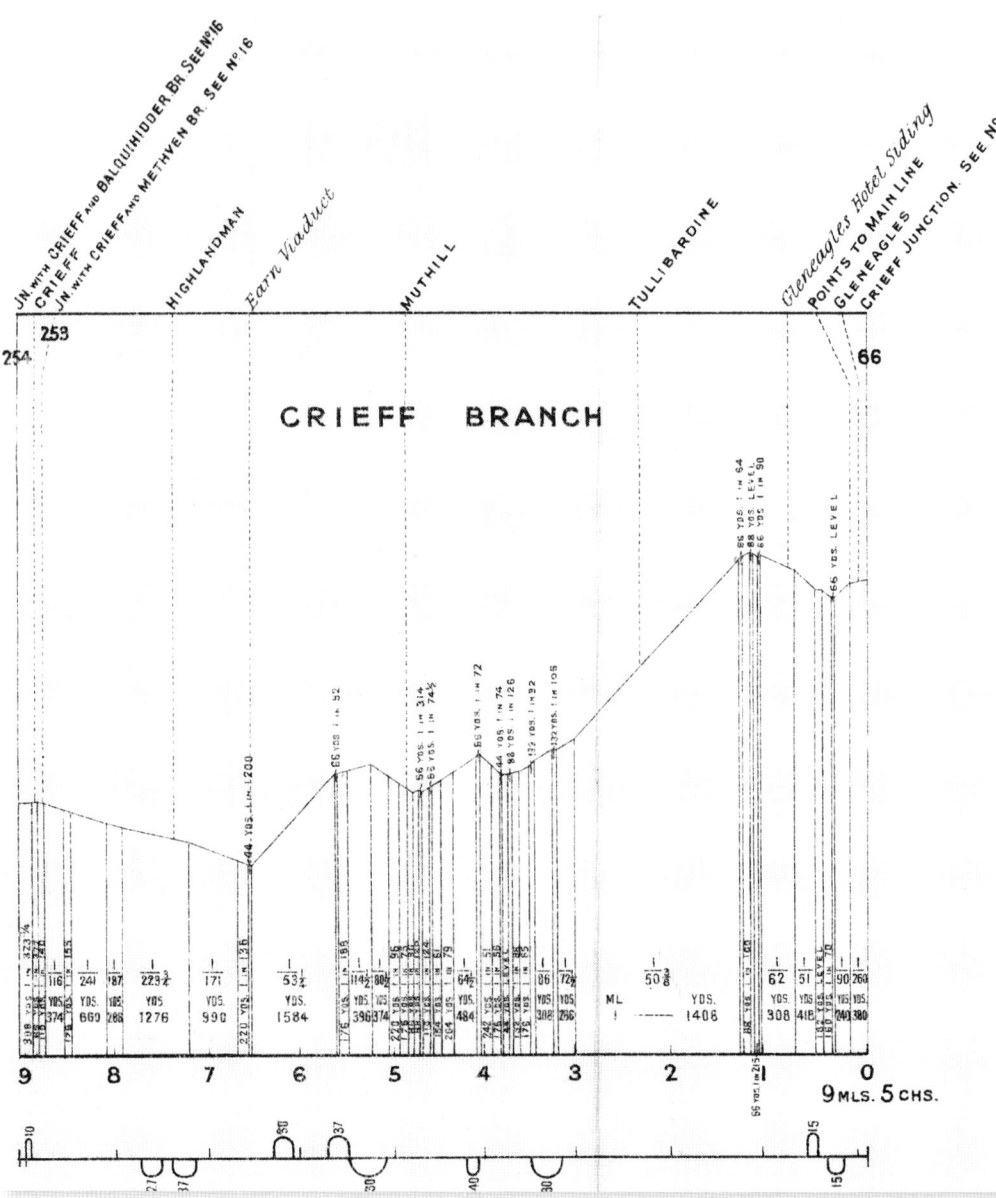

CHAPTER 3: GLENEAGLES TO CRIEFF – THE LINE DESCRIBED

Plate 3.13
The bridge over the A9 trunk road viewed from the east. Prior to the remodelling in 1919, the original line crossed this road by means of a level crossing which was sited roughly where the bush can be seen on the right by the line-side. The clearance under the bridge was only 15 feet and high loads had to be routed by way of the Orchil Road and Muirton, past the hotel. The two taller telegraph poles are where the GPO wires running alongside the main road are carried over the railway telegraph wires. Note the direction sign for Gleneagles Hotel. *Author*

RIGHT: **Plate 3.14**
The junction of the branch line to Gleneagles Hotel just beyond Greenwells Farm seen from the north. The hotel line made a trailing connection with the Gleneagles to Crieff line as seen here. The signal on the left is the Gleneagles Up Branch Home Distant signal which was a 'fixed' signal. The small hut on the left was the pointsman's hut dating from the installation of the hotel siding in 1914. The branch line up to the hotel can be seen curving away to the right through the field gate provided to prevent livestock straying onto the line. *Author*

Part way up this incline the line crossed over the occupation crossing on the track leading to Greenwells Farm. After a short way, and just beyond the fixed Up Distant signal, there was a trailing connection with the Gleneagles Hotel branch line which is described in more detail in Chapter 7. Past the junction with the hotel branch the line continued to climb at 1 in 62 on a gentle left-hand curve to pass under the A823 Auchterarder to Crieff road on the outskirts of town. This stretch of line passed through a shallow cutting across part of the White Muir, with Auchterarder Golf Course to the east and the woods of the Muir to the west. Steam locomotives heading towards Crieff had to work hard up this incline, and lineside fires caused by sparks from the locomotives' chimneys were a perennial problem. This caused considerable concern in the early years, as recounted in Chapter 1, but was still a nuisance right up to the time of closure. The line then passed under the Auchterarder to Muirton road, known as the Orchil Road. This was the site of the suggested platform which was requested both in the 1880s and again in the late 1950s following the introduction of the railbus as being the closest point of the branch line to Auchterarder, but the platform was never built.

Shortly after this the line reached the summit for this part of the route. It was not uncommon for steam hauled trains to come to a standstill on this final stretch until the engine could get up enough steam to reach the top. After passing through a cutting next to Auchterarder Cricket Club to the west, the line started the descent towards Tullibardine at 1 in 64. Continuing to curve to the left, the line passed under the Auchterarder to Tullibardine road and another farm track to Easthill, then straightened out for the final run to Tullibardine. This stretch over a mile and a quarter on a falling gradient of 1 in 50 was one of the fastest parts of the line; this was the scene of the accident at the user worked occupation level crossing to East Third Farm, described in Chapter 9. Just prior to reaching Tullibardine station the line passed over a substantial girder bridge over the Tullibardine road.

This small wayside station was typical of the thousands of isolated wayside stations spread liberally along the length of rural branch lines throughout the country. Sited over half a mile from the small hamlet from which it took its name, the station was not fully opened to passengers until 2nd May 1857, nearly a year after the original line, being the subject of an agreement between Viscount Strathallan and the Crieff Junction Railway. Perched along the embankment to the north end of the road bridge, the station had a single low platform on the Up side. Gravel surfaced and with a timber coping, it could accommodate a four-coach train at the most. The station house, fronting onto the platform, also incorporated the booking and parcels offices, and in addition had a wooden porch running along part of its length. The waiting rooms – and there were two even here – were in a separate adjacent building of wooden construction.

The goods facilities comprised one short siding and a loading bay with a scotch derrick. As the station was on the falling gradient of 1 in 50 towards Crieff, the siding connection facing in the Up direction to avoid wagons running away onto the main line. The crane was provided to deal with the moderate flow of agricultural and sawmill traffic from the nearby estate and farms. In later days, these modest facilities were more than adequate, but in Victorian times Tullibardine was a busy little station, and there were even calls for an increase in goods facilities which were never realised. In the early days, Tullibardine had a covered ground frame in a small wooden hut at the north end of the platform, which masqueraded as a signal box. This closed as early as 1921, being replaced by a small 2-lever ground frame beside the points leading from the branch line.

Beyond the station the line continued to descend before passing over Buchanty Water some quarter of a mile on. This was the section of line which presented the biggest challenge to southbound (Up) trains, and where they sometimes stalled. It was also the stretch of line most prone to snow drifts during heavy snowstorms. From here the line started to climb for a short distance, following a twisting route, passing through a rock cutting flanked by woods before dropping down once again to cross Prestney Burn. Climbing again to cover the final mile to Muthill station, the line traversed a tortuous

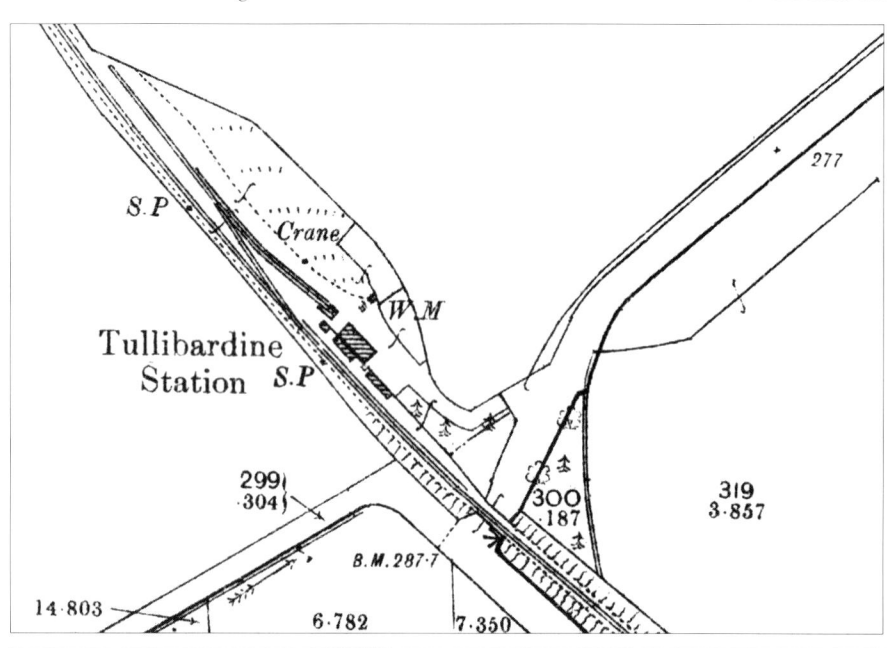

Figure 3.5
Map of Tullibardine station, showing the simple track layout with a single siding alongside the loading dock. Two signal posts are shown, as at this time (1901) Tullibardine was still a block post – although it did not have a signal box as such, only a covered ground frame which was housed in the small building at the north end of the platform. The alterations to the road layout can be seen clearly. Prior to the building of the railway, the road from Tullibardine Chapel off to the left ran straight through to the village which is off to the right. The road was slewed to the south and the junction altered so that the siting of the bridge allowed sufficient room for the passenger platform. Scale 1:2,500.
Image courtesy of Kinross & Perth County Archive

Plate 3.15
Tullibardine station from the north in LM&SR days, although the station has retained its Caledonian Railway livery and signage. On the right is the 2-lever ground frame which replaced the original signalling installation in 1921. Although it was listed as a block post it never had a signal box as such, but a covered ground frame, which was possibly housed in the wooden hut opposite the 2-lever ground frame which replaced it. The falling gradient of 1 in 50 is evident here.
CRA collection

CHAPTER 3: GLENEAGLES TO CRIEFF – THE LINE DESCRIBED

Plate 3.16
Tullibardine station from the south showing the large British Railways running in board. Tullibardine was the only station on the line to be equipped with the ubiquitous British Railways totem signs, of which it was supplied with the grand total of three. The falling gradient is evident here, as the line curves round to the right. The single platform was quite low, and boarding or alighting from trains was usually tricky, although there was a set of wooden steps for passenger use.
HB Priesley

Plate 3.17
The Caledonian Railway leather cash bag for Tullibardine station. Although in better condition than the LM&SR example at Plate 3.2, it is a much earlier relic, dating from the late 19th century. This bag was found when the booking office was cleared out after the line closed in 1964.
Author

Plate 3.18
This Caledonian Railway hand lamp being Tullibardine station No. 1, it would probably have been issued to the stationmaster. Although it is not certain how many lamps the station had, this was one of two hand lamps found in the booking office when it was cleared out in 1964. Unusually, both this lamp and the oil can at Plate 3.19 had copper rather than the conventional brass labels.
Author

Plate 3.19
A Caledonian Railway oil can from Tullibardine station. The copper plate specified that it belonged to the passenger department, although for such a small station this appellation was superfluous. The compound burning oil referred to would have been the type of oil required for hand, office and platform lamps.
Author

stretch through Machany cutting. Passing through the cutting, which was blasted from solid rock, the line negotiated a reverse curve, whilst at the same time the gradient changed from 1 in 73 rising to 1 in 66 falling. Emerging from this cutting, the line swung north and crossed Machany Water, to reach Muthill station, some 5 miles from Gleneagles.

Muthill station was situated at a level crossing on the Muthill to Millearn road and was over 2 miles to the east of the village from which it took its name. Being roughly halfway between Gleneagles and Crieff it was provided with a passing loop, the only one on this section of line. The station was therefore laid out on a scale which would not otherwise have been justified by the level of traffic it handled. As originally laid out, Muthill was a more modest affair than in its latter days. It had a shorter passing loop north of the level crossing and only a single platform on the Up side. Only when the line was resignalled in 1892 was the signal box added and the loop lengthened, such that the level crossing was laid out for double track. At the same time a platform was added on the Down side and a footbridge provided at the north end of the station to connect the two platforms.

In its new form, the station boasted a 400 yard long passing loop, and an adequate goods yard of five sidings. The station itself was immediately north of the level crossing, and as rebuilt was equipped with both Up and Down line platforms originally connected by a footbridge. When built, both platforms were plain gravel surfaces with timber coping and ran the full length of the loop. In the 1950s the Down platform was shortened at the north end and rebuilt with brick facing and coping of concrete slabs. The footbridge was removed at the same time so that thereafter access to the Down platform was by the wicket gates next to the level crossing. The Up platform remained unaltered, and this was also used for the various steam specials which traversed the line in later years. The stationmaster's house was on the Up platform, and again this incorporated the various offices. There were, in addition, three wooden buildings housing waiting room, stores and lamp room, while the Down platform had a single waiting room.

Being a passing station, Muthill was important enough to merit a signal box, and this was situated at the south end of the Up platform where it commanded a good view of the level crossing it controlled. The box was a brick structure of standard Caledonian Railway design, dating from 1892 when it replaced the original box under a resignalling scheme for the whole line. The goods yard was equipped with cattle pens, a scotch derrick and loading bays – originally built to encourage *'Private Horse and Carriage'* traffic, an early form of Motorail. A simple wooden shed, capable of accommodating three goods vans, completed the facilities. For many years an interesting relic existed here in the form of a 'Caley' van body which lay next to the shed. Still resplendent in its original red rust livery, with the letters 'CR' on the sides and the number '5468' on the ends, it survived in remarkably good condition until the final demolition of the line in 1964, over forty years after the Caledonian Railway had ceased to exist.

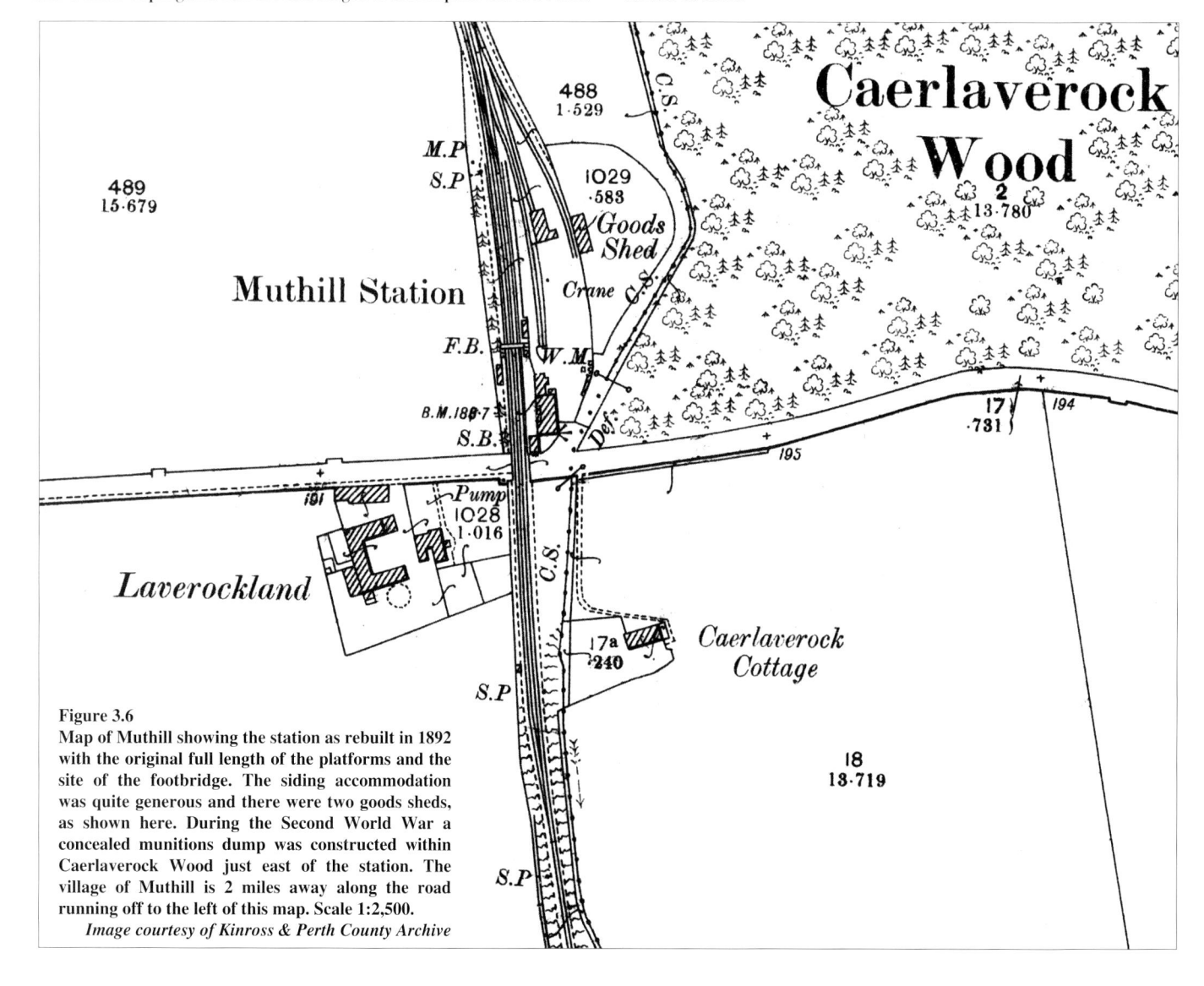

Figure 3.6
Map of Muthill showing the station as rebuilt in 1892 with the original full length of the platforms and the site of the footbridge. The siding accommodation was quite generous and there were two goods sheds, as shown here. During the Second World War a concealed munitions dump was constructed within Caerlaverock Wood just east of the station. The village of Muthill is 2 miles away along the road running off to the left of this map. Scale 1:2,500.
Image courtesy of Kinross & Perth County Archive

ABOVE: **Plate 3.20**
Muthill station from the south showing the level crossing with the adjacent signal box and the station beyond. This was the only passing station between Gleneagles and Crieff. The level crossing was on a minor road between Tullibardine and Muthill which was approximately 2 miles to the west of the station, or to the left in this photograph. The poster beside the signal box advertising the new railbus service dates this photograph from post 1958.
Author

LEFT: **Figure 3.7**
A British Railways (Scottish Region) transfer label for a platform oil lamp. These labels replaced the yellow and black lamp labels issued by the LM&SR and were in use until the line closed. Muthill, in common with most other small stations, was still lit by oil lamps in 1964. These labels measured 8½ inches by 3 inches, with white lettering on a light blue ground, and had a white border around the edge.
Author's collection

Plate 3.21
The station house at Muthill, seen shortly after the line closed. This building incorporated both the stationmaster's residence and the booking office, while the wooden building to the left housed the waiting room and another office. The heraldic shields on the two gable ends were blank and would appear to have been purely ornamental. The poster on the right is the one announcing the closure of the line, and the rusty rails indicate the line is already out of use. The deserted station now awaits the demolition contractors.
Author

LEFT: Plate 3.22
A view of Muthill station from the north, late in British Railways days and after the removal of the footbridge which was located roughly where the photographer was standing. Most of the station buildings were on the Up side with the signal box in the background. The Down platform had been shortened by this time, and completely rebuilt with brick facing and concrete slab coping. The wooden waiting shelter on the Down platform is just off to the right of the photograph. *Author*

RIGHT: Figure 3.8
A British Railways Annual Season ticket issued at Muthill in August 1958, just prior to the introduction of the new railbus. Issued to Miss Donna Forbes to travel to and from school in Crieff, this was valid until the end of the summer term in 1959. The 'Half Rate' stamp indicated that it was issued to a child, and the 'W', as was customary in those days, indicated that it had been issued to a female. *Author's collection*

Beyond Muthill, the line curved to the west, climbing gently at first and skirting thick pine woods. At this point it crossed the course of the old Roman road from Ardoch Camp to the nearby fort to the west, the gradient stiffening to 1 in 80, before descending to cross the Muthill to Strageath road on the level. Originally only a manned level crossing, Strageath's relative proximity to Muthill – just over a mile as opposed to two in the case of the station – led to the creation of a halt here with the introduction of the railbus in 1958. Although Strageath Halt was provided as a closer alternative to the original station at Muthill, the latter remained open as it served a wider community than just the village of Muthill. Strageath also lacked any parking facilities for passengers wanting to leave their cars. A rudimentary affair of concrete slabs was laid to provide a small platform at rail level for passengers using the halt, which had a brief life of only six years before the line closed in 1964.

The final goal of Crieff was now in sight as the gradient continued to fall and, turning north, the line crossed over the River Earn. The line was carried over the river at this point by the largest engineering structure on this section of line – a bowstring girder bridge of four spans measuring some 270 feet in length which had replaced a

Plate 3.23
The goods yard at Muthill handled considerable traffic in its day, much of it related to agriculture as one might expect in a rural community. The station was well equipped with two long sidings either side of the loading bank, a scotch derrick, and a modest goods shed on the right. It is ironic that after the station closed the site was redeveloped to house a large seed potato marketing business, with all the potatoes being shipped out by road. *Author*

CHAPTER 3: GLENEAGLES TO CRIEFF – THE LINE DESCRIBED

Plate 3.24
One interesting relic which was photographed in 1964 was this old Caledonian Railway van body, still bearing the initials 'CR' after nearly forty years. It was being used for storage by the local coal merchant, and bags of coal can be seen stacked ready for delivery. Despite close inspection there were no wagon plates or other means of identification left at this stage. The van body disappeared along with everything else when the station was demolished only a year or so later. *Author*

Plate 3.25
Strageath level crossing and halt, with Crieff and the Grampians in the distance. This crossing over a minor road only a mile from the village of Muthill was operated by a crossing keeper. With the introduction of the railbus in 1958, it was selected as the site for a halt as it was closer to the village. The facilities provided amounted to no more than the concrete slabs which can be seen to the left of the far crossing gate. Later a set of wooden steps were provided for use with conventional carriages if the railbus broke down, which it often did. The trespass notice, which is still of LM&SR vintage, has been re-sited beyond the new platform. *Author*

Plate 3.26
The principal engineering structure on this section of line was the four-span bowstring girder bridge over the River Earn. This replaced the original wooden viaduct built when the Crieff Junction Railway was opened. It was just upstream of the ford at Dalpatrick which drovers used to get their cattle across, the Highlanders who brought their cattle down giving their name to the settlement of Highlandman. This bridge was dismantled after the line closed in 1964, but the massive piers remain to this day.
Author

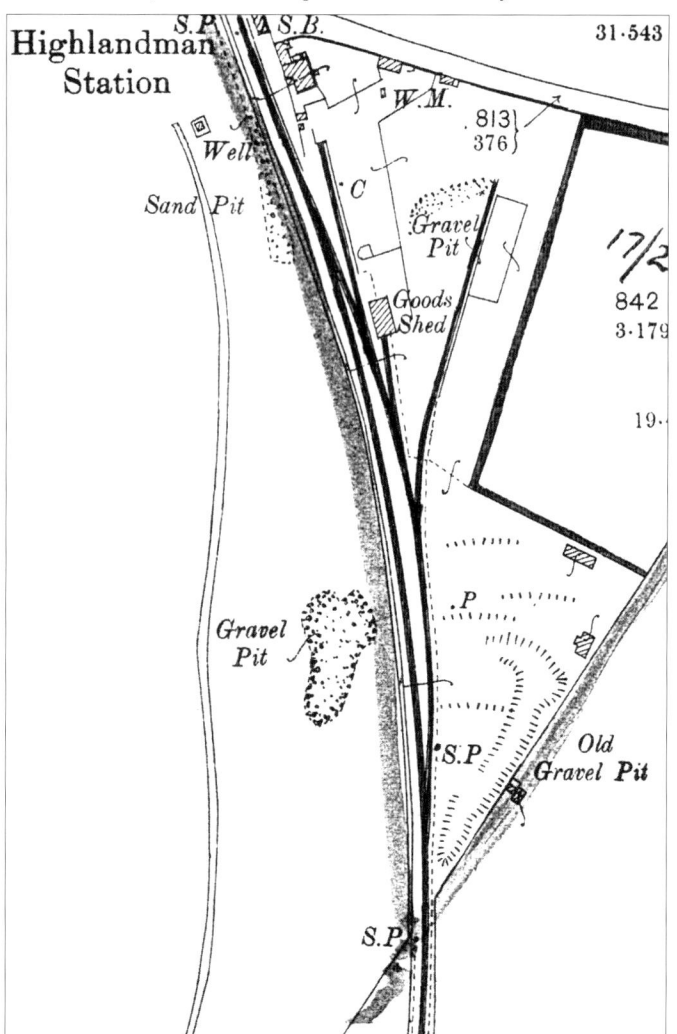

FACING PAGE: **Figure 3.9**
A selection of tickets from Highlandman station. This station appears to have had a low turnover in tickets, and subsequently very few tickets were printed to specific destinations. Even tickets to the adjacent stations of Muthill and Crieff had to be written out. All these LM&SR tickets were issued some years after nationalisation in 1948; the bicycle ticket to Glasgow was issued on 29th September 1951, almost the last day of service before passenger services were withdrawn from the Perth to Crieff line.
Author's collection

LEFT: **Figure 3.10**
Map of Highlandman station including the layout of the goods yard, with a short cattle dock siding, goods shed and a longer siding for mineral and other traffic. The length of the goods loop is well illustrated here, and explains why a separate ground frame was necessary at the south end. The field to the right marked '17/2' was later the site of the large saw mill which generated considerable timber traffic for the railway. Scale 1:2,500.
Image courtesy of Kinross & Perth County Archive

much earlier wooden structure in 1885. Each pier consisted of two cylinders, each 6 feet in diameter, cast in 4-foot segments, bolted together by inside flanges and filled with Portland cement. The average depth from rail level to the rocks on which they rested was 56 feet, with rubble around the columns to prevent scouring. The piers also had cutwater fenders, formed of 12 inch square piles protected with wrought iron plates and filled with concrete, to protect the piers against ice. This substantial structure, designed by Mr Thomas Barr, the Caledonian Railway Resident Engineer in Perth and built by Messrs Henderson Matthew & Co of Musselburgh, required over 300 tons of cast and wrought iron in its construction.

Curving gently to the left, the line skirted Highlandman Golf Course, climbing at 1 in 171 to cover the last mile to Highlandman station. This delightfully named station lay just south of the level crossing by which the line crossed the Crieff to Millearn road. This level crossing appeared to be the main justification for a station at this point, for there was no community of any size for it to serve, although it handled considerable goods traffic from the adjacent sawmill and local farms. Highlandman was indeed one of those

CHAPTER 3: GLENEAGLES TO CRIEFF – THE LINE DESCRIBED

RIGHT: Plate 3.27
A general view of the little wayside station at Highlandman taken from the south. The main building was the station house which incorporated the booking office. The wooden building beyond it housed the waiting room, which in the 1920s was used as a Sunday school for local children attending Crieff Parish Church. The small ground frame on the right was one of two installed after the signal box was closed and demolished in 1948. *Author*

ABOVE: Plate 3.28
A closer view of the station platform at Highlandman. As with Tullibardine, it was low, with a wooden edge and gravel surface, and steps were provided for passengers boarding and alighting from trains. Even as late as 1960, the station retained its Caledonian Railway running in board and three different types of oil platform lamps.
HC Casserley

LEFT: Plate 3.29
Highlandman station house, seen here in 1964. Of a similar design to Tullibardine and Muthill station houses, it also sported a heraldic shield on the gable end, and again it was blank. The wooden building housed the booking office to the right, with a clock above the window, and the booking hall and waiting room to the left, with a fire at the far end. The stone building served as accommodation for the porter signalman and, in the final years, the family of Mr Doig, the signalman at Crieff. *Author*

sleepy, picturesque little wayside stations where time stood still, and which could easily have been 'Buggleskelly' of Will Hay's celebrated comedy *Oh, Mr Porter!* of the 1930s.

The platform was again on the Up side just to the south of the level crossing, with the station cottage as a backdrop. In this instance, however, the offices were in a wooden building which adjoined the north end of the cottage. The overall appearance was neat and well proportioned, with the possible exception of the running in boards which, by virtue of the length of the name, tended to dominate the scene. The goods yard consisted of three sidings, making a trailing connection with the branch line in the Up direction. These coped adequately with the agricultural traffic which existed and, in latter days, the large sawmill adjacent to the goods yard.

Originally, Highlandman too had a signal box, but this was reduced to a gate box in 1948 and finally demolished in 1951, being replaced by a ground frame. From Highlandman, the line from Almond Valley Junction could be seen coming in from the east and the Gleneagles line swung west to come alongside it at Pittentian level crossing.

The lines then ran parallel over the last mile to Crieff, passing on the way over Pittenzie crossing, the second of the request halts introduced with the advent of the railbus in 1958. The actual junction between the two lines was only just outside the eastern end of the station, a hangover from the days of the two separate companies which originally constructed the two lines. Just over 9 miles from Gleneagles, the line reached Crieff which is described in detail in Chapter 5.

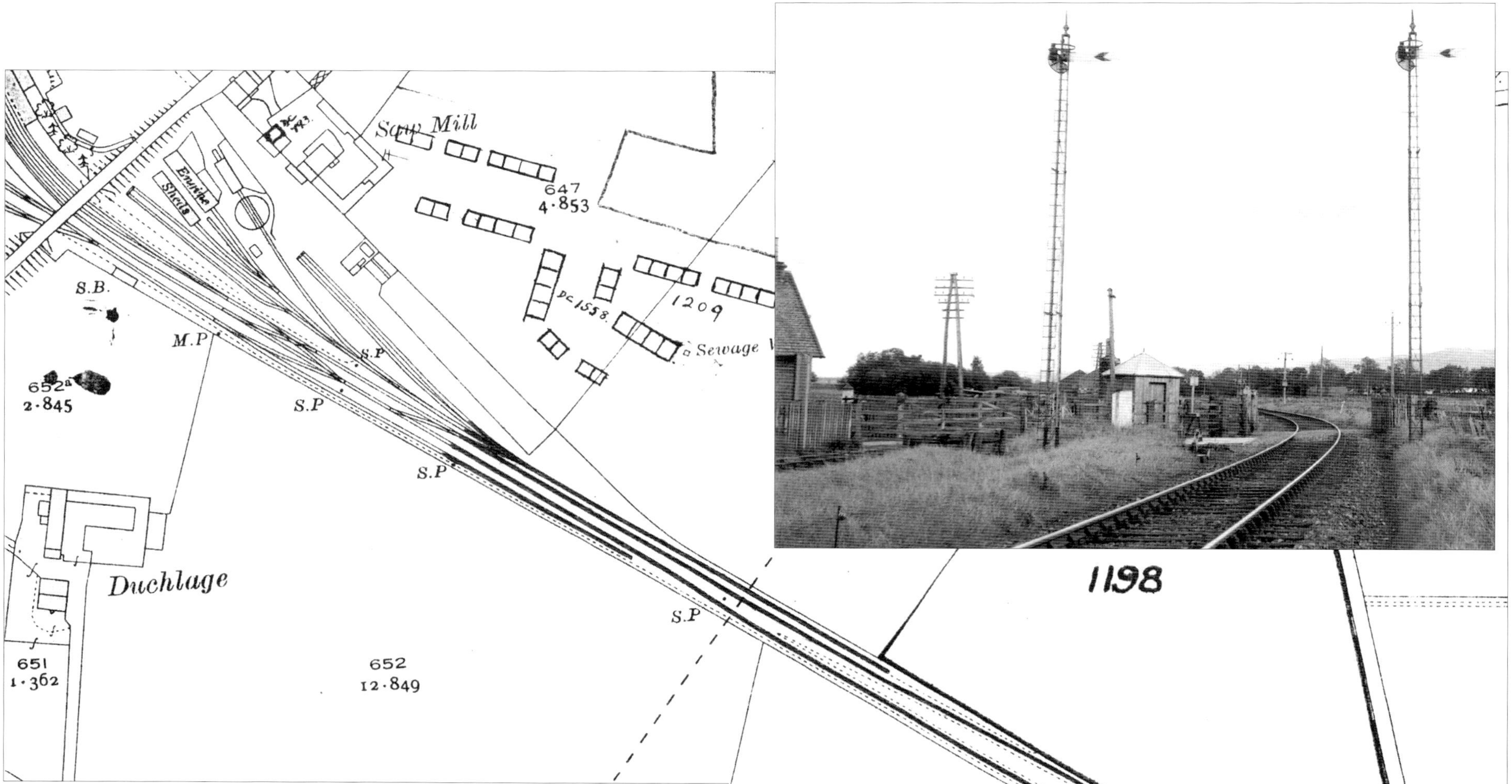

Figure 3.11
The approaches to Crieff from the east showing the two separate lines running parallel, the lower one being the original Crieff Junction Railway line from Gleneagles and the upper one being the later Crieff & Methven Junction line. The level crossing at the lower right corner was Pittenzie, which was the site of the halt opened with the introduction of the railbus in 1958. The three engine sheds are just to the east of the Duchlage Road bridge and the original Crieff & Methven Railway goods yard can also be seen. In later years these sidings were often used for storing spare carriages and wagons, all goods traffic being handled at the original Crieff Junction Railway yard. Scale 1:2,500. *Image courtesy of Kinross & Perth County Archive*

INSET: Plate 3.30
Pittenzie level crossing on the approach to Crieff. The Almond Valley line can just be seen on the left. From here both lines ran parallel to Crieff, hence the two separate Distant signals. The small wooden building between the two sets of lines was the crossing keeper's box. Pittenzie was also chosen as a halt when the railbus was introduced due to its proximity to the outskirts of Crieff – the low platform can be seen just to the left of the Gleneagles line. *Author*

Chapter 4
Almond Valley Jct to Crieff – The Line Described

Travelling out of Perth on the main line to Inverness and the north, you pass the site of the relatively new gravity marshalling yard on the Down side of the old Caledonian line, just on the outskirts of the city. Beyond this, and just before the line crosses the old A9 Perth to Inverness trunk road, can be discerned the course of a single line railway curving westwards on a high embankment. This is now all that remains of the former Perth to Balquhidder branch line to remind us that this was once the site of Almond Valley Junction.

This was the point at which the former Perth Almond Valley & Methven Railway diverged from the main line, originally part of the Scottish North Eastern Railway. The original signal box and connection survived until 1962, in which year the new Perth marshalling yard was built on the flat ground immediately south of the junction. The new track layout incorporated the junction as part of the yard, and Almond Valley Junction was one of the seventeen mechanical signal boxes closed on the opening of the new Perth power box near St. Leonards Bridge to the south of the city. Although named Almond Valley Junction, and known as that on the railway, it was sometimes referred to by locals as 'Muirton Junction' after the locality of that name to the east of the main line at that point.

The line followed an almost straight course over the 16-mile stretch to Crieff, running along the northerly edge of Strathearn. By following this route it passed through flat, undulating farmland and,

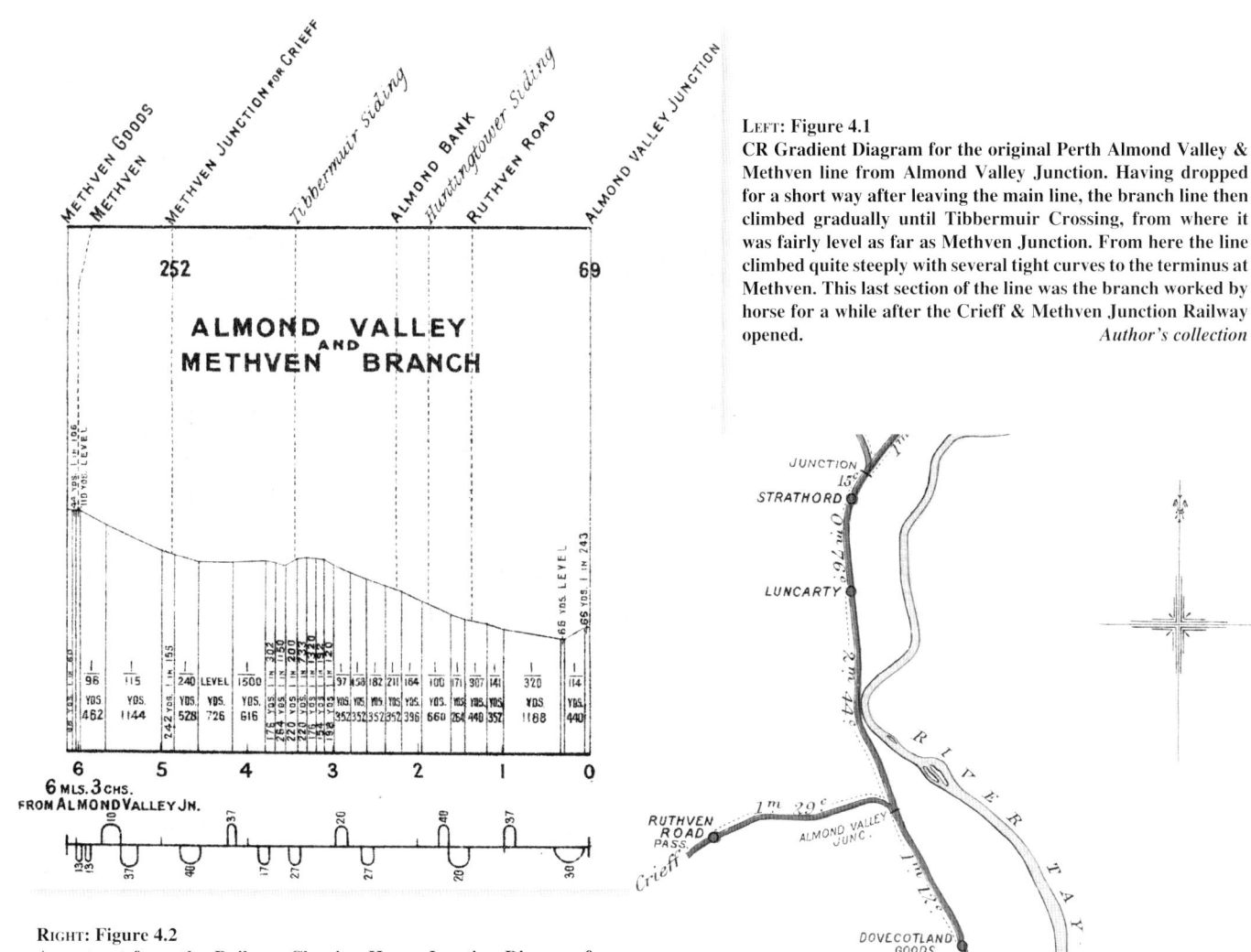

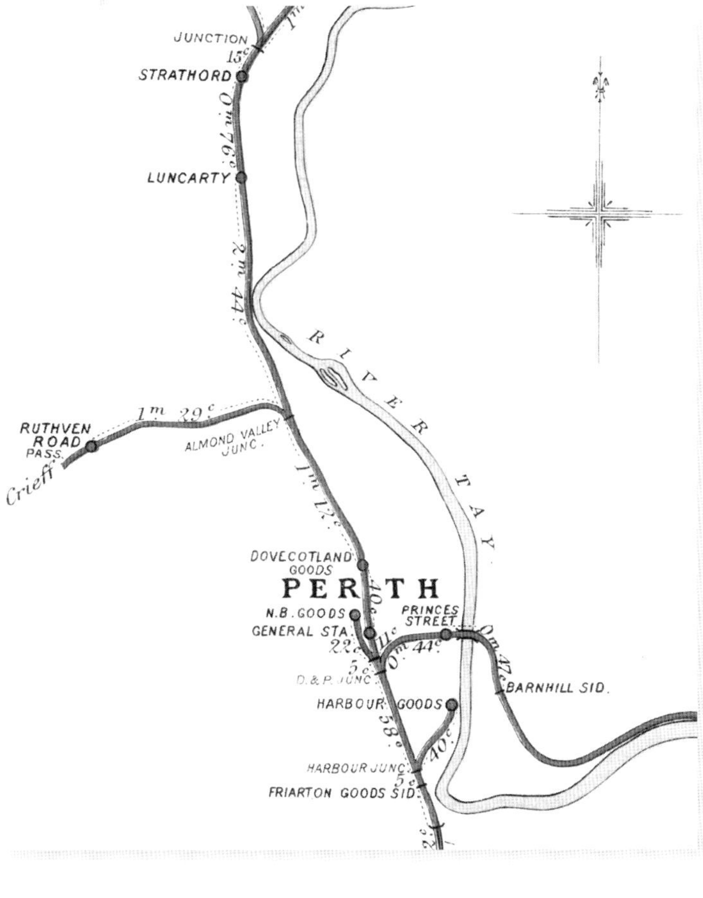

Left: Figure 4.1
CR Gradient Diagram for the original Perth Almond Valley & Methven line from Almond Valley Junction. Having dropped for a short way after leaving the main line, the branch line then climbed gradually until Tibbermuir Crossing, from where it was fairly level as far as Methven Junction. From here the line climbed quite steeply with several tight curves to the terminus at Methven. This last section of the line was the branch worked by horse for a while after the Crieff & Methven Junction Railway opened.
Author's collection

Right: Figure 4.2
An extract from the Railway Clearing House Junction Diagram for the Perth area. These diagrams, with precise mileages and accurate depiction of all the stations and lines of the various companies, were essential for accounting purposes, being the basis by which the apportioning of cost and income between the railway companies was calculated. On this section all the lines belonged to the Caledonian Railway, with the exception of the short spur to the NBR goods station at Perth and the Highland Railway whose main line to Inverness diverged at Stanley Junction. Almond Valley Junction, the start of the Strathearn lines, is shown as 1 mile 62 chains north of Perth General station.
Author's collection

Plate 4.1
The Crieff branch line diverged from the Caledonian main line to Aberdeen at Almond Valley Junction, just over a mile north of Perth. The main line to Inverness and Aberdeen curves away to the right to cross the A9 Perth to Inverness road in the background, while the branch line curves off to the left. Almond Valley Junction was a standard Caledonian Railway signal box which was closed when the new Perth power box opened in 1962. *Courtesy SRS/Kidderminster Railway Museum*

except for the spur to Methven itself, was easily graded – the high point of the line being only 150 feet above sea level. Interestingly, this line was one of only three on the whole of the Caledonian Railway system to have specially cast mile post plates bearing the name of the point from which the mileage was measured, in this case referred to as 'Almond Junction'; the other two lines were the West Coast Main Line, with mile plates from 'Carlisle' all the way to Aberdeen, and the Perth to Dundee line with plates from 'Dundee'. The Almond Junction mile plates were only provided as far as Crieff (Milepost 16), after which the standard Caledonian Railway mile plates, bearing a number only, were used. Why such a minor line as the Almond Valley to Crieff branch should be singled out for such treatment remains a mystery.

ABOVE: **Figure 4.3**
The only known example of a Caledonian Railway luggage label printed to the tiny halt at Ruthven Road. Luggage labels were printed to most of the stations on the Strathearn branch lines, particularly tourist destinations such as Crieff, Comrie, St. Fillans and Lochearnhead, but others were less common. This example from Perth is faded (Caledonian labels were purple in colour) and water stained, but has never been used, the gummed back being intact. *Author's collection*

ABOVE RIGHT: **Plate 4.2**
About a mile and a half from the junction, the line crossed the minor road from Lawgrove (near the Inverness to Perth road) to Huntingtower, a short distance from Ruthven House. The first station on the line, a small halt, was built here to serve the nearby Ruthvenfield Bleach Works just to the north. This view from the east shows the level crossing and the crossing keeper's cottage, with Ruthven Road Halt in the background. *CRA collection*

CHAPTER 4: ALMOND VALLEY JCT TO CRIEFF – THE LINE DESCRIBED

Plate 4.3
The tiny halt of Ruthven Road seen here in LM&SR days. The platform was considerably shortened at a later date, but both it and the station building survived intact up to closure in 1965, some fourteen years after passenger services were withdrawn. A ground frame controlling the signals protecting the level crossing was located just next to the gate at the base of the telegraph pole. *J Alsop collection*

Figure 4.4
An LM&SR transfer label for Ruthven Road for use on platform lamp glasses. The standard LM&SR labels were 8 inches long to fit the normal platform lamps, with black text on a yellow background, and where, as in this case, the station name was too long, it was placed on two lines. The LM&SR were clearly methodical in providing such signage for all their stations, however small, as Ruthven Road had at most only two platform lamps. *Author's collection*

Having left the main line, the line turned westwards, initially descending at 1 in 114 to the valley floor. From here it began climbing gently, to follow roughly the course of the Lade Burn. A mile and a half from the junction, the line crossed the Huntingtower to Lawgrave road on the level. Just west of this level crossing was Ruthven Road Halt. Built primarily to serve the workers of the nearby Ruthvenfield Bleach Works a quarter of a mile down the road, this was never more than a request halt – as such, the barest minimum of facilities were provided. A short platform, long enough to accommodate a two-coach train, was sited on the Up side of the line, adjacent to the crossing keeper's cottage. A small wooden building with an ornate canopy was the sole amenity, being a combined booking office and waiting room. There were no sidings or goods facilities here, but although it did not merit a signal box, the crossing was protected by Up and Down Distant signals, worked from a small 2-lever ground frame.

Leaving Ruthven Road, the railway curved to the left, running alongside the road, and followed a straight course toward the point at which the Almondbank village road meets the main Perth to Crieff road. Halfway along this stretch, and about 2 miles from Almond Valley Junction, the line crossed a minor road leading to Huntingtower Bleach Works, a few hundred yards to the north on the banks of the River Almond. The proximity of this level crossing to the bleach works provided a suitable access point to the railway, and a public siding, known as Huntingtower Siding, was provided just to the west of the level crossing on the south side of the line. Some 300 feet long and with a loading bank, this siding was under the charge of the stationmaster at Almondbank a little under half a mile away.

The traffic generated by the bleach works was such that in 1911 a private line was constructed to serve the various works of

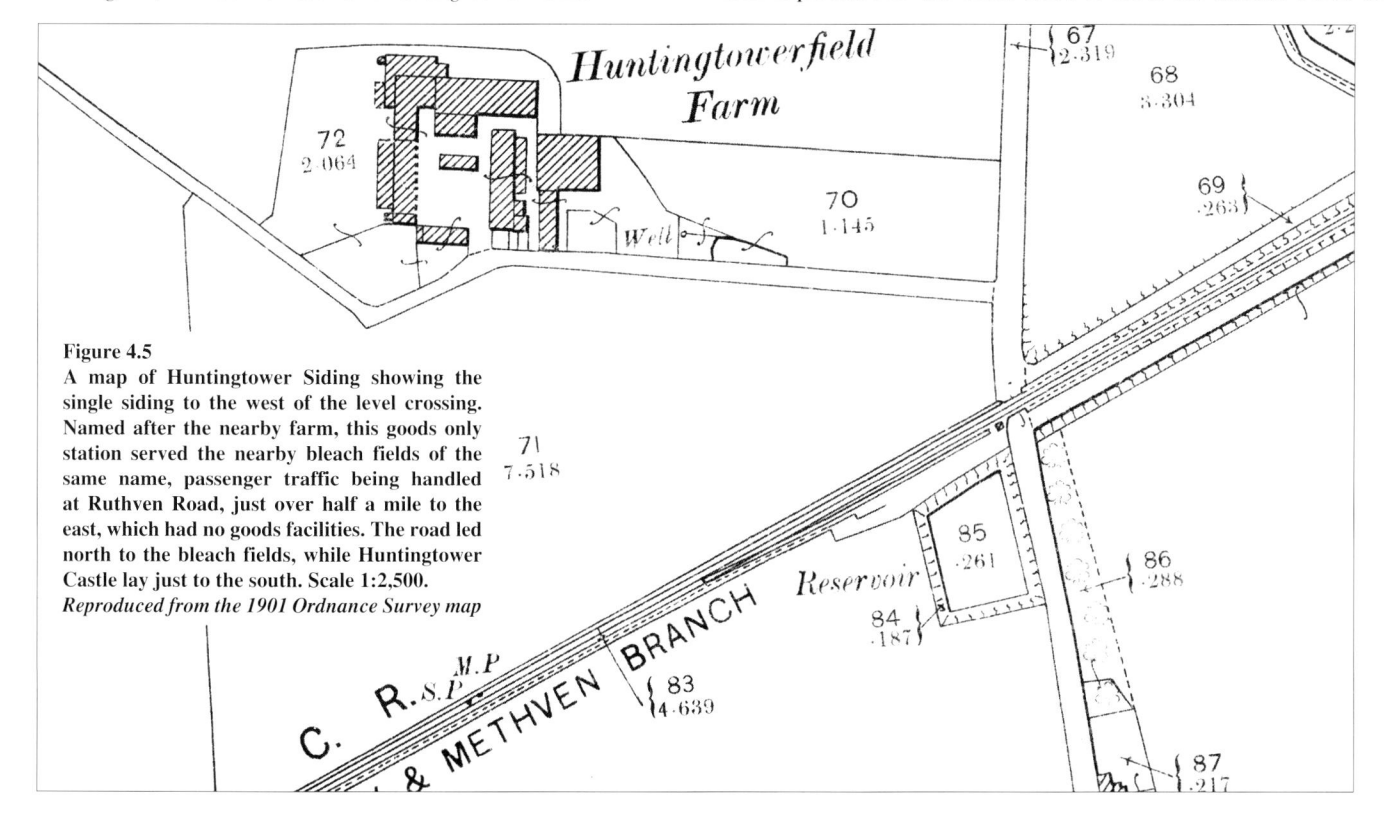

Figure 4.5
A map of Huntingtower Siding showing the single siding to the west of the level crossing. Named after the nearby farm, this goods only station served the nearby bleach fields of the same name, passenger traffic being handled at Ruthven Road, just over half a mile to the east, which had no goods facilities. The road led north to the bleach fields, while Huntingtower Castle lay just to the south. Scale 1:2,500.
Reproduced from the 1901 Ordnance Survey map

Plate 4.4
The siding serving the complex of Huntingtower Bleach Works, which can be seen in the background, made a trailing connection with the branch line some 100 yards east of Almondbank station. The signal shown is the Huntingtower Up Distant, so close were the two stations. The poles on either side of the sidings carried the overhead wires for the 500V DC system used for the works shunting locomotive. *Author*

Plate 4.5
Another view of the private siding into the bleach works and the RN Stores Depot, seen here from the road bridge over the railway at Almondbank station. The proximity of the siding to the station can be seen from the remains of Almondbank station platform visible alongside the track on the left. This cutting was also the principal engineering challenge for the original Perth Almond Valley & Methven Railway. The level crossing in the far distance is that at Huntingtower. *CRA collection*

Lumsden & MacKenzie. A noteworthy feature of this line was that it employed electric traction, something of an innovation in 1911. Originally a water turbine at Cramwell Park, about 2 miles to the north-east on the River Almond, generated electricity at 3,300 volts, this being carried to a transformer and rectifier at Huntingtower Bleach Works to provide a 500 volt DC output. Later, additional power was generated by stationary steam engines augmented by a mains supply from the Hydro Electric Board. The 500 volt supply was carried on overhead wires supported by simple wooden poles on either side of the track. Subsequently, during the Second World War, the Royal Navy built a depot just to the east of the road leading from Almondbank station to the village.

The entrance to these sidings made a trailing connection with the branch line about 300 feet east of Almondbank station, just near the Up Distant signal protecting Huntingtower level crossing. After passing through a gate on the railway boundary, the line curved to the left to run north towards the river. Some 300 yards from the junction a spur curved off to the left to the Royal Naval Stores Depot (RNSD Almondbank), and at this junction there was a run-around loop and three long sidings for the interchange of goods traffic. The line then continued, to run alongside the River Almond before curving round the northern edge of Huntingtower Bleach Works. Here there was another loop and a reverse spur which led across a bridge over the river to Pitcairnfield Bleach Works. This spur was abandoned after the Second World War, and the remaining system ceased operation in 1962, being dismantled the following year.

Less than a quarter of a mile beyond this sidings complex, the branch line passed under the main Perth to Crieff road to reach Almondbank station. Situated near the road junction from which the road to Almondbank village itself runs north, this was the only intermediate station on the original Perth Almond Valley & Methven

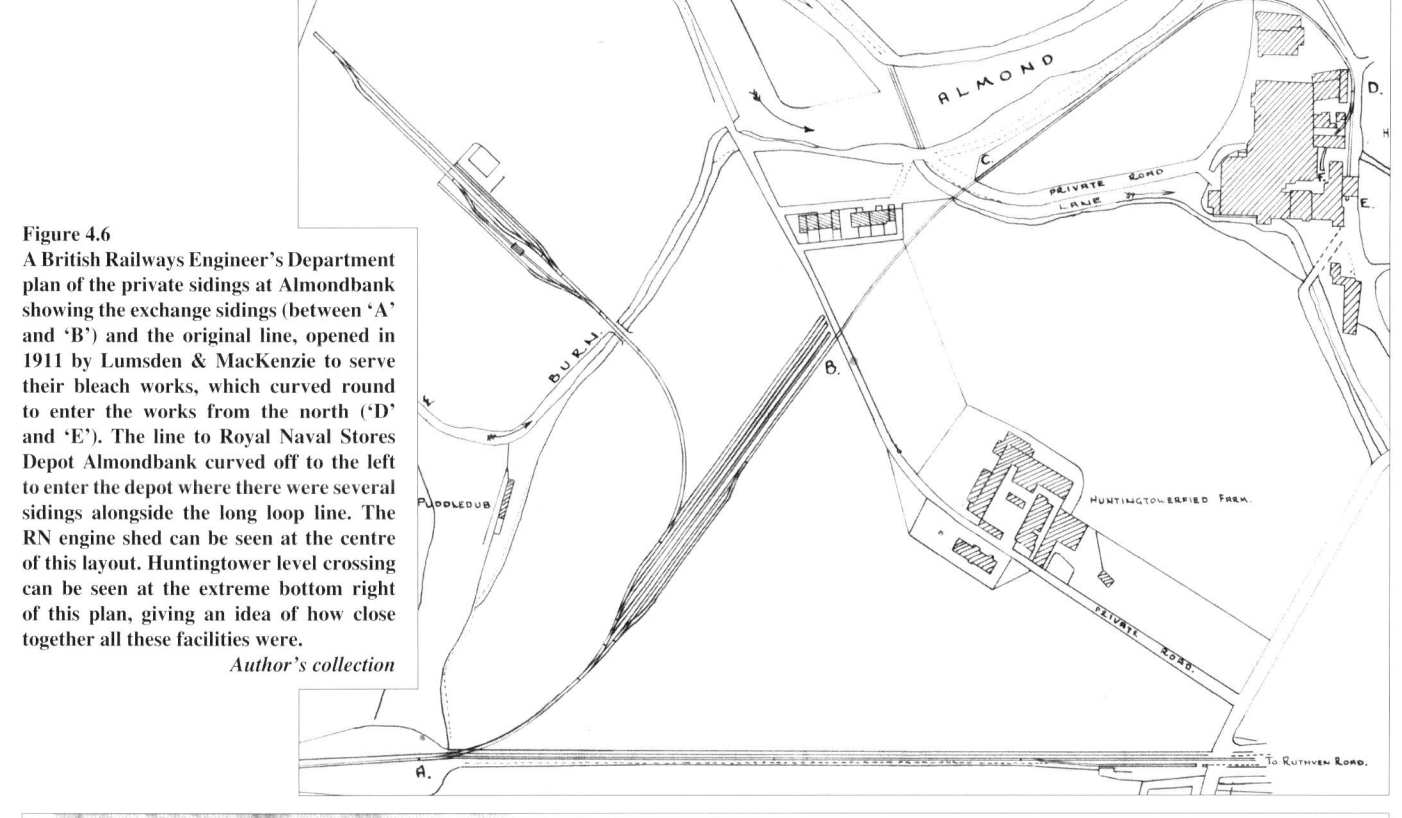

CHAPTER 4: ALMOND VALLEY JCT TO CRIEFF – THE LINE DESCRIBED

Figure 4.6
A British Railways Engineer's Department plan of the private sidings at Almondbank showing the exchange sidings (between 'A' and 'B') and the original line, opened in 1911 by Lumsden & MacKenzie to serve their bleach works, which curved round to enter the works from the north ('D' and 'E'). The line to Royal Naval Stores Depot Almondbank curved off to the left to enter the depot where there were several sidings alongside the long loop line. The RN engine shed can be seen at the centre of this layout. Huntingtower level crossing can be seen at the extreme bottom right of this plan, giving an idea of how close together all these facilities were.
Author's collection

Plate 4.6
Almondbank passenger station in LM&SR days looking east. The platform continued through overbridge No. 3, which carried the A85 Perth to Crieff road over the line; unusually, the inside of the bridge arch was whitewashed to improve lighting. The entrance to Huntingtower Bleach Works sidings and Huntingtower Up Distant can be seen in the background. The ground frame on the right was one of two installed after the signal box closed in 1930.
J Alsop collection

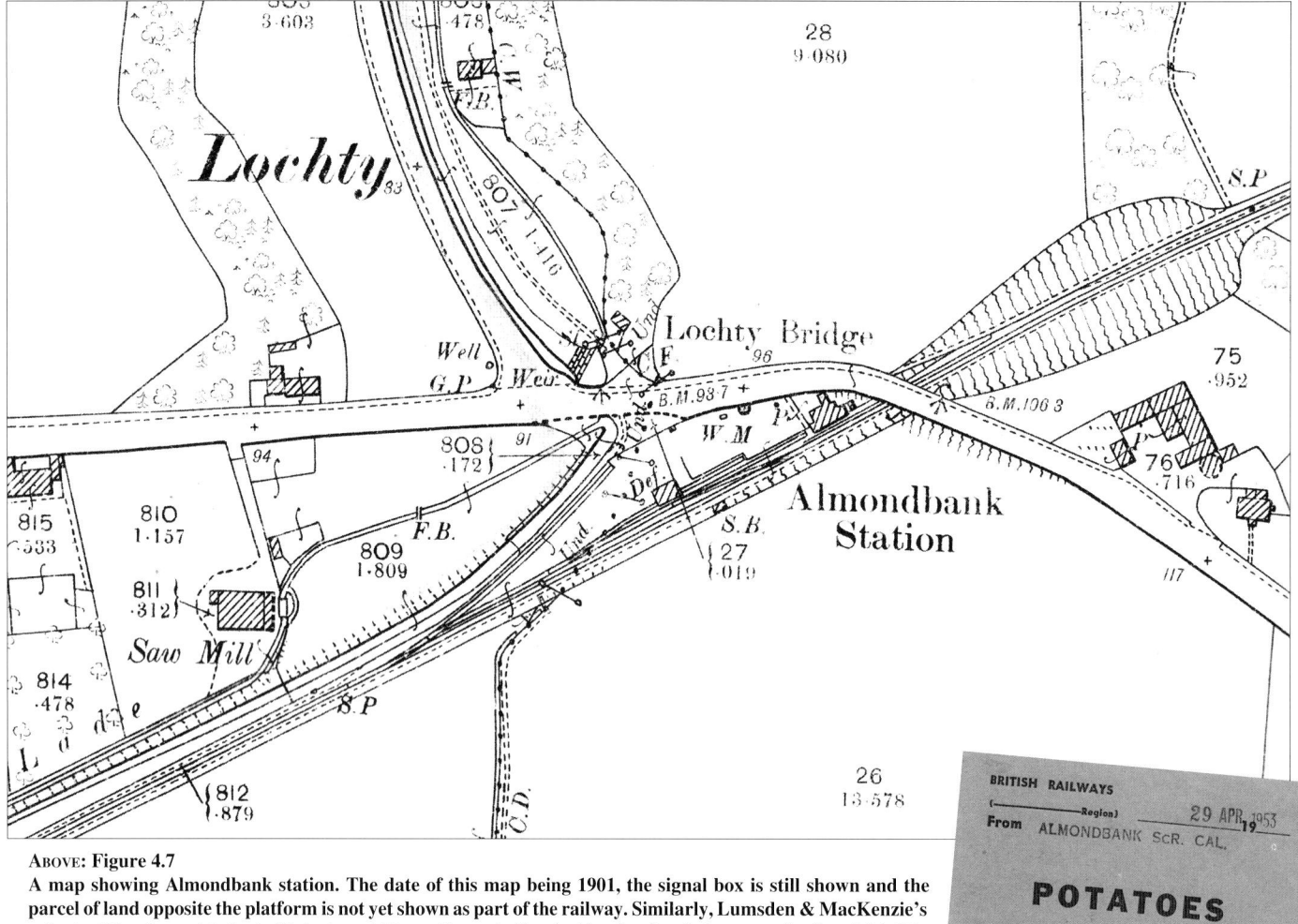

ABOVE: Figure 4.7
A map showing Almondbank station. The date of this map being 1901, the signal box is still shown and the parcel of land opposite the platform is not yet shown as part of the railway. Similarly, Lumsden & MacKenzie's private siding has yet to be built, but would leave the main line just by the signal shown on the far right, this being the Up Distant signal for Huntingtower, as visible in Plate 4.4. Scale 1:2,500.
Reproduced from the 1901 Ordnance Survey map

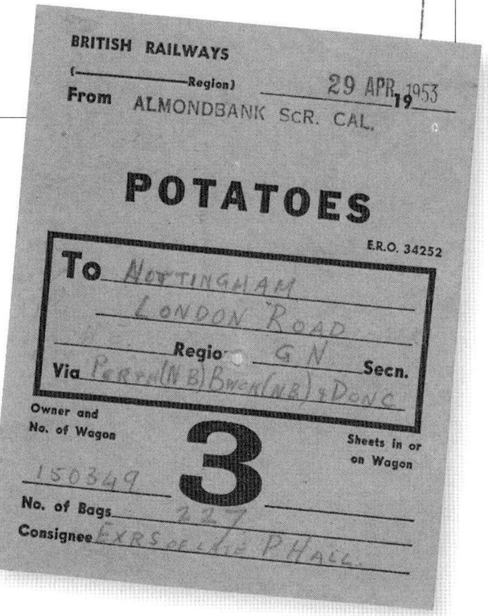

RIGHT: Figure 4.8
A British Railways 'Potatoes' wagon label from Almondbank for a consignment of seed potatoes to Nottingham dated 29th April 1953. This was the standard size wagon label, 4 inches by 5 inches, used in later years. The reference number E.R.O. 34252 indicates that this was an LM&SR design perpetuated by BR. It should be noted that the rubber-stamp 'ScR' denoted the Scottish Region of British Railways, which had been created in 1948 when the railways were nationalised; however the 'Cal' indicated that Almondbank was a former Caledonian Railway station, this still being used thirty years after the Caledonian became part of the LM&SR. Similarly, the routing via Perth and Berwick indicated that the wagon was to travel over these former North British lines. 227 bags was about a full van load of potatoes. *Author's collection*

Railway. As such, the architecture was not that of the more usual Caledonian stations to be seen elsewhere on the Strathearn lines. The platform, sited on the Up side, was originally a short affair some 115 feet long on the west side of the road overbridge. At a later date, this was extended under the bridge a further 65 feet, as the split level suggested, most probably when the line was extended through to Crieff. The section of platform under the bridge was extremely narrow and dark despite the platform oil lamps at each end of the bridge portal. In an attempt to improve light levels, both the wall behind the platform and the wall opposite were whitewashed.

The station building itself was on the original part of the platform, nestled between the line and the road embankment to the north. It was of an unusual design, being two stories, all of brick construction, with sharply sloped gables. The upper floor served as the stationmaster's house, while the ground floor contained the booking office, waiting room and so forth. To the west of the station there was a small goods yard with three sidings, although latterly two were removed and the third converted into a loop with a short loading bay.

In the 1880s the Caledonian Railway acquired further land to the south of the line to extend the station facilities. Judging from the elongated fan shape of the area involved it was almost certainly intended to lay out further sidings, for which there was no further room alongside the existing goods yard by nature of its cramped site. This work was never carried out; although the land remained in railway ownership, it was only ever used as a landscaped garden and washing green for the occupants of the station house. Occasionally timber awaiting loading was stored on part of it as space in the goods yard was limited.

Originally there was a signal box at Almondbank, opened in 1892 when the whole line was resignalled. Sited opposite the platform at the west end of the station, it was listed as a block post, but was limited by the fact that there being no passing loop, trains could not cross here. Few details of it survive, although it appears in early photographs of the station. Unsurprisingly, it was an early casualty of the rationalisation of signalling in the area carried out by the LM&SR, being closed in 1930. It was replaced by a ground frame,

CHAPTER 4: ALMOND VALLEY JCT TO CRIEFF – THE LINE DESCRIBED

LEFT: Figure 4.9
An LM&SR transfer label for platform lamps for Almondbank. The lettering on this label has been condensed in order to fit the station name within the standard 8 inch long label. It is worth noting that the station name is given as Almondbank, the name by which it was correctly referred to, and not 'Almond Bank' as is sometimes quoted. *Author's collection*

LEFT: Plate 4.7
The crest of the Royal Naval Stores Depot at Almondbank. Constructed during the Second World War, this was an aircraft repair and maintenance depot supporting airfields such as the Royal Naval Air Station at Edzell. Being a naval establishment, albeit a shore establishment (termed a 'stone frigate'), it had a unit crest, in this case the propeller indicating its aviation role. *Author*

ABOVE: Plate 4.8
Another view of Almondbank station in LM&SR days, looking west. The goods yard with carriage dock and goods shed can be seen beyond the platform. The land on the left was acquired by the Caledonian Railway; from the profile it was probably intended to provide additional sidings, but this development was never carried out. The station dog has appeared to pose in this photograph! *Photograph by Hugh Davies/Photos from the Fifties*

RIGHT: Plate 4.9
A view of the area opposite the station at Almondbank. As mentioned above at Plate 4.8, this piece of land was probably intended for sidings, including an access route to the main road, as can be seen here. However, it was never developed, being used as a garden and washing green for the station house. This view of the daily goods shunting in the 1950s shows the well-kept lawn and station sign, despite the fact that Almondbank had closed to passengers some years earlier.
Hugh Davies/Photos from the Fifties

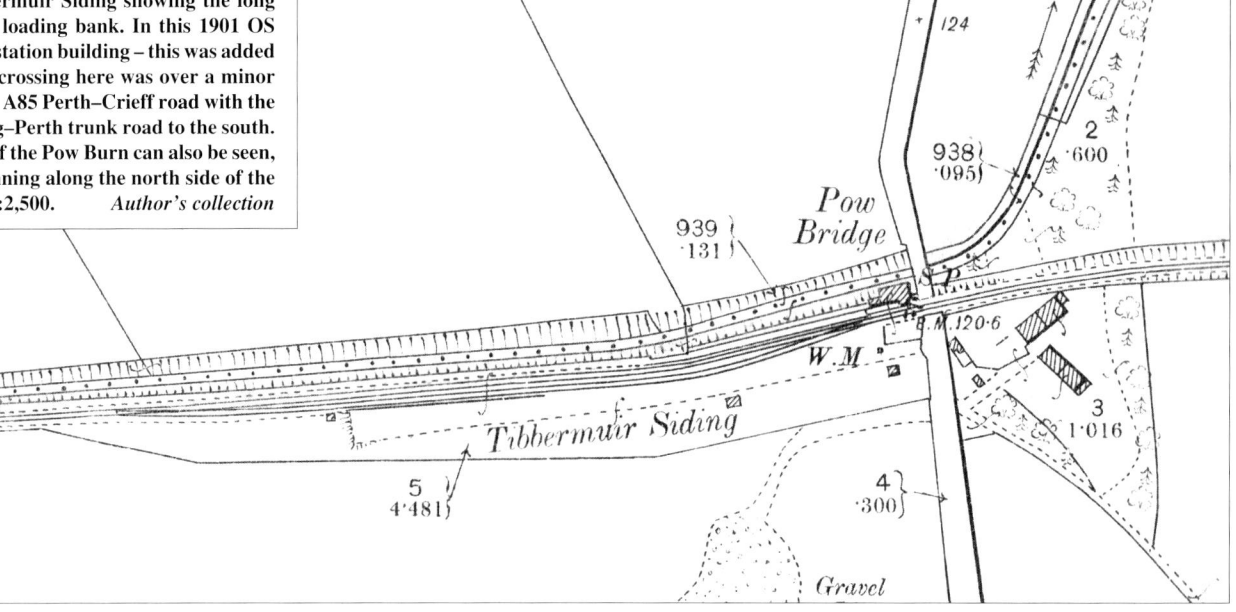

Figure 4.10
A map of Tibbermuir Siding showing the long goods loop and loading bank. In this 1901 OS map there is no station building – this was added later. The level crossing here was over a minor road linking the A85 Perth–Crieff road with the main A9 Stirling–Perth trunk road to the south. The proximity of the Pow Burn can also be seen, at this point running along the north side of the railway. Scale 1:2,500. *Author's collection*

controlled by the Almond Valley Junction–Methven Junction tablet, which operated the points to the goods yard sidings.

From Almondbank the line continued westwards, again climbing gently, and after a mile and a half crossed the Almondbank to Findo Gask road. At this level crossing there was another small wayside halt. This was Tibbermuir, sometimes spelt 'Tibbermore', which served the small community of the same name some three-quarters of a mile to the south near the site of the battle of Tippermuir, fought in 1644.

Originally simply called 'Tibbermuir Siding' or plain 'Tibbermuir', it was finally renamed Tibbermuir Halt by the LM&SR in 1938. Again, there was a short platform on the Up side next to the crossing keeper's cottage. A narrow timber affair, squeezed between the line and Pow Burn just to the north of it, it sported a solitary wooden shelter of the same design as that at Ruthven Road. In this case, however, half the building was used as a goods office, with the added luxury of a coke stove.

LEFT: **Plate 4.10**
Tibbermuir Halt was another small wayside station, albeit with goods facilities in the form of a single siding as seen here. The platform, station building and crossing keeper's cottage were similar to Ruthven Road. Unlike the latter, the platform at Tibbermuir was never altered, but retained its timber platform until closure. This view in 1963, twelve years after closure, shows it in a dilapidated state. *Author*

RIGHT: **Figure 4.11**
Another LM&SR transfer label, this one for Tibbermuir. Again, the lettering on this label has been condensed in order to fit the standard size of 8 inches by 3 inches. The LM&SR experimented with various colour combinations as part of their standardisation programme before deciding that black lettering on a yellow background provided the most visible contrast, and they subsequently used this for their transfer labels and other signage. These examples from the Perth to Crieff line were part of a stock of unused labels which came to light many years after the line closed. *Author's collection*

CHAPTER 4: ALMOND VALLEY JCT TO CRIEFF – THE LINE DESCRIBED

Plate 4.11
The station building, for want of a better word, at Tibbermuir in 1963. Of similar design to that at Ruthven Road, this shelter had the additional benefit of a stove, the flue of which can be seen on the left. The canopy provided a degree of protection to passengers, but facilities were rudimentary. Note the Caledonian Railway '½' milepost plate just to the left of the building. *ND Mundy*

To cater for goods traffic – in the main, seasonal loads of seed potatoes, common to this area – there was a loop some 550 feet long on the Down side of the line, together with a large storage shed. The level crossing was protected by signals in both directions, these being controlled from a ground frame in the garden of the level crossing keeper's cottage.

From here the line continued due west on the level for 2 miles to the isolated outpost of Methven Junction. There was no station at this site when the original line ran direct to Methven – it was constructed only when, on the opening of the Crieff & Methven Junction Railway, the line was carried through to Crieff, leaving the original Methven section as a short spur. Intended merely as an exchange platform for Methven traffic (similar to Killin Junction on the Callander & Oban Railway) the station had no direct access save a footpath from Tippermallo Farm and was in fact over a mile from the nearest road.

The track layout incorporated running loops on both the Methven and Crieff branches, although Methven trains had to cross to the Down Crieff loop before re-crossing the Up line to reach the branch

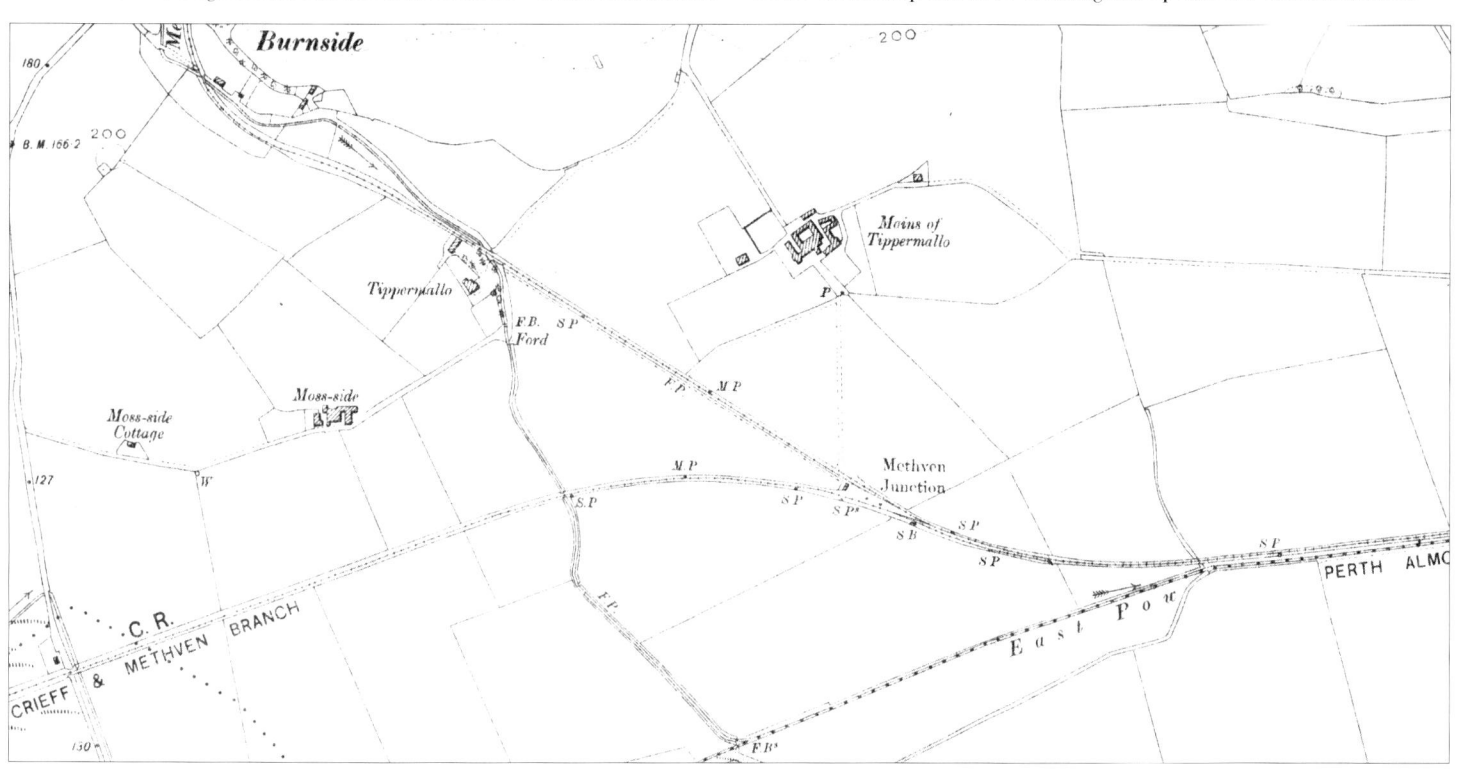

Figure 4.12
This map of Methven Junction shows clearly the remote location of this junction situated as it was in the middle of farmland. The original Perth Almond Valley & Methven Railway ran in from the east and then continued straight on uphill past Tippermallo Farm to Burnside and thence to Methven. The Crieff & Methven Junction Railway line curved away to the left and ran straight to cross a minor road at Methven Moss level crossing, which can be seen on the far left. This map also shows how close the railway ran to the Pow Burn for much of the route along the valley bottom. Scale 6 inches:1 mile.
Author's collection

ABOVE: **Plate 4.12**
Methven Junction was little more than a passing loop with platforms for Up and Down lines and the branch to Methven. There was no road access to this station and this view looking west gives an idea of its isolated location in the middle of open farmland. Taken in 1963, this shot shows the junction after the signal box closed and Methven Junction ceased to be a passing place. The track layout has been simplified, but the footbridge and station buildings are already long gone. *Author*

BELOW: **Plate 4.13**
This view of Methven Junction, taken in 1958 on the occasion of a rail tour hauled by CR 4-2-2 No. 123, shows the station from the east end. The line to Crieff curves off to the left, while the branch line to Methven which had been the original Perth Almond Valley & Methven line can be seen on the right. Although passenger facilities were minimal, goods traffic was also handled here, the short siding through the gate to the right being Tippermallo private siding which served the adjacent farm. *WAC Smith/transporttreasury.co.uk*

ABOVE: **Figure 4.13**
A selection of tickets issued from Methven Junction. The two Third Class Monthly Return tickets to Crieff and to Perth (LM&SR) are both endorsed 'RB', which indicates that they were available for use on buses for the return journey. This attempt at providing greater flexibility for travellers was probably a double-edged sword, as it gave them the opportunity to become familiar with the competing bus services. There could have been little call for tickets such as the Third Class Single from Perth, as Methven Junction was an isolated exchange platform in the middle of nowhere. *Author's collection*

CHAPTER 4: ALMOND VALLEY JCT TO CRIEFF – THE LINE DESCRIBED

platform. There was a refuge siding at the Perth end of the loop and on the Methven line there were two short sidings. One of these was a private siding serving Mains of Tippermallo Farm about half a mile north of the station, across whose land the original Methven railway had been built.

There were three platforms, one on the Down side and an island platform in the 'vee' serving Up main and Methven trains. A passenger bridge connected the two. There were waiting rooms on both platforms, but no station offices as all passengers were originally through booked. The signal box serving this busy little complex was of standard Caledonian Railway red-brick design housing a 36-lever frame. Opened in 1892, it was closed in 1962, when both loops and sidings were removed, with the remaining points to the Methven branch being hand worked.

THE METHVEN BRANCH LINE

On leaving the junction, the Methven branch started to climb at 1 in 115, and continuing on a straight north-westerly course until it reached the Methven road. Here the line swung sharply right to follow the road up to the village and the gradient stiffened to 1 in 98. The line reached its terminus on the southern outskirts of Methven about a quarter of a mile from the centre of the village.

Despite the fact that this was the original headquarters of the Perth Almond Valley & Methven Railway, Methven was a decidedly unimpressive station. Passenger facilities amounted to a short low platform on the Down side with a solitary single-storey brick building of the 'lean to' variety. The station was, however, well equipped to handle the not inconsiderable volume of freight traffic. There was a

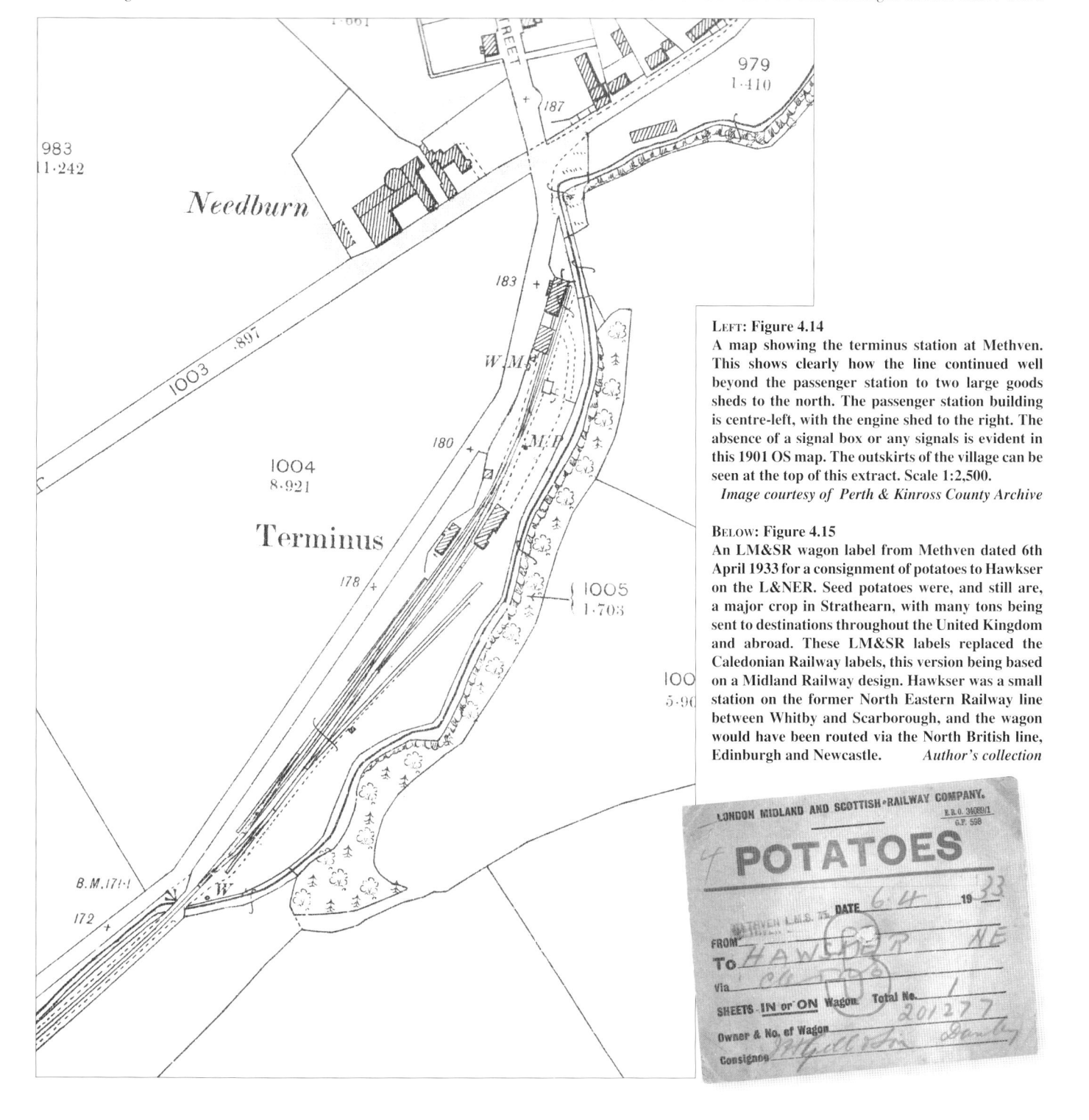

LEFT: Figure 4.14
A map showing the terminus station at Methven. This shows clearly how the line continued well beyond the passenger station to two large goods sheds to the north. The passenger station building is centre-left, with the engine shed to the right. The absence of a signal box or any signals is evident in this 1901 OS map. The outskirts of the village can be seen at the top of this extract. Scale 1:2,500.
Image courtesy of Perth & Kinross County Archive

BELOW: Figure 4.15
An LM&SR wagon label from Methven dated 6th April 1933 for a consignment of potatoes to Hawkser on the L&NER. Seed potatoes were, and still are, a major crop in Strathearn, with many tons being sent to destinations throughout the United Kingdom and abroad. These LM&SR labels replaced the Caledonian Railway labels, this version being based on a Midland Railway design. Hawkser was a small station on the former North Eastern Railway line between Whitby and Scarborough, and the wagon would have been routed via the North British line, Edinburgh and Newcastle. *Author's collection*

ABOVE: Plate 4.14
The terminus at Methven was hardly a grand affair, as can be seen from this view of the passenger station. The booking office was on the right of the platform building, with the station clock on the wall, while the waiting room was on the left. There was never any canopy or awning to provide protection for passengers. The line continued beyond here to a number of goods sheds, and the layout included a number of sidings to handle goods traffic. The small engine shed shown on the right was a sub shed of Perth and closed in 1931. There was no signalling at Methven, the branch from Methven Junction being worked on the 'One engine in Steam' principle throughout its lifetime.
N Forrest/transporttreasry.co.uk

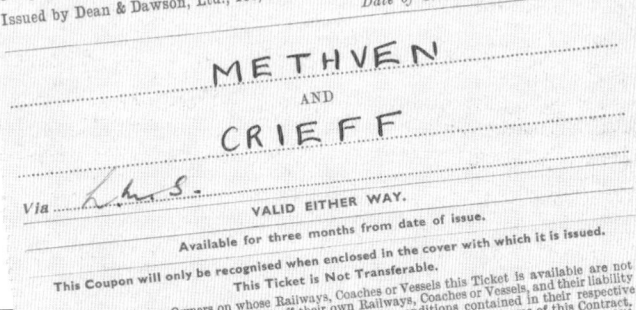

ABOVE: Figure 4.16
An interesting paper ticket issued by Dean & Dawson of London in 1937. This London & North Eastern Railway tours ticket was one of a pair issued, the other being from Perth to Methven, which were never used. This may have been for several reasons: first, there was no First Class in the Sentinel steam railcar which was then in use on the Methven line, and second was that although this ticket, issued on 30th July 1937, was valid for three months, the Methven Junction to Methven line closed less than two months later on 29th September 1937, which could have left the intending traveller stranded at Methven Junction.
Author's collection

LEFT: Plate 4.15
Following withdrawal of passenger services in 1937, the modest station building was retained to serve as the goods office, and is seen here in 1961.
Author

long siding alongside coal staithes and a loading bank on the Down side, while two other sidings branched off the reversing loop on the Up side.

One of the sidings was the engine shed road. The engine shed, built when the line opened in 1858, was of brick construction, capable of housing two tank engines or one tender locomotive. There was also a water column, the only one on the PAV&MR section. Originally the branch line engine, usually a tank engine from Perth, was stabled here, working the first train out in the morning and the last train back in the evening. This practice ceased in 1927 with the introduction of the Sentinel steam railcar which replaced the locomotive-hauled trains. Methven shed then closed as the railcar was based at Perth South Motive Power Depot. Early photographs show the building with an arched door, but at some later stage this was rebuilt with a plain

Left: Plate 4.16
A closer view of Methven engine shed in later years. Following closure, it was used as an additional goods shed. By 1963, when this photograph was taken, it was starting to show signs of neglect, such as the damage to the doors. The three smoke louvers were unaltered, although some of the windows had been bricked in. *Author*

Below: Plate 4.17
A general view of the goods yard at the south end of Methven station showing the fairly extensive layout of sidings. The branch line leading to the passenger station passes to the right of the coal wagons in the siding on the left. The engine shed road is also in use as a siding, while some of the trackwork had already been simplified by the time this photograph was taken in 1963. *Author*

rectangular door. After the Methven branch closed to passengers in 1937 the shed continued to be used for many years for goods traffic, surviving until the line closed completely in 1965.

The line continued beyond the passenger station for a short distance to branch into two more sidings. A cattle dock was provided on the Down side of the long siding, which continued beyond the goods shed to a large granary. The other shorter siding ran alongside these two buildings. There were no signals or signal box at Methven, the line being worked from the outset on the 'One Engine in Steam' principle.

From Methven Junction, the line of the Crieff & Methven Junction Railway continued westwards towards Crieff some 11 miles away. Largely crossing open farmland along the valley, this section of line was easily graded, being level for much of its length. The line crossed the Methven to Madderty road on the level a mile after leaving Methven Junction. Beyond this the line was carried through Methven Moss and, following Pow Burn, reached Balgowan station, just under 3 miles to the west. Here the line passed over Cowgate Burn and, at the west end of the station, crossed the private road leading to Balgowan House, from which the station took its name.

The usual timber-coped platform was on the Down side, and there was a heterogeneous collection of buildings housing various offices and stores. The line at this stage curved fairly sharply to the north-west and all the sidings fanned out to the south of the station. Although the passenger facilities were modest, Balgowan was well equipped to handle goods traffic, including horses and private carriages. The layout comprised a running loop with two short sidings to loading bays and three other sidings of just over 300 feet. As in the case of Tullibardine, the bulk of the traffic emanated from the nearby estate – in fact Mr Thompson of Balgowan was one of the original directors of the Crieff & Methven Junction Railway. In latter days considerable traffic was generated by the large sawmill which was constructed adjacent to the goods yard, and during the Second World War a large army stores depot was established here. Originally, Balgowan had some form of signal box, of which no details survive, although, as with Almondbank, it was never a block post.

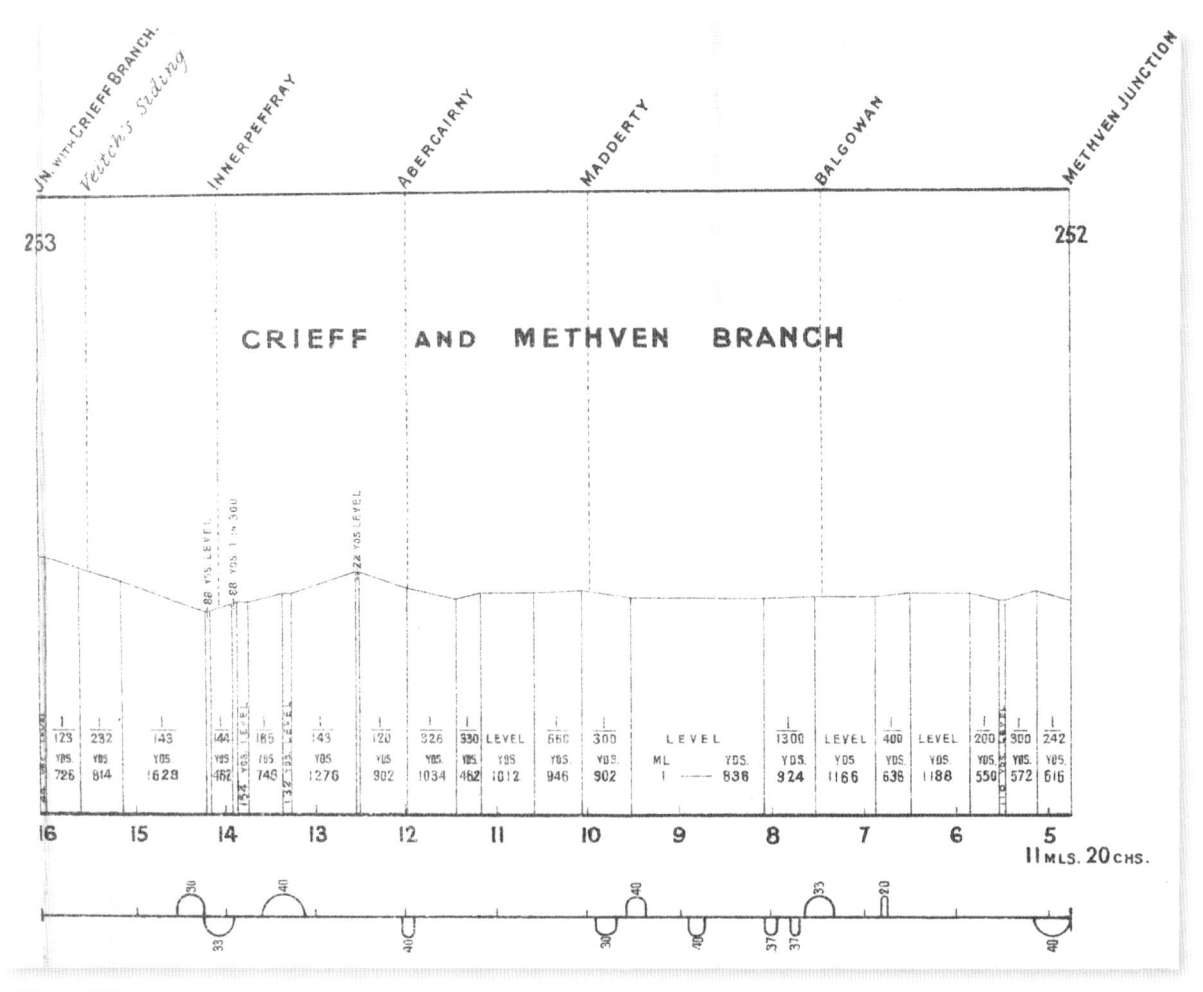

Figure 4.17
CR gradient diagram for the Crieff & Methven Junction section of the line, showing the gentle gradients on this stretch of the line which ran on the level for much of the way, although it climbed for the final approach to Crieff. Note also Veitch's Siding shown here, just under half a mile from Crieff. This chemical manure works later became the Strathearn Manure Works and had a siding off the main line.
Author's collection

Plate 4.18
Less than a mile west of Methven Junction, the line crossed the minor road running south from Methven village before continuing east across Methven Moss. This view shows the daily goods train from Crieff approaching the level crossing in the 1960s, hauled by Perth based 0-6-0 No. 44253, which was a frequent visitor to Crieff both on this duty and on the Gleneagles to Comrie passenger service. The crossing keeper's cottage is just out of shot to the right of the telegraph pole.
Hugh Davies/ Photos from the Fifties

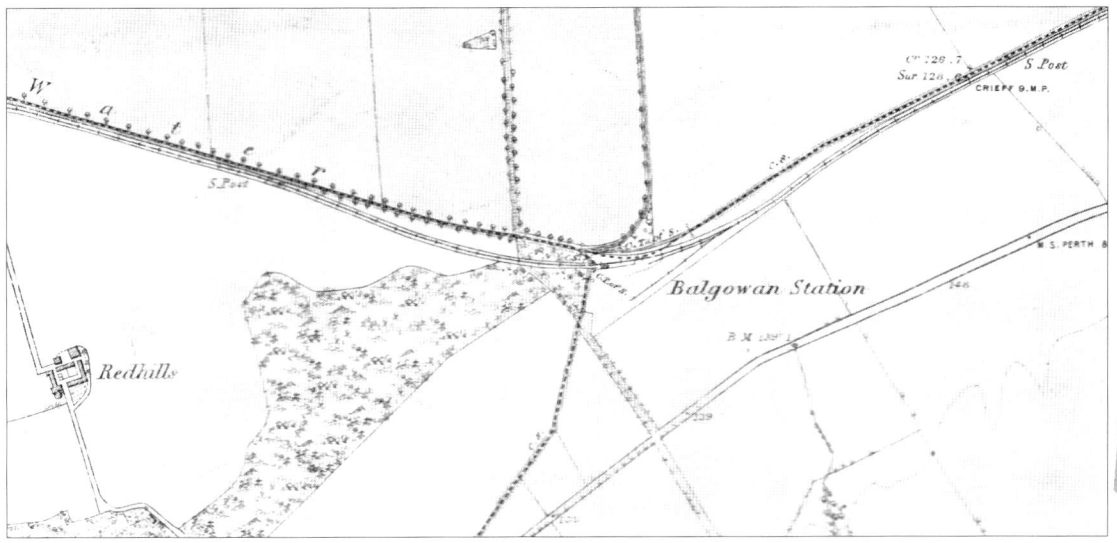

CHAPTER 4: ALMOND VALLEY JCT TO CRIEFF – THE LINE DESCRIBED

ABOVE: Figure 4.18
A map of Balgowan station showing well how this station appears to have been built in the middle of nowhere. It was, however, convenient to Balgowan House, just under a mile north of here and the residence of Mr Thompson, one of the original Directors of the Perth Almond Valley & Methven Railway. The road over the level crossing to the west of the station was the drive up to the house. In this 1901 OS map, the large sawmill which occupied much of the wedge shaped area of land adjacent to the station has yet to be built. Scale 6 inches:1 mile.

Reproduced from the 1901 Ordnance Survey map

RIGHT: Figure 4.19
A selection of tickets issued at Balgowan. All three of these are British Railways tickets printed during the brief three years prior to closure in 1951; unusually, none have been dated or used, and the cancellation clips indicate that these were unused stock returned to the Audit Office after closure. Nonetheless they are interesting, and the Third Class Single is another example of two destinations with the same fare, so one ticket type sufficed. The very low serial number of the First Class Cheap Day Return to Crieff would indicate that they were little used.   *Author's collection*

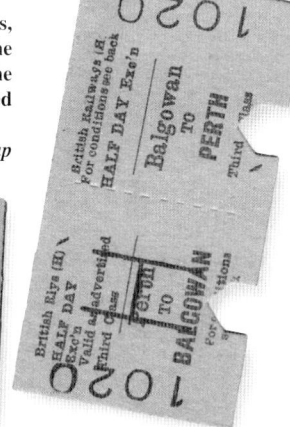

Plate 4.19
Balgowan station from the east showing the goods yard and extensive sawmill operation on the left. The fixed Distant signal protects the level crossing just beyond the station, there never having been a signal box at this location. The buildings on the extreme left were built during the Second World War for a large army supply depot. Balgowan was the nearest station to Findo Gask, some two miles to the south, where a large camp for the Polish Army was established in 1940.   *Author*

ABOVE: Plate 4.20
Balgowan passenger station was a simple affair with a waiting shelter and a number of small buildings lining the single low platform. The original station building had been demolished by the time this view was taken. The sharp curve through the station is evident from the use of a 'check rail', as can be seen here. It is hard to believe that in its heyday Balgowan frequently won prizes – six first class and one third class – in the Best Kept Station competition. The crossing keeper's cottage can be seen in the background.
Author

Plate 4.21
The level crossing to the east of Balgowan station, where the private road to Balgowan House crossed the line. In the 19th century this was the residence of Mr William Thompson, who was both the Vice Chairman of the Perth Almond Valley & Methven Railway and one of the promoters of the Crieff & Methven Junction Railway. The stationmaster's wife was the crossing keeper, and on one memorable occasion had to open the gates no less than ninety-five times in one day for carts from nearby Redhill Farm! The crossing keeper's cottage is of a similar design to those at Ruthven Road and Tibbermuir.
Author

This was removed as early as 1895, less than thirty years after the line opened, to be replaced by a ground frame. As was customary, this ground frame controlling the level crossing and signals was situated near the crossing keeper's cottage.

The whole stretch of line was very easily graded, for the most part being around 1 in 200. It is easy to see how the line followed the most economical route possible by threading its way up the valley towards Crieff avoiding any requirement for heavy, and thus costly, engineering. Continuing along the banks of the Pow Water, the line passed to the south of Balgowan estate to reach Madderty 3 miles to the west.

The station here was sited just to the east of the bridge which carried the Crieff to Perth road into the village, just to the south of the ruins of the ancient Inchaffray Abbey. Conveniently, Madderty was almost halfway between Crieff and Methven Junction and was therefore a logical choice as a crossing point for trains running over that section. As such, the layout was on a somewhat grander scale than would otherwise have been justified by the domestic traffic from the two small communities of Madderty and St. David's.

There was a running loop capable of passing the longest trains anticipated on the line, together with two sidings on the Up side. One of these was a spur along the north side of the goods yard, while the other ran the length of the loading bank which formed an island platform with the Up platform. Both Up and Down platforms were stone faced and a fence ran along the back of the Up platform to separate it from the loading bank. The station house – an attractive villa-style two-story stone building, incorporating the offices on the ground floor – was on the Down side, whilst there was a wooden waiting shed on the Up platform. A passenger footbridge connected the two. Being a block post, Madderty had a signal box, another of standard Caledonian Railway brick design, which was sited on the east end of the Up platform. Opened along with others on the line in 1892, it was closed in 1962 and thereafter the remaining points worked by hand.

Once under the bridge to the west of the station, the line passed through a half mile long cutting, one of the few substantive earthworks on the line. Madderty manse lay to the north of the line, and halfway along this cutting the private access road was carried over the line on an unusual iron girder bridge, not unlike a military 'Bailey bridge' in design.

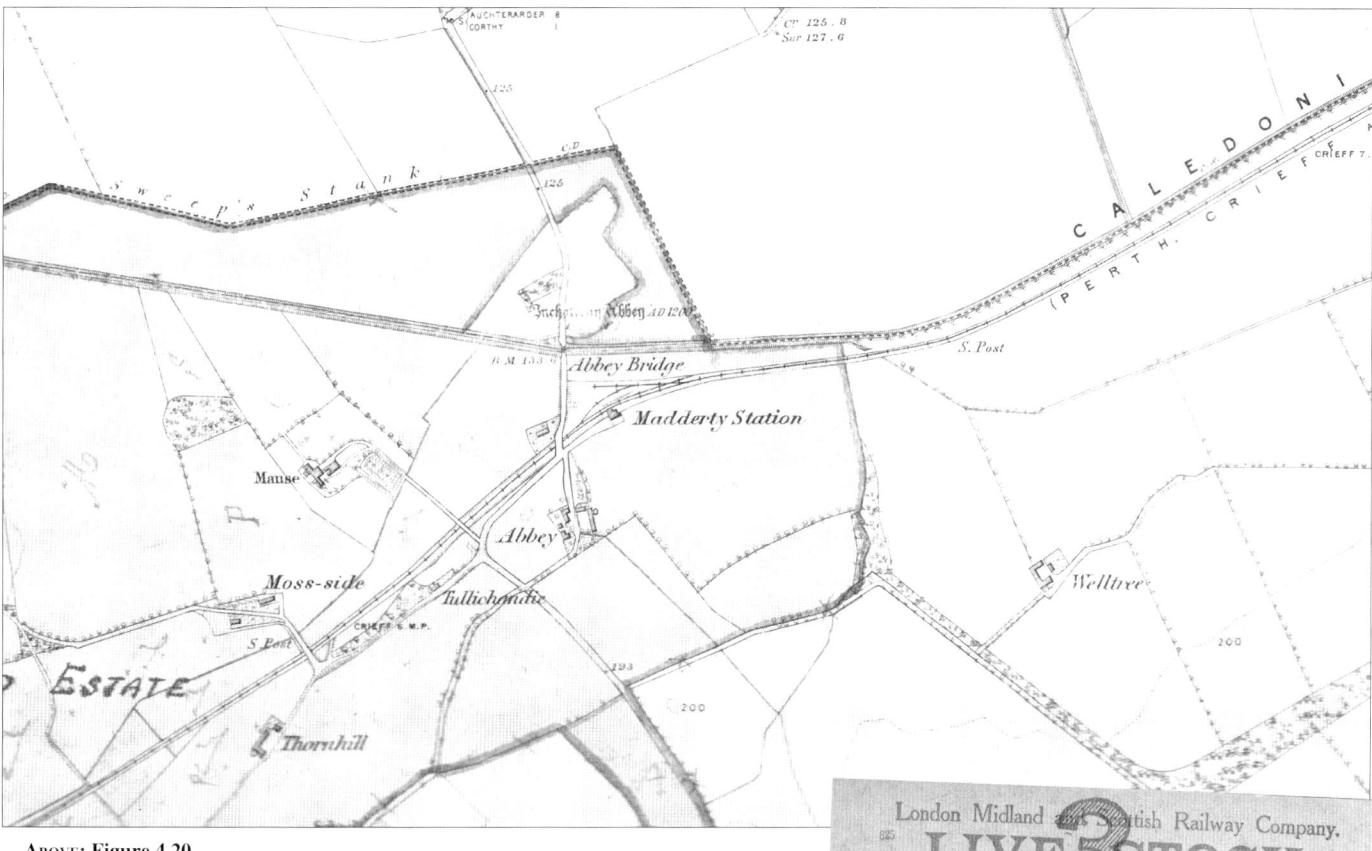

CHAPTER 4: ALMOND VALLEY JCT TO CRIEFF – THE LINE DESCRIBED

ABOVE: Figure 4.20
A map of Madderty showing the station and, outlined in red, the extent of the Woodend Estate. The site of the 11th-century Inchaffray Abbey can be seen just north of the station and the three bridges over what was called the 'Abbey Cut' are also evident. The Pow Water, which ran alongside the railway from its source near Methven Moss, turned north of the high ground through which the railway ran. Scale 6 inches:1 mile.
Reproduced from the 1901 Ordnance Survey map

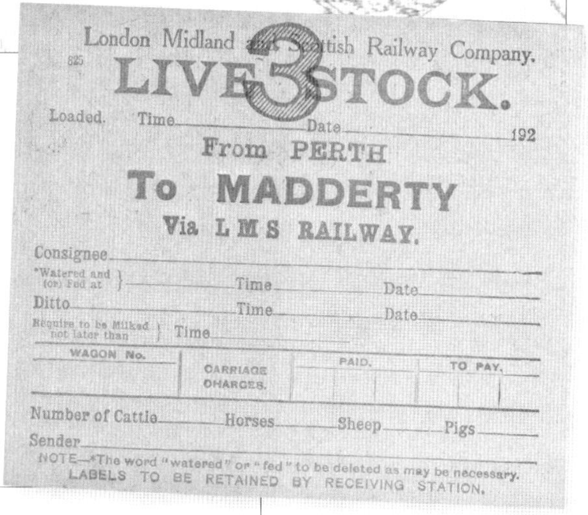

RIGHT: Figure 4.21
An early LM&SR wagon label for livestock printed 'From PERTH To MADDERTY'. The use of pre-printed labels such as this would indicate a regular level of such livestock traffic. The routing 'Via LMS Railway' was superfluous in this case – as the only routes were via Almond Valley Junction or Gleneagles, all part of the LM&SR system – but were included as part of the standard layout for such labels. These were large labels, measuring 6 inches by 5 inches rather than the later standard size of 4 inches by 5 inches.
Author's collection

LEFT: Plate 4.22
A general view of Madderty station from the east, with the line curving round towards Crieff. Madderty was the only station between Methven Junction and Crieff equipped with a passing loop and signal box, both of which closed in 1962, having survived almost until the final closure of the line in 1965. The small goods yard to the right had two sidings, the one on the left being a long siding alongside the loading bank. The Caledonian-pattern double telegraph poles can still be seen on the right. *Author*

Beyond a third bridge, to Woodend Farm, the line traversed open flat farmland on a straight and almost level route to Abercairny. This isolated wayside station was named after the nearby estate – the main reason for its existence, there being no actual village of that name. Situated at the point where the Fowlis Wester to Kinkell Bridge road crossed the railway, it was also intended to serve the numerous farming communities in the area.

The layout at Abercairny was neat and compact. The platform and station building was on the Up side, being another of the villa-type stone buildings incorporating the stationmaster's residence on the upper story with the booking office on the ground floor. A wooden waiting room shed adjoined the main building. The goods yard lay on the Down side, and again was designed to handle predominantly agricultural traffic. To this end there were two loops running either

Plate 4.23
Madderty passenger station in LM&SR days looking east towards Perth. The fence dividing the passenger platform area from the goods platform behind it can be clearly seen, while the standard Caledonian Railway wooden footbridge dominates the scene. Unusually, there are no enamel advertising signs to be seen, and passenger facilities could best be described as spartan. *Lens of Sutton/CRA*

Plate 4.24
Madderty station looking east, as seen from the approach road. In this view taken in 1963, the footbridge and the fence between the passenger and goods platforms have been removed, although the waiting shelter on the Up platform remains. There is evidence of goods traffic, probably seed potatoes, whilst the hurdle set against the signal box steps would suggest that cattle traffic was still being handled at this time. *Author*

CHAPTER 4: ALMOND VALLEY JCT TO CRIEFF – THE LINE DESCRIBED

side of a substantial loading bay which effectively formed an island platform. In addition, a short siding was laid between the loops at the western end to provide a loading dock for carriages and trucks; a further spur branched off the outer loop and handled the mineral traffic.

An attractive stretch followed as the line passed under the road bridge and continued through the thick woods which form the southern part of Abercairny estate. Having crossed over the Crieff to Madderty road the line climbed slightly on an embankment and emerged from the woods to cross the farm track to Muir of Dollerie and Woodburn farms at an occupation crossing which, sadly, was the site of a fatal accident (featured in Chapter 9). Negotiating a gentle curve, the line followed a north-westerly course towards Crieff, now visible only 3 miles away. After a short distance it crossed the Pow

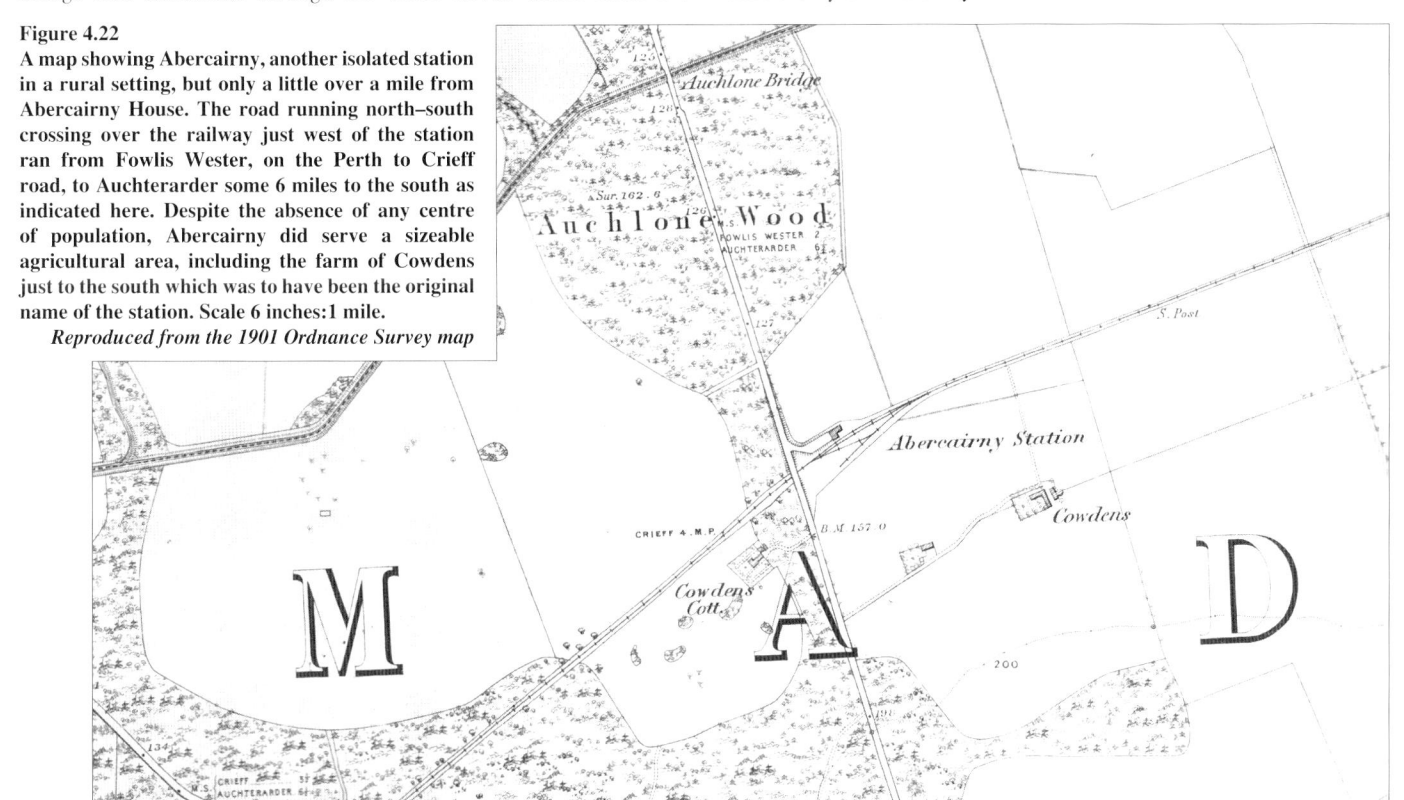

Figure 4.22
A map showing Abercairny, another isolated station in a rural setting, but only a little over a mile from Abercairny House. The road running north–south crossing over the railway just west of the station ran from Fowlis Wester, on the Perth to Crieff road, to Auchterarder some 6 miles to the south as indicated here. Despite the absence of any centre of population, Abercairny did serve a sizeable agricultural area, including the farm of Cowdens just to the south which was to have been the original name of the station. Scale 6 inches:1 mile.
Reproduced from the 1901 Ordnance Survey map

Plate 4.25
Abercairny station was a neat station with a stone building similar in design to the other 'villa' houses at Madderty and Innerpeffray. This served as the stationmaster's house and booking office, with passenger facilities in the adjoining wooden structure seen on the right. The station gardens are well kept and the topiary along the back of the platform would indicate a keen interest in gardening.
Lens of Sutton/CRA

Burn on a single-arch masonry bridge, then crossed over the Dollerie to Highlandman road to come to the last intermediate station before Crieff, that of Innerpeffray.

Another extravaganza of the railway mania of the nineteenth century, Innerpeffray station served a tiny community and was barely a mile from the existing station at Highlandman. However, the building of a separate station here probably owed more to influential local connections. The ruins of Innerpeffray Castle, built by the first Lord Madderty in the 16th century, were close by, as was the famous Innerpeffray Library. The oldest lending library in Scotland, this was founded in 1680 by David Drummond, third Lord Madderty, whose wife was the youngest sister of the renowned Duke of Montrose. Among other treasures housed here are an inscribed bible from 1540, and the nearby St. Marys Chapel is the burial place of the Drummonds.

The layout of the station was similar to Abercairny, with the platform and an almost identical villa-style building on the Up side. The single loop and two loading dock sidings were likewise sited on

Plate 4.26
Abercairny station from the east, showing the ample siding layout which, even in this 1963 view, is being well used. The predominance of covered vans would again indicate seed potato traffic for which the area was, and still is, renowned. Access to the sidings was controlled by a ground frame which was just behind the photographer, at the end of the rodding run to be seen on the right. It is worth noting that this is still laid out with round rodding which probably dated from Caledonian Railway days.
Author

RIGHT: Figure 4.23
An LM&SR wagon label for livestock printed 'From PERTH To ABERCAIRNY'. These labels could be used for consignments of cattle, horses, sheep or pigs as indicated; they also included details of the times and dates on which the livestock were fed and watered, and the time by which cows were required to be milked. All of these were reminders that the animal husbandry of such livestock was the responsibility of the railway company from the time the animals were received until they were collected at their destination. The reverse of the label has been used by someone at Perth North goods yard to record the holdings of wagon stock on 10th January 1940.
Author's collection

LEFT: Plate 4.27
Abercairny station from the west in 1963. Although the passenger service had been withdrawn twelve years previously, the station still looks in fair condition with well-tended shrubs. Next to the van standing at the loading dock is the short carriage dock siding, while the siding curving off to the right is the other end of the loop seen on the left in Plate 4.26.
Author

the Down side. Originally there was also a signal box here, adjoining the west end of the station building. Opened in 1892 when the line was resignalled, it was in effect a covered ground frame. It closed in 1917 as part of the economy measures during the First World War but was never reinstated. The lever frame remained in situ until it was finally removed in 1949 to be replaced by a pair of ground frames released by the section tablet.

Covering the final two miles to Crieff, the line was soon joined from the left by the Gleneagles line and the two ran side by side for the last mile to Crieff, with level crossings across both lines at Pittentian and Pittenzie. Shortly after Pittentian there was a single siding on the Up side which served the Strathearn Manure Works, formerly called Veitch's Siding, but this was removed shortly after the Second World War.

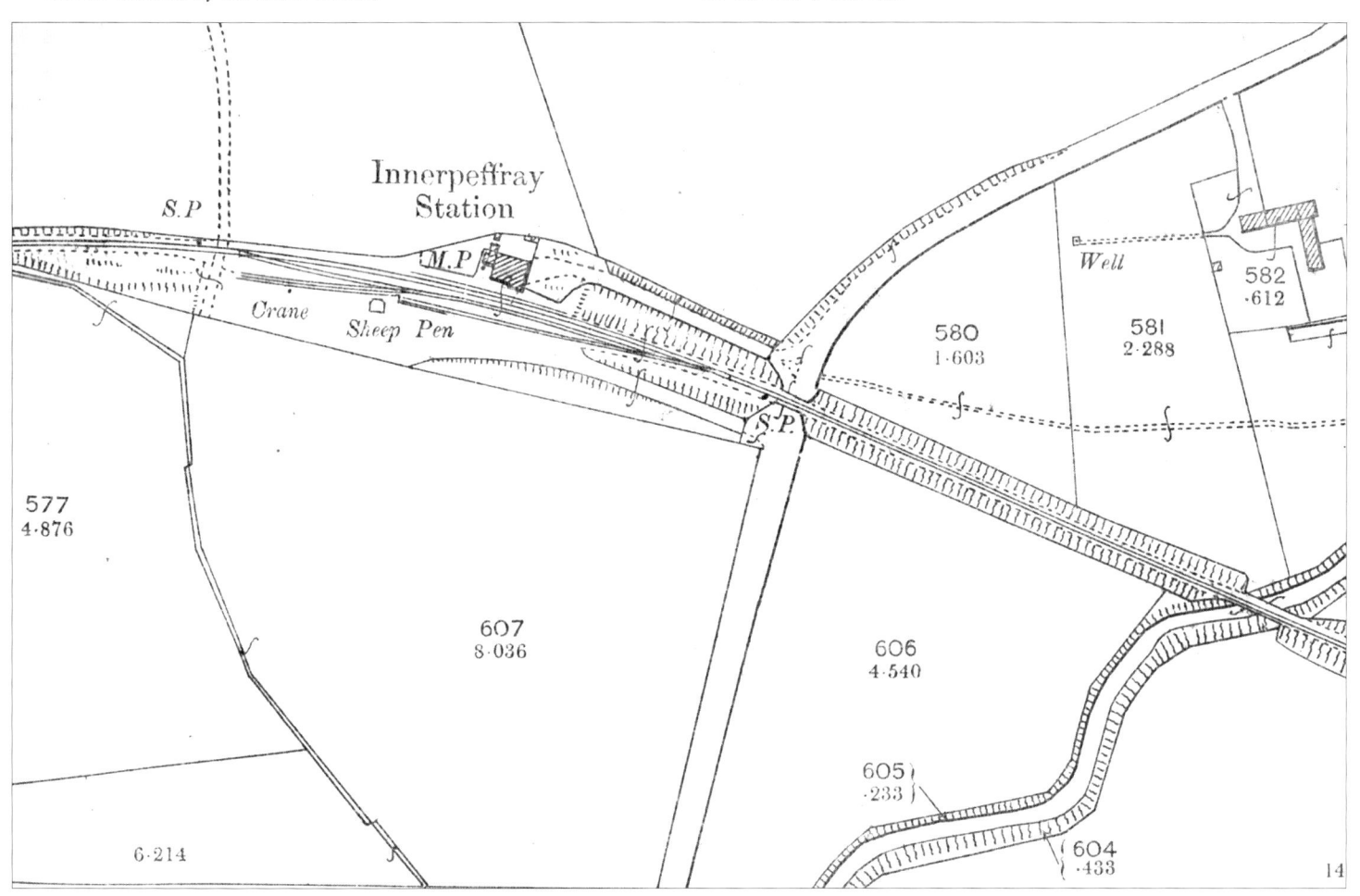

Above: Figure 4.24
Map of Innerpeffray station showing the passenger station to the north of the line and the goods yard to the south, both with their own approaches from the Dollerie to Highlandman road which passed under the railway at the east end of the station. The site of the scotch derrick can be seen alongside the loading bank, and the sheep pen at the west end of the main siding. Scale 1:2,500.
Reproduced from the 1901 Ordnance Survey map

Plate 4.28
Innerpeffray station looking west. By the time this photograph was taken in 1963, Innerpeffray had closed to goods traffic and the sidings in the foreground had been lifted. The booking office and passenger shelter was at the far end of the station house, as at Abercairny, and is hidden from view here. *Author*

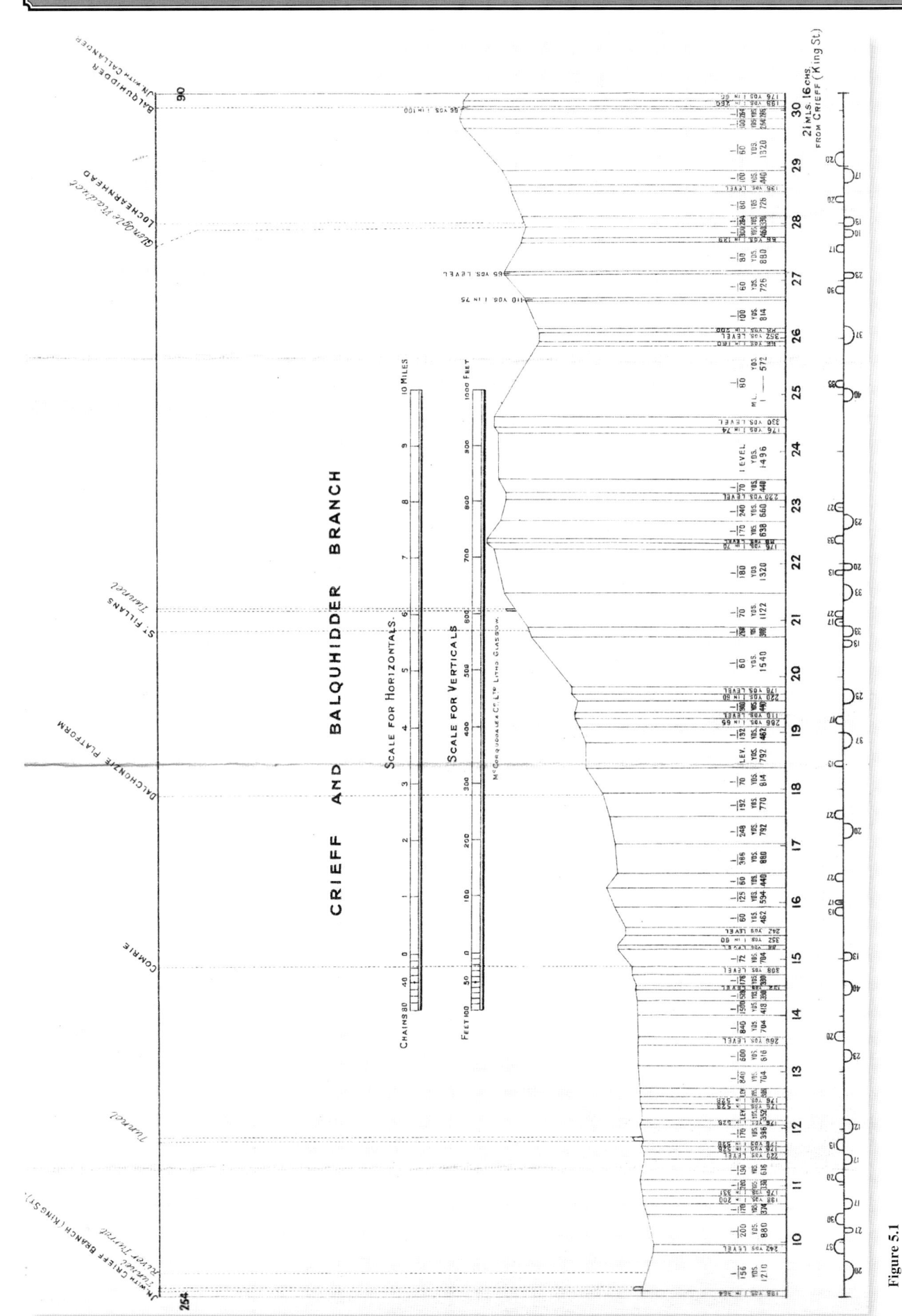

Figure 5.1
The Caledonian Railway gradient diagram for the Crieff to Balquhidder line. This covers the entire line from the King Street bridge in Crieff to the junction with the Callander & Oban line, a distance of 21 miles 16 chains. The mileage shown along the bottom of the diagram is the distance from Gleneagles, and the figure 254 at the top left refers to the adjoining gradient diagram for the Gleneagles to Crieff section. All three tunnels are shown, but the only bridges are the one over the River Turret and Glen Ogle viaduct. The steep ascent through St. Fillans and the final climb to Balquhidder are evident here.

Author's collection

Chapter 5

Crieff to Balquhidder – The Line Described

Crieff was the centre of the network of branch lines in Strathearn, with the lines from Gleneagles and Perth, described in the preceding chapters, running in parallel to each other from the east, and the line to Balquhidder heading west towards Comrie. The original station, described in Chapter 1, had been a terminus, originally for the Crieff Junction Railway and later expanded to accommodate the Crieff & Methven Junction Railway when that opened in 1866.

With the opening of the long-awaited Crieff & Comrie Railway in 1893, a completely new passenger station was built and much of the existing layout altered. It is this enlarged station layout, which survived until final closure, that is taken as the starting point for the description of this stretch of line. The three main areas of the station were the passenger station, the goods yard, and the engine sheds and carriage sidings to the east of the station.

The new passenger station was much grander than the one it replaced, perhaps reflecting the pre-eminence of rail travel in the late-Victorian era, and the prosperity it had brought to Crieff. It was an impressive affair with extensive wooden buildings on both Up and Down platforms. Although these were of generous proportions, the use of wood and concrete rather than dressed stone was viewed by the local paper as being rather down-market compared with the new Crieff of villas, the Hydro and Morrison's Academy. The use of wooden construction to keep down costs was an economy measure whose shortcomings became evident later in life. By the late 1950s the buildings were starting to look careworn and large sections of the canopy had to be dismantled on safety grounds. The situation was not helped by the lack of investment in maintenance by British Railways in later years, and it could be speculated just how much longer the buildings would have lasted had the line not closed in 1964.

This new station was built on what had been part of the Crieff Town Muir, an open space just to the north of the existing terminus which had been used in the past as bleaching greens by the many weavers in the town. The actual station was sited in the East Meadow, while the cutting leading to the Burrell Street tunnel ran through the old West Meadow. Originally it had been mooted that the latter

Plate 5.1
A view from Duchlage Road bridge in Crieff looking east, showing the Perth and Gleneagles lines running in parallel to each other. On the far left are the goods sidings built by the Crieff & Methven Junction Railway and next to them the sidings leading to the locomotive depot. The railbus is arriving on the Down line, and on the right is the headshunt for the goods yard which is behind the photographer. Crieff signal box, originally 'Crieff East', can just be seen on the right.
Author

Plate 5.2
An overall view of Crieff station from the east end, looking under the Duchalage Road bridge, showing the goods yard – formerly the terminus of the Crieff Junction Railway – to the left and the later 1893 station built for the opening of the Crieff & Comrie Railway to the right. This bridge was the one which caused such a stir when it was installed in 1893, as recounted in Chapter 2. The photographer is standing close to the site of the original level crossing over the Crieff Junction line which it replaced.
AG Ellis

Plate 5.3
A good view of the passenger station at Crieff taken from the Duchlage Road bridge at the east end of the station giving a good impression of the full length of the platforms, the twenty-four cast iron columns supporting each canopy, and the spacious nature of the covered area. At this stage the footbridge is still covered and both platform canopies are intact. Ex-LM&SR 2-6-4T No. 42199 stands in the Up platform with a Gleneagles train.
AG Ellis

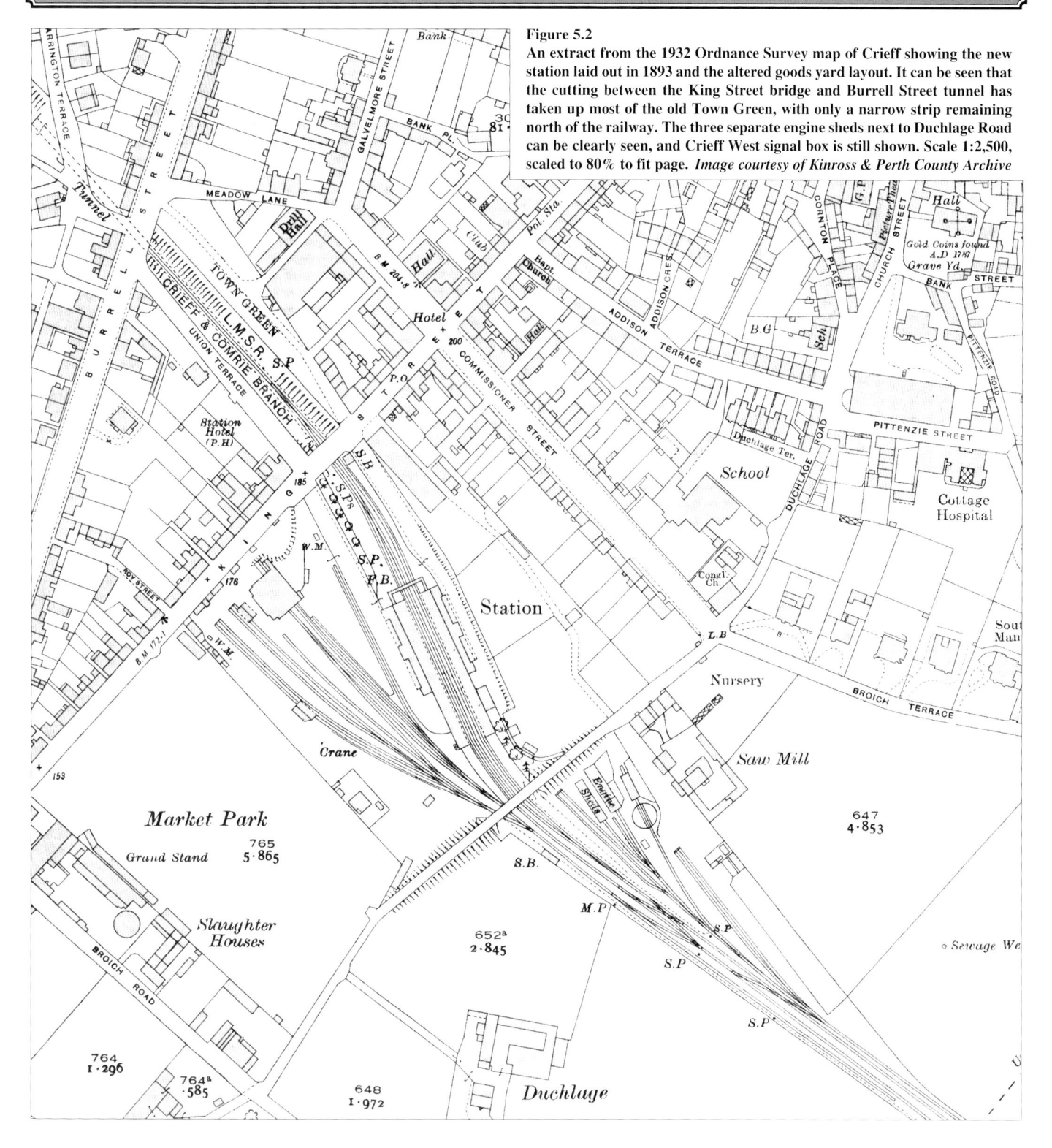

CHAPTER 5: CRIEFF TO BALQUHIDDER – THE LINE DESCRIBED

Figure 5.2
An extract from the 1932 Ordnance Survey map of Crieff showing the new station laid out in 1893 and the altered goods yard layout. It can be seen that the cutting between the King Street bridge and Burrell Street tunnel has taken up most of the old Town Green, with only a narrow strip remaining north of the railway. The three separate engine sheds next to Duchlage Road can be clearly seen, and Crieff West signal box is still shown. Scale 1:2,500, scaled to 80% to fit page. *Image courtesy of Kinross & Perth County Archive*

would also be a tunnel constructed on a 'cut and cover' basis, but this was never done. The new station layout was generous, having two long platform lines with an additional third running line, known as the 'Mid Road', which could be used as an engine release road, for shunting, or to store rolling stock. Substantial canopies carried on handsome cast iron columns covered over half the length of the platforms, which were connected by a covered footbridge at the western end. Booking offices were provided on both platforms, together with waiting rooms and other office accommodation. The remaining length of the canopies had wooden walls running along the back of the platforms. These provided additional space on which to display the many noticeboards advertising railway services and other commercial products. Carriage driveways ran down from King Street to circulating areas behind the buildings on both the Up and Down sides, in addition to which there was also a footpath on the Up side affording pedestrian access to Duchlage Road. The station was equipped throughout with gas lighting, and lamp standards and flower beds completed the attractive appearance of this important country junction.

Goods facilities were extensive to cater for the volume and range of traffic handled. The goods yard occupied the site of the original Crieff Junction Railway terminus, with a number of the original

Plate 5.4
A view of the Up platform buildings taken from the rear showing the extensive accommodation provided. The station approach road sloped down from King Street, off to the left. The ornate iron canopies, and equally ornate ridge tiles and bargeboards, are well illustrated here. Despite its impressive size, the building was of all-wood construction and was completely demolished shortly after closure. *Author*

Plate 5.5
A view of the west end of the station from the King Street bridge, giving a good idea of the overall size and layout of the new station – although by the time this photograph was taken the footbridge had lost its covering roof. The centre road was used for running round trains, the west end being controlled by the small ground frame which replaced Crieff West signal box when it closed in 1934. The water column was one of a pair provided at the station at the platform ends. *AG Ellis*

Plate 5.6
Crieff goods yard seen from under Duchlage Road bridge showing the extensive layout. To the left several long sidings handled the coal and mineral traffic, whilst those on the right led to the cattle docks. In this view taken in 1963, at least three goods sheds can be seen, the larger two-bay building in the centre being the original Crieff Junction Railway passenger station. *Author*

CHAPTER 5: CRIEFF TO BALQUHIDDER – THE LINE DESCRIBED

facilities adapted to suit. The original combined passenger station and goods shed became the goods shed – the larger of the two loading banks was retained, with a second smaller loading dock being extended and a carriage dock added. This northern set of sidings on the site of the old passenger station was referred to as 'No. 1 Group' and handled mainly general merchandise and livestock traffic. Much of the original goods yard, including the engine shed, stables and carriage sheds, was remodelled and four long sidings laid out, these being referred to as the 'No. 2 Group'. A large scotch derrick was provided alongside these sidings which handled, in the main, mineral and bulk traffic. In addition to the two original goods sheds, two further prefabricated buildings were added in later years. This yard survived the passenger station by several years, as the Crieff to Perth line remained open for freight traffic after the closure of the Crieff to Gleneagles line in 1964, not closing until 1967.

Crieff station had no less than four different engine sheds during its existence, and their history is more than a little complex. The first of these was the original Crieff Junction Railway shed. Reputedly ordered to the design of their engineer Thomas Bouch, it was a small brick building just south of the then level crossing over Duchlage Road. This shed was subsequently demolished during the remodelling of the goods yard in 1893. With the opening of the Crieff & Methven Junction Railway in 1866, a second and separate shed was provided; this was also brick built and was sited just east of Duchlage Road bridge, flanked by six sidings laid out to handle the Crieff & Methven Junction traffic. This shed also had a 45-foot turntable immediately outside it. Following the opening of the Crieff & Comrie Railway, two further sheds were added, one on either side of the existing shed. The southernmost was a longer wooden shed, while that to the north was a shorter wooden affair with a siding running through it. In 1895 the brick shed was extended to almost double its length. In 1910, not long after the line opened through to Balquhidder, a 50-foot turntable lying spare at Aberdeen was sent to Crieff. This replaced the shorter turntable outside the original shed but, probably in order to accommodate the extra length, it was installed outside the northernmost small wooden shed. Originally built by Cowans Sheldon in 1888, this balanced unit was later extended to 52 feet in length. The later wooden sheds did not wear well and deteriorated over the years. The southernmost shed was demolished not long after the Second World War and the turntable shed succumbed in 1961. Thus, by the time the line closed to passengers in 1964, the only shed remaining was the 1866 brick structure.

The two sidings on the south side of the engine sheds, together with two longer sidings alongside the Perth line, originally handled the goods traffic from the Methven Junction line, having their own crane and weighbridge. Latterly, goods traffic was concentrated in the main goods yard and these sidings were largely used to store wagons or to stable coaching stock. Their origins, however, continued to be reflected in their name, right up to the time of closure, being referred to as the 'Methven Sidings'.

With the opening of the new station, two signal boxes were constructed at Crieff – replacing the original box at Duchlage Road level crossing, of which little is known. The main and larger of these was Crieff East, which was just to the east of Duchlage Road bridge; this controlled not only the approaches of the two lines from Gleneagles and Perth, but also the east end of the passenger station, the goods yard, engine sheds and the complex of adjacent sidings. Crieff West was a much smaller installation, controlling only the west end of the passenger station and the approach from Comrie, and of an unusual design due to its location – it was sited at the extreme west end of the Up platform, being squeezed between the platform edge and the retaining wall of the approach road from King

ABOVE: Plate 5.7
At one time, Crieff boasted three separate engine sheds, two of which are shown above, together with the 52-foot turntable. The brick shed was the original, having been erected on the opening of the new station, while the two wooden sheds, the second of which is off to the left, were later additions. The original turntable, replaced in 1910, was in front of the main brick shed.
On the end of the ventilator of the brick shed was a stag's head, revealed by increasing the contrast in the greatly enlarged image on the left.

CRA collection

Plate 5.8
The line to Comrie heading west from Crieff through the cutting on the site of the old Town Green towards the tunnel under Burrell Street which can be seen in the background. Little sign remains of this cutting, which was filled in following closure and the site redeveloped for a supermarket.
JR Hume

LEFT: **Figure 5.3**
A pair of early LM&SR carriage destination boards for use on passenger trains between Crieff and Comrie. These small wooden boards, measuring 3 inches by 28 inches, were slotted into holders on the side of the carriage at just below the roof line at one end of the vehicle. The boards were reversible so that they could simply be turned round for the return journey. Similar boards existed for other parts of the Strathearn network, such as the Gleneagles to Crieff line.
Author's collection

Street. This box was an early casualty of the LM&SR rationalisation programme and closed in 1932, the signals being taken over by Crieff East while the points at the west end of the 'Mid Road' were controlled by a ground frame. Crieff East was thereupon renamed simply 'Crieff' and survived until 1965 when all remaining signals were dispensed with.

Passing under the King Street bridge, the line entered a deep cutting through what had been part of the Town Green before entering a short tunnel under Burrell Street. This was the first of three tunnels on this stretch of line, the only such structures on the lines around Crieff. Shortly after emerging from the tunnel the line descended gently at 1 in 156 and curved to the left, crossing Turret Water, before running alongside the north bank of the River Earn. A little over two miles from Crieff, and just after passing Baird's Monument

Plate 5.9
Bridge over River Turret to the west of Crieff. The Turret is one of the larger tributaries which flows into the River Earn, and this was the only bridge of any significance on the Crieff to Comrie section.
Photograph by B Connell/ Photos from the Fifties

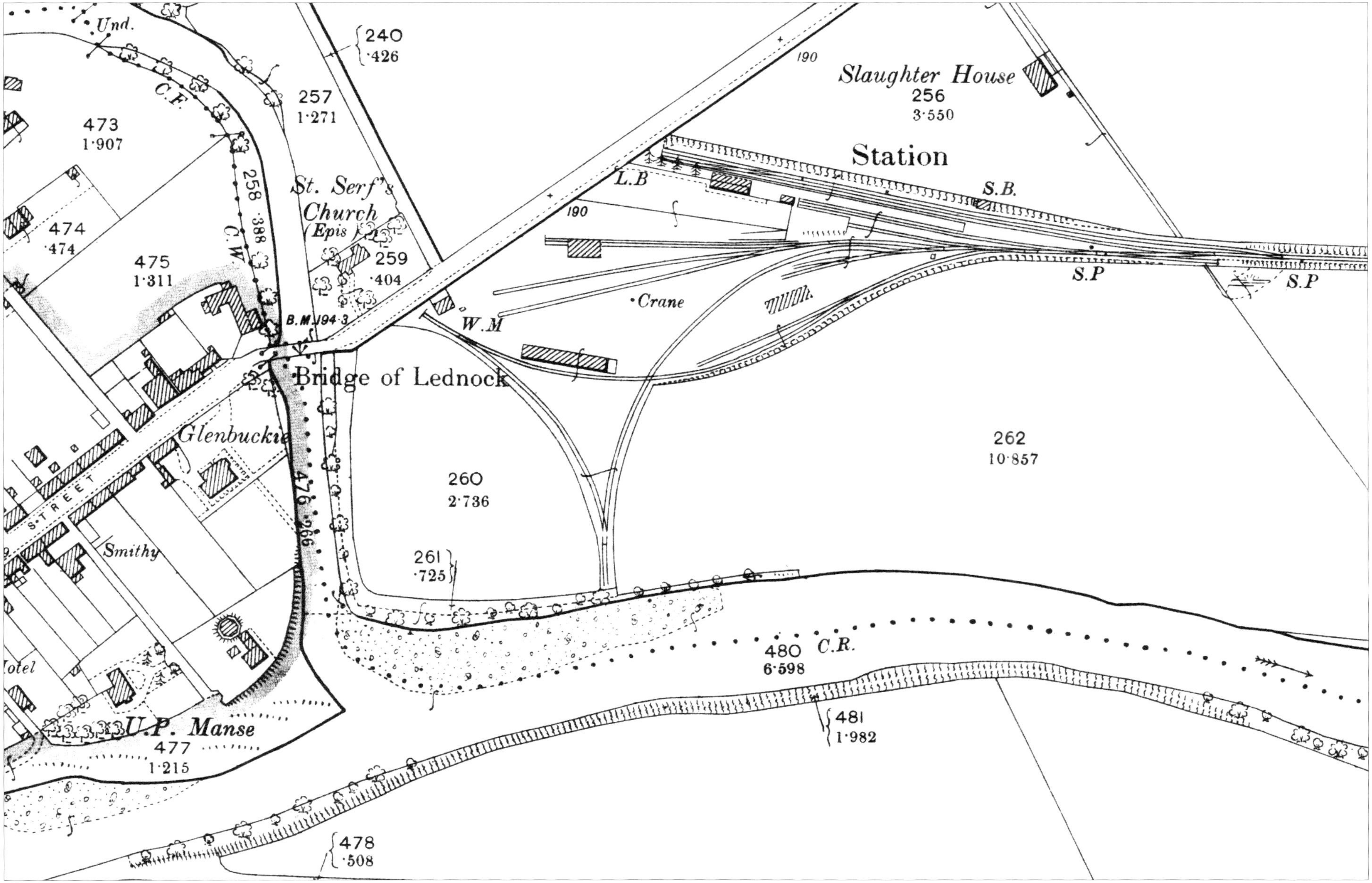

Figure 5.4
A plan of Comrie station taken from the 1901 Ordnance Survey map. This shows the original terminus layout for the Crieff & Comrie Railway, including the triangle for turning locomotives which obviated the need for a turntable. This was later removed after the line was extended through to St. Fillans. At that time, the two tracks in the station became the Up and Down lines and a second platform and station building was added opposite the one shown. The allotments shown at the top left were on the route taken by the extension to St. Fillans and were one of the reasons for some of the opposition to the proposed route. Scale 1:2,500.

Image courtesy of Kinross & Perth County Archive

on the right, the line swung sharply north through the short tunnel at Strowan. Emerging from the tunnel the line again curved sharply, this time to the west to resume its course along the north bank of the Earn. This curve of only 12 chains radius was one of the sharpest on the line and in later years resulted in a severe speed restriction of 15 mph. Skirting along the southern side of the Carse of Lennoch, and climbing gently at an average gradient of about 1 in 800, the line curved gently to the left to enter Comrie station in Laggan Park, just to the south of the Crieff to Lochearnhead road.

Prior to the opening of the Lochearnhead, St. Fillans & Comrie Railway in 1901, the line terminated here just short of the road, but a bridge was built to carry the road over the railway when the line was extended. Comrie had two platforms, the Down line being the original, while the site of the Up platform had previously served as a livestock loading siding during the days of the Crieff & Comrie Railway – the main station building was therefore on the Down platform. Although the Up platform building and footbridge were added when the line through to St. Fillans was opened in 1901, the Up side booking office and waiting room were not added until 1906, when stairs up to the road level were provided. The iron footbridge connecting these two platforms was a few yards south of the road overbridge.

The signal box, opened in 1901 when the line was extended, was sited at the southern end of the Up platform. This box was burned down in 1950 and replaced by a rather plain wooden shed, which was in effect a covered ground frame of the type favoured on the Callander & Oban line. This closed in 1961 after the introduction of the railbus, when all signals were removed.

The goods yard included a large wooden goods shed, loading bank and several sidings. Originally this layout included a turning triangle, but this became largely disused when Comrie became a through station, obviating the need to turn locomotives. A small water tank on a raised wooden base was provided with outlets on both sides to enable locomotives in the sidings to draw water as there were no water columns at the station itself. A scotch derrick, loading bank and carriage sidings completed the goods facilities. During the Second World War a large army stores building was erected in connection with the nearby camp at Cultybraggan. In later years the loading bay adjacent to the Down platform was used for a camping coach, of which there were a number along this popular tourist route.

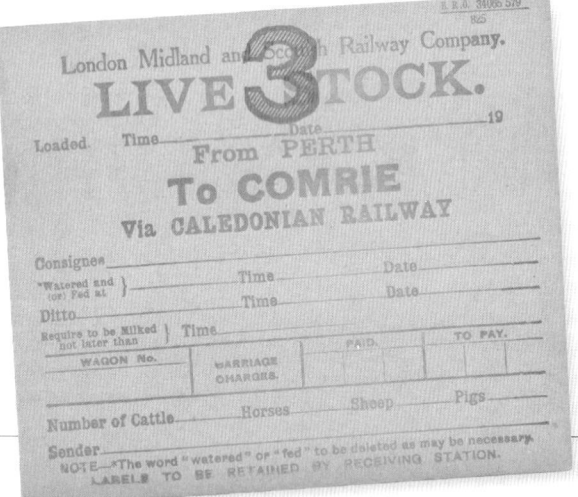

LEFT: Figure 5.5
Another of the LM&SR livestock wagon labels printed for traffic from Perth. It appears that the printer was having a bad day, for he has failed to update the routing information which still shows it to be 'Via CALEDONIAN RAILWAY', despite the fact that this label was printed in the 1930s, a good ten years after that railway had ceased to exist. Either that or it was a case of 'old habits die hard'.
Author's collection

BELOW: Plate 5.10
A fine view of Comrie station from the west showing the station as rebuilt after the opening of the line through to St. Fillans in 1901, including the original wooden footbridge. The Down platform on the right was the original Crieff & Comrie Railway terminus, while the Up platform on the left was added when the line was extended. This view also shows the original signal box, which was burned down in 1950.
CRA collection

CHAPTER 5: CRIEFF TO BALQUHIDDER – THE LINE DESCRIBED

TOP RIGHT: Plate 5.11
The Down platform building at Comrie housed the main booking office and other accommodation. It had a canopy with cast iron supports similar in design to that at Crieff. After closure of the line to St. Fillans in 1951 this served as the only station building, although the disused one on the Up platform survived until final closure in 1964. A British Railways camping coach can be seen in the bay siding in the background of this 1963 view. *Author*

BOTTOM RIGHT: Plate 5.12
The approach road and forecourt at Comrie, showing the Down platform building. This was the original station entrance – although the Up platform buildings with their own entrance were added in 1906, there was only pedestrian access to that side of the station. The A85 road from Crieff is just off to the left, and the goods yard away to the right. By the time this photograph was taken the wooden footbridge had been replaced by an iron one, as seen here.
Photograph by B Connell/ Photos from the Fifties

BELOW: Plate 5.13
The Down platform building at Comrie as seen from the station forecourt. A wooden structure, it was similar in design but on a much more modest scale to that at Crieff. The presence of the Caledonian Railway coaches just visible through the gate date this view to the 1960 Scottish Railtour, with railway enthusiasts taking the opportunity for photography while the train prepares to return to Crieff. The camping coach can also be seen in the bay siding on the right. *CRA collection*

Plate 5.14
Comrie goods yard from the east, showing the layout which existed in 1963. The former engine turning triangle, which was removed in 1902 when the line was extended to St. Fillans, was off to the left of this photograph. In addition, two short engine sidings which ran either side of the water tower were also later removed, leaving the water tower too far from the remaining siding to supply locomotives, although it was retained as a domestic water supply. The goods shed is in the background and the resident camping coach is in the bay siding, where a sleeper has been laid across the rails as an *ad hoc* scotch block. *Author*

After passing under the road bridge, the line swung sharply left on another tight curve – this one of 13 chains radius behind the main street – and climbed at 1 in 72 to cross both the St. Fillans road and the River Earn on a lengthy viaduct. This was one of the early mass concrete structures for which this line was renowned and which were the subject of much publicity by the railway. The viaduct comprised two concrete arches followed by a steel girder bridge over the main road, a further six arches before crossing the River Earn on an impressive iron girder bridge, and two more arches before continuing on a high embankment. The line then swung sharply to the right, crossing two minor roads, descending at 1 in 60 to re-cross the River Earn before climbing again at 1 in 60 to run alongside the Comrie to St. Fillans road. Following the line of this road, it continued to climb gently and swung left once more to come to Dalchonzie Platform.

Dalchonzie was unusual in that it had one of the combined signal box cum station house buildings which were also a feature of the Callander & Oban line, at places such as Drumvaigh and Glenoglehead. The signal box controlled both a short siding to the east of the platform and the level crossing over the minor road to Dalchonzie House. Continuing through the woods at the base of

Plate 5.15
This impressive concrete and steel viaduct at the west end of the village was one of a number of innovative mass concrete structures on the Comrie to Balquhidder section. The nearer steel span carries the railway over the River Earn, while the shorter span on the right was the bridge over the A85 Comrie to Lochearnhead road. A similar view of the viaduct showing an Engineer's special train hauled by CR 4-2-2 No. 123 was used for publicity purposes. *Aberdeen University GW Wilson collection*

ABOVE: **Plate 5.16**
The only intermediate station between Comrie and St. Fillans was that at Dalchonzie. Termed a Siding, it was classed as a halt and had only basic amenities, as can be seen here. There was no booking office, tickets being issued by the guard. The signal box controlled the level crossing and the single goods siding to the east of the halt.
CRA/Lens of Sutton

Plate 5.17
Equally impressive with the viaduct in Plate 5.15, this concrete and steel girder bridge over the River Earn at Tynriach was another of the major structures on the line which merited a publicity photograph. Being built on a skew to accommodate the course of the line, this bridge was of considerable proportions. It survives to this day serving as a roadway for the local estate.
CRA/National Railway Museum

Plate 5.18
This general view of St. Fillans station, taken from the hillside to the south shortly after it opened, gives a good idea of how the railway had to be carved out of the lower slopes of Little Port Hill. The new station approach road can be seen running from right to left up towards the bridge under the line. The stationmaster's house was on the left, while just to the right of it are two staff cottages. The A85 Crieff to Lochearnhead road runs alongside the River Earn in the foreground.
Author's collection

Mor Rheinn, the line crossed the River Earn, for the final time, at Tynriach on a substantial bowstring girder bridge, which survives to this day, and began the final climb to St. Fillans at 1 in 60.

The gradient eased to 1 in 260 for the short stretch through St. Fillans station which sat well above the village from which it took its name. St. Fillans was a delightful station well suited for the tourist traffic which was anticipated to form a significant element of the passengers arriving in this renowned locality. Being the principal passing place between Comrie and Lochearnhead, it had a long loop with Up and Down platforms. An attractive brick and timber building with ornate canopy on the Down side housed the booking office, waiting rooms and other facilities, while a more modest wooden building on the Up side served as a waiting room. An iron footbridge spanned the tracks at the mid-point of the station, whilst the signal box was sited on the western end of the Up platform. Opened on 1st October 1901 when the initial section from Comrie to St. Fillans was finished, it was closed exactly fifty years later on 1st October 1951 with the full closure of the Comrie to Balquhidder section.

A running loop passed behind the Up platform, which although it appeared to be an island platform was never used as such, with a wooden fence running along the back of the platform. The loop was useful for shunting purposes or as an engine release line for the various trains, both timetabled and excursion, which terminated or turned around at St. Fillans. The small goods yard lay to the north of

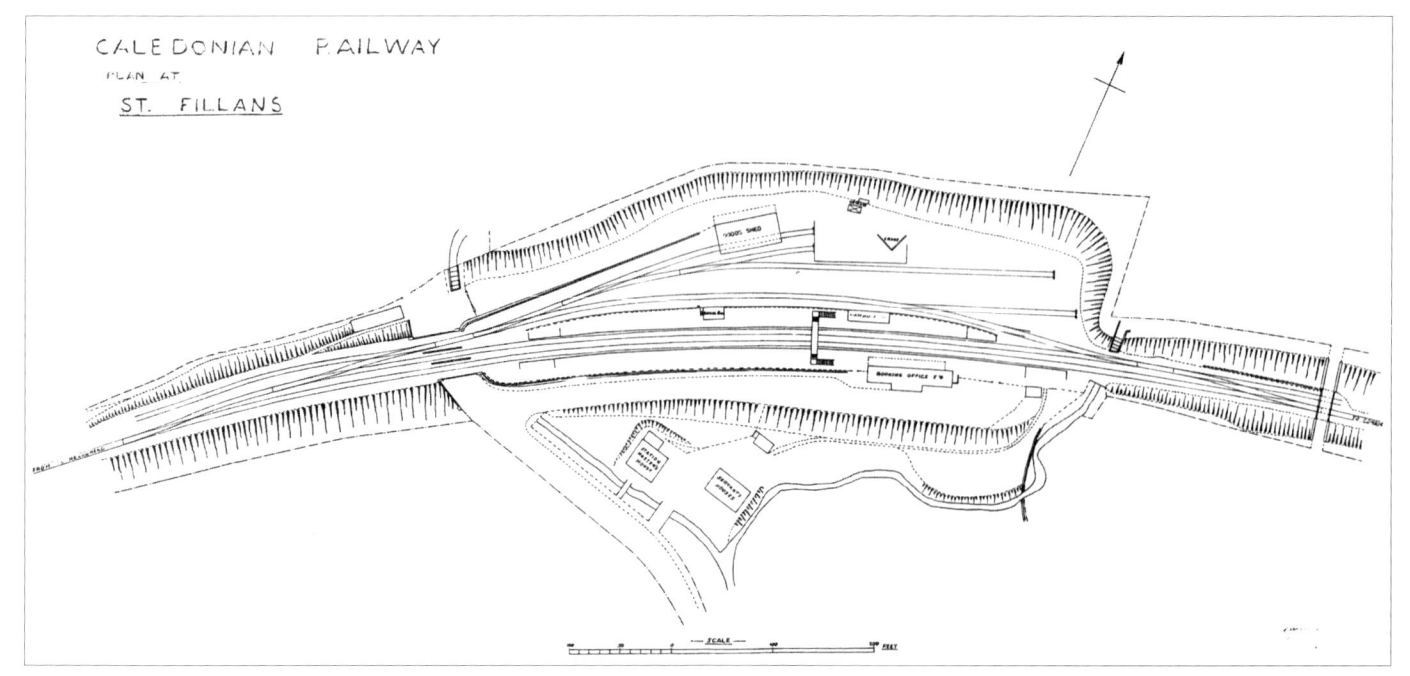

Figure 5.6
A Caledonian Railway plan of St. Fillans. Having had to be carved out of the hillside, the layout was compact although adequate, but with little scope for expansion. The running loop behind the Up platform, which can be seen here, provided additional operational flexibility which would have been welcome at busy times, particularly when dealing with the many summer excursion trains. The narrow rock cutting to the east of the station, on the extreme right of this plan, was the scene of the serious accident in 1921.
Courtesy David Ferguson

ABOVE: **Plate 5.19**
A view of St. Fillans from the west in the early 1920s, by which time the station flower beds and the foliage round the signal box, itself adorned with plants and hanging baskets, had matured. The station won many Best Kept Station prizes in its day. The Up loop line ran along the back of the platform, just behind the white picket fence on the left. The mass of Little Port Hill can be seen in the background. *HA Ruffell*

BELOW: **Plate 5.20**
St. Fillans station in LM&SR days, looking from the east, showing the principal station building on the Down platform, the substantial platforms and the smaller waiting shelter on Up side. The two platforms were connected by a footbridge, while the signal box on the Up platform can be seen in the background. In this view the original Caledonian Railway signs are still in place. *CRA/Lens of Sutton*

the station and, in addition to the short headshunts at each end of the loop, there were four sidings. The longer of these had a loading bank and scotch derrick, while the shorter one ran through the goods shed. The fourth siding ended in a carriage loading dock. In LM&SR days this was another station where a camping coach was sited.

For the next 7 miles the line clung to the southern slopes of the hills above the northern shore of Loch Earn, climbing almost 200 feet from the valley floor to run along the hillside. On leaving St. Fillans it continued to climb at 1 in 70, curving round the side of the hill before passing through a short tunnel cut through solid rock. The tunnel portals were constructed of mass concrete to the same design as the principal viaducts along the line. Thereafter the line ran along the hillside above the St. Fillans to Lochearnhead road, providing spectacular views of the loch. After about 4 miles, the

Left: Plate 5.21
St. Fillans Up platform seen from the footbridge in 1956, five years after closure. Remarkably, not only the track but also the signals are still in situ, although the Up line platform has been taken out of use and blocked with a sleeper. This view shows how only the areas in front of the buildings were paved, the remainder of the platform surfaces being gravel with concrete edges. The trap points at the east end of the Up loop had been removed by this date. The site of the 1921 derailment described in Chapter 9 was just under the bridge in the background. *FH Dyson*

Below: Plate 5.22
The only tunnel on this section of line was just to the west of St. Fillans station, where the line cut through the rocky outcrop at the base of Monadh a Phuirt Mhoir. The line can be seen snaking its way westwards along the hillside above Loch Earn. The village of St. Fillans, with its many villas and the Drummond Arms Hotel, lies in the foreground.
Authors collection

CHAPTER 5: CRIEFF TO BALQUHIDDER – THE LINE DESCRIBED

line began to descend at 1 in 80 to cross the Beich Burn where it runs into Loch Earn at the southern end of Glen Beich. The line began to climb again at 1 in 100 to skirt round the southern slopes of Meall a Mhaddaidh before descending again at 1 in 80 to the mouth of Glen Ogle. Here the line curved left on an embankment and entered a sharp curve of only 10 chains radius, the sharpest on the whole line, to cross Glen Ogle on an impressive nine-arch concrete viaduct. Continuing on a short embankment, the line crossed the main Callander to Crianlarich road before it reached Lochearnhead station. This station, built on the hillside, supplanted the original Lochearnhead station, sited nearly two miles away on the Callander and Oban line, which was rebuilt and renamed Balquhidder when the Lochearnhead line was completed in 1905.

The road which runs down Glen Ogle was originally one of those built by General Wade for pacifying the Highlands after the first Jacobite rebellion of 1715. Known locally as 'Wade's Roads', they were described in the famous couplet:

'Had you seen this road before you was made
You would hold up your hands and bless General Wade'

LEFT: Plate 5.23
A view from the hillside above Lochearnhead station, looking east along Loch Earn, showing the line as it curves around the lower slopes of Meall a Mhaddaidh and crosses Glen Ogle on the viaduct. The bridge towards the centre of this scene carried a farm track across the railway to the fields above it – this was another example of the mass concrete construction used on the Comrie to Balquhidder section.
Neil Parkhouse collection

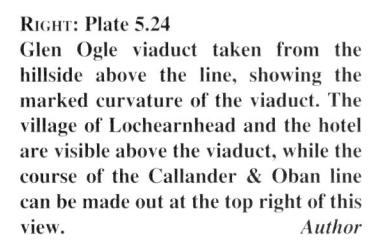

RIGHT: Plate 5.24
Glen Ogle viaduct taken from the hillside above the line, showing the marked curvature of the viaduct. The village of Lochearnhead and the hotel are visible above the viaduct, while the course of the Callander & Oban line can be made out at the top right of this view. *Author*

LEFT: Plate 5.25
The Glen Ogle viaduct seen from the A95 road, showing the full length of this nine-span structure. Although taken in 1963, some twelve years after the line closed, the viaduct remained in good condition. The mass concrete has mellowed such that it now blends in well against the backdrop of mountains of Breadalbane visible in the background, in contrast to the view at Plate 5.26. *Author*

Plate 5.26
Lochearnhead station taken from the hillside to the west of the station looking back towards St. Fillans. In this view, taken shortly after the station opened, the farm overbridge in the foreground and the viaduct over Glen Ogle stand out starkly although the earthworks have started to grass over. The goods yard is visible on the left, while the signal box dominates the station building in the centre. *Author's collection*

Plate 5.27
A postcard featuring the grounds of the Lochearnhead Hotel, showing the station in the background. Despite the claim that there was a private path to the station, this is highly unlikely as hotel guests would have had to cross the Down line before climbing onto the station platform. It is possible that the purpose of the path leading from the greenhouse towards the railway has been embellished. Because of the raised embankment, the station could only be accessed by means of the subway up to platform level. *Author's collection*

CHAPTER 5: CRIEFF TO BALQUHIDDER – THE LINE DESCRIBED

Figure 5.7
A selection of tickets from Lochearnhead. The Third Class Single to St. Fillans would enable the passenger to travel along the most picturesque section of the line high above the north shore of Loch Earn. The LM&SR Third Class Privilege Single to Crieff would enable a member of the railway staff to travel at the reduced rate; this ticket was another issued on 29th September 1951, the day before the station closed. The LM&SR Third Class Single is a rare example where it could be used to get to one of three different destinations, all having the same fare of 2s 5d, in this case Callander or Killin on the Callander & Oban line, or Comrie. *Author's collection*

Lochearnhead station consisted of a single island platform with pedestrian access through a subway under the Down line. The single brick building with double canopy housed all the station facilities, while a full-size signal box was sited towards the western end of the platform. This was over-generous given the layout and traffic handled, but necessary during the brief period before the final section of line to Balquhidder opened in 1905, when trains from the Crieff direction terminated here. Once the line was fully opened the station had largely outlived its usefulness and was closed as a wartime economy measure in 1917. Unlike Innerpeffray, it reopened briefly after the war in 1919, only to close for good in 1921. Thereafter it ceased to be a block post, the signals were dispensed with and sidings controlled by a ground frame. Lochearnhead was, and still is, a tourist destination and in later years there were often two camping coaches in the siding next to the goods shed. This pretty station survives largely intact and is used today as a Scout Station.

From Lochearnhead the line passed under a road bridge at the west end of the station to continue along the side of Glenogle for a short distance before crossing the Kendrum Burn at Edinchip on another impressive viaduct. This structure combined the use of mass

Plate 5.28
A good view of Lochearnhead from the east, showing the line crossing the Glen Ogle viaduct in the foreground, then passing through the station before heading west towards Balquhidder. Kendrum viaduct can be seen in the distance, while the line of the Callander & Oban line can be discerned midway up the hillside behind Lochearnhead.
Author's collection

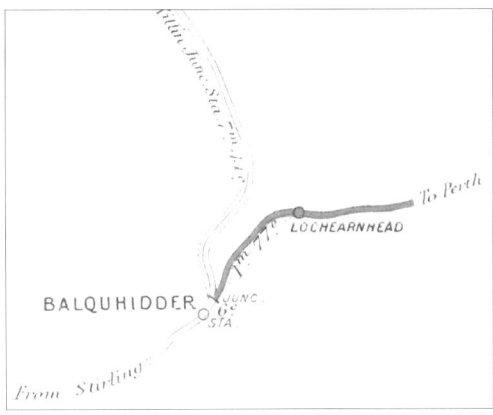

ABOVE: Plate 5.29
To the west of Lochearnhead station the line crossed the river Kendrum on another impressive viaduct at Edenchip. This was a seven-arch viaduct with a central steel girder span over the river. In this view of a Caledonian train heading towards Balquhidder, the postcard calls it 'Kendrum' rather than 'Edenchip' viaduct. The road in the foreground is the main road from Callander to Crianlarich, now the A85, while the large house in the background is Edenchip, which was the residence of Lady Margaret McGregor who objected to the construction of the line when the Bill went before Parliament in 1899. *Author's collection*

LEFT: Figure 5.8
An extract from the Railway Clearing House map for the junction at Balquhidder. This shows very clearly not only the distances from Lochearnhead and Killin Junction, but also the distance of 6 chains between the junction where the branch line joined the Callander & Oban line and the actual station. This was pertinent for accounting purposes, for although the Callander & Oban line was operated by the Caledonian Railway, it remained an independent company until it became part of the LM&SR in 1924. *Author's collection*

concrete with a single-span girder across the river, there being two arches on the north bank and five on the south side. At this stage the line climbed steadily at 1 in 60, crossing the Callander to Crianlarich road again, skirting the slopes of Ben Vorlich to join the Callander and Oban line at Balquhidder.

As already mentioned, prior to 1905 the modest station here, the original Lochearnhead, was a small wayside station of little significance. The arrival of the Lochearnhead, St. Fillans & Comrie Railway changed all that. A completely new station with three platforms, two signal boxes and an engine shed was built. To achieve this, the main road was diverted and a hefty retaining wall built alongside it where the land was built up to provide sufficient level space for the new station. The Down platform ran along the top of this structure while the island platform served Up trains and branch line trains and housed the main station buildings. Access to the main station was, as at Lochearnhead, by a subway beneath the line leading to stairs up to the island platform.

The engine shed, a sub shed of Perth, was a wooden structure with a brick base, capable of housing a single locomotive. It was equipped with a 60-foot turntable but, unusually, had no water supply of its own. Locomotives needing to take water had to do so at one of the three water columns at the station – one each for the Up Main, Down Main, and Branch Line platforms. This shed was closed in the early years of the Second World War, following which the branch line service was worked by Crieff locomotives. The shed was demolished but the turntable survived, albeit increasingly overgrown, until well after the war.

The layout at Balquhidder required two signal boxes, Balquhidder West and Balquhidder East, although geographically they were actually north and south of the station. These two signal boxes remained in use after the closure of the Crieff line in 1951 to serve the main Callander to Oban line, finally closing in March 1965, a few months prior to complete closure of the Dunblane to Crianlarich section of the Oban line.

Plate 5.30
Balquhidder station shortly after it was rebuilt and renamed. The two tracks in the foreground were Callander & Oban railway Down and Up lines, while the branch line from St. Fillans used the far side of the island platform. The single station building was of a similar design to that at Lochearnhead and housed the offices and waiting rooms. The wooden structure on the foreground is the covered steps leading down to the subway access to the main road. Unlike Lochearnhead, however, the platforms here were of timber construction with gravel surfaces, only the areas alongside the station building being paved.

Courtesy of Perth Museum & Art Gallery, Perth & Kinross Council

ABOVE: Plate 5.31
The northern end of Balquhidder station showing the Callander & Oban line curving off to the left as it started the heavy gradient to the summit of Glen Ogle, and a branch line train approaching on the line from Crieff off to the right behind the signal box. Confusingly, this box was called Balquhidder West although it was north-east of the station. The wooden Balquhidder engine shed can also be seen behind the water column on the Down platform. *J Alsop collection*

RIGHT: Plate 5.32
The south end of Balquhidder station showing the main double line Callander & Oban line platforms, with the Crieff branch line platform to the right curving round the island platform. This view gives an idea of the extensive layout provided when the junction was created and the station rebuilt in 1905. The cottages on the left are part of the staff accommodation provided by the railway. *CRA collection*

Plate 5.33
Balquhidder looking south towards Callander from the end of the Up platform, showing Balquhidder East signal box. The main line loop continued some distance beyond the overbridge in the background, as did the headshunt for the branch line on the left. The main signal is the Up Main Starting signal, while the lower signal is an elevated shunting signal from the Up Main line into the headshunt. *CRA collection*

CHAPTER 6

THE GOLDEN AGE OF THE CALEDONIAN RAILWAY

The Caledonian Railway opened the first main line between Carlisle and Glasgow in 1848, linking with the Lancaster & Carlisle Railway. The latter was worked by the London & North Western Railway which took it over in 1879. The Caledonian and London & North Western railways thus formed the through route from London to Glasgow known today as the West Coast Main Line. The Caledonian went on to spread its operations throughout the industrial heartland of Scotland, particularly in Lanarkshire and the surrounding areas, before embarking on a programme of expansion to the north and other parts of the country. In 1865 it absorbed the Scottish Central Railway to reach Perth, and the following year amalgamated with the Scottish North Eastern Railway to acquire the route to Aberdeen, eventually becoming the pre-eminent railway company in Scotland.

It was as a result of these later amalgamations that the Caledonian took control of the branch lines in Strathearn. It took over the Crieff Junction Railway through the Scottish Central Railway and the following year it acquired the Perth Almond Valley & Methven Railway by amalgamation with the Scottish North Eastern Railway. The Crieff & Methven Junction Railway had been worked from the outset by the Scottish North Eastern Railway, which then became part of the Caledonian only two months after the line opened.

Thus, by 1869, all three of the original branch lines in Strathearn formed part of the growing Caledonian Railway system. This was to remain the status quo for over half a century until the Grouping of the British railway companies in 1923, seventy-five years after the Caledonian first opened. In these days of rapid and constant change in the commercial world, it is difficult to appreciate that for many Scots in the 19th and early 20th centuries the Caledonian Railway would have been a constant for the whole of their lives.

The two remaining branch lines in Strathearn were even more beholden to the Caledonian Railway. As described in Chapter 2, the Caledonian subscribed half the capital of the Crieff & Comrie Railway and, when it was eventually built, worked it from the outset, taking it over fully only five years later. The Lochearnhead, St. Fillans & Comrie Railway had to be rescued by the Caledonian before it had even opened, so was part of the Caledonian system from the outset. With the opening of the final section to Balquhidder, the whole network of branch lines in Strathearn formed part of the mighty Caledonian Railway.

The Caledonian Railway soon set about putting its stamp on these local lines. The Caledonian Railway Rule Book superseded earlier versions, and their management and operating procedures prevailed. The Strathearn lines were included in the Caledonian Railway Time Tables, although it is interesting to note that in the first timetable issued following amalgamation with the Scottish Central Railway, the timetable was in two sections, one for the former Scottish Central lines and the other for what was termed the '*Caledonian Railway proper*'.

The 1865 edition of the Caledonian Railway Time Table included the timetable for the Crieff branch line as it appeared in the Scottish Central section. It showed a service of six trains each way per day, with an average journey time of 23 minutes. The first two trains each day were 'Parliamentaries' – that is, those trains which every railway company was obliged by Act of Parliament to run, to provide a minimum service of trains with First, Second and Third Class accommodation.

The situation did not change overnight, but the Caledonian Railway sought to expand the existing traffic on the lines and inherited some of their ongoing problems. In some respects, life continued very much as before. Thus, for example, summer excursions to Crieff continued as in previous years. In June 1866, Messrs Young & Co of Perth organised a trip for their employees, with 500 workers and sweethearts arriving for the day on the 8.5am train. Unfortunately, as the *Strathearn Herald* reported:

> *'We cannot speak favourably of the party, most of whom being drunk in the street by 10.0am. Many spent the day verbally abusing or physically assaulting innocent members of the public.'*

On a more positive note, however, the paper carried a report on 22nd February that year that a site was being sought for a Hydropathic Establishment, and a month later were able to report

TOUR No. 3, 20TH JUNE.—Tickets available for three days. To Crieff, St. Fillans, Lochearnhead, and back same route.

Route.—To Crieff by railway, from Crieff to Lochearnhead by coach; return journey by same route.

Fares.—From Edinburgh, 1st class by railway and outside of coach, 19s.; from Glasgow, 1st class by railway and outside of coach, 17s.

The journey may be broken at Crieff, St. Fillans, or Lochearnhead.

This tour enables passengers to visit the celebrated Gardens of Drummond Castle, the Grounds of Ochtertyre, the Falls of the Turret, Glenturret, &c.

TOUR No. 4, 20TH JUNE.—Tickets available for four days. To Crieff, St. Fillans, Lochearnhead, Callander, Dunblane, and back.

Route.—To Crieff by railway, from Crieff to Callander, *viâ* Lochearnhead, by coach; from Callander by railway.

Fares.—From Edinburgh, 1st class by railway and outside of coach, 22s.; from Glasgow, 1st class by railway and outside of coach, 20s.

The journey may be broken at Crieff, St. Fillans, Lochearnhead, or Callander.

The tour enables passengers to visit the celebrated Gardens at Drummond Castle, the Grounds of Ochtertyre, the Falls of the Turret, Glenturret, St. Fillans, Lochearnhead, the Pass of Lenny, and Callander.

It may be accomplished in fifteen hours from Edinburgh and Glasgow. By leaving per first train in the morning passengers are taken forward from Crieff to Callander, *viâ* Lochearnhead, in time to join the 6.30 P.M. train from Callander to Edinburgh and Glasgow.

TOUR No. 5, 1ST JULY.—Tickets available for three days. To Crieff, Amulree, Aberfeldy, and back same route.

Route.—To Crieff by railway; from Crieff to Aberfeldy by coach; return journey same route.

Fares.—From Edinburgh, 1st class by railway and outside of coach; 20s.; from Glasgow, 1st class by railway and outside of coach, 18s.

The journey may be broken at Crieff, Amulree, or Aberfeldy.

This tour enables passengers to visit Drummond Castle Gardens, the Grounds of Ochtertyre, the Grounds of Monzie, the "Sma' Glen," Glenalmond, Glenquiech, the Falls of Moness, Taymouth, &c.

Figure 6.1
An extract from Measom's *Official Illustrated Guide to the London & North Western and Caledonian Railways* dated 1859 giving details of excursions to Crieff. At this time the Crieff Junction Railway was still an independent concern, but the excursions were marketed through the Caledonian. Tours 3 and 4 would form the basis for the Circular Tour which would become a feature of the Caledonian excursion programme from 1872 onwards. Interestingly, this extract also includes details of a round trip coach excursion to Aberfeldy, the branch line to that town not being opened until 1865. Local beauty spots and attractions are also listed. *Author's collection*

Plate 6.1
A colourised postcard of Methven passenger station, seen here with the station staff on the platform and the Methven branch tank engine standing on the loop line. The station is shown as it was when it opened, in unadorned red brick which was later whitewashed overall. The engine shed is also as originally built, with an arched doorway, later replaced by a rectangular one; the water tank to the right was demolished after the shed closed in 1937. The title 'Kildrummie Station' refers to the depiction of Methven with that name in the novels of Ian Maclaren. *Author's collection*

that arrangements for it to be built were almost finalised. On 22nd June a further report mentioned that the mason was busy carting material to the site from Crieff station, so construction was evidently underway.

On 1st August 1866, the former Perth Almond Valley & Methven Railway became part of the Caledonian Railway by virtue of the amalgamation of the Scottish North Eastern Railway with the latter, and on 7th August an instruction was issued to all former Scottish North Eastern stationmasters to operate the Caledonian system. One unfortunate situation which the Caledonian inherited was the operation of the short branch line from Methven Junction to Methven, which since the opening of the line through to Crieff had been worked by horse, as referred to in Chapter 2. The local paper reported that rumours had been circulating that *'a proper engine'* had been acquired for the Methven line, but that these were subsequently found to be untrue; the Methven line was still being worked by a couple of horses, much to the chagrin of the local passengers. The paper complained that the local traffic was being lost to the railway, and a committee was appointed to agitate for a locomotive to replace the horses.

Progress was evidently made, for on 1st March 1867 a locomotive was provided to work the Methven branch line, with horse haulage being permanently consigned to the history books. On a less happy note, however, it was reported in June that year that the Free Pass issued by the old Perth Almond Valley & Methven Railway to the local 'carrier' entitling him to free travel between Methven and Perth two days per week had been withdrawn by the Caledonian Railway. As a consequence, the aggrieved local carrier had now reverted to transporting his goods by the turnpike road to Perth rather than by rail. The Caledonian Railway, having flexed its muscles over these historic local arrangements, would appear to have been unmoved. The privileges enjoyed by Mr Drummond Moray of Abercairney, referred to in Chapter 1, probably suffered the same fate but no details of this have survived.

The summer of 1867 saw a return of the excursions to Crieff with a report of one such at the end of July being an outing of

Plate 6.2
A closer view of the 0-4-4 tank engine on an Up train at Methven station. This was possibly the locomotive provided by the Caledonian Railway to replace the horses used at first after the Crieff & Methven Junction opened. Some of the Methven station staff stand proudly in front of No. 1157. *ARG collection*

'several hundred tanners and nailers from the Stirling area also accompanied by a fine brass band'. Evidently these excursionists were better behaved than some of those of the previous year.

On 10th August, the *Strathearn Herald* reported that the firm of Herron & Co, Chemical Manure Manufacturers of Crieff, were moving out of town to a new site alongside the railway at Pittenzie, and that the works would have a coke tower. These works would later have rail connection, referred to in the 1895 Appendix to the Working Time Tables as 'Veitch's Siding', and much later, in the 20th century, would eventually become the Strathearn Manure Works.

August was not all positive news, for it had been a disastrous season for grouse which had been decimated by grouse disease. It was reported that fewer than 400 brace had been despatched south by rail compared with an impressive 6,000–7,000 brace the previous year. The loss of this lucrative traffic affected the railway in other ways, for shooting parties, their servants and luggage were also an important source of revenue.

On 5th October the *Strathearn Herald* reported a rather amusing incident in Crieff, when '*the inhabitants of the lower town thought they had heard the Fire Bell being rung*'. It turned out that the new bell for the United Protestant Church in Comrie had arrived at Crieff station by rail en route to its final destination and '*thoughtless youths had rung it*'. One can only imagine the alarm and consternation that caused!

That December, the same newspaper carried a report that Mr James Taylor, stationmaster at Highlandman, had been appointed to be stationmaster at Craigo on the main line to Aberdeen near Montrose. It was commented that '*Mr Taylor has for several years been stationed at Highlandman and has by his kindness and obliging manner been respected by all*', so his promotion to a more important station was probably well merited.

A significant event in 1868 was the opening of the Strathearn Hydropathic Establishment, known locally just as 'the Hydro', on 11th August, just the day before the grouse season started, the 'Glorious Twelfth'. The building was as yet unfinished, but was reported to have many guests already. The opening of the Hydro, in addition to the many other villas and lodging houses in Crieff, led the *Strathearn Herald* on 12th September to claim that '*Crieff is now famed throughout Europe as a place of resort for invalids and others during the summer months*', reflecting the view that Crieff was now a spa resort of some note.

1868 also saw a resurgence of the perennial problem of lineside fires on the section of the line which passed through a shallow cutting alongside Auchterarder Common Muir. This was near the summit of the stiff climb from Crieff Junction and, with locomotives working hard, was prone to sparks being emitted from their chimneys. On 31st March the *Strathearn Herald* reported that the young plantation at Auchterarder Muir had been partly burned after hot ashes from the locomotive had ignited dry grass and whin. The fire was reportedly put out with great difficulty.

On 7th July the newspaper reported that the plantation, only planted four years previously, had all but been destroyed by fire, over 4 acres being burned out. A week later it was agreed at a meeting of Auchterarder Muir Commissioners to dig a trench alongside the railway, presumably to act as a fire break. Despite this, barely two weeks later, another 2 acres of the plantation were set on fire by a spark from a locomotive.

This problem rumbled on into the following year, for on 8th May 1869 it was reported that sparks from an engine had again ignited whins and dry grass on the Muir, and that in the space of two hours fire had engulfed 6 acres of excellent young fir trees. The sparks had apparently been carried over the trench which had been dug 10-12 yards from the railway. Later that same month another fire started by sparks from an engine destroyed nearly two acres of woodland before being put out. It is clear that the Auchterarder Muir Commissioners were not happy about these recurring fires and pursued the railway company for compensation, for on 7th August it was reported that at their recent meeting they had received £52 14s 6d from the Caledonian Railway in respect of damage to the plantation.

They were not the only ones to cross swords with the railway company. On 24th July the *Strathearn Herald* reported that the new autumn timetable was the cause of some dissatisfaction locally. This matter was raised at a meeting of Crieff Town Council, where the complaint was that it was not more trains which people wanted, but cheaper tickets. A committee was appointed by the council to lobby the Caledonian Railway on this issue, and there the matter appears to have rested for the time being.

An interesting exchange of correspondence appeared in the *Strathearn Herald* in October, when a suggestion was made that a platform be made near the Orchil Road in Auchterarder, where the railway passed under the road. This, it was argued, would be far more convenient than the stations at either Auchterarder, Tullibardine or Crieff Junction, pointing out that it was silly to have to walk 1½ miles alongside the Crieff Junction line to reach a station.

However, a response in the newspaper a few weeks later pointed out that such a facility would only benefit those living at the west end of the town, and nothing came of the idea. It is worth noting that a similar suggestion was to be made nearly ninety years later when the new diesel railbus service was introduced between Gleneagles and Comrie in 1958, for a halt at the Orchil Road similar to those provided at Strageath and Pittenzie. This idea again met with a marked lack of success.

An interesting aspect of local history was reflected in a report in the *Strathearn Herald* on 6th November that the wooden Free Church of Monzie had been purchased by Stoddart & McGregor, Joiners of Crieff, to be erected in the neighbourhood of the station as a workshop. The disruption of the Church of Scotland which had been triggered by the 'Auchterarder case' in 1848, resulted in the creation of the United Free Church with the little church at Monzie being one of the first erected.

1870 saw the first ever Crieff Highland Games. The event was held on 18th August, and it was reported that '*railway arrangements are to be liberal*'. Indeed, the Caledonian Railway, perhaps mindful of the lobbying by the town council, offered return tickets at the single rate from Dundee, Perth, Stirling, Glasgow, Edinburgh and all intermediate stations. Doubtless this experiment was worthwhile, for, although no figures exist for 1870, the following year was even more successful, with some 4,000 visitors arriving by train at Crieff for the Highland Games of 1871.

A mark of the growing importance of the Hydro was the establishment in October 1870 of a direct telegraph link between it and the railway station. This private line was something of an innovation, coming, as it did, only four years after the telegraph first arrived in Crieff. The Hydro thereafter had an arrangement with the Caledonian Railway to advise it in advance of the arrival of guests, so that coaches and carts could meet them at the station and convey them and their luggage to the Hydro without delay. This was reflected in the Train Telegraphing Arrangements listed in the Appendix to the Working Time Tables. The earliest available copy, dated 1889, stated:

'*Crieff Junction Signal Box will telegraph all Passenger trains and say how many passengers for Strathearn Hydropathic Establishment. Crieff to telegraph this information to the Hydropathic Establishment. Crieff Branch Guard will telegraph from Perth how many passengers for the Strathearn Hydropathic Establishment in each train. Crieff to telegraph this information to the Hydropathic Establishment.*'

Some improvements were also made at the other end of the line, where the platform at Crieff Junction was extended eastwards.

However, it was observed that the junction still lacked a proper entrance and that passengers still had to cross a set of rails where shunting went on. Clearly safety arrangements on the old Crieff Junction Railway still had some way to go.

The summer of 1871 was again a busy one for tourism to Crieff, with several noteworthy events. At the beginning of August, over 1,000 passengers travelled from Crieff via Methven Junction to Perth for the Highland Games Show. It was commented that there were no mishaps – a credit to the railway officials concerned. A week later an excursion conveyed the employees of John Shields, Manufacturer of Perth, to Crieff for the day. Over 600 passengers were accompanied by the Perth Volunteer Band, later parading through the streets with flags and banners, and carrying a model loom and *'other devices'*. These presumably related to the nature of John Shields business.

The second Crieff Highland Games was held at the end of August, with large numbers travelling to Crieff by train. One special train conveyed the workers of Hally & Co of Auchterarder. The 400-500 passengers were accompanied by *'a splendid brass band and banners flying'*.

The 1871 Caledonian Railway passenger timetable contained few changes over the previous year for the Crieff Junction line, the service being maintained at six trains each way per day, although all six now conveyed First, Second and Third Class passengers compared with only four such trains the previous year. The service between Perth and Crieff via Methven Junction had only four trains each way, the journey time being 45-50 minutes.

The timetable also listed the two horse-drawn coaches run each day between Crieff and Comrie, with an additional run on Mondays:

Comrie	Dep	8.45am	2.45pm	6.30pm
Crieff	Arr	9.45am	3.45pm	7.30pm
Crieff	Dep	10.25am	6.50pm	
Comrie	Arr	11.25am	7.50pm	

In addition to this, a local coach met trains at Crieff Junction, for, under Auchterarder, it also stated that *'Omnibus runs between the station and the town to meet every train'*, thus enabling the townsfolk to access Crieff Junction without the long walk referred to earlier.

One logistical problem created by the boom in tourism was raised at a meeting of Crieff Town Council Water Scheme in September, when mention was made of the need for a well for *'the many horses which are regularly coming in large numbers to the railway station'*. These horses were in addition to the yearly average of around 600 horses and 900 wagon-loads of livestock received or dispatched by rail.

The water supply for the station became an ongoing issue between the town council and the Caledonian Railway. The following year a proposal was made for a branch pipe to be laid down Duchlage Road to meet the potential requirements for water for Caledonian Railway engines. The railway company made an offer of £35 per annum for the supply of 'surplus' water, but the town council wanted £50 per annum with the proviso that the Caledonian Railway pay for the cost of the connection. Negotiations dragged on for the next two years until, finally, in June 1873 the Caledonian Railway increased their offer to £37 per annum. They also agreed to provide two tanks at Crieff station and to lay and maintain the necessary pipes. The total equivalent value of this offer was calculated to be £44 9s 6d, and was accepted by the town council. The settlement did not come a day too early, for by 1875 it was estimated that the railway was using up to 10,000 gallons of water daily.

The following year, 1872, saw the introduction by the Caledonian Railway of a new circular tour through Loch Earn. A report on 20th July mentioned that this new and popular tour to St. Fillans and Lochearnhead (renamed Balquhidder in 1905), thence round by the Callander & Oban line, was a complete success. Two coaches left Crieff station heading west, while two more coaches left Lochearnhead station heading east, all meeting up at St. Fillans. Forty to fifty passengers, and sometimes more, were carried. The Caledonian Railway Tourist, Excursion, Pic-nic and Pleasure Parties Programme for the summer of 1872 included details of the new tour (see Figure 2.7), In addition to details of the new tour (Figure 2.8), the booklet also included prices of the monthly return tickets available from Edinburgh (Waverley) to Crieff: First Class 17s 6d, Second Class 13s 3d, and Third Class 8s 9d.

In July the *Strathearn Herald* commented that *'The new and popular tour to St. Fillans, Lochearnhead and round by Callander and Dunblane has been a complete success'*, and its editorial of 5th October was highly complementary:

'No one has need to complain of railway arrangements this season. The Caledonian Railway to give them all credit have this year done justice, both to the inhabitants of Crieff, to tourists, and to visitors, and, we doubt not, from the vast increase in traffic, to themselves also. The cheap return tickets, the numerous trains daily, and the incomparable circular tours that they have this year opened up, via Comrie, St. Fillans, and Lochearnhead, have all united to greatly benefit all parties, and proving to a demonstration that Crieff and its surroundings have only to be thoroughly known, and the cheap facilities offered, to make it one of the most popular resorts in summer.'

The paper went on to press the case for a tour from Crieff to Dunkeld via the Sma' Glen, extolling the wild romantic nature of the glen. All was not sweetness and light, however, as the paper raised the hoary old subject of the present Crieff station, with some prophetic words of advice:

'There is one thing however, in connection with our railway arrangements and the great increase in traffic, especially passenger traffic at Crieff, that ought at once to be looked in to by the Caledonian Railway and that is the need for a new and more commodious railway station. The present building is not only utterly inadequate for the traffic that is done at it, but it is a perfect disgrace to the town. The Caledonian Railway should at once convert the whole of the present station into a goods station, and build a new one, worthy alike of the Caledonian Railway and the town of Crieff, on the company's ground to the north of the present station, known as the Easter Meadow.'

On a more poignant note, the *Strathearn Herald* recorded on 23rd November that Mr Edmund Haggart, an engine driver on the Crieff Junction line, was moving to Glasgow, he being the last of the original employees of the Crieff Junction Railway. It is noteworthy that such changes in even the most junior staff on the railway were reported, and only 15 months later an article appeared regarding Mr Robert Young, a parcels clerk at Crieff, who was moving to *'a more important position in Perth'*.

Following the success of the first season of the circular tour, the Caledonian was keen to further exploit the tourist potential of the district to the full. Back in October 1872 the *Strathearn Herald* had reported that plans were in hand to erect wooden stables and coach house accommodation just south of the original Crieff Junction Railway engine shed. Work on these was started in April 1873 and they were completed in time for the start of the new season on 22nd May.

In March the North British Railway opened its own booking office at Crieff station to facilitate through bookings to stations on its own system and destinations in England reached via Edinburgh, Berwick and the East Coast Main Line. When the new station was built twenty years later, this booking office was in the building located on the

CHAPTER 6: THE GOLDEN AGE OF THE CALEDONIAN RAILWAY

Down platform, whereas the main Caledonian Railway booking office was on the Up side most convenient to the town.

The 1873 season proved to be even better than the previous year, with reports of the Hydro being well patronized, lodging houses full, and accommodation in Crieff being in short supply. The coaches to Lochearnhead were said to be frequently crowded, and it was estimated that by early August there had been between 4,000 and 5,000 more visitors than in 1872. Unfortunately the year did not end well, for in December a fierce storm struck Crieff and the *Strathearn Herald* reported that the wooden stables and coach houses so recently erected were '*totally wrecked by the wind*'. No doubt, however, they would have been rebuilt in good time for the 1874 season.

As an established spa town, tourist traffic to Crieff was evidently not confined to the summer months, for on 28th February 1874 the *Strathearn Herald* reported, in the language of the day, that the Hydro was doing well, that for several weeks the number of '*inmates*' numbered between 70 and 100, and that the previous Sunday there had been no less than 100 '*patients*', fifteen of whom had arrived at Crieff on a single train, the 3.40pm.

The opening of the 1874 season on 1st June was greeted with enthusiasm by the *Strathearn Herald*, who even reported the Caledonian Railway was contemplating putting a steamer on Loch Earn and in effusive terms stated:

'*No greater attraction could be added to the popular tour supplying as it would do to the inland tourist in one day a trip by rail, coach and steam boat through scenery the most romantic and grand that Perthshire can offer.*'

Sadly nothing more was heard of this grand idea, but nonetheless the season soon proved to be a success. During the Dundee holiday at the end of June, it was reported that seventy-one Dundonians went on the circular tour on one day, with seventy-six the following day and another forty the day after that. The following month, two, and sometimes even three or four coaches were being run each way per day, and the Hydro and the hotels were busy. In total, 7,532 passengers had arrived by rail at Crieff during July, representing an average of over 300 per day.

However, not all the traffic was incoming; for example, in mid-August the CU Sunday School excursion travelled to Crieff Junction, where a Mrs Cameron of Millhill put her park at their disposal for the day and an enjoyable day was had by the children. Traffic of a different kind travelled over the Methven Junction line earlier in the month, when on 1st August the two Crieff Companies of the 'Volunteers', as they were then known, took part in a Brigade drill at Perth.

On 26th the *Strathearn Herald* commented that another successful season '*reflects great honour on the able District Superintendent, Mr Currer, Glasgow, who – we believe – organised the tour.*' Despite the undoubted success, all was not plain sailing. In August, complaints about shortcomings of Crieff station were such that a visit was made by no less a person than the General Manager of the Caledonian Railway, Mr Smithells, accompanied by his Chief Engineer, Mr Graham. Some changes were planned, including the passenger platform to be extended to the east and covered, the goods shed to be covered and a loading bank for wool traffic to be built on the north side of the station site. However, even if this '*patchwork*'

Plate 6.3
One of the Caledonian Railway's horse-drawn coaches used on the Lochearnhead to Crieff excursion. This coach is probably standing at the end of the approach lane to the original Lochearnhead station on the Callander & Oban line which can be seen in the background. A Caledonian Railway pattern platform lamp stands by the fence on the left together with two sets of ladders, possibly used to assist passengers on and off the coaches.

David Ferguson collection

were carried out it was still considered inadequate. In December, Crieff Town Council discussed a proposal to move the steelyard in James Square to the station to obviate the need for potatoes, coal and other goods to be carted up the hill to be weighed.

To add to this, there were vigorous complaints about the new winter timetable. It was considered that this was worse than the Crieff Junction Railway service of ten years earlier, with only three trains each way per day. The service between Crieff and Perth was reduced to two trains each way per day, and the through carriage to Methven withdrawn altogether. The town council sent a delegation to see Mr Smithells at the Caledonian Railway offices in Glasgow, which resulted in a letter from him on 26th November announcing the introduction of a new train departing Crieff at 1.55pm and returning at 3.40pm. There was, however, no change to the Crieff to Perth service, but the town council was probably satisfied that their direct approach to the head man had paid off.

1875 started somewhat inauspiciously for the railway. On the first Sunday after the New Year, the roof of the engine shed at Crieff caught fire. Fortunately, the flames were soon put out and damage was confined to the roof.

Other than that misfortune, 1875 heralded another bumper season for tourism. Keen to promote this, Provost MacRosty (who later bought and paid for the park which bears his name and which he gave to the people of Crieff), taking a robust approach, secured another interview with Mr Smithells. The result of this was that the Caledonian Railway agreed to run an extra train to Crieff Junction from 1st July onwards, departing from Crieff at 10.35am and returning at 11.50am. Mr Smithells was no doubt becoming familiar with Crieff and the proactive nature of the town council, much to their credit.

The circular tour season commenced on 1st June, and by 6th July the *Strathearn Herald* was able to report that the number of passengers arriving daily by rail at Crieff during June had risen from 5,291 in 1874 to 5,705 in 1875, an increase of almost 8%. The circular tour was extensively advertised by the Caledonian Railway, as can be seen from the example shown in Figure 6.2.

This tourist traffic reached a peak at the beginning of August when it was reported that the Hydro and all the hotels were busy. Indeed, on the previous Wednesday, the first train of the day, the 9.45am, was met by no less than twenty coaches for passengers and eight carts for their luggage. This involved some forty-eight horses, so the comments a few years previously relating to the water supply were well founded. Sadly, the summer heat and the strain placed on the horses was not without consequence, and on 31st July one of the stage coach horses dropped down dead at the station. The only hint of regret, however, would appear to have been the fact that it had been bought some time ago by the Caledonian Railway for the not inconsiderable sum of £80.

Such coach travel was not without its hazards: only a couple of years later a coach running between Crieff and Lochearnhead capsized a few yards short of the bridge over the Ogle Burn near Lochearnhead. The horses had shied at a heap of lime lying next to the road and had pulled the coach into a ditch; the coach had, in the words of the newspaper report, *'turned on its side and relieved itself of its human freight safely in a field.'* Happily no one was injured and the coach was soon on its way.

CIRCULAR TOUR—No. 1.

LOCH-EARN, ST. FILLANS AND COMRIE.

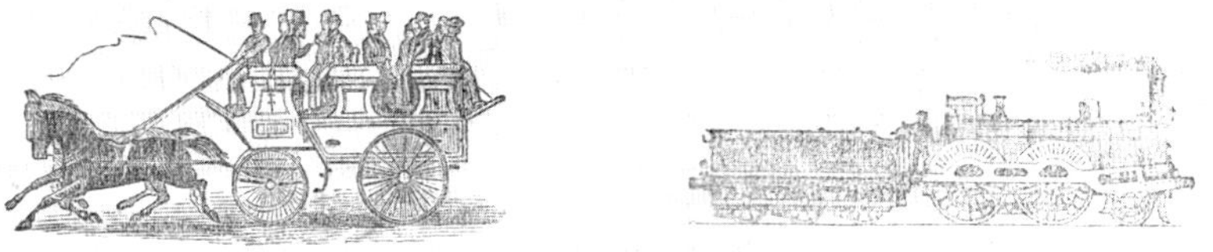

VIA CRIEFF AND LOCHEARNHEAD.

GOING VIA CALLANDER AND RETURNING VIA CRIEFF.

		A.M.	A.M.	
Carlisle,	leave	3 55	6 0	...
Coatbridge,	„	6 30	9 5	...
Glasgow, Buchanan St.,	„	7 25	9 30	...
Edinburgh, Waverley,	„	6 30	8 35	...
Stirling,	„	8 34	10 33	...
Bridge of Allan,	„	8 41	10 40	...
Dundee,	„	6 45	7 40	...
Perth,	„	8 0	8 30	...
Dunblane,	„	8 55	10 48	...
Callander,	„	9 35	11 25	...
Lochearnhead,	arrive	10 11	11 59	...
Coach. Lochearnhead,	leave	12 5		...
Coach. Do. Hotel,	„	12 25		...
Coach. St. Fillans,	„	2 15		...
Coach. Comrie,	„	3 10		...
Coach. Crieff,	arrive	4 10		...
Crieff,	leave	4 25	...	...
Do. (via Perth),	„	...	5 50	...
Perth,	„	...	6 50	...
Dundee,	„	...	8 15	...
Dunblane,	arrive	5 38	8 59	...
Callander,	„	6 20	...	...
Bridge of Allan,	„	5 48	9 9	...
Stirling,	„	5 54	8 31	...
Edinburgh, Waverley,	„	7 40	10 4	...
Glasgow, Buchanan St.,	„	7 15	10 30	...
Coatbridge,	„	9 31	9 31	...
Carlisle,	„	12 37	12 37	...

GOING VIA CRIEFF AND RETURNING VIA CALLANDER.

		A.M.		
Carlisle,	leave	3 55		...
Coatbridge,	„	6 30		...
Glasgow, Buchanan St.,	„	7 25		...
Edinburgh, Waverley,	„	6 30		...
Stirling,	„	8 34		...
Bridge of Allan,	„	8 41		...
Callander,	„	7 45		...
Dunblane,	„	8 50		...
Crieff,	arrive	10 5		...
Via Methven. Dundee,	leave	7 40		...
Via Methven. Perth,	„	9 35		...
Via Methven. Crieff,	arrive	10 35		...
Coach. Crieff,	leave	10 40		...
Coach. Comrie,	„	11 5		...
Coach. St. Fillans,	„	1 25		...
Coach. Lochearnhead Hotel,	„	2 40		...
Coach. Lochearnhead,	arrive	3 0		...
Lochearnhead,	leave	3 7	6 7	...
Callander,	„	3 50	7 15	...
Dunblane,	„	4 22	7 47	...
Perth,	arrive	6 40	9 30	...
Dundee,	„	8 15	10 55	...
Bridge of Allan,	„	4 32	7 56	...
Stirling,	„	4 40	8 3	...
Edinburgh, Waverley,	„	6 25	10 4	...
Glasgow, Buchanan St.,	„	5 53	9 15	...
Coatbridge,	„	5 50	9 31	...
Carlisle,	„	12 15	12 37	...

Passengers going via Callander will obtain a good view of Ben-Ledi (2,882 feet). The Pass of Leny, Loch-Lubnaig, on the opposite shore of which the Chapel of St. Bride will be seen (see Sir Walter Scott's "Lady of the Lake"), thence past the Braes of Balquhidder, the burial place of Rob Roy (parties may visit the spot by asking the Railway Guard to put them down or take them up at Kingshouse Station). At Lochearnhead Station Tourists join the Coach, and immediately after starting Glen-Ogle is seen, a wild and narrow defile; Ben-Voirlich (3,300 feet), Loch-Earn, along the shores of which the Coach passes for 7 miles; St. Fillans, Comrie and Crieff.

From Crieff, Drummond Castle and its famous Gardens may be visited.

Passengers going via Crieff will see those places in the reverse order.

Fares for the Round, including Coachman's Fees:—

Available for One Month, with liberty to break the journey at any place on the Route.

Passengers breaking their journey at places between Crieff and Lochearnhead must take their chance of finding room in the Coach.

FROM	1st Class. s. d.	3rdClass. s. d.	FROM	1st Class. s. d.	3rdClass. s. d.	FROM	1st Class. s. d.	3rdClass. s. d.
Aberdeen,	36 6	18 6	Crieff,	10 0	6 6	Hamilton,	17 3	9 9
Annan,	40 7	19 10	Cumbernauld,	14 0	8 0	Lanark,	23 0	11 6
Arbroath,	19 0	10 0	Denny,	12 6	7 6	Larbert,	11 4	7 0
Beattock,	32 2	16 0	Doune,	10 0	6 6	Lockerbie,	36 0	18 3
Belfast (via Larne),	45 3	25 6	Dumfries,	40 3	20 0	Motherwell,	18 6	9 6
Biggar,	25 9	12 9	Dunblane,	10 0	6 6	Paisley,	16 9	9 6
Bridge of Allan,	10 0	6 6	Dundee,	15 0	8 0	Peebles,	30 0	15 0
Callander,	10 0	6 6	Edinburgh,	18 6	9 6	Perth,	12 6	7 0
Carlisle,	43 3	21 9	Glasgow,	15 3	8 6	Stirling,	10 0	6 6
Coatbridge,	16 10	8 6	Greenock,	17 9	10 0			

Figure 6.2
Details of Circular Tour No. 1 as depicted in a Caledonian Railway Tourist & Excursion Guide of 1875. This was the third season of this popular tour, which had been inaugurated in 1872 as mentioned in Chapter 2 (Figure 2.2). The table of fares illustrates the range of stations from which this tour could be booked, which even included Belfast. As was often the case, this page depicts a well patronised Caledonian Railway stage coach on the left and a period Conner 2-4-0 locomotive on the right.
Author's collection

The usual programme of special excursions also took place that summer. At the beginning of July, a train carrying workers from the Caledonian Tube Works and Tinplate Works in Coatbridge brought 600 passengers to Crieff. Accompanied by '*two excellent bands, a piper and several banners*', they paraded through the town. Later that same month, the Fleshers of Glasgow arrived on their annual excursion. An impressive train of twenty-three carriages was needed for the 500 passengers accompanied by the '*splendid band of the 31st Lanarkshire Volunteers*'.

Theirs was not the only movement of military personnel that summer, for at the beginning of July the 8th (Crieff) Company under Capt McNab and the 19th (Crieff) Company commanded by Lt Meikle had travelled by a special train to Perth for the Annual Inspection of the 1st Administrative Battalion of the Perthshire Volunteer Rifles. The total contingent numbered around 140.

One incident in August was reminiscent of the numerous fires at Auchterarder Muir which had plagued the railway some years earlier, when fire broke out on Methven Moss between Methven Junction and Balgowan. As the newspaper reported, '*Smoke was observed coming from Methven Moss, but as this is a frequent event during the summer months, it was not at first much thought about.*' The fire, however, eventually reached the railway where it burned several telegraph poles, sleepers and a hut. In this instance it would seem to have been a case of the biter bitten!

The holiday season culminated with the Fifth Crieff Highland Games at the end of August. It was estimated that between 8,000 and 10,000 people attended, with reports that '*Train after train in the morning poured thousands into the town*'. The circular tours concluded for the season on 9th October and the winter timetable came into effect on 1st November, but, unlike previous years, it would appear that there were no complaints regarding the winter service.

On the commercial side, ground had been staked out for a new chemical works near Highlandman. This was probably similar to the chemical manure works planned near the railway at Pittenzie.

Various other improvements to the Strathearn branch lines were planned or carried out during the late 1870s. Rumours that the wooden bridge over the River Earn at Highlandman was to be replaced circulated during 1877, but that November a '*large squad of workmen*' thoroughly overhauled the existing bridge, much to the chagrin of the locals. The following year the Caledonian Railway included in its Additional Powers Act (1878) provision for the acquisition of a parcel of land on the south side of the line opposite Almondbank station. This wedge of ground extended 470 yards from the bridge by which the Perth to Crieff turnpike road crossed the railway. It included a slope up to the road and stopped up a local footpath which crossed the railway. This land was probably intended for additional sidings and goods facilities, but as described in Chapter 4, was never developed.

In November 1879 the Methven branch line was closed for a day to allow all three wooden bridges to be replaced. Scheduled to last two days, the work was completed in just a day. The following month, in a railway related matter, it was reported that the Perth District Roads Committee had had to spend £500 during that year on repairing 4 miles of road between Craiglea slate quarry and Methven station as a result of the damage caused by the traction engines of Messrs Anderson. Slate was one of the many commodities sent out by rail from Methven, but there was no suggestion that the Caledonian should contribute towards the cost of these repairs.

Unfortunately the year ended much as it had begun, with yet another fire, when at the beginning of October, the sawmill near Muthill station owned by a Mr Miller, Wood Merchant of Balloch in Dunbartonshire, burned down. Then, just before Christmas, a severe storm blew down the large wooden shed which had almost been finished at Highlandman station. This was in all probability the chemical works referred to earlier.

During the winter, outside the main tourist season, train services on both lines had by now been more or less standardised on four trains each way per day. Leitch & Leslie's Perth Time Tables for August 1878 showed the services for the lines as in Figure 6.3.

On the Crieff Junction line, all trains other than the 7.35am were 'mixed' trains, that is to say they conveyed goods wagons as well as passenger carriages. Consequently journey times were around 30 minutes as opposed to 25 minutes for the 7.35am. For the Perth to Crieff line, a note in the 1879 Working Time Table stated that the 4.25pm and 7.30pm departures from Perth would set down passengers at Tibbermuir and Ruthven Road halts, and that similarly the 8.0am and 10.50am departures from Crieff would pick up passengers at those halts when signalled to do so by the gatekeeper. The guard

ABOVE: Figure 6.3
Leitch & Leslie's Perth, Methven and Crieff timetable for August 1878.
Author's collection

Plate 6.4
Madderty station in Edwardian days showing the station house on the Down platform with several of the staff and two schoolgirls, one of whom is pushing her bicycle. Of particular interest here is the Caledonian Railway crest in the bottom right-hand corner of the photograph. This elaborate display was typical of the pride both in the company and individual stations being created by the station staff as part of the landscaping which made these small stations so attractive.
CRA collection

Plate 6.5
A heavily laden coal train passing Almondbank heading for Crieff hauled by an unidentified 0-6-0 in 1906. Shown clearly in the foreground of this view is the additional area of land acquired by the Caledonian Railway for sidings, but never used. A part of it near the road has already been utilised as an allotment, while at the far end a good deal of timber would seem to be stacked awaiting removal. This shot also shows distinctly the station name painted on the station building as 'Almond Bank', which style was used in some railway printed material, but for the most part the station was called simply 'Almondbank'.
Courtesy Perth Museum & Art Gallery, Perth & Kinross Council

LEFT: **Plate 6.6**
An early colourised postcard of the railway station at 'Abercairney', showing the neat flower beds and borders. The station name was often spelled thus after the local Abercairney House, but more usually it was referred to as 'Abercairny', which is the spelling used on the station nameboard in this photograph. The telegraph poles seen along the north side of the line carried the first telegraph link to reach Crieff, in addition to railway circuits and signalling.
John Alsop collection

would issue tickets, but passengers were warned that he would not provide change.

The 1879 Working Time Table also made mention of the fact that public telegrams would be forwarded from the following local stations at public rates: Abercairney, Almondbank, Madderty and Methven. These facilities were often provided where no public telegraph, such as a local Post Office, existed. It is significant that all these stations were on the Perth to Crieff line, along which ran the first telegraph to Crieff which was laid in 1866. Later, in 1894, Balgowan and Crieff Junction would be added to this list. Another useful facility for travellers was the information that return tickets between Crieff and Perth and all stations north of Perth could now be used either via Methven Junction or via Crieff Junction.

The tourist season that year got off to a slow start, with even the circular tour suffering a decline in numbers – on one day in July the coach having only four passengers. Matters improved in August, and following the Glorious Twelfth some 700 brace of grouse and other game were dispatched south by rail. By the end of the month all available accommodation was reportedly full and the Crieff Highland Games attracted between 6,000 and 7,000 visitors.

CHAPTER 6: THE GOLDEN AGE OF THE CALEDONIAN RAILWAY

A rather charming story which underscored the rural nature of the lines around Crieff was recounted by the *Strathearn Herald* at the end of November, when it reported that:

'A setter dog belonging to Mrs Mercer, Huntingtower, may be seen every morning regularly awaiting the passing of the 9.35am train from Perth to Crieff, and as soon as the morning newspaper ('The Scotsman') is thrown out, takes it in its mouth, and runs home some 600 yards from the line with his errand. It is remarkable that this sagacious animal is always – in all weathers – at its post awaiting the train; and those who wish to observe such a proof of canine sagacity for themselves can do so any morning when passing between Perth and Almondbank.'

1879 ended much as the previous year with a serious fire – this time it was the premises of Messrs Stothard & McGregor, joiners, in the Duchlage Road next to the railway. Not only were the entire workshops burned down, but also the old Monzie Church mentioned earlier, which had been used as a workshop, and the roof of the Caledonian Railway weigh house.

The 1880 tourist season apparently got off to a sluggish start, for in early June it was observed that the Caledonian Railway coaches on the circular tour had thus far had a very moderate season and a large number of lodging houses were still unlet. However, things picked up and by late August it was reckoned that between 1,200 and 1,500 visitors were in lodgings, the Hydro was well patronised and coach hirers were doing a roaring trade.

As usual, some large excursions were noted. The first being on the Queen's birthday in May when 500 Juvenile Good Templars from Perth travelled by special train to Almondbank and spent the day at Methven Castle, courtesy of Mr Smythe. In mid-July, another large excursion from Coatbridge brought between 700 and 800 visitors to Crieff, and at the end of August nearly 2,000 visitors travelled to Crieff for the Highland Games.

Summer was also the season for Army Volunteer exercises. In mid-July the 1st Perthshire Rifles, 504 strong, held their 'united drill' at Ochtertyre courtesy of Sir David Murray, the outlying companies travelling by train to Crieff. Later that month the same battalion travelled by special train from Crieff to Crieff Junction, where they marched to a field near Auchterarder for drill practice.

Goods traffic, too, continued to flourish. In October it was noted that Messrs William Anderson, Slate Merchants of Edinburgh, who held the tenancy of Craiglea Slate Quarries near Fowlis Wester, were sending large quantities of slate out through Methven station. They now had a pair of traction engines each hauling two wagons carrying 4-5 tons of slate each, on a regular basis. Methven must have been a busy place, for a few weeks later Mr Crighton of Burrelton set up a saw mill at the station.

Timber also featured in a report in November, when Dunira Estate near Comrie dispatched thirty massive larch trees by rail; each being about 65 feet long, they needed five wagons to accommodate their length. Perhaps the strangest traffic noted was in December when about 4,000 rabbits and hares were sent from Crieff to the English markets. Such traffic was not uncommon in Strathearn and the railway quoted rates for *'Rabbits, dead, per Cwt'*.

By the mid-1870s, the Caledonian Railway had firmly established

Crieff as a holiday resort and as a base for its coach operations to Upper Strathearn. The extension of the railway to Comrie would take another twenty years, and the final link-up with the Callander & Oban line at Balquhidder a further ten, but in the interim the Caledonian promoted tourism to the area by a variety of means. In conjunction with its partner on the West Coast main line, the London & North Western Railway, the Caledonian published a series of joint promotional guides.

Pre-eminent among these was the Caledonian and L&NWR Tourist Guide, running to around 209 pages. It was a copiously illustrated book which included details of the various Caledonian Railway tours, together with maps. This was later re-branded as 'Scotland for the Holidays'. There was also an illustrated descriptive guide, titled Through Scotland by the Caledonian Railway, which ran for many years. These publications were updated and issued annually, although in the case of the latter only minor changes were usually necessary. Later, special editions of some of these guides would be produced for the American market and some publicity was produced specifically for the USA.

In these guide books, such as the 1881 edition of the Tourist Guide, the circular tour was now referred to as 'Tour No. 1'. It is significant that while the Caledonian Railway ran upwards of sixty different numbered tours, it was the one via Crieff that had pride of place, rather than the many tours on the Clyde or through the Trossachs. The other tours via Crieff also enjoyed top billing, these being:

Tour No. 2   Crieff, Loch Earn, and Loch Tay
Tour No. 3   Crieff, St. Fillans, Loch Earn, Crianlarich, Loch Lomond, Loch Katrine, and the Trossachs

The 1881 guide shows the coach timetable as being:

Crieff	Dep	10.40am
Comrie	Dep	11.45am
St. Fillans	Arr	12.40pm
St. Fillans	Dep	1.25pm
Lochearnhead Hotel	Dep	2.40pm
Lochearnhead station	Arr	2.55pm
Lochearnhead station	Dep	12. 5pm
Lochearnhead Hotel	Dep	12.30pm
St. Fillans	Arr	1.40pm
St. Fillans	Dep	2.35pm
Comrie	Dep	3.25pm
Crieff	Arr	4.20pm

The guide included the cautionary wording, perhaps the equivalent of today's 'small print', that *'Passengers breaking their journey at places between Crieff and Lochearnhead must take their chances of finding room on the coach'*. With the risk of being stranded in the

Figure 6.4
A copy of one of the first Caledonian Railway posters advertising Crieff as a holiday destination and promoting it as the 'Montpelier of Scotland'. The welcoming Highlander and the text 'Glad to see you again' all hinted at the hoped-for repeat business brought by people who returned to Crieff each year for their holidays. A delightfully romantic image, with more than a hint of artistic licence.

Author's collection

Figure 6.5
The Caledonian Railway Tourist Guide and Pleasure Parties Programme for the summer of 1881. This A5-sized volume ran to 140 pages together with 70 pages of advertisements. The cover depicted a typical Highland scene and is overprinted 'GRATUITOUS' at the bottom, indicating that it would have been handed out free of charge.

Author's collection

middle of nowhere in the days before telephone or even telegraph, this warning carried some weight! The tour could be taken either clockwise by Callander or anti-clockwise by Crieff. Timings were shown from Edinburgh, Glasgow, Dundee, and even the most southerly Caledonian station on the main line, Carlisle:

		Via Callander	Via Methven	
Carlisle	Dep	4.18am	5.15am	
Lochearnhead	Arr	9.47am	12 noon	
Lochearnhead	Dep		12. 5pm	
Crieff	Arr		4.20pm	
Crieff	Dep	5.10pm	6.55pm	5.50pm
Glasgow	Arr	8. 0pm	9.55pm	9.55pm
Edinburgh	Arr	8.35pm	9.55pm	9.55pm
Carlisle	Arr	---------	12. 8am	12. 8am

		Via Crieff	
Carlisle	Dep	5.15am	
Crieff	Arr	10. 0am	
Crieff	Dep	10.40am	
Lochearnhead	Arr	2.55pm	
Lochearnhead	Dep	3.19pm	6.47pm
Glasgow	Arr	5.50pm	9.45pm
Edinburgh	Arr	6.30pm	9.55pm
Carlisle	Arr	8.40pm	12. 8am

The tour via Callander allowed passengers an extra two hours if they travelled by the earlier train, and a varied amount of time in Crieff before catching the train home, while that via Crieff allowed passengers an extra three hours at Lochearnhead if they so wished. For travellers from Carlisle this was a long day, leaving as early as 4.18am in the morning and returning just after midnight – not a journey for the faint-hearted.

In addition to Tours 1, 2 and 3, Tour 52 also brought tourists through Crieff, being a tour via St. Fillans, Loch Earn, Dalmally, Inverary, and the Kyles of Bute. This complete journey involved six stages:

Train	Glasgow to Crieff
Coach	Crieff to Lochearnhead
Train	Lochearnhead to Dalmally
Coach	Dalmally to Inverary
Boat	Inverary to Weymss Bay
Train	Weymss Bay to Glasgow

The boat element was aboard the Glasgow & Inverary Steamboat Company's steamer *Lord of the Isles*. There was an advertisement for the Lochearnhead Hotel placed alongside this tour in the guide book, proudly stating that the hotel '*had been twice visited by the Queen, and was under Royal Patronage*', the proprietor being a Mr R Dayton. Elsewhere, there were also advertisements for four of the hotels in Crieff: the Drummond Arms, the Commercial, the Strathearn House Hydro and Mitchells, formerly the Temperance Hotel.

All of this publicity helped to swell the number of visitors to the district. On one day at the end of August 1881, for example, it was reported that the Caledonian Railway coaches carried over 150 visitors from Crieff to Lochearnhead, while 109 passengers travelled from Lochearnhead to Crieff. The coaches could not manage the numbers, and some 40 passengers were left behind, not finally reaching Crieff until 8.0pm. There they were fortunate to be able to travel south on a train which had just brought the Volunteers back from a Royal Review in Edinburgh.

By October it was reported that Lochearnhead had had the best season since the circular tour started in 1872, and the following month, in an article to mark the 25th anniversary of the *Strathearn Herald*, the benefits of the railway were highlighted. It was said that in 1856 there had been about fifty visitors each summer to Crieff, whereas the figure were now between 1,000 and 1,500 per year.

This increase in passenger traffic, however, further highlighted the inadequacies of Crieff station, and in June the *Strathearn Herald* ran an editorial complaining about the state of the station, comparing it with the new Glasgow Central station, saying of it:

'*The accumulation of wooden booths which constitute what is called Crieff Station being a disgrace to the town, a source of inconvenience and a danger to all, while the company spends tens of thousands of pounds on one station in Glasgow.*'

Passengers using Tullibardine station were more fortunate, for a new entrance porch on the platform side was erected to provide protection from the weather, and the appearance and tidiness of the station was said to be a great credit to the stationmaster, Mr Donald.

Such additional protection would have been welcome, for the weather in that area could be pretty wild. The previous November a sever gale had blown down a tree onto a train between Muthill and Tullibardine, smashing through the carriages and bringing the train

Figure 6.6
The London & North Western and Caledonian railways' guide for 1889. A slightly larger format than the Caledonian Railway guide at Figure 6.5, this promoted summer tours in both England and Scotland by the West Coast route. Here a slightly wistful Scottish lassie sits high above a loch while steamers, presumably Caledonian Steam Packet vessels, ply their trade.
Author's collection

to a stand. Again, in March that year a severe snowstorm blocked the line at Auchterarder Muir and, for the first time ever, all traffic was completely stopped. Traffic was re-routed via Perth and the Methven Junction line, but even then the Perth to Crieff train got stuck at Pittentian.

1882 marked another good tourist season for Strathearn. At the end of May another special took 1,100 Good Templars from Perth to Almondbank on the Queen's birthday, and in late July there was a repeat excursion from Coatbridge, bringing 600 merchants to Crieff. Earlier that month 170 High Constables of Edinburgh arrived at Crieff on their annual excursion. Seven coaches were needed to take them on the circular tour, with lunch at St. Fillans. From Lochearnhead they took the train to Callander for dinner, and thence back to Edinburgh.

There were the usual complaints in June about poor numbers on the tours, but by the end of the season it was again reported that they had carried more than usual. It was also noted that there had been an influx of visitors to Crieff, with *between 1,400 and 1,500 strangers residing in the town*.

One less happy event was recorded at the end of October 1882, when the body of the late Lieutenant Graham Stirling, who had fallen at the storming of Tel-el-Kebir on 13th September, arrived at Crieff from Portsmouth. Colonel Williamson had gone out to Egypt to bring home the remains of his young friend for burial at the family burial ground at Strowan. The Crieff Company of the Perthshire Rifles lined the route from the station for this solemn event.

Not all the reported events connected with the railway were as sad as this, however, and from time to time more light-hearted happenings were reported. In August 1880 there was an altercation between two passengers on a train between Crieff and Almondbank. Mr Black, a ploughman from Madderty was accused of assaulting James McArthur, also a ploughman, by pulling his whiskers and striking him. Black pleaded guilty to pulling the whiskers and was fined 20 shillings or to serve six days imprisonment.

Then in December that year, a hen was observed perched on top of a carriage of a Perth train on arrival at Crieff. The newspaper stated that: *'Unable to give a reason for being in that queer position and failing to produce a ticket, "Miss Hen" was taken in charge by the Ticket Collector'*.

It is possible that the hen had in fact boarded the train while it was stopped at the ticket platform prior to entering the station, for Mr John Crerar, the pointsman at Duchlage Road level crossing had a hen-run there. In another amusing incident a couple of years later, in March 1883, the hen-house was broken into and three hens and a cockerel stolen. The police visited the house of a known individual, Murray Kirkwood, in East High Street *'where they found 4 fowls, plucked, skinned, and undergoing the operation of cooking'*! Murray was found guilty of theft and sentenced to three months in prison.

The 1884 Tourist Guide included two new tours. The first of these, Tour 2B, although not following the route suggested many years earlier through the Sma' Glen, involved a joint enterprise with the Highland Railway, for it was routed via Aberfeldy, Loch Tay, Oban, Loch Earn and Crieff. Again, this tour could be taken clockwise or anti-clockwise:

Glasgow		6.50am	Glasgow		6.50am
Aberfeldy		10.55am	Crieff		10. 0am
Oban	Arr	6.15pm	Lochearnhead		2.55pm
		-------	Oban	Arr	6.15pm
Oban	Dep	8. 5am			-------
Crieff		4.20pm	Oban	Dep	8. 5am
Dundee		7.30pm	Dundee		8.10pm
Glasgow		7. 7pm	Glasgow		9.55pm

As can be seen from the timings, this tour involved an overnight stay at Oban. The schedule was even more complicated than that for Tour No. 52, being:

Train	Glasgow to Aberfeldy (via Perth)
Coach	Aberfeldy to Kenmore
Steamer	Kenmore to Killin Pier
Coach	Killin Pier to Killin
Train	Killin to Lochearnhead
Coach	Lochearnhead to Crieff
Train	Crieff to Glasgow

In addition to the change at Perth, this journey also included changes at Ballinluig, Killin Junction and Crieff Junction.

The other new tour, No. 65, went by way of the Kyles of Bute,

Plate 6.7
A colourised postcard of the new station at Crieff, opened with the Crieff & Comrie Railway in 1893, on a busy day in Caledonian Railway times – with trains in both the Up and Down platforms and coaching stock standing in the centre road. A good proportion of the rolling stock seen here is still the old short 4-wheel carriages. The Up train is headed by an unidentified 0-4-4T, one of the tanks engines which were used extensively on these lines. *Author's collection*

the Crinan Canal, Oban, Loch Earn, and Crieff, again involving an overnight stay in Oban:

Via Greenock

Edinburgh (Princes St)		6.40am
Glasgow (Central)		8. 0am
Oban	Arr	4.45pm

Oban	Dep	8. 5am
Lochearnhead		12. 5pm
Crieff		4.20pm
Edinburgh (Waverley)		8.35pm
Glasgow (Buchanan St)		8. 0pm

Via Crieff

Glasgow (Buchanan St)		7.10am
Edinburgh (Waverly)		6.10am
Crieff		10.40am
Lochearnhead		2.55pm
Oban	Arr	6.17pm

Oban	Dep	8. 0am
Greenock		4.50pm
Glasgow (Central)		5.45pm
Edinburgh (Princes St)		8.33pm

For this tour, the seaborne part of the journey, between Oban and Greenock, was on board the Hutchenson & Co and David MacBrayne steamer *Columbia*. It should be noted that because of the route travelled, passengers departed from and arrived at different stations both in Glasgow and Edinburgh. In the guide book, advertisements were placed next to the tour details for the Royal Hotel in Comrie, stating that 'Caledonian Railway coaches en route from Crieff to Lochearnhead call at the hotel 4 times daily'.

Important as these summer tours and excursions were, they could not sustain the railway all year round and it was the daily passenger traffic and, more importantly, the goods traffic which were the lifeblood of these rural lines. The 1883 Working Time Table, which included all trains, not just the publicly advertised passenger trains, reflected the proportion of passenger and goods traffic. Of the ten trains run over the Crieff Junction branch, only one was a passenger-only train:

		Pass	Mixed	Goods	Mixed	Mixed
Crieff	Dep	7.30am	10.35am	10.40am	1.55pm	5.15pm
Crieff Jct	Arr	7.55am	11. 5am	11.20am	2.33pm	5.45pm

		Mixed	Mixed	Mixed	Mixed	Mixed
Crieff Jct	Dep	9.30am	11.25am	12.25pm	3. 5pm	6.25pm
Crieff	Arr	10. 0am	11.55am	1.20pm	3.35pm	6.55pm

The instructions stipulated that no wagon was to be conveyed to and from intermediate stations on the Crieff branch by mixed train. To avoid any delay to trains conveying passengers, all shunting at Muthill and Highlandman was performed by the goods train which was allowed a more generous 40-45 minutes for the journey, wagons from the junction to these stations travelling via Crieff.

A curious arrangement was made for Tullibardine, where the stationmaster was required to notify the driver and guard of the 7.30am train from Crieff when wagons were to be collected. The engine from this train, together with the guard and brake van would then set off from Crieff Junction at 8.30am to collect any wagons from Tullibardine which were ready. The instructions stipulated that the engine had to be back at Crieff Junction in time to work the 9.30am train back to Crieff. One probable reason for this system was the fact that the steep gradient at Tullibardine presented problems for the regular goods train shunting where wagons would have had to be left standing on the main line.

The equivalent timetable for the Methven Junction line reflected a similar proportion of goods traffic, although traffic on this line, with one or two exceptions, was conveyed by separate passenger and goods trains rather than mixed ones:

		Goods	Pass	Pass	Pass	Goods	Pass
Crieff	Dep	--------	7.50am	10.45am	2.40pm	2.50pm	5.50pm
Methven	Dep	7.20am	8.15am	11. 5am	3. 5pm	--------	6.15pm
Perth	Arr	8. 0am	8.50am	11.40am	3.40pm	4.25pm	6.50pm

		Goods	Goods	Pass	Pass	Pass	Pass
Perth	Dep	6. 5am	6.20am	9.35am	12.25pm	4.25pm	7.30pm
Methven	Arr	--------	7. 0am	10. 5am	12.55pm	4.55pm	8. 0pm
Crieff	Arr	7.45am	--------	10.30am	1.25pm	5.25pm	8.30pm

The instructions laid down that the 7.50am from Crieff was to call at Huntingtower Siding and Tibbermuir Halt to pick up and set down goods wagons, and that any livestock wagons for Perth from Crieff and Balgowan stations were to be attached to the 10.45am train from Crieff. It also stated that the Methven Branch engine was to make a special run with goods wagons from Methven to Methven Junction at 2.30pm, returning from Methven Junction at 2.45pm. This traffic would then be attached to the 2.50pm from Crieff which left Methven Junction at 3.45pm.

Another interesting instruction, which alluded to the safety standards and signalling then in use (covered in Chapter 9), related to the 6.20am goods train from Perth. It stated that:

'The driver of the 6.20am Goods train from Perth to Methven Junction must be prepared to stop before reaching Huntingtower, Almondbank, Tibbermuir or Methven Junction, should the 6.5am Goods train from Perth to Crieff not be clear away.'

In other words, if the 6.5am train was still shunting at any one of these stations, the driver of the 6.20am was required to make a swift brake application to prevent any collision. It seems that footplate crews in those days were required not only to be quick witted, but to have nerves of steel!

The relative importance of goods traffic is borne out by the revenue statistics for the stations on the line recorded on the Traffic Books maintained by the Caledonian Railway as part of their financial management tools. These showed, for each station, annual figures for the following:

– Passengers – numbers booked
– Passengers – number of tickets collected
– Parcels
– Horses
– Carriages
– Milk – gallons
– Goods – tons forwarded
– Goods – tons received
– Minerals – tons forwarded
– Minerals – tons received
– Livestock – wagons forwarded
– Livestock – wagons received
– Receipts – coaching
– Receipts – goods
– Total receipts
– Increase or decrease for coaching
– Increase or decrease for goods

The receipts for each station were broken down into 'Coaching', which included passenger fares, parcels and milk traffic as well as

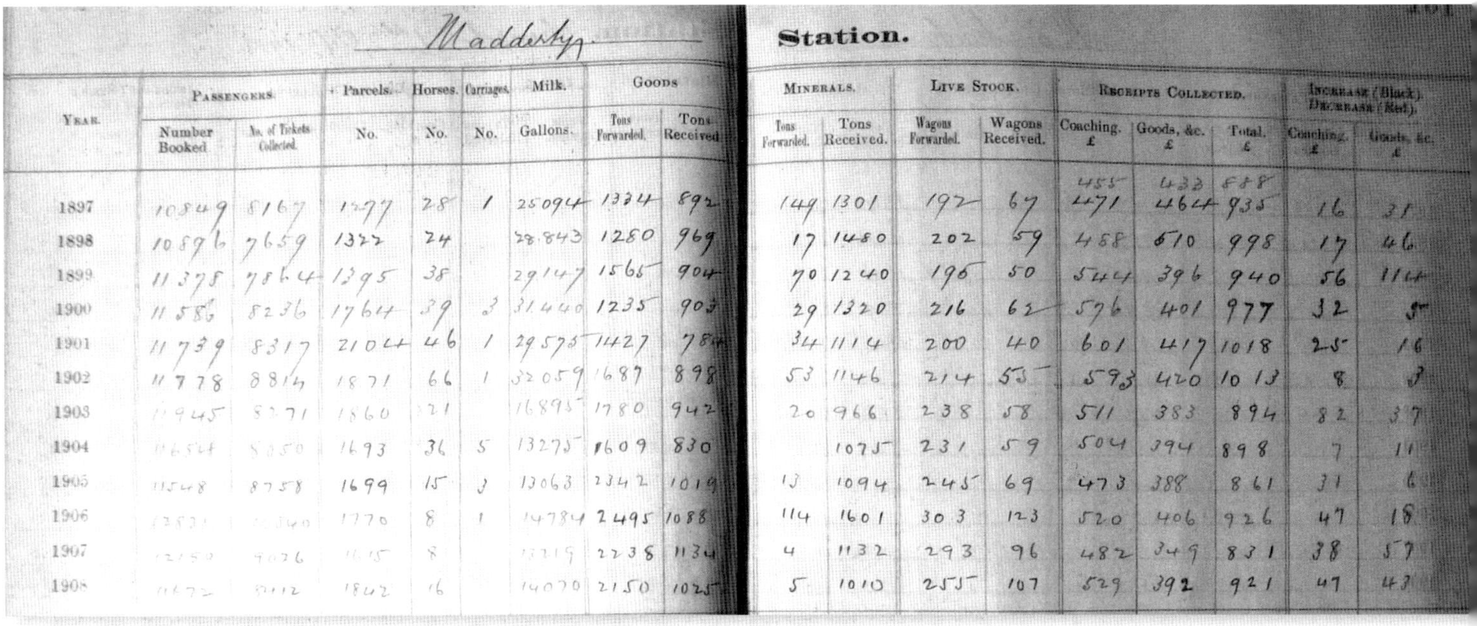

Figure 6.7
An extract from one of the Caledonian Railway Traffic Books. This volume covered the twelve-year period from 1897 to 1908. All Caledonian Railway stations were listed in alphabetical order, two to a page, and in this example Madderty was at the top of the page. Of particular interest to the accountants were any increases, shown in black, or, more importantly, decreases, shown in red, in the two right-hand columns. One figure which stands out on this page was the amount of milk sent out by Madderty, the highest figure being an impressive 32,059 gallons in 1902. *CRA collection*

horses and carriages, while 'Goods' receipts included minerals and livestock. For 1883, for example, the receipts for Crieff and the ten intermediate stations on the branch lines, ranked in order of their results, were as follows:

Station	Coaching	Goods	Total
Crieff	£8,054	£11,036	£19,090
Almondbank	£648	£3,008	£3,656
Methven	£806	£1,377	£2,183
Muthill	£578	£922	£1,500
Madderty	£455	£496	£951
Abercairny	£379	£489	£868
Tullibardine	£293	£437	£730
Highlandman	£114	£606	£720
Balgowan	£337	£379	£716
Innerpeffray	£115	£221	£336

As expected, Crieff was in a league of its own, generating over five times as much revenue as the runner-up, Almondbank. Even here, the figures should really be adjusted as Almondbank was the accounting station for all traffic generated by Huntingtower Siding and both Ruthven Road and Tibbermuir halts.

After Crieff and Almondbank, the next most productive stations were Methven and Muthill. The remaining five stations of Madderty, Abercairny, Tullibardine, Highlandman and Balgowan were in the middle order, while little Innerpeffray came a very poor tenth.

Crieff Junction has not been included as the Traffic Books did not differentiate between receipts generated by traffic on the main line and that from the branch line. It is worth noting that in all cases, revenue generated from goods traffic exceeded that from coaching traffic, only a proportion of which represented passenger revenue. Indeed, in the case of Innerpeffray, even the modest goods revenue was nearly double that for coaching, while for Almondbank the ratio was nearly 5 to 1.

In terms of the number of 'Passengers Booked' from each station, the results were not dissimilar, although Madderty, Abercairny and Innerpeffray fare slightly better with Highlandman trailing in last place:

Station	Passengers
Crieff	55,587
Almondbank	30,467
Methven	19,467
Madderty	10,121
Abercairny	9,861
Muthill	7,968
Balgowan	7,915
Tullibardine	7,233
Innerpeffray	4,975
Highlandman	3,008

After Crieff, Almondbank and Methven were in a class of their own, with Madderty, Abercairny, Muthill and Balgowan in the middle quartile, and Innerpeffray and Highlandman well behind. The figure for Crieff represented over 1,000 passengers per week throughout the whole year, or nearly 180 per day, there being no Sunday service. The figure for all the stations on the Crieff Junction line, together with a proportion of the 9,363 booked at Crieff Junction, represented 251 passengers a day. By comparison, the passenger traffic some ninety years later, quoted in the Beeching report of 1962, showed an average of only five passengers per train, giving at most eighty passengers per day.

The figures for 'Tickets Collected' have not been included here as they can be misleading. In the days before corridor coaches allowed travelling ticket collectors to inspect tickets en route, tickets were sometimes collected at stations prior to the final destination. So, for example, as from 4th May 1888, tickets for Crieff were collected at Highlandman or Innerpeffray, for certain trains at Muthill, and in one case tickets for Crieff Junction were collected at Crieff before the train even started. In the case of Crieff this avoided the need for all trains to stop at the ticket platform prior to entering the station.

Thus, for example, Innerpeffray collected 4,013 tickets in 1883, slightly less than the 4,975 passengers booked, but in 1895 collected a staggering 44,736 tickets with only 9,013 passengers booked, the majority of these tickets being from passengers to Crieff. Likewise, at its peak in 1899, Highlandman collected 62,827 tickets with just over 3,000 passengers booked.

In terms of other traffic, Crieff was again head and shoulders above the other stations in all areas except one, that being milk traffic. Here, Madderty was a clear leader, sending out an impressive 30,106 gallons, all of it in churns, compared with only 742 gallons from Crieff. Milk was the one form of traffic which fluctuated wildly. Abercairny recorded no milk at all for twenty years, then sent out 12 gallons in 1899, with a peak of 8,599 gallons in 1919. Muthill sent out a solitary gallon in 1908, but in 1918 a record 8,632 gallons. The significance of such figures for the war years will be mentioned later.

Crieff also handled a huge number of parcels. The 1883 total was 28,696, although this would be more than doubled in later years. An impressive 500 horses and 101 carriages were also handled that year, nearly ten times that of the next busiest station Muthill. Many of these horses and carriages would have been related to the tourist trade during the summer months, so the numbers were probably not spread evenly throughout the year. Some of the stations generated little or no horse or carriage traffic – indeed three of them, Abercairny, Methven and Tullibardine, were not among those stations listed in the 1889 Appendix to the Working Time Tables as '*Stations that can load and unload horses and private carriages*'. Despite this, all three of these stations handled a handful of horses and the odd carriage in 1883.

'Goods Forwarded', which might include anything from timber, potatoes, wool or manufactured goods, was generally greater than the amount of 'Goods Received', although there were a few exceptions. The reverse was the case for minerals, where 'Minerals Received' was far higher than 'Minerals Forwarded', due in the main to the amount of coal imported. Coal was an important traffic – it was not unusual for the stationmaster to also be the coal agent, and, indeed, some made a good deal of money from it. There were also private coal merchants, with up to four in Crieff, as well as individual merchants at Almondbank, Crieff Junction and Muthill.

'Live Stock' was also an important class of traffic, with considerable amounts being handled at all the stations on the Methven Junction line except Almondbank, less so the Crieff Junction stations. Livestock was recorded as wagon loads, so the actual number of animals could vary depending on whether cattle, pigs or sheep were being carried. Nonetheless, the 853 wagons handled by Crieff was substantial, and even such small stations as Abercairny handled an impressive 257 wagon loads.

The railway company was responsible for any livestock from the time it was delivered to a station until it was collected at the destination station, so animal husbandry was important. Animals had to be fed and watered, and in some cases even milked, as necessary; details of this were included in the wagon label affixed to the wagon, as shown in some of the examples illustrated in Chapters 3, 4 and 5. The 1889 Appendix included an instruction relating to water for animals:

'*The following is a list of stations on the Caledonian Railway at which water for animals carried, or about to be carried, or have been carried, on the railway is provided:*'

Only fifty-four stations were listed, but significantly these included Almondbank, Crieff, Highlandman, Methven and Tullibardine.

The 1880s saw a continued increase in tourism, and in 1883 it was estimated that there were over 6,000 visitors to Crieff. For the first time a North British Railway excursion from Edinburgh was noted. Two years later, large numbers of tourists were reported in August, with the station being busy with both Caledonian and North British specials. One such excursion in early August needed two trains to bring about 1,000 employees of Messrs Pullers of Perth to Crieff.

Tourism was not the only season traffic, for in August large quantities of game would be sent south. In 1883, over 350 boxes of grouse were dispatched from Crieff in addition to hampers from game dealers, a total of 2,000 brace of grouse in all.

The following year, the enterprising postmaster at Crieff, Mr Learmonth, arranged for a direct parcel basket service to London, dispatched by the 6.55pm train from Crieff to arrive in London the following morning. Game boxes from St. Fillans and Comrie received at Crieff by 6.0pm were sent on the same train. A few months earlier, Mr Learmonth had also introduced a letter bag service to Glasgow and Edinburgh, whereby letters posted by 7.10am were made up in bags by 7.30am and arrived in the cities in time for the forenoon delivery. Replies could then be received in Crieff that evening, a remarkable same day service.

In 1885, traffic levels at Crieff during August were said to be the largest on record with over 12,000 passengers arriving by rail. This included a special conveying some 400 children, parents and friends from Sunday Schools at Almondbank, Pitcairngreen and Huntingtower to Crieff. On arrival, they marched to the market park to play football and games.

Crieff Highland Games continued to attract large numbers of visitors by rail each year, and the figures given for the period were:

1883	1884	1885	1886
2,212	1,894	2,186	2,290

In June 1887, Queen Victoria's Jubilee was celebrated in Crieff and the railway played its part. The station was decorated with banners and an arch of evergreen spanned the railway at Duchlage Road level crossing. The engine on the Crieff Junction line was decorated with birch, broom and flowers, while that on the Methven Junction line was similarly decorated with flowers.

A notable event the following year was an excursion in connection with the British Medical Association annual meeting which was held that year in Glasgow. Between 100 and 120 members of the association, together with a number of ladies, visited Crieff. Arriving by train at Lochearnhead, they were conveyed in a series of horse-drawn brakes and carriages to Crieff, stopping on the way for tea at Cowden near Comrie. They then had dinner at the Hydro before

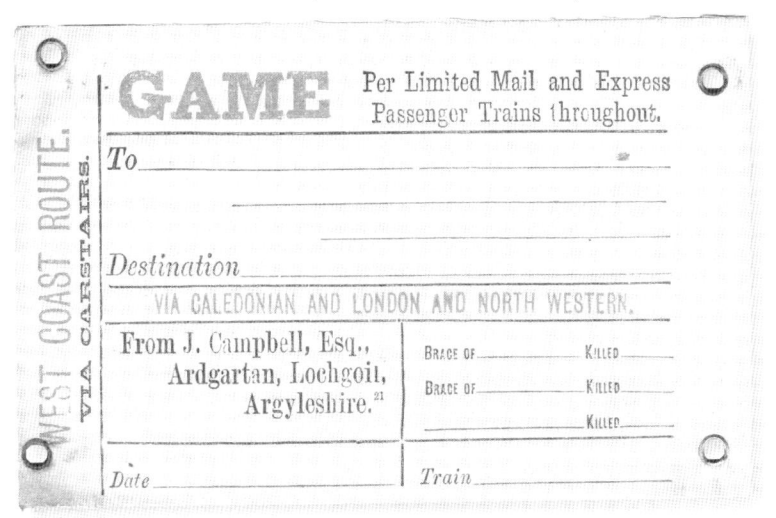

Figure 6.8
An example of the special labels supplied for boxes of game being sent south. Although this example was printed for Mr Campbell of Lochgoil, similar labels would have been used for the many estates in Strathearn. These labels had metal eyelets at each corner so they could be nailed to the wooden boxes, and were made of linen to avoid the effects of moisture. The label ensured that this perishable traffic was not delayed and that it was only routed via the West Coast route. *Author's collection*

departing from Crieff at 7.0pm in a special consisting entirely of First Class saloons.

Figures published in 1889 illustrated the impact of tourism in the district, comparing the growth in the number of lodging houses with the previous year:

PLACE	1888	1889
Crieff	151	187
Comrie	29	30
St. Fillans	14	14
Muthill	13	16

A useful facility introduced that autumn at the initiative of Mr Morrison, stationmaster at Crieff, was the inclusion of through Composite carriages on the 10.40am and 2.10pm trains to Edinburgh and Glasgow. These carriages contained lockers for luggage enabling passengers and their luggage to travel through to those cities without changing.

Despite such improvements in passenger facilities, there were still complaints about goods facilities. In June 1889, Colonel Williamson presided over a meeting of agriculturalists in Crieff where complaints were raised over the inadequate loading facilities for cattle and sheep. A deputation subsequently met with the Directors of the Caledonian Railway who assured them they would look into matter.

At the other end of the line there were also calls for more accommodation at Tullibardine for loading farm produce, and in May 1890 a public meeting was held at the Girnal House in Auchterarder. Not only was more loading accommodation needed, but requests were also made for two trains per day to call at Tullibardine to lift and set down wagons.

As traffic continued to grow, so the services on both lines were expanded. By 1889 – by which time the Crieff & Comrie Railway was finally becoming a distinct possibility – the service on both of the lines to Crieff had already been increased significantly. The service on the Crieff Junction branch had risen to eight trains each way per day with nine on Saturdays, as shown in Figure 6.9.

The timetable included four new trains, the 2.10pm and 8.5pm (Saturdays Only) from Crieff, and the 1.52pm and 8.50pm (Saturdays Only) from Crieff Junction. Journey times were also reduced, being 25 minutes or less for passenger trains, the two express trains taking only 16 minutes for the 9-mile journey. In both cases, tickets were collected at the start of the journey. Interestingly, the 8.45am from Crieff called at Highlandman on Wednesdays only, while the 5.0pm from Crieff only called at intermediate stations to set down passengers on request. The 5.34pm from Crieff Junction now also conveyed a 'through carriage' from Glasgow which left Buchanan Street at 4.5pm; this also called at Highlandman on Wednesdays only, and also at Tullibardine provided due notice was given to the guard at Crieff Junction.

By this date, however, the complicated arrangements for collecting wagons from Tullibardine had been dropped, for the 1889 instructions stated that '*When wagons are shunted on to Up trains at Tullibardine station, the Guard must put sufficient brakes firmly on to prevent a break away.*'

Two years later, the 1891 Working Time Table showed through carriages on the 7.30am from Crieff to Dunblane, and on the 8.40am from Crieff to Glasgow. The Dunblane through working would have provided a connection to Edinburgh, such that it was possible by then to commute daily from Crieff to Scotland's two major cities. The service on the Methven Junction line had been similarly enhanced, although in this case mainly with additional goods and cattle trains.

The instructions relating to the new livestock trains were quite complex. On Fridays, the engine and guards van to work the 8.15am train from Crieff left Perth attached to the 6.5am goods train so that they reached Crieff just in time to work their train back to Perth. On

CRIEFF BRANCH.

To CRIEFF, Via Crieff Junction.	a.m.	a.m.	p.m.	a.m.	p.m.	p.m.	Sats. only. p.m.
Carlisle ....leave	4 22	6 12	...	9 15	...	1 12	*5 10*
Glasgow (Buchanan St.) ,,	7 15	9 30	12 15	12 45	4 5	......	*7 0*
Edinburgh (Waverley) ,,	6 25	8 30	12 0	12 25	3 35	4 10	*6 40*
Stirling .... ,,	8 8	10 19	1 12	2 2	4 52	5 21	*7 56*
Perth .. .. ,,	8 45	10 30	...	1 50	...	5 15	*7 55*
CRIEFF JUNCT. leave	**9 13**	**11 20**	**1 52**	**2 58**	**5 34**	**6 5**	*8 50*
Tullibardine .... ,,	9 21	11 28	...	3 6	✱	6 13	*8 58*
Muthill .... ,,	9 27	11 34	......	3 12	5 45	6 19	*9 3*
Highlandman .... ,,	9 35	11 42	...	3 20	...	6 27	*9 10*
CRIEFF ....arrive	**9 40**	**11 47**	**2 8**	**3 25**	**5 54**	**6 32**	*9 15*

✱ Calls at Tullibardine to set down Passengers on notice being given to the Guard at Crieff Junction.

From CRIEFF, Via Crieff Junction.	a.m.	a.m.	a.m.	p.m.	p.m.	p.m.	p.m.	Sats. only. p.m.
CRIEFF ....leave	**7 35**	**8 45**	**10 40**	**1 15**	**2 10**	**5 0**	**6 45**	*8 5*
Highlandman .... ,,	7 39	✱	10 44	1 19	......	5 4	6 49	*8 9*
Muthill .... ,,	7 45	8 53	10 51	1 26	...	5 11	6 55	*8 15*
Tullibardine .... ,,	7 52	8 58	10 59	1 34	......	5 19	7 2	*8 22*
CRIEFF JUNCT. arrive	**8 0**	**9 4**	**11 7**	**1 42**	**2 26**	**5 27**	**7 9**	*8 30*
Perth......................arrive	9 10	9 40	......	2 20	3 35	6 40	......	*9 25*
Stirling .... ,,	8 40	9 40	12 6	...	3 20	6 46	7 48	*9 5*
Edinburgh (Waverley) ,,	9 45	11 7	1 50	......	5 3	8 38	9 55	......
Glasgow (Buchanan St.) ,,	9 50	10 30	1 20	...	4 35	8 0	9 5	*10 15*
Carlisle .... ,,	......	12 28	4 25	......	7 45	......	1154	......

✱ Calls at Highlandman on Wednesdays.

CRIEFF and METHVEN BRANCH.

To METHVEN and CRIEFF, Via Perth.	a.m.	a.m.	p.m.	p.m.	
41 | Dundee (West)...........leave	8 50	11 20	3 30	6 40	...
PERTH ....leave	**9 22**	**12 5**	**4 25**	**7 30**	......
Almondbank .... ,,	9 34	12 17	4 38	7 43	...
Methven ....arrive	9 50	12 33	4 55	8 0	......
Methven ....leave	9 30	12 15	4 35	7 40	...
Balgowan.................... ,,	9 47	12 30	4 53	7 58	......
Madderty.................... ,,	9 53	12 36	5 0	8 5	...
Abercairny .... ,,	9 59	12 42	5 6	8 11	......
Innerpeffray .... ,,	10 7	12 50	5 15	8 20	...
CRIEFF ....arrive	**10 12**	**12 55**	**5 20**	**8 25**	......

Passengers by 4.25 and 7.30 p.m. Trains from Perth wishing to be set down at Ruthven Road or Tibbermuir Crossings will require to inform the Guard at Perth.

From CRIEFF and METHVEN, Via Perth.	a.m.	a.m.	p.m.	p.m.	
CRIEFF ....leave	**7 50**	**10 25**	**2 50**	**6 0**	...
Innerpeffray .... ,,	7 55	10 30	2 55	6 5	......
Abercairny .... ,,	8 1	10 35	3 1	6 11	...
Madderty.................... ,,	8 7	10 41	3 7	6 17	......
Balgowan.................... ,,	8 13	10 47	3 13	6 23	...
Methven ....arrive	8 30	11 3	3 30	6 40	......
Methven ....leave	8 10	10 45	3 10	6 20	...
Almondbank .... ,,	8 28	11 1	3 28	6 38	......
PERTH ....arrive	**8 42**	**11 15**	**3 40**	**6 50**	...
40 | Dundee (West) ....arrive	9 40	11 55	4 35	7 35	......

The 7.50 and 10.25 a.m. Trains from Crieff will stop at Tibbermuir or Ruthven Road Crossings to take up Passengers when signalled by the Gatekeeper to do so. The Guard will issue Tickets, but will not provide change.

Figure 6.9
An extract from the Caledonian Railway Public Time Table for 1889, prior to the opening of the Crieff & Comrie Railway. Neither Ruthven Road nor Tibbermuir Crossing were shown in the timetable although they were mentioned in the footnotes. Methven Junction did not appear at all, as at that stage it was still only an interchange platform. Almost all trains had connections to and from Glasgow, Edinburgh and Dundee, and quite a number with Carlisle. ***Author's collection***

Mondays, however, the engine and guards van left Perth at 9.00am, just ahead of the 9.22am passenger train. The 7.30am passenger train from Perth took five empty livestock wagons up to Crieff – except on Fridays when it only took three, but only if the 4.40pm cattle train did not run. These flexible arrangements were necessary to meet the sometimes unpredictable nature of the livestock traffic, and to get the required number of empty special livestock wagons to the right place at the right time.

1891 did not start well for the railways of Scotland, there being a widespread strike, although fortunately it had little effect on Crieff, and the Caledonian Railway employees on both lines remained at work. However, the strike further afield did bring the important potato business at Crieff Potato Market to a complete halt and coal was difficult to acquire. Fortunately the supply was maintained through the efforts of the local coal merchants – two special trains were organised, one bringing back eighteen wagons of coal and another a further twenty-four wagon loads.

Later that year it was recorded that Colonel Colquhoun of Clathick had donated £5 to be divided among the men at Crieff station in recognition of their loyalty during the strike.

Despite this unpromising start, 1891 proved to be another good year for tourism in the district. By the end of the year it was reported that Crieff had had a '*bumper season*'. One drawback, was that there were complaints about a shortage of porters at Crieff, and this had been exacerbated by the exceptionally busy season. Typical of the specials that summer was an excursion in early July which brought 1,000 porters from Leith on their Shopkeepers' Holiday.

The Army too put in another appearance when that same week a detachment of twenty men and their horses from the Fife and Perth Light Horse arrived at Crieff station. Having paraded through the town they then carried out sword exercises in a field near Pittentian before leaving again by special train at 5.50pm.

Increases in passenger traffic and corresponding increases in goods traffic sometimes resulted in the need to juggle priorities, not always successfully. A case in point was the complaints raised in October 1891 about the persistent delays to the 4.25pm Perth to Crieff and Methven train, which was frequently shunted into a siding at Almond Valley Junction to allow the goods train from Crieff to pass.

In fact, as revealed during a discussion regarding the roads of the district at Crieff Town Council the following March, 1891 had been a busy year for goods traffic at Crieff. Some 3,180 tons of timber had been handled, and 1,000 tons of potatoes and 900 tons of hay and grain sent out. Added to that was the '*enormous and constant traffic between Glen Turret Distillery and the station*'.

1893 was a landmark year for Crieff, marking as it did the final completion of the Crieff & Comrie Railway. However, before that happened, the town celebrated the coming of age of Mr William Murray, son of Sir Patrick Murray of Ochtertyre, in April. The railway joined in the celebrations, with a large banner across the station entrance reading '*Caledonian Railway St. Rollox Works Glasgow 1872*', and locomotives and carriages being decorated with evergreens and flowers.

The main event of the year was, however, the opening of the Crieff & Comrie Railway that summer, heralding the next major development in terms of the traffic arrangements on the line. The Crieff & Comrie section was operated mainly as an extension of the Crieff Junction line, although services did also connect with trains on the Methven Junction line to Perth.

With the opening of the new line, Crieff station underwent a huge expansion programme, as described in Chapter 2, with the previous passenger terminus station being relegated to being the goods station, and the brand new station being constructed to the north of it.

The redevelopment of the station also involved enhancements to the facilities for locomotives, as more fully described on page 99. The three separate engine sheds formed a locomotive depot which was a 'sub-shed' of the main Caledonian Railway shed in Perth. Several locomotives were based at Crieff, generally going to Perth at intervals for boiler wash outs and minor repairs. In the early days, Connor 2-4-0s and, later, Drummond 'Jumbo' 0-6-0s handled the branch line trains. These were eventually replaced by McIntosh 0-4-4 tank engines, initially No. 439, then also No. 440 and No. 448. When these locomotives went to Perth they would be relieved by 0-4-4Ts No. 458 or No. 154, and even the occasional 'Jumbo' 0-6-0.

The 0-4-4Ts survived throughout Caledonian days and even into the LM&SR era, not being replaced until just before the Second World War. Later, when the line opened through to Balquhidder, a solitary 0-4-4T was based at the new shed there. This was subsequently replaced by a 'Jumbo' 0-6-0 which, in addition to working the branch line trains, also served as a pilot engine when required for heavy trains on the Callander & Oban line that needed assistance up the steep climb to Glenoglehead.

The 8.0am through train from Crieff to Glasgow (Buchanan Street) and the corresponding 4.0pm Glasgow (Buchanan Street) to Crieff were hauled by more prestigious locomotives as befitted their status as the 'Strathearn Express'. Originally handled by 'Dunalistair III' 4-4-0s No. 890 or No. 894, these were later replaced by Pickersgill 4-4-0s, either No. 934, No. 935, No. 76, No. 77, or No. 83. Once the

Plate 6.8
Comrie station not long after the opening of the extension to St. Fillans, showing the new Up platform and building, the wooden footbridge and on the far left the access stairs from the main road. The goods yard with water tower and extensive livestock facilities can be seen in the background. Judging from the number of vehicles in the forecourt, a train has not long arrived, as various buses, carts and even an early motor car are collecting passengers.
Courtesy Bernard Byrom

CRIEFF and COMRIE BRANCH.

To COMRIE, Via Crieff Junction.	p.m.		p.m.		p.m.	p.m.	Daily ex. Sats. night	Sats. only, night	p.m.	p.m.	a.m.		p.m.
London (Euston) leave	8 b 0	....	8 50	....	10 0	....	12 0	12‡0	....	....	5 15	....	....
Liverpool (Lime St.) ,,	10 b 50	....	12 45 a	....	2§40a	....	2 d 35 a	....	....	....	10 § 5	....	....
Manchester (Exchange) ,,	11 b 0	....	1 0	....							10 0	....	....
Carlisle ,,	2 c 30 a	....	4 22	....	6 12	....	9 10	9 10	....	....	1 12 p	....	....
GLASGOW (Bu. St.) ,,	5 † 10	....	7 10	....	10 0	12 10	12 40 p	1 30			4 5	....	4 30
EDINBURGH(Prin.St.) ,,	4 45	....	6 45	....	9 40	11 25	11 25 a	1 35			3 30	....	4 30
Stirling ,,	6 22	....	8 5	....	10 45	1 8	1 47 p	2 35			4 57	....	5 27
Perth ,,	6 5	....	....	....	10 30	....	1 50	1 50	Saturdays only.		....	....	5 5
CRIEFF JUNCT. leave	a.m. 6 55	....	a.m. 9 8	....	11 23	p.m. 1 40	p.m. 2 45	3 15		p.m.	p.m. 5 36	p.m.	6 3
Tullibardine ,,		....	9 16	....	11 31	....	2 51	3 22		....	5 43	....	6 11
Muthill ,,	7 7	....	9 22	....	11 37	1 52	2 57	3 28		....	5 48	....	6 17
Highlandman ,,		....	9 30	....	11 45	....	3 5	3 35		....	5 55	....	6 25
CRIEFF {arrive	7 20	....	9 35	....	11 50	2 0	3 10	3 40		....	5 59	....	6 30
{leave	7 25	....	9 58	....	11 55	....	3 15	3 45	4 15	5 15	6 1	....	....
COMRIE arrive	7 40	....	10 13	....	12 10	....	3 30	4 0	4 30	5 30	6 19	....	....

NOTES.

† Starts from Central Station.
§ Exchange Station.
b Daily except Saturday and Sunday nights.
c Daily except Sunday and Monday mornings.
d Mondays only.
e Friday, midnight.
f Victoria Station.
‡ Friday night.

COMRIE BRANCH.

From COMRIE, Via Crieff Junction.	a.m.		a.m.		a.m.		p.m.		p.m.	p.m.	p.m.		Sats. only. p.m.	
COMRIE leave	7 10	....	8 20	....	10 20	....	1 40	....	4 40	5 37	6 30	....	7 10	....
CRIEFF {arrive	7 25	....	8 35	....	10 35	....	1 55	....	4 55	5 52	6 45	....	7 25	....
{leave	7 30	....	8 40	....	10 45	....	2 0	....	5 0	....	6 50			
Highlandman ,,	7 34	....	8 44	....	10 49	....	2 4	....	5 4	....	6 54			
Muthill ,,	7 39	....	8 50	....	10 55	....	2 11	....	5 11	....	6 59			
Tullibardine ,,	7 44	....	8 55	....	11 1	....	2 19	....	5 19	....	7 5			
CRIEFF JUNCT. arrive	7 49	....	9 1	....	11 8	....	2 27	....	5 27	....	7 10			
Perth arrive		....	9 35	....	11 35	....	3 20	....	6 30	....	....			
Stirling ,,	8 29	....	9 38	....	12 8p	....	3 20	....	6 46	....	7 47			
EDINBURGH(Prin.St.) ,,	10 17	....	11 2	....	1 40	....	4 30	....	8 0	....	9 35			
GLASGOW (Bu. St.) ,,	9 15	....	10 25	....	1 20	....	4 30	....	8 0	....	8 55			
Carlisle ,,		....	1230p	....	4 5	....	8 35	....	....	....	11 54			
Manchester (Exchange) ,,		....	3 53	....	7 6	....	12 † 10 a	....	....	....	3 15 a			
Liverpool (Lime St.) ,,		....	3 § 22	....	7 § 0	....	12 0	....	....	....	3 30			
London (Euston) ,,		....	7 0	....	10 45	....	3 50	....	....	....	7 20			

NOTES.

† Arrives at Victoria Station, Manchester.

§ Arrives at Exchange Station, Liverpool.

ABOVE: Figure 6.10 and Figure 6.11
An extract from the Public Time Table for 1894, the first full year of operation of the Crieff & Comrie Railway, showing trains on the Crieff Junction to Comrie line. The number of stations for which connections are shown has increased considerably, with Manchester, Liverpool and London now being included. Connections were also shown to Perth despite the existence of the service using the direct route via Methven Junction. *Author's collection*

BELOW: Figure 6.12 and Figure 6.13
The section of the 1894 Public Time Table for the Crieff & Methven Junction line showing connections to Dundee. In most cases, passengers to and from Comrie would have had to change at Crieff. As in the 1889 timetable, Tibbermuir and Ruthven Road crossings are mentioned only in the footnotes. *Author's collection*

59 COMRIE, CRIEFF and

To METHVEN, CRIEFF and COMRIE, via Perth.	a.m.		a.m.	Sats. only p.m.	p.m.	p.m.		p.m.					
Dundee (West) leave	8 20	....	11 40	2 30	3 30	....	7 0	....	....				
PERTH leave	9 5	....	12 15	3 27	4 20	....	7 35	....	....				
Almondbank ,,	9 16	....	12 27	3 41	4 32	....	7 48	....	....				
Methven arrive	9 30	....	12 43	....	4 50	....	8 7	....	....				
Methven leave	9 5	....	12 17	....	4 20	....	7 38	....	....				
Balgowan ,,	9 28	....	12 40	....	4 45	....	8 3	....	....				
Madderty ,,	9 34	....	12 46	....	4 51	....	8 10	....	....				
Abercairny ,,	9 40	....	12 52	....	4 57	....	8 16	....	....				
Innerpeffray ,,	9 48	....	1 0	....	5 5	....	8 25	....	....				
CRIEFF arrive	9 53	....	1 5	4 10	5 10	....	8 30	....	....				
COMRIE arrive	10 13	....	3 † 30	4 30	5 30	....	....	....	....				

NOTES.

Passengers by 4.20 and 7.35 p.m. Trains from Perth wishing to be set down at Ruthven Road or Tibbermuir Crossings will require to inform the Guard at Perth.

† 30 minutes later on Saturdays.

METHVEN BRANCH. 60

From COMRIE, CRIEFF, & METHVEN, Via Perth.	a.m.		a.m.		p.m.		p.m.		Sats. only. p.m.			
COMRIE leave	7 10	....	10 20	....	1 40	....	5 37	....	7 10	....		
CRIEFF leave	7 50	....	10 40	....	2 50	....	5 55	....	7 30	....		
Innerpeffray ,,	7 55	....	10 45	....	2 55	....	6 0	....	....	....		
Abercairny ,,	8 0	....	10 50	....	3 1	....	6 5	....	....	....		
Madderty ,,	8 6	....	10 56	....	3 7	....	6 10	....	....	....		
Balgowan ,,	8 12	....	11 2	....	3 13	....	6 15	....	....	....		
Methven arrive	8 30	....	11 18	....	3 30	....	6 30	....	....	....		
Methven leave	8 10	....	11 0	....	3 10	....	6 10	....	....	....		
Almondbank ,,	8 26	....	11 16	....	3 26	....	6 28	....	8 5	....		
PERTH arrive	8 40	....	11 30	....	3 40	....	6 40	....	8 20	....		
Dundee (West) arrive	9 37	....	12 10	....	4 32	....	7 15	....	9 40	....		

NOTES.

The 7.50 and 10.40 a.m. Trains from Crieff will call at Tibbermuir or Ruthven Road Crossings to take up Passengers when signalled by the Gatekeeper to do so. The Guard will issue Tickets, but will not provide change.

The 2.50 p.m. Train from Crieff will call at Ruthven Road Crossing on Saturdays only to take up Passengers.

line opened through to St. Fillans, the 'Strathearn Express' started from there, with the locomotives being turned on the triangle at Comrie.

A variety of other locomotives visited the Strathearn lines, particularly hauling the many excursion trains, including on one occasion the ex-Highland Railway 4-6-0 *River Ness*. Other visitors included the famous Caledonian Railway 'Single' 4-2-2 No. 123 on an Engineer's inspection train and even Pickersgill 4-6-0 No. 956, equipped with an indicator shelf on a test train.

A less welcome development was the introduction of a new bus service between Muthill and Crieff during the summer months. The *Strathearn Herald* commented that '*Mr Fotheringham deserves to be well supported, the village being so far from the station*', which, of course, it was. The year ended with another coal strike, this one being in the west of Scotland, which created difficulties in getting coal supplies. Some coal was obtained from Fife, as yet unaffected by the strike, but predictably the Fife coal mines increased their prices.

With the 1893 development, Crieff became a true junction with connections being made between trains coming from three different directions. The revised passenger timetable for 1894, the first full year of operation of the Comrie line, included several enhancements, as can be seen in Figures 6.10-6.13. This provided Comrie with a generous service of seven trains each way per day, with an extra train each way on Saturdays. The 5.37pm and 7.10pm (Saturdays Only) departures from Comrie ran through to Perth via the Methven Junction line. The goods service was similarly enhanced, with the morning cattle train to Perth now starting from Comrie at 7.50am, and on Mondays an additional cattle train at 9.15am. The afternoon goods train from Crieff to Crieff Junction now also started from Comrie at 3.30pm.

The circular tour (Tour No. 1) was amended to show Comrie as the new railhead, with the coach times adjusted accordingly. The 1894 Tourist Guide showed them as:

Comrie	Dep	10.30am
St. Fillans	Arr	11.20am
St. Fillans	Dep	11.40am
Lochearnhead Hotel	Arr	12.45pm
Lochearnhead Hotel	Dep	1.45pm
Lochearnhead station	Arr	2. 5pm
Lochearnhead station	Dep	12.25pm
Lochearnhead Hotel	Arr	12.40pm
Lochearnhead Hotel	Dep	12.50pm
St. Fillans	Arr	2. 0pm
St. Fillans	Dep	3.15pm
Comrie	Arr	4.10pm

Thus, coaches from Comrie allowed a short break at St. Fillans and a lunch break at Lochearnhead Hotel, while those in the opposite direction stopped only briefly at Lochearnhead Hotel, but for over an hour at St. Fillans. These breaks also allowed the horses to be fed, watered and rested. Passengers arriving at Comrie could catch either the 4.40pm, 5.35pm, or 6.30pm train depending on how long they wanted to stay in the village.

Timings for Tours 2, 2B, 3, and 52, 65 and 65B were also modified accordingly. Interestingly, the guide included the usual advertisements for local hotels, but that for McNeils Commercial Hotel in Comrie had now been modified to state that '*McNeil's is the closest hotel to the railway station*'.

One consequence of the opening of the line to Comrie was a drop in water consumption by the railways in Crieff, an issue which was raised with the town council. The four coaches and ten horses employed on the circular tour until the end of the 1892 season had now been moved to Comrie, and the Caledonian Railway Locomotive Superintendent produced figures showing that locomotives were now using a third less water at Crieff. As ever, the matter was referred to the Water Committee where it appears to have sunk without trace.

The Traffic Books show that 1895 was a good year for the branch lines of Strathearn, with increasing revenue at nearly half the stations on the network. As might be expected, traffic at Comrie continued to grow, as referred to in Chapter 2. However, Crieff saw an increase in Revenue of £1,353, representing an increase of 7% over the previous year, while at Almondbank, goods traffic revenue was up £767, an impressive 21% increase. Methven also had a good year, but the star performer was Innerpeffray, where an increase in goods traffic resulted in a staggering increase of 251%, or £503, in receipts. This, however, was an exceptional year and over the next few years most of this gain was lost.

The tourist season for 1895 saw the return of all the tours except No. 65B, which had been dropped from the itinerary. Advertisements for hotels were again different, these being:

– Royal Hotel, Comrie
– Drummond Arms Hotel, Crieff
– Commercial Hotel, Crieff
– Victoria Temperance Hotel, Crieff

The advertisement for the Royal Hotel stated that '*a bus awaits all trains*', while Mr Stodhart reminded patrons that the Victoria Temperance Hotel was opposite the new Crieff station. The 1895 edition of the Tourist Guide also included, for the first time, details of golf courses served by the Caledonian Railway. Those listed for the Strathearn branch lines were:

Station	Course	Holes
Comrie	Comrie Ladies	6
Comrie	Comrie Gents	9
Comrie	St. Fillans	6
Crieff	Ochtertyre	9
Highlandman	Dornoch	9
Lochearnhead	Hotel	9

Tourist arrangements for the following year, 1896, were similar, although Tour No. 65B, dropped the previous year, had now been reinstated. The passenger and goods services had by now reached maturity, three years after the opening of the Crieff & Comrie Railway, and the Caledonian Railway Working Time Table for 1896 reflected the complexity of the operations over the three branch lines in Strathearn.

Although the new passenger station at Crieff opened in 1893, the conversion of the old terminus station and expansion of goods facilities was not completed until 1896. That year, four new sidings were laid, increasing capacity from 54 wagons to between 140 and 150 wagons, and a 5-ton crane was added. The Crieff & Methven Junction Railway engine shed was enlarged and another shed added, together with a 17,000 gallon water tank near to the turntable. The former Crieff & Methven Junction Railway East station was closed to goods traffic, which was now dealt with at the King Street goods yard. One retrograde step was the proposed removal of the cart weighing machine, and representations were made to the Caledonian Railway to retain it.

A good example of the level of service provided for goods traffic was noted in the local newspaper at the time. A number of coal agents had their own wagons, and in one case three wagons left Crieff on a Wednesday night, arrived at the pits at dawn on the Thursday, were loaded and dispatched that evening, to arrive back at Crieff on Friday morning, only 36 hours later. '*This is smart work*' the paper commented, as indeed it was.

Over the next few years, the tourist arrangements remained very much the same, although by 1899, Tour 65B had again been dropped,

Plate 6.9
A six-coach Crieff-bound passenger train pulling away from Almondbank station around the turn of the century. The signal box was still extant at that time, and the cramped position of the station buildings next to the main road can be seen here. The good yard is well stacked with timber awaiting loading. The total absence of any road traffic on what is now the A85 Perth to Crieff main road makes an interesting contrast with the same view today.
Author's collection

not to reappear for several years. That year, special Tourist tickets from Dundee were advertised:

To	First Class	Third Class
Comrie	8s 9d	4s 5d
Crieff	7s 6d	3s 8d

Several new advertisements also appeared in the Tourist Guide that year, including the Ancaster Arms at Comrie, the new name for McNeils Hotel, and the Bridgend Hotel, also in Comrie, which boasted among its other facilities, '*a Photographer's Dark Room*'.

For the first time, an advertisement promoting the tourist potential of Methven appeared, in the form of one for the Methven Hiring Establishment of Mr R Donaldson. This advertised landaus, broughams, brakes, wagonettes and dog carts, while mentioning that Methven was the nearest station to Trinity College, Glenalmond, the renowned public school founded in 1848. It also promoted circular drives round 'Drumtochty', stating that '*Parties arriving by the 12.43pm train can do the round and return to Perth by the 6.0pm train*'. Methven achieved a certain fame thanks to the novels of Ian Maclaren (pseudonym of the Rev. John Watson) who published novels based on Methven and its worthies when he served as Minister of Logiealmond. He sold 750,000 copies of his first novel, published in 1894. Methven was the fictitious Kildrummie in these novels, whilst the fictitious Drumtochty was a community nearby.

One development, which although at the time may have appeared to be insignificant but was to have a dramatic effect on the local railways in the years to come, occurred on 20th July 1896 when the first 'horseless carriage' passed through Auchterarder. The owner, a Mr Eliot of Kelso was on his way to the Highland Show in Perth. A little over a year later, on 16th September 1897, the first motor car passed through Crieff.

For now, however, the railways continued to prosper, and with them the district. At the annual supper for the station staff at Crieff in early March, the stationmaster extolled the benefits the railways had brought to the town, pointing out that when the Crieff Junction Railway opened in 1856, the valuation of Crieff Parish was £12,000 whereas forty years later in 1896 it had tripled to £36,000.

1896 proved to be another good year for tourism. At the end of the holiday season on 31st August, traffic was unprecedented as large numbers of visitors headed home after their holidays. The 8.38am train from Crieff that day had to be 'double headed', and on two days special relief trains had to be run to Glasgow and Edinburgh, the longest of these needing fourteen carriages.

A special of an altogether different nature arrived at Madderty in early December, conveying a Mr Hair, a farmer from Glenfarg, with all his cattle, farm equipment and furniture. This was to have been a routine farm move by rail, an event which happened quite often in those days. Mr Hair was the new tenant of nearby Newbigging of Gorthy Farm but, unfortunately, the existing tenant, Mr Methven Robertson, refused to move. Having been a tenant there for some 48 years, he was in dispute with his landlord and barricaded himself in. Eventually the Estate Factor and a lawyer were called to sort it all out and the train could eventually be unloaded.

Goods traffic was generally heavier along the Methven Junction line than that to Crieff Junction, with most traffic being forwarded on around the country from Perth. In May 1897, for example, another load of large larch trees was dispatched from Abercairny, the smallest being 60-70 feet long. Later that same month it was reported that 3,500 tons of slate were now being taken annually from Craiglea quarries to Methven station, and that more could be moved if the roads were better.

The tourist season started well that year with large numbers visiting Crieff over Easter. The train from Glasgow and Edinburgh, due at Crieff at 6.0pm, had to be run in two portions, one of ten carriages, another of eight, to accommodate the numbers travelling. On Easter Monday there were two specials, a ten-coach train from Glasgow, and an eight-coach train from Edinburgh. Even the timetabled train from Perth had to be strengthened to fourteen carriages.

In June, Queen Victoria's Jubilee was celebrated in Crieff, and again the railway played its part, with the station being decorated with flags and even the Caledonian Railway stage coaches being bedecked with evergreens and flowers.

Another milestone in terms of the Strathearn branch lines was reached in 1901, when on 1st October the new line opened as far as St. Fillans, although, as described in Chapter 2, it would be another three years before the final section to Balquhidder opened. After all their efforts the Caledonian was keen to exploit the potential of St. Fillans, and the 1902 Public Time Table carried a prominent notice stating:

'The attention of the public is respectfully directed to the increased Service of Express Trains between Glasgow (Buchanan Street), Edinburgh (Princes Street) and Callander, Crieff and St. Fillans.'

The various trains remained the same, except for the termination of the trains at St. Fillans rather than Comrie. Tour No. 65B was once again reinstated. The shortened coach journey now became:

St. Fillans	Dep	12.35pm
Lochearnhead Hotel	Arr	1.40pm
Lochearnhead Hotel	Dep	2.40pm
Lochearnhead station	Arr	3. 0pm
Lochearnhead station	Dep	11.55am
Lochearnhead Hotel	Arr	12.15pm
Lochearnhead Hotel	Dep	12.35pm
St. Fillans	Arr	1. 5pm

The 1902 edition of Through Scotland by the Caledonian Railway was amended to reflect the extension of the line to St. Fillans, enthusing that:

'St. Fillans where the Earn pours out of the Loch and the new railway begins remains one of the most rustic spots in the Highlands. City dwellers passing through may justly envy the dwellers in such a sequestered Arcadia.'

The initial passenger service provided six Up trains each day, with an additional evening train on Saturdays, and five Down trains daily, with an additional afternoon train on Saturdays. All of these made connections at Crieff Junction with trains to or from Glasgow and Edinburgh. Dalchonzie Platform between Comrie and St. Fillans did not appear in the timetable at this stage, and, being only a halt, was a request stop.

Options for passengers were further extended, for the 1902 edition of the Caledonian Railway brochure produced exclusively for the American market included the following note:

'Passengers for Perth, Dundee, and stations north thereof by the Caledonian Route have the option of travelling via Crieff Junction and Crieff, and Crieff and Methven Junction in addition to the direct route, either coming or going, and to break their journey at any intermediate station en route without extra charge.'

Crieff and Comrie, although not St. Fillans, were even shown in the timetable of through trains between London and Scotland in a brochure produced for the US market. Further details of these services were available from the Caledonian Railway and L&NWR Agent in America, a Mr AG Wand of 852, Broadway, New York.

All of this promotion of St. Fillans did little for Comrie, which had now lost its status as the railhead for Upper Strathearn, and this was reflected in the traffic figures for 1902, the first full year after St. Fillans opened. Passenger numbers dropped from 45,340 in 1901 to 31,593 in 1902, a fall of some 13,749, or just over 30%. The effect on revenue was not quite as dramatic, being a drop of £226, which was just over 5%.

All of these losses, however, were more than offset by the gains at St. Fillans, which in 1902 booked 26,258 passengers and generated a total revenue of £1,418. Much of the horse and carriage traffic also transferred to St. Fillans, so whereas the number of horses handled at Comrie fell from 186 to 166, St. Fillans handled 48 horses in 1902. Similarly, carriage traffic at Comrie fell from 67 to 60 in 1902, but in the same year St. Fillans dealt with 15. The opening of the final section of line to Balquhidder would, however, have a more dramatic effect on these figures as we shall see.

1902 was not a good year for Balgowan station, for at the beginning of July the booking office was burgled. Not only was the office ransacked, but the safe was blown up using dynamite or some similar explosive. The thieves, who were never caught, must have been very disappointed for the safe had only £1 in it.

While construction of the line forward to Balquhidder continued, a significant event in 1903 was the visit of the King and Queen to

Figure 6.14
The colourful cover of the Caledonian Railway guidebook Through Scotland by the Caledonian Railway. This book was produced for nearly twenty years; written by George Eyre Todd, the text was updated annually where necessary. Various editions were produced, some included details of the principal tours, others did not, and there were special editions aimed at the North American market.

Author's collection

Edinburgh on the 15th May that year. Part of the programme was a full review of Army Volunteers, including 4th Battalion, 42nd Highlanders (The Black Watch). A whole programme of special trains was run to convey troops to and from this event, including the fifteen officers and 400 NCOs and men of the 4th Volunteer Battalion based at Perth. This included the outlying companies at Crieff and Auchterarder, the latter being commanded by the author's grandfather. The special train was to include a horse box for the officer's horses and a saloon for the officers themselves.

1904 saw the further extension of the line as far as Lochearnhead, which acted as a temporary terminus until the line was carried through to Balquhidder. The station opened on 1st July 1904, and that year's edition of the guide book Through Scotland by the Caledonian Railway was updated to reflect this. The section on Strathearn then read:

'By extending the Caledonian line from Comrie to Lochearnhead, one of the most beautiful and interesting regions in Scotland has been brought in to simple connection with the outside world. Before long, when the extension is completed between Lochearnhead and Lochearnhead station, the quiet region will form part of a new highway between east and west, and it will be possible to travel without a break from Oban to Perth, through the most storied and picturesque valleys of the Highlands. Meanwhile the charm of variety is lent to the route by the coach drive around the head of the loch.'

This last sentence was making a virtue of necessity because any passenger wishing to travel onwards over the Callander & Oban line in either direction was forced to take the coach for the final few miles to the original Lochearnhead station. To describe this as 'a charm of variety' was putting something of a gloss on it to say the least, and it is doubtful if many of the passengers had time to appreciate this as they bumped their way along to the station. The fact that the original Lochearnhead station was not renamed 'Balquhidder' until 1st May 1904 also explains the slightly confusing comment 'when the extension is completed between Lochearnhead and Lochearnhead station'.

1905 heralded the opening of this final section of the line between Lochearnhead and Balquhidder, thus completing the network of branch lines in Strathearn. The complete passenger service for 1905 is shown at Figures 6.17 and 6.18. In comparison with the more than adequate service on other parts of the system, that between St. Fillans and Lochearnhead was rather thin, amounting to five trains in the Down direction, but only three Up trains, with an additional train each way on Mondays, Wednesdays and Saturdays. Thus, for example, on Tuesdays, Thursdays, and Fridays, the first train of the day from St. Fillans for Lochearnhead was not until 10.44am. Similarly, on those days the last train of the day to St. Fillans left Lochearnhead at 3.20pm. All this tended to point towards the tourist, and largely seasonal, nature of the passenger traffic.

The 1905 edition of the L&NWR and Caledonian Railway guide, now titled 'Scotland for the Holidays', included a revised description of the section on Strathearn:

'Balquhidder station forms the junction of the new branch line which makes the charming and storied tour by Loch Earn, St. Fillans, Comrie, and Crieff. The line passes Edinchip, residence of the Chief of McGregor, and beyond Lochearnhead village, it sweeps along the loch side, and affords a view, on the opposite shore, of Edinample Castle, a Breadalbane seat, and of Ardvorlich.'

The guide also contained fare tables from the principle stations served by the L&NWR – London (Euston), Birmingham (New Street), Liverpool (Lime Street), and Manchester (Exchange). All of these had fares to Crieff, Comrie, and St. Fillans.

As with the opening of St. Fillans three years earlier, the opening of the new section to Lochearnhead led to a drop in traffic figures at existing stations on the line, as passengers extended their journeys to the new terminus. That said, the traffic figures for Lochearnhead were not impressive. Receipts for 1905, the first full year of operation, were only £693, which put it in the same league as the smaller stations elsewhere on the branch line, such as Balgowan. The number of passengers carried, 7,652, placed Lochearnhead only just ahead of small stations such as Highlandman, Innerpeffray and Tullibardine. Lochearnhead also handled a modest eighteen horses and six carriages that year.

Revenues fell at both St. Fillans and Comrie by £661 and £226 respectively, so, overall, revenue on this stretch of line fell by £194. Passenger numbers at St. Fillans went down by 2,482 and at Comrie by 2,546, so overall the numbers rose by 2,524. In terms of both horses and carriages, numbers handled fell overall. Horse traffic at St. Fillans fell by a little over half from 39 to 18, and at Comrie from

Plate 6.10
A view of Balquhidder showing the main station building on the island platform in Caledonian days. The cover to the ramp leading down to the subway entrance is in the background. This view shows clearly the extensive use of timber for the platform edges and coping. The waiting room here was used for Parish Meetings, among other community activities.
Author's collection

CHAPTER 6: THE GOLDEN AGE OF THE CALEDONIAN RAILWAY

Plate 6.11
A view looking down on Lochearnhead station with a Caledonian Railway 0-4-4T standing in the Up platform with a train consisting of a solitary coach. This postcard gives a good view of the front of Lochearnhead signal box. *Author's collection*

155 to 115, the total reduction of 61 outstripped the modest total of 16 horses handled at Lochearnhead. Similarly, carriage traffic at Comrie fell by 13, although that at St. Fillans actually increased by two. The overall reduction of 11 was still nearly double the new traffic at Lochearnhead.

Overall, Lochearnhead never enjoyed any great prosperity, and it was unsurprising that it was one of the small stations closed as an economy measure during the First World War.

It is worthwhile noting that the figure for tickets collected at Lochearnhead in 1905 was 19,632, compared with the 7,652 passengers booked. As mentioned previously, the number of tickets collected was often distorted by the ticket collecting arrangements in force at any one time. Staff at stations where such ticket collection or inspection was carried out used special ticket nippers or punches for this purpose. The impressions or cuts made by these punches were unique to a particular station and took the form of a variety of letters, numbers, or symbols. Intriguingly, Comrie, used a boot. The various punches used at stations on the Strathearn line were:

Station	Symbol
Balquhidder	14
Comrie	(boot)
Crieff	(hat)
Crieff Junction	
Highlandman	★
Innerpeffray	N
Lochearnhead	241 ▲
Muthill	

After the opening of the line through to Balquhidder, one significant event of 1905 affecting the Strathearn lines was another royal visit to Edinburgh on 18th September that year. On this occasion a Royal Volunteer Review was held in honour of King Edward VII. This involved the mass movement of troops to Edinburgh by forty-two special trains. Indeed, the demand on the Caledonian Railway for rolling stock was such that it had to borrow 240 carriages from the North Eastern Railway, made up of 176 Third Class, 32 Brake Thirds, and 32 Composite (First and Third Class) carriages.

Train No. 37 conveyed the 24 officers and 420 men of the 4th (Perthshire) Volunteer Battalion, Royal Highlanders in three portions. It was an early start for everybody, with the main body leaving Perth at 3.30am. The Crieff companies enjoyed an extra ten minutes in bed, leaving Crieff at 3.40am to arrive at Crieff Junction

Figure 6.15
The later version of the London & North Western Railway and Caledonian Railway tourist guide, now titled 'Scotland for the Holidays'. The printing style was very much that of the L&NWR, although the sequence of the title for the two railways alternated each year. This view of the Scott Monument in Edinburgh cleverly avoids any inclusion of the rival North British Railway's Waverley station, part of which should have been visible in the bottom left-hand corner.
Author's collection

Figure 6.16
An extract from the CR Public Time Table for 1905, shortly after the opening of the line through to St. Fillans, listing express train services.
Author's collection

EXPRESS SERVICE OF TRAINS BETWEEN PRINCIPAL STATIONS.

6 GLASGOW (Buchanan Street) AND EDINBURGH (Princes Street) WITH CALLANDER, OBAN, AND BALLACHULISH.

	a.m.	a.m.	a.m.	a.m.	noon	p.m.	p.m.	p.m.	p.m.	p.m.
Glasgow (Buchanan St.)....leave	...	7 20	9 15	10 0	12 0	2 d0	4 5	4 45	6 10	10 0
Edinburgh (Princes St.).... ,,	...	7 5	B	9 25	11 20a	1 25	3 35	...	4 25	9 45
Callander............arrive	...	8 52	10 43	10 55	11 35	1 41p	3d33	5 30	5 58	6 6	7 40	12 40a
Oban............ ,,	...	12 0	...	2 10p	...	4 52	6E35	...	9 5	9 5	...	4 45
Ballachulish............ ,,	...	1 1p	...	...	...	6 4	...	...	...	...

	a.m.	a.m.	a.m.	p.m.	p.m.	a.m.	p.m.	p.m.
Ballachulish............leave	...	...	...	6 40	...	11 27	...	3 5	...	4 25
Oban............ ,,	...	6 0	...	7 55	...	12 35p	...	4 15	...	7 0
Callander ,,	8 0	...	8 50	10 35	12 5	2 0	3 40	...	7 20	...	9 48
Edinburgh (Princes St.) arrive	9W45	...	10 30	...	12 20	2 30	4 35	5 30	...	9 27	...	B
Glasgow (Buchanan St.) ,,	9 20	...	10 20	...	12 5p	2 5	4h33	5 15	...	8 55	...	11 15

GLASGOW (Buchanan Street) AND EDINBURGH (Princes Street) WITH CRIEFF, COMRIE, AND ST. FILLANS.

	a.m.	a.m.	a.m.	B	p.m.	p.m.	p.m.	p.m.
Glasgow (Buchanan St.)............leave	4c20	7 40	10 0	12 0n	...	12j15	4 5	...	4 45	6 10	...
Edinburgh (Princes St.)............ ,,	4 0	7 5	9 25	11 20a	...	1 25	3 35	...	4 25	6W8	...
Crieff............arrive	6 28	9 32	11 43	1 19	...	3 30	5 41	...	6 28	8 38	...
Comrie............ ,,	6 48	10 20	12 2p	2 8	...	...	6 0	...	6 45	...
St. Fillans............ ,,	7 10	10 44	12 18	3 37	...	...	6 16	...	...	...

St. Fillans............leave	...	...	7 45	8 47	...	12 15	B	3 36	...	...
Comrie ,,	...	6 50	8 0	9 5	...	12 35	2 50	3 52	...	7 15
Crieff ,,	...	7 10	8 20	10 40	...	1 50	3 10	5 23	6 40	7 32
Edinburgh (Princes St.)............arrive	9W45	...	10 30	2 30	...	4 35	5 30	8 8	9 27	9 38
Glasgow (Buchanan St.) ,,	9k10	...	10 2	1 10	...	4 33	5 15	8 10	8 55	9 25

LOCHEARNHEAD, and BALQUHIDDER.

From BALQUHIDDER, Via Crieff Junction.	a.m.	Mons only. a.m.	a.m.	a.m.	a.m.	p.m.	p.m.	p.m.	p.m.	p.m.	p.m.	p.m.	p.m.
BALQUHIDDER......leave	...	7 5	...	8 25	...	11 40	...	2 15	...	3 14	...	...	7 0
LOCHEARNHEAD...... ,,	...	7 11	...	8 31	...	12 0	...	2 21	...	3 20	...	...	7 6
ST. FILLANS .... ,,	...	...	7 45	8 47	...	12 15	...	...	...	3 36	...	...	7 22
COMRIE { arrive	...	...	7 59	9 3	...	12 33	...	...	...	3 52	...	7 15	7 40
{ leave	6 50	...	8 0	9 5	...	12 35	...	...	3 5	3 54	...	7 30	7 55
CRIEFF { arrive	7 5	...	8 16	9 20	...	12 50	...	...	3 10	4 9	5 23	6 40	7 32	8 0
{ leave	7 10	...	8 20	9 23	10 40	...	1 50	...	...	4 14	5 27	6 44	7 36	...
Highlandman ,,	7 14	...	...	8 23	10 44	...	1 54	...	3 18	...	5 33	6 49	7 41	...
Muthill ,,	7 19	...	...	8 28	10 49	...	2 0	...	...	...	5 39	6 54	7 47	...
Tullibardine ,,	7 24	...	...	8 34	10 55	...	2 6	...	3 27	...	5 45	7 0	7 53	...
CRIEFF JUNCTION arrive	7 29	...	...	8 39	11 0	...	2 12	...	...	...	...	...	...	8 40
PERTH............arrive	8 30	10b55	10 0	11 34	...	3 0	...	...	5 35	5 0	6 32	...	8 35	...
EDINBURGH (Princes St.)...	9W45	...	10 30	...	2 30p	...	4 35	...	5 30	...	8 8	9 27	9 38	...
GLASGOW (Bch. St.)...	9f10	...	10 2	...	1 10	...	4 33	...	5 15	...	8 10	8c55	9 25	...

b Arrives at 9.45 a.m. on Mondays, Fridays, and Saturdays.   c Arrives at 8.34 p.m. on Saturdays.   f Arrives Glasgow (Buchanan Street) at 8.55 a.m. on Mondays during June.   W Waverley Station, Edinburgh, *via* Stirling and Larbert.
Any of the Trains from St. Fillans will call at Dalchonzie Platform (between St. Fillans and Comrie) to set down Passengers on their intimating to the Station Master at St. Fillans their desire to alight, and to take up Passengers on their intimating to the Signalman at Dalchonzie at least 5 minutes before the Train is due to leave St. Fillans.

COMRIE, CRIEFF, and METHVEN.

From BALQUHIDDER, COMRIE, CRIEFF, and METHVEN. *Via* Perth.	a.m.	a.m.	a.m.	p.m.	a.m.	p.m.	p.m.	p.m.	NOTES.
OBAN............leave	...	...	6 0	...	7 55	12 35	...	4 15	The 7.50 a.m. and 10.30 a.m. Trains from Crieff will call at Tibbermuir or Ruthven Road Crossings to take up Passengers when signalled by the Gatekeeper to do so.
BALQUHIDDER ,,	...	...	8 25	...	11 40	3 14	...	7 0	
LOCHEARNHEAD ,,	...	...	8 31	...	12 0n	3 20	...	7 6	
ST. FILLANS ,,	...	7 45	8 47	...	12 15p	3 36	...	7 22	
COMRIE { arrive	...	7 59	9 3	...	12 33	3 52	...	7 38	
{ leave	6 50	8 0	9 5	...	12 35	3 54	...	7 40	The 2.30 p.m. Train from Crieff will call at Ruthven Road Crossing on Saturdays only to take up Passengers.
CRIEFF { arrive	7 5	8 16	9 20	...	12 50	4 9	...	7 55	
{ leave	7 50	8 40	9 23	10 30	2 30	4 14	5 50	8 0	
Innerpeffray ,,	7 55	8 44	...	10 35	2 35	4 19	5 55	...	
Abercairny ,,	8 0	...	B	10 40	2 40	4 24	6 0	B	The Guard will issue Tickets but will not provide change.
Madderty ,,	8 5	...	...	10 46	2 47	4 29	6 5	...	
Balgowan ,,	8 11	...	...	10 52	2 53	4 34	6 10	...	
METHVEN { arrive	8 30	...	B	11 10	3 19	4 50	6 25	8 30	B Trains marked (B) will call at Stations between Crieff and Perth when required, to set down Passengers from Stations on the Callander and Oban Line.
{ leave	8 8	...	...	10 50	2 0	2†47	4 25	6 5	8 12	
Almondbank ,,	8 26	...	...	11 6	2 10	3 6	4 46	6 22	8 27	
PERTH............arrive	8 42	9 15	10 0	11 20	2 20	3 21	5 0	6 35	8 40	† Daily except Saturdays.
DUNDEE (West)............arrive	9 35	9 45	1030	12 10p	3 20	4 25	5 35	7 15	9 20	

Figure 6.17
An extract from the Caledonian Railway Public Time Table for the summer of 1905, showing the full service of Up passenger trains for the branch lines of Strathearn following opening of the final section from St. Fillans to Balquhidder. Being only halts, Ruthven Road Crossing, Tibbermuir Crossing and Dalchonzie Platform are not shown in the timetable, although mention is made of them in the notes at the side.
Author's collection

at 3.55am. Here their carriages were added to the Perth special which arrived two minutes later, departing at 4.5am.

At Stirling, the final portion which had left Callander at 4.0am was added to the special which departed at 4.38am to arrive at Edinburgh (Morrison Street) at 6.0am. Morrison Street was used as a Reception Depot to avoid disruption to the regular passenger services using Princes Street station. Other specials terminated at Pilrig on the Leith North branch line, where a temporary signal box was erected for the event.

The battalion returned by Special Train No. 200, which left Morrison Street at 6.30pm arriving at Perth at 9.10pm. No arrival time is shown for Crieff, but the Crieff companies would have returned at about 9.30pm. The comprehensive instructions issued by the Caledonian Railway made clear that there were to be no mix ups, stating sternly that:

'No exertion will be spared by the Railway Company to ensure the comfort and due accommodation of the several Corps, but in order to preserve this, it is absolutely necessary that the above regulations be strictly adhered to; and no deviation therefrom can be permitted, nor can any proposal to that effect be entertained. First Class accommodation for officers will be provided in each Special Train.'

Clearly no dissent was to be tolerated, and if anything went wrong, heads would roll. It may only be a pure coincidence, but Mr Guy Calthrop resigned as General Manager of the Caledonian Railway twelve days later, after less than two years in post.

The branch line through Upper Strathearn, although only as far as St. Fillans, achieved a new elevated status in the 1905 Public Time Table, when it featured under a special table entitled *'Express Service of Trains between Principal Stations'*. The train arriving at St. Fillans at 3.37pm, and that starting from Comrie at 2.50pm, ran during the summer months only, starting on 1st June, and the former ran only on Saturdays.

A notable event on August 1906 was a visit by the King and Queen of Spain to Drummond Castle. The Royal Train was routed from Perth via Almond Valley Junction and, having arrived at Methven Junction in the very early hours of the morning, was stabled there for three hours before proceeding to Crieff. There the Crieff Company, 4th Battalion the Royal Highlanders formed the Guard of Honour as the royal couple arrived at the station and proceeded on to Drummond Castle.

Their Majesties were among a number of royal visitors who had arrived at Crieff station over the years. When the then stationmaster, Mr Morrison, finally retired in 1914 after twenty-eight years in the post, he recalled visits by His Majesty King George V and Queen Mary when they were the Duke and Duchess of York, the Duke and Duchess of Teck, Queen Mary's parents, the kings of Italy and Siam, and even the Crown Prince of Germany.

Over the following years, various amendments were made to the initial 1905 timetable. Thus, for example, in 1907 the 8.47am,

CRIEFF, COMRIE, ST. FILLANS,

To BALQUHIDDER, *Via* Crieff Junction.	a.m.	a.m. (Mons. only—Commences 5th June.)	a.m.	a.m. (Runs on Mondays, Wednesdays, and Saturdays only.)	a.m.	a.m.	a.m.	p.m.	p.m.	noon. (Commences on 1st June.)	Sats. only. (Commences on 3rd June.)	p.m.	p.m.	p.m.	p.m.	
											p.m.					
GLASGOW (Buch. St.) leave	4 f 20	......	......	......	7 40	......	10 0	......	......	12 0	......	1*g15	4 5	4 45	6 10	......
EDINBURGH (Princes St.) „	4 0	...	...	...	7 5	...	9 25	...	...	1120a	...	1 25	3 35	4 25	6 w 8	...
PERTH „	...	......	...	7 45	8 d 0	......	10 20	12 20	......	....	2 25	1 50	......	5 10	7 40	......
	a.m.	a.m.	a.m.	a.m.	a.m.	a.m.	a.m.	p.m.	p.m.	p.m.	p.m.	p.m.	p.m.	p.m.	p.m.	
CRIEFF JUNCTION ... leave	6 8		......	......	9 8	......	11 20	......	......	1 31	......	3 5	5 24	6 5	8 15	......
Tullibardine „	...		...	...	9 14	...	11 26	...	...		...	3 11	...	6 11	8 21	...
Muthill „	6 20		......	......	9 20	......	11 32	......	......	1 41	......	3 18	5 33	6 17	8 27	......
Highlandman „	...		...	..	9 25	...	11 37	...	...	...	...	3 23	B	6 22	8 32	...
CRIEFF arrive	6 28		......	8 15	9 32	......	11 43	12 50	......	1 49	2 59	3 30	5 41	6 28	8 38	......
CRIEFF leave	6 33		...	8 19	10 5	...	11 47	12 55	...	1 53	3 5	...	5 45	6 31	...	...
COMRIE arrive	6 48		......	8 34	10 20	......	12 2	1 10	......	2 8	3 20	......	6 0	6 45	......	......
COMRIE leave	6 50		...	8 35	10 30	...	12 4	1 12	...		3 23	...	6 2	...	...	...
ST. FILLANS „	7 10		......	8 49	10 44	......	12 18	1 26	......	......	3 37	......	6 16	......	......	......
LOCHEARNHEAD „	...	7 20	8 0	9 5	11 7	11 15	12 35	1 44	2 50	...	3 55	...	6 32	...	...	...
BALQUHIDDER arrive	......	7 27	8 7	9 13		11 22	12 45	1 53	2 57	......	4 5	......	6 40	......	......	......

B Calls at Highlandman at 5.36 p.m. on Saturdays. *d* Mondays, Fridays, and Saturdays only. *f* Starts from Central Station, Glasgow. *g* Connection from Glasgow at 1.15 p.m. on Saturdays. *w* Waverley Station, Edinburgh. Any of the Trains to St. Fillans will call at Dalchonzie Platform (between Comrie and St. Fillans) to set down Passengers, on their intimating to the Station Master at Comrie their desire to alight. * Saturdays only.

BALQUHIDDER, LOCHEARNHEAD, ST. FILLANS,

To METHVEN, CRIEFF, COMRIE, and BALQUHIDDER, *via* Perth.	a.m. (Runs on Mondays, Wednesdays, and Saturdays only.)	a.m.	a.m.	a.m.	Sats. only. p.m. (Commences on 3rd June.)		Sats. only. p.m.	p.m.	p.m. (Commences on 1st June.)	p.m.	
DUNDEE (West) leave	7 10	8 15	11 35	11 35	1 45	...	1 45	3 30	4 30	7 0	...
PERTH leave	7 45	9 5	1220p	12 50	2 25	......	2 40	4 20	5 5 b	7 40	......
Almondbank „	B	9 16	...	12 59		...	2 52	4 32		7 52	...
METHVEN arrive	......	9 30	......	1 15		......	3 10	4 50		8 7	......
METHVEN leave	...	9 10	...	12 58		...	...	4 25		7 45	...
Balgowan „	......	9 27	......	1 11		......	......	4 45		8 5	......
Madderty „	B	9 33	...	1 17		...	...	4 51		8 11	...
Abercairny „	......	9 38	......	1 22		......	......	4 57		8 17	......
Innerpeffray „	...	9 42	...	1 27		...	...	5 2	5 31	8 22	...
CRIEFF arrive	8 15	9 50	12 50	1 35	2 59	......	......	5 10	5 36	8 30	......
CRIEFF leave	8 19	10 5	12 55	1b53	3 5	...	...	5 45	5 45	...	...
COMRIE arrive	8 34	10 20	1 10	2b8	3 20	......	......	6 0	6 0	......	......
COMRIE leave	8 35	10 30	1 12	...	3 23	...	...	6 2	6 2	...	...
ST. FILLANS „	8 49	10 44	1 26	......	3 37	......	......	6 16	6 16	......	......
LOCHEARNHEAD „	9 5	11 7	1 44	...	3 55	...	...	6 32	6 32	...	...
BALQUHIDDER arrive	9 13	11 22	1 53	......	4 5	......	......	6 40	6 40	......	......
OBAN „	12 0	2C10p	4 52	...	6 35	...	...	9 5	9 5	...	...

NOTES.

B Calls at Stations between Perth and Crieff, when required, to take up Passengers for Callander and Oban Line.

C Connection to Oban—Commencing on 1st June.

b These times apply from 1st June only.

The 2.40 p.m. Saturday Train, Perth to Methven, calls at Ruthven Road.

The 4.20 p.m. and 7.40 p.m. Trains from Perth call at Ruthven Road and Tibbermuir Crossings to set down Passengers on notice being given to the Station Superintendent at Perth.

Figure 6.18

An extract from the Caledonian Railway Public Time Table for the summer of 1905 showing the equivalent full service of Down passenger trains for the branch lines of Strathearn. In the case of the Crieff Junction line, connecting services from Edinburgh, Glasgow and Perth are shown, while for trains on the Methven line, times are shown from Dundee. Train times to and from Oban via Balquhidder and the Callander & Oban line are also shown.

Author's collection

12.15pm and 3.36pm departures from St. Fillans were all re-timed to later departures of 9.14am, 1.8pm and 4.34pm respectively, while a new train was added leaving St. Fillans at 5.0pm. This latter replaced the 6.40pm from Crieff. At the same time, a number of further relaxations were introduced relating to the availability of tickets. Thus, Return tickets to Highlandman from Crieff and stations to the west were also available to Innerpeffray, and tickets from Perth to Methven were also available to Balgowan.

The most significant improvement in 1907 was the introduction of 'slip coaches' on certain express trains from Edinburgh and Glasgow. Slip coaches avoided the need for express trains to stop at particular intermediate stations, thus permitting faster running and reduced timings. The 9.30am and 1.17pm trains from Edinburgh each slipped a coach at Crieff Junction for Crieff. The coach, which had its own guard, was simply uncoupled from the rear of the train as it approached Crieff Junction and was slowed to a stop by the guard under its own brake power. It was then attached to the branch line train to continue its journey to Crieff. These coaches were worked back to their original station the following day. The 7.45am from St. Fillans included a slip coach destined for Edinburgh which was slipped from the Glasgow train at Larbert.

Plate 6.12
A detailed view of the Down platform at Crieff showing the cast iron columns and spandrels, the generous provision of gas lighting and the profusion of hanging baskets and plants. On the left, rolling stock is stabled in the centre road and one of the old fashioned weighing machines is on the extreme right. It can be seen that although the canopy was supported by cast iron columns, much of the rest of the roof structure was of timber, which gave problems later in life as can be seen in Chapter 10. *CRA collection*

Another innovation that year was the introduction by the London & North Western Railway of a Composite Sleeping Carriage which was added to the 8.0pm train from London (Euston). This was a through carriage to Crieff, arriving there the following morning, providing a direct link from the nation's capital.

In the following year, 1908, further changes were made to the timings for some trains, but, significantly, the 1.31pm and 3.5pm afternoon trains from Crieff Junction now ran through to St. Fillans, arriving at 2.20pm and 4.5pm respectively. A new evening train on Saturdays was introduced, leaving Methven for Perth at 8.55pm, returning from Perth at 10.20pm.

A considerable number of trains to and from Edinburgh, Glasgow and elsewhere conveyed through carriages from St. Fillans, Comrie and Crieff which were attached to or detached from main line trains at Crieff Junction. The 1908 instructions illustrate the extent of these workings:

From Crieff	From Comrie	From St. Fillans
7.10am Glasgow	6.50am Glasgow	7.45am Edinburgh
8.20am Edinburgh	8. 0am Edinburgh	7.45am Glasgow
8.20am Glasgow	8. 0am Glasgow	8.57am Dundee
8.40am Dundee	9. 9am Dundee	2.30pm Edinburgh
9.25am Dundee	2.50pm Glasgow	2.30pm Glasgow
9.55am Glasgow	3.50pm Glasgow	7.22pm Dundee
3. 8pm Edinburgh	3.50pm Dundee	
3. 8pm Glasgow	7.40pm Dundee	
4.14pm Dundee		
6.28pm Glasgow		
8. 0pm Dundee		

These workings would be balanced by similar through carriages from Edinburgh, Glasgow and Dundee. Such services did encourage commuter traffic from Strathearn to these major cities. The through carriages included the slip coach workings referred to earlier, and in 1908 a further slip coach was added – the 5.0pm from Glasgow (Buchanan Street), the 'Granite City', which had previously stopped to detach a through coach to Comrie, now slipped this coach at Crieff Junction.

1908 was probably the peak year for slip coach operation at Crieff Junction, with three workings daily, for by 1910 this had been reduced to just one. This was the slip coach for St. Fillans which formed part of the 1.25pm from Edinburgh; the coach, having been slipped at Crieff Junction, was attached to the 3.5pm train to Crieff and St. Fillans. This coach was then returned to Crieff where it was attached to the 6.0pm train to Perth via Methven Junction. Having spent the night at Perth, the vehicle was then returned to Edinburgh by the 7.46am train the next day.

On Saturdays an additional slip coach for Crieff was added to the St. Fillans coach. This spent the weekend at Crieff before being returned to Edinburgh by the 3.4pm train on Monday. These slip coach workings were still being operated during the First World War, and the 1915 Working Time Table reveals that the 10.0am express from Glasgow (Buchanan Street) slipped a coach for St. Fillans at Gleneagles at 11.11am, while the 1.25pm from Edinburgh (Princes Street) also included a slip coach for St. Fillans, although this was detached at Stirling, to be attached to the 2.51pm and slipped at Gleneagles at 3.14pm. The Gleneagles station referred to here was the old Crieff Junction station which had been renamed Gleneagles in 1912, rather than the new station which was not opened until 1919.

The spring of 1909 saw the resumption of special excursions, one of the largest being that organised by Mr John Campbell of Auchterarder to Fort William. Three special trains conveyed nearly 900 passengers via Crieff, Comrie and Lochearnhead to Crianlarich and then onto the West Highland line. From Fort William the trippers

CHAPTER 6: THE GOLDEN AGE OF THE CALEDONIAN RAILWAY

took a steamer to Kinlochleven to visit the aluminium works there.

This excursion was dwarfed, however, by one the following year bringing members of St. Cuthbert's Cooperative Society from Edinburgh to Crieff. No less than six trains were needed for the 3,000 passengers who were accompanied by the Musselburgh and Fisherrow Band. Crieff was an exceptionally busy station that day, as can be seen from the timetable of special trains which were in addition to the normal timetabled services:

Crieff Arr	9. 3am	9.20am	9.32am	9.50am	10.15am	10.25am
Crieff Dep	6.55pm	7.10pm	7.20pm	7.30pm	8.10pm	8.45pm

1910 saw a radical overhaul of the Caledonian Railway excursion programme which had survived in basically the same format since the 1880s. The number of advertised tours was drastically curtailed, with Strathearn Tours Numbers 2, 2B, 3, 52 and 65 having all disappeared. Tour No. 1, the original and most popular tour, survived, and was now renamed the 'Grand Circular Tour', so remaining one of the most, if not *the* most prominent tour in the Caledonian Railway programme.

Tourism continued to be an important source of traffic and revenue for the railway, and, as part of this, station staff were encouraged to make their stations attractive and welcoming to the travelling public. There was always a great sense of pride in the appearance of stations, the staff often willingly gave their own time and even sometimes their own resources to maintain high standards. The images of some of the stations in this chapter reflect the standards achieved. The results of the Caledonian Railway Best Kept Station awards of 1909 give an idea of how well the stations of the Strathearn branch lines were rated. Ten stations, headed by little Tullibardine, won prizes that year:

STATION	STATIONMASTER	%
FIRST CLASS PREMIUM (£5)		
Tullibardine	William Ross	86¼
SECOND CLASS PREMIUM (£4)		
Comrie	Peter Taylor	78¾
Crieff Junction	Thomas Bayne	78¾
THIRD CLASS PREMIUM (£2)		
Madderty	William McLean	73¾
Abercairny	James Laing	71¼
Innerpeffray	George Allan	71¼
FOURTH CLASS PREMIUM (£1)		
Highlandman	George Durward	67½
Crieff	William Morrison	65
Muthill	David Smith	66¼
St. Fillans	David Thompson	63¾

The competition was evidently stiff, with even a quarter of one percent making all the difference. The marking at that time would appear to have been quite strict with 80% being sufficient to win a First Class Premium, whereas in later years this sort of mark would only earn a Third Class Premium, as illustrated in the results for 1917 and 1918.

Two years later, of the fifteen stations on these lines – including the two junction stations – only three, Almondbank, Balgowan and Crieff Junction failed to win a prize. Methven Junction could be discounted as at that stage it was only an interchange platform.

Nor was the war allowed to interfere with such activity. The results of the competition judged in the summer of 1917 and published that October again showed that despite the temporary closure of Innerpeffray and Lochearnhead, the Strathearn stations were well placed, again scoring highly:

STATION	STATIONMASTER	MARKS	MAX	%
FIRST CLASS PREMIUM (£5)				
Crieff	William Miller	690	700	98
Comrie	Peter Taylor	620	650	95
SECOND CLASS PREMIUM (£4)				
Madderty	William McLean	460	500	92
THIRD CLASS PREMIUM (£2)				
Gleneagles	Walter Walker	445	500	89

A special prize was also awarded to Mrs Ogilvie, gate keeper at Dalchonzie for the fine floral display. Three stations, Abercairny, Balquhidder and St. Fillans were ineligible for awards under the rules, having won prizes for several years in a row, this despite St. Fillans having scored 100%. Clearly Strathearn stations were in danger of sweeping the board year on year. However, all three were again eligible to enter the following year, 1918, with predictable results:

STATION	STATIONMASTER	MARKS	MAX	%
FIRST CLASS PREMIUMS. 20 STATIONS AT £5 EACH				
St. Fillans	Thos Buchanan	550	550	100
Crieff	William Miller	600	595	99
Balquhidder	D McDiamid	550	525	92
SECOND CLASS PREMIUMS. 30 STATIONS AT £4 EACH				
Balgowan	John Mawer	550	514	94
Comrie	Peter Taylor	600	550	94
THIRD CLASS PREMIUMS. 50 STATIONS AT £2 EACH				
Tullibardine	James Hill	550	495	90
Abercairny	James Irvine	550	490	89
FOURTH CLASS PREMIUMS. 50 STATIONS AT £1 EACH				
Muthill	DC Clark	550	485	88
Gleneagles	Walter Walker	550	475	86

It was pleasing to note that the gate keeper at Dalchonzie Level Crossing was again one of three awarded a special prize for '*the fine floral displays at these places*'.

Even the last year in which the Caledonian Railway ran the competition, 1922, two stations, St. Fillans and the new flagship station of Gleneagles, won First Class Premiums. Unfortunately only partial results were published in the *Railway Gazette*, but it included the comment that:

'*The Caledonian scheme is more comprehensive than many schemes, as it not only covers floral displays at stations and their general appearance, but also office and depot cleanliness, station books and other matters.*'

Caledonian Railway Best Kept Station awards were well deserved and much coveted. Interestingly, the prizes of £5, £4, £2 and £1 for the four categories remained unchanged for well over ten years.

Strathearn received further recognition in 1911 with the introduction of its own named express train, the 'Strathearn Express'. This was a new fast service between Crieff and Glasgow and Edinburgh. Leaving Crieff at 8.18am, it had portions for Edinburgh and Glasgow, while a new train left Glasgow at 4.35pm arriving at Crieff at 6.0pm. The Edinburgh portion departed at 4.50pm, cutting 21 minutes from the journey time, while the new Glasgow train made only one stop, at Crieff Junction.

A less welcome development that year was the approval by Perth City Council of a motor bus service between Perth and Almondbank using a 26-seat omnibus. However, when the operator attempted to

Plate 6.13
The stationmaster at Crieff in 1922, Mr RW Millar, seen here at the west end of the Down platform. This view shows the extensive and neatly kept flower beds and borders, with King Street bridge in the background and Crieff West signal box in the far corner of the Up platform. The young man stood somewhat reverently at the foot of the Down starting signal is Robert Millar, one of William Millar's sons. Both he and his brother, William Junior, were employed as clerks in the goods office.
CRA collection

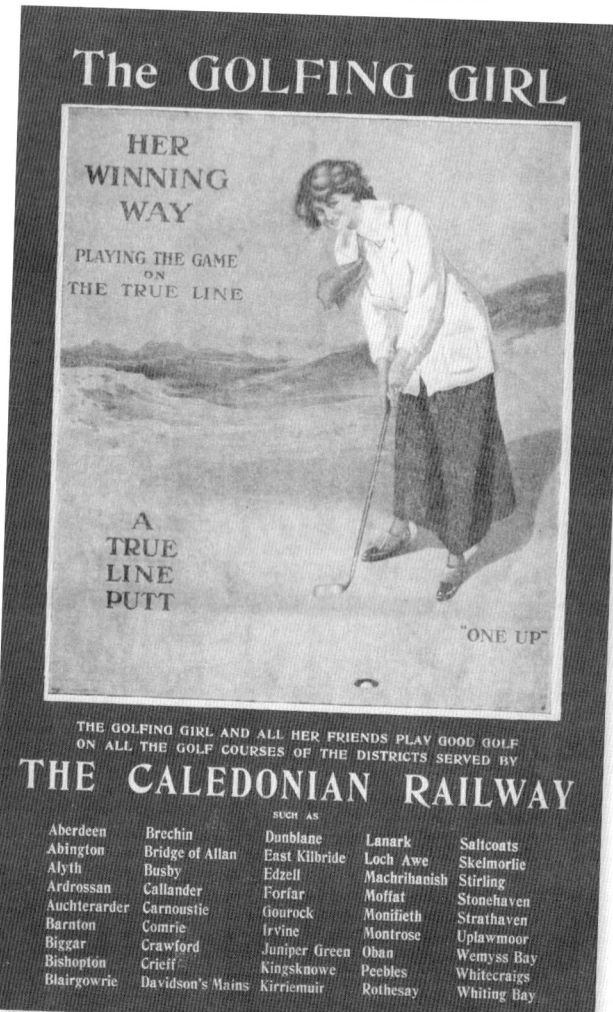

Figure 6.19
One of the Caledonian Railway Company's own advertisements in the 1912 Public Time Table. The 'Caley' had always promoted its service to '*The Royal and Ancient Game of Golf*' but this advertisement first appeared in 1912, the year in which plans were being laid for the golf course and hotel at Gleneagles. Consequently, Gleneagles does not appear on this list of courses, although Auchterarder, Comrie and Crieff do. The image of the 'Golfing Girl' was one which was subsequently much used in the promotion of Gleneagles Golf Course when it opened in 1919.
Author's collection

extend the service to Methven the following March because the train service was suspended owing to another miners' strike, local carriers objected on the grounds that the Corporation Order limited the bus service to a 3-mile radius of Perth. The Sheriff upheld this objection and awarded costs against the bus operator.

The 1911 edition of the Caledonian Railway Tourist Guide was a hefty volume running to 238 pages, and included much new information, including a list of all the fishing resorts which could be reached by the Caledonian Railway. An impressive twenty-one rivers and lochs were listed against stations on the Strathearn lines, and a full list of these is shown in Appendix 7.

Golf courses were again shown, but in more detail. All were now 9 holes, as shown below. Auchterarder was described as '*A sporting green, in splendid order, with numerous hazards*', with the Secretary shown as Thomas E Young, the author's grandfather. Comrie course was similarly described, somewhat menacingly, as '*Grand old turf with sporting hazards*'.

STATION	COURSE	HOLES
Auchterarder or Crieff Junction	Auchterarder	9
Comrie	Comrie	9
Crieff	Crieff	9
Highlandman	Dornoch	9
Lochearnhead	Hotel	9
St. Fillans	St. Fillans	9

The 'Grand Circular Tour' was again advertised, but with the additional option of pleasure sailing on Loch Tay by the saloon steamer *Lady of the Lake*. Tourist tickets from Dundee, West Ferry, and Broughty Ferry, to Crieff, Comrie and St. Fillans were promoted, as were tickets from London.

Interestingly, the Tourist tickets from London were also available to Tullibardine and Muthill, both unlikely tourist destinations.

There was a significant expansion of the freight facilities at Almondbank in 1911, not in the form of development of the additional land acquired in 1877, but a new siding to serve the bleach works. The Caledonian Railway entered into an agreement with Lumsden & MacKenzie to construct and maintain a private siding to their Bleachfield Works. The Caledonian agreed to install a connection and a short spur from their line at a point 146 yards east of the centre of Almondbank station, The Caledonian also undertook to construct and maintain the siding for an annual interest rate of 5% of the cost of the permanent way materials – these to be supplied by Lumsden &

CRIEFF AND LOCH EARN CIRCULAR TOUR.

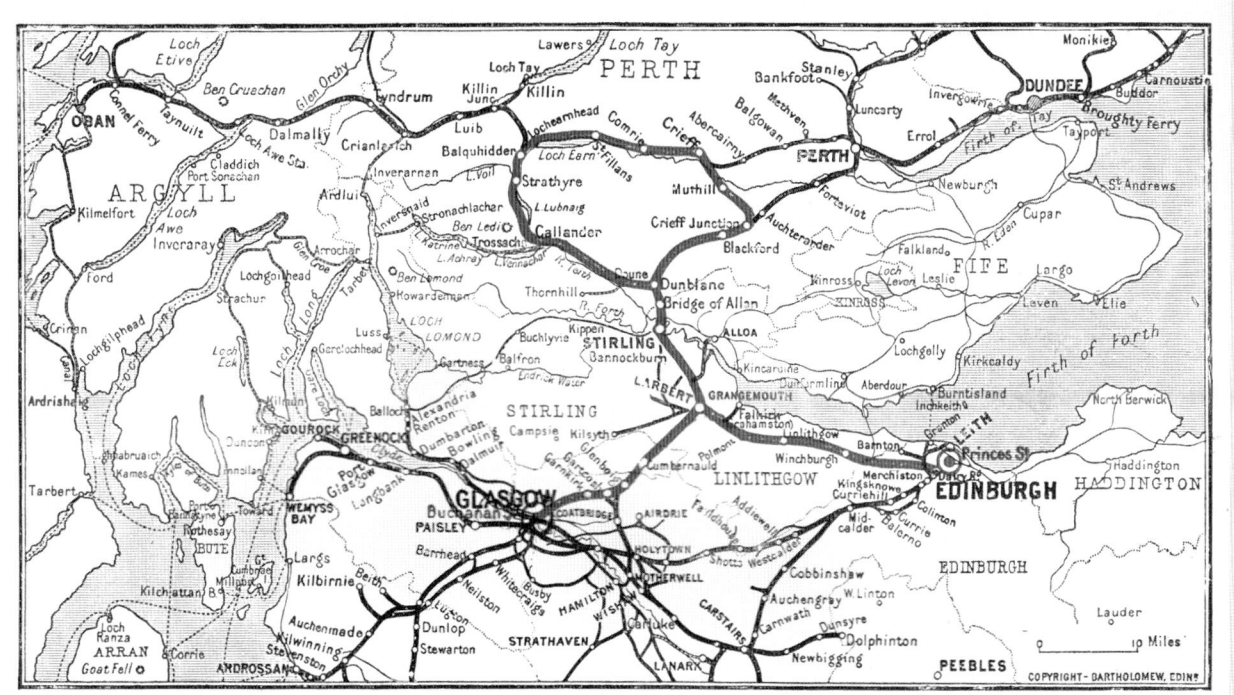

Route.—Rail from GLASGOW (Buchanan Street), or EDINBURGH (Princes Street), to Lochearnhead and Balquhidder, via Stirling, Crieff, Comrie and St Fillans; thence to Glasgow or Edinburgh respectively, via Callander; or the route may be reversed. Tickets available for break of journey at Callander, Crieff, and one other point which must be declared at time of booking.
Fares for the Round—From GLASGOW, 1st Class, 12/8; 3rd Class. 7/-.   From EDINBURGH, 1st Class, 17/2; 3rd Class, 8/10.

Figure 6.20
The map depicting the 'Crieff & Loch Earn Circular Tour', also referred to as the 'Grand Circular Tour' which appeared in the Caledonian Railway guide book from 1905 onwards. This gives prominence to the route from Glasgow and Edinburgh round through Strathearn. As indicated, this tour could be taken either clockwise or anti-clockwise.   *Author's collection*

MacKenzie, who were also required to supply a locomotive to operate the line inside their boundaries.

The 1912 Tourist Guide was a more modest affair, with only half the number of pages of the previous edition. The 'Grand Circular Tour' remained, however, and the guide book now included a full-page photograph of Lochearnhead station. It would seem that efforts were still being made to promote tourism in the area, for the guide included an advertisement for the Caledonian Railway official publications, one of which was '*CRIEFF & STRATHEARN. A well written book on Holiday Resorts and attractions in the Central Highlands (Illustrated) 2d*'. Unfortunately, unlike a companion volume, the well-known Homes and Haunts of Scott and Burns, no copy appears to have survived.

Various alterations were made to the passenger timetable in 1912, with the 12.50pm Crieff to Balquhidder and the 3.5pm Crieff Junction to Crieff trains being discontinued, and the 11.40am cut back from Balquhidder to start from St. Fillans at 11.40am. However, two new trains were introduced, an 11.00am from Comrie to Crieff and the 4.56pm St. Fillans to Crieff. On the Methven Junction line, the 12.50pm from Perth to Crieff train was also discontinued. One other minor but significant point was that this timetable also reflected the renaming of the station at Crieff Junction to 'Gleneagles' with effect from 1st October 1912. This was one of the preliminary steps in the development of Donald Matheson's ambitious plan for a luxury hotel and golf course resort, which is described more fully in the next chapter.

This matter of the station name had been raised with Auchterarder Town Council back in February when the Caledonian Railway proposed the name change on the grounds that 'Crieff Junction' was confusing, although it had evidently taken over fifty years to find

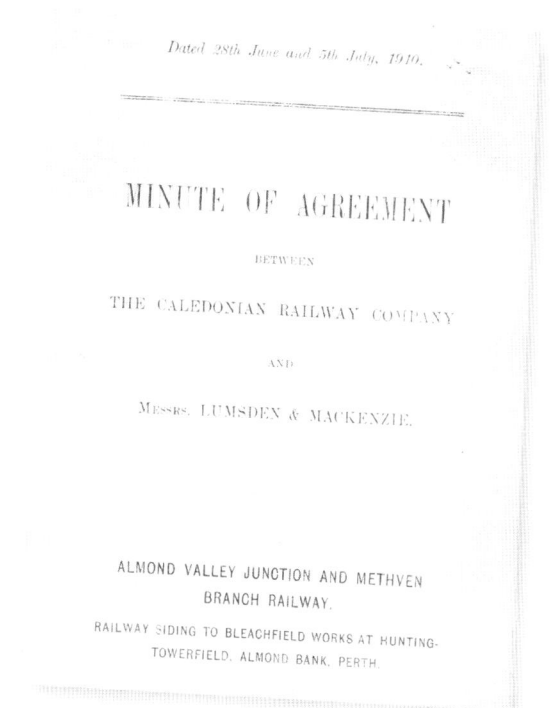

Figure 6.21
A copy of the legal agreement drawn up between the Caledonian Railway and Lumsden & MacKenzie relating to the construction, maintenance and operation of their private siding to the bleach works at Almondbank. Note that in this case the document refers to 'Almond Bank'.   *Author's collection*

Plate 6.14
CR 0-4-4T No. 439 with a train standing in the branch line platform at Balquhidder. This shot shows clearly that the platform surface was only paved for the length of the building, the remainder being simply a gravel surface. Being only a short two-coach train, this could have been one of the return workings to Lochearnhead. The engine's coal bunker is well stacked, and sacks of what are probably wool lie in the foreground. *CRA collection*

Plate 6.15
Abercairny station in Caledonian days with the station staff posing on the platform. The stationmaster on the left is easily distinguished by his distinctive frock coat. This view shows well the profusion of enamel signs which adorned stations during that era, including one for the Caledonian Railway's two hotels, and wooden notice boards, two of which carry advertisements relating to golf. The well-tended border and creepers demonstrate why Abercairny regularly featured in the prize list for Best Kept Station awards. *CRA collection*

that out. 'Auchterarder West' was proposed, but was also considered to be confusing. The name 'Gleneagles' was not favoured by the town council on the grounds that it would be known only to the locals, but the Caledonian went ahead with the name change anyway.

Unfortunately, 1912 was also a notable years for less positive reasons, seeing a marked downturn in traffic and revenue over the Strathearn lines. In fact six of the thirteen stations on the branch lines showed a decrease in revenue compared with 1911. Comrie saw a drop of £220, mainly attributable to a reduction of 3,575 in the number of passengers booked, while all the other reductions were due to falls in the all-important goods traffic. Crieff saw revenue fall by £893, which was a modest 4%, but at Muthill it fell by £308 or 22%, and worst of all was Balgowan where revenue plummeted by £169, or 26%. Methven too witnessed a fall in goods traffic, but this was offset by an increase in coaching revenue, mainly due to healthy parcels traffic.

CHAPTER 6: THE GOLDEN AGE OF THE CALEDONIAN RAILWAY

LEFT: Plate 6.16
The colour party of 1st/6th (Perthshire Volunteer) Battalion The Black Watch on the Down platform at Crieff station in the summer of 1913. The battalion annual camp that year had been held at Monzie Castle near Crieff and it is likely that this photograph shows part of battalion headquarters about to entrain at Crieff for their return to Perth. The group of nurses in the background may or may not have been connected with the annual camp.
Author's collection

RIGHT: Plate 6.17
The Officers and NCOs of the Auchterarder Company of 1st/6th Battalion The Black Watch under canvas at Monzie Castle in 1913. Monzie Castle grounds were used for the annual camps of such local Territorial Army units in 1912, 1913, and 1914. The author's grandfather, Captain TE Young, who commanded this Company, is in the centre, and behind him is Lieutenant Halley who was killed in France in 1916.
Author's collection

Plate 6.18
The Auchterarder Company setting off from Monzie Castle at the end of their annual camp in 1913 to march to Crieff station where they would catch a train to Gleneagles. They were preceded by the colour party who are depicted in Plate 6.16. A quarter of a century later the extensive grounds at Monzie were used as the venue for the third World Rover Scout Moot, as recounted in Chapter 8.
Author's collection

1913 saw a number of further changes to the timetable. The 3.4pm Balquhidder to Crieff train was cut back to St. Fillans, departing at 5.0pm. The 7.45am Perth to Balquhidder train was discontinued, although a new Saturdays Only train from Balquhidder to Comrie at 6.5pm was introduced. The 'Grand Circular Tour' appeared as usual in the 1913 Tourist Guide, although the map was a little out of date as it still showed Crieff Junction rather than Gleneagles. A new advertisement for the Commercial Hotel in Crieff stated that *'Boots with conveyance meets all trains'*.

Boots of a different nature were in evidence again in July that year when the Royal Highlanders returned to Monzie Castle for their annual camp. Some fifteen special trains arrived at Crieff from Edinburgh, including at least four North British Railway trains bringing the troops to their camp. There were 5,000 soldiers camped under canvas at Monzie, including the Auchterarder Company of 6th Battalion, commanded by the author's grandfather, Captain TE Young.

That year also saw much initial planning of the development of Gleneagles Hotel and Golf Courses. The current Crieff Junction station, by now renamed Gleneagles, was considered quite unsuitable for such a prestigious project and was to be completely remodelled. One associated bone of contention had been the long delays caused by the level crossings at both Blackford on the main line and the Auchterarder Road level crossing by which the Crieff branch line crossed the same Stirling to Perth main road.

As early as 1908, a traffic survey had been conducted at Blackford of the number of vehicles delayed at the level crossing on certain dates during July and August that year. Between 7am and 10.0pm on 9th August, for example, 488 motor cycles, 304 motor vans, 786 light vehicles and 439 heavy vehicles were delayed at the level crossing. The total duration of the stoppages at the crossing had been 169 minutes or 2 hours 49 minutes, with the length of stoppage varying from 5 to as much as 18 minutes.

The majority of this traffic would also have had to cross the Auchterarder Road level crossing at Gleneagles, although the degree of stoppages would have been a good deal less due to the smaller number of trains on the branch line. Nonetheless, with the ever increasing number of motor vehicles taking to the roads – the number of registered motor vehicles in the United Kingdom having risen from 18,000 in 1904 to some 306,000 by 1913 – Perthshire County Council were keen for something to be done.

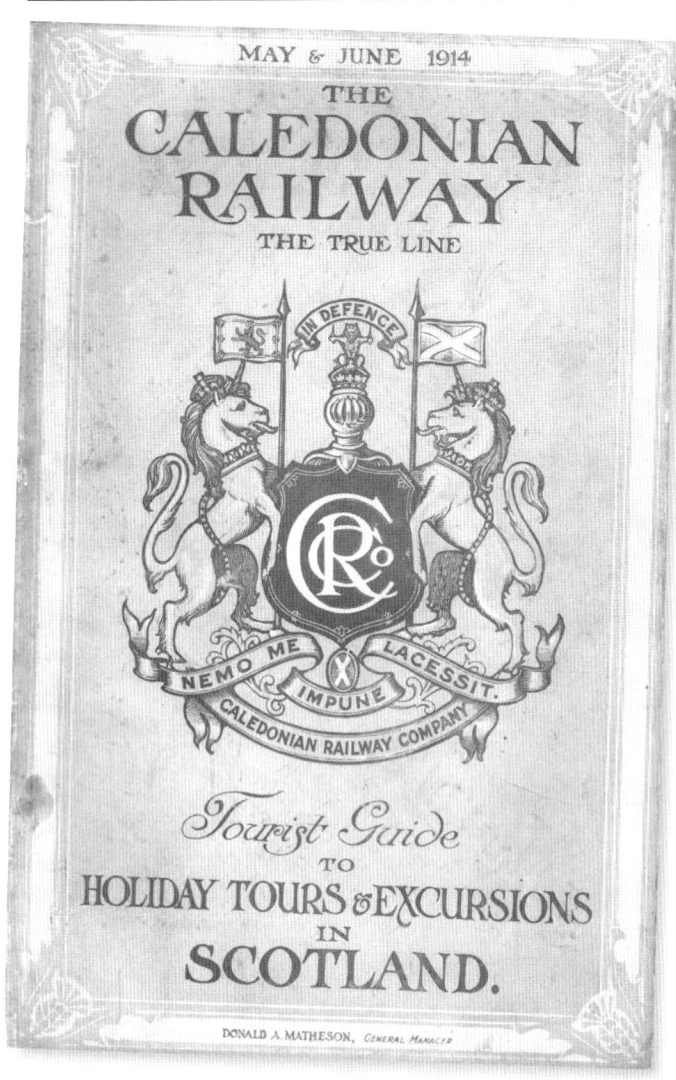

The county council applied to the Imperial Road Board for a grant to erect bridges at Blackford and Gleneagles, but were turned down. Subsequently they entered into negotiations with the Caledonian Railway, which in the case of the Gleneagles level crossing responded by offering to contribute half the estimated cost of £4,000 for the bridge. The county council declined this offer, despite the fact that the bridge had been their initiative, but agreed that the railway company could carry out the improvements at their own cost. The Caledonian had little option but to proceed on these grounds, which they duly did.

There was no hint of the impending war when the 1914 Tourist Guide for the summer season was issued in May of that year. This was one of the first guides to include the promotion of Gleneagles as a tourist destination, work having started on the hotel at Easter.

The title of the 'Grand Circular Tour' was altered to include Gleneagles and the name of Crieff Junction was finally corrected on the map. The table of Tourist Fares included fares to Gleneagles from sixteen English stations, including, in addition to the principal cities, such places as Alderley Edge, Bristol, Preston and Warrington.

Surprisingly, promotion of Gleneagles continued through 1915 despite the fact that construction on the hotel had been suspended the previous autumn, for the 1915 edition of the Caledonian Railway Tourist Guide included the following glowing reference:

> 'Gleneagles district is about to become one of the finest holiday centres in the country. A great new hotel is being built with all the features of modern luxury. While a superb golf course is being laid out – the finest inland course in the kingdom – and with the glorious air of the place, lying high on the watershed between East and West, there will be health and entertainment of the very best for the exacting holiday maker.'

The advent of the motor car as a vehicle for tourism was reflected for the first time in several of the advertisements in the 1914 guide, including one for Harold Barrington of Crieff, whose later 1916 advertisement is illustrated below, and reference was made in the advertisements for the Drummond Arms Hotel at St. Fillans of the availability of a garage and petrol.

The outbreak of the First World War on 4th August affected the branch lines of Strathearn as it did all the railways of the United Kingdom. The Territorial Army was mobilised on the 5th August and

ABOVE: Figure 6.22
The Caledonian Railway Tourist Guide for May and June 1914, the penultimate issue prior to the outbreak of the First World War. This less colourful and simpler cover depicted one of the various versions of the Caledonian Railway crests used by the company. This A5-size booklet was much slimmer than in previous years, running to only 174 pages. *Author's collection*

Figure 6.23
One of a number of advertisements for garages in Crieff which appeared in the 1916 edition of the Caledonian Railway Tourist Guide. These advertisements were aimed at the railway passenger arriving in Crieff, but the range of vehicles and services offered were a portent of the increasing competition which was emerging from the advent of the motor car. Eventually it would be the increasing use of cars and buses which would bring about the demise of the Strathearn lines. Interestingly, the content of the 1916 guide gave little hint that there was a war on. *Author's collection*

the 4th Battalion Perthshire Volunteers, by now renamed 6th Battalion The Black Watch under the 1908 reforms of Lord Haldane, deployed to their war station. Although no documentary evidence survives, the Crieff Companies would have travelled by train from Crieff to Inverkeithing in Fife to take up their war station; this was at Carlingnose near North Queensferry, part of the defences of the naval base at Rosyth.

One notable change in traffic in 1914, other than a fall in passenger numbers which was to be expected, was a significant increase in horse traffic. At that early stage of the war, virtually all British Army transport was horse drawn, and large numbers of additional horses were required as the army rapidly expanded. A great number of horses were used on the land and in rural areas such as Strathearn. The movement of horses by stations on the Strathearn lines in 1914 rose to 1,404 and, although no breakdown exists, it is reasonable to assume that most of this traffic related to horses for the army.

Most stations recorded an increase in horse traffic, including even small stations such as Balgowan where the number nearly doubled from twelve to twenty-two. The biggest increase was credited to Muthill, where horse traffic rose by nearly 80% from fifty-two to ninety-three. The only station to record a fall was Comrie, but this was probably due to the curtailed tourist season, as carriage traffic also fell by over 50%. The distribution of horse boxes in the 1909 Caledonian Railway instruction on this subject allocated fifteen to Perth to cover all the stations between Almond Valley Junction and Lochearnhead, and six to Stirling to cover the Crieff Junction line, so they would have been kept busy.

By 1915, when it had become obvious that the war was not going to be over quickly, railway services began to be pruned. In Strathearn, the effect was most keenly felt in Upper Strathearn, where the 6.35am Comrie to Crieff, 10.22am Balquhidder to Crieff Junction and the 11.45am St. Fillans to Crieff were discontinued, and the 12.20pm and 4.30pm trains from Balquhidder were both cut back to start from St. Fillans, reducing the number of Up trains per day between Balquhidder and St. Fillans to only three. The 1.31pm passenger train from Gleneagles to Crieff was also discontinued, although an additional goods train was run in its place, leaving Gleneagles at 1.25pm.

Some aspects of life continued unaltered, thus, for example, the Working Time Table included an updated version of the instructions relating to Crieff Hydro:

'The Stationmaster at Gleneagles, or the Chief Ticket Examiner at Perth will ascertain if there are any passengers in the Crieff train for Strathearn Hydropathic Establishment, Crieff, and if so, will telegraph or telephone the same to the Hydropathic Establishment so that the necessary conveyance may be provided for the passengers.'

Other changes in traffic patterns continued to emerge. The volume of goods traffic forwarded by station in Strathearn rose steadily during the war. The peak goods traffic figures over a forty-year period were achieved by ten out of the thirteen intermediate stations at some stage during the period 1914-19. Some spectacular increases were recorded, such as at Abercairny, where traffic rose from a pre-war level of 700-800 tons to 6,999 tons in one year. Revenue figures for Madderty rose from £1,526 to £7,052, while even Lochearnhead achieved a ten-fold increase in revenue from £245 to £2,637.

Much of this increase was probably due to timber traffic in aid of the war effort, in addition to traditional traffic such as pit props for coal mines. Indeed, the Canadian Forestry Corps established a camp near Methven station during the war years. It was not unusual for timber to be loaded directly onto wagons from the lineside closest to the area where it had been cut, rather than the nearest station. An example of this was a Caledonian Railway Weekly Instruction Notice dated 24th November 1918:

'Messrs D Wishart & Co, Timber Merchants, Kirkcaldy, will load a quantity of timber from the line side between Balquhidder and St. Fillans at a point about a mile from Balquhidder (West) signal box, and the line between Balquhidder West and St. Fillans will be blocked from 6.40am to 6.40pm. For this purpose an Engine and Brake Van with 5 bogie wagons will leave Balquhidder at 6.40am, return to Balquhidder for empty wagons, leave again at 10.35am with 5 bogie wagons and return at 1.30pm for more wagons and relief Trainmen, leave again for site of operations at 2.10pm with 6 bogie wagons, returning to Balquhidder when work is finished, which is expected to be about 5.30pm. The wagons must be propelled in each case from the point of loading so that the engine will be on the lower end of the incline. The Balquhidder engine and Brakesman will commence the work and carry on to 2.0pm when they will be relieved by an Engine and Brakevan which will leave Stirling at 12.00 noon. The Signalman at Balquhidder (West) must draw the tablet for the section to St. Fillans.'

Fortunately this work did not interfere with normal operations, as there was no service over the line on a Sunday. Lochearnhead signal box was closed at this time, so the token section was Balquhidder (West) to St. Fillans as indicated above.

Livestock traffic also saw some dramatic increases during this period. Muthill dealt with 153 wagon-loads in 1917 compared with a pre-war average of around 40 wagon-loads a year. A peak day for traffic was Friday, when livestock was dispatched to Perth for the weekly sale, and the 1915 Working Time Table included new instructions relating to such traffic. All stationmasters at stations between Comrie and Perth were required to inform the District Traffic Superintendent of details of livestock to be conveyed, and how many wagons, full or part, were required.

1916 saw further trimming of services, with the 8.0am Lochearnhead to Balquhidder, 3.5pm Gleneagles to St. Fillans, and the 3.30pm mixed train from Balquhidder to Crieff all being withdrawn, and the 10.0am Crieff to Balquhidder cut back to

Plate 6.19
An official portrait of Donald Alexander Matheson in 1905 when he was still the Chief Engineer of the Caledonian Railway, which position he held from 1899 until September 1910 when he was appointed General Manger in succession to Guy Calthrop. Born in Perthshire and educated at Perth Academy, he was apprenticed to Mr John Young MICE of Perth from 1887 until 1891, before embarking on a railway career which culminated in his joining the Caledonian Railway. It was as General Manager of the Caledonian that Matheson was able to turn his vision for Gleneagles Hotel and Golf Courses into reality. *Author's collection*

St. Fillans. The one new train introduced was a 12.50pm passenger working from Balquhidder to Gleneagles.

Work on the Gleneagles Hotel remained suspended, but that on the golf courses went on. Traffic continued to be handled over the hotel siding, and the local instructions contained in the Working Time Table specified that:

> 'Wagons must be propelled from Gleneagles to the siding, and drawn from the Siding to Gleneagles, the object being to have the engine always at the lower, or Gleneagles end of the wagons. The rounding of the wagons must be performed in the loop line inside the Catch Points. Stations forwarding traffic in wagon loads for the New Hotel, Gleneagles Ltd, or any of the contractors in connection therewith must label the Wagons to "Gleneagles Hotel Siding". All such traffic carried on the 1.40am from St. Rollox must be detached at Greenloaning and worked forward from there by the 9.0am Goods Train, Stirling to Auchterarder, the engine of which will work the siding until further notice.'

Despite the war, tourism was still being promoted by the Caledonian Railway and the 1916 edition of their Scottish Holiday Resorts included an updated paragraph on Crieff which makes interesting reading:

> 'Crieff, the capital of Strathearn, might, for all the world be some little old-world town on the Rhine, with a luxurious hydropathic, instead of a grim medieval stronghold, towering on the hillside at its head, and the little narrow street slopping down by well and square to the Earn flowing silvery at its feet.'

This ill-concealed reference to what could be construed as *'the dastardly Hun'* probably reflected popular feeling at the time, as well as contemporary prose. The guide also contained a glowing reference to the projected Gleneagles Hotel, although work on the main building remained suspended:

> 'In the same Strathearn, a few miles to the south, there is being built the most modern and luxurious of all Scottish Spas. Where the famous pass of Gleneagles debouches through the

Plate 6.20
A formal studio photograph of Mr William Millar, the stationmaster at Crieff, taken in 1922 showing the detail of his Caledonian Railway uniform. He wears his frock coat with embroidered epaulettes, a waistcoat and his cap, also with embroidered badge and band. This photograph was taken by Mr Mackenzie at his studio in Ferntower Road, Crieff.
CRA collection

Plate 6.21
A team photograph of Mr Millar, the stationmaster at Crieff, with most of his staff, at the west end of the Down platform. Only nineteen staff are shown here, but as these include only two signalman, others would have been on duty or days off. William Millar's two sons are seated on the ground in the front row, Robert being second from the left and his brother William on the far right. On the far left of the second row, William Marshall, one of the ticket collectors, can be seen carrying his ticket nippers in a special pocket, while on the far right of the same row, Robert Amos, passenger guard, wears the distinctive cross belt of his grade.
CRA collection

Ochils, and the height of the watershed in a rare upland of heathery moors, and old moraines, a great hotel is being built under the aegis of the Caledonian Railway Company, and what will be the finest golf course is being laid out at its doors. With tennis courts and a swimming pond, the finest angling waters in the country within easy reach, and every modern luxury within doors, and around, Gleneagles promises to be the very last word in the modern British spa.'

This particular format of guide book included comprehensive lists of accommodation and local facilities. The entry for Crieff listed no fewer than fifty-five establishments, mostly villas or private hotels. Each stressed their attractions, including views, gardens and being near the station, golf course or bowling green. Most were *'with attendance'*, and Laurel House on the Comrie Road even boasted a telephone (Crieff 68). There were also advertisements for the Cinema (Manager Mr P Crerar) and four garages or motor agents, one example being that shown at Figure 6.23.

The entry for Comrie listed hotels and a more modest six private residences. Most claimed to be *'beautifully situated'* and to be near the golf course or the fishing. An advertisement for the Ancaster Arms helpfully stated: *'bus meets all trains'*. In this section there was a whole range of advertisements for local Comrie businesses, including Duncan Comrie, Stables, W Drummond, Coal Merchant, and M McNab, Motors and Cycles.

St. Fillans also figured in the list, although, interestingly, there was no mention of either Lochearnhead or Balquhidder. The St. Fillans entry listed seventeen establishments, although there were no actual advertisements. Most of those listed stated that they had a boat on the loch, and one claimed to be near the station and golf course, while seven establishments mentioned that they had a piano. It would seem that evening entertainment in St. Fillans in those days was somewhat limited!

As the war entered its third year, the effects began to be reflected in the traffic patterns on the Strathearn branch lines. Lochearnhead was closed entirely from 1st January 1917 as a wartime economy measure, while Highlandman and Innerpeffray stations were both closed to passengers from the same date for similar reasons. Passenger figures for other stations reached all-time lows in 1917, including Almondbank (5,032), Comrie (27,117) and St. Fillans (6,684). Even Crieff recorded an all-time low of only 62,286, only just over half that for its best ever year. One station to buck the trend was Balgowan, whose passenger figures increased during the war years, probably reflecting nearby military activity.

In some cases the war had the opposite effect on traffic, as already mentioned, with increases in goods, livestock, milk and, at times, horse traffic. Balgowan saw a marked increase in goods traffic, reaching a peak of 5,991 tons in 1919, while livestock traffic was also healthy. Muthill recorded substantial milk traffic, starting from 1,436 gallons in 1916 to a high of 8,632 gallons in 1918. Abercairny too became a significant milk exporter, with a maximum of 8,599 gallons sent out in 1919.

From these figures it is evident that a considerable amount of goods and other non-passenger traffic was still being handled as the war drew to a close in 1918, and even into 1919. Indeed, horse traffic increased in these two years, almost certainly reflecting the return of horses from the army during the large-scale demobilisation which followed the Armistice on 11th November 1918.

The end of the war also heralded the resumption of work on the Gleneagles project, although initially only on the rebuilding of the station and the elimination of the troublesome Auchterarder Road level crossing. The new station opened on 1st October 1919 and, as illustrated in Chapter 3, this was commemorated by a stone set into the wall below the bay window.

Over the next couple of years the railways struggled to overcome the effects of the war and, in this respect, the branch lines of Strathearn were no exception. Traffic, other than that already mentioned, began to return, but barely reached pre-war levels. Methven, Lochearnhead and Highlandman stations reopened on 1st February 1919, but Innerpeffray did not reopen until 2nd June 1919, and then only after representations by Crieff Town Council.

One further post-war change occurred in 1920, when the last of the women who had been employed by the Caledonian Railway as signalwomen at local stations to make good the shortage of manpower during the war now lost their jobs. Miss June Buchan and Miss Margaret Thompson, who had worked Crieff West signal box for four years, received presentations from the stationmaster, while Miss Mary McPherson who had been a signalwoman at Comrie subsequently emigrated to Canada.

The 1920 Caledonian Railway Time Table was a very much slimmed down version of its pre-war equivalent, running to only 68 pages. Despite this, the Gleneagles to Crieff line now enjoyed a service of eleven trains each way per day with an additional mid-afternoon train on Saturdays. The Crieff to Balquhidder section had seven trains each way per day, although three of these terminated at St. Fillans, such that the St. Fillans to Lochearnhead section was only served by four of these. At the western end, however, there was one additional train which made a return trip from Balquhidder to Lochearnhead each morning.

As previously mentioned, Dalchonzie Platform did not appear in the timetable as such, but notes were added to the effect that passengers were required to notify the guard at either Comrie or

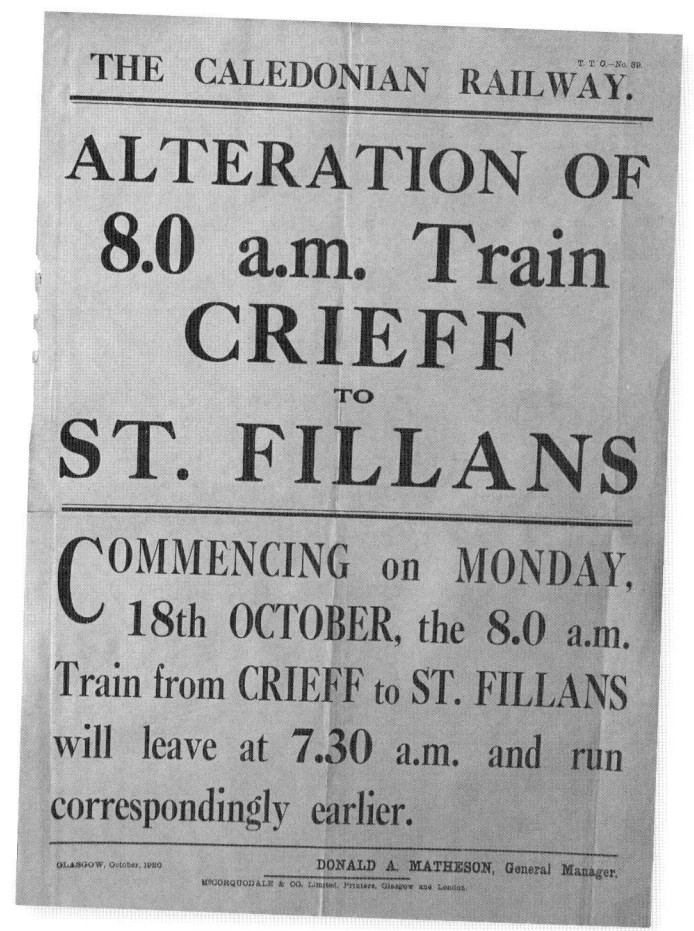

Figure 6.24
A Caledonian Railway poster dated October 1920 announcing the changed timing of the 8.0am train from St. Fillans to Crieff. As the only intermediate stations were Dalchonzie Platform and Comrie, there cannot have been a great demand for this particular poster, and very few copies would have been printed. This example comes from one of McCorquodale's printer's proof books. *Author's collection*

Plate 6.22
The north end of Gleneagles station in late Caledonian days with Caledonian Railway 4-6-0 No. 905 on an Up train and an unidentified 0-4-4T on a train for Crieff in the branch line platform. Both the Down Main and Down Branch signals are off in this striking pose of the two trains ready to depart. The landscaping and new trees visible along the approach road indicate that this view was taken not long after the station opened. Part of the sign for Gleneagles Golf Courses can just be seen on the extreme left.
BRB Residuary

St. Fillans of their desire to alight at Dalchonzie. Passengers wishing to join the train at Dalchonzie were advised to notify the signalman at least 5 minutes before the train was due that they wished to do so. Dalchonzie Platform being an unstaffed halt, the notes also stated that no bicycles or heavy luggage would be taken into or put out of trains there.

The Perth to Crieff line via Methven Junction fared less well than the others, with only five trains each way per day. However, there was an additional train each way on Saturdays, and two further Saturdays Only trains to Methven. Various trains were listed to call at Ruthven Road and Tibbermuir, some by request when signalled to do so by the gatekeeper. The 8.45am through train from St. Fillans and the 12.5pm train from Perth to Balquhidder were both annotated to the effect that they may pick up vehicles en route, so they may run a few minutes late. A curious specification was that the 7.50am from Perth was to call at Madderty: '*Only when required to pick up passengers for the Callander & Oban line*'.

The 1921 Caledonian Railway Time Table reverted to something akin to the pre-war edition, with additional information regarding fares and tickets. Of more interest to the Strathearn lines was the list of 'Through Carriages' to and from the principal cities in Scotland. Crieff had a number, and Balquhidder had just one, but significantly there was no mention of Comrie or St. Fillans. These workings were:

From Crieff
8. 8am	Edinburgh (Princes Street)
8. 8am	Glasgow (Buchanan Street)
8.30am	Dundee

From Edinburgh (Princes Street)
4.25pm   Crieff

From Dundee
1. 5pm   Crieff (Saturdays Only)
4.45pm   Crieff
4.45pm   Balquhidder

Perhaps the most dramatic event affecting the railways in 1920 was the miners' strike in October that year. This not only robbed the Caledonian Railway of a considerable volume of mineral traffic, but also led to a coal shortage. To reduce coal consumption, various contingency measures were planned and put in place to curtail train services. The Caledonian Railway instructions relating to this situation stated:

'*In consequence of the Strike of Coal Miners, a revised Time Table was brought in to operation on 20th October 1920. This remained in operation until Sunday, 7th November, and resulted in a decrease in mileage of 33.49% on Weekdays, 34.26% on Saturdays, and 22.48% on Sundays. Special Time Table leaflets and posters were produced and distributed.*'

The effect on the Strathearn branch lines was significant. The various passenger services were reduced as follows:

– Gleneagles to Crieff	From 7 to 6
– Crieff to St. Fillans	From 7 to 4
– St. Fillans to Balquhidder	From 6 to 2
– Crieff to Perth	From 6 to 3

One anomaly was that the Methven branch line appeared to have retained its full service of six trains each way per day, some of which now had no connecting service to Crieff or Perth from Methven

CHAPTER 6: THE GOLDEN AGE OF THE CALEDONIAN RAILWAY

Plate 6.23
Caledonian Railway McIntosh 4-4-0 'Dunalastair III' Class No. 889 on a north-bound stopping train at Gleneagles in the early 1920s. Standing next to the signal box on the Up Main platform, the crew appear to be waiting for the 'right away' from the guard before setting off on the falling gradient through Auchterarder and Dunning towards Perth. *KG Young*

RIGHT: **Plate 6.24**
Caledonian Railway Pickersgill 4-4-0 No. 82 on a Stirling-bound stopping passenger train standing in the Up platform at Gleneagles in the early 1920s. Trains starting from here did so on the climbing gradient towards the summit a mile or so to the west before reaching Blackford. No. 82 was nearly new when this photograph was taken. A Perth-bound train stands in the Down platform.
KG Young

Junction. All goods services on the Strathearn branch lines were also suspended during this period.

The revised timetable had a knock-on effect on the marshalling of trains, particularly main line passenger workings, and a special instruction was issued. This, for example, revealed the composition of the 8.8am train from Crieff as:

Crieff to Glasgow	**Return working**
Brake Composite	4.15pm Glasgow to Stirling
Composite	thence 5.50pm Stirling to Crieff
Third Class	
Brake Third	
Crieff to Edinburgh	**Return working**
Brake Composite	4.25pm Edinburgh to Stirling
	thence 5.50pm Stirling to Crieff
Stirling to Glasgow	**Return working**
Brake Third	6.10am Glasgow to Crieff
Composite	
Brake Third	

Further contingency timetables reflecting another reduction of 3% in mileage were prepared but never issued, and yet another provisional timetable reflected a further reduction of 10%, almost halving many normal services. This too was never issued, but it would not have had any further impact on the Strathearn branch lines.

Despite the effect of the coal miners' strike which lasted over two weeks, 1920 was a good year for the Strathearn stations, seven of which recorded increased revenue over 1919, which had also been a good year for most of them. Balgowan booked a record 10,278 passengers and Highlandman 5,132, while Madderty achieved 15,051. Crieff increased revenue by £17,927, largely due to an increase in goods traffic with 15,594 tons dispatched and 10,475 tons received. Lochearnhead also recorded increased goods traffic, while for stations such as St. Fillans and Muthill, increases in revenues were due to better figure for various classes of traffic. In the case of Tullibardine, passenger numbers rose and a record 9,278 gallons of milk was sent out.

By 1921, golf at Gleneagles was in full swing. That year's edition of the Caledonian Railway Tourist Guide included a revised description:

But it is the golf courses, stretching along the high lying ridge to the left, and unseen from the railway which have given Gleneagles its world-wide fame … The war, and post war conditions have of necessity delayed completion of the palatial hotel alongside the courses, but meanwhile, and until such time as the hotel is finished and available, an excellent service of express trains at convenient hours between Glasgow, Edinburgh, Bridge of Allan, Dunblane, Perth, Crieff etc makes light of the lack of hotel accommodation at immediate hand.'

It is doubtful if the golfers who had to struggle off the train with their clubs and catch a bus to the course would have agreed with this sentiment, and it would seem that the wording used was another case of the Caledonian Railway making a virtue of necessity! The guide also included a prominent advertisement for golf at Gleneagles, but, interestingly, there was no advertisement for the 'Grand Circular Tour'.

Work on the hotel was now well in hand, as described in the next chapter, with material being delivered by rail to the site by the hotel branch line. A small goods yard with several sidings was laid down adjacent to the level crossing over the Dunfermline to Crieff road as can be seen on the map at Figure 7.33. The instructions for the use of the line were now revised yet again to read:

'All wagons for the siding will be propelled from Gleneagles to the entrance to the siding, where the Engine will round them in the loop, and again propel them to the short siding at the Crieff to Glendevon road, and while propelling along the hotel siding the Driver must frequently sound the Engine whistle to warn all concerned of the approach of the engine, or engine with wagons.

The speed of the Engine passing over the Hotel Siding must not exceed 8 mph.'

The 1921 timetable included a number of changes to services on the Strathearn branch lines, with six new trains being introduced. These were the 9.50am Gleneagles to Crieff, the 10.22am express

T.T.O. No. 50.

CALEDONIAN RAILWAY.

MINERS' STRIKE

RESTRICTED PASSENGER TRAIN SERVICE,

Commencing Wednesday, 20th October, 1920.

Crieff, Comrie, St. Fillans, Lochearnhead, and Balquhidder.

						P						
		a.m.	a.m.	a.m.		a.m.	p.m.	p.m.	p.m.	p.m.		p.m.
Gleneagles .... leave	...	6 45	...	8 56	...	11 18	...	3 5	...	6 32	...	8 35
Tullibardine . . ,,	.	.	.	9 2	.	11 24	.	3 11	.	6 38	.	8 41
Muthill .... ,,	..	6 56	..	9 9	..	11 31	..	3 18	..	6 45	..	8 46
Highlandman ...... ,,	...	...	...	9 16	...	11 38	...	3 25	...	6 52	...	...
Crieff . . . . . arrive	.	7 4		9 20	.	11 42	.	3 29	.	6 56	.	8 56
Crieff leave	.	.	7 46	.	.	.	12 47	3 32	5 55	7 0	.	.
Comrie .... arrive	..	..	8 1	..	..	..	1 2	3 47	6 10	7 15	..	..
Comrie leave	..	..	8 3	..	..	..	1 3	3 48	6 11	...	..	..
St. Fillans ....arrive	...	...	8 18	...	...	..	1 16	4 0	6 23	...	...	...
Lochearnhead . . leave	.	.	.	.	.	.	1 32	.	6 39	.	.	.
Balquhidder ......arrive	..	..	..	..	..	..	1 38	..	6 45	..	..	..

Any of the Trains to St. Fillans will call at Dalchonzie Platform (between Comrie and St. Fillans) to set down Passengers on their intimating to the Station Master at Comrie their desire to alight. No Heavy Luggage or Bicycles will be taken into or put out of the Trains at Dalchonzie Platform.

								P				
	a.m.	a.m.	a.m.	a.m.		p.m.	p.m.	p.m.		p.m.		
Balquhidder . . . leave	.	6 50	.	.	.	.	1 50	.	.	.	.	.
Lochearnhead .... ,,	..	6 57	..	..	..	..	1 57	..	..	..	..	..
St. Fillans .... ,,	...	7 16	...	8 45	...	..	2 10	4 25	...	...	...	...
Comrie . . . . arrive	.	7 28	.	8 57	.	.	2 22	4 37	.	.	.	.
Comrie leave	.	7 30	.	8 59	.	.	2 24	4 39	.	7 30	.	.
Crieff.......... arrive	..	7 45	..	9 14	..	..	2 39	4 54	..	7 45	..	..
Crieff leave	7 15	..	8 8	9 25	...	1 35	..	4 56	..	7 47	...	..
Highlandman ...... ,,	7 19	...	8C12	9 29	...	1 39	...	5 0	...	7 51	...	...
Muthill . . . . . ,,	7 24	.	8 17	9 34	.	1 45	.	5 6	.	7 57	.	.
Tullibardine .... ,,	7 30	..	..	9 40	..	1 51	..	5 12	..	8 3	..	..
Gleneagles ....arrive	7 36	...	8 30	9 47	...	1 58	...	5 19	...	8 10	...	...

Any of the Trains from St. Fillans will call at Dalchonzie Platform (between St. Fillans and Comrie) to set down Passengers on their intimating to the Station Master at St. Fillans their desire to alight, and to take up Passengers on their intimating to the Signalman at Dalchonzie at least 5 minutes before the Train is due to leave St. Fillans. No Heavy Luggage will be taken into or put out of the Trains at Dalchonzie Platform.

C—Calls at Highlandman at 8 12 a.m., only when required, to pick up Passengers for Larbert or beyond.

P—Trains marked **P** attach Vehicles *en route*, when required, and may run a few minutes later.

Figure 6.25
One of the leaflets specially printed and distributed showing the reduced passenger train service in operation during the miners' strike in October 1920. This shows the reduced service for the Gleneagles–Balquhidder service. Details of the Perth–Methven–Crieff services were on the reverse side. This was the only emergency timetable which was actually implemented, although several more contingency timetables were drawn up in case further reductions were necessary. *Author's collection*

from Gleneagles to Balquhidder, which left Glasgow at 8.45am, the 8.45am St. Fillans to Gleneagles and a mixed train from Balquhidder to Lochearnhead at 7.25am. The 6.45am from Gleneagles now terminated at Crieff rather than St. Fillans, with the result that the 11.15am mixed train from St. Fillans to Crieff was now retimed to 12 noon and ran as a goods train.

After the encouraging results of 1920, a number of Strathearn stations saw a drop in revenue in 1921. Almondbank, Innerpeffray and St. Fillans all had a poor year, while revenue at Crieff fell by £10,217, in large part due to a drop of nearly 25% in livestock traffic.

Lochearnhead recorded a reduction of £149 in coaching revenue, but Innerpeffray bucked the trend that year, recording an increased revenue of £343, largely due to an increase in mineral traffic and a record 107 horses.

The final year of the Caledonian Railway, 1922, saw further changes to the timetable. In the main these affected the Upper Strathearn section of the line, with the 8.45am from Gleneagles now terminating at Comrie, and the 9.20am cut back to Crieff. The 8.25am from Balquhidder now started from St. Fillans, and there were no runs between Balquhidder and Lochearnhead. This reduced the passenger service between St. Fillans and Balquhidder to only three trains each way per day.

The popularity of the golf courses at Gleneagles continued to grow. The 1922 Public Time Table made first mention of the bus service provided from Gleneagles station, stating: 'Motor buses meet the trains with which golfers usually travel at Gleneagles station and convey golfers to and from the Club House.'

Mention was also made in this timetable of the bus service between Auchterarder Town and Gleneagles station. Motor buses met twelve trains each day at Gleneagles to convey passengers to Auchterarder, while there were thirteen departures from Auchterarder to connect with trains from Gleneagles. At least two buses were employed as some of the departure times coincided.

The final year was also a poor one for quite a number of Strathearn stations, with revenue falling. On the Methven Junction line, Madderty saw revenue fall by £146, largely due to a collapse in goods traffic to pre-war levels, at only 2,558 tons. At the other end of the line, goods traffic fell heavily at Lochearnhead with revenue down £408, or nearly 33%. On the Crieff Junction line, revenues dropped at both Tullibardine and Muthill due to falls in traffic across the board, with goods traffic at Muthill halved to its pre-war level. Receipts at Crieff itself continued to slide, being £6,688 less than 1921, due mainly to falls in mineral and goods traffic. In fact goods traffic in 1922 was only a third of that two years previously. That said, passenger numbers at Crieff held up with 100,996 booked in 1922. The same could not be said of Almondbank, however, where the figure of 16,446 was just half that of 1883, the earliest year covered by the records.

It is evident from the traffic figures for the stations on the branch lines of Strathearn that the railways were starting to feel the pinch. Passenger traffic was holding up reasonably well, aided by the summer tourist trade, but an increasing proportion of the all-important goods traffic was gradually being lost to road haulage. The railways were also still recovering from the austerity and under-investment of the war years, and in this respect the Strathearn was

Figure 6.26
All Caledonian Railway guards usually carried a rubber stamp to frank or endorse waybills and invoices of traffic carried on the train for which they were responsible. This waybill for a hamper containing five live fowls dispatched from Muthill to Coupar Angus by the 12.5pm train on 14th April 1903 has been stamped by Robert Amos. For twenty-five years he was one of the guards stationed at Crieff and appears in the staff photograph illustrated at Plate 6.21.   *Author's collection*

Plate 6.25
A rare view of Caledonian Railway 0-4-4T No. 459 on a Crieff-bound branch line train, seen in the branch platform at Gleneagles in the early 1920s. The locomotive is standing almost adjacent to the signal box at the east end of the platform. Unfortunately the background details have been lost from this rather primitive view. Nonetheless, it can be seen that No. 459 is in smart condition and has a full bunker of coal.
    KG Young

Plate 6.26
An unusual view of Caledonian Railway Pickersgill 4-6-0 No. 956 standing in the branch line platform at Gleneagles in the early 1920s. This train may either have come off the Crieff branch line or been run into the branch loop to attach through carriages from Crieff to a southbound train. These locomotives were occasional visitors to Crieff so either scenario may apply. No. 956 was only a year or two old when this shot was taken, and probably excited the interest of the photographer, the author's father. The new station nameboard can be seen in the background carrying the lettering 'GLENEAGLES For AUCHTERARDER WEST' as preferred by the Caledonian Railway. In later years the word 'west' was dropped. *KG Young*

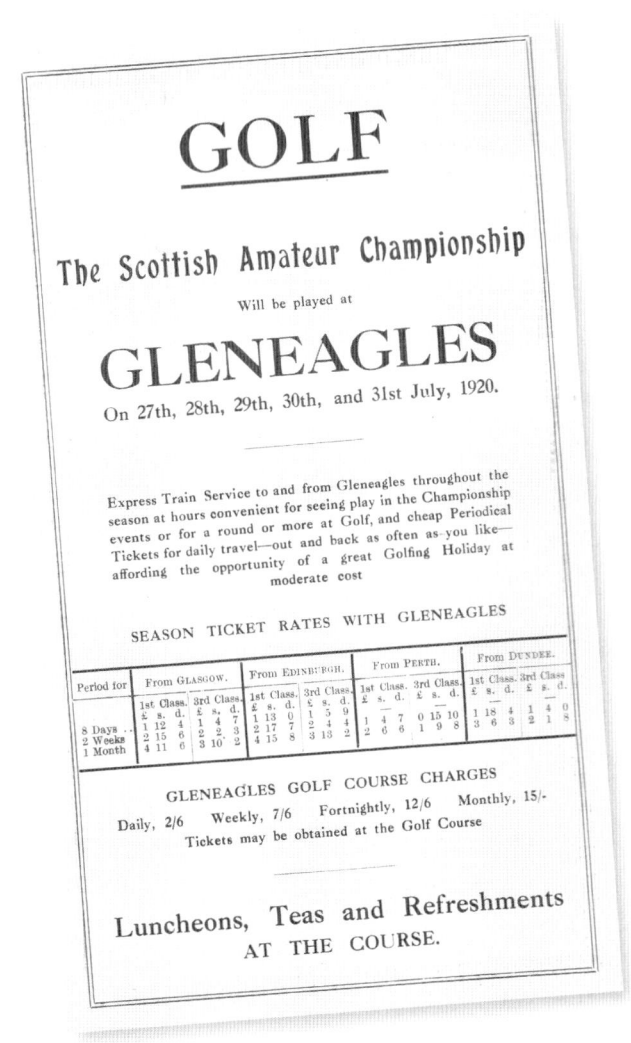

no exception. The one project which was under way again was the completion of the much heralded Gleneagles Hotel, but it would not be ready to open until 1924, and then as part of the London Midland & Scottish Railway, not the Caledonian Railway, as described more fully in the next chapter.

The Caledonian Railway became part of the London Midland & Scottish Railway under the reorganisation of the railways of England, Scotland and Wales on 1st January 1923, although as the result of a rear-guard action by disgruntled shareholders it remained a separate legal entity until 1st July 1923. To all intents and purposes, however, it became part of the Northern Division of the LM&SR from 1st January that year, together with the Glasgow & South Western and Highland railways.

For the original branch lines of Strathearn this represented the first change in ownership in nearly sixty years, but the LM&SR era was destined to last only less than half this time. The halcyon days of the Caledonian were over and a new era of reality was about to dawn.

Figure 6.27
An advertisement which appeared on the inside cover of the Caledonian Railway Tourist Guide for 1920. The Scottish Amateur Open was one of a number of golf tournaments hosted by Gleneagles in the years before the hotel was opened when only the golf course was available. The catering facilities referred to were available from the Club House which had been completed. The season ticket rates offered correspond to the various period tickets available for golf. There was no annual season ticket at this stage. *Author's collection*

Figure 6.28
A Caledonian Railway Company advertisement promoting Gleneagles Golf Courses which appeared in the 1922 edition of the Public Time Table, this being the last year of operation before the Caledonian became part of the London, Midland & Scottish Railway Company in 1923. By 1922 the Caledonian Railway had already had to bail out and take over Gleneagles Ltd and work was in hand to complete the hotel. The annual subscription of guineas shown here had increased considerably by 1939. *Author's collection*

Chapter 7
Gleneagles Hotel

By the turn of the century, the reputation of Strathearn as a tourist destination was already well established and, as described in Chapter 6, the Caledonian Railway had promoted it vigorously for many years. With the completion of the final section of the Comrie, St. Fillans and Lochearnhead line in 1905, the network of branch lines serving the Strath was complete and its reputation as a place to visit further enhanced.

The virtues of the district are extolled in the book *Golf at Gleneagles* by RJ MacLennan, published on behalf of the Caledonian Railway to promote the new golf courses at Gleneagles and the planned hotel. He quotes Sir Walter Scott as writing that *'Amid all the provinces of Scotland if an intelligent stranger were asked to describe the most varied and the most beautiful, it is probable he would name the County of Perth'* adding *'Perthshire forms the fairest portion of the Northern Kingdom'*.

That Perthshire, and Gleneagles in particular, was an ideal location for such a resort as Gleneagles Hotel and its golf courses is therefore self evident. However, the vision and drive to create it is often ascribed to one man – Donald Matheson. Matheson was a career railwayman who rose to become General Manager of the Caledonian Railway in 1910 by which time it was arguably the leading railway company in Scotland.

It is recorded that in that year Matheson spent a holiday in the area and as a result was inspired to create *'a Georgian Hotel or country house, built in the style of a palace, to attract and cater for the British travelling class'*. This vision was probably not some sudden 'Road to Damascus' transformation as it is sometimes portrayed, but an opportunity presented by Matheson's promotion that year to the post of General Manager. Matheson was familiar with the area – he was born in Perth in 1855 and attended Perth Academy. In 1877 he was then apprenticed to John Young Chartered Engineer (no relation to the author) who a few years later became the engineer for the Crieff & Comrie Railway. Following service with the London & North Western, Lanarkshire & Ayrshire and Glasgow Central railways Matheson joined the Caledonian Railway as Divisional Engineer for the Western District. He was subsequently appointed Engineer-in-Chief of the Caledonian in 1899, which post he held for eleven years. During that time he would have travelled over most, if not all, of the Caledonian lines, and almost certainly the Comrie to Balquhidder section which was opened in stages from 1901 to 1905.

That Matheson was familiar with the area is therefore beyond doubt, but prior to his appointment as General Manager he was an engineer with little or no responsibility for marketing or development within the company. With his elevation to General Manager that changed, and he would probably have had this in mind when he took his holiday in 1910. The rest, as they say, is history.

Matheson lost no time in bringing his vision to the Caledonian Board and worked hard to convince his fellow directors of the merits of his scheme. The site chosen was near the existing junction of the Crieff branch line with the Caledonian main line at Loaninghead to the west of Auchterarder. The area known as the White Muir was some 2 miles from the town, part of it having been vested in the Auchterarder Muir Commissioners in 1866 for the benefit of the townsfolk, while other land formed part of various local estates.

Despite the attraction of the location, the name of the existing station – Crieff Junction – was considered hardly inspiring as a holiday destination and one of the first actions was to adopt a new name for the whole scheme. The Caledonian favoured the use of the name Gleneagles, taken from the nearby historic estate of that name. The origins of the name Gleneagles is still a matter of debate. Popularly considered to be associated with the eagle which features prominently on the Gleneagles Hotel crest, there are those who hold that it was an adoption of the words *'Glen de l'eglise'*, because many years ago there was a Kirk of St. Mungo in the glen, supported by the fact that 'Gleneglais' is the Gaelic for Kirk Glen. Whatever its origins, there is no doubt that, as McLennan puts it: *'Gleneagles has a rare romantic ring to it'*. So Gleneagles it was to be.

However, the adoption of the name was not as simple as that, for the Haldane family ownership of the estate dated back over 600 years to around 1284. The then Laird took a dim view of the use of the name by the railway company and objected vigorously. Protracted negotiations between the railway company and the family resulted in agreement being given for Crieff Junction station to be renamed 'Gleneagles', although no mention was made of the hotel. Following this, the company formally approved the name change which became effective on 1st October 1911.

This was by no means the end of the story and as late as 1928 Mr Chinnery Haldane wrote to the *Daily Record* in Glasgow complaining:

Figure 7.1
The front cover of the promotional book *Golf at Gleneagles* produced by the Caledonian Railway circa 1922. Running to 144 pages, it included not only detailed descriptions of each hole on the King's and Queen's courses but the history of golf at Gleneagles since it opened officially in 1919. There was also a fold-out map of the courses and numerous advertisements. This copy was presented by Donald Matheson, General Manager of the Caledonian Railway to the author's grandfather, Major TE Young who opened the Union Bank of Scotland branch in the hotel. *Author's collection*

'I am well aware that, owing to the outrageous and uncalled for attempt made by the officials of the late Caledonian Railway Company and by what the LMS have succeeded to, the public have been led to think that the LMS company own Gleneagles. Our family have owned Gleneagles since the 12th century and you will appreciate that we very much resent being mixed up with a modern railway hotel.'

Even Donald Matheson incurred the displeasure of the laird, for Mr Haldane continued:

'Mr Matheson, who more than anyone else was responsible for the misuse of my name, wrote more than once to assure me that "nothing was further from the minds of the company than to take the honoured name of Gleneagles", yet he actually had the audacity to mark the forks and spoons made for the railway hotel with the plain word "Gleneagles" – not "Hotel".'

Agreement was finally reached whereby the railway undertook to always refer to their establishment as Gleneagles Hotel, Auchterarder. For many years this was reflected in the AA guide book which listed Gleneagles Hotel as the only 5* establishment in Auchterarder. This distinction is still made today and when you take the slip road from the A9 at Loaninghead to the junction with the A823, one sign points to Gleneagles Hotel while another points in the opposite direction to Gleneagles – this being the estate.

GLENEAGLES LTD

In view of the scope and magnitude of the whole scheme, it was decided to establish a separate company, Gleneagles Hotel & Golf Courses Ltd (subsequently shortened to Gleneagles Ltd). For their part, the Caledonian would remodel and rebuild Gleneagles station, while Gleneagles Ltd would build the golf courses and hotel. At a meeting on 30th October 1913, the outline plans called for a hotel with 175 rooms, comprising 80 single bedrooms, 60 double bedrooms, 35 double bedroom suites, and 100 bathrooms. Three golf courses were initially planned – a first class main course of 18 holes, 6,800 yards long, a very good relief course of 9 holes, 3,500 yards long, and a beginners course of 9 holes some 1,800 yards long.

The opening was planned for Easter 1915, with the contract being awarded to Messer P&W Anderson of Glasgow. The architect was to be Mr J Miller, while Mr Ferguson, a civil engineer of Forman's & McCall was to be superintendent. James Miller was the favourite architect of the Caledonian Railway, having designed many of their stations – he also had a pedigree as an architect of large hotels, having previously designed the Peebles Hydro and the Glasgow & South Western Railway's Turnberry Hotel, both in the period 1904-5. Although Miller designed Gleneagles Hotel, Matthew Adam deputised for him in the completion of the project after the First World War. The original estimates for the construction were:

Hotel Buildings including central heating	£78,500	
Swimming Pool and Shooting Range	£4,000	
Garage and Stables	£3,500	
Electric Power Station	£4,000	
Entrance Gates and Lodges etc	£2,000	
Water and Drainage Works	£7,000	
Roads and Paths	£5,000	
Grounds, Gardens, Tennis Courts etc	£3,500	
Golf Courses, Club House etc	£10,000	
Sub Total		£117,500
Land (350 acres from Blackford Estate)	£5,750	
Compensation to shooting tenant	£1,200	
Professional Fees	£6,550	
Furnishings and General Equipment	£20,000	
Underwriting Registration and Issuing Fees	£15,000	
Working Capital	£10,000	
Sub Total		£58,500
Overall Total		£176,000

A decision was made to hold over plans for a swimming pool and shooting range, and instead allocate £2,500 towards the cost of a laundry. It was noted that *'The architect was instructed that these estimates were not to be exceeded'* – a phrase which has a familiar ring to it to anyone who has been involved with building contracts.

ABOVE: Figure 7.2
A Caledonian Railway poster advertising the promotional book *Golf at Gleneagles* illustrated at Figure 7.1. Copies of this book are still much sought after and can command considerable prices on ebay and elsewhere. *J Paton collection*

ABOVE RIGHT: Figure 7.3
Originally produced in colour, this Caledonian Railway poster advertising Gleneagles Golf Courses featured the iconic 'Golfing Girl' used in much of their promotional material for golf, such as that at Figure 6.19. *J Paton collection*

Figure 7.4
A Caledonian Railway poster of the 'Howe o' Hope', the 15th hole on the King's course. Originally produced in colour, this view depicts the real Gleneagles in the background, with Glendevon in the distance. *J Paton collection*

Figure 7.5
A simple Caledonian Railway letterpress poster advertising Golf at Gleneagles, stressing the excellent train service. This included the overnight sleeping car services from and to London (Euston) which stopped at Gleneagles. The 'London Sleeper' still calls at Gleneagles. *J Paton collection*

Figure 7.6
A Caledonian Railway letterpress poster advertising the 'Glasgow Herald' Tournament held at Gleneagles in June 1921. *J Paton collection*

It was resolved that options on the land should be exercised and the necessary areas should be acquired for the least possible price from Captain Moray's Blackford Estate, Captain Johnstone Browning's Kincardine Estate, and Sir James Roberts Strathallan Estate. An additional 323 acres of land from Kincardine Estate and 74 acres from Strathallan Estate were to be acquired at a cost of £403 and £74 respectively. This land was not to be used for the hotel, but possibly for building purposes, subsequently becoming the basis for the present day private road unsurprisingly named 'Caledonian Crescent'.

Work on the golf courses was to start immediately, with initially only the first class and beginners courses. The relief course was only to be constructed when requirements necessitate it. It was also recognised that the services of a golf architect, as well as a professional and good amateur golfer may be required. Mr James Braid, together with Captain Hutchinson, was to be employed to design and direct the construction of the courses.

Work started almost immediately and continued at a rapid pace during 1913. However, financial pressures were already being felt, and before the year was out it was agreed to reduce the expenditure from £179,470 down to £165,000. Savings of £14,470 were found from across the board, including £3,000 on the hotel, £2,500 on the golf courses and £500 on the garage. By early 1914 work on the golf courses was sufficiently advanced for a green keeper to be appointed from 1st March. In June a siding linking the hotel with the Gleneagles–Crieff line near Easter Greenwells Farm was opened for traffic. Despite the progress being made, all was not well, and on 11th March the architect, Mr Miller, resigned. Why he resigned is not known, but it took a further month of negotiations before his severance package was finally agreed.

By the middle of 1914, following the assassination of the Austrian Archduke Ferdinand, the situation in Europe deteriorated, and war broke out on 4th August. Work on the project continued, but it soon became apparent that the war would not be over by Christmas and, faced with the economic reality that there was no place for a luxury hotel resort in wartime together with competing pressures on manpower, work was suspended in the autumn. By then work on the golf courses was well advanced, but only the main walls of the hotel were up, and this is how they then remained for another eight years until work restarted in 1922.

In the intervening period it became apparent that Gleneagles Ltd was in financial difficulty and had insufficient funds to complete the project. This is succinctly summarised in the Caledonian Railway Act 1923, the last Act promoted by the Caledonian before it was swallowed up by the LM&SR, which was specifically intended to transfer the assets of Gleneagles Ltd to the Caledonian:

'And whereas for financial and other reasons Gleneagles Limited are unable to complete erection and laying out of the said hotel and golf course and it is expedient and would be to the advantage of the company and the public that the Company should be authorised to acquire the lands so

ABOVE: Figure 7.7
The second of the pair of Caledonian Railway posters depicting one of the holes at Gleneagles Golf Courses. This one shows the 'Witches Bowster' on the Queen's course. This was the 5th hole on the original 9 hole course, subsequently becoming the 14th hole on the rebuilt 18 hole course. *J Paton collection*

LEFT: Figure 7.8
A Caledonian Railway letterpress poster advertising the special train service between Glasgow (Buchanan Street) and Gleneagles for the International Golf Week in June 1921. Two trains each way were offered depending on how much time the spectator wanted to spend at Gleneagles.
J Paton collection

RIGHT: Figure 7.9
Another Caledonian Railway letterpress poster from June 1921, this one for the train service between Edinburgh (Princes Street) and Gleneagles. Although only one special train was shown, the timings still allowed the visitor over six hours at the golf course.
J Paton collection

RIGHT: Figure 7.10
A Caledonian Railway poster, originally produced in colour, promoting Gleneagles golf courses. Mention of the train services and the Caledonian Railway's existing hotels is in line with the Caledonian Railway Tourist Guide for 1921 mentioned in the previous chapter. The 'Golfing Girl' again features. *J Paton collection*

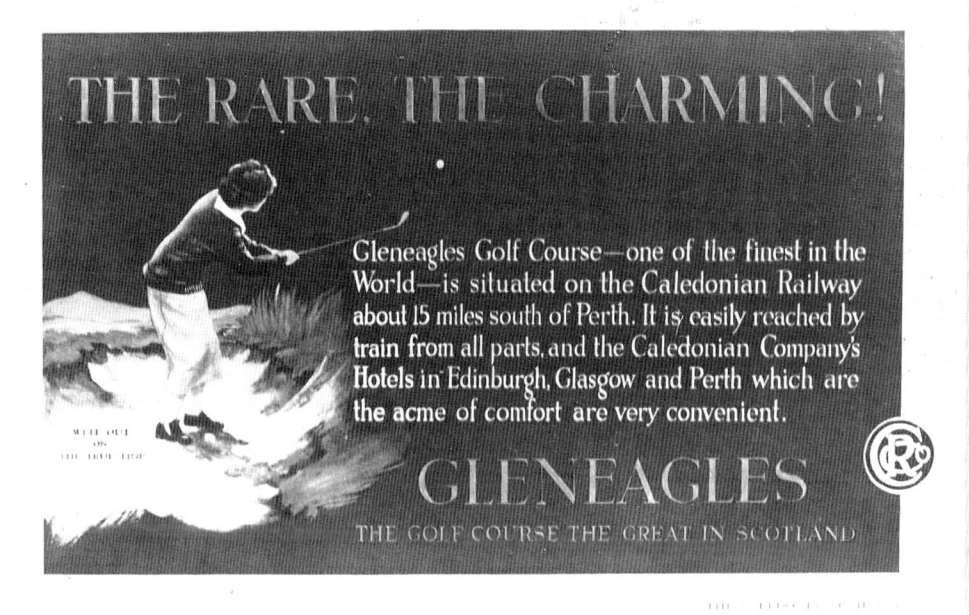

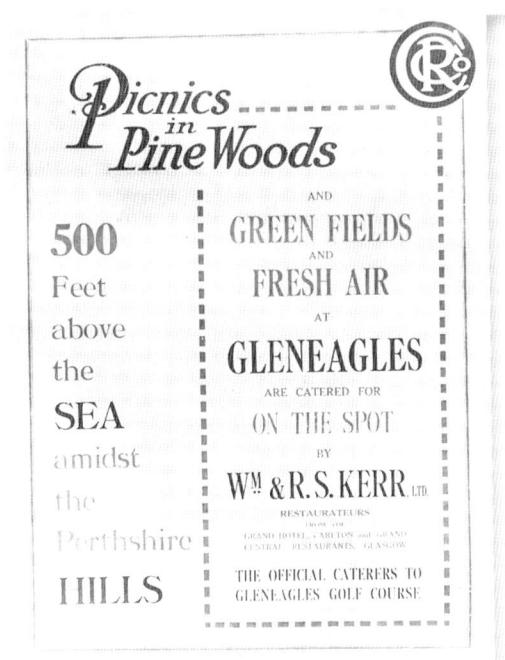

LEFT: Figure 7.11
Golf was not the only draw to Gleneagles as this Caledonian Railway letterpress poster shows. The Club House, which opened at the same time as the golf courses, was the only catering available until the hotel finally opened, and at this stage was operated by Wm & RS Kerr Ltd of Glasgow, as shown here. *J Paton collection*

RIGHT: Figure 7.12
A rather distressed Caledonian Railway letterpress poster for the 'Glasgow Herald' Tournament in 1921 which reflects the international nature of these events, with competitors from as far afield as Australia, Canada and the United States – referred to as America – in addition to the continent of Europe. These events drew large crowds to see the top golfers of the day, and in the days before television and with only limited newsreels at the cinema, this was the only way to see them in action.
J Paton collection

purchased by Gleneagles Limited as aforesaid and to complete the erection and laying out of the hotel and golf course and to carry on and maintain the same when completed as part of their undertaking.'

The Caledonian Railway took over the entire undertaking on 7th December 1922 and continued the work necessary to complete the hotel. The Caledonian itself was taken over by the LM&SR, not on 1st January 1923 as the other pre-Grouping companies, but on 1st July 1923, after further legal wrangles. Gleneagles Ltd was finally wound up on 6th November 1928, over four years after the hotel finally opened.

GOLF COURSES

Golf was a key component of Matheson's plans for Gleneagles. The 'Royal and Ancient' game of golf, as it was referred to, had long been promoted by the Caledonian Railway and their timetables regularly included a list of golf courses *'adjacent to stations of the Caledonian Railway Company, or of companies with which Caledonian trains run in direct connection'*. These included courses served by the Highland Railway and Great North of Scotland Railway (GNoSR) companies, but of course not those of the Caledonian's arch rival the North British – so did not include St. Andrews. Some fifty-seven golf courses were listed including eight on islands served by the Caledonian Steam Packet Company's ships. Local courses listed, all of 9 holes, included:

STATION	GOLF COURSE
Auchterarder	Auchterararder
Comrie	Comrie
Crieff	Ochtertyre
Highlandman	Dornock
Lochearnhead	Lochearnhead Hotel

As one of the foremost golfers of his generation and five times winner of the Open Golf Championship, James Braid was a top proponent of his profession. As previously mentioned, Matheson, determined that Gleneagles was to be the best golf course in Britain, engaged Braid, together with Captain Cecil Hutchinson, a prominent amateur golfer, to design the Gleneagles courses. Braid and Hutchinson visited Gleneagles in December 1913 to begin preliminary work. Messrs James Carter & Co, Seed Merchants of London, who are still in business today, were contracted to undertake the formation of the golf courses, particularly trees and greens, under Braids direction. Work started in the New Year, and on 1st March approval was given to appoint a Green Keeper, Mr McFarlane, the then Assistant Green Keeper at Bruntsfield near Edinburgh. His initial salary to be 35 shillings per week with an additional 5 shillings per week until a house could be provided. At that stage it was planned that both the hotel and the golf courses would be completed the following year, in the spring of 1915.

Gleneagles was considered by experts to possess the natural features required of a golf course – *'fine resilient turf on gravelly sub-soil readily drained'* – and therefore unaffected by heavy rain. There was also *'infinite variety of the ground for golf, the undulating character of the surface, the natural plateaux, the sandy ridges and hillocks, the rough hollows and ravines, the heather, the whin and the broom, the bracing air and the magnificence of the surroundings'* – all of which led them to consider that *'Gleneagles could be made to be absolutely unrivalled among countryside courses'*. Indeed, Captain Hutchinson was delighted with the potential of the place and described it as being *'the finest natural golfing ground he had ever seen'*.

Construction of the courses was well in hand by the time war broke out in August 1914, and although work on the project was slowed by the war, it was not halted as was the case with the hotel. What were described as *'Circumstances of War'* compelled Captain Hutchinson to withdraw from the work, but he returned after hostilities ceased and now as Major Hutchinson was involved in the final completion of the courses in 1918 and 1919. Braid however remained and pressed on with completion of his work. Although the original target date of spring 1915 was missed by several years due to the war, the courses were playable by 1918. At that stage the courses were not officially open, but it seems that some, including locals, took advantage of their availability to play informally. The well-known photograph of one such group on the King's course shows the half-built hotel in the background.

Two courses were laid out by Braid. The first-class main course named the King's was an 18 hole, bogey 80 course of 6,125 yards, with colourful names for the holes:

1.	Dun Whinny	355	5
2.	East Neuk	390	4
3.	Silver Tassie	360	5
4.	Broomy Law	440	6
5.	Het Girdle	145	3
6.	Blink Bonnie	455	5
7.	Kittle Kink	420	5
8.	Whaup's Nest	155	3
9.	Heich o' Fash	350	4
10.	Westkin Wyne	430	5
11.	Deil's Creel	185	3
12.	Tappit Hen	395	5
13.	Braid's Brawest	435	5
14.	Denty's Den	245	4
15.	Howe o' Hope	445	5
16.	Wee Bogle	125	5
17.	Warlin' Lea	365	5
18.	King's Hame	450	5

The relief course, named the Queen's was a 9 hole, bogey 36 course. As originally laid out this was:

1.	Trystin' Tree	375	5
2.	Needle E'e	140	3
3.	Heather Bell	400	5
4.	Warlock Knows	340	4
5.	Witches' Bowster	170	3
6.	Leddy's Ain	200	4
7.	Lover's Gait	365	4
8.	Hinny Mune	190	4
9.	Queen's Hame	325	4

With the war over and the courses playable, the Caledonian Railway was keen to capitalise on the facilities now available even if the hotel was not yet ready. Both courses were officially opened on 1st May 1919, although temporary facilities had to suffice as the Club House had not yet been built. Approval had been given the previous month for work to start, but this would not be completed until December the following year. The Caledonian launched a publicity campaign to

Plate 7.1
Although the hotel did not open until 1924, the golf courses were completed and officially opened in 1919. However, locals were known to take advantage of the course even before that, and this view shows golfers circa 1918. The shell of the hotel can be seen in the background, very much as it was when work was halted in late 1914, including a crane, scaffolding and other plant abandoned at the time.
Author's collection (Courtesy Dr J Grant)

promote Gleneagles as a destination for golfers. Three poster designs were produced, bearing the slogan *'There is no better golf course in Great Britain than Gleneagles'*. One depicted the 15th hole on the King's course (How o' Hope), another the 5th hole on the Queen's course (Witches Bowster), and probably the most famous one of a female golfer described by the press as being that of *'a winsome lass playing well out of bunker'*.

The first major championship to be played at Gleneagles was held in May 1920 with a prize of £150 being offered by the North British Rubber Co. of Edinburgh. One novel aspect was the advertisement of flights from Renfrew, and later also from Robroystoun, to Gleneagles – the designated aeroplane landing ground being alongside the Braco Road to the west of the hotel. That same month the first international tournament at Gleneagles was sponsored by the *Glasgow Herald* newspaper, when George Duncan beat the Frenchman Arnaud Massy in the final.

From 1920 onwards, major tournaments were held regularly at Gleneagles and these were all widely promoted by the Caledonian. All stressed that Gleneagles was served by a convenient train service, and in some cases, such as the International Golf Week in June 1921, special trains were laid on. By this time Gordon Lockhart from Prestwick St. Nicholas had been appointed Professional. Lockhart was another pre-eminent golfer who had won the Scottish Amateur Championship at Gleneagles the previous year, and was to enjoy a long and illustrious career at Gleneagles.

The Hotel

While work on the golf courses continued throughout the First World War, as already mentioned, construction work on the hotel was stopped in the autumn of 1914. By that stage the outer walls were largely complete, although they were not yet finished, and the majority of the internal walls were complete. The structure had the ghostly look of some long abandoned mansion sat amid a tangle of undergrowth and builders equipment. It was to remain like this for eight long years.

With the war over and the golf courses open, the Caledonian were keen for work on the hotel to press ahead, but it was recognised by Gleneagles Limited that they lacked the capital to see the project through. In fact the company had been borrowing capital from the Caledonian Railway at intervals throughout the war to keep the project afloat. At a meeting of the company's directors on 28th May 1919 it was agreed that they should approach the Caledonian to bale them out. The Caledonian paid off the remaining directors of the company and finally took it over on 7th December 1922, allowing work to restart.

As already mentioned, this takeover necessitated the Caledonian Railway to seek Parliamentary Authority. This they gained by the promulgation of a Provisional Order in December 1922. One response this did provoke was from the Aucherarder Town Council as the proposed Act called for the stopping up of private rights of

Plate 7.2
Work on the hotel was halted in late 1914 and it lay unfinished until 1922. This view is of the front entrance and west frontage. The brickwork has been largely completed, together with the cornerstones, lintels and mullions, but the stone facing had yet to be added. Vegetation has grown back, adding to the eerie, abandoned, feel of the building.
Author's collection (Courtesy Dr J Grant)

Plate 7.3
Another view of the half built hotel as left in 1914. Scaffolding adorns part of the structure and piles of construction material lie about. Little work had been done on the roof so the whole building was left open to the elements for nearly eight years. It is a testament to the materials used and the workmanship involved that it was still in such good condition when work recommenced in 1922.
Author's collection (Courtesy Dr J Grant)

way across the land to be acquired and they were keen to ensure that this would not be extended to include public rights of way. Meetings were held with the Caledonian Railway's solicitors to seek assurances to this effect, with one of the local delegates being Major TE Young, the author's grandfather, who at that time was a county councillor. The main concern related to a path which ran from the Muirton, a small settlement to the west of Auchterarder, to the parish church at Blackford. As a result of these negotiations, the future of the Auld Kirk Road or the 'Coffin Road' as it was known locally, was secured. Today this public footpath, which starts from the car park near the club house, still passes through the midst of the King's and Queen's courses.

The promotion of this Act was one of the last actions of the Caledonian Railway, for under the Railways Act of 1921 it became one of the constituent companies of the LM&SR. It therefore fell to the LM&SR to bring the Gleneagles Hotel project to full fruition. That said, under the terms of the 'Grouping', as it was known, Donald Matheson became the Deputy General Manager (Scotland) of the LM&SR and thus remained fully involved in bringing his original vision to reality.

Work on the hotel continued apace throughout 1922 and 1923, with some 400 men employed on construction work, many of them living in wooden huts and old coach bodies on site. Photographs of this period show a hive of activity with a mass of cranes and machinery. The temporary service railway extended behind the hotel and comprised numerous sidings, which were lifted when work was completed, augmented by a narrow gauge railway system which is also visible in some of the photographs. In addition to completion of the main hotel buildings, much work was carried out to complete the terraces, walls, roadways and entrances. The Caledonian Railway, ever conscious of the need to keep down costs found a ready source of good stone for much of this work from one of its redundant viaducts. Built in 1841, the Jerviston viaduct on the Wishaw and Coltness line in Lanarkshire was demolished during 1922/3 and much of the stone recovered and shipped by rail to the hotel.

Some twenty-three sub-contractors were employed on the site covering all aspects of work from kitchen equipment to marble tiling. Electrical work was undertaken by the prestigious firm of Metropolitan Vickers of Glasgow. All this was before electricity became widely available and, there being no local electricity supply, it had to be brought from Bridge of Allan, 16½ miles away near Stirling. A substation, which survives to this day, was built at Bridge of Allan station and an overhead pole route brought the 33,000 volt supply alongside the main line to Gleneagles station, from where an underground cable ran up to the hotel.

By the spring of 1924 construction work was almost complete and

Plate 7.4
A view from the roof of the hotel during construction looking north. The temporary narrow gauge railway network in the foreground was used to move materials brought in by rail around the site and was removed once work was completed. Also visible is part of the standard gauge siding with a wagon from the Caledonian's great rival, the North British Railway. The Auchterarder to Braco road can just be seen in the background.
Author's collection (Courtesy Dr J Grant)

Plate 7.5
A view of work on the second story at the rear of the hotel showing some of the many cranes used. Visible in the back right is a siding which later formed the hotel branch line which ran down to connect with the Gleneagles to Crieff branch line to the east. The curve in the line just visible through the jib of the crane became the site of the sidings and small goods yard. Also in the background is the Braco road from Auchterarder and beyond it the site of the much later riding school and shooting school. *Author's collection (Courtesy Dr J Grant)*

attention turned to fitting the hotel out. Although Donald Matheson had continued to oversee the project, once the hotel was complete operational control would pass to Arthur Towle, Controller of Hotel Services for the LM&SR. It was agreed that the handover would take place on 30th May 1924, a little under a week prior to the planned opening on 5th June. Matheson, however, continued to be involved in all manner of final detailed preparations, even such things as bedroom and bathroom door locks. Arrangements were agreed to acquire the old railway coaches being used by the contractors for use as male staff sleeping accommodation, and an offer was made to purchase the wood hut for the same purpose. That *some cheap mattresses and bedding* were to be acquired for these was something of a contrast with the opulence planned for guests. Some forty-two different firms were due to deliver all manner of furnishings and equipment to the hotel, including some famous names such as Harrods and Mappin & Webb, and some, such as the Buoyancy Upholstery Company and the Scottish Folk Fabrics, possibly less well known. All supplies, however, would have been of the highest quality.

Arthur Towle selected Mr RW Turier, the then manager of the Adelphi Hotel in Liverpool, another of the LM&SR hotels, as the first General Manager of Gleneagles. Gordon Lockhart, as the Professional was responsible for the golf courses, but all other sports came under the care of the newly appointed Sports Secretary, Captain GF Davies.

The opening date of 5th June 1924 had been set some time previously and was included in LM&SR publicity material in April that year. The first guests were due to arrive that day, although the Grand Opening Gala was set for 7th June, which sometimes causes confusion over the actual date on which the hotel opened. Even then some parts of the hotel were not quite ready. The West Wing was not available for guests, and temporary décor and fittings had to suffice in the sun lounge until it was completed.

The hotel was planned to accommodate 350 guests, and sometimes more, in sumptuous surroundings. To cater for such numbers and to look after their every need, the hotel employed over 400 staff in addition to those who serviced the golf courses. As well as the sporting facilities, Gleneagles was equipped with the most modern amenities, including a range of shops and even an in-house bank; this

ABOVE: **Plate 7.6**
A general view of the construction work at the rear of the hotel with four cranes visible and work up to roof level well in hand. Wagons on the siding in the foreground include a Caledonian Railway 5-plank wagon and one from the Midland Railway. The former reflects the fact that tenders for the work specified that materials from around the country should be delivered via the Caledonian Railway wherever possible.
Author's collection (Courtesy Dr J Grant)

RIGHT: **Plate 7.7**
Another view of the rear of the hotel shows work well advanced. The long low building visible is one of the huts used to accommodate the many workmen involved on the site. Over 400 workmen were employed, with work proceeding at a rapid pace in order for the hotel to be ready for the 1924 season. It is possible that this was one of the huts which were used initially to house some of the hotel staff, but it is unlikely to have remained so for long as it was on the site of the large garage which, it was boasted, could accommodate 100 cars.
Author's collection (Courtesy Dr J Grant)

Plate 7.8
A view of Jerviston viaduct on the Wishaw to Coltness line in Lanarkshire being prepared for demolition in August 1922. A double set of narrow gauge rails, known as the 'Bogie Road' have been constructed alongside the viaduct to remove the stonework after demolition. Two cable-hauled wagons can be seen near the base of the incline which leads up to the original rail level. A set of rail constructed buffer stops can be seen at the top of the approach pier, this being the truncated part of the original line along which the stone was to be removed.
Author's collection (Courtesy R Pidgeon)

Plate 7.9
The final pier to be demolished was No. 3 pier, here seen on 15th March 1923, starting to fall, just after the detonation of the demolition charge. Although No. 1 pier was demolished as early as 29th August 1922, the remaining two piers were not demolished until the following spring, during which period the stonework from No. 1 pier was cleared and transported to Gleneagles. Each pier would have produced a considerable volume of stone for use on the boundary walls, terraces and landscaping of the hotel.
Author's collection (Courtesy R Pidgeon)

Plate 7.10
The remains of No. 3 pier lying on the ground after the explosion shown in Plate 7.9. Only a small portion of the base remains to be demolished by hand. The remaining short approach pier was probably also demolished by hand. The Bogie Road can be seen in the foreground, having been laid just far enough for the stone from No. 3 pier to be removed up to the line at the other end of the viaduct.
Author's collection (Courtesy R Pidgeon)

Plate 7.11
A view of the remains of Nos 2 and 3 piers taken from the other end of the viaduct, showing how the piers have been felled neatly along the line of the railway. No stones appear to have fallen into the adjacent cemetery to the left, although the Bogie Road has taken a bit of battering and would probably have had to be repaired after it had been cleared before it could be used to remove the stone. A few blocks have even ended in the river!
Author's collection (Courtesy R Pidgeon)

LEFT: Figure 7.13
A page from the LM&SR (Northern Division) Excursions leaflet for June, July and August 1924, published in April that year, announcing the opening date for the hotel and inviting bookings. The leaflet was published under the joint authority of HG Burgess, the General Manager of the LM&SR and Donald Matheson, by then Deputy General Manager (Scotland). It must have given Matheson some satisfaction to see his cherished dream come to fruition some fourteen years after embarking on the project.
Author's collection

ABOVE CENTRE: Figure 7.14
The first LM&SR publicity booklet published for the American market, it was produced as early as January 1924 in anticipation of the opening of the hotel later that year. Extolling the virtues of the new hotel, it was aimed specifically at the potentially lucrative US market, and included details of Mr John Fairman, LM&SR General Passenger Agent located at 200 Fifth Avenue, New York.
Author's collection

ABOVE RIGHT: Figure 7.15
'The Gleneagles Map', also produced in 1924 for both the home and overseas market. Case bound on linen, it opens to some 3½ feet square depicting the central region of Scotland, it was a magnificent map made to impress the visitor. The map is reproduced on page 8.
Author's collection

was a branch of the Union Bank of Scotland in Auchterarder where the author's grandfather was the agent. In addition to the sun lounge, the hotel boasted a large ballroom, and other facilities including a billiard room and library. Donald Matheson was determined that Gleneagles would be equipped with the most up-to-date facilities, and other modern conveniences including a cold-storage plant, bakery and the latest in kitchen appliances.

Central to Gleneagles were its excellent sporting facilities and, in addition to the famed golf courses, other attractions included:

- 10 tennis courts (modelled on Wimbledon)
- 18 hole putting course
- 3 croquet lawns
- a bowling green
- a children's playground
- an aeroplane station
- the Laich Loch for boating, skating and curling

The aeroplane landing ground, alongside the Braco Road to the west of the main avenue, was shown on the earliest maps of Gleneagles. It had been in use since the opening of the golf courses and was now available for hotel guests. In 1926 a Mr and Mrs Butler flew up from Suffolk in their own aeroplane in only 3 hours and 40 minutes, and a few years later a Mr Cramond flew up from Croydon airport to join his parents for lunch. Flights to Gleneagles became common place, and when the Gleneagles Air Rally was staged in 1929, pilots arrived with their golf bags strapped to the outside of the aircraft.

Another first for Gleneagles was the inauguration of BBC broadcasts from the hotel in the days when radio was in its infancy. Some time prior to the opening of the hotel, Arthur Towle, who had been the Director of Hotels on the Midland Railway, and had by then become Controller of LM&SR Hotel Services, heard a performance by a young pianist at the Midland Hotel in Manchester. He was so impressed by the young man, one Henry Hall, that he asked him if he would like to conduct the orchestra at the new LM&SR hotel in Scotland. Hall accepted and the Gleneagles Hotel Band was born, with programmes being broadcast from the hotel twice-weekly for many years. Henry Hall became a household name and the fame of the Gleneagles Hotel Band spread worldwide. The band recorded a number of records and the LM&SR even produced a handsome book of music entitled *The Gleneagles Collection of Old Scottish Dance Tunes*. Perhaps somewhat diplomatically, the first foursome reel was named 'Miss Haldane of Gleneagles'.

The LM&SR marketed the hotel widely and as early as January 1924 they produced a booklet aimed specifically at the US market. Describing Gleneagles as '*A Resort of distinction*' it waxed lyrical

(Continued on page 172)

ABOVE: Plate 7.12
A view of the front of the hotel not long after it opened, indicating that parking was an issue even in the very early years. The gardeners have been busy and both the roundabout and verges have been well laid out, although the trees and shrubs have yet to fully mature. Note the Union flag flying above the main entrance, although some early photographs also show the Scottish Lion Rampant flag.
Author's collection

BELOW: Plate 7.13
One of the series of LM&SR official postcards published shortly after opening in 1924 to promote the hotel, this view of the tennis courts with Glendevon in the background shows play in full swing with lady players in the fashion of the day. Modelled on Wimbledon, the hotel originally boasted nine tennis courts, but these fell into disuse during the Second World War and in post-war years only the three courts in the centre block were still in use, the remainder having been landscaped as a grass area.
Author's collection

CHAPTER 7: GLENEAGLES HOTEL

THIS HOTEL IS EQUIPPED WITH A COLD STORAGE AND ICE MAKING PLANT BY THE BRITISH REFRIGERATING COMPANY, BURY ST. EDMUND'S.

GLENEAGLES HOTEL.

ABOVE: Plate 7.14
Gleneagles was equipped with the latest technology, including in the kitchen area, and the suppliers of such equipment were keen to be associated with this prestigious hotel. This LM&SR official postcard showing the front of the hotel from the Laich Loch has been overprinted with a promotional message from the British Refrigerating Company of Bury St. Edmunds in Suffolk. The LM&SR also used other cards depicting Gleneagles Hotel for routine correspondence while at the same time promoting the hotel. *Author's collection*

RIGHT: Plate 7.15
These LM&SR postcards all bore the Gleneagles Hotel crest on the back, together with details of how to contact the hotel. The early postcards show the postal address as Gleneagles despite the dispute with the Haldane family, although the hotel did have an early Auchterarder telephone number. This was in the days before Subscriber Truck Dialling (STD) when all calls were connected through the operator. The author's home telephone number was Auchterarder 88 while his grandmother was privileged to have Auchterarder 2 – probably because the telephone exchange was built on land bought from the family. *Author's collection*

FAR RIGHT: Figure 7.16
One of the many advertisements published in US magazines, this one from 1925 would probably not be considered appropriate today, but nonetheless reflects the exotic prose used at the time to promote this new golfing 'Mecca'. Mention is made of the sleeping car service from London and readers are directed to enquire of Mr John Fairman, the LM&SR Agent in New York, or of Thomas Cook & Son, the well-known travel agents. *Author's collection*

POST CARD
COMMUNICATION   ADDRESS

The postal address is "Gleneagles Hotel, Gleneagles, Perthshire"; the Telegraphic Address is "Gleneagles Hotel;" and the Telephone Number is Auchterarder 70

THE AMERICAN REVIEW OF REVIEWS

Hadji Golfer

IN THE EAST a man who has made a pilgrimage to Mecca has the right to stain his beard with henna, wear a green turban, and put Hadji before his name.

A golfer who has made a pilgrimage to Scottish links shows no outward and visible sign (even in the cut of his plus fours) of the inward exaltation that is his; but let him meet a fellow-pilgrim, another "Golf Hadji"—then indeed the floodgates of eloquence are opened and the tide is at full. The talk is all of Gleneagles, of amazing turf, of natural hazards that brought down Sir Plus Four, of approach shots that lay dead where they fell, and eighteen holes that served only to kindle desire for another round.

Scotland is the ancestral home of golf: Gleneagles is the shrine whither all good golfers make pilgrimage.

Gleneagles is a night's sleep from London, via Carlisle, in the best sleeping cars in the world.

Gleneagles Hotel, built by the London Midland and Scottish Railway, and opened last year, will bear comparison even with the wonderful hotels of New York. Yet it stands on a Scottish hillside in the heart of Perthshire at the gate of the Highlands.

Literature and advice from John Fairman, L M S Agent, 200 Fifth Avenue, New York, or from any office of Thos. Cook & Son

LMS

EUSTON STATION & ST. PANCRAS STATION · LONDON

ABOVE: Plate 7.16
An aerial view of the hotel in 1931, showing the full layout with the main building and the garage, with the circular vegetable garden and the nine tennis courts on the east side in the foreground. Also clearly visible is the hotel branch line with passing loop for shunting. Several wagons can be seen in the loop with the coal stockpile to their left, and others at the loading bay at the rear of the hotel itself. The small triangular area between the railway and the tennis courts was used by the gardeners and maintenance staff as a works yard.
RCAHMS Aerofilms collection

RIGHT: Figure 7.17
The LM&SR also produced colourful luggage labels promoting the sporting facilities at Gleneagles. This label, probably produced for the US market, again refers to the 'Mecca' of sport. It locates it in Europe although it fails to mention that Perthshire is in Scotland. Measuring a full 5 inches (130 mm) in diameter, it would have been a distinctive label which was instantly recognisable. A later Art Deco version termed Gleneagles 'Britain's Unrivalled Resort'.
Author's collection

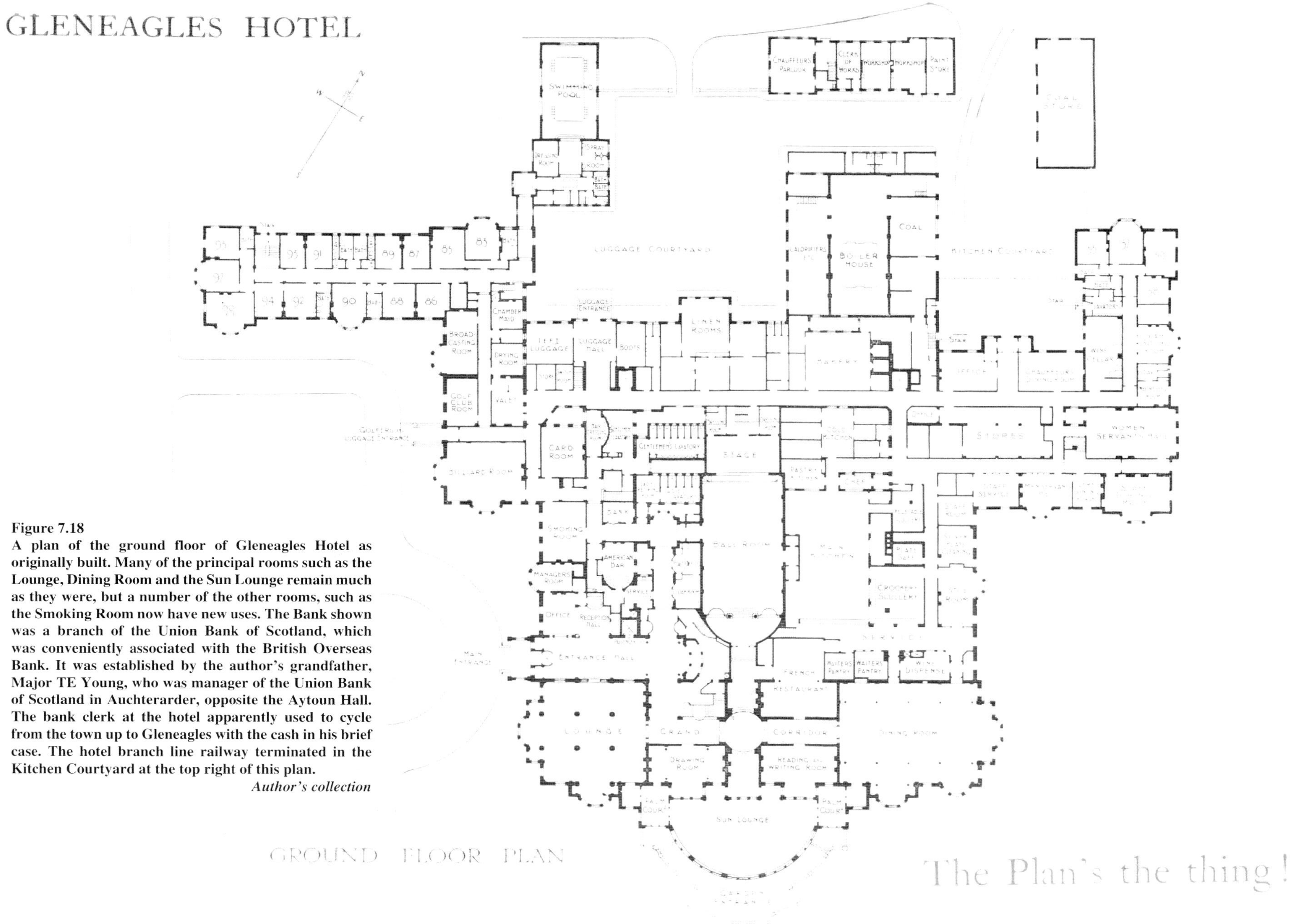

GLENEAGLES HOTEL

Figure 7.18
A plan of the ground floor of Gleneagles Hotel as originally built. Many of the principal rooms such as the Lounge, Dining Room and the Sun Lounge remain much as they were, but a number of the other rooms, such as the Smoking Room now have new uses. The Bank shown was a branch of the Union Bank of Scotland, which was conveniently associated with the British Overseas Bank. It was established by the author's grandfather, Major TE Young, who was manager of the Union Bank of Scotland in Auchterarder, opposite the Aytoun Hall. The bank clerk at the hotel apparently used to cycle from the town up to Gleneagles with the cash in his brief case. The hotel branch line railway terminated in the Kitchen Courtyard at the top right of this plan.
Author's collection

BELOW: Figure 7.19
The 1932 LM&SR brochure depicting the hotel with the grounds yet to fully mature. The daily tariff for a double room was 25s (about £64.35 today) in the low season (April to June) and 30s (£77.22) in the high season (July to September). Lunch cost 5s (£13.37) and dinner 8s 6d (£21.85). A round of golf cost 3s (£7.50) and mention was now made of the Wee course which had been laid out in 1928. Saddle Hacks were also available for hire in the summer months. *Author's collection*

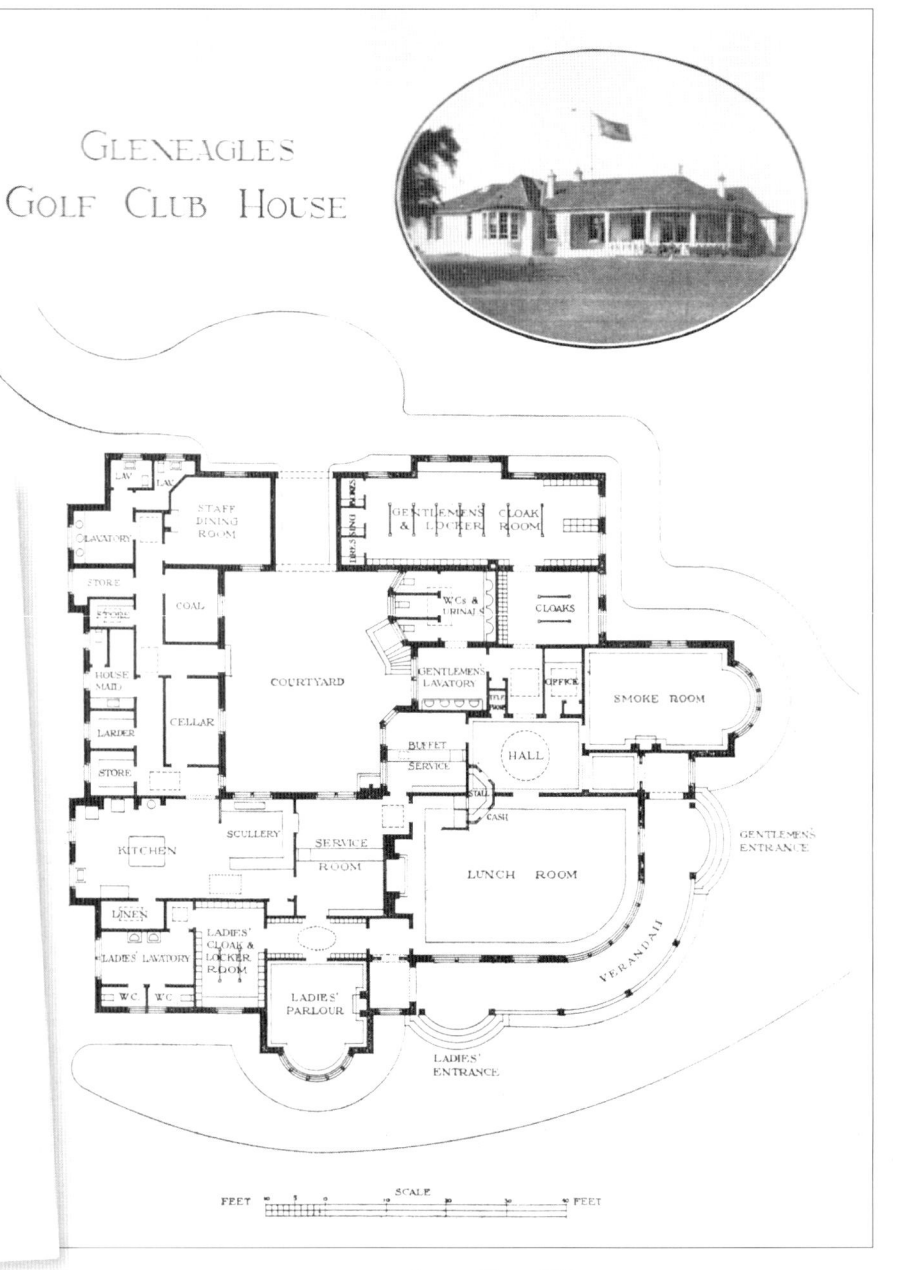

ABOVE: Figure 7.20
The plan of the original Club House at Gleneagles Golf Course which appeared in the book *Golf at Gleneagles*. Until the hotel was completed and opened, this served as the sole catering establishment for golfers and visitors to the courses at Gleneagles. Ladies and gentlemen had separate entrances and lounges, termed respectively the 'Ladies Parlour' and 'Smoke Room'. Significantly, the Gentlemen's Cloak and Locker Room was three time the size of that for the ladies. *Author's collection*

LEFT: Plate 7.17
Staff posing by the Gleneagles Hotel bus circa 1935. The service provided some fifteen trips each day to take hotel guests to Gleneagles station and to meet passengers by train. The booklet at Figure 7.30 included two vouchers valid for the bus from Gleneagles Station to the hotel and back again. Luggage was loaded into a separate lorry and taken up to the hotel to be collected by guests on arrival. *Author's collection (Courtesy Dr J Grant)*

CHAPTER 7: GLENEAGLES HOTEL 171

RIGHT TOP: Figure 7.21
Traffic dispatched to the hotel by rail was carried free of charge, termed 'OCS' (On Company's Service), using preprinted labels such as the one shown. This early 1920s LM&SR label is addressed to the Resident Manager, again using the simple address of 'Perthshire'. *Author's collection*

RIGHT BOTTOM: Figure 7.22
The Club House was a separate accounting entity for which different labels were printed. The label shown here dates from post 1948, the year in which the railways were nationalised. All the railway hotels were grouped under The Hotels Executive, a part of the nationalised railway, and in this case 'OBRS' on the label stands for 'On British Railways Service'. Centre No. 74 refers to the system of internal mail centre originally established by the LM&SR and perpetuated by British Railways. *Author's collection*

BELOW LEFT: Figures 7.23 and 7.24
The LM&SR printed score cards for each course. This 1930s card shows the King's course after lengthening from the original 6,125 yards to 6,340 yards. The rear of the card lists the local rules for both the King's and Queen's courses and the general rules, which include reference to 'rabbit scrapes' which would appear to have been a hazard. This card was used in the 1930s and completed by a foursome who have used a single card to record the scores for all four players. Although complete in all other details, the one piece of information missing is the date. *Author's collection*

BELOW CENTRE: Figures 7.25 and 7.26
This LM&SR 1930s score card for the Queen's course shows it after it had been extended in 1925 from a 9 hole course of 2,505 yards to an 18 hole course of 5,810 yards. The back cover of the scorecards for the Queen's course listed a handicap chart as shown here rather than the rules listed on the back of the score card for the King's as shown at Figure 7.23. The card was completed by the same foursome as shown at Figure 7.24, who again have used a single card to record the scores for all four players. This example is also missing the date. *Authors collection*

BELOW RIGHT: Figures 7.27 and 7.28
An LM&SR score card from the original Wee course, opened in 1928 as a 9 hole course of 2,625 yards. Being only 9 holes, the card was not folded, unlike those for the King's and Queen's, and lacked the note about the distances from the forward and back tees as there was only one set length for each hole. Score cards for the Wee course are much rarer than those for the other courses. The reverse of the score card for the Wee course was completed by the same foursome shown on the King's and Queen's score cards at Figures 7.24 and 7.26. All these cards bore both the Gleneagles Hotel crest and the logo of the LM&SR. After nationalisation, British Railways continued the same style but without the LMS logo and altered the title slightly to refer to 'Gleneagles Golf Courses'. *Authors collection*

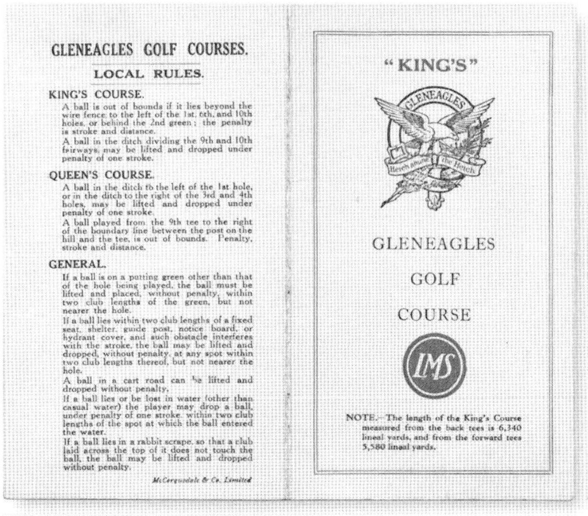

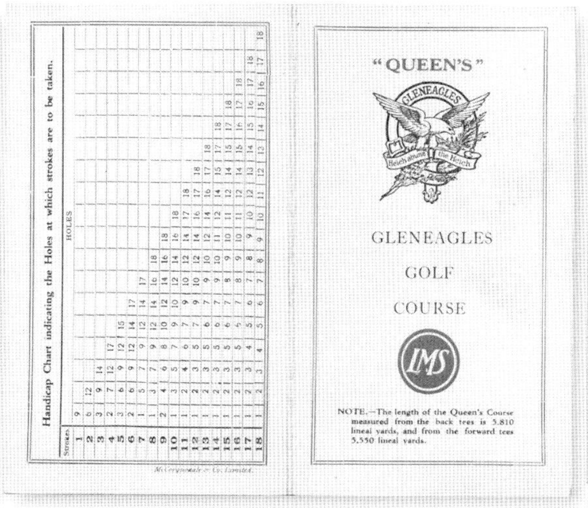

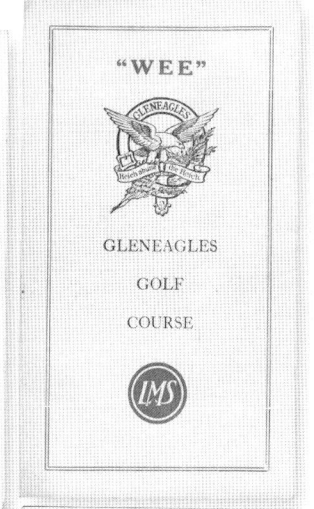

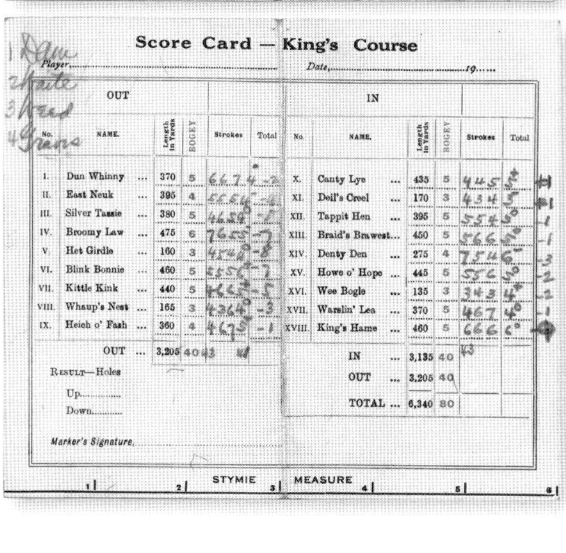

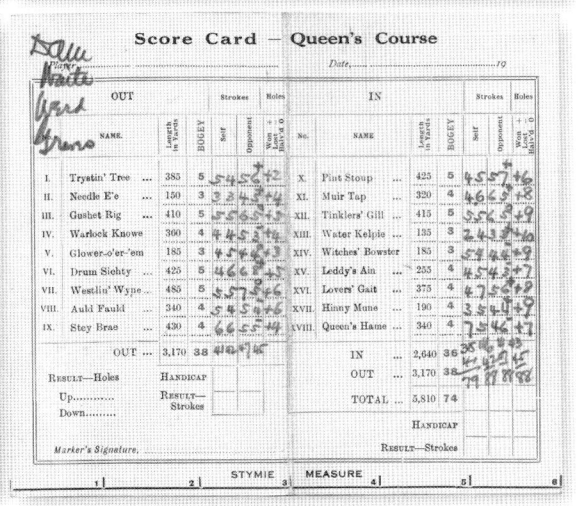

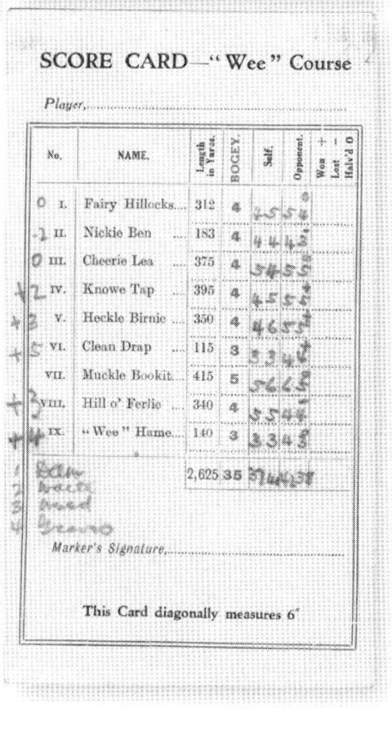

(Continued from page 165)

about the facilities stating that: *'Of their kind they are among the finest in Europe. None is better'* and about the surroundings as being: *'the Countryside of a thousand delights'*. The public rooms were described as *'stately in their elegance'*, the Grand Corridor as *'well and truly named'*, and the kitchen *'unique'*. Guests were even reassured that the Chief Cook would be *'a person of importance'*.

Much was also made of the *'motor runs'*, as the scenic drives were referred to, around the local area, facilities having been provided for up to 100 cars in the garage, while details were provided of nearby fishing rivers and lochs. To top it all the booklet boasted that *'The briskness and crispness of the air about Gleneagles has the exhilarating effect attributed to champagne'*. The LM&SR continued to market the hotel extensively in the US, regularly placing advertisements in American publications. One even compared the pilgrimage made by a golfer to Gleneagles with that made by a Moslem to Mecca, terming the visitor a *'Haji Golfer'*. It is doubtful if such comparisons would be used today, but in 1925 it reflected the pre-eminent place held by Gleneagles in the golfing world, claiming that *'Gleneagles is the shrine whither all good golfers make pilgrimage'*.

Golf was still the main attraction of Gleneagles, and the LM&SR continued to improve and develop these facilities. The Queen's course was extended to 18 holes in September 1925 with a length of 5,550 yards and a par of 74. About the same time the King's course was lengthened to 5,580 yards but remained a par 80 course. Three years later the third of the originally planned courses, the Wee course was opened. This was a 9 hole course of 2,625 yards with a par of 35, designed and laid out by the head greenkeeper, George Alexander. Championships were played regularly at Gleneagles with up to six major events each year. Hotel guests could purchase tickets for play on a daily or weekly basis, and for those lucky enough to live close by, annual season tickets were available. The LM&SR also promoted weekend excursions to Gleneagles which included travel, accommodation and play over the golf courses.

Throughout the 1920s and '30s, Gleneagles gained a worldwide reputation as the place to visit and featured regularly in society pages on both sides of the Atlantic. Many famous visitors, including royalty, passed through the front door, and it was described as *'golden times for golden people, a mecca for high society, a temple for the game of golf'*. This high life continued until the late 1930s by which time the threat of war once again loomed.

ABOVE LEFT: Figure 7.29
An LM&SR Hotel Residents Daily ticket issued in August 1938, the cost of 3s per day (£7.72 today) having remained unaltered since the opening of the hotel in 1924. These paper tickets were issued from a counterfoil book, as can be seen from the serial number printed in the top left corner. Many would have been issued, but as is often the case with such incidental ephemera, few have survived. *Authors collection*

ABOVE RIGHT: Figure 7.30
The LM&SR promoted Gleneagles as a weekend destination and this booklet includes tickets for Third Class travel from and to London, including sleeping car berth, the hotel bus from Gleneagles station to the hotel and back, vouchers for a two-day stay at the hotel and a voucher to play the golf courses on a Saturday and Sunday. All that for £7 10s (around £415 today). *Authors collection*

RIGHT: Figures 7.31 and 7.32
A rare LM&SR Annual Subscriber's season ticket for 1939. These season tickets were usually only issued to those who had access to the course throughout the year, so their use was largely limited to players who lived locally. This was probably the last year in which these were issued as the hotel was requisitioned by the government from 1940 to 1947. In 1947 it reopened for only one season under the LM&SR before being nationalised in 1948. This particular annual season ticket was issued to the author's father, Mr KG Young. Although valid until 31st December 1939, he was unable to make full use of it, as he was mobilised on 28th August on the eve of the outbreak of the Second World War. It is understood that he never received a refund for the missing four months!
Authors collection

The Second World War Years

On 3rd September 1939 war broke out, and for a second time in the history of the hotel a world war had a major impact on life at Gleneagles – but this time it was quite different. There was little call for luxury resorts such as Gleneagles during wartime and in common with many hotels, stately homes and even schools, it was requisitioned for war work. Initially the hotel was converted into a hospital. Its size and facilities, added to the fact that it was rail served and relatively safe in the event of invasion or bombing, being some distance from the major cities, made it highly suitable for this purpose.

The hospital had a large staff of Royal Army Medical Corps (RAMC), Voluntary Aid Detachment (VAD) personnel headed by a matron and two assistant matrons in addition to domestic staff and even its own Military Police detachment. Wards A & B and C–L were upstairs with ten to twelve rooms per ward and between two and four beds per room. The Dining Room became Ward C, the convalescent ward with eighty beds in it, while the Lochnagar Suite became a seven-bed ward for officers. Ward D, the ward for female patients, was in the suite previously used by Henry Hall; the Barony Room became the operating theatre. The Ballroom floor was covered with a false floor and used for entertainment, while one of the suites was converted into an office for the matrons. There was even a NAAFI (Navy Army & Air Force Institute) in the main corridor, and the French Restaurant housed the Red Cross library.

Some patients arrived by road but when large numbers arrived it was often by the special hospital train which was brought up the hotel branch line to the rear of the hotel. Termed 'Hospital Evacuation Train 101', the coaching stock was stabled at Gleneagles station. When required it was staffed by members of the medical team from the hotel and, it is presumed, a locomotive was supplied by Perth Motive Power Depot. In April 1940, for example, a trainload of wounded from Narvick arrived at the hotel. They had been brought by sea to Glasgow and there loaded onto the hospital train. The wounded included British and French soldiers and even German prisoners of war, many of whom spoke no English. Many of these were suffering from frostbite and exposure from the harsh weather conditions in Norway. Other hospital trains arrived after the fall of France in May 1940, and on one occasion 100 Polish wounded soldiers arrived and were detrained and admitted in only 20 minutes. This hospital train remained for a number of years after the war and the coaching stock was still stored out of use at Gleneagles as late as the early 1950s.

All the staff, particularly the nursing staff, worked long, hard hours. Day shifts were from 7.00am to 9.00pm with a short break, and night shifts were 9.00pm to 7.00am five nights a week. That said, there was a tremendous team spirit and the standard of care was extremely high. By all accounts the nursing staff looked back on their time at Gleneagles with a sense of achievement and pride, as well as with great fondness.

By the end of 1941 the need for such auxiliary hospitals as Gleneagles was less pressing, and in 1942 the hotel took on a new role as a recuperation centre for miners. Coal production was essential to the war effort and as a result miners were working longer and harder than in peacetime and suffering a higher rate of industrial injuries.

Plate 7.18
By 1944 the hotel had ceased to be used as a hospital by the Army and RAF and had been converted into a rehabilitation centre for Scottish miners. Here a group of miners are led by a physical training instructor from the main entrance on a morning 'walk', one of the compulsory aids to convalescence. Taken on 23rd August 1944, this photograph appeared in some newspapers in the USA under the headline '*Scotch miners at swank hotel*'!

Author's collection

A rehabilitation centre was considered important to return miners to full health and thus to help maintain coal output.

Again, Gleneagles was adapted to its new role. Upstairs wards became dormitories; the public rooms downstairs were fitted out as gymnasiums and as occupational therapy and physiotherapy departments. The Sun Lounge, for example, had exercise bars fitted to the walls, mattresses wrapped around the pillars and wire cages to protect the ceiling light fittings. The miners could use the swimming pool and the one functioning golf course (the King's) and were taken for fitness walks around the grounds. The age of miners ranged from seventeen to seventy, which reflected the manpower needs of the industry from the young 'Bevin Boys' who were conscripted for work down the pits to miners who were well past the normal retirement age. This role as a recuperation centre continued well after the war ended in 1945 – by which time industrial workers other than miners were also being treated – and the last patients did not leave until February 1947.

The Post-War Period

With the departure of the last miners, the hotel was returned to the LM&SR. The pre-war practice of opening only from Easter to October was resumed. However, after the miners' departure, only a few months were left before the hotel was due to open for the season and there was a flurry of activity to convert Gleneagles from the war-time austerity of a rehabilitation centre back to its original role as a luxury hotel. Much of the furniture and fittings had been stored on the fourth floor, and this had to be unpacked, cleaned, and redistributed. Such was the pressure of work that the junior staff were employed to assist the gang of workmen employed for the task. Even this was not enough, and they were joined by groups of German prisoners of war from the POW Camp 21 at Comrie, referred to in more detail in Chapter 8. In the event everything was ready in time for the reopening. Amazingly, the crystal chandeliers in the ballroom were found to be still intact, having been carefully protected during the room's time as a gymnasium.

Although largely restored to its pre-war splendour, Gleneagles was not immune from some other aspects of post-war austerity, including food rationing, which was then still in effect. Menus were restricted, choices being annotated 'A' or 'B', and bore the instructions from the Ministry of Food that *'not more than one dish marked "A" and one marked "B" or alternatively two dishes marked "B" and not more than three courses in all may be partaken at any one meal'*.

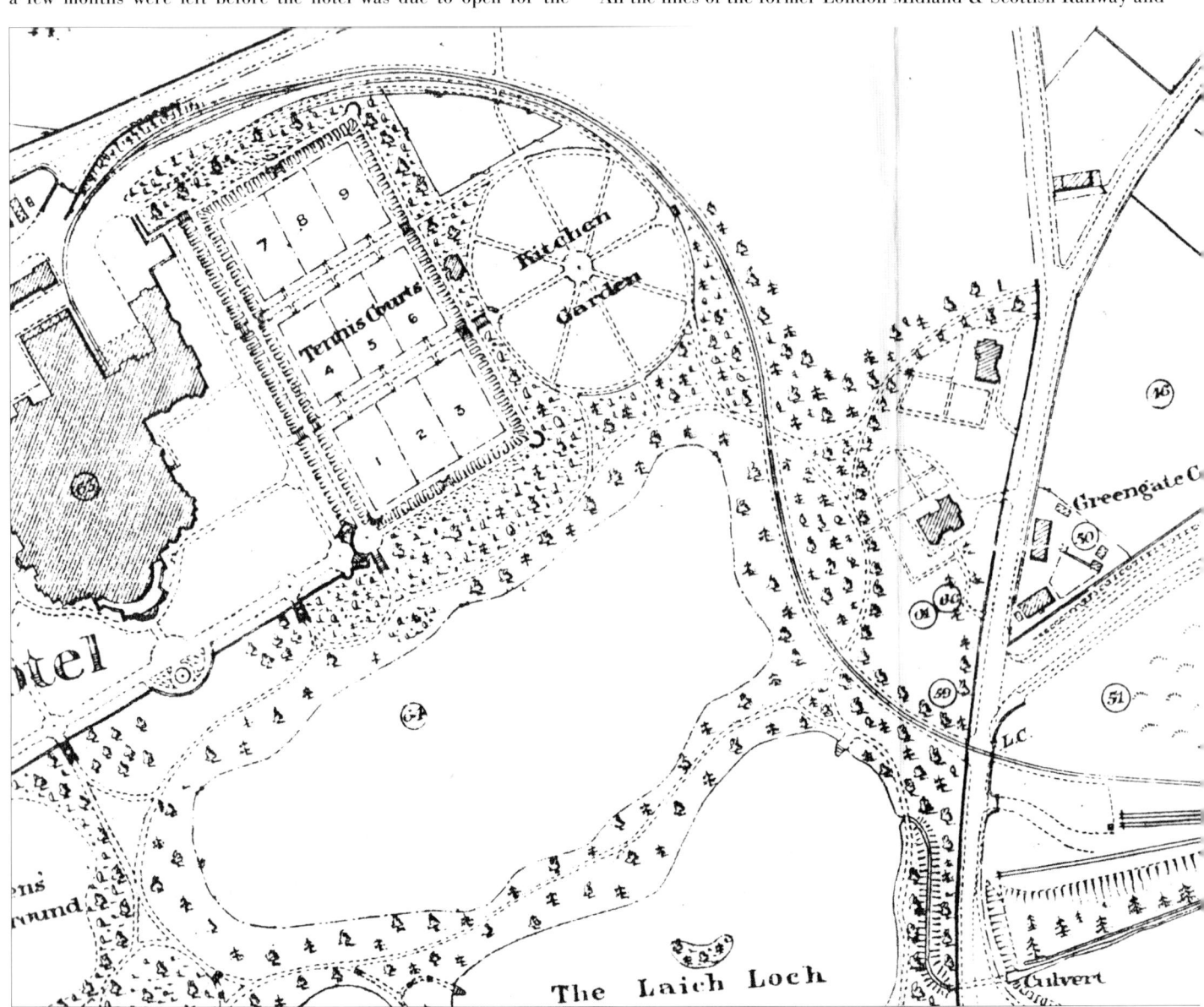

The 1947 season was to be the first and last post-war at Gleneagles under the LM&SR, for under the sweeping nationalisation of industries by the new Labour government, the railways of the United Kingdom became part of British Railways from 1st January 1948. All the lines of the former London Midland & Scottish Railway and the London & North Eastern Railway in Scotland became part of the Scottish Region of British Railways, and all the railway owned hotels became part of The Hotels Executive.

Gleneagles continued to operate as a seasonal hotel, advertised as being open from *'Easter to October'*. In fact the hotel usually opened on the Thursday nearest to the 12th of April. This seasonal nature of operation presented the management with various problems, including that of what to do with the hotel staff when the season ended and how to ensure they returned the following year. In LM&SR days this was largely resolved by moving staff to other hotels owned or operated by the company during the November to April interregnum. Some staff were only employed for the season and they, or their replacements, would be re-employed at the start of the following season.

During the closed season, the opportunity was taken to carry out repairs, maintenance and improvements to the hotel, but the golf courses and Club House continued to operate as usual. In fact the Club House operated as a more or less independent entity as is reflected in the address label reproduced in Figure 7.22. During the winter months locals used the Laich Loch for skating and curling, and unofficially people would ski and sledge on the slopes of the golf courses. The author fondly recalls the 2nd hole of the King's course as being good for tobogganing.

The hotel continued to flourish during the 1950s and '60s and, in addition to the traditional guests, from the 1970s it began to grow the conference business for which Gleneagles was well suited. The Wee course was extended to 18 holes in 1974 and was renamed the Prince's course; in recent years the name of the Wee course has been

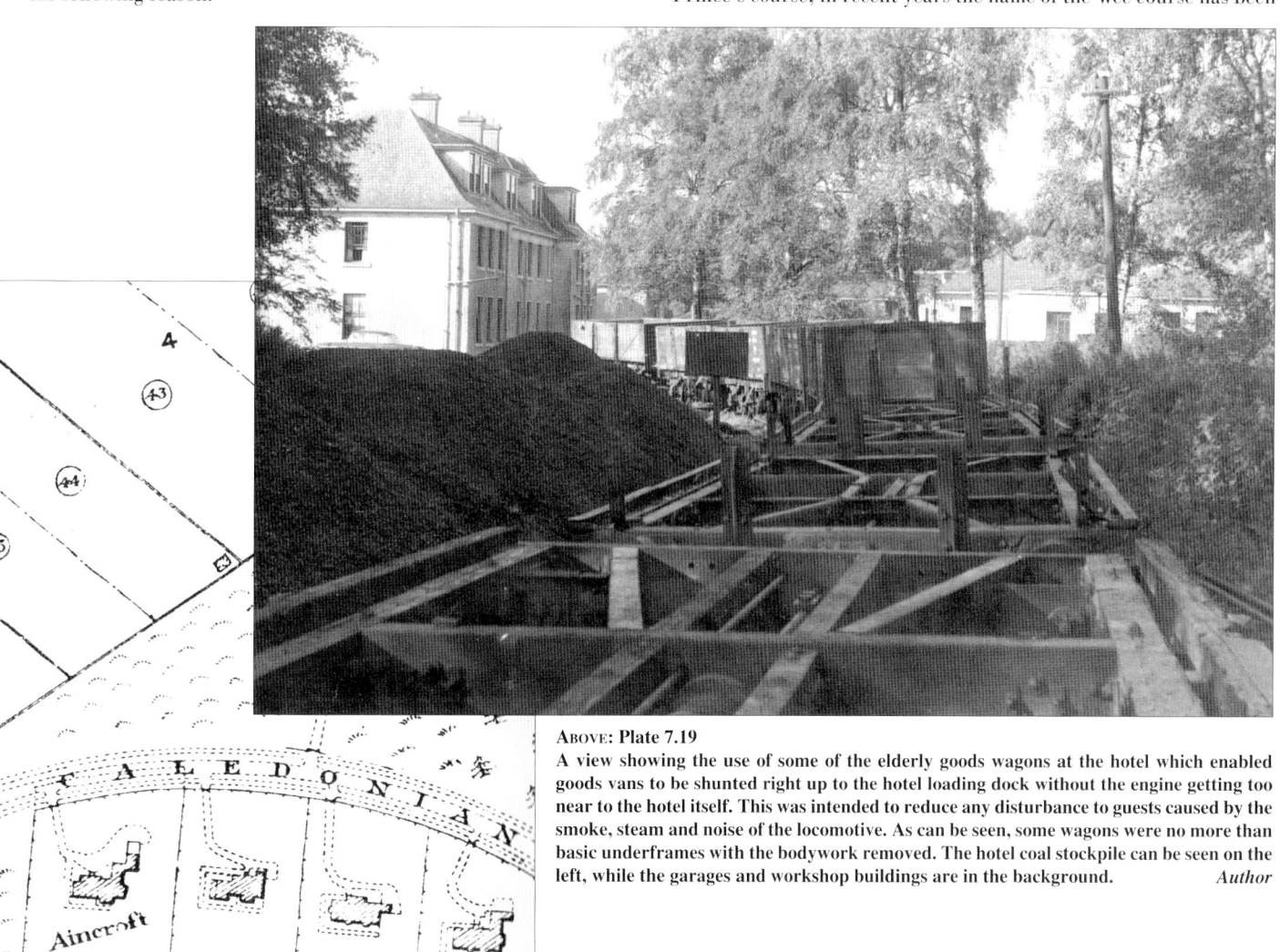

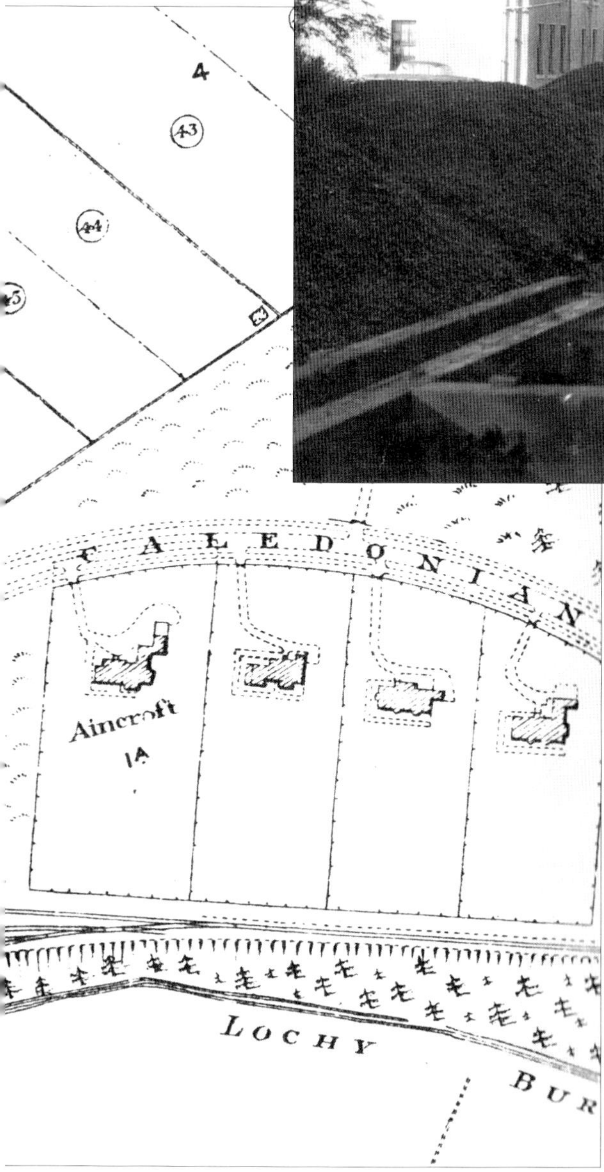

ABOVE: **Plate 7.19**
A view showing the use of some of the elderly goods wagons at the hotel which enabled goods vans to be shunted right up to the hotel loading dock without the engine getting too near to the hotel itself. This was intended to reduce any disturbance to guests caused by the smoke, steam and noise of the locomotive. As can be seen, some wagons were no more than basic underframes with the bodywork removed. The hotel coal stockpile can be seen on the left, while the garages and workshop buildings are in the background. *Author*

Figure 7.33
A plan showing the route of the hotel branch line in the 1930s. The line ran across the rear of the villas in Caledonian Crescent to cross the Crieff to Dunfermline road and then curved north to swing round the kitchen garden to the small goods yard loop at the rear of the hotel. Also clearly visible here is the fan of three sidings south of the line just east of the level crossing. These sidings were almost certainly where the stone from Jerviston viaduct was brought in, as much of it was used to build the adjacent walls and entrances. *Authors collection*

reused for a completely new course. A highlight of this period was the Commonwealth Prime Ministers' Conference which was held at Gleneagles in the summer of 1977.

However, the advent of privatisation of state assets under the Conservative government led by Margaret Thatcher spelt the end of Gleneagles as a railway hotel, for the railway hotels were one of the first groups to be denationalised. Thus in 1981 Gleneagles hotel ceased to be a railway hotel after fifty-seven years and, together with the North British Hotel in Edinburgh, became part of Gleneagles Hotel plc. It was ironic that this company should bring together the two flagship hotels of the Caledonian and its 'auld enemy' the North British Railway. Quite what Donald Matheson would have thought of that one can only imagine.

The hotel continues to this day, now as 'The Gleneagles', a part of Diageo plc. Although no longer a railway hotel, it continues to be served by Gleneagles station where the London sleeper express still stops daily as it has done, except during the war years, since the hotel first opened.

THE HOTEL BRANCH LINE

The hotel being part of a scheme promoted by the Caledonian Railway, it was logical that it should be rail served. This aspect was addressed at an early stage of the planning when it was resolved – at a meeting at the Caledonian Railway offices at Buchanan Street on 25th November 1913 – that a temporary railway should be constructed from Crieff Junction. In fact the topography of the area made this impractical and thus the hotel branch line was built as a trailing connection with the Crieff branch line just north of Easter Greenwells Farm.

The branch line was constructed like any other private siding on the Caledonian system. The points entering the branch line were operated by a small ground frame, controlled by a tablet lock. Beyond the trailing connection was a set of trap points to prevent runaway wagons, or even locomotives, from running onto the main line. The branch line then passed through a wooden gate which was normally closed across the rails. This not only marked the boundary between the Caledonian Railway and Gleneagles Limited, but also served to prevent livestock from straying onto the main line as the hotel branch line passed over an ungated level crossing further on.

Beyond the gate there was a short passing loop to allow locomotives to run round a train. Because of the severe gradient leading up to the hotel the regulations required that all wagons be propelled up the branch line with the locomotive at the lower end. On the return journey the locomotive, being at the lower end, had to run round the wagons to propel them onto the Crieff line such that it could then pull them down to Gleneagles. From this loop the branch line climbed steadily alongside the wood which formed part of the White Muir and then crossed the private road at Caledonian Crescent. This was an ungated crossing; the procedure was for the train to be brought to a stand while the guard walked ahead to the crossing to ensure that

ABOVE: Plate 7.20
Elderly goods wagons, no longer fit for commercial use, were used on the hotel branch line in the 1950s and '60s. Strictly restricted for this purpose, they were stencilled '*To be worked between Gleneagles Station and Gleneagles Hotel*' as shown here. They were not used to convey goods but mainly for shunting purposes at the hotel. These were often relics of the early pre-Grouping railways, including the Caledonian, the Midland, and the London & North Western. *Author*

Plate 7.21
All wagons on the hotel branch had to be propelled uphill towards the hotel such that the locomotive could prevent runaways on the steeply falling gradient. Here ex-Caledonian Railway Pickersgill 0-6-0 No. 57679 propels a wagon of coal and a van of laundry across the ungated level crossing on Caledonian Crescent in 1963 while the guard with his red flag checks that the crossing is clear of road traffic. The steep gradient of the line leading up to the hotel is evident in this photograph. *Author*

Plate 7.22
During the 1920s and '30s, the hotel branch line was worked by a small tank engine. During the week this was based at Gleneagles, but returned to Perth each Friday for maintenance and a boiler washout. This was usually one of the ex-Caledonian Railway 0-4-0 saddle tank engines. In this rare shot taken from Johnnie Matthie's bridge, it is seen here racing down the 1 in 100 main line near Auchterarder one evening in 1922. The opportunity to run at speed on the main line would have been a rare opportunity for the crew to show what the locomotive could do.
KG Young

Plate 7.23
The branch line entered the hotel grounds over a level crossing on the A823 Dunfermline to Crieff road. Looking more like conventional domestic gates, they were painted dark green, presumably to make them more aesthetically pleasing, although they did have red warning triangles. Here, ex-Caledonian Railway 0-6-0 No. 57679 propels its two-wagon load into the hotel grounds in 1963. Although the level crossing is long gone, the gate pillars can still be discerned where the wall has now been infilled.
Author

the road was clear. He held up a red flag to stop any road traffic and hand signalled the engine driver to proceed over the crossing.

A short distance beyond this crossing on the south side of the line was the site of a small goods yard with a fan of three sidings. This was used for the delivery of building materials during construction of the hotel and was left *in situ* for a number of years after it opened, finally being lifted some time before the Second World War. The site was still visible up to the time of closure of the line in 1964, being delineated by the telegraph pole route which followed along the south side of the line. The line then curved north to cross the A823 Dunfermline to Crieff road at a gated level crossing. This led into the hotel grounds so the stone pillars were made to match all the other entrances to the hotel, and green painted metal gates were used rather than the conventional white painted wooden level crossing gates. Despite the fact that they had red diamonds on them, the gates were not easy to see when closed across the road and would probably have been frowned upon these days, but as the line was only used during the hours of daylight (except in emergencies during the war) this was not regarded as a problem. The gates were not interlocked in any way and were hand operated and, because of their width, overlapped when opened across the roadway.

Having entered the grounds of the hotel proper, the line curved sharply north and climbed to skirt round the circular vegetable garden and the tennis courts after which it levelled off. Here there was another longer loop, between the tennis courts and the Braco Road to facilitate shunting operations and unloading of wagons. Generally one line was used to store wagons including the open framed wagons used as 'spacers'. These wagons, which were usually ancient rolling stock no longer fit for revenue traffic, were only permitted to be worked between Gleneagles station and the hotel. In the 1950s and '60s it was not unusual to see ex-L&NWR, Midland and Caledonian wagons still being used for this purpose. They bore specially painted stencils indicating their restricted use. So decrepit were they that when a wagon once derailed near the level crossing it literally fell apart and the component pieces were simply stacked at the side of the line for scrap. The purpose of these wagons was to allow the laundry and other vans to be propelled to the loading bay at the rear of the hotel without the steam locomotive getting too close to the hotel, presumably so that distinguished guests were not inconvenienced by the noisy dirty steam engine.

In the early days, when rail-borne traffic was quite heavy, a small shunting locomotive was provided to work the hotel branch line. The loco worked the line during the week, returning to Perth at the end of the week for maintenance and a boiler wash out. This practice ceased in the 1930s as the proportion of traffic carried by rail reduced and thereafter the branch line was operated by a locomotive from one of the goods trains calling at Gleneagles.

The amount of traffic to and from the hotel by rail was still substantial, and this is evidenced by the one serious accident to occur on this branch line, which happened in May 1932. A locomotive was propelling seventeen wagons up the line and had reached the steep curves near the top end when the load proved too heavy for it. The driving wheels began to slip and then the train started moving backwards downhill. The brakes were unable to hold the weight of the train which started to gather speed, at which juncture the fireman, John Lynoch, leapt from the footplate and ran down the line in an attempt to open the gates on the Glendevon to Crieff road. He had only managed to open them partway when the train, by now estimated to be travelling at over 40 mph, ran through the gates and continued downhill. Seeing there was nothing he could do, the driver, William Lee, then also leapt from the engine, leaving the crewless train to continue down over the Caledonian Crescent level crossing. It negotiated the points at the loop and then ran into the buffer stops at the end of the headshunt. The tender buried itself in the bank behind the buffers while the wagons telescoped together in a jumble on top of the locomotive. As a result of this accident, a set of 'catch points' was installed to protect the level crossing on the Glendevon to Crieff road. Sited uphill from the crossing, within the hotel grounds, they could be run through in the trailing (uphill) direction, but when a train returned down the hill, they had to be held over by the ground frame lever provided. As an added precaution, the speed of trains on the hotel branch line was limited to 8 mph.

In the post-war years the hotel branch train was usually worked by one of the locomotives from the two daily goods trains which crossed at Gleneagles each morning. These were known locally as the 'Stirling bogies' and the 'Perth bogies' and worked local stations between Bridge of Allan and Blackford, and Forgandenny and Auchterarder respectively. The locomotive from the Stirling bogies would assemble wagons for the hotel and then take them up the branch line, returning with any outgoing wagons. The surviving logbook indicates that this train left Gleneagles anywhere between 9.00am and 11.15am, returning after about 35 to 45 minutes. Sometimes the journey took as long as one and a quarter hours to allow for the regular passenger service on the Crieff branch line to pass. The trip operated six days a week.

It is noteworthy that on 29th and 30th June 1964 two trips were made, presumably to withdraw all the wagons from the line prior to closure. The last trip was made on the morning of 4th July 1964, the last day of operation as the section of line between Gleneagles and Muthill closed to all traffic the following day.

In September, a little over two months after the hotel branch line closed, the track was lifted and the level crossings removed. Gleneagles station closed to goods traffic two months later, and thereafter all goods for the hotel were delivered by road. Although the hotel remained in railway ownership for a further seventeen years, the closure of the branch line removed one of the unique aspects of its operation and one of the most tangible symbols of its railway origins.

Plate 7.24
Ex-Caledonian Railway 0-6-0 No. 57679 shunting at the hotel goods yard in 1963. This locomotive would have been the train engine on the local goods trip from Stirling to Perth which would spend about an hour at Gleneagles working the daily goods train up to the hotel and back again. The engine stands at the east end of the loop which was quite close to the Auchterarder to Braco road, the fir trees in the background being part of the wood on the north side of the road.
Author

Chapter 8
The Challenging Years Under the LM&SR

The First World War had put a considerable strain on the railways of Great Britain, the Caledonian Railway included. The heavy use of the railways in support of the war effort coupled with a shortage of manpower, lack of maintenance and under-investment, had left them in a poor state. In the years following the peace of 1919, the future of the railways was the subject of considerable debate. The main thrust of this was to group the large number of railways, some quite small, into fewer large companies which would be economically more viable. Full scale nationalisation was dismissed at this stage, and various grouping models proposed.

Originally there were to be seven groups, with one of these covering the whole of Scotland. In the event, this was amended and the Railways Act 1921 called for two groups to share the lines in Scotland. One group of the East Coast companies – which was to become the London & North Eastern Railway – included the Great Eastern, Great Northern and North Eastern railways in England together with the North British and Great North of Scotland railways north of the border. A similar grouping of the West Coast companies included the London & North Western, Midland, North Staffordshire and Lancashire & Yorkshire railways, and in Scotland, the Caledonian, Highland and Glasgow & South Western railways. The 'Grouping', as it was referred to, was to come into effect on 1st January 1923.

That said, as mentioned in Chapter 6, all did not go smoothly in respect of the Caledonian Railway or, in England, the North Staffordshire Railway. This stemmed from a disagreement over the number of shares in the new London Midland & Scottish Railway allocated on the basis of the number of shares held in the Caledonian Railway. The calculation was based on the Caledonian Railway Company's profits for 1913, the last full year of operation prior to the outbreak of war. Unfortunately for the Caledonian (and the North Staffordshire) this had been a particularly poor year, reflected in the dismal traffic results for 1912/13 for the branch lines of Strathearn.

As a result, the Caledonian Railway did not formally become part of the LM&SR until 1st July 1923, although for all practical purposes, it operated as part of what became the Northern Division of the LM&SR from 1st January 1923. A Scotland Committee was formed in December 1922 which took full control of the Highland and Glasgow & South Western railways, and in the interim, exercised considerable influence over Caledonian Railway matters.

The headquarters of the new LM&SR was at Euston in London, and it was quite evident from the outset where the centre of power and influence was to lie. No less than twenty of the twenty-six Board members of the LM&SR came from the London & North Western and Midland railways, while only two came from the Caledonian. The same was true at an operational level, where nine out of ten chief officers came from the three largest English companies, the one exception being Donald Matheson, formerly General Manager of the Caledonian Railway, who became the LM&SR General Manager for Scotland.

This one appointment was particularly significant for Strathearn, as it meant that Matheson was in the best possible position to see his vision for Gleneagles Hotel and golf courses come to fruition. The post-war resumption of construction was well in hand when the LM&SR took over, and Matheson was able to oversee the final completion of the work and fitting out of the hotel, which opened on 5th June 1924.

At a local level, two long-standing Caledonian Railway railwaymen retired. One was Guard Robert Amos, mentioned in Chapter 6, who had started his career with the Caledonian Railway back in 1877 as a lampman at Perth. Promoted to guard in 1892, he came to Crieff in 1899, and for the next quarter of a century was a well-known figure on the Crieff branch lines. He was over seventy years old when he retired after forty-five year service, and was presented with a wallet of notes by the stationmaster at Crieff at a ceremony to mark his retirement. The other was William Wishart, a signalman, and ancestor of David Ferguson, who retired in April 1924 after an impressive forty-seven years' service. Having lost a leg in an accident at Brechin in 1880, he came to Duchlage Road Crossing as a nightwatchman, and then spent ten years in Crieff West signal box before becoming gate keeper at Pittentian.

One other staff move of note was the appointment of Mr HH Ward, who had been manager of the LM&SR Railway Hotel in Inverness

Plate 8.1
The Gleneagles Hotel golf courses had been open for four years before the LM&SR took over, and continued to be a popular venue until the hotel opened in 1924. This view of Broomy Law, the 6 hole on the King's course, gives a good idea of the crowds attracted to this prestige course that summer.
Author's collection

LEFT: Figure 8.1
An early LM&SR brochure advertising Gleneagles Hotel along the lines of the 'Eighth wonder of the World'. This publication dates from 1925-28 as the Queen's course is shown as an 18 hole course having been extended from 9 holes in 1925, but the Wee course which was added in 1928 is not listed. The various facilities of the hotel are outlined in colourful prose including equating Gleneagles to Robert Louis Stephenson's description of Fontainebleu as *'There is no place where the young are more gladly conscious of their youth or the old better contented with their age'*.
Author's collection

RIGHT: Figure 8.2
A rather colourful tariff card for the new Gleneagles Hotel showing the rates for various sporting and recreation activities in the hotel. Printed in red and black on white, besides golf this cover illustrates shooting, fishing, swimming, horse riding and dancing. These small folding cards were placed on tables in the lounge. *Author's collection*

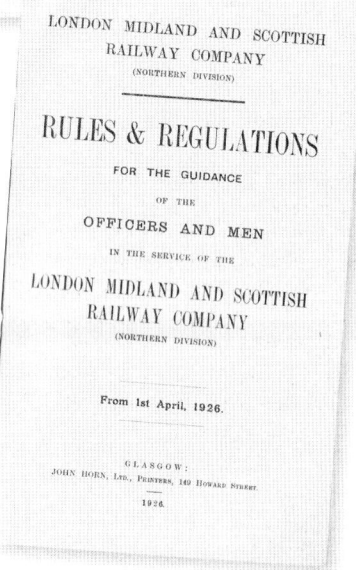

RIGHT: Figure 8.3
Frontispiece of the LM&SR (Northern Division) Rule Book of 1926. This superseded the various rule books of the constituent companies. Printed in Glasgow, this was still very much the Scottish edition of the Rule Book. Subsequent editions, used for the whole of the LM&SR, were printed in Derby. *Author's collection*

ABOVE: Figure 8.4
An LM&SR (Caledonian Section) Luggage Label. This label was to the standard Caledonian Railway design except for the change in the heading showing it was now part of the LM&SR. These 'transitional' labels were used until the new company produced its own standardised design. This is a nice example of a local label between two Strathearn stations. *Author's collection*

for twenty-one years, to be the first manager of the newly opened Gleneagles Hotel. His tenure was brief, however, for he was replaced the following year by Mr Frank Fisher, who remained at the helm until 1930 when he left to become manager of the Metropole Hotel in London, being succeeded by Mr Gordon Yates.

Some things did change overnight, but the LM&SR faced huge challenges in bringing together the many and disparate railway companies which formed the new company. It was not until three years later that a new Rule Book was introduced, and then on 1st April 1926, hardly the most auspicious of dates. The introduction to the new Rule Book spelled out:

'*The following Rules & Regulations supersede The Rules & Regulations formerly in operation on the London Midland & Scottish Railway (Northern Division) and as contained in the following Rule Books and Appendices:*

Caledonian	*1921*
Glasgow & South Western	*1917*
Glasgow Barrhead	
& Kilmarnock Joint Line	*1917*
Highland	*1920*
Portpatrick & Wigtown Joint	*1922*'

Other matters such as printed material and stationery also evolved slowly. Initially much stationery continued to be printed in the old Caledonian Railway house style, and it was not replaced until the LM&SR, after much study, introduced its own standard range of stationery, bearing ERO (Executive Research Office) stock numbers, in the early 1930s. Much Caledonian Railway material continued to be used on a waste out basis, and it was not unusual, for example, to find Caledonian Railway luggage labels, such as that at Figure 4.3, being used in the early 1960s, well into the British Railways days.

ABOVE: Plate 8.2
A postcard of the main entrance at the newly opened Gleneagles Hotel taken from the Dunfermline to Crieff road. The recently laid out grounds have yet to mature in this view of the pristine gates and sign. The stonework was part of the works carried out using material from the demolished Jerviston Viaduct pictured in Chapter 7. *Author's collection*

RIGHT: Plate 8.3
A view of a pristine looking Gleneagles station from the east end in 1923, the year in which the Caledonian Railway became part of the LM&SR. The rebuilt station had been open for just over four years at this point, allowing the vegetation to grow back and the borders and flower beds to mature. The station was well equipped with the large distinctive Caledonian Railway seats, and still has the original wood-post oil lamps which were later replaced. Note also the extensive point rodding alongside and between the main running lines. *Author's collection*

In many areas, the Caledonian Railway legacy lived on, in its stations, structures and signalling to name but a few. Other than changes in signage and livery, little was done to the branch lines of Strathearn, which retained their essentially Caledonian Railway feel right up to the day they closed in 1964 (Plate 10.37). A few cosmetic changes were made in British Railways days, but the LM&SR carried out little more than routine maintenance during its stewardship, although some economies, rather than changes or improvements, were made in later years.

Much the same could be said of the Caledonian Railway locomotives and rolling stock in use on the branch lines, although inevitably they were replaced as they wore out or new and improved stock was introduced across the LM&SR. Former Caledonian Railway locomotives in particular continued to work many of the trains throughout Strathearn during LM&SR days, and a few goods services were still being hauled by ex-Caledonian Railway engines until the Gleneagles to Crieff line closed in 1964.

Another major asset to be transferred to the LM&SR were the staff who became employees of the new company. Many, such as Robert Amos and William Wishart already mentioned, had been with the Caledonian 'man and boy', and remained fiercely loyal to their old company. In those days it was not unusual for a man to join the Caledonian Railway at the tender age of fourteen and to spend his entire working life with the company, retiring at 65 with fifty-one years' service. When Mr James Smith retired as stationmaster at Comrie in October 1931 for example, he had forty-five years of railway service, having joined the Caledonian Railway in 1886. Prior to his nine years at Comrie he had been stationmaster at Muthill for sixteen years, so had spent a quarter of a century in Strathearn. Two months later, Mr John McGregor, a goods porter at Comrie was presented with '*a handsome Waltham gold watch*' on completion of thirty-seven years' service, and the following year, Mr Thomas McPherson, a traffic porter at the same station retired also after thirty-seven years as a railwayman. Having started with the Caledonian Railway at Bridge of Allan in 1895, he had worked at Stanley, Luncarty and Strathord prior to coming to Comrie. Such service was not exceptional, and a good many railwaymen who started work with the Caledonian Railway outlasted the LM&SR to become employees of British Railways in 1948, not retiring until the 1960s.

In terms of services and traffic over the Strathearn branch lines, the Grouping brought few significant changes in the early years of the LM&SR. In terms of commercial sustainability, the LM&SR continued to tailor local services to meet local demand and to actively promote the tourist potential of the district. On the other side of the coin, they made a number of economies to reduce costs wherever possible. The opening of Gleneagles Hotel on 5th June 1924 amid

Plate 8.4
An unusual view of the main station buildings at Gleneagles taken from the approach road in the early 1920s. Surprisingly this view was even published as a postcard. The trackwork in the goods yard still looks clean and tidy in comparison to the same view in later years. A solitary Caledonian Railway vintage coach stands in the long carriage siding.
Author's collection

RIGHT: **Plate 8.5**
Gleneagles station in early LM&SR days with a heavy doubled-headed goods train passing through on the Up line. The well-manicured gardens and lawns are looking most attractive and the trees planted on the bank in the foreground are maturing. The short head-shunt from the long carriage sidings, which is just visible on the extreme left, was removed in later LM&SR days. The station is still equipped with the original signage in Caledonian Railway livery and wooden post platform lamps and a generous number of the large Caledonian Railway style platform seats. *Author's collection*

Figure 8.5
The LM&SR Time Table for 1926 showing the services between Glasgow and Edinburgh to stations in Strathearn via Gleneagles. This was always shown as the principal route to Crieff and Upper Strathearn, and enjoyed what through services there were. The route from Crieff to Perth via Methven Junction was regarded as the secondary passenger service.
Author's collection

CHAPTER 8: THE CHALLENGING YEARS UNDER THE LM&SR

much publicity afforded the LM&SR an opportunity to promote travel not only to Gleneagles, but to the surrounding district, and this they were not slow to do.

Other developments, were, however, less welcome. At the end of February 1925, Mr Peter Crerar began operating a bus service between Crieff and Perth. The return fare of 3s 6d was 10d cheaper than the train fare, and he offered late night buses on Wednesdays and Saturdays. The *Strathearn Herald* saw this as healthy and much needed competition for the railway, and ended their article with the advice that: *'we confidently appeal to the public to give this new venture their support'*. By 1927, this bus service had been extended through to St. Fillans.

One of the economies of scale achieved under the LM&SR was the marketing of tourism to a much wider public than the pre-Grouping companies, an example being the LM&SR 1926 Tourist Guide. This included a table of Tourist fares from London (Euston), St. Pancras, Kensington (Addison Road), Broad Street and Moorgate Street to what were termed 'Scotch Stations' including:

DESTINATION	FIRST CLASS	THIRD CLASS
Balquhidder	166s 9d	100s 0d
Comrie	167s 0d	100s 3d
Crieff	167s 0d	100s 3d
Gleneagles	162s 3d	97s 6d
Lochearnhead	166s 9d	100s 0d
St. Fillans	171s 0d	102s 9d

It is difficult to appreciate in today's climate that you could go to a booking office at one of these London stations, that they would know where a little village such as St. Fillans was, and moreover could sell you a through ticket to it, and all that without the aid of the internet. Interestingly, the pooling arrangements between the LM&SR and the L&NER meant that you could also purchase tickets to destinations on the L&NER in Scotland including obscure little stations such as Rumbling Bridge, about 10 miles south of Auchterarder.

One nationwide event which had an impact on the Strathearn lines was the National Strike of 1926. Starting off as a strike by miners, it spread rapidly, and a General Strike was called for 1st May. By 4th May between 1.5 and 1.75 million workers were on strike, the railways being badly affected. The *Strathearn Herald* reported that:

'some 33 Porters, Clerks, Engine Drivers, Firemen and Surfacemen etc. employed at Crieff ceased work on Tuesday. The train service for the first 2 days of the strike composed of one or two trains to Perth, Dundee, and the South, but this was increased on Thursday to 2 trains. 5 trains were running yesterday to and from Crieff. The service today (Saturday) it is anticipated will be much the same.'

The General Strike lasted until 12th May, after which most men went back to work – but the majority of miners stayed on strike throughout the summer, the last strikers not returning to work until November. This continued action by the miners led to coal shortages and the need for reduced train services as had been the case in the past, but Strathearn was not too badly affected as can be seen from the timetable at Figure 8.7.

The following year, 1927, saw an example of the fruits of promoting Gleneagles Hotel when, on 15th June, the 11.5pm Sleeping Car train from London (Euston) to Perth was duplicated, with a special Sleeping Car train for a large party from the Sun Life of Canada Assurance Company. The train, No. 163, ran slightly behind the 11.5pm timetable:

Carlisle	5.34am
Gleneagles	8.51am
Perth	9.13am

The train also stopped at Larbert and Dunblane, if required, to set down Sleeping Car passengers only. The Sun Life party returned to London on the evening Sleeping Car train from Gleneagles on 18th June.

The LM&SR proved keen to exploit any potential for attracting new custom, and the early years saw a regular pattern of specials for the likes of football matches and other events. Thus, in October 1926, when Scotland played Wales at football in Glasgow, cheap Excursion tickets were sold and extra carriages were added to strengthen trains from Crieff.

Similarly, whenever St. Johnstone were playing at home at Perth,

Figure 8.6
The LM&SR Time Table for 1926 showing the services between Perth and Crieff via Methven Junction, including the Methven branch. This reminds passengers that the 'Steam Rail Coach' between Methven Junction and Methven is Third Class only. Also shown are the connections through to Dundee. *Author's collection*

Crieff, Comrie, St. Fillans, Lochearnhead and Balquhidder.

		a.m.	a.m.	a.m.		a.m.	p.m.		Ex. Sats. p.m.	Sats. only p.m.		p.m.	p.m.	p.m.	
Gleneagles	dep.	6 35		8 50		11 40			3 5	3 15			6 40	8 20	Any of the Trains to St. Fillans will call at Dalchonzie Platform (between Comrie and St. Fillans) to set down Passengers on their intimating to the Station Master at Comrie their desire to alight. No Heavy Luggage or Bicycles will be taken into or put out of the Trains at Dalchonzie Platform.
Tullibardine	"			8 56		11 46			3 11	3 21			6 46		
Muthill	"	6 45		9 4		11 55			3 20	3 30			6 55	8 29	
Highlandman	"			9 10		12 1			3 26	3 36			7 0		
Crieff	arrive	6 54		9 14		12 5			3 30	3 40			7 5	8 41	
	dep.	7 10				12 10		1 9	3 32	3 42	6 0		7 6		
Comrie	arrive	7 25				12 25		1 24	3 47	3 57	6 15		7 21		
	dep.		7 55			12 27		1 26	3 48	3 58	6 16				
St. Fillans	"		8 7			12 39		1 38	4 0	4 10	6 28				
Lochearnhead	dep.							1 52			6 44				
Balquhidder	arrive							2 0			6 50				

		a.m.	a.m.		a.m.			p.m.		p.m.		p.m.	p.m.	
Balquhidder	dep.	7 5											7 30	Any of the Trains from St. Fillans will call at Dalchonzie Platform (between St. Fillans and Comrie) to set down Passengers on their intimating to the Station Master at St. Fillans their desire to alight, and to take up Passengers on their intimating to the Signalman at Dalchonzie at least 5 minutes before the Train is due to leave St. Fillans. No Heavy Luggage will be taken into or put out of the Trains at Dalchonzie Platform
Lochearnhead	"	7 12											7 37	
St. Fillans	"	7 31			8 45			1 10		5 0			7 50	
Comrie	arrive	7 43			8 57			1 22		5 12			8 2	
	dep.		7 50		8 59			1 25		5 14		7 28	8 4	
Crieff	arrive		8 5		9 14			1 40		5 29		7 43	8 19	
	dep.		8 10		9 25			1 43		5 34		7 45		
Highlandman	"		8C14		9 29			1 47		5 38		7 49		
Muthill	"		8 19		9 34			1 53		5 47		7 55		
Tullibardine	"				9 40			1 59		5 53				
Gleneagles	arrive		8 30		9 47			2 5		6 0			8 7	

C—Calls at Highlandman, only when required, to pick up Passengers for Larbert or beyond.

Perth, Methven, Crieff, Comrie, St. Fillans, Lochearnhead and Balquhidder.

		B a.m.	B p.m.			B p.m.			
Perth	dep.	9 15	12 20			5 5			B—Calls at Ruthven Road and Tibbermuir Crossings.
Almondbank	"	9 27	12 32			5 17			
Methven	arrive	9 45	12 47			5 40			
	dep.	9 20	12 20			5 15			
Methven Junction	"	9 33	12 38			5 26			
Balgowan	"	9 39	12 44			5 32			
Madderty	"	9 45	12 50			5 38			
Abercairny	"	9 51	12 56			5 44			
Innerpeffray	"	9 57	1 2			5 50			
Crieff	arrive	10 2	1 7			5 54			
Crieff	dep.		1 9			6 0			
Comrie	arrive		1 24			6 15			
	dep.		1 26			6 16			
St. Fillans	arrive		1 38			6 28			
Lochearnhead	"		1 52			6 44			
Balquhidder	"		2 0			6 50			

		a.m.	a.m.	a.m.	a.m.	B p.m.	p.m.		
Balquhidder	dep.		7 5					7 30	
Lochearnhead	"		7 12					7 37	
St. Fillans	"		7 31	8 45		5 0		7 50	The 7.42 a.m. Train from Crieff calls at Tibbermuir or Ruthven Road Crossings to take up Passengers when signalled by the Gatekeeper to do so.
Comrie	arrive		7 43	8 57		5 12		8 2	
	dep.		7 50	8 59		5 14		8 4	B—Calls at Tibbermuir and Ruthven Road Crossings.
Crieff	arrive		8 5	9 14		5 29		8 19	
Crieff	dep.	7 42			10 20	6 3	8*22		
Innerpeffray	"	7 47			10 25	6 7			† Daily except Saturdays.
Abercairny	"	7 52			10 30	6 12			* Saturdays only.
Madderty	"	7 58			10 37	6 17	8*36		
Balgowan	"	8 3			10 42	6 23			
Methven	arrive	8 23			10 58	6 45			
	dep.	8 0			10 35	6 15			
Methven Junction	"	8 10			10 48	6 30	8*47		
Almondbank	"	8 18			10 55	6 38	8*55		
Perth (Ticket Platform)	arrive	8 28			11 7	6 48			
	dep.	8 30			11 10	6 50			
Perth	arrive	8 32			11 12	6 52	9* 7		

Methven Branch.

		a.m.	a.m.	a.m.	p.m.			p.m.		p.m.				
Methven Junction	dep.	8 18	9 40	10 53	12 42			5 35		6 40				
Methven	arrive	8 23	9 45	10 58	12 47			5 40		6 45				

		a.m.	a.m.	a.m.	p.m.	p.m.		p.m.						
Methven	dep.	8 0	9 20	10 35	12 20	5 15		6 15						
Methven Junction	arrive	8 5	9 25	10 40	12 25	5 20		6 20						

Bankfoot Light Railway.

		a.m.				p.m.					a.m.				p.m.		
Strathord	dep.	7 20				4 50			Bankfoot	dep.	7 45				5 15		
Bankfoot	arrive	7 35				5 1			Strathord	arrive	7 56				5 26		

Figure 8.7
An extract from the LM&SR (Northern Division) emergency timetable published in the summer of 1926 following the General Strike of that year. Although by the time this was published the strike had largely collapsed, the continued strike by the miners affected coal supplies and a reduced service was still necessary. At least the Strathearn lines fared better than the poor little Bankfoot branch which was reduced to two trains each way per day with a 10-hour interval between trains. *Author's collection*

CHAPTER 8: THE CHALLENGING YEARS UNDER THE LM&SR

special trains were run. On January 1927, for the St. Johnstone v Kilmarnock match, a special train left Comrie at 12.50pm for Perth. Again, in December 1928, a special train was laid on for the St. Johnstone v Hibernians match, with a forecast load of 130 passengers, and on 2nd January 1929, another special left Comrie, again at 12.50pm with an estimated 150 passengers.

Sunday schools and choirs were another source of regular excursion traffic both to and from the district. The abbreviation 'SS' for Sunday school used in the instructions for such traffic did not then have the unfortunate cache it later acquired in Nazi Germany. The numbers concerned were impressive, and the figures for one busy Saturday, 11th June 1927, give some idea of this:

Organisation	From	To	Passengers Adult	Child
St Michael's Parish SS	Crieff	St Fillans	40	90
Comrie UF SS	Comrie	Lochranza	40	70
Congregational SS	Perth	Methven	90	140
Baptist SS	Perth	Almondbank	60	100
St Leonard's Parish SS	Perth	Almondbank	100	170
Mannofield Parish Church Choir	Aberdeen	St Fillans	40	
St Paul's UF Choir	Aberdeen	Crieff	50	
Ferryhill Free Church Choir	Aberdeen	St Fillans	63	

The Crieff and Comrie parties travelled by the timetabled train, strengthened, while the three Perth Sunday Schools took a special train leaving Perth at 2.5pm and returning from Methven at 7.5pm. Another special was laid on for the three choirs from Aberdeen, leaving there at 1.30pm, returning from St. Fillans at 7.15pm. All in all, 483 adults and 570 children, a total of over 1,000 passengers, travelled on these excursions that day.

Some two months later, at the end of August, an innovative development by the LM&SR saw the introduction of a new Rail-Motor service on the Methven branch line between Perth and Methven. A Sentinel Cammel steam railcar replaced the steam locomotive and carriages which had previously been used to operate this service. This railcar was operated as a *'self-propelled steam carriage'*, being 56 feet long, with a steam locomotive enclosed at one end and a driving compartment at the other. The carriage had one compartment with 44 seats, the cushioned backs of which were reversible, and was all Third Class. The vehicle had electric lighting, steam heating and large picture windows. With a maximum speed of 35mph the journey time between Perth and Methven was 25-30 minutes. In another new development, the railcar had no guard, station staff being responsible for operating the doors and seeing off the train.

Although the accommodation of the Steam Rail Motor was limited to 44 seats, it could be used to make additional trips where the occasion required, one example being New Year 1929 when it made an extra evening trip to Perth on 29th December and again on 5th January 1929:

Methven	Dep	8.20pm
Perth	Arr	8.46pm
Perth	Dep	10.40pm
Methven	Arr	11. 5pm

In addition to this, a number of other trains were strengthened that New Year, with extra coaches being added, on 29th and 31st December, and again on 1st, 2nd and 3rd of January 1929:

7.50am	Comrie to Glasgow	2-3 carriages
12.50pm	Balquhidder to Gleneagles	1 coach at Crieff
4.50pm	St Fillans to Gleneagles	2 coaches

The additional loads were such that pilot assistance was required on these trains between Crieff and Gleneagles.

This practice was repeated a few months later to cope with the traffic expected on 15th April 1929 from the Edinburgh Spring Holiday and both the Crieff and Muthill Spring Holidays. Again, pilot assistance, in the form of an additional locomotive to double head the train, had to be provided between Crieff and Gleneagles. In addition to this, specials were also run, including a seven-coach train which left Edinburgh (Princes Street) at 8.24am arriving at St. Fillans at 10.55am, while an extra train was laid on from Crieff to connect with the 8.0am from Glasgow which arrived at Gleneagles at 9.38am. This special left Gleneagles at 9.45am, called at Muthill at 9.57am to arrive at Crieff at 10.7am. Similar arrangements were made the following month for the Comrie Merchants Holiday, when on 22nd May an additional late night train was laid on, leaving Gleneagles at 9pm.

Figure 8.8
An example of the standard LM&SR Edmondson card tickets specially printed for particular excursions, in this case the Unionist Association GF outing from Perth to Almondbank on 25th June 1932. The quantity printed was dictated by the expected load as they were only valid on the day, so could not be re-used. This ticket was never issued and has survived intact. *Author's collection*

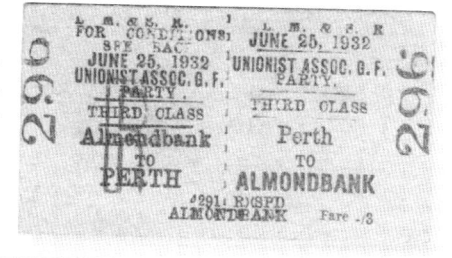

Figure 8.9
The working instructions for a typical group of Sunday school trips from Perth to Almondbank and Methven on 11th June 1927. In this case they travelled from Perth by the ordinary train with extra coaches added, and then returned by a special train leaving Methven at 7.5pm. The instructions included details of rolling stock, ticket prices and anticipated load. The total load, which in this case was 250 adults plus 410 'juveniles', gave an impressive total of 660 passengers. Controlling 410 excited children must have been a challenge!
Courtesy David Ferguson

Plate 8.6
The Sentinel steam railcar, seen here at Methven. The railcar floor level was lower than the standard carriage and below platform level at Perth, but nonetheless, box steps were still needed for the very low platform at Methven, as can be seen here. The railcar was intended to run as a single unit so had no buffers, although it was equipped with couplings at both ends for use in emergencies.
David Ferguson collection

That same week, the Crieff South United Free Church Choir, numbering fifty, made an excursion to Aberdeen, travelling out via Methven Junction, but returning by Gleneagles. Other groups included forty members of the Dundee Shipping Golf Club who travelled to Gleneagles, the Dundee Highland Society who visited St. Fillans and a group of 110 from the Sandyfield Burns Club who visited both Perth and Crieff. Some of the more esoteric groups included a party of twenty from the Master Court of the Incorporation of Skinners and Glovers from Glasgow, who visited Crieff on 11th June 1929.

Methven was a popular destination for the Sunday Schools, but the single coach Steam Sentinel Railcar which operated the normal services had only limited capacity. On excursion days such as 8th June 1929, the railcar would be withdrawn and substituted by a steam locomotive and two carriages – a Third Class and a Brake Third Class. This would then be strengthened as required for the Sunday school parties. On this date, the 1.15pm from Methven was augmented by three Third Class carriages and one Brake carriage for a party of 170 children of St. Serfs United Free Church in Almondbank who went to Dunkeld for the day, while Bridgend United Free Church Sunday school in Perth numbering forty adults and fifty children came to Methven. The 1.42pm Perth to Methven train was strengthened by two carriages, these returning on the 7.0pm train from Methven to Perth. This operation was repeated again the following year in June 1930, although the numbers involved were slightly less.

Special trains were not limited to passenger traffic, for there was a large amount of seasonal freight traffic, mainly agricultural, such as livestock and potatoes. In particular, large numbers of sheep were carried at specific times of the year, there being an annual migration from the Highlands to wintering quarters in the Lowlands and the eastern parts of Scotland in the autumn, and back again to the Highlands the following spring. Typical of these was the traffic in late 1930 when a special livestock train was run from Balquhidder to Perth on 14th September with seventeen trucks of sheep – three for Abercairny, five for Balgowan, one each for Methven and Bankfoot, three for Stanley, and four for Perth. A week later, on 26th September, another special from Oban to Laurencekirk with seventeen trucks of sheep travelled via Crieff, joining the Strathearn line at Balquhidder at 8.25am and passing Almond Valley Junction at 10.4am. The following week yet another special, this time from Comrie, conveyed eighteen trucks of sheep to Cupar in Fife.

At the same time of year, Messrs Hay & Co of Crieff held regular livestock sales. These were held weekly between mid-August and the end of October, and the numbers involved were impressive, with 2,000 to 2,500 and sometimes as many as 6,000 sheep being offered for sale on a single day. On these days, an Empty Truck Train (ETT) of some thirty to forty cattle trucks would leave Perth at 2.0pm. Having been loaded with livestock sold at the Auction Mart, this train would then leave Crieff at 6.20pm, detaching wagons at various stations as required.

This whole process was reversed in the spring when the sheep returned from wintering, and again a succession of livestock trains were run. One such was a consignment of sheep from Brechin in April 1929. Nineteen cattle trucks were attached to the 11.5pm freight train from Aberdeen, arriving at Perth in the middle of the night. The special livestock train left Perth at 4.45am, passing Crieff at 5.38am to arrive at Balquhidder at 6.33am. The train then reversed direction to continue up the Callander and Oban line, dropping off eight trucks at Luib, and taking the remaining eleven trucks on to Oban.

Not all such specials involved livestock alone. From time to time, farmers moved from one tenancy to another, sometimes a fair distance away, as was the case with Mr Hair, recounted in Chapter 6. In such cases the railway would lay on a special train for 'Farmers Removal'. On 22nd May 1929, one such special moved a farmer with all his impedimenta and animals from Comrie to Caldarvan near Balloch on the L&NER line from Stirling. Comprising three wagons of implements, three cattle trucks, and one horse box, the special left Comrie at 8.50am, passed onto the main line at Gleneagles at 9.48am to reach Stirling at 10.25am, where it was handed over to the L&NER, finally arriving at Caldarvan at 12.30pm.

Similar special trains were also arranged for the annual agricultural shows which are a feature of such rural areas as Strathearn. Typical of these were the Strathearn Agricultural Show at Crieff at the end of July 1930 and the Perthshire Agricultural Show at Perth three days later.

On the morning of the Strathearn show, a livestock special ran from Perth to Crieff via Blackford and Gleneagles, '*calling where required to attach Show traffic*'. Another special started from Glencarse for Crieff at 7.0am. A shunting engine was provided at Crieff all day to handle show traffic. Interestingly, the instructions stipulated that '*Engines on Specials must take a full supply of water before reaching Crieff as supplies there are limited*' – clearly the water supply problems raised back in 1871 were still an issue. After

CHAPTER 8: THE CHALLENGING YEARS UNDER THE LM&SR

Plate 8.7
A good view of the Down platform at Crieff station showing the profusion of notice boards and advertising hoardings along the full length of the back wall. The large number of floral hanging baskets which helped Crieff to win so many Best Kept Station awards over the years can be seen on both platforms. The station appears to be deserted apart from one person outside the bookstall on the Up platform.
GH Robins

the show, three specials left Crieff for Perth, a horse box special at 5.28pm followed by two livestock specials at 5.50pm and 6.15pm.

On the staff side, 1929 marked the retirement of the much respected stationmaster at Crieff, Mr William Millar, after 52 years' service, having joined the Caledonian as a lad in 1877. Mr Millar had been at Crieff for many years, and his two sons both worked at the station. At his retirement presentation, he recalled that his first knowledge of Crieff was during the railway strike of 1890, when at the time he was a reliefman at Mossend near Coatbridge. His predecessor as stationmaster, Mr Morrison, together with a Mr McOwan, a coal merchant in Crieff, arrived with two engines and two guards '*in search of coal*'. He took charge of them to Strathaven Junction near Hamilton, where they picked up thirty-two wagons of coal for Crieff and district. Despite a coupling breaking while going through Barncluwith tunnel, they reached Gartsherrie safely, and there Mr Millar sent them on their way to Crieff. The arrival of thirty loaded wagons at coal-starved Crieff saved the day, and one can imagine this being akin to the 'Relief of Mafeking'.

Mr Millar was regarded as being 'at the top of the tree' in terms of awards for the Caledonian Railway and LM&SR (Scotland)

Plate 8.8
A view of the Up platform at Crieff in LM&SR days, with two coaches standing in the platform. The canopy and roof is already starting to show signs of ageing, and the cost of repairs would eventually lead British Railways to remove the overall roof of the footbridge and, later on, dismantle whole sections of the canopy on both platforms.
Author's collection

Plate 8.9
An undated view of Crieff station from the west end in LM&SR days showing the extensive footbridge which was still covered in those days. Three coaches stand in the Up platform, and a Comrie bound train awaits departure in the Down platform. *AG Ellis*

Best Kept Station competitions. Since coming to Crieff in 1914, the station had won seven First Class and three Special awards under his management.

It is pleasing, therefore, to record that Mr Millar deservedly left on a high note, for in the week before he retired, he was responsible for making arrangements for the annual excursion of some ninety members of the LM&SR Engineer's Office at St. Enoch in Glasgow, who arrived at Crieff by train, lunched at the Star Hotel, and then departed by charabanc for Dunblane via Loch Earn. His efforts were rewarded by the presentation of a gold mounted pencil in a case. In his last week of duty he was also responsible for ensuring that the flower beds were planted out, and that the hanging baskets were placed in position, in readiness for the Best Kept Station competition, such was his pride in his beloved station.

Other work of a more practical nature was carried out earlier in the summer when, in late May, the water pipes supplying the tank at Crieff Station were cleaned out. This took five days, working from 9.30am until 4.30pm, during which time no water was available at Crieff. The main tank was, however, filled every night. The water supply at Crieff, or rather the lack of it, would seem to have been a constant source of concern, as was mentioned earlier, but later in the year the line suffered from rather too much of it in the form of flooding. In late August, heavy rain caused a landslide about 600 yards west of Crieff station, when large parts of the embankment on either side of the mill lade gave way. Fortunately the track was not directly affected, but for several days, trains had to pass over the embankment at a much reduced speed until repairs could be effected.

Only a few weeks later, rain caused even more serious disruption when a landslide blocked the Callander & Oban line at Craig-a-

Plate 8.10
Ex-Caledonian Railway Class '179' 4-6-0 No. 17913 standing in the Up platform at Crieff in the early years of the LM&SR looking rather less splendid than it would have done in Caledonian blue livery. The first coach of the train would appear to be an equally vintage Caledonian Railway carriage.
Author's collection

CHAPTER 8: THE CHALLENGING YEARS UNDER THE LM&SR

Coilleach, 5 miles north of Callander. All trains between Callander and Oban had to be diverted via Crieff until the blockage was cleared the following day, proving the value of this alternative route and causing much excitement at Crieff. Prophetically, it would be a similar landslide in Glen Ogle which would result in the premature and final closure of the Dunblane to Crianlarich section of the Callander & Oban line in 1965.

Despite these minor interruptions, 1929 was a busy year for tourism, with a full programme of excursions. The range of these demonstrated one of the benefits of the Grouping, for the LM&SR ran trips to Strathearn not only from the usual cities of Edinburgh, Glasgow, Dundee and Aberdeen, but also from such places as Blackpool and even Bacup and Littleborough on the former Lancashire & Yorkshire Railway.

A regular excursion was that from Dundee to Oban, usually with a forecast load of 300 to 400 passengers. Dundee was responsible for providing the train of corridor stock together with one of the Pullman Cars to provide dining facilities. The usual timetable would be:

Dundee		10.20am
Crieff		11.37am
Balquhidder		12.25pm
Oban	Arr	2.50pm
Oban	Dep	6. 5pm
Balquhidder		8.20pm
Crieff		9.10pm
Dundee		10.27pm

That summer, such excursions from Dundee ran on 21st April, 5th May, 19th May, and 2nd June. In most cases, the Pullman Car was 'Diana Vernon', but on 2nd June 'Mauchline Belle' was rostered. The use of the Pullman Cars on the Caledonian and later LM&S railways originated from an agreement signed back in November 1913 whereby the Pullman Car Company agreed to supply seventeen vehicles to run on the Caledonian Railway system. The Pullman Car Company met the construction costs, while the Caledonian Railway was responsible for hauling them free of charge on their trains. The Pullman Car Company made their money from the profits on catering and supplementary fares. Unfortunately only ten of the planned seventeen vehicles had been built before the First World War broke out in 1914 and delivery of the remainder was delayed until after the war. All these Pullman Cars were given names of famous Scottish heroines, some historical, but others fictional. The Pullman Cars known to have run over the Strathearn lines during this period were:

Name	Built	Withdrawn
Fair Maid of Perth	1914	Dec 1927
Diana Vernon	1922	Mar 1955
Mauchline Belle	1923	Apr 1961
Meg Dodds	1923	May 1961
Queen Margaret	1927	May 1961
Helen of Mar	1927	Jul 1958
Kate Dalrymple	1927	Apr 1961

All of the 1914-vintage Pullmans had been withdrawn by the LM&SR before the Second World War, but later vehicles survived into British Railways ownership until the early 1960s – with the last two, both of which had run over the Strathearn lines, not being withdrawn until May 1961.

Weekends were a particularly busy time over the summer period, so, for example, on Saturday 5th May 1929 the Dundee to Oban excursion passed through Strathearn and one of the special excursions from Aberdeen to St. Fillans ran the following day. These excursions also included a Pullman Car, in this case the 'Fair Maid of Perth', the outline timetable being:

Aberdeen	Dep	11.00am
Almond Valley Jct		12.54pm
St Fillans	Arr	2.10pm
St Fillans	Dep	7.25pm
Almond Valley Jct		8.22pm
Aberdeen	Arr	10.30pm

The Aberdeen excursions were routed over the Strathmore line

Plate 8.11
An ex-Caledonian Railway Class '766' 4-4-0 No. 14328 on an Up train at Crieff in the 1930s. This view must be after 1932 as Crieff West signal box has already been removed. Note the running in board to the right of the locomotive which is still painted in the Caledonian Railway colours of chocolate and cream with a double band part way up the posts. *RJ Buckley*

through Forfar, so did not even enter Perth, being able to take the Crieff line from Almond Valley Junction, although this did involve the locomotive running round the train to reverse direction. Where these excursions were run on a Saturday, the return working would take up the path of the 7.55pm (Saturdays Only) Crieff to Perth train which would be cancelled. In order to maintain balanced working, the coaches from the latter would be attached to the 6.5pm Crieff to Perth train, while the locomotive would run to Perth as a light engine.

The excursions from Bacup and Littleborough in Lancashire were ambitious affairs. Run by a local firm called Parkinsons, they conveyed around 400 passengers, and must have left at a late hour, for the timetable for the Caledonian section was:

Carlisle	Dep	3.34am
Balquhidder		7.35am
St Fillans	Arr	8.18am
St Fillans	Dep	9. 0am
Crieff	Arr	9.50am
Crieff	Dep	10.25am
Gleneagles		10.45am
Edinburgh	Arr	1.44pm

The schedule over the Upper Strathearn section was more sedate than that for normal services to allow passengers to enjoy the scenery for which the district was famed. An extra 6 minutes was allowed between Lochearnhead and St. Fillans, 8 minutes more between St. Fillans and Comrie, and another 3 for the Comrie to Crieff section. Instructions were also given for the train to be restocked with towels and to be '*charged with gas*' at Crieff, a reminder that gas-lit rolling stock was still a feature of rail travel in those days. Just under three quarters of an hour was allowed at St. Fillans, and a little over an hour at Crieff to allow for the train to be serviced.

The summer of 1929 also saw the usual crop of Sunday school outings over the Strathearn lines. One such was a special from Perth to Balgowan conveying 40 adults and 70 children from Castlegable Mission Sunday School along with 120 adults and 200 children from St. Andrews Church Sunday School. Quite how the tiny hamlet of Balgowan absorbed this influx of 430 people, and what they found to do in Balgowan, history does not record, but it was probably their annual picnic. Leaving Perth at 2.10pm, the special disgorged its passengers at Balgowan at 2.37pm and then continued on to Madderty, which had a passing loop, as empty stock. The train remained there until 6.32pm when it set off back to Balgowan to collect the day trippers at 6.40pm to arrive back at Perth at 7.8pm.

Despite the best efforts of the LM&SR to promote the tourist traffic, one of the first hints that the railways were beginning to feel the pinch was revealed in an editorial in the *Strathearn Herald* on 6th July 1929:

'*Regretfully one notices the change that has come over Crieff Railway Station in recent years. The half empty trains due to the keen bus competition to and from Crieff tell their own tale. The bustle and excitement on the platforms at train times seem to have for the most part disappeared, and there is a quietude which, somehow is disturbing. Something drastic – either in the cheapening of the fares or in some other way – will require to be done by the respective companies if the railways are to prosper – and the sooner the better.*'

That said, the LM&SR continued to provide a good service, which more than matched that of the Caledonian Railway in the years leading up to the First World War. The Gleneagles to Crieff service enjoyed thirteen trains each way per day with an additional Down train on Saturdays, while there were six Up and eight Down trains each way per day on the Perth to Crieff line, also with additional trains on Saturdays. The service between Crieff and St. Fillans had ten Up and nine Down trains, with six of these running through to Balquhidder, and an extra train each way on Saturdays. Most trains continued to be hauled by ex-Caledonian Railway 0-6-0 goods locomotives, although ex-Caledonian Railway 4-4-0s and 0-4-4Ts were employed from time to time.

The 1930 season saw the resumption of a full programme of special excursion trains, with the majority of these being from Aberdeen, with half day excursions as far as St. Fillans and whole day excursions to Lochearnhead. Some travelled over the Strathearn lines to Oban, and at least one went to Callander. The Dundee to Oban excursions featured, and there was also one from Perth to Oban which called at local stations, as well as the usual excursions from Edinburgh. The

Plate 8.12
A Crieff bound train heading along the side of Loch Earn having just crossed over the Glen Ogle viaduct in the foreground. This view from the hillside above Lochearnhead station gives a good idea of the impressive scenery through which this stretch of line passed, and the insignificant size of the railway set against the mass of Meall a Mhaddaidh in the background. There is little evidence of much traffic in the goods yard, and the solitary six-wheeled coach in the foreground is probably the camping coach.
ES Morten

one special from Aberdeen and Callander which was most definitely not a tourist outing was that on 19th July 1930, which conveyed eight officers, 150 men and eight horses of a Divisional Engineer Company. This train was joined at Almond Valley Junction by another special from Dundee conveying two officers and 130 men of 237 Field Company Royal Engineers.

The LM&SR also provided facilities for local events, such as the Comrie Highland Gathering on 5th July 1930 when the 9.30am Perth to Crieff train was extended to Comrie arriving at 10.30am. In the evenings, the 6.55pm Crieff to Perth train started from Comrie at 6.30pm while the 7.10pm Comrie to Gleneagles service was extended through to Glasgow and strengthened to eight carriages. The following day, the LM&SR laid on an excursion to the seaside, possibly to do with the same celebrations. The probable load was given as 300 passengers, but how many hardy souls made it for the early start from Comrie is not recorded:

Comrie	Dep	8. 0am
Gleneagles	Dep	10.38am
Girvan	Arr	1.55pm
Girvan	Dep	6.15pm
Gleneagles	Arr	9.36pm
Comrie	Arr	10.17pm

At the end of July, a special was laid on from Crieff to Perth which connected with another excursion from Dundee to Inverness. This left Crieff at a more respectable 10.35am, returning at 11.15pm that evening. A few days later, another special was laid on to Gleneagles in connection with an excursion to Dumfries Highland Show.

Despite this, tourists were increasingly taking the bus to Crieff rather than the train. At the beginning of the Glasgow Fair Holiday at the end of the month, some 2,000 people arrived at Crieff by bus, the normal hourly service having to be augmented. It was not only visitors who opted for the bus, for earlier in the year it was reported that of the 1,000 people who left Crieff for their annual Victoria Day outing, 700 of these went by bus. The *Strathearn Herald* commented somewhat ominously that: *'It is only too evident how the local railways are being hit hard – and hit badly'*.

Towards the end of the season, a half day excursion from Edinburgh to St. Fillans was expected to carry 500 passengers. Routed via Gleneagles, this special was programmed to combine at Crieff with the scheduled 12.30pm from Perth. The instructions included the specific requirement that the local train *'must consist of dual stock on this date'*. This was a reminder that while some of the older coaching stock from the Caledonian era was fitted with the Westinghouse air brake, the more modern LM&SR stock was all vacuum brake fitted. Some of the old Westinghouse fitted stock

Plate 8.13
An unidentified ex-Caledonian Railway 4-4-0 on a short goods train at Balquhidder. The assorted rolling stock includes a vintage Caledonian Railway guards van. The cold frame next to the barrow crossing was probably for plants used to enhance the borders and flower beds; the enamel Caledonian Railway trespass notice next to it appears to be on its last legs.
ES Morten

Plate 8.14
An unidentified ex-Caledonian Railway 'Jumbo' 0-6-0 on an Up passenger train on the Callender & Oban main line at Balquhidder. The seven-coach train consists of an eclectic variety of rolling stock, while the locomotive does not appear to be in the best of condition. Note the running in board on the right which is still in Caledonian Railway colours. *ES Morten*

Plate 8.15
Another view of the unidentified ex-Caledonian Railway 4-4-0 seen in Plate 8.13, now taking water at Balquhidder from the column at the south end of the island platform. No water was available at the engine shed, so locomotives had to fill up at one of the platform columns before setting off back to Crieff. *ES Morten*

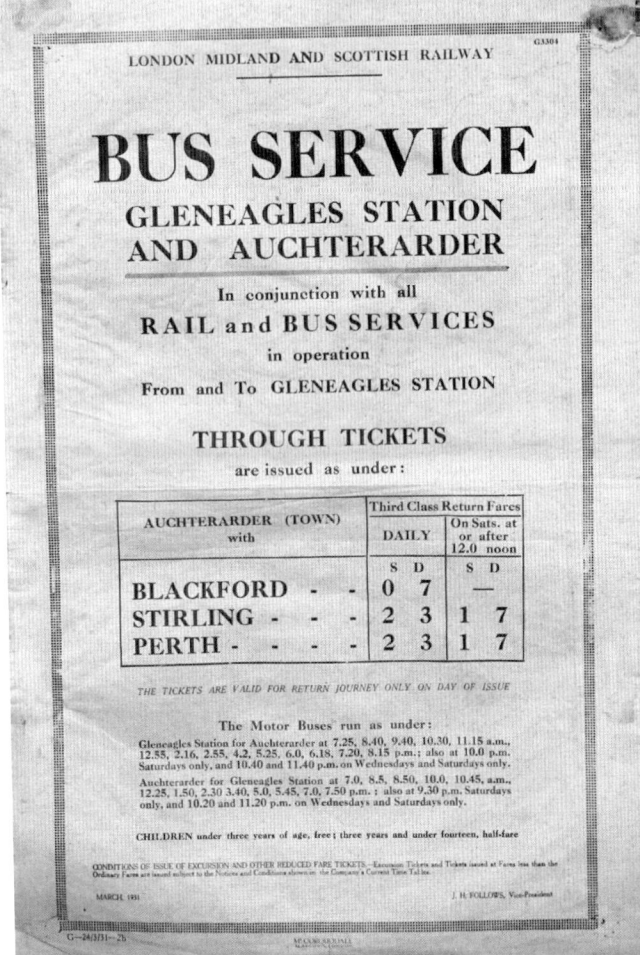

Figure 8.10
A 1931 poster advertising the bus service between Auchterarder and Gleneagles station. The poster specified Auchterarder town to avoid any confusion with Auchterarder station. The service was contracted out to a local garage – Paterson's Motors, and the town bus stop was outside the Aytoun Hall at the same stop used by Alexander's buses.
Author's collection

had been equipped with the vacuum system in addition, so that they could operate either braking system, and this was the requirement in this case.

However, while all this activity was taking place, the gloomy portends expressed in the *Strathearn Herald* the previous summer were beginning to manifest themselves. In April 1930, the Scottish Motor Traction Co – an associated company of W Alexander & Co, of which much more will be heard – acquired the Scottish General Omnibus Co's bus section of Dunfermline Tramways. Through this they gained 300 to 400 buses, plus garage accommodation at Larbert, Stirling, Kirkcaldy and, most significantly, Crieff. At Easter it was noted that although a special train brought in many visitors, a large number also arrived by the hourly bus service from Glasgow to Crieff which had to be augmented to cope with the demand.

On Victoria Day at the end of May, 700 people left Crieff by bus, and although some 350 passengers took advantage of the cheap fares, this was far fewer than in previous years. The Glasgow Fair Holiday at the end of June saw some 2,000 trippers arrive at Crieff by bus, and there were regular observations in the press about the number of charabanc tours throughout the district, and the number of cars on the roads. None of this was good news for the railway. That this was not just a phenomenon in Strathearn is reflected in a press report in September that the gross receipts for the railway companies for the first thirty-six weeks of 1930 were down by £6 million compared with the previous year, with a warning that the railways might be forced to cut wages.

The LM&SR was already starting to tighten its belt, and one of the first signs of this locally was the closure of the carriage & wagon works at Crieff in June. This workshop, a relic of the old Crieff Junction Railway, had continued to carry out light repairs and maintenance. However, after seventy-four years, it was now closed and the Inspector, Mr David Petrie, transferred to Perth.

Elsewhere in Strathearn, the decision was made in November that Gleneagles Hotel, hitherto open all the year round, would now close from January to March 1931, for what was termed the 'quiet season'. This was to be experimental to see if it was cheaper to close the hotel during this period rather than keep it open all year. In the event, this became a permanent feature of the hotel calendar, the hotel only being open from Easter to the end of October, a practice which

LEFT: Figure 8.11
A set of LM&SR tickets used on the Auchterarder town to Gleneagles station bus service. Two of these are return halves of through tickets issued at Perth and Stirling, while the third is a return half of a ticket issued from Auchterarder, although the amount of detail shown has resulted in the first letter of Auchterarder being obscured. *Author's collection*

RIGHT: Figure 8.12
The 1924 edition of the LM&SR holiday brochure Scotland for the Holidays, the successor to the Caledonian Railway publication of the same name. This was a much more modest affair running to only twenty-three pages. Folded, it opened to A4 size. This brochure for the Central Highlands was one of a series covering the whole of the LM&SR. *Author's collection*

continued, except for the war years when it was a hospital, until it was privatised in 1981.

On a brighter note, it was announced in April that plans had been approved for alterations to the hotel in respect of the layout whereby two bedrooms shared one bathroom. The plan made provision to link each bedroom directly with the bathroom to avoid the need for the guests to go via the hallway. Perhaps this was one of the initiatives of the new manager, Mr Gordon Yates, who took over from Mr Frank Fisher in February.

Railway traffic in Strathearn in 1931 followed a similar pattern, with a programme of special excursions – such as a repeat of the excursion of Messrs Parkinsons from Bacup at the beginning of June. Again this excursion arrived at an early hour, being routed via Callander to Balquhidder, with stops at St. Fillans and Crieff, but on this occasion the return route was via Gleneagles to Gourock, presumably to enable passengers to take a trip on the Clyde before heading back to Lancashire.

Later that same month, some 200 passengers took advantage of the cheap excursion fares on the occasion of the Crieff Merchants Holiday to travel by train to Glasgow and Edinburgh. However, considerable numbers also travelled by bus and charabanc. Interestingly, the previous month, when two railway staff outings from the LM&SR Estates Department and the District Engineer's Department, both in Glasgow, visited Crieff, they travelled by train, but chose to tour the local area by bus.

Road traffic was on the increase, and at the beginning of July there were calls for a policeman to sort out the traffic jams in Crieff, and later than month, there were reports that:

'There has been an appreciable increase in the amount of motor traffic on Strathearn's roads. Charabancs and motor coaches from the South and Midlands of England are seen on the roads every other day.'

This trend towards long distance touring would have been particularly unwelcome for the railways.

The continued growth of competing bus services locally was reflected in developments such as that in September, when W Alexander & Sons announced the introduction of a new service from Perth via Crieff to Callander, while in October they introduced another new service on Wednesday evenings from Crieff to Perth for theatre goers. More significantly, in November, Alexander's advertised their new parcel delivery service.

Although buses in general represented unwelcome competition for the railways, the LM&SR were not averse to using them for its own ends. One example was the bus service provided between Auchterarder town and Gleneagles station (Figure 8.10). Ever since local objectors in 1844 had compelled the Scottish Central Railway to follow a more southerly route, the good folk of Auchterarder had been saddled with a station nearly a mile from the town on the other side of the steep valley through which Ruthven Water flowed. Auchterarder station also enjoyed a much less frequent service than Gleneagles, and later lost its passenger service altogether in 1956. The frequent bus service consisted of thirteen round trips daily (fourteen on Wednesdays and fifteen on Saturdays), with through ticketing available to Blackford, Stirling and Perth (Figure 8.11). This service continued to operate for sixteen years until the end of September 1940, by which time the hotel had been requisitioned. Pattersons had continued to operate the service at a loss during the first year of the war, but then called it a day.

While these developments focussed on passenger services, the railway continued to dominate the freight market, particularly the mass movement of livestock. The annual sheep sales at Oban generated such traffic, so, for example, on 27th September, two special freight trains were run from Perth to Oban via Crieff, one at 11.00am and another at 11.30am, each conveying thirty empty cattle trucks. The following day, two specials left Oban, one at 9.30am with twenty-four trucks full of sheep for Laurencekirk, and another at 3.00pm with another twenty trucks for Laurencekirk and three for Brechin. A few days later another special conveyed twenty truckloads of sheep from Balquhidder to Perth as the annual movement of wintering sheep got under way, while the following month a more modest trainload left Comrie with seven trucks for Almondbank and three for Perth.

Throughout October, a succession of such specials ran over the Strathearn lines. One such train ran from Crianlarich to Boat of Garten on the former Highland line north of Aviemore, conveying twenty-four trucks of sheep from Glenfinnan to Craigellachie L&NER station on the old Great North of Scotland line. Another special a few days later took sixteen trucks of sheep from Comrie to Cupar in Fife. The schedule for this train included an eight minute stop at Almondbank for the sheep to be watered. This was presumably to ensure that they were well cared for until the LM&SR handed them over to the L&NER at Perth for the onward journey.

Meanwhile, the football season was in full swing and the usual specials were run to Perth whenever St. Johnstone were playing at home. These included the match against Alloa on 14th November, Armadale on 12th December, King's Park the following week, and Queen of the South on New Year's Day 1932. All these except that on 14th November started from Comrie at 12.50pm, with some stopping at Abercairny, Madderty and Balgowan – whereas, somewhat curiously, some only stopped at Innerpeffray and Almondbank. An interesting instruction also noted that the service from Methven was suspended until 11.00am on New Year's Day – probably a pragmatic decision!

Happily, 1931 ended on a bright note for the Strathearn lines with yet more major successes being announced in December in the Best Kept Station competition. In all, nine of the thirteen local stations won prizes:

– Gleneagles   Special Award
– St. Fillans   Special Award
– Crieff   1st Class
– Comrie   2nd Class
– Madderty   3rd Class
– Muthill   3rd Class
– Abercairny   4th Class
– Highlandman   5th Class
– Innerpeffray 5th Class

The award of a 1st Prize to Crieff must have been particularly pleasing for the former stationmaster, Mr Millar, and reflected the great pride taken by the staff, particularly the stationmasters, in their station. Two of the other stationmasters in Strathearn were on the move early in the year on promotion to stations on main lines. In February, Mr George Stewart moved from Methven to Glasterlaw (between Arbroath and Montrose), while, at the end of the same month, Mr Charles Robertson moved from St. Fillans to be stationmaster at Dunning. Mr Robertson typified the place a stationmaster held in the community in those days, being secretary and treasurer of the parish church, a member of the Kirk Session, the choir and the golf club.

It would seem that the talents of such men were wide and varied, for on 9th February, Mr Durward, stationmaster at Madderty, gave a talk to the local Women's Institute on 'The Passion Play of Oberammagau'. Mr and Mrs Durward were well known in Madderty, having the previous year presented prizes at the village school – Mr Durward presented a prize for the most distinguished child in school sports, while Mrs Durward presented one for the best collection of flowers and collection of leaves correctly named.

Mr Durward was a classic example of the 'railway family' of those days. He was born in the railway cottage at Ruthven Road where his mother was the crossing keeper and his father was a porter at Almondbank station. Having joined the Caledonian Railway at an early age, he returned to Strathearn as stationmaster at Highlandman in 1906, serving there for seventeen years before moving to Madderty in 1923. He retired in 1932, but sadly died less than three years later. A measure of his popularity was reflected in the fact that the local Jubilee celebrations for King George V were retimed to allow villagers to attend his funeral.

A major sporting event early in the year was the Scottish Cup Tie between St. Johnstone and the mighty Celtic at Perth. This time the estimated load for the football special was 300, three times the normal number, and it started from St. Fillans. Exceptionally, the timetable even included a scheduled stop at Dalchonzie Platform. 1932 saw the usual programme of other excursions, including Sunday school parties, along Strathearn to various destinations such as St. Fillans and Strathyre. In June a special train conveyed St. Michaels Church Sunday School to Broughty Ferry for a day by the sea, while the choir of the Old Parish Church travelled by train to Montrose for their annual outing.

The railway, however, faced growing competition from the local buses, such that although 400-500 passengers arrived by train at

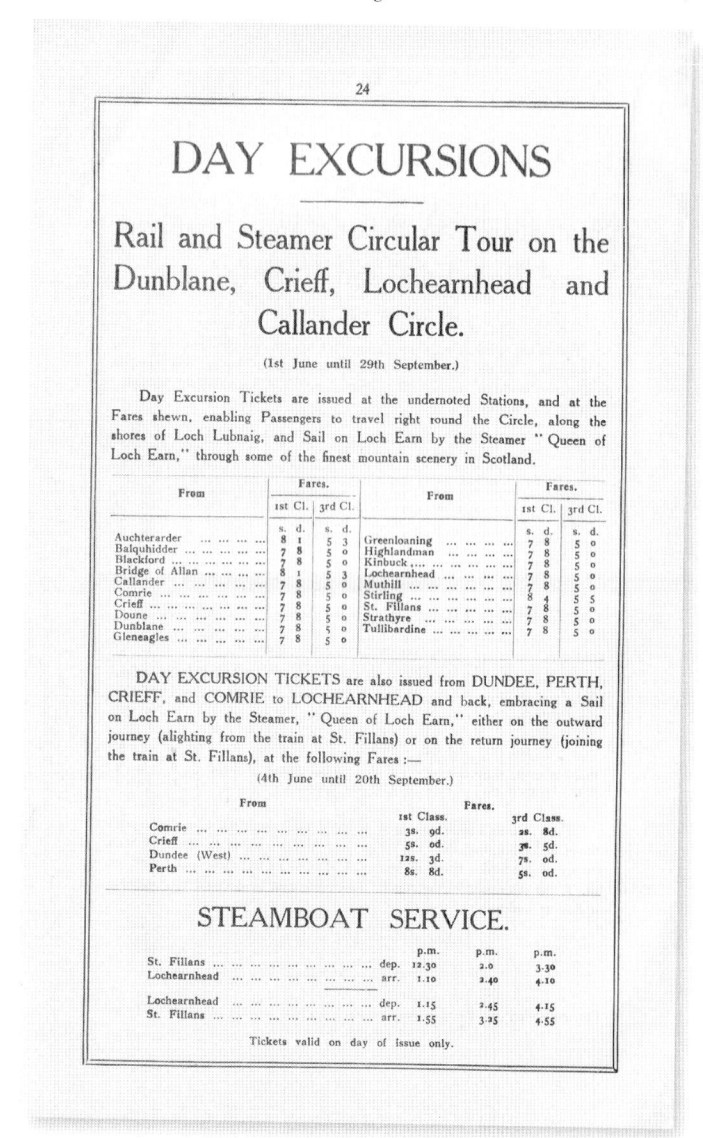

Figure 8.13
A 1928 advertisement for the circular tour via Crieff and Balquhidder. This was the route followed by the popular tours run from Glasgow and Edinburgh. The advertisement also included details of excursions on the steamer *Queen of Loch Earn* between St. Fillans and Lochearnhead.
Author's collection

Crieff at Easter, large numbers also came by bus, necessitating the use of several double deckers. In April, W Alexander & Son applied for licences to run two new routes – Crieff to Dunfermline, and a special school bus from Crieff to Muthill. Buses were not the only threat to the railways, and on the occasion of the Edinburgh Holiday at the end of April, it was reported that there had been an almost continuous procession of cars on the Comrie to St. Fillans road.

The LM&SR, however, did not take these developments lying down, and a number of advertisements appeared for cheap fares and excursions. In May it was announced that certain bus and train tickets were now interchangeable. The LM&SR and L&NER between them controlled 50% of Scottish Motor Transport (SMT) which operated mainly in the lowlands, but seemed not to have exploited their position. At any rate, bus competition was here to stay, so it was noted at Whitsun that although 300 passengers left Crieff by train, many others made use of the excellent bus service to Stirling, while many English visitors used Stirling as a base for charabanc tours of Strathearn.

One notable excursion in 1932 was a day outing on 5th August that year for passengers from the cruise liner SS *Doric* from Oban to Crieff. This was a joint venture with W Alexander & Sons, and the LM&SR even went to the extent of printing a special brochure with a fold-out map of the route (Figure 8.14). The *Doric* had been built by Harland & Wolff and launched in Belfast in 1922. A White Star liner of 16,484 tons, she was initially used on the trans-Atlantic run between Liverpool and Montreal and Quebec, but from 1932 was used solely for cruising, so this was her first season. Sadly she did not last much longer, being involved in a collision off Cape Finisterre on 5th September 1935, and was scrapped two months later.

Another small sign of the railway tightening its belt was the rationalisation of signalling at Crieff at the beginning of April. Crieff West signal box closed on 3rd April 1932 and was demolished. The layout at the west end of the station was controlled by a ground frame and operation of the signals transferred to Crieff East, which was now renamed simply 'Crieff'.

1933 saw the introduction of what would prove to be the enormously popular evening excursions from Dundee and elsewhere. A contemporary report in the *Strathearn Herald* recorded:

'Remarkable scenes were witnessed at St. Fillans last night when 3,000 Dundee people descended upon the Perthshire hamlet. They arrived in 4 crowded special trains, and as the city horde passed through the street of the little village the entire population of 200 came to their doors.

The solitary shop was besieged by the visitors and in a few minutes the entire stock of 500 bottles of lemonade was sold. A fruit cart and 2 ice-cream barrows which were fortunate enough to be on the road when the trains arrived were speedily "sold out".

The excursionists had been transported from Dundee for 1/6d to the heart of the Perthshire hills in little more than an hour. Each train comprised over 12 carriages, and every compartment and corridor was crammed. There were several cases of fainting in the heat.

From 4 o'clock there was a steady stream of gaily-attired trippers to Dundee West Station, and from that hour until the last excursion train left the platforms presented a colourful and animated spectacle, comprising factory girls to office chiefs. The great majority were family parties with picnic cases.

As the trains moved off they were accorded hearty cheers by the railway workmen – a welcome to the new-found prosperity of the railway excursion business.

All the little townships along the Carse of Gowrie seemed to be watching for the "specials" and platforms were lined with people.

A few hundreds joined the trains at Perth and most of the excursionists went right through to St. Fillans. A few left the train at Crieff and Comrie.

On the arrival of the trains at St. Fillans the small station personnel got down to the colossal task of collecting 2,500 tickets. In a "breather" between his strenuous exertions, the

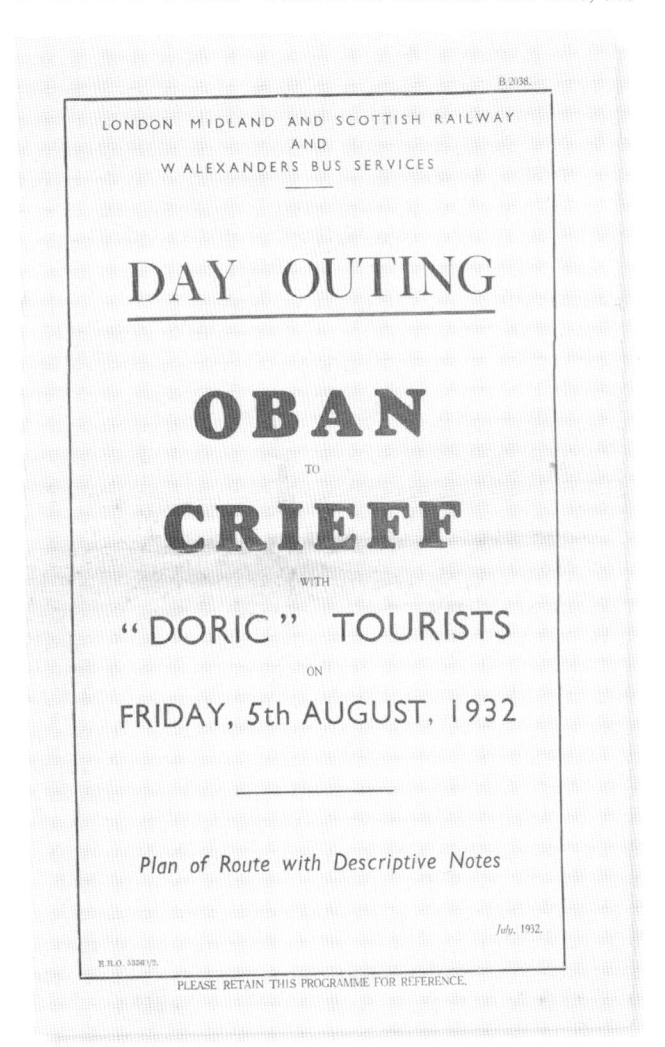

Plate 8.16
A White Star Line postcard of the SS *Doric* in her days as a transatlantic liner before being relegated to being a cruise liner. Her time in this role was due to be short-lived. *Author's collection*

Figure 8.14
The specially printed leaflet for the tour by passengers from the SS *Doric* during her visit to Oban on 5th August 1932. This fold-out leaflet included both a map of the tour and details of places of interest on the way. The trip was a joint enterprise with W Alexander & Sons, but the publicity was provided by the LM&SR, as shown here.
Author's collection

Plate 8.17
The station staff at Almondbank pose for the photographer in LM&SR days. This shows the station looking neat and tidy, with the whitewashed arch of the road bridge clearly visible, and a profusion of notice boards. Pride of place, however, goes to the extensive and well-kept garden on the embankment opposite the platform where it could be most appreciated by the passengers waiting for their train. *David Ferguson collection*

Station-Master, Mr. George Maxwell, told a reporter that the station had never had a crowd anything like this before. "We have had a hundred or two occasionally," he said, "but thousands – never. We even had to remove the flowers and plants to make way for them".'

At the end of the month, the LM&SR ran an equally popular excursion from St. Fillans. This also attracted a full report in the *Strathearn Herald* which conveys something of the sense of excitement and adventure:

'Strathearn's first venture into the evening excursions recently made popular by the LMS Railway Co., was marked by unprecedented scenes. The special which was run from St. Fillans to Broughty Ferry, Carnoustie and Arbroath, arrived at Crieff with 11 coaches, and 4 additional carriages had to be put on these to cope with the exceptionally large number of passengers.

There was a great bustle at Crieff Station long before the train drew in. A steady flow of excursionists queued past the Booking Office window for over ½ hour. Before the train arrived there would be over 600 people on the platform, all of whom were unable to secure accommodation on the train and extra carriages were added, as already stated.

The booking to the various sea-side resorts proved Broughty Ferry to be the most popular, over 300 Crieff folks leaving the train there. Over 200 visited Carnoustie and Arbroath.

As the usual service train was being run in conjunction with the special, a stop had to be made at Tullibardine, situated on a steep incline. The heavy load of 15 full carriages made too heavy a demand on the 2 engines here, and after a long delay the train was pulled to Gleneagles Station in 2 portions. Still another 3 coaches were added to the train there as a result of information received from Auchterarder that nearly 200 passengers were waiting to join the train.

The train was scheduled to leave the "Junction" at 6pm, but owing to the delay was over an hour late in departing.

The stoppage of the excursion train at Tullibardine caused a block in the line for the Gleneagles to Crieff train, which is due to arrive at 6:55pm. When the excursion arrived at Gleneagles west-going passengers found that they had not only lost time, but also literally lost their train! The coaches were attached to the excursion and passengers for Crieff did not arrive until 8pm.

Owing to the delay in the outward journey, the excursionists were allowed longer at the various places, and the return trip was made in 2 trains, which arrived in Crieff after 1am on Thursday morning.'

The manoeuvre at Tullibardine must have been interesting, as to split a fifteen-coach train on the 1 in 50 gradient was no easy task. One locomotive would have had to uncouple and reverse back into the short goods siding, and the train then divided. The other locomotive would have taken the first portion forward to Gleneagles, and the remaining engine would have had to come out onto the branch line and reversed onto the remaining coaches and then proceed to Gleneagles. However, as the token section was Muthill to Gleneagles, additional precautions would have been needed to move the train in two separate portions.

The fate of the passengers waiting to board the 6.33pm train to

Crieff is even more amazing, and they cannot have been impressed to see their coaches disappear on the excursion to the seaside! The load of eighteen coaches must have been quite a spectacle. Unfortunately no photographs appear to have survived of this mammoth ensemble.

The 1934 tourist season saw the return of special excursions to and from Strathearn with events such as an excursion carrying the employees and families of Gartsherrie Ironworks from Coatbridge to Crieff. 350 adults and 400 children travelled on that train in late June, while that same week, 300 members of the Sunday school in Comrie went to Carnoustie for the day. The nature of road competition is reflected in a report a few weeks later of an excursion by workers and families from Messrs Coats, Ferguslie Mills, Paisley who made a trip to Braemar, and on their return journey stopped in Crieff for a *'High Tea'*. This large party travelled in forty-seven *'luxurious motor coaches'* provided by W Alexander & Sons.

Again, the LM&SR did not remain idle in the face of such competition, and one innovation particular to Strathearn was the introduction during the summer months of regular 'cruise trains'. Cruises could be taken either clockwise via Dunblane, Balquhidder, Crieff and Gleneagles, or anti-clockwise by way of Gleneagles, Crieff and Balquhidder back to Dunblane. These evening excursions from Edinburgh, Glasgow, Perth and Dundee proved extremely popular, and it was not unusual to find two long trains from Glasgow going round the circle clockwise and squeezing past a train from Dundee and another from Edinburgh taking the trip anti-clockwise.

The inaugural 'Evening Cruise Train' from Glasgow was so successful that it had to be run in three portions, with about 1,000 passengers booked. Further trips were run during the summer months, and they became a regular feature of summer traffic over the Strathearn branch lines. These excursion trains often included a Dining Car and, not missing any opportunity to promote the district, the LM&SR even printed napkins advertising their Holiday Runabout tickets over these lines (Figure 8.15). These tickets allowed unlimited travel over a given area for one week. A number of these included all or part of the branch lines of Strathearn:

C 7   Dundee to Perth, Gleneagles, Crieff, Dunkeld, Aberfeldy and sailings on Loch Tay (steamer service on Loch Tay from 1st June to 9th September).
C 8   Stirling to Bridge of Allan, Dunblane, Gleneagles, Crieff and Callander.
C 9   Edinburgh to Grangemouth, Stirling, Callander, Crieff, Lanark, Biggar and Peebles.
C 14 Perth to Dundee, Crieff, Gleneagles, Pitlochry and Struan.
C 18 Dundee, Perth, Callander via Dunblane, Balquhidder, St. Fillans, Crieff and Dundee via Methven Junction and Gleneagles.

The operation of these circular cruises was often quite complex. On Saturday 18th May for example, two excursions arrived at St. Fillans, the first from Arbroath, and an hour later another from Dundee. The coaching stock from the Arbroath train was then taken forward empty to Balquhidder. Here it was passed by a cruise train from Johnston and Paisley heading clockwise for St. Fillans where it stopped from 7.20pm to 9.0pm. The empty train then returned to St. Fillans, leaving for Arbroath at 9.40pm followed 15 minutes later by the Dundee excursion. In between all this excursion traffic was the Saturdays Only local train which reached St. Fillans at 9.14pm, returning to Crieff at 9.20pm. St. Fillans must have been a hive of activity on such evenings, and the station staff, most of all the signalman, kept on their toes.

Not all these cruise trains went the full circle, and at the beginning of May, Messrs Parkinsons ran another of their long-distance excursions from Bacup and Littleborough. This travelled by way of Dunblane and Balquhidder to St. Fillans, returning by the same route to head for Edinburgh, resulting in another marathon of a day:

Carlisle	Dep	3.25am
Balquhidder		7.35am
St. Fillans	Arr	7.55am
St. Fillans	Dep	9.15am
Edinburgh	Arr	1.38pm

These timings allowed the passengers an hour to sample the Highland air, albeit at a fairly early hour, while the instruction regarding the scenic part of the journey stipulated: *'Train to make slow run from Stirling to St. Fillans and St. Fillans to Stirling, but must not be allowed to delay other trains'*.

The LM&SR Guide to Scottish Holiday Resorts for 1935 contained glowing references to the Strathearn destinations. This hefty tome, running to 400 pages, included descriptions of places of interest, detailed listings of accommodation and numerous advertisements. The copy writers of the LM&SR Publicity Department waxed lyrical about the charms of the district, describing Crieff thus:

'The capital of Strathearn slopes pleasantly to the sun on the woody side of the Knock. It has charming walks and famous drives in all directions, and the River Earn wimpling at its feet. Many of the famous spots in Scotland, like Drummond Castle and the Falls of Turret lie around. There are several golf courses, the best of angling, tennis courts and bowling greens, and one of the finest express train services in the country, to and from Edinburgh (Princes Street) and Glasgow (Buchanan Street) and all places southward to London by the West Coast route. It is a gay, picturesque, delightful little town, with the best of accommodation in Hydropathics, hotels, and private lodgings. There are motor bus tours through the Sma' Glen which are most delightful.'

Twenty-eight lodgings were listed, and there were in addition twenty-one advertisements, including eight for hotels and, less welcome, two for garages. Interestingly, the Drummond Arms and Sealladmohr Hotels also promoted golf at Gleneagles in their advertisements.

ABOVE: **Figure 8.15**
An LM&SR table napkin, almost certainly used in one of the Buffet or Restaurant cars which ran on the 'Circular Tours'. This napkin advertised the seven-day 'Holiday Runabout' ticket for area C 8 which included the Gleneagles to Balquhidder line. This rare survivor, albeit used, dates from the late 1930s. *Author's collection*

The description of Comrie was equally effusive:

'Nestling in the heart of Strathearn with the "Bonnie Earn" clear winding at its side and bosky glens running in to the heart of the hills, this is one of the most delightful and convenient resorts in the Highlands. There is capital angling on every side, beautiful roads, and endless spots of the highest interest to see, while by way of the railway to St. Fillans and Lochearnside access is given to the Oban line and all the famous places on the West Highlands. Gleneagles, with its superb golfing facilities is within half an hours train journey, and there is a local 9-hole course.'

Fifteen bed and breakfast establishments were listed, three of which boasted baths, but strangely there was no mention of any of the hotels, and the only advertisement was for the Cuilt B&B.

The description of St. Fillans was briefer if no less enthusiastic:

'A pretty little village pleasantly situated at the foot of Loch Earn. Delightful motor boating and fishing. Fine train service to and from all parts of Scotland and England by LMS Railway. Numerous interesting cheap excursions may be made from St. Fillans. The scenery in the district is among the loveliest in Scotland. 9-hole golf course. Good fishing.'

Again, sixteen establishments offering accommodation, two mentioned that they had a boat on the loch, while six still had pianos. This was only one less than in 1916, so it would seem not a lot had changed in twenty years, even with the advent of modern entertainment inventions such as the 'wireless'.

Finally, Lochearnhead also merited a mention:

'This pretty little village approached by the railway from Callander and St. Fillans, is situated at the western extremity of Loch Earn and the southern end of Glen Ogle. Loch Earn presents the perfection of lake scenery – a retiring mountain boundary on either side, with here and there rich woodlands. It abounds with trout. The highest mountains in the neighbourhood are Ben Vorlich (3224 feet) and Struc-a-Chroin (3189 feet). The Braes of Balquhidder – Rob Roy's country are at hand.'

Seven lodgings were listed, one maintaining a boat on the loch, but again there was no mention of the hotel.

In addition to promoting the Strath and attracting visitors, the LM&SR also continued to do its bit serving the local community. On 8th March 1935, a special train was run from Crieff to Perth in connection with the Perth Music Festival, conveying parties from Comrie, Crieff and Madderty, totalling 27 adults and 135 children.

LEFT: 8.16
An LM&SR Holiday Contract ticket for area C 18 for the week 31st July to 6th August 1937. This First Class ticket was issued to Miss Catherine Scott-Wier. Area C 18 covered the whole of the branch lines of Strathearn while other tickets in this series only covered parts of them. This illustration shows the front of the ticket. *Author's collection*

BELOW LEFT: 8.17
The reverse of a similar LM&SR Holiday Contract ticket for area C 18. This shows the lines and stations for which the ticket was valid, which in this case included the main line between Dunblane and Dundee in addition to the Callander & Oban line as far as Balquhidder. The Methven branch is not shown although it was still open at this time. *Author's collection*

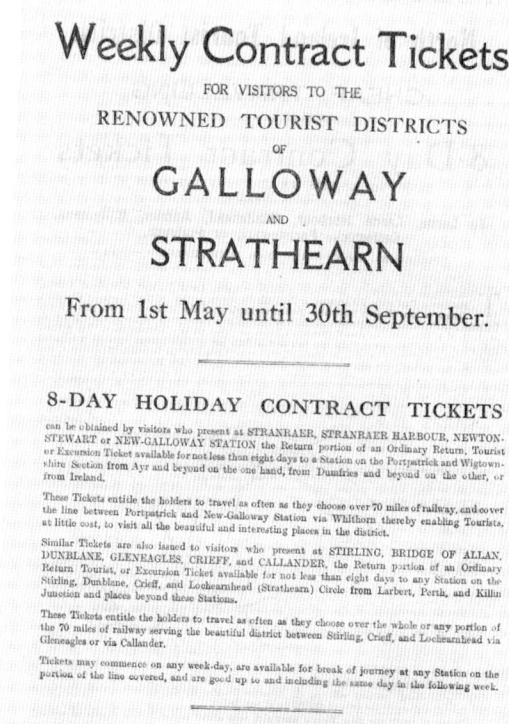

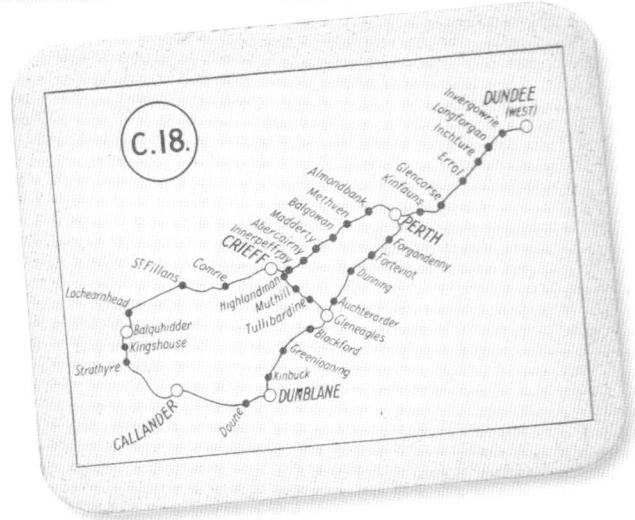

ABOVE: Figure 8.18
An advertisement for LM&SR eight-day Holiday Contract tickets. The forerunner of the Holiday Runabout tickets, these tickets allowed unlimited travel over the lines specified for a period of eight days. The main condition being that passengers had to present a ticket for travel to one of the stations in the area covered. This was not the case with the later Runabout tickets. *Author's collection*

Some returned by ordinary trains, but the following day another special left Perth for Crieff at 10.40am with an estimated 120 passengers.

Having played Celtic in January, it was now the turn of St. Johnstone to play their arch rivals, Rangers, on 23rd March. A football special was laid on, but from Crieff rather than Comrie, with an expected load of 250 supporters. Unusually, the instructions specified that this train, although an Up train, was to depart from the Down platform at Crieff. On 6th April, arrangements were also made for the Scotland v England match in Edinburgh. The 12.20pm Crieff to Gleneagles was retimed to start from Comrie, and the 10.40pm Gleneagles to Crieff train was extended to Comrie. Beyond Gleneagles, supporters travelled by ordinary train over the main line.

Seasonal Sunday school traffic was also in evidence – on 22nd June, specials conveyed parties from Crieff and Methven to Broughty Ferry or Carnoustie, while a party from St. Fillans travelled to St. Andrews by way of Newburgh. Other events such as the Muthill Merchants Holiday on 10th April and the Victoria Day Holiday on 17th May merited the strengthening of trains or their extension beyond their normal destination.

One special visitor that summer was Queen Wilhelmina of the Netherlands, who, accompanied by her daughter Princess Juliana, later Queen Juliana, arrived by Royal Train at Crieff at the start of a holiday in Strathearn. Unusually, she then went on by car to St. Fillans where the party stayed at the Drummond Arms Hotel.

In the autumn, in another initiative to win local traffic, the LM&SR ran a whist drive special from Crieff to Glasgow on 8th October. The train travelled via Balquhidder and Callander on the outward leg, returning via Gleneagles. The timings allowed four hours in Glasgow, to allow *'ample time to visit a place of entertainment.'* No further details were given on this score, but it was made clear that the playing of whist was not compulsory!

Similarly, the agricultural community was served by the usual seasonal special trains returning wintering sheep to the Highlands. Some were local trips such as a special freight train from Tullibardine on 1st April 1935 conveying two trucks of sheep from there, plus three trucks from Muthill to Crieff, while on the same day a special train ran from Luncarty to Balquhidder. This started with just two trucks from Luncarty, but then picked up two more at Methven, three at Abercairny and two at Crieff, to which were added a further seven from Tullibardine and Muthill. By contrast, the following day a special freight made a coast to coast journey from Laurencekirk to Oban. This train, with twenty-nine trucks of sheep, passed through Strathearn in the early hours of the morning:

Perth	Dep	4.30am
Almond Valley Jct		4.35am
Balquhidder		6.25am
Oban	Arr	10.55am

The following day a similar special conveyed twenty-three trucks from Glencarse to Taynuilt on the Callander & Oban line. All this mass movement of livestock was then repeated in the opposite direction during the autumn months.

1935 saw a number of other initiatives by the LM&SR, both nationally and locally, to generate new traffic. One of these was the introduction of Camping Coaches throughout the LM&SR, with twenty-three sites in Scotland including one each at Comrie and St. Fillans. These Camping Coaches were essentially holiday homes on wheels which could be rented out on a weekly basis. Elderly carriages, which might otherwise have been scrapped, were converted to sleep up to six people, with washing and toilet facilities, and a kitchen and living room cum dining area. They were usually located at picturesque stations in sidings which were no longer used, and connected to mains water and drainage systems. The benefit to the railway was not only the rent charged, but the revenue generated by the fares of those travelling to and from the Camping Coaches, and local rail travel from the station where it was located. The Camping Coaches evidently proved a success, for in the following years up to 1939, the LM&SR nearly doubled their number, including eleven more in Scotland. One of these sites was Lochearnhead which was allocated not one but two Camping Coaches.

1935 would seem to have been a typical British summer with its unpredictable weather, for on 24th June a heavy cloudburst damaged the railway bridge over the River Ardoch between Dunblane and Doune, severing the Callander & Oban line yet again. All through traffic was diverted by way of Crieff and two cruise excursions on 26th June were also re-routed. Being the middle of the tourist season, repairs were carried out as quickly as possible and the line was open for traffic by the following Saturday, 29th June.

Figure 8.19
A working instruction for two typical livestock specials in the spring of 1937. As usual, it shows details of the locomotive and rolling stock working and any alterations to the existing timetable to accommodate the special. The Luib to Cargill train is an example of those specials which were routed over the Strathearn lines, while the Balquhidder to Perth train is typical of the local specials serving stations on the branch lines. *Courtesy David Ferguson*

SPECIAL FREIGHT TRAIN—LUIB TO CARGILL.
Conveys 6 Trucks Sheep Perth, 2 Brechin, and 7 Cargill.

	65 p.m.		65 p.m.
Luib ....dep.	12 5	Crieff .... arr.	2 12
Killin Junction	12 18	Do. dep.	2 19
Glenoglehead	12 26	Madderty	2 34
Balquhidder ...... arr.	12 44	Methven Junction	2 47
Do. dep.	1 11	Almond Valley Jct. ...	3 2
St. Fillans .... arr.	1 35	Perth (North) ... arr.	3 7
Do. dep.	1 42	Do. dep.	3 25
Comrie	1 57	Stanley	3 43
		Cargill .... arr.	3 53

Light Engine and Guard to leave Perth for Luib *via* Methven Junction at 7.20 a.m.
Stirling to provide Trucks and Brake Van by Ordinary Train.

SPECIAL FREIGHT TRAIN—BALQUHIDDER TO PERTH (North).
Conveys 21 Trucks Sheep, Balquhidder to Perth, and 7 Trucks, Comrie to Almondbank.

	66 a.m.		66 a.m.
Balquhidder ....dep.	9 30	Madderty	10 58
St. Fillans .... arr.	9 57	Methven Junction	11 10
Do. dep.	10 3	Almondbank........ arr.	11 17
Comrie .... arr.	10 18	Do. dep.	11 25
Do. dep.	10 28	Almond Valley Jct. ...	11 33
Crieff	10 43	**Perth** (North) ...... arr.	11 38

10.40 a.m. Mixed Train, Crieff to St. Fillans, to leave at 10.44 a.m.

Plate 8.18
A view of Glen Ogle viaduct and the line towards St. Fillans from the hillside above Lochearnhead station. Although taken in post-war years, this shows the two camping coaches occupying one of the sidings in the foreground which were reinstated after the war. Significantly, at least one family appear to have travelled by car rather than by train.
Author's collection

In the years leading up to the Second World War, the LM&SR continued to promote tourism in the district, and the ever popular cruise trains were maintained. Excursions from Edinburgh, Glasgow, and Dundee featured regularly in the programme, while others came from Arbroath, Johnston and Strathaven in Lanarkshire. The main purpose of these cruise trains being to give the passengers a leisurely and enjoyable trip through the attractive scenery of the district, instructions were often issued related to relaxed running times. The excursion from Johnston to St. Fillans on 15th May 1937 being a case in point. Instructions were given that *'Train will make a slow run from Callander to St. Fillans and St. Fillans to Crieff but must not be allowed delay ordinary trains'*.

The following month similar instructions were issued for the marvellously titled *'Glasgow & District Churches Badminton*

ABOVE: **Figure 8.20**
The cover of a booklet of vouchers marketed by the LM&SR for a weekend at Gleneagles Hotel and Golf Courses. The combined charge for First Class passengers was £12 15s 0d, but in this case had been amended to £12 5s 9d, a reduction of 9s 6d, which may have been some form of special offer. The comparable Third Class charge was £7 10s 0d as illustrated in the previous chapter. This booklet was date stamped for use on 2nd July 1937, but never used. *Author's collection*

RIGHT: **Figure 8.21**
The set of eight vouchers issued in the booklet shown at Figure 8.20 for a weekend at Gleneagles. The four yellow vouchers covered the First Class travel from London (Euston) to Gleneagles and return, while the four pink vouchers covered the return trip in the hotel bus, the two-night stay at the hotel, and three days golfing. The outward journey was to have been used on the 10.40pm departure from London (Euston) on 2nd July 1937. *Author's collection*

League Evening Cruise Train' to make a slow run from Callander to Strathyre and from Balquhidder to Crieff. The excursion returned to Glasgow via Gleneagles, and so ran at normal speed from Crieff, through the less spectacular scenery of lower Strathearn.

The usual load for such trains was anywhere between 250 and 400 passengers, although 250 to 350 was the norm. Trains were quite long, being on average eight or nine coaches, but on one occasion a Glasgow excursion had twelve coaches, near the maximum which could be accommodated in the passing loops at places such as Comrie and St. Fillans. A variety of locomotive power was employed, including LM&SR 'Moguls' and Class '4' 0-6-0s. The Dundee and Oban excursions were often hauled by ex-Highland Railway 'Castle' Class locomotives, including *Brodie Castle*, *Duncraig Castle* and *Beaufort Castle*.

Meanwhile, ordinary branch line trains continued to be hauled by a mix of ex Caledonian Railway 0-6-0s, 4-4-0s and 0-4-4Ts. The 4.0pm through train from Glasgow to Crieff was always hauled by a Glasgow engine, usually an ex-Caledonian Railway Pickersgill 4-4-0. However, from 1933 onwards when four ex-Midland Railway 4-4-0 'Compounds' were transferred from Carnforth to Balornock, these locomotives were regularly used on this run. They were said to be popular with crews, being faster on the level and light on coal consumption, although they were less powerful, particularly uphill.

One unfortunate experiment in 1938 was the introduction of one of the new Stanier 2-6-2 tank engines on the Perth to Balquhidder run. Despite its capacity of 3 tons of coal and 1,500 gallons of water, it was not popular with drivers who considered it inadequate for the duties it had to perform. Needless to say this experiment does not appear to have lasted long and the traditional motive power was reinstated.

Besides the excursion traffic mentioned above, the LM&SR continued to run special trains for the local population. Excursions from Comrie to Glasgow and St. Fillans to Arbroath were run in 1937, while on 7th June, an ambitious excursion was laid on for the Crieff Public Schools to Tobermory. This train ran from Perth to Oban with an anticipated load of 200 passengers. It was a long day:

Perth	Dep	7. 5am
Crieff	Dep	7.42am
Oban	Arr	11. 4am
Oban	Dep	7.35pm
Crieff	Arr	10.36pm
Perth	Arr	11.14pm

Sunday schools continued to use the railway for their summer excursions, with 5th June 1937 being a particularly busy day. A half day excursion for Trinity Church Sunday School brought 140 adults and 120 children from Stanley to Crieff, while the combined Sunday Schools of York Place and Wilson Church in Perth, totalling 160 adults and 160 children, travelled to Almondbank. Meanwhile, St. Serfs Sunday School at Almondbank, with 100 adults and 150 children, headed in the other direction for a day excursion to Forgandenny. To top it all, 80 adults and 130 children from Methven Parish Church travelled to Perth to join an excursion from there to Moniefieth near Broughty Ferry.

Sadly, for the Methven contingent this would be the last time they would be able to take their annual outing by rail, for on 26th September 1937, the LM&SR withdrew the passenger service, operated by the Steam Rail Motor, between Methven and Methven Junction.

This economy measure deprived Methven of its railway after nearly eighty years, and was yet another indicator of the financial pressures on the railway and the effects of competition from the buses. Although Methven closed to passengers, it remained open for the all-important goods traffic, and this was to continue for another twenty-eight years until 1965, just before the line closed completely.

One change brought about by this withdrawal of passenger service was that Methven Junction, previously only classed as an exchange platform was now elevated to the status of a station in its own right. Quite what passenger traffic the LM&SR hoped to attract to this isolated spot in the middle of farmland and with no road access is hard to imagine, but tickets were printed for journeys from Methven Junction to Perth and Crieff (Figure 4.13). For hardy souls it was still possible to access the station by a public footpath which ran down from Methven village through Tippermallo Farm, but they were probably few in number.

Methven disappeared from the timetable for the Perth to Crieff line, and in its place a note was inserted, of the type which was to become all too familiar in the 1960s era following the 'Beeching cuts':

'Methven Junction and Methven

The Passenger Train Service between Methven Junction and Methven has been discontinued. Messrs W Alexander & Sons Ltd operate an hourly service of omnibuses daily between Perth (General Station) and Methven. For times see local omnibus Time Tables.'

Not long after this the siding serving the Strathearn Manure Works near Crieff was taken out of use and lifted, and the following year the LM&SR instructions for signal boxes at Balquhidder were amended to indicate that at certain times of the day both signal boxes were to be operated by only one signalman.

The Munich crisis of 1938 was a portend of things to come, and as the possibility of another war increased, the railways, among others, did not remain idle. Having learned the lessons of the First World War, they began their preparations in good time. The 'Big 4', including the LM&SR, began contingency planning for a possible war and as early as 1938 issued instructions relating to air raid precautions and gas attack. These measures had little direct impact on the branch lines of Strathearn, where life continued very much as normal.

The 1939 edition of the LM&SR Guide to Scottish Holiday Resorts contained all the usual information and listings including the Strathearn resorts. The texts had been updated, but were no less fulsome in their praise of the district. Crieff now boasted no less than forty-one listings for accommodation, including five hotels, although interestingly, the Drummond Arms was not among them. In addition there were some twenty advertisements for hotels and lodgings.

Comrie had a respectable twenty-two listings for lodgings, but there was only one advertisement, that for the Commercial Temperance Hotel. St. Fillans had a modest ten listings, but only three now claimed to have a piano. Of more concern to the LM&SR was that three of them were listed as having a garage – and this in a railway guide!

Lochearnhead managed eight listings, one of which announced that it now had '*an inside convenience*' – an interesting commentary on the times. However, the summer of 1939 was destined to be the last tourist season for a number of years, and one of the last under the LM&SR.

One of the major events held locally prior to the outbreak of war was the Third World Rover Scout Moot held at Monzie Castle from 15th to 29th July 1939. A huge tented camp for 3,500 Rover Scouts from 48 countries was established in the grounds of the castle by courtesy of the Laird, Mr Douglas Maitland-Makgill-Crighton. The scouts arrived from various parts of the world, the last leg of their journey being by rail to Crieff. In addition, 400 tons of camping equipment also arrived by rail. When they left on the final day, they did so en masse for a short break in Edinburgh, and special trains were laid on for them. This was a busy day as can be seen in Plate 8.19.

One of the first calls on the railways following the outbreak of the Second World War on 3rd September 1939 was the mass movement of hundreds of thousands of evacuees being sent from the cities to safer places around the country. Three special trains conveyed over 2,000 women and children from Glasgow to Crieff and a further train took a large contingent to Comrie. Another group of between 200 and 300 women and children also spent a night in Gleneagles Hotel before being transported onward to their final destinations.

Other than these activities, the war did not have an immediate impact on the branch lines of Strathearn beyond the various measures including air raid precautions brought about by the government control of railways, but over the next few years the effects of the war would be increasingly felt. One of the first changes was the requisitioning of Gleneagles Hotel when it closed at the end of the 1939 season. Initially this became a hospital, and later a recuperation centre, not being handed back to the LM&SR until May 1947 for one final season. A fuller account of the hotel during this period has already been given in the previous chapter, but the main effect on the railway was the stationing of Hospital Train No. 101 in the carriage sidings at Gleneagles.

Not only was the tourist traffic severely curtailed during the war years, but the regular passenger service was gradually and considerably pruned. A comparison of the timetables for 1939 and 1943 show a marked decrease in the number of trains on the Strathearn lines. On the Gleneagles to Balquhidder via Crieff section, six weekday and two Saturday trains had been withdrawn by October 1943, reducing the service between Gleneagles and Crieff from nine to six Up trains and eleven to seven Down trains, a reduction of roughly one third. The section between Crieff and Balquhidder was hardest hit, with the service reduced to just two trains each way per day, with one additional train each to and from St. Fillans.

The Perth to Crieff line fared no better, with six Down and seven Up trains, mostly Saturdays Only services, having been withdrawn. This reduced the weekday services from four trains to three each way per day, and removed all Saturdays Only services except one. Added to this, the priority accorded to troop trains and other military traffic had a knock-on effect

By the beginning of the Second World War, the ex-Caledonian Railway 0-4-4Ts which had served the lines around Crieff for many years were replaced by ex-Caledonian Railway Pickersgill 4-4-0s. However, war time exigencies meant that local trains were often hauled by whatever locomotive Perth had available, Thus branch line trains were often hauled by ex-Midland Railway 4-4-0 'Compounds',

ABOVE: Plate 8.19
A busy scene on the Up platform at Crieff station in August 1939 as Scouts who had been attending the Third World Rover Scout Moot at Monzie Castle board a special train to take them to Edinburgh for a brief visit before they returned to their home countries. In addition to the Scouts, a fair crowd of passengers can be seen on the Down platform awaiting a train to Comrie. *Author's collection*

Plate 8.20
One of the rooms at Gleneagles Hotel which was requisitioned as a hospital during the Second World War. The basic nature of the hospital beds and lockers contrasts with the opulent décor of their surroundings. His Majesty King George VI and Queen Elizabeth visited Gleneagles in the summer of 1943 when it was being used as an RAF recuperation hospital.
Author's collection

LM&SR '4F' 0-6-0s, and even, on occasion, the L&NER 'D49' Class *Invernesshire*.

The early morning mail train from Stirling was often hauled by an L&NER 'V1' 2-6-2 tank engine. The morning stopping goods from Stirling was hauled by a variety of locomotives, almost all L&NER classes including 'J35', 'J36', 'J37' and even 'J39' locomotives, in addition to the ex-North British Railway 'Scott' and 'Glen' Class 4-4-0s.

Military traffic undoubtedly passed over the Strathearn lines as it had done in the First World War when the utility of the east–west link was proved. The Gleneagles to Perth via Crieff section also had an important role as the primary diversionary route should the important choke point of the Moncrieffe tunnel be bombed and put out of action. Additional military traffic was generated by the various camps and depots established throughout the district. An ammunition dump was established in the wood next to Muthill station and another near Balquhidder station. It was later estimated that in excess of 110,000 tons of high explosive and 8,000 tons of gas munitions were concealed in ammunition dumps across Perthshire, with much of it still being in situ nearly three years after the war ended.

By 1943 a large Royal Army Service Corps (RASC) storage depot had been established at Balgowan station. A number of large Nissen-type huts were erected and a special siding laid to this depot which was rail served. This storage facility was probably associated with the various camps established in the woods near Trinity Gask to house large numbers of Polish troops who had escaped from Europe to continue the fight under British command.

About the same time work began on a Royal Navy Stores Depot (RNSD) at Almondbank. Most of the construction material arrived by rail at Almondbank station which was kept open seven days a week to deal with this surge in vital war traffic. The station continued to serve the depot until the private siding to RNSD Almondbank was completed. This siding formed a spur from the original private siding to Lumsden & MacKenzie's bleach works just east of Almondbank station. The full layout of the naval depot shown in Figure 4.6 included a number of sidings, a run-around loop and its own locomotive shed for the depot shunter.

Perhaps one of the best known military camps was the notorious Prisoner of War Camp 21 at Comrie. Laid out at a site called Cultybraggan about a mile south of Comrie, work on its construction began in the summer of 1941. No. 249 (Alien) Company of the Royal Pioneer Corps (RPC) were employed on this work. This unit was formed mainly of Austrian Jewish refugees who had volunteered to join the British Army, but who at that stage in the war were not permitted to serve in combat units. The camp was completed by the end of October 1941 and thereafter the guard force consisted mainly of Polish troops under British command.

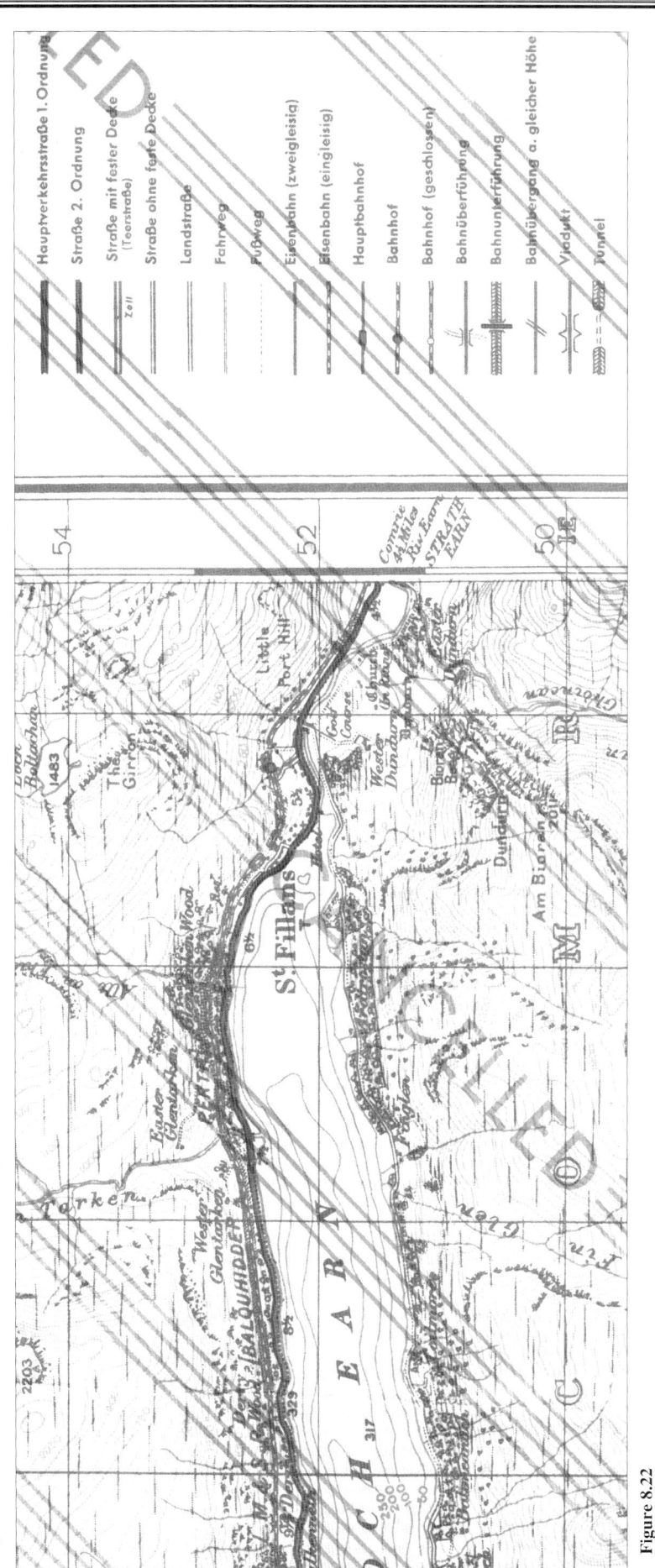

Figure 8.22
An interesting version of the Ordnance Survey map covering Upper Strathearn. This map was originally printed by the German Wehrmacht as part of their preparations for the invasion of England in 1940. They reprinted the British OS map to a larger scale and added their own key, on the right, to the map symbols. This map was probably part of the stock of a German map depot in France which was captured by the Allies in 1944. Map paper was high quality and it has been reused, hence the overprint 'CANCELLED' in blue. The reverse was used by the War Office to print Sheet 3516 of their 1:25,000 series covering the town of Lempforde, north west of Minden in Germany. Fortunately the invasion never took place, but it shows the extent of the detailed planning which was carried out if such maps of Scotland were prepared.
Author's collection

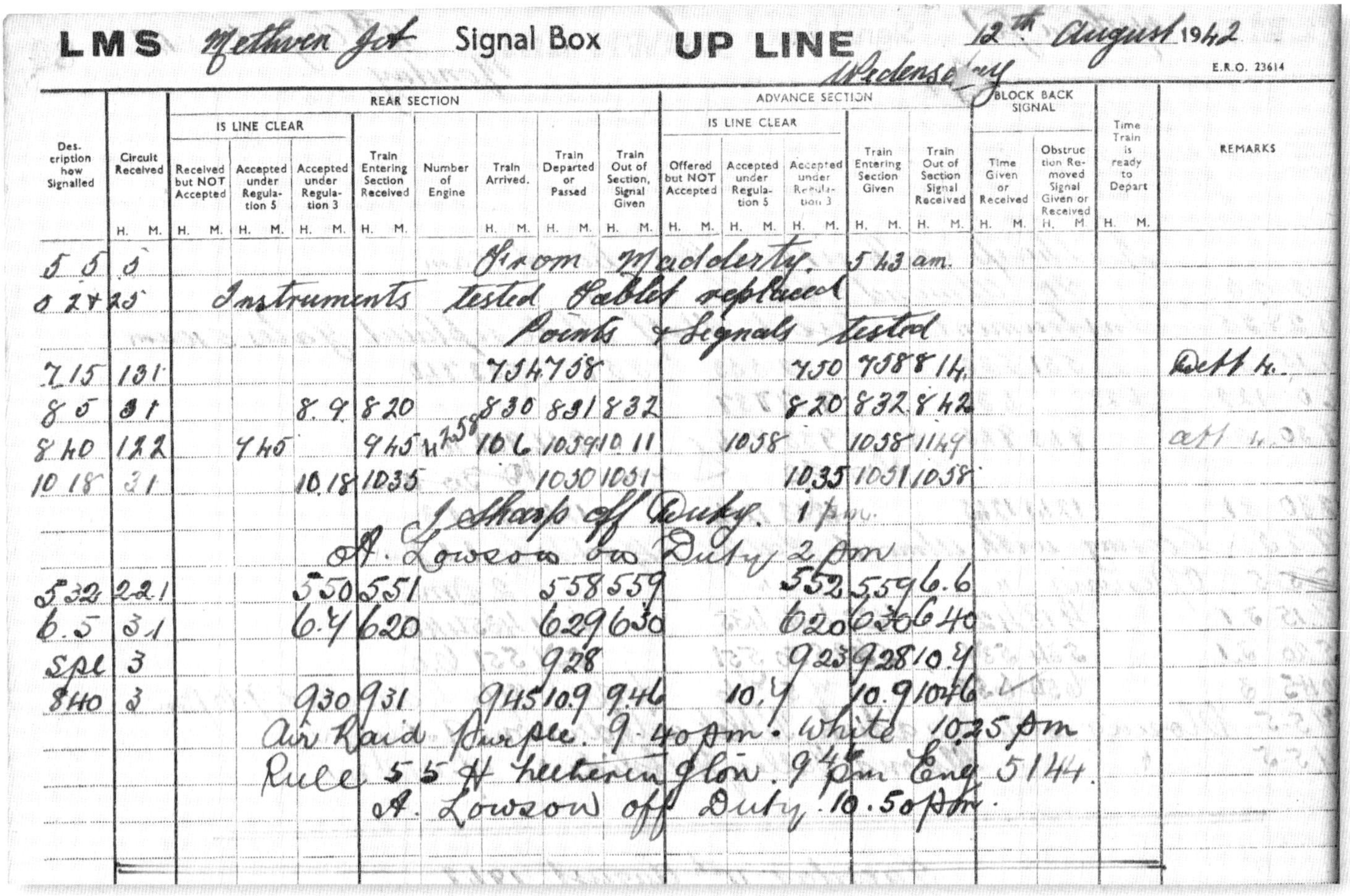

Figure 8.23
A page from the Train Register Book in use at Methven Junction on 12th August 1942. These entries for the Up Line show that Madderty signal box opened at 5.43am and from then on the day was pretty normal until 9.40pm when Air Raid Message 'Purple' was received. This would normally have been preceded by Air Raid Warning 'Yellow' – the 'Preliminary Caution', but not in this case. The 'Purple' warning was the 'Lights Warning' which required all lights except those in the special exempt categories to be extinguished. Fortunately, in this case, it was not followed by the Air Raid Warning 'Red' – the 'Action Warning'. The Air Raid Warning 'White' – the 'All Clear' was received at 10.25pm without further incident. *Author's collection*

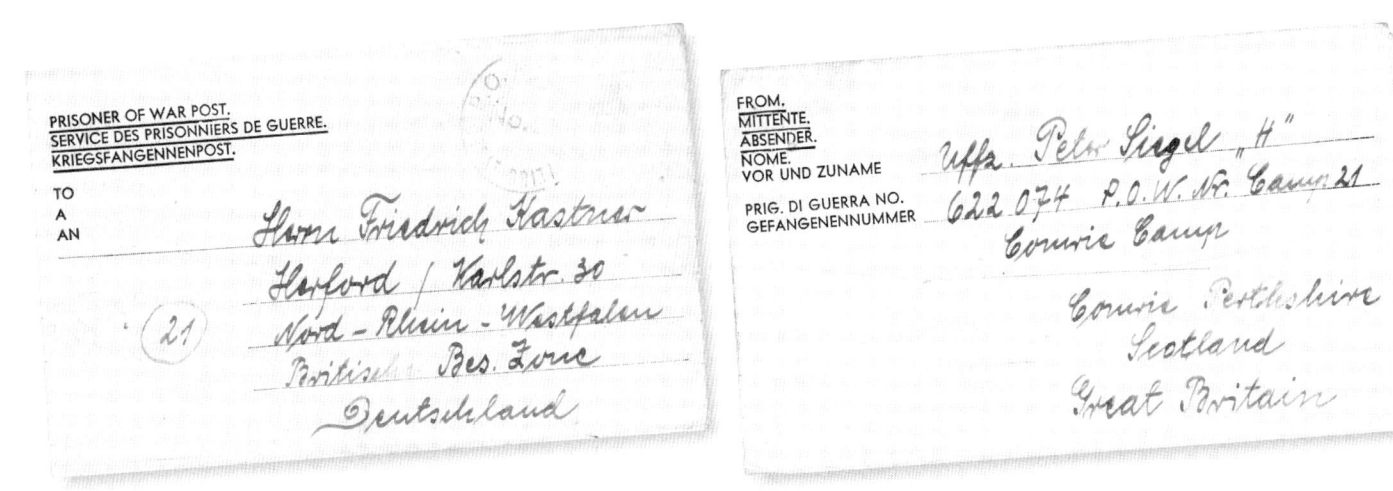

Figure 8.24
A Prisoner of War letter sent by a German prisoner at Comrie. Addressed to Herr Friedrich Kastner of Herford in the British Zone of Occupation in Germany, the letter is postally franked 'POW Camp No. 21 Great Britain'. The sender has added '21' in ink. This letter was dated 21st January 1947, over a year and half after the war ended. The last prisoners left the camp later that year. *Author's collection*

Figure 8.25
The rear of the Prisoner of War letter at Figure 8.24 showing the details of the sender, which in this case was Under Officer Peter Siegel. He lists the camp as 'POW Camp Nr 21, Comrie Camp. The term Cultybraggan was the name given to the camp in post-war years when it became a British Army Training Camp. The address is written in English as it was also intended as the return address should the letter not be delivered, which was a distinct possibility in war-ravaged post-war Germany. *Author's collection*

Plate 8.21
Cultybraggan Camp seen here in post-war years, was established as a Prisoner of War Camp in 1941, and was known as Camp 21 or 'Comrie Camp'. A sprawling collection of corrugated iron Nissen huts, the camp was originally divided into a number of compounds. By the 1960s, when the author was there, most but not all of the barbed wire had gone, as had the guard towers, but much of the camp remained unchanged from its wartime days.
Author's collection

German Prisoners of War (PoWs) were classified as 'White', 'Grey' or 'Black' depending on their political outlook. Most committed Nazis were classified 'Black' and Comrie was called the 'Black camp of the North'. It housed some 4,000 German NCOs and soldiers, airmen and U boat crews regarded as hard-line Nazis. There was also a sub camp at Cowden where 500 were housed. PoWs would arrive by train at Comrie and then be marched under guard to Cultybraggan.

The Strathearn lines did not suffer any damage as a result of enemy action, although they were subject to air raid warnings from time to time as Luftwaffe bombers flew over to bomb Clydeside. The only event of note was a lone German bomber, possibly lost or heading for home, which jettisoned its bomb load into a field near Muthill cemetery, 2 miles from the station, resulting in nothing more than some impressive craters and a few windows blown out in the village.

Apart from the 'Blackout', rationing and other wartime austerity measures, the work of the branch lines of Strathearn carried on much as usual, and as if to underline this, one of the events in May 1944 while the allied world was eagerly awaiting 'D-Day' was a visit from the Engineer's weedkilling train. This train was en route from Oban to Forfar, spraying certain specified sections of line as it went. The timetable followed was:

Balquhidder	Dep	8. 0am	
Gleneagles	Arr	9.40am	
Gleneagles	Dep	9.55am	Start spraying
Crieff	Arr	10.35am	Stop spraying
Crieff	Dep	10.55am	
Madderty	Dep	11.13am	Start spraying
Almond Valley Jct	Arr	11.45am	Stop spraying

The length of track to be sprayed was specified at 8 miles and 1,100 yards between Gleneagles and Crieff and 11 miles 280 yards between Madderty and Almond Valley Junction, the other sections being deemed not to require spraying that year. The instructions stipulated that *'a speed of 20-25 mph was to be maintained to enable the apparatus to work properly'*, thus accounting for the extended timings shown above. The train included rail tank wagons containing concentrated chemical, two specially constructed tenders containing one-third chemical and two-thirds water, and a saloon fitted with spraying apparatus.

By late 1944, with the end of the war in sight, life slowly began to return to normal. Leisure travel once again became possible, and during the autumn holidays, 150 day trippers travelled from Crieff to Perth on 4th October, with many going on to Glasgow and Edinburgh. Later that same month, the annual cattle sales were under way with a record 8,000 head of cattle being sold at Oban. This resulted in 412 loaded cattle trucks being dispatched by rail, many of them routed as usual via Strathearn.

The war of course was not over by Christmas, and during this period London and the South East was subjected to a second 'blitz', this time by V1 Flying Bombs and the more deadly V2 rockets. The *Strathearn Herald* of 14th February 1945 recorded that the residents of Crieff contributed 1,200 items of furniture in response to an appeal on behalf of the bombed-out victims of the London Borough of Stepney. This furniture would have been sent south by rail. Meanwhile, the PoW camp at Comrie was still in operation although the number of PoWs had fallen to just over 3,000, but many of them would remain until the camp finally closed in 1947. Indeed, some would be employed on snow-clearing work during the severe

Plate 8.22
A mixed train on the Crieff to Comrie line headed by one of the ex-Caledonian Railway 0-4-4 tank engines which were regularly used on the Strathearn lines during the LM&SR period.
Courtesy Bernard Byrom

winter of 1947 as recounted later. When the POWs eventually left, the British Army converted Cultybraggan into a training camp as mentioned in Chapter 10.

Six years of war had taken its toll on the railways and, as in 1919, by the time the war had ended, they were in a rundown state. Even the relief at the end of hostilities was tempered by the large number of ex-military vehicles which were declared 'war surplus'. This led to a number of small firms setting up in business as carriers providing yet more competition for the hard-pressed railways.

In Strathearn, the poor state of the LM&SR finances manifested itself in news which leaked out in October 1945 – that they wanted to close the entire line between Crieff and Balquhidder. This led to a public outcry, and the swift formation of the Strathearn Railway Committee (SRC). A public meeting was attended by 300 people, presided over by Sir Robert Dundas of Dunira, while another 200 people could not even get into the hall. At the suggestion of Mr McNair-Snaddon MP, the SRC were authorised to approach both the LM&SR and the Ministry of Transport (War).

It was reported that the residents of Comrie, St. Fillans, Lochearnhead and Balquhidder were up in arms and that 120 people from the Lochearnhead area had signed a petition stating that '*It would cause great hardship to the whole community*'. Their case was supported by Kinross & Perthshire County Council.

In a written reply to a Parliamentary Question by Mr McNair-Snaddon, the Minister stated that '*No decision has been take to close the branch line, but I understand that the LMS have the matter under consideration.*' This classic example of weasel wording did little to reassure the public, and in an interesting letter to *The Scotsman* on 20th October, complaining about the train service, the Rev Hanmer was closer to the mark when he asked if it was '*the usual practice of a railway to provide a service of a most inadequate and inconvenient type and then declare that there is not sufficient traffic to maintain it*'.

The SRC continued to press for a meeting with the LM&SR which consistently declined to do so. With apprehension in Strathearn growing, they finally issued a statement on 15th December that '*they are examining all branch lines in Scotland to improve and to justify the service in conjunction with the rise in road transport*'.

Meanwhile, in another effort to return to pre-war normality, the LM&SR were pressing the government to de-requisition Gleneagles Hotel. Here, however, they were opposed by the National Union of Mineworkers who insisted that if Gleneagles were to be handed back to the LM&SR then alternative facilities for the treatment of injured miners must be provided. Not surprisingly, a new Labour government was in no rush to hand back such a playground for the rich at the expense of the injured miners, and nearly a year of wrangling would ensue before the future of Gleneagles was settled. However, although the hotel remained closed, the LM&SR were able to announce at the end of May 1946 that the Club House and the King's course were now open.

Eventually, in October 1946, it was announced that Bridge of Earn Hospital, a wartime hospital originally earmarked as an orthopaedic and TB centre, would now be shared with the miners. The report recorded that 2,200 patients, including 1,930 miners, had been treated at Gleneagles, and that 102 patients remained under treatment. Matters continued to move slowly, and by 11th January 1947, no date had yet been set for the handover over of the hotel which was being negotiated by the Department of Health (Scotland).

Meanwhile, Strathearn, in common with much of the country, experienced the worst winter weather for many years. On 15th February, snow was 18 inches to 2 feet deep at rail level, but the snow ploughs from Perth were able to clear the Crieff to Balquhidder line. At the beginning of March further heavy snow falls caused delays to trains. A snow plough from Perth was able to clear the line from Gleneagles to Crieff, but the Perth to Crieff road was closed for a week until roadmen aided by fifty German PoWs were able to reopen it.

On 15th March, more heavy snow blocked the line at Tullibardine, and although it was cleared, it became blocked again the next day. This time the snow plough got stuck in the drifts and it took several days to extricate it. Throughout all this, however, the buses came off worst, adding an extra burden on the railways.

Finally at the end of March it was announced that Gleneagles Hotel would be handed back to the LM&SR on 11th April, and that it was hoped that it would reopen at Whitsuntide. Large numbers of tradesmen and workmen were employed on renovation and redecoration of the building to meet this deadline. On 10th May the LM&SR were able to confirm that the hotel would reopen on 22nd May, which it duly did.

On 9th February 1947, a meeting finally took place between Crieff Town Council and Mr Malcolm Spier, Chief Operating Officer for the LM&SR in Scotland. He confirmed that there was no truth in the rumours of closure of the line west of Crieff. He explained that, although the May timetable would still be 24% below the pre-war standards due to shortages of manpower, rolling stock and coal, a number of improvements were planned.

CHAPTER 8: THE CHALLENGING YEARS UNDER THE LM&SR

LEFT: Plate 8.23
A good action shot of another ex-Caledonian Railway Pickersgill 4-4-0 on a Down train having just exchanged tablet hoops at Crieff signal box. Note that the signalman is standing at ground level, which made such exchanges rather awkward. Later, elevated stands such as that shown in Plate 9.24 were provided to make this a less hazardous operation. *ES Morten*

BELOW: Plate 8.24
A smart looking Highlandman station in the post war years. Although taken just after nationalisation, the station retained its essential LM&SR character with its two running in boards and well-tended flower beds.
J Paton collection

The early morning train from Crieff would now have a connection at Stirling for Edinburgh, and there would be two extra late-night trains from Glasgow on Wednesdays and Saturdays. In addition, the Saturday afternoon train from Crieff to Perth would now call at Muirton Halt, near the St. Johnstone football ground, which had been opened in October 1936 for the benefit of football supporters.

Sadly, these modest improvements could not stem the ebb of passengers away from rail to road. In June it was reported that members of Madderty Women's Institute travelled to Oban by bus, and the following month, Forteviot Women's Guild toured Crieff and Lochearnhead by bus rather than train. During the Perth holiday in July, W Alexander & Sons employed forty extra buses, while the traffic on road routes, including the Crieff area, was the heaviest since 1939. Even the choir from the author's own church, St. Andrews in Auchterarder, went by bus to St. Fillans, Lochearnhead and Callander. Back in January, Alexander's had introduced a new school bus between Auchterarder and Crieff, and now in September they announced additional buses to Almondbank on Sundays.

The LM&SR fought back by introducing Cheap Day tickets at the Single fare to '*Populous towns*', such as Perth and Dundee, on Tuesdays, Wednesdays, and Saturdays, and to market towns, including Crieff, one day a week, presumably market day. On 22nd

Plate 8.25
An unidentified ex-Caledonian Railway 4-4-0 shunting next to the Balquhidder West signal box. The point rodding appears to have been recently refurbished and, although the original Caledonian Railway Stevens 'Flap' ground signals are still much in evidence, a new disc ground signal among the stores in the immediate foreground indicates that some signalling renewals are probably imminent.
CRA collection

Figure 8.26
The final LM&SR timetable for the Strathearn branch lines dated '*6th October 1947 Until Further Notice*'. The service was still at such a reduced level that both the Gleneagles to Balquhidder and Perth to Crieff lines could be accommodated on one page of the timetable. Methven Junction had by now become effectively a request stop with notice being required if passengers wanted to be set down or picked up there.
Author's collection

September, the *Strathearn Herald* published an article highlighting the problem of rising costs on the railways, pointing out that in the seven years since 1939, costs had risen as follows:

Salaries & Wages	60%
Coal	137%
Sleepers	70%
Rails	200%

Overall cost had therefore risen by 70%, yet fare increase had been limited to 37% of 1939 prices. Despite the fact that fare increases covered only half this increase in costs, railways were still uncompetitive. The return trip by train from Crieff to Glasgow now cost 15s 6d, having for many years been just 5s 10d, but was nearly three times the comparable bus fare of 5s 6d.

It was strange that despite Mr Spier's excuses regarding shortages of manpower, it was reported that by the end of October the Perth District of the LM&SR had dispensed with the services of 100 women who had covered the jobs of some 150 men during the Second World War. These women had been employed as porters, guards, signalwomen, ticket collectors, clerks and crossing keepers. As well as dispensing with the services of these women, other changes in local staff included re-instating the post of stationmaster at Highlandman. At the end of August, Mr John McDonald, stationmaster at Johnston, was appointed to this post, and Mr Roger, stationmaster at Crieff, who had been covering both stations now only had Crieff. The railway was still a major employer in Crieff, and this was reflected in the turnout on 21st December, when the station staff and friends enjoyed a social and dinner dance at the Star Hotel, when eighty-six sat down to dinner.

CHAPTER 8: THE CHALLENGING YEARS UNDER THE LM&SR

LEFT: Plate 8.26
An ex-Caledonian Railway Pickersgill 4-4-0 about to run around the train it has just brought into St. Fillans station. Although taken in 1950, this whole scene retains its LM&SR flavour. A young railway enthusiast stands proudly beside the footplate crew in this nicely posed shot. *Author's collection*

BELOW: Figure 8.27
The working instruction for the last LM&SR Engineer's Inspection train to run over the Strathearn branch lines on 8th October 1947. This included several slow runs over sections such as Gleneagles to Tullibardine where 25 minutes were allowed rather than the usual 6 minutes, again between Innerpeffray and Abercairny and Almondbank and Almond Valley Junction. Extra time was also allowed at Crieff and Balgowan where a new siding had been added during the war. The train did not however make a run over the short branch to Methven. *Author's collection*

ENGINEER'S INSPECTION SPECIAL TRAIN—OBAN TO GLENEAGLES (via Comrie) AND GLENEAGLES TO PERTH (via Crieff).

	N120 ST a.m.			N120 ST p.m.	
Oban ....dep.	GW 8 35	Crieff ....arr.	12 46
Glencruitten........arr.	8 45	Do. dep.	12 54
Do. dep.	8 49	Highlandman	12 57
Connel Ferry.........	8 56	Muthill.................	1 7
Taynuilt................	9 9	Tullibardine	1 12
Awe Crossing	9 17	Gleneagles ....arr.	1 42
Loch Awe	9 26	Do. dep.	1 45
Dalmally ....arr.	w9 31	Muthill.................	1 55
Do. dep.	9 36	Crieff ....arr.	w2 3
Glenlochy	9 52	Do. dep.	2 8
Tyndrum	10 1	Innerpeffray	2 12
Crianlarich Jct.	10 9	Abercairny	2 30
Luib ....arr.	10 22	Madderty	2 33
Do. dep.	10 33	Balgowan ....arr.	2 45
Killin Jct.	10 41	Do. dep.	2 49
Glenoglehead	10 46	Methven Jct.	2 53
Balquhidder ......arr.	w10 57	Almondbank	2 57
Do. dep.	11 20	Almond Valley Jct.	3 19
St. Fillans ....arr.	11 50	**Perth** (General) ..arr.	3 23
Do. dep.	12 15p		
Comrie	12 27		

C—Inspection Saloon No. 45020.
GW—Saloon to be gassed and watered to capacity.
Saloon to be attached front of 3.45 p.m., Perth to Glasgow (Buchanan Street).

Time allowed for Inspection Purposes.	Minutes
Between Balquhidder and St. Fillans	14
Between Comrie and Crieff	7
At Crieff	8
Between Highlandman and Muthill..............................	6
Between Tullibardine and Gleneagles	25
Between Innerpeffray and Abercairny	15
Between Madderty and Balgowan	8
At Balgowan...	4
Between Almondbank and Almond Valley Junction	18

The autumn of 1946 saw the usual increase in livestock traffic to deal with wintering sheep. On one ten-day period, at least five livestock specials were run from Oban, Tyndrum, Luib and Killin, to various destinations in the east and central highlands. Typical of these was one from Luib to Boat of Garten on 3rd October, conveying twenty-seven trucks of sheep:

From Crianlarich to Carr Bridge	3
From Luib to Carr Bridge	3
From Killin to Grantown-on-Spey	9
From Killin to Grandale	7
From Killin to Broomhill	5

By this time, however, the Labour government's policy of nationalising major industries was well under way. The railways were in a parlous state – partly as a result of minimal maintenance during the war and having had to turn over large parts of their engineering production capacity to munitions work, coupled with increasing competition from road transport – and ripe for nationalisation, and the LM&SR was no exception. The 1946 Transport Bill received the Royal Assent on 6th August 1947, and from then on the days of the four main railway companies were numbered.

In many ways, life on the Strathearn branch lines continued as normal. Work on dispersing the huge stocks of ammunition secreted around Perthshire continued, although at the rate of one train a week carrying about 400 tons, it was reckoned it would take some time to clear the estimated 110,000 tons remaining. On 1st October, it was reported that a series of special trains were run by the LM&SR and the L&NER to bring 1,700 Glasgow school children to hostels in Perthshire to help overcome the manpower shortage to lift the potato harvest. However, the LM&SR were obviously hampered by the continued shortage of rolling stock, for at a meeting of the local National Farmers Union farmers complained that the movement of seed potatoes was at a standstill due to a lack of wagons. It was said that 174 wagons were needed to transport this vital traffic.

On 8th October, the LM&SR Engineer's inspection special made what would be its last trip over the Strathearn lines. Starting from Oban at 8.35am, it left Balquhidder at 11.20am, travelling to Gleneagles to arrive at 1.42am, where it reversed direction to return to Crieff. Leaving Crieff at 2.3pm, it arrived at Perth at 2.32pm. The instructions for the Inspection Saloon No. 45020 were that it was to be gassed and watered to capacity, and specified that it was to be propelled between Gleneagles and Crieff.

The winter timetable issued on 6th October was the last published by the LM&SR, and contained services, which for the Strathearn lines, were little better than those at the end of the war. The Gleneagles to Crieff and Comrie service was reasonable, while that to St. Fillans was sparse, and beyond there only two trains each way per day ran over the section to Balquhidder, with about 10 hours between them! The Crieff to Perth line had only three trains each way per day, with an extra one on Saturdays, but again with gaps of up to 5 hours between some trains. Not surprisingly, these latter two sections had only four years life left in them, but their final demise, which took place in British Railways days, is described in the next chapter.

1947 ended on a disappointing note for the branch lines of Strathearn, with only four successes that year for local stations in the LM&SR Best Kept Stations competition, and of these all bar Gleneagles would be closed less than four years later:

– Gleneagles   Special Class
– Almondbank   1st Class
– St Fillans   1st Class
– Madderty   2nd Class

When the clock struck midnight on 31st December 1947, the relatively brief reign of the LM&SR over the railways in Strathearn came to an end, and from the following day the branch lines became part of the Scottish Region of British Railways.

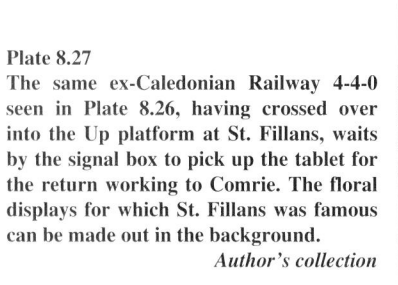

Plate 8.27
The same ex-Caledonian Railway 4-4-0 seen in Plate 8.26, having crossed over into the Up platform at St. Fillans, waits by the signal box to pick up the tablet for the return working to Comrie. The floral displays for which St. Fillans was famous can be made out in the background.
Author's collection

Plate 8.28
Ex-Caledonian Railway Pickersgill 4-4-0 No. 14476 on an Up train at Comrie. The line to St. Fillans can be seen beyond the road bridge, curving to the left and starting the climb up to the embankment and viaduct which carried it behind Comrie.
Author's collection

CHAPTER 9

SAFETY AND SIGNALLING

In the early days of railways, speeds were relatively low and trains infrequent, and it was usually sufficient for drivers to keep a sharp lookout and to control the speed of their trains accordingly. If they saw another train or an obstruction ahead, they slowed down or stopped. In darkness or poor visibility, engines carried a white light at the front to warn of their approach, and a red light was carried at the back of the train to warn drivers of following trains.

Trains operated on a 'Time Interval' system – that is, they ran to strict timetables with a set time between trains – to avoid the possibility of collisions between following trains. Despite these rudimentary safety rules, there were relatively few fatalities in the early years. In 1842 and 1843, for example, only one passenger was killed in each year out of a total of over 20 million passengers carried. Given the harsh living conditions of the time, accidental deaths and injuries in many walks of life, and low life expectancy, this was extremely low and, not unnaturally, there was little call or need for improved safety.

However, by the time the Crieff Junction Railway opened in 1856, matters had moved on significantly. By 1850, there were 6,083 miles of railway open, and such was the rate of expansion that in just ten years this had risen by 50% to 9,069 miles. Passenger traffic tripled to 62 million passengers by 1850, and nearly tripled again to 163 million in 1860.

This dramatic increase in traffic levels in particular led to the need for additional safety measures. The basic method of timetabling trains at adequate intervals to keep them apart, and the punctual working of trains could only afford a certain level of safety. Trains often broke down, ran slow, or were delayed at stations, so the first early signals were provided to protect trains at stations. This was particularly the case at junctions, such as Crieff Junction, where there was an increased danger of collision.

The very early signalling was by policemen using hand signals, but this was soon replaced by the use of flags, usually green for all clear and red for caution or danger. The Crieff Junction Railway Rule Book of 1855, however, used a slightly different system as shown in Figure 9.1. The 'All Clear' was indicated by the policeman standing erect with his flags in his hand, and only exhibiting a green flag to indicate caution. The 'Stop' signal was given by waving the 'Danger Signal', a red flag, up and down. The flaw in this system was that it did not 'fail safe', for if the policeman forgot to exhibit a flag, or the driver did not see a flag, the assumption was that the line was clear.

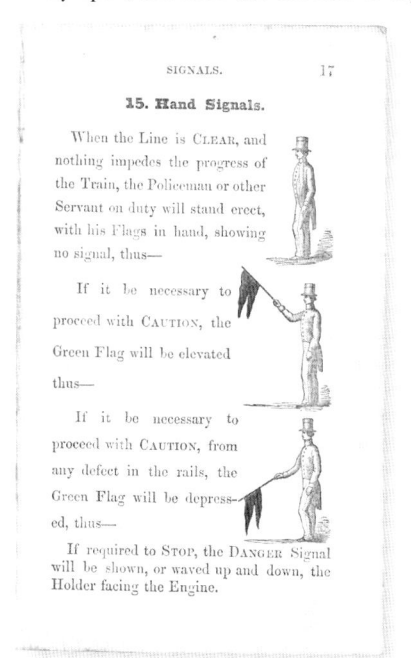

Figure 9.1
Page 17 of the Crieff Junction Railway Rule Book published in 1855. The Policeman depicted is wearing what was standard dress for the era, complete with frock coat and distinctive top hat. The images demonstrate how the various signals were to be given. Note that two types of caution signal were used, one relating to defects in the rails, which given the technology of the day and the number of derailments, was probably necessary. The green flag used was of a pennant design rather than a standard rectangle. The danger signal is not illustrated but would almost certainly have been a standard red flag. *Author's collection*

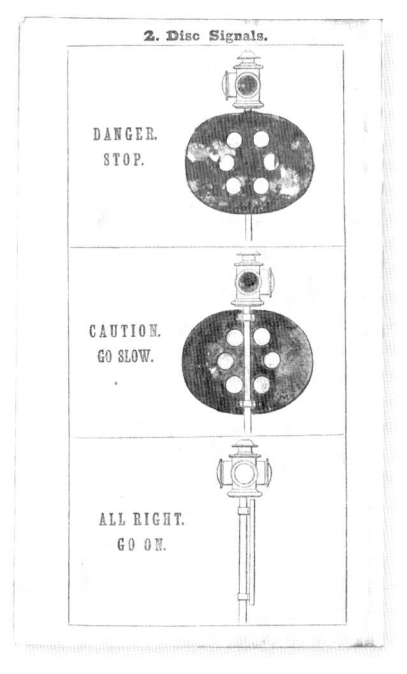

Figure 9.2
The Disc signals illustrated in the Crieff Junction Railway Rule Book at page 12. The size and shape was the same for 'Danger' or 'Caution', but were painted red or green and displayed a corresponding coloured light at night. In the case of the 'All Right' signal, the disc was turned end on and a white light displayed. This followed the system in use for flags, and was far from 'fail safe'. It is worth noting that these illustrations were coloured, possibly by hand, and that in the intervening 160 years some of the ink has run or smudged. *Author's collection*

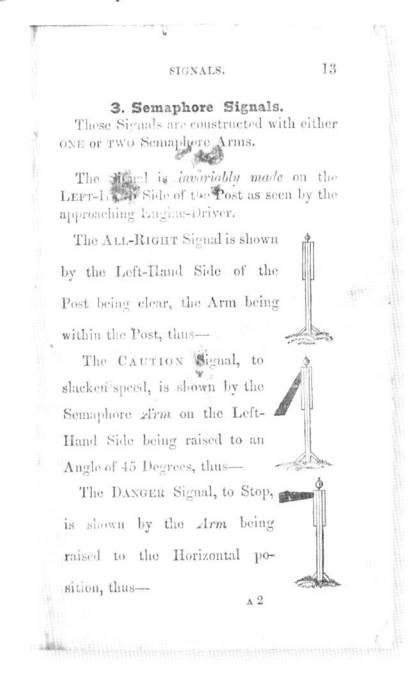

Figure 9.3
The early semaphore signals illustrated in the Crieff Junction Railway Rule Book. These signal posts were quite short and would have been operated by a turn lever and rod. The wooden post was slotted such that the signal arm was free to move in and out of it, and in the case of the 'All Right' indication, the arm was out of sight within the post. Although the indications were slightly different, the North Eastern Railway continued to use these 'slotted' signal posts until the 1920s, and some survived until the 1990s. The discolouration on this page is from the illustrations on page 12 shown in Figure 9.2. *Author's collection*

The Crieff Junction Railway Rule Book illustrated both the rotating disc signals and semaphore signals (Figures 9.2 and 9.3), although it is not clear if both types were used on the line. These signals were similar to those used by the Scottish Central Railway at the time, which made sense, and specific instructions were laid down regarding Junction Signals.

The signals at the stations were under the charge of the station agent, or stationmaster as he became known, but were operated by the 'pointsman', who also worked the points as the title implied. In those days, however, the points and signals were not interlocked, and so could be operated independently, with all the attendant risks. Pointsmen were the forerunner of signalmen, although it is interesting that the Caledonian Railway were still using the term 'pointsman' well into the 1890s. The colloquial term for signalmen was often 'Bobbies', harking back to the days of the policeman, and it is a term still in use today.

Responsibility for obeying any signals rested firmly with the footplate crew as defined in Section IV of the Crieff Junction Railway Rule Book. Elsewhere it stated at Rule 50 that:

'No engine, with or without Wagons or Carriages, shall pass from the Crieff line on to the Scottish Central line until the Pointsman at the Junction Points signals the Scottish Central line clear; and in Foggy Weather the Engineman must ascertain "When the preceding Train has passed" before entering the Scottish Central line.'

The rules also laid down that the speed over the junction was to be no more than six miles an hour. Nevertheless, the whole concept of just checking that the preceding train has gone before proceeding onto the junction would have appeared a risky business, although it was standard practice in 1856.

Signals would have been provided at all the stations on the Crieff Junction line, while those at Muthill, Highlandman and Crieff (Duchlage Road) also protected the level crossings at these stations. Although no details of these early signalling layouts have survived, it is known that by 1886, by which time the line to Perth was also open, Crieff had a total of just five signals. The other level crossings – at Auchterarder Road, Strageath, Pittentian and Pittenzie – may also have had signals, but again no details of these have survived. Despite the rudimentary nature of this signalling, it served its purpose, for in his report to the Board of Trade in 1857, one of the Inspectors, Captain David Dalton, was able to report that there had been no accidents to passengers on the Crieff Junction Railway between 1850 and 1857.

CRIEFF JUNCTION TO CRIEFF LINE

In those early years, most of the accidents or incidents on the line were due to the primitive and unreliable nature of the technology of the day. Typical of these was a derailment at Crieff in September 1860 when *'owing to the points working a little loose, the locomotive came off the rails'*. The main concern of all involved was that passengers might miss their connection with the Scottish Central Railway train at Crieff Junction. However, *'by placing rails under the driving wheels the locomotive was got on the rails 30 minutes later'*. The passengers made their connection so all was well!

Problems with early locomotives and rolling stock were also a recurring theme. In February 1863, the 4.5pm train from Crieff was brought to a standstill near Crieff Junction when *'the engine broke'*. Fortunately all the passengers were disembarked and a telegraph message sent to Perth for a replacement engine, but they were delayed for 3 hours until it arrived. Just over two years later, in July 1865, one of the axles on the tender of an engine broke as it approached the Earn viaduct between Muthill and Highlandman. Passengers were again disembarked, and had to walk the half mile to Highlandman station where they were taken to Crieff by horse-drawn coach. The 7.35pm from Crieff was also delayed until the line could be cleared.

Three years later, in April 1868, a Down mixed train was approaching Muthill when a spring in one of the wagons broke and brought the train to a standstill. In this case the passengers were luckier, being transferred to an open truck in which they arrived at Crieff *'very little behind time'* if a little windblown. Life as a Victorian railway traveller would seem rarely to have been dull!

Later that same year, another Down train was derailed just south of Muthill, the locomotive and tender being off the rails. This time passengers and mail were sent back to Crieff Junction, and thence to Perth and on to Crieff via the recently opened Crieff & Methven Junction line, arriving just one and half hours late. A large gang of men were dispatched to Muthill and re-railed the locomotive in 2 hours, the line being reopened the following day.

1875 was not a good year for safety on the Crieff branch, starting on 9th January when the 10.30am goods train from Crieff came to a standstill at Muthill. The train derailed while entering the sidings blocking the branch line. Another engine was sent from Crieff and the locomotive was re-railed. Then, in late June, the 6.30pm Crieff Junction to Crieff train encountered a problem when starting off. According to the report *'It appears that owing to some oversight, the points were misadjusted so that on starting, the 3rd Class carriage next to the engine went off the rails, causing a half hour delay'*. No doubt words were exchanged between the pointsman and the train crew.

Finally, in August there was yet another derailment, this time at Tullibardine when a cattle truck on a passing goods train became derailed. Services were suspended for several hours and passengers again rerouted via Perth.

A more serious incident occurred at the end of May 1879 when a Crieff-bound passenger train was restarting from Muthill. The coupling between the engine and the leading carriage, in the words of the contemporary account, *'became disconnected in some way. The engine driver, not observing the mishap, drove to near Highlandman station before he discovered he had left the carriages behind'*. Although the primary cause of the incident was some form of mechanical failure, the lack of diligence of the train crew was somewhat alarming. To have driven on for two miles or more without realising they had not got their train behind them must have left them with some explaining to do to the management.

In October 1890, the engine of an excursion train broke down near Highlandman and passengers were again obliged to walk to Crieff. All, that is, except one passenger, *'probably fuelled by alcohol'*, who refused to be moved and insisted on transport to Crieff. Eventually a special was organised for the *'spirit inspired tanner'*. It was reported that the good-natured stationmaster at Crieff considered this the best way to handle the situation, fulfilling the proverb that *'it is better to flatter a fool than to fight him'*.

An unusual accident occurred in November 1893 at Crieff Station while an engine was marshalling the 4.20pm train. The regulator jammed open while backing some wagons onto the carriages, and the resulting collision caused the last carriage to run up against the embankment. A number of vitriol bottles in one truck were broken, but, more seriously, in another truck full of whisky, one of the casks was damaged.

In January 1897, the engine of the 2.0pm train from Crieff to Crieff Junction broke down at Tullibardine and a replacement locomotive had to be sent. Just two years later, in 1899, a goods train from Crieff to Crieff Junction came to grief near the same place when one of the axles of the brake van broke. The van derailed and nearly 200 yards of track were torn up. The brakesman gamely remained in his van until the bottom was torn out, at which juncture he jumped out, luckily being only slightly injured. Traffic was re-routed via Methven Junction while repairs were effected by a gang from Perth.

The accident having occurred around 10.30am, they worked with commendable speed, for the line was reopened by 3.30pm, only four and half hours later.

These incidents of mechanical failure diminished in later years as materials, technology and manufacturing processes improved, but there were still the odd occasions when such failures resulted in accidents.

Even the main line was not immune from such incidents, and in September 1909 an Up goods train was climbing on the 1 in 100 gradient from Auchterarder to Crieff Junction in the early hours of the morning, when one of the connecting rods broke. This resulted in one of the driving rods coming adrift to land on the Down line, thus blocking both lines. The London mail train was diverted by Crieff and the Methven Junction line, which probably caused some consternation.

The Strathearn lines were used on a number of occasions as a diversion route for trains to reach Perth and, just five years later, in October 1914, when a lengthy goods train, mostly of coal wagons, derailed at Hilton Junction, northbound trains were again routed by way of Crieff. Southbound passengers were apparently bussed to Bridge of Earn where they joined North British trains.

Shunting was always a more hazardous manoeuvre, and back in December 1863, a driver was shunting trucks of coal at Crieff when they derailed, blocking the station. Passengers had to alight at the ticket platform and walk the last few hundred yards, although their luggage was carried for them. The *Strathearn Herald* commented that: *'But justice to say that accidents of any kind are a rare occurrence on the railway owing to the careful and cautious management of servants'*, which was much to the credit of the Crieff Junction Railway.

Unfortunately, only four months later, a number of wagons were once again derailed during shunting at Crieff. The platform at the engine house *'was smashed to pieces'* and one of the porters narrowly escaped being run over. The platform referred to was probably the 'ticket platform' mentioned earlier, which was the point at which trains entering Crieff stopped for all tickets to be checked before the train entered the station proper.

Some years later, in 1885, a goods train was shunting at Tullibardine when the engine and tender became derailed. The line was blocked for four hours before the damage was repaired. However, shunting was not the only times when derailments occurred – other incidents being due to track and other defects. Five years previously, at the end of July 1880, for example, an Up goods train derailed at Highlandman tearing up a considerable length of track. Seven years later, the engine of a goods train from Perth became derailed at Duchlage Road level crossing. As often happened, a large crowd gathered to watch the recovery operations, but unfortunately one little six year old girl, Helen McKendrick, had her head through the gap between the gate and the gate post when it was opened and her skull crushed. Sadly there is no record as to whether or not she survived.

A less serious collision occurred a number of years later at Methven Junction when, in the words of the *Strathearn Herald*:

'Last Saturday afternoon, while the engine of a Glasgow excursion train was moving off the loop line at Methven Siding (sic), the passenger engine of the Crieff and Perth railway moved forward to where the loop line joins the main road, the result being that both grazed and collided with each other. The footboards of both engines were smashed to pieces and part of the ironwork also broken, while the front wheels of the Glasgow engine were thrown off the metals. After a short time the engine was got back on the line and both were able to resume their journeys.'

Fortunately this was a slow-speed side-on collision and there were no reports of any injuries. From the description given it seems likely that one of the drivers, most probably that of the Crieff train, misread the signal and moved forward into the path of the other train.

Not all staff were as fortunate as the porter at Crieff mentioned earlier, and it is a reflection of the dangers of the workplace in Victorian times that there were often reports of accidents to staff. In December 1857, one of the staff at Crieff injudiciously attempted to pass between two wagons while a train was in motion. Unfortunately he slipped and fell between the wagons, the wheel of one passing over him, severely fracturing his arm and leg.

Late in August 1865, a workman using a horse to shunt wagons at Highlandman was injured. More seriously, the following year Porter McKillop of Highlandman was badly injured when he was caught between the buffers of two carriages while coupling them up. One of his legs *'was smashed in the most dreadful manner. Doctor Thom rendered all help. The man lies in a most precarious state'*. Sadly for Mr Mckillop his days as a porter were probably over.

Barely a year later, Porter Thomas Brown fell while trucks were being shunted at Crieff. The wheel of a wagon ran over one of his legs which was subsequently amputated at Perth Infirmary. The newspaper reported that *'He is now improving'*, which was probably a relative term given his injuries. Two years later, in 1868, another porter at Crieff, by the name of Comrie, was *'violently'* thrown to the ground during shunting operations and suffered serious external and internal injuries. Another two years later, a labourer called Robin slipped and broke his leg while unloading a wagon-load of stones.

Railway staff were not the only ones at risk at stations, for in mid-August 1868, a plumber working at Culdees Castle was looking for a parcel of tools at Crieff station when he unwisely attempted to pass between two coal trucks while they were being shunted, and his right arm was crushed between two buffers. The *Strathearn Herald* reported that *'Before assistance could be got the poor fellow had lost a good quantity of blood'*.

The newspapers of the day were not squeamish in describing such injuries in lurid detail, and when a number of years later, in a mysterious incident in November 1875, a body was found on the line east of Crieff Junction it was reported that *'The head was terribly smashed and the brains scattered about the line'*. A Return ticket from Crieff to Tullibardine was found in the pocket, and the unfortunate victim was later identified as Andrew Salmond, a tenter, of Auchterarder. How he came to be on the main line when his ticket was to Tullibardine remains a mystery.

Thankfully, injuries to passengers were relatively rare, but one incident in January 1870 was in the nature of a tragic comedy. When the 9.30am mixed train from Crieff Junction arrived at Tullibardine, the carriages were left standing on the bridge just south of the station while the engine shunted some wagons in the siding further up the line. Then, as the *Strathearn Herald* reported:

'An old woman from Blackford, thinking the train had reached the platform, stepped out of the carriage, and fell headlong over the bridge. Officials and a few passengers immediately ran to her aid, but she was not so seriously injured as might have been expected.'

It is doubtful if the unfortunate lady who had just fallen over 20 feet into the road would have agreed with this sanguine assessment, but she was indeed lucky not to be killed.

Animals sadly also came to grief on the railway from time to time. In June 1862, some cattle on Barns Farm just south of Crieff Junction got out of the field in which they were grazing through a gate onto the Crieff Junction branch which had been left open. They wandered onto the Scottish Central Railway main line where they were run down by a heavy goods train, although fortunately only one cow was killed.

More tragic was an incident seven years later in 1869, when the 4.10pm mixed train from Crieff was approaching Muthill. One wagon contained nine fat swine and three calves destined for the Edinburgh markets. Unfortunately a spark from the engine ignited the litter or straw in the wagon. The draught from the speed of the train caused a fierce fire and, as the report stated, *'Before it was spotted the swine were literally roasted and one calf so badly injured that it had to be destroyed'.*

With numerous horses employed on all manner of tasks in rural Strathearn, it is not surprising that there were a number of accidents involving such animals – quite apart from the common practice in those days of using horses for shunting, as reflected in the incident at Highlandman recounted later.

An accident of a quite different and almost comical nature occurred in July 1880, when a horse and dog cart was coming down Pittenzie Street in Crieff and the driver lost control. The horse dashed down Duchlage Road and, in true Grand National style, jumped the level crossing gate at the bottom, leaving the wheels of the cart behind. It then dragged the remainder of the cart along the railway line until it disintegrated, and kept on going. It was eventually found three miles away between Innerpeffray and Abercairny.

As with cattle, horses straying on the line rarely ended on a happy note, and only a year later, an evening train from Edinburgh was approaching Muthill when it struck and killed two horses on the track. Several carriages were derailed, and traffic was delayed for an hour until the mess had been cleared up.

In 1887 there was another sad incident when a horse on a cart being used to deliver potatoes at Tullibardine was frightened by the engine engaged in shunting. The horse backed over the loading bank and was run over and killed while the cart-load of potatoes was completely demolished.

None of these accidents in the early years were due to signalling failures, or the failure of staff to follow the Rule Book, but one incident just before Christmas 1872 illustrated how things could go wrong when procedures were not followed. Fortunately the only casualty was probably the driver's reputation in an event which would not have been out of place in an Ealing comedy. As a result of a derailment in Moncrieffe Tunnel just south of Perth, the main line between Stirling and Perth was blocked. A decision was taken that the 4.05pm Crieff to Crieff Junction train should continue through to Stirling, there being no southbound main line connection. Off went the train to Stirling, but unfortunately so did the train staff for the Crieff to Crieff Junction section! The passengers for the next train were delayed for two hours as recounted in the paper:

'The cause of this was the want of the Train Staff which had been carried off by the 4.5pm train from Crieff to Crieff Junction, and did not return until 7.45pm. so that it was impossible for the Station Master to dispatch the Limited Mail until it was returned.'

The stationmaster, of course, was absolutely right in refusing to let the train go until the driver was in possession of the train staff. All the lines to Crieff were operated under the 'train staff and ticket' regulations in those days, and this continued to be the case until the introduction of the Tyer's electric train tablet system in 1892. The sections listed in the 1889 Appendix to the Working Time Tables No. 29 were:

Crieff–Crieff Junction	Train staff & tickets (Red)
Almond Valley Jct–Methven Jct	Train staff & tickets (Red)
Methven Junction–Crieff	Train staff & tickets (Blue)
Methven Junction–Methven	Train staff only (Red)

In November 1873, the Caledonian Railway announced that it was to introduce interlocking of signals with points on the section from Crieff Junction to Perth and between Perth and Dundee. This would have resulted in an upgrade of the signalling at Crieff Junction, but not, as yet, the other stations on the branch lines. The following year improvements were carried out north of Perth, for a Board of Trade report in 1875 noted that the signalling at Almond Valley Junction was renewed in June 1874, but again the Crieff branch line was unaffected.

In the early 1890s, in order to meet new Board of Trade requirements, the Caledonian Railway embarked on the wide-scale introduction of the Tyers electric train tablet system which had been trialled on the Callander & Oban Railway some years earlier. In September 1891 it was noted that an additional telegraph wire had been laid between Crieff Junction and Crieff in preparation for the introduction of this new system, and by the end of April 1892 the tablet system was in use on both the Crieff Junction and Perth to Crieff lines.

A pair of these tablet instruments was provided for each section of line, one in the signal box at each end, and were electrically connected. They operated in such a way that only one tablet could be withdrawn from one pair of instruments at any one time. Both instruments were then electrically locked until the tablet was inserted in one of the instruments and both instruments restored to normal. The tablet was handed to the driver and was his authority to proceed along that particular section of line. Provided this system was operated correctly, it ensured that only one train could be in one section at any one time.

At the same time, the Caledonian Railway took the opportunity to carry out a major programme of resignalling of the Strathearn lines,

Figure 9.4
Prior to the introduction of the Tyers electric train tablet system in 1892, the branch lines of Strathearn were controlled by the train staff & ticket system. The Caledonian Railway used small card tickets similar to the one shown here. Tickets were kept in a locked box which could only be opened by a key attached to, or part of, the train staff. When a ticket was issued it was filled in as shown here and handed to the driver as his authority to proceed. He had also to be shown the train staff at the same time to prove that the ticket was valid. Tickets were printed with the name of the section concerned and were of different colours, usually the same colour as the train staff. This particular ticket was used on New Year's Eve 1872. *Author's collection*

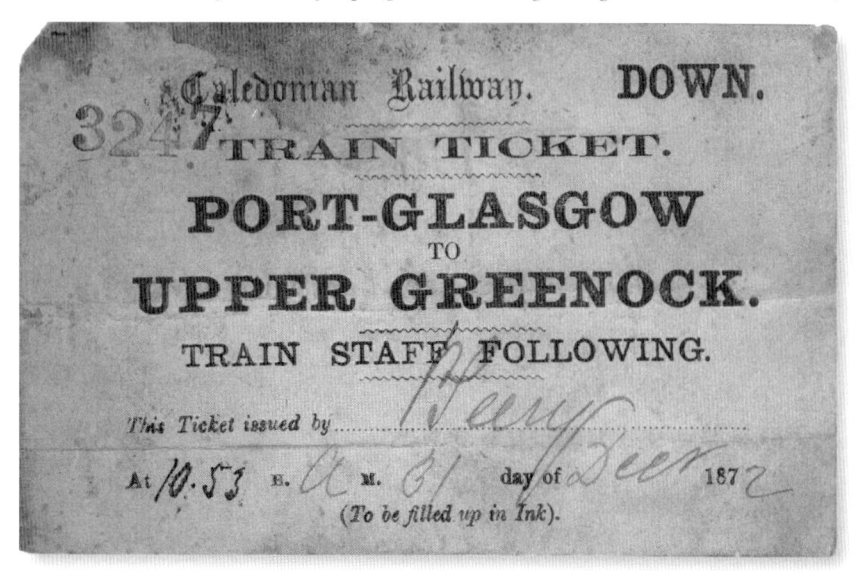

CHAPTER 9: SAFETY AND SIGNALLING

and most of the original signal boxes which survived until closure of the lines dated from that period. On the Crieff Junction line, new boxes were opened as follows:

- Crieff Junction   8th November 1892
- Tullibardine   22nd April 1892
- Muthill   22nd April 1892
- Highlandman   22nd April 1892

Crieff Junction signal box was a tall brick structure sited in the 'Y' of the junction, and had a 50-lever frame. The only surviving image showing the signal box is the well-known postcard of the station reproduced in Chapter 1. This box was renamed Gleneagles on 1st April 1912 and was replaced by the new Gleneagles signal box, as part of the complete rebuild of the station, on 28th March 1920.

The first signalling installation on the branch line was originally Auchterarder Road level crossing. This was simply a 2-lever ground frame controlling Up and Down Distant signals, as shown in the diagram (Figure 9.9), but was not a block post. This was also abolished in 1920 as part of the remodelling of the track layout at Gleneagles, when the level crossing was replaced by a bridge over the Stirling to Perth road, later the A9 trunk road.

The first station on the line, Tullibardine, was originally a block post, although, in common with a number of smaller stations, there was no actual signal box. The signalling instruments were housed in the booking office while the lever frame was on the platform in a small wooden building at the north end of the station. Tullibardine ceased to be a block post on 11th May 1921 from which date the tablet section became Gleneagles–Muthill. The lever frame was replaced by a ground frame controlled by the section tablet from the same date.

Muthill signal box was another brick building to a standard Caledonian Railway design dating from the 1892 resignalling. In addition to the improvements carried out to the station as already described in Chapter 3, the signalling layout was completely upgraded. The signal box, with a 20-lever frame also controlled the level crossing gates, which had previously been hand worked, and wicket gates. The provision of a passing loop and the introduction of tablet working was seen as a great improvement, as late-running trains, for example, could pass, rather than having to wait at Crieff or Crieff Junction for the train staff, as apparently frequently happened in the summer season. This signal box survived until the closure of the line in 1964, not closing until 2nd November that year, although the Gleneagles to Muthill section had been taken out of

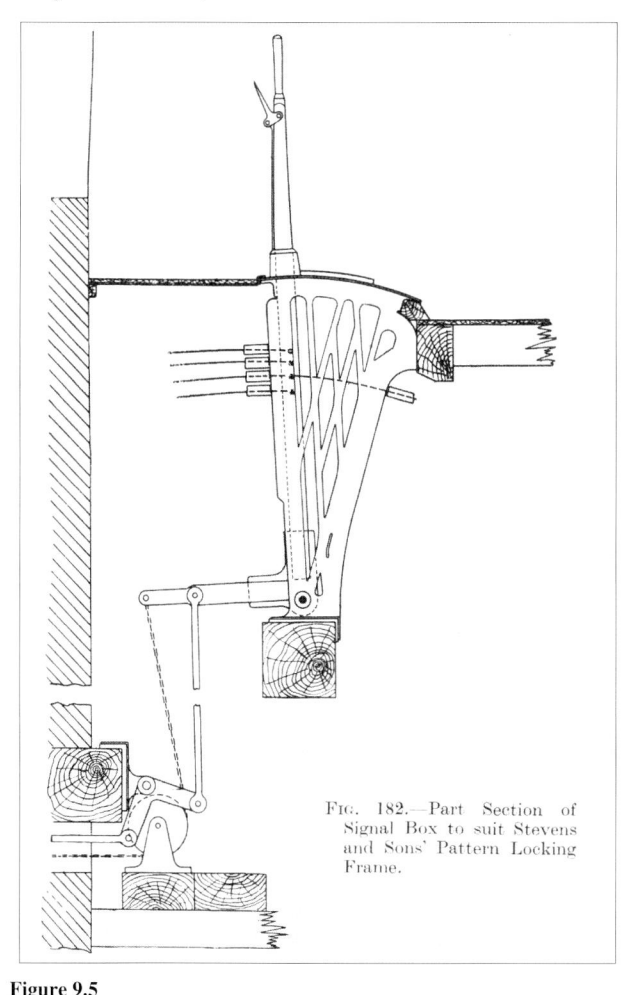

Figure 9.5
A cross section of a Stevens lever frame. These frames were adopted as standard by the Caledonian Railway, who later manufactured their own lever frames to this design after the patent expired. The very long levers, over 9 feet from the bearer to the top, made them comparatively easy to pull, with only about a third of the lever being above floor level. The locking employed a simple direct tappet system as shown in the diagram, which also shows how the levers could be used to operate either wires to signals, or rods to points and locking bars.
Author's collection

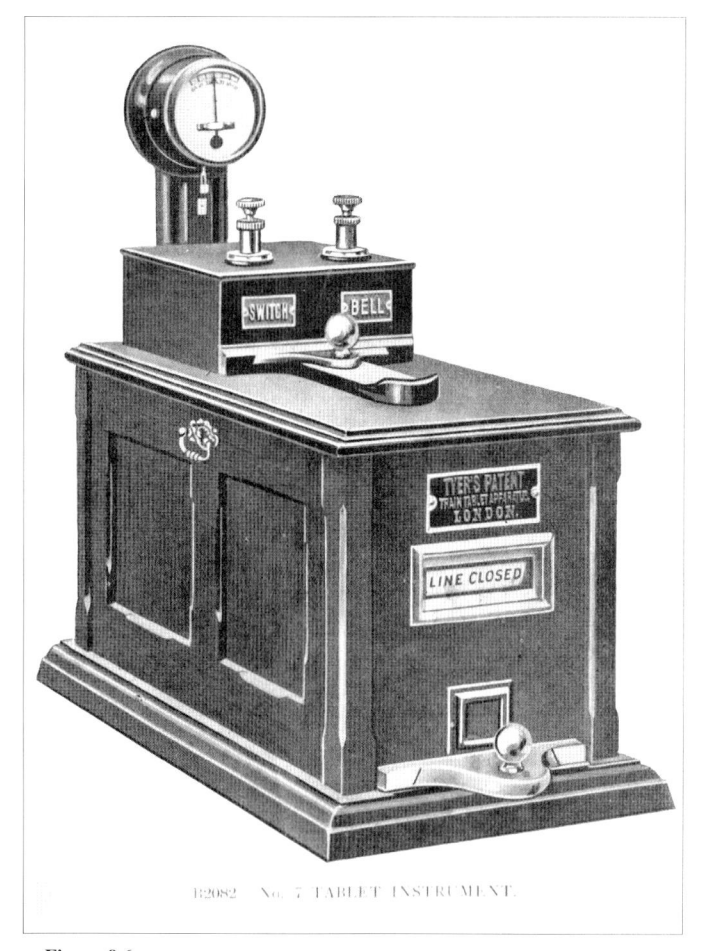

Figure 9.6
Tyers No. 7 train tablet instrument as used on the branch lines of Strathearn. The Switch plunger was used to operate the instrument, while the Bell plunger was used to send bell signals. Tablets were withdrawn from the slide at the bottom of the instrument when it was released, and were replaced in the slide just below the plungers. The aperture reading 'LINE CLOSED' indicated the state of the instrument, while the galvanometer at the top indicated the direction and strength of the current. They were complex and heavy instruments, but very reliable – which was crucial in their role as part of the safe working of the railway.
Author's collection

CRIEFF JUNCTION

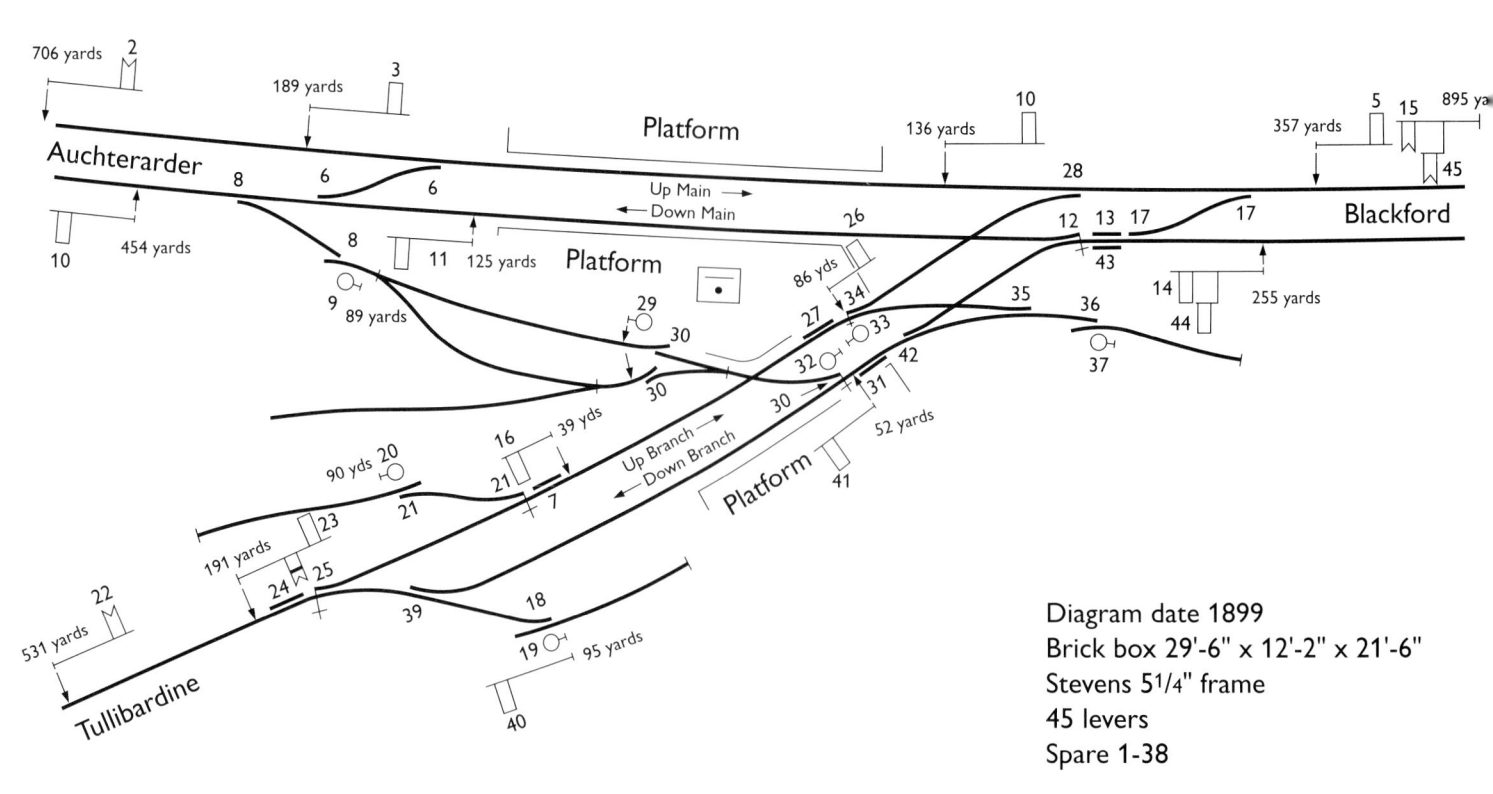

Diagram date 1899
Brick box 29'-6" x 12'-2" x 21'-6"
Stevens 5¼" frame
45 levers
Spare 1-38

Above: Figure 9.7
The signalling at Crieff Junction in 1899 showing the rather complex track layout which had evolved over the years. It is hardly surprising that the Caledonian Railway found it necessary to completely remodel the layout when Gleneagles was planned.

Plate 9.1
The impressive signal gantry at the east end of Gleneagles station mounting the signals for the branch line platform and goods loops. Unlike the upper quadrant main line signal in the background, the signals in the goods yard were never converted from their original Caledonian Railway lower quadrant style as shown here. Note that although the weight distribution of this gantry was well placed, it still required an additional signal post with bracing struts to strengthen the structure. *Author*

GLENEAGLES

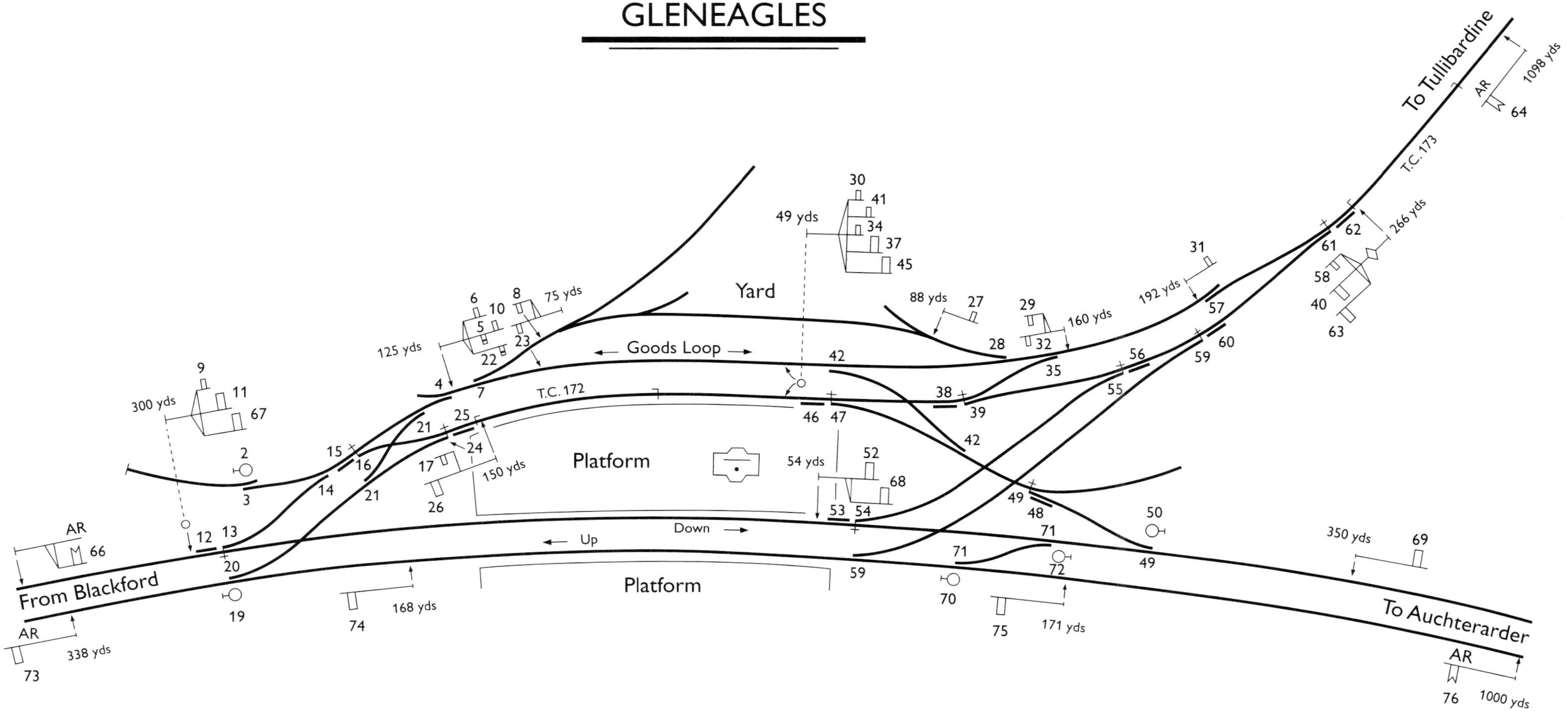

Diagram date - 1920
Opened - 28/3/1920
Closed - 14/8/1966
Brick box 44'-0" x 12'-0" x 7'-0"
Stevens N.P. 51/4" frame
76 levers
Spaces - 46-47-48
Spare - 1-18-33-36-43-44-51-65

Figure 9.8
Gleneagles was the largest box on the Strathearn lines with a 76-lever frame. The track layout included a double junction at each end of the station to and from the branch line. The gap between levers 35 and 37 was to allow the signalman to cross from one side of the box to the other without the need to walk round the frame. The short siding above ground signal No. 50 led to the tip or 'coup' where there were several sidings.

use on 1st September. No signalling was provided at Strageath level crossing which simply had hand worked gates.

Highlandman had another small brick signal box similar to that at Muthill, situated at the north end of the station, which again controlled the level crossing gates and wicket gates. The points controlling access to the southern end of the goods loop were beyond the limit which could be worked from the signal box, so were controlled by a ground frame released by a key which was held in the signal box. The tablet section to Crieff was a relatively short one, and Highlandman was reduced to gate box status in 3rd October 1948 as an economy measure, the tablet section becoming Muthill–Crieff. Just three years later, on 11th July 1951, the signal box was abolished altogether and demolished, to be replaced by a ground frame on the west side of the line near the level crossing, the gates of which then became hand worked.

As mentioned earlier, the line was originally worked by train staff & ticket system for the whole line from Crieff Junction to Crieff. This was replaced by the Tyer's electric tablet system in 1892. Originally Tyer's No. 3 instruments, and latterly Tyer's No. 7 instruments, were installed. The original sections were:

– Crieff Junction–Tullibardine
– Tullibardine–Muthill
– Muthill–Highlandman
– Highlandman–Crieff East

These four sections were later reduced to two when Tullibardine and later Highlandman, were deleted. Originally, and as listed in the 1889 Appendix, the signalling instruments on the line were maintained by a telegraph lineman, Mr Jones, who was based in Stirling, while Mr W Mitchell looked after the instruments on the Perth to Crieff and Methven lines. By 1915, all the Strathearn lines were maintained by two telegraph linemen based in Perth. William Ramsay, who covered the main line from Perth to Dunblane, looked after the Gleneagles to Balquhidder line, while James Nolan, who covered the Perth to Kirriemuir section, looked after the Almond Valley Junction to Crieff line. Eventually this arrangement was tidied up and the 1921 Appendix showed a single telegraph lineman, Peter Whyte, based at Crieff, covering all the branch lines between Gleneagles, Almond Valley Junction and Balquhidder.

The lever frames and all mechanical signalling was the responsibility of the Signal Department, whose Inspector, Mr McPherson, covered all the lines from Gleneagles to Aberdeen. The majority of the mechanical signalling retained its Caledonian Railway flavour right up to the date of closure. At Gleneagles, the signals on the main line were converted from lower quadrant to upper quadrant in British Railways days, but the remainder retained their Caledonian Railway vintage lower quadrant arms to the end. Muthill remained untouched, and the lower quadrant signals at Highlandman were only changed to upper quadrant some time after the signal box closed.

Plate 9.2
Gleneagles signal box from the east end. This well-proportioned box was sited at the east end of the island platform, and was glazed all round giving clear views of the main and branch lines and the goods yard. Bay windows in the centre of the north and south sides further enhanced the signalman's views. The short steps at the west end onto the island platform were convenient for the signalman handing over or receiving the single line tablet. *Author's collection*

Plate 9.3
The interior of Gleneagles signal box taken from the door at the west end, showing the standard Caledonian Railway Stevens pattern lever frame. There was a gap in the centre of the frame to allow access to the back of the box, while the block shelf was mounted behind the frame at the right-hand end. The signalman worked with his back to the main lines, as was Caledonian Railway practice in their later signal boxes. The signalman's desk is in the bay window to the right, as is the ubiquitous armchair which was a feature of most signal boxes. *Author*

RIGHT: **Plate 9.4**
One of the groups of shunting signals at Gleneagles. This one at the west end of the goods yard mounted no fewer than five signals in a compact design. These short shunting arms were used extensively at Gleneagles in preference to the ground mounted shunting signals used elsewhere. Two further examples can be seen in the background. *Author*

ABOVE: **Plate 9.5**
The Tyers No. 7 tablet instrument in Gleneagles signal box for the section Gleneagles–Muthill. Originally this instrument would have worked to Tullibardine until the latter was abolished in 1921. This instrument was mounted on a cabinet at the back right-hand corner of the signal box behind the lever frame. The goods yard is just visible behind it in this 1960s view. The telephone on the right was the 'Block' telephone to Muthill signal box, and the small device hung on the left of the instrument was a lever collar used as a reminder device when the section tablet was taken out for the morning shunting train which went up the branch line to the hotel. *Author*

RIGHT: **Plate 9.6**
The pointsman's hut at the junction for the branch line up to Gleneagles Hotel. This structure was installed in 1914 when the line was opened for construction traffic, but by the 1960s had fallen into disrepair as can be seen here. The lead roof was similar to those on the early Caledonian railway signal boxes. The point rodding in the foreground led from the 2-lever ground frame, which was released by the Gleneagles–Muthill section tablet, to the trailing points leading from the branch line proper to the hotel branch line. *Author*

AUCHTERARDER ROAD L.C.

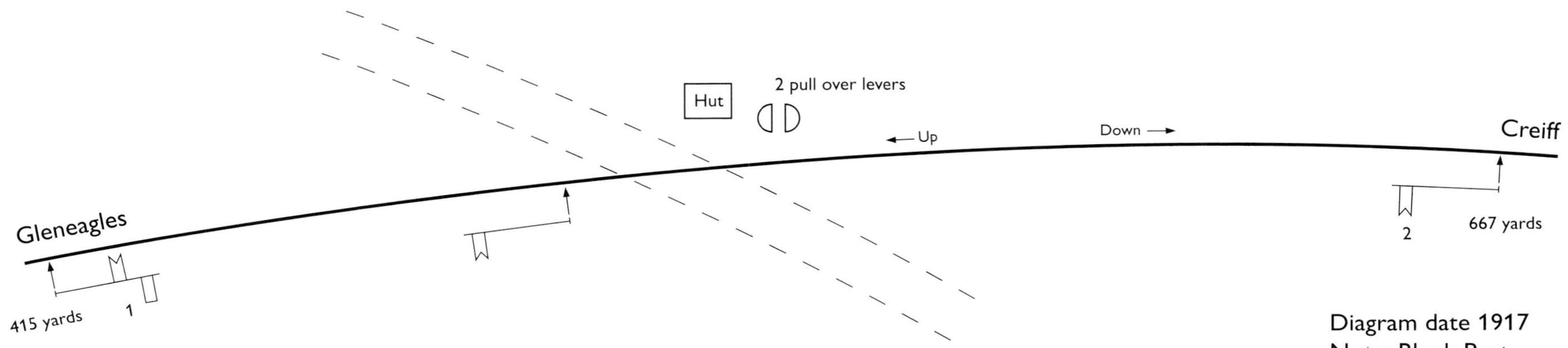

Figure 9.9
This diagram shows the signalling at the Auchterarder Road level crossing, shortly before it was abolished in 1919 when the level crossing was replaced by a bridge. The Down Distant signal on the far left was on the same post as the Gleneagles Up Home signal, while the un-numbered signal near the crossing was the Gleneagles Up Distant signal.

Diagram date 1917
Not a Block Post
2 levers

TULLIBARDINE

Figure 9.10
The 1892 resignalling resulted in Tullibardine being equipped with a 7-lever frame, mounted, as can be seen, on the platform. In 1921 when Tullibardine ceased to be a block post this was replaced by a 2-lever ground frame.

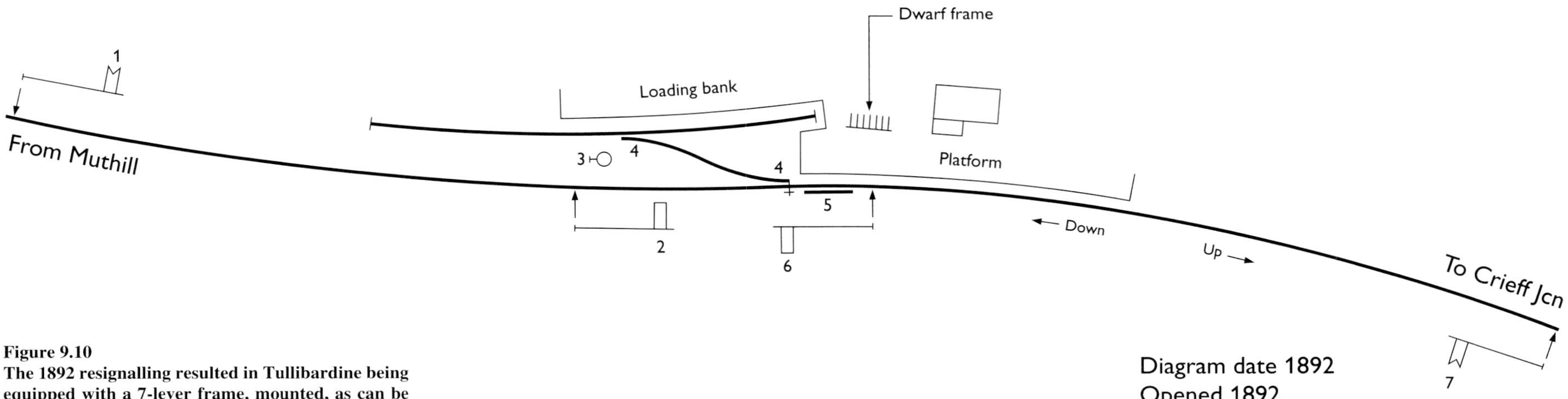

Diagram date 1892
Opened 1892
Closed 11/5/1921
7 levers

MUTHILL

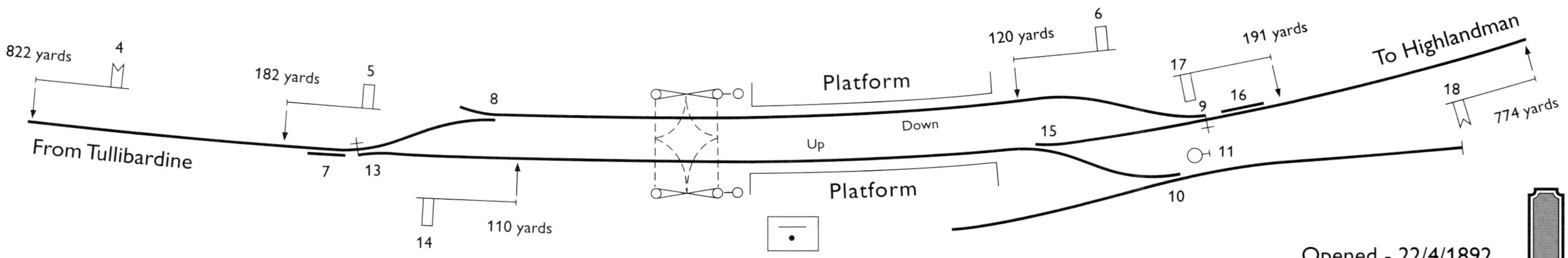

To Highlandman — 774 yards

Opened - 22/4/1892
Closed - 2/11/1964
Diagram date - 1892
20 levers
Spaces - 19-20
Spare - 12

Wickets - 1
Gate locks - 2
Gate lock - 3

From Tullibardine

Figure 9.11
Muthill signalling diagram showing the signalling provided following the remodelling in 1892, which included extending the Down loop well south of the level crossing. This signal box had a 20-lever frame although only 18 levers were fitted.

LEFT: Plate 9.7
A good close up view of the Down Starting signal at Muthill. As mentioned in the main text, Muthill retained its original Caledonian Railway signals until closure in 1964. This is a good example of a standard Caledonian Railway Stevens pattern signal of lattice steel construction with a cast iron ball finial at the top. The counterbalance was mounted well up the post to provide the required clearance, as this signal was originally at the north end of the Down platform which was subsequently shortened.

Author's collection

Plate 9.8
A view of the neat little brick-built signal box at Muthill. The design of the arched windows in the locking room beneath the operating floor is clearly visible here, as are the steps at the side of the box. What is missing is the signal box sign which was already in the boot of the photographer's car! This had been purchased from British Railways and, although it was painted in the light blue colours of the Scottish Region, careful removal of this paint revealed that it was the original Caledonian Railway dark blue enamel sign installed in 1892. *Author*

HIGHLANDMAN

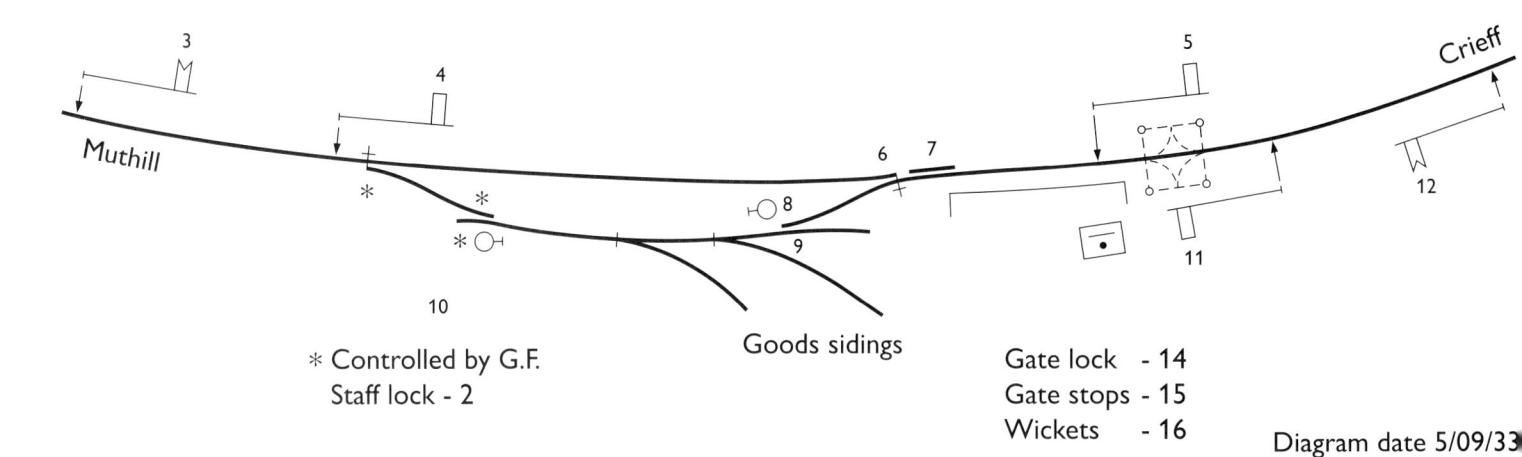

* Controlled by G.F.
Staff lock - 2

Gate lock - 14
Gate stops - 15
Wickets - 16

Diagram date 5/09/33
Space - 1
Spare - 13

ABOVE: **Figure 9.12**
The signalling at Highlandman with its 16-lever frame, showing the separate ground frame at the southern end of the goods loop, necessary because the points were too far from the signal box to be worked directly.

Plate 9.9
The original signal box at Highlandman was almost exactly the same design as that at Muthill, with the steps nearest the level crossing and two windows in the locking room. Because of the angle and width of the road, the level crossing gates were too long to close over the railway, so overlapped as shown here. The Down Starting signal shown in this view is still the original Caledonian Railway lower quadrant design.
Lens of Sutton(CRA)

PERTH TO CRIEFF LINE

The safety record of the Perth & Crieff line followed a similar pattern to that of the Crieff Junction line. Early incidents tended to be the result of mechanical failure and other causes rather than any deficiencies in the signalling.

The Perth Almond Valley & Methven Railway unfortunately got off to a poor start, for on 14th December 1857, only six weeks after the line opened for goods traffic, a member of staff suffered a fatal accident. As the local newspaper reported:

> 'He was endeavouring to pass from one wagon to another while the train was in motion; he unfortunately slipped his footing and fell between two wagons, where the wheel of the last wagon passed over him and severely fractured his leg and arm. He was conveyed to the Infirmary without delay.'

Sadly it was reported the following week that he had died a few days later as a result of the accident. He was not the first, and nor would he be the last person to suffer as a result of rashly attempting to pass between two wagons in motion. It was doubly unfortunate for the Perth Almond Valley & Methven Railway which was due to be re-inspected by the Board of Trade Inspector only five days later, on 19th December 1857, as recounted in Chapter 2.

The next untoward incident on the Perth to Crieff line occurred on 25th June 1872 when Crieff trains were delayed at Almond Valley Junction by an accident on the main line just south of the junction. The contemporary report makes intriguing reading, stating that: 'A travelling crane with wagons loaded with parts of a locomotive which had recently exploded at Bridge of Dun were derailed through an axle breaking'.

Unfortunately no further details of the explosion at Bridge of Dun have come to light, but these were not unknown in the early days of steam locomotives.

This was followed in April 1873 by an incident on the line itself involving the Perth to Crieff train due to arrive at about 5.30pm. Again, the contemporary report is worth quoting verbatim: 'The train suddenly came to a standstill through the engine going out of order'. As a result of this, the late train to Perth could not proceed and the mail bags were sent, in true 'Wild West' style by a man on horseback, to Greenloaning station on the main line between Crieff Junction and Dunblane.

CHAPTER 9: SAFETY AND SIGNALLING

Plate 9.10
A view taken from the platform at Highlandman looking north towards Crieff in the 1960s showing the layout after the signal box was demolished in 1948. The signalling was then controlled by a ground frame to the left of the line in this view, and the lower quadrant signal arms replaced by upper quadrant arms on the original posts. The level crossing gates have also been replaced with sets of gates of different lengths which now meet and lock as shown here.
John Boyes

Four years later, in late August 1877, it was the Crieff and Perth line's turn to suffer a derailment, when the last passenger train on a Saturday left the rails at Madderty. The engine derailed and dragged two carriages with it, effectively blocking the line. This time the passengers escaped with '*a good shaking*', and damage to the permanent way was described as '*trifling*'. The passengers were on their way two hours late, a repair gang from Perth arrived on Sunday morning, and the line was opened for traffic on the Monday. The regularity with which such incidents were reported seems to indicate that while they may not have been common place, they were not out of the ordinary.

Over a decade later, in 1887, another Perth to Crieff train broke down between Almondbank and Tibbermuir Crossing, when the front axle of the locomotive failed and it became derailed. Over 100 yards of track was damaged; while repair work was under way, the engine and carriage from the Methven branch was used to work traffic between Tibbermuir and Crieff.

An unusual derailment occurred in September 1894 when some wagons on a Crieff to Perth goods train derailed as it set off. The reason for this was that the load included some exceptionally long larch trees among a consignment of timber from Comrie. Measuring 80 feet in length, they were loaded along no less than six wagons, and two of them derailed on a sharp curve leading from the siding to the main line. As well as damage done to the new signalling installation, 150 yards of track were also torn up.

Apart from mechanical failures, there were also accidents in the early years due to errors by the railway staff, one potentially quite serious. In October 1871, while assembling the 10.45am Crieff to Perth service, the train reversed into the sidings to pick up extra carriages. In ran too far and collided violently with the first extra carriage. Again the poor passengers were '*severely shaken*'; one suffered internal injuries not noticed at the time, and he lost consciousness before the train reached Perth. Fortunately he was seen by a doctor and subsequently recovered.

Level crossings, especially those user worked level crossings such as farm crossings, were always a potential hazard in those early days, and with much of the Crieff & Methven Junction line being on the flat, there were plenty of them, at least eleven in all. This was highlighted early on when, in September 1859, a local farmer left the level crossing gates open at Ruthven Road, allowing his livestock to wander onto the line.

A year later, the Perth Almond Valley & Methven Railway

complained about certain individuals improperly attempting to cross the line at Ruthven Road when a train was approaching, in other words opening the gates after the crossing keeper had closed them. The railway company eventually took legal proceedings against the farmer, Mr William McKenzie, but withdrew them following his apology and promise not to repeat the offence, which was published in the *Perthshire Advertiser*:

'Mr W.C.Henderson
Secretary to the Perth Almond Valley
& Methven Railway Company, Perth.

Sir,
On your withdrawing any prosecution against me or my servants, for having according to my order, improperly opened the gates at the crossing at Ruthven Road when the same were shut by the gatekeeper, on approach of a train; I hereby express my great regret at having given such an order, and promise that the offence will not be repeated by me or any of my servants. I also agree this order be published in the newspapers if the Directors see fit.

Yours &c
(Signed) William McKenzie'

Two years later, in January 1862, the body of a Mr Andrew Honey of Methven was found on the line at Tippermallo level crossing, and although he had been run over by a train, there was no conclusive evidence that he was on the crossing. However, six years later, in 1868, Mr James Jackson, a weaver, was driving his cows across the same level crossing when the Methven train came along and knocked him down. Despite being dragged along some distance, he was lucky to escape with bruises.

Four years later, on 29th February 1872, in a more bizarre incident, the level crossing gates at Pittenzie were demolished by a runaway wagon, during a severe storm, in the most unusual circumstances, as recorded in the *Strathearn Herald*:

'A cattle truck standing in the Methven Railway sidings was propelled on to the main line, and as it travelled east it increased in speed, and smashed to pieces the level crossing gates at Pittenzie Road. The wagon ran on with great fury past Innerpeffray station, a distance of 2 miles. It appears that some people coming along the railway to Crieff to church, had a very narrow escape of being run over by the truck at Pittachar.'

It was worrying enough that the wagon would appear to have been left without the brakes pinned down and in a siding without the scotch block in place, but the habit of the local churchgoing fraternity of using the railway as a convenient footpath reflects an even more hazardous custom of those times.

Five years later, in 1877, the replacement gates at Pittenzie suffered the same fate as their predecessors when the level crossing keeper was slow off the mark and forgot to open the gates for the first train of the day, the 6.30am Crieff to Perth service. Being a dark morning, this was not noticed by the driver until the last moment, and the train ran through the gates, '*smashing them to pieces*'. One unconfirmed report indicated that the engine was '*much damaged, and put out of action until repaired*'. It was not be the first and would not be the last such accident at a level crossing.

A further six years later, the gates at Methven Moss level crossing just west of Methven Junction were victims of a similar error. The contemporary account reflects the scene of panic well:

'The gatekeeper, or rather his wife, remembered that the way was barred only when she heard the approaching train. At imminent risk to her life she had time to get one of the gates opened, and the train coming up, bore away the remaining obstruction on its buffers.'

Pittenzie level crossing was again the scene of an accident, this time particularly tragic, in October 1895, when seven-year-old Robert Graham was killed. Robert had been standing on the Crieff Junction line watching the 5.55pm train from Crieff to Perth pass by when he was run down by the 4.5pm train from Glasgow coming in the other direction along the Crieff Junction line from Highlandman. It was pointed out that the wicket gates were not locked and that anybody could stray onto the line when the road gates were closed. There were calls for a footbridge across both lines, but this was never built, and this hazard persisted for the next seventy years.

Just two years later, in January 1897, Pittenzie level crossing was the scene of yet another accident when the 5.55pm Crieff to Perth train ran through the gates which had been left across the railway. The night gatekeeper had just arrived to take over from the day gatekeeper and neither appear to have noticed that the gates were closed. The one unfortunate casualty was Mr Taylor who was sitting in his crossing keepers house when a piece of the demolished gates crashed through the window and struck him a heavy blow in the back.

More serious than any of these level crossing mishaps were two accidents at Almond Valley Junction, both as a result of the lack of vigilance by the driver of the branch line train. The first of these was in late July 1866 when the 9.5am train from Crieff to Perth ran into the 6.50am mixed train from Forfar on the main line just south of the junction.

The main line train had left Aberdeen at 2.0am as a goods train, but had been combined to become a mixed train at Forfar. It had stopped at Almond Valley Junction where the train engine was shunted off and a pilot engine came to take the passenger portion forward to Perth. At this juncture, '*the Crieff & Methven Junction train came up and dashed right in to the other*'. Fortunately both trains were moving slowly at the time of the impact and the passengers escaped with the customary '*severe shaking and a few cuts and bruises*'. No record exists of any formal Board of Trade report on this accident, but this was not the case nine years later with a similar but potentially more serious accident at the same place.

On 4th September 1875, an excursion train from Crieff overran signals at Almond Valley Junction and twenty passengers were injured in the resultant collision. Lieutenant Colonel CS Hutchinson RE conducted the Inquiry into this accident and his report published on 30th September 1875 was unequivocal:

'An excursion train, returning from Crieff to Perth, was approaching the main line at Almond Valley Junction at about 9.30pm, the driver failed to stop at the Branch Home Signal which was at danger against him, and ran with considerable speed in to some wagons which were standing on a siding leading on to the branch, for which the sidings were open. Up to the present time 20 passengers have complained of having been injured. This collision was due to the extraordinary want of care on the part of Driver Smith in approaching Almond Valley Junction.'

In the Annual Report on accidents for the year 1875, produced by Captain Tyler RE for the Board of Trade, he further commented that the driver had also passed the Distant signal which was also at danger, at too high a speed. However, in commenting on the fact that the collision occurred 180 yards beyond the Home signal he also observed that '*there was only one break van to nine carriages, but that had the train had continuous breaks under the engine driver's control the collision might still have been prevented.*'

In his evidence, the driver stated that he saw the Distant signal

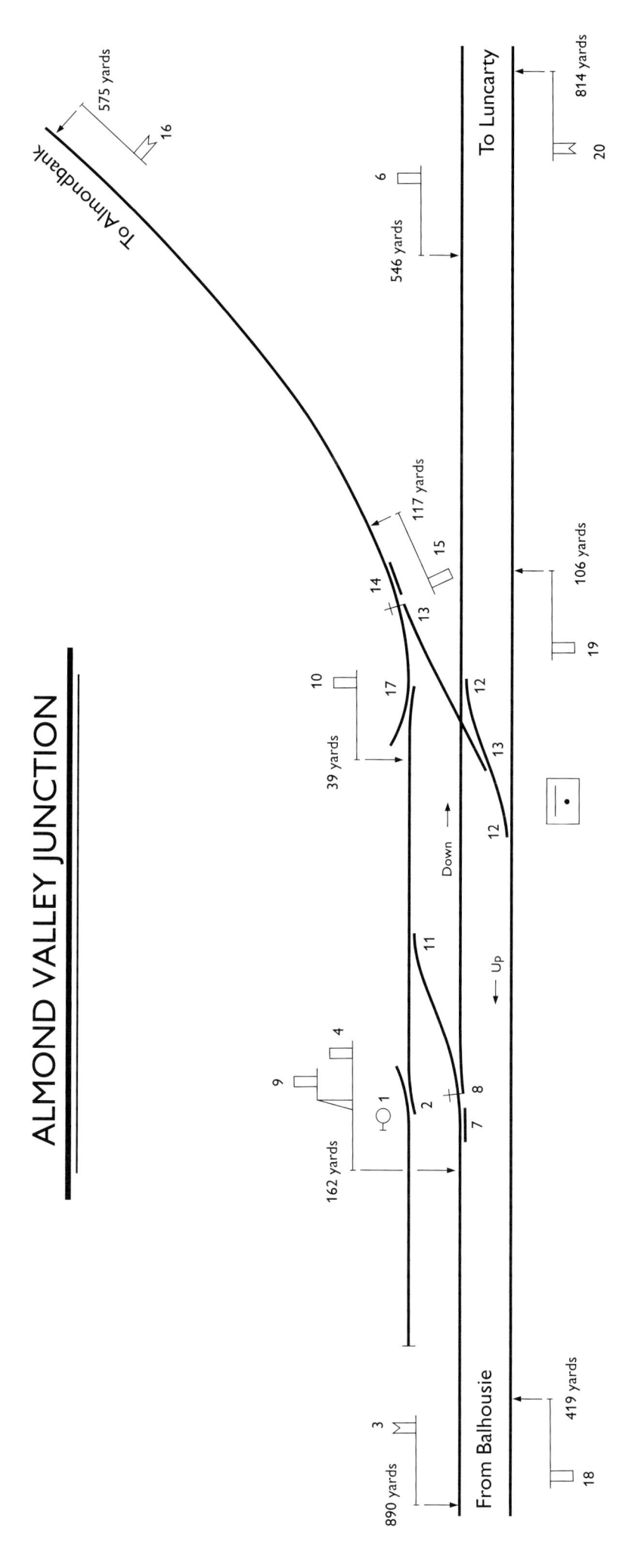

Closed - 25/2/1962
Diagram date - 1917
Brick box 16'-3" x 8'-9" x 6'-6"
Stevens 5¼" frame
20 levers
Spare - 5

Figure 9.13
The signalling layout at Almond Valley Junction showing the Crieff line coming in from the top to join the main line. The siding was the site of the accident in 1875 when the driver went past signals 16 and 15. The trap points at No. 17 were added after that date to prevent runaways entering the siding.

showing a red light and eased off the regulator, and 100 yards later though he saw the Branch Home signal showing a green light. However, the fireman having reached to get the train staff ready to hand over at the junction, looked up and said *'The Branch Home signal is at danger'*. The driver thereupon reversed his engine but seconds later it struck the wagons. Twelve of the twenty-one wagons in the siding were derailed, one fell foul of the Up main line, two were foul of the Down main line, and four were catapulted into the field beyond the buffer stops.

The signalman at Almond Valley Junction had just accepted an Up train on the main line and lowered his signals when the accident happened. However, with great presence of mind, when he saw the excursion train pass the Branch Home signal at danger he threw all his main line signals back to danger, anticipating, as was the case, that the line would be blocked with wreckage. Had he not done so, a much more serious second collision would have resulted, and he was rightly praised in the official report for his quick thinking.

Other than these accidents, there was one incident when a passenger was injured as a result of rather strange happenings. In May 1868, the forenoon train had just left Balgowan for Crieff *'when the cry was raised that a man had just fallen out. When the train reached Crieff, a doctor was speedily got and go to the spot where he found him with severe bruises across the forehead.'* When it says that a doctor was speedily got, what is perplexing is why the train went on to stop at Madderty, Abercairny and Innerpeffray, the doctor not being summoned until it arrived at Crieff some 20 minutes later!

The hazards of shunting were not confined to the early years of the Crieff & Methven Junction section, for in October 1883 there occurred one of the few fatal accidents to staff on the Perth to Crieff line. Goods guard James Stanton was engaged in shunting at Madderty when he was crushed between the train and the loading bank. He was subsequently taken to Perth where he died on arrival at Perth Infirmary. A rather more harrowing account appeared in the *Strathearn Herald* to the effect that he was not taken directly to Perth but *'was put in the Guards van and left to writhe in agony as shunting was carried out between Madderty and Perth, including a quarter of an hour at Almondbank'*, which, if true, paints a disturbing image of the lack of concern shown by the Caledonian Railway for one of its staff.

Other than the unfortunate James Stanton, there does not appear to have been the same casualty rate among the staff as befell the Crieff Junction line in the early days. The only other serious accident having been in June 1879 when a signal fitter fell 20 feet off a signal post at Abercairny. He was *'severely bruised but otherwise uninjured'* and, having been carried to the waiting room, was *'sent home by the first train to Perth, where he resides'*, which sounds very like a Victorian version of what is now called 'care in the community'.

It was not just the signal fitters who were at risk in climbing signal posts. Most oil-lit signal lamps required to be changed once a week and the old lamp brought into be serviced and refilled. This duty of lampman was not particularly popular and was often allocated to any available member of staff. In January 1896, Porter Duncan Farquharson of Crieff was performing the duty at Crieff East signal box when he fell 20 feet off a signal post and suffered a *'severe shaking'*, although his fall was broken by landing on a staging a few feet from the ground.

Both of these were lucky they did not fall off the Up Home signal at Madderty, which at 60 feet was reckoned to be the tallest signal in Perthshire. The extra height was deemed necessary for sighting purposes because of the deep cutting and three bridges just west of Madderty station. This was part of the signalling installed at the opening of the Crieff & Methven Junction Railway in 1866. At that time there were only two intermediate signal boxes at Methven Junction and Madderty.

The line was operated by train staff & tickets, the two sections being Almond Valley Junction to Methven Junction and Methven Junction to Crieff. The short branch line from Methven Junction to Methven was worked by train staff coloured red, there being no requirement for train staff & ticket working. This staff, later termed a 'one engine in steam' (OES) staff, survived until the Methven line closed in 1965.

As with the Crieff Junction line, the Almond Valley Junction to Crieff line was completely resignalled by the Caledonian Railway in 1892, and four new signal boxes were opened:

– Almondbank   22nd April 1892
– Methven Junction 21st April 1892
– Madderty   22nd April 1892
– Innerpeffray   22nd April 1892

In addition to these there were ground frames at Ruthven Road, Huntingtower Siding, Tibbermuir, Balgowan and Abercairny. Those at Pittentian and Pittenzie controlled the level crossings on both the lines approaching Crieff from the east. There was no actual signal box at Innerpeffray, rather a covered ground frame on the platform similar to that at Tullibardine. Balgowan had a similar installation, but this was replaced by a ground frame as early as 1895.

Again, as with the Crieff Junction line, Tyer's electric train tablet working was also introduced in 1892. Initially the tablet stations were:

– Almond Valley Junction
– Almondbank
– Methven Junction
– Madderty
– Innerpeffray
– Crieff East

Innerpeffray ceased to be a tablet station on 8th March 1917 as a wartime economy measure, although the platform lever frame was retained. This was dispensed with on 30th November 1949, being replaced by a ground frame released by the Crieff–Madderty tablet. Almondbank signal box was another early casualty, being closed by the LM&SR on 22nd September 1930 when it too was replaced by two ground frames (East and West). The remaining signalling on the line was largely untouched until the final years prior to closure.

Plate 9.11
A good view of the cramped interior of Almond Valley Junction signal box, showing the lever frame in the foreground, the block shelf and the signal box diagram in the background. The Tyers No. 7 tablet instrument for the section to Methven Junction is in the far corner. The block shelf has an interesting array of Caledonian Railway instruments including two **single beat bell units**, a Tyers Train Describer and a Tyers Caledonian Railway pattern block instrument. The signal repeaters including that mounted on a stand are all standard LM&SR instruments.
Courtesy SRS/Kidderminster Railway Museum

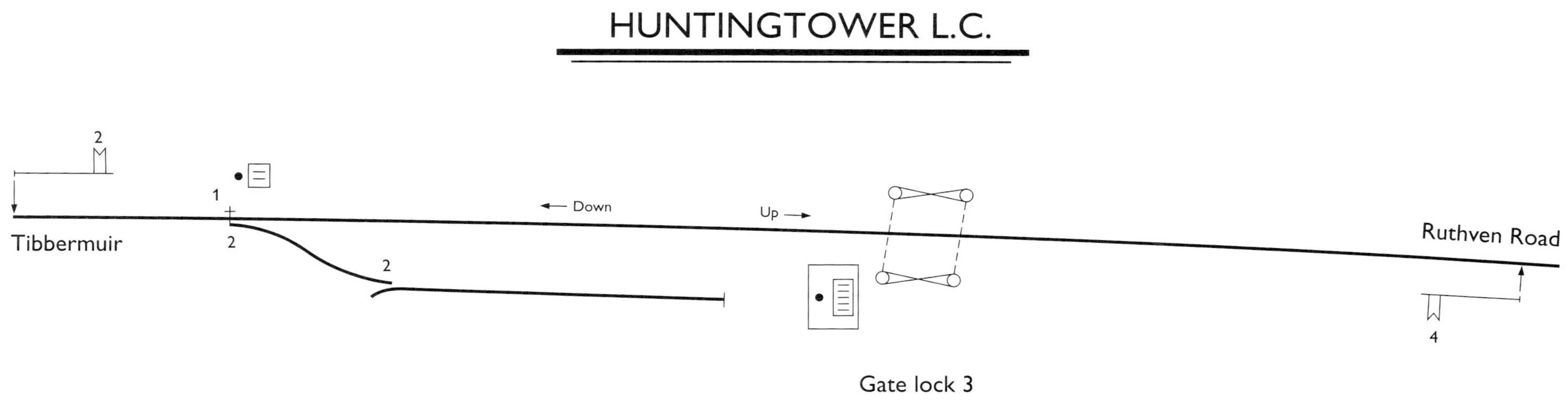

CHAPTER 9: SAFETY AND SIGNALLING

HUNTINGTOWER L.C.

Spare 1-5

Gate lock 3

Figure 9.14
Huntingtower Siding had a 5-lever ground frame next to the level crossing and a separate 2-lever ground frame at the entrance to the siding controlling the points there; this ground frame was unlocked by the section tablet or key.

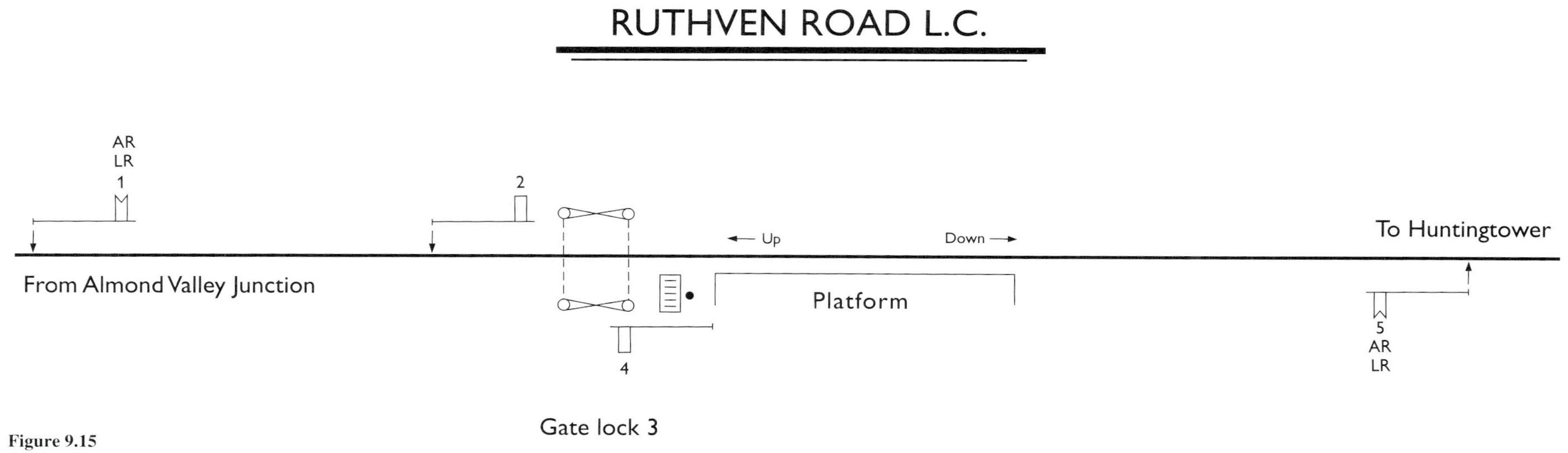

RUTHVEN ROAD L.C.

Gate lock 3

Figure 9.15
Ruthven Road was a simple layout with no sidings, so it had only one 5-lever ground frame to work the gate locks and signals protecting the level crossing.

228 BRANCH LINES OF STRATHEARN

ALMONDBANK

Plan dated 12/11/1908 for proposed siding to be worked from cabin. Not done:
Siding installed but worked from 2-lever G.F.

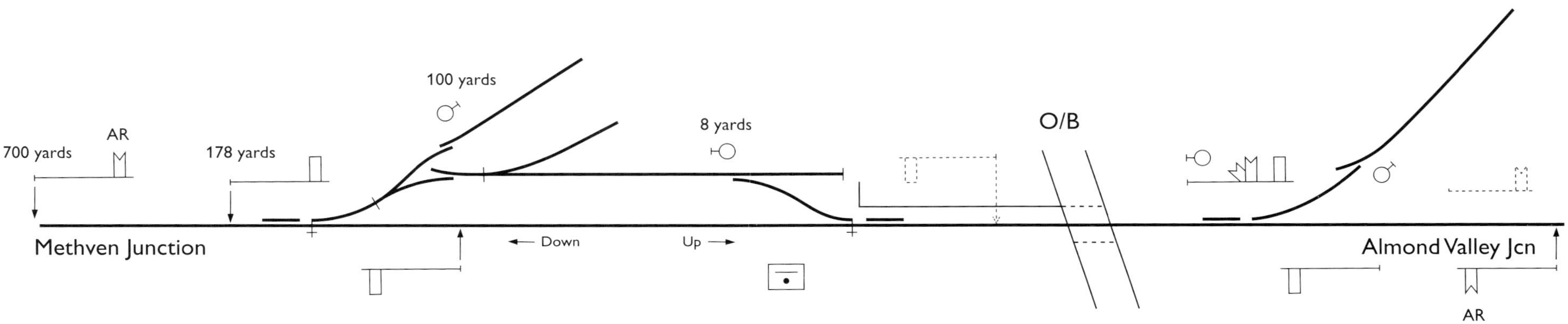

Almond Valley Jcn

Opened - 22/4/1892
12 levers
10 working, 2 spare

Methven Junction

Figure 9.16
Almondbank was a small signal box with only 12 levers, and was the only intermediate box on the old Perth Almond Valley & Methven line. Although it was a block post, it had no facility to cross trains. The siding on the right led to Lumsden & MacKenzie's bleach works sidings and latterly also the Royal Naval depot.

TIBBERMUIR L.C.

To Methven Jcn.

Spare - 3

From Almondbank

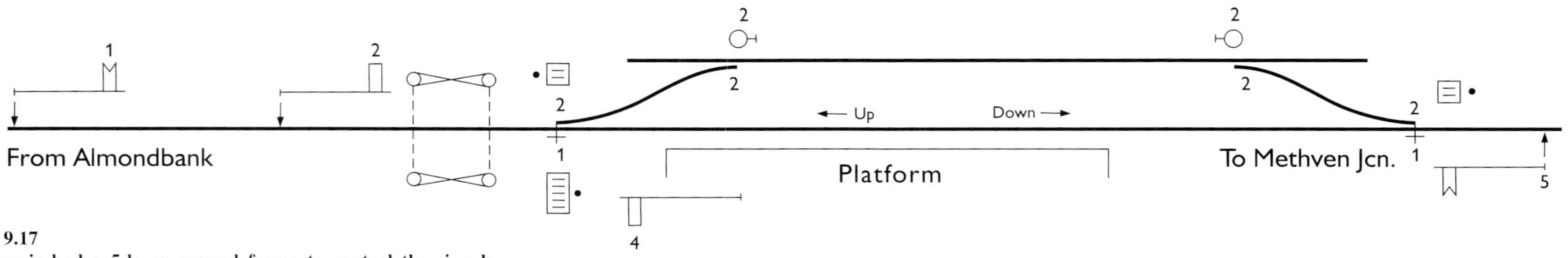

Figure 9.17
Tibbermuir had a 5-lever ground frame to control the signals protecting the level crossing, in addition to which it had two 2-lever ground frames, one at each end of the long goods loop, to operate the points there.

CHAPTER 9: SAFETY AND SIGNALLING

Plate 9.12
A view of a Down passenger train pulling away from Almondbank station in Caledonian days, with the signal box in the background. The signalman is holding the hoop for the train tablet for the Almond Valley Junction–Almondbank section which he has just received from the driver and will now restore in the instrument for that section. In this view the station name had been painted as 'ALMOND BANK', which was later corrected to 'ALMONDBANK'. Note the North British Railway advertising board and the interesting signal on the far right.
Courtesy of Perth Museum & Art Gallery, Perth & Kinross Council

BRANCH LINES OF STRATHEARN

Plate 9.13
Methven Junction signal box in later years. This box was considerably larger than others on the line, controlling, as it did, the junction to Methven, a crossing loop and several sidings. Of standard Caledonian Railway design, it had two full size windows in the locking room and had a weather porch at the head of the stairs. Note the supply of coal for the signal box fire, stored under the stairs. This box survived until well after withdrawal of passenger services in 1951, not closing until 1962, after which the points for the Methven branch were hand worked.
N Forrest/transporttreasury.co.uk

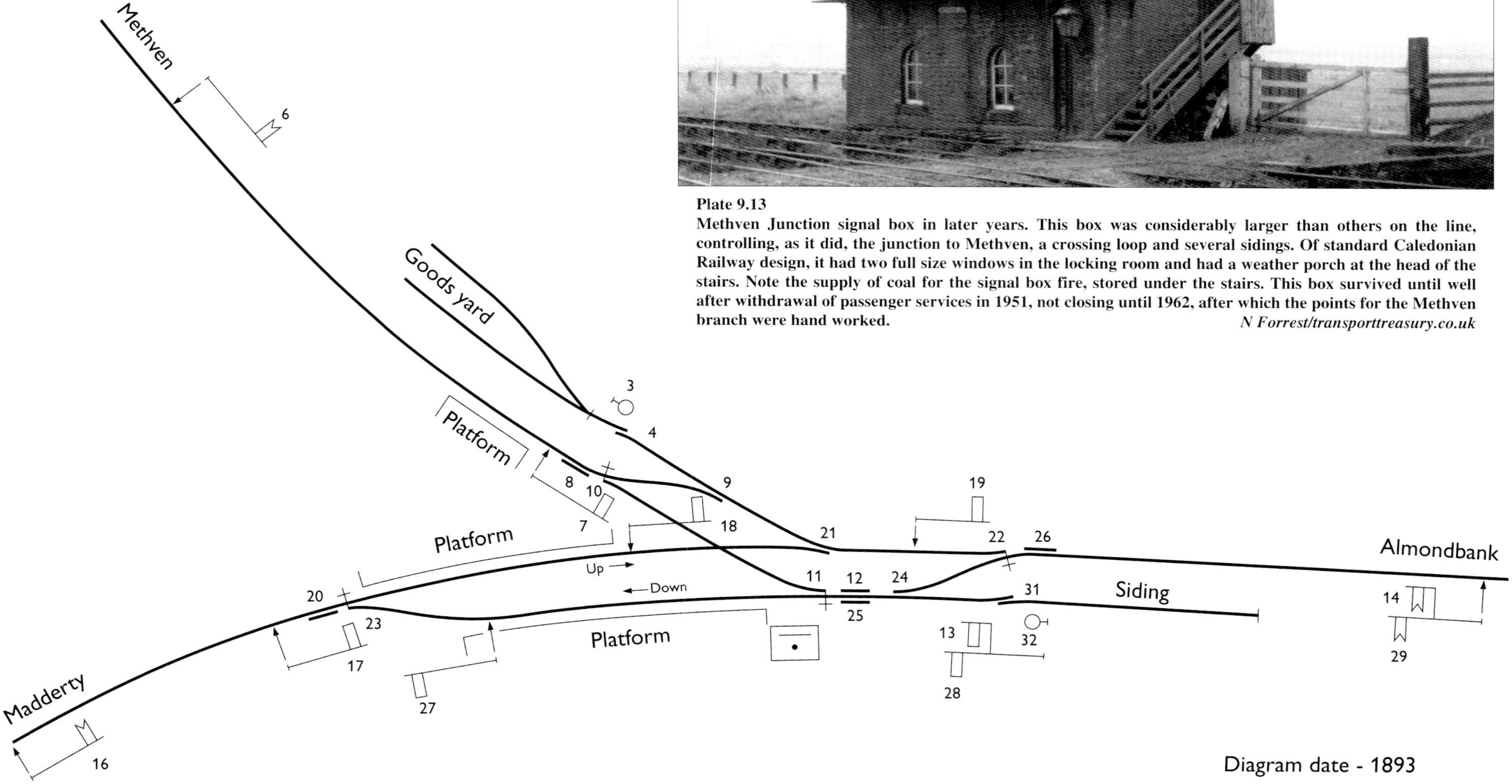

Figure 9.18
The layout at Methven Junction, which included a double junction for the Methven branch line. The goods yard at the centre was referred to as Tippermallo Sidings and served the nearby farm of that name.

Diagram date - 1893
36 levers
Spaces - 1-2-33-34-35-36
Spare - 5-15-30

CHAPTER 9: SAFETY AND SIGNALLING   231

Plate 9.14
A view of the interior of Methven Junction signal box, showing Signalman Doig standing at the lever frame, a standard Stevens pattern. This shows well the rather Spartan nature of this remote signal box, with bare wooden floor and functional furniture. The signalman's desk is in the background, while the two Tyers tablet instruments can just be seen on the right, one working to Almond Valley Junction and the other to Madderty. The signal box diagram which can just be seen on the left now resides in the author's collection. After Methven Junction signal box closed, Mr Doig transferred to Crieff and lived in the station house at Highlandman.

*Photo by Hugh Davies/
Photos of the Fifties*

Plate 9.15
A nicely posed shot of Signalman Doig at work. Standing in front of the two Tyers No. 7 tablet instruments, he is holding a tablet for the Methven Junction–Almond Valley Junction section which he has just withdrawn from the lower slide of the instrument on the left and is about to place in the pouch of the tablet hoop ready to be handed to the driver of an Up train. The instrument to the right for the Methven Junction–Madderty section is showing 'Normal' as he will have just restored the tablet handed to him by the driver in the upper slide.

Photo by Hugh Davies/Photos of the Fifties

Plate 9.16
The One Engine in Steam (OES) train staff for the Methven Junction–Methven branch line. Although shown here in the 1960s, this was a Caledonian Railway pattern 'A' configuration train staff. The wooden handle is round in cross section and was painted red. Other Caledonian train staff configurations were painted black, blue, green or yellow and had different shapes. The two nibs on the lower side of the train staff would have operated locks on ground frames or level crossing gates if there were any. The position of these nibs was different on each configuration of train staff so that only the correct one could be used on a particular section of line. As the term 'OES' implied, only one train could travel over the section from Methven Junction to Methven at any one time, but this basic system was quite adequate for the traffic on that short branch line.

Photo by Hugh Davies/Photos of the Fifties

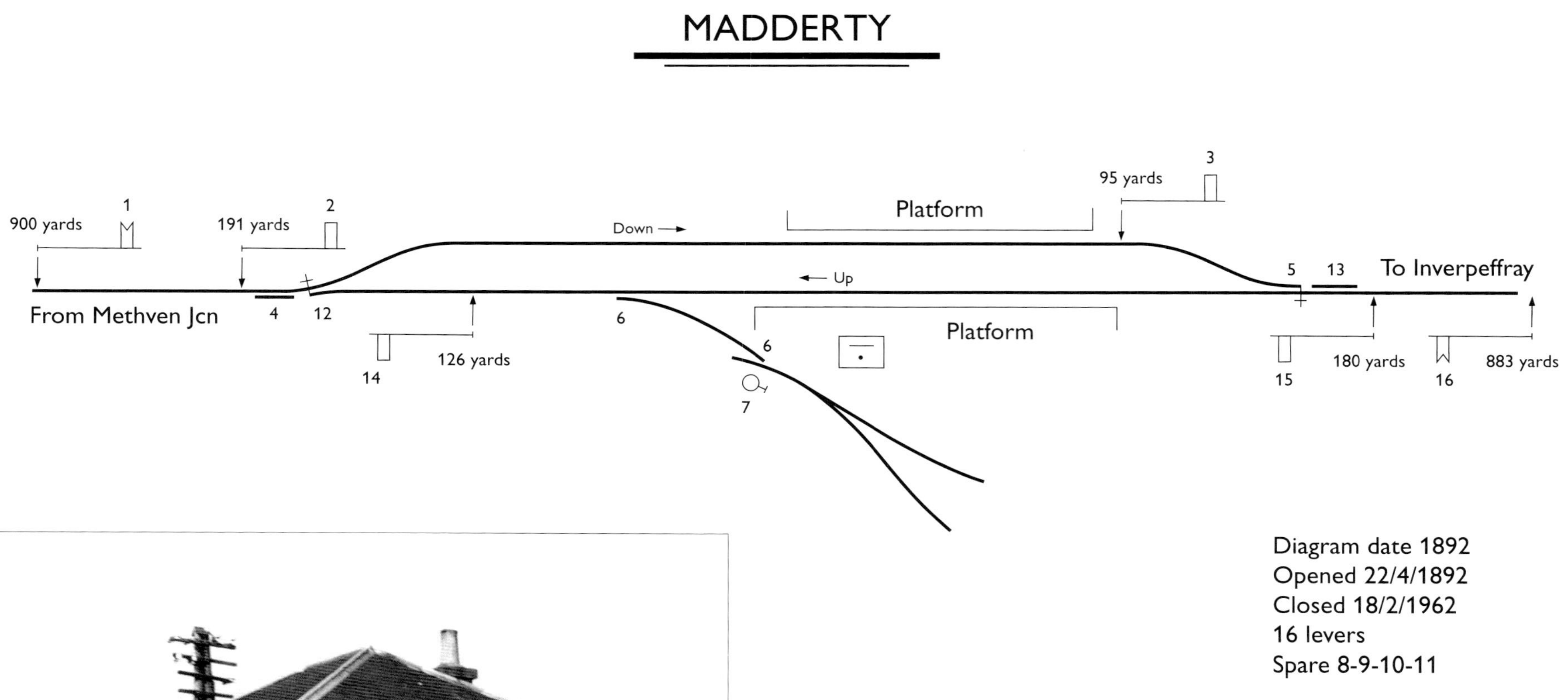

MADDERTY

Diagram date 1892
Opened 22/4/1892
Closed 18/2/1962
16 levers
Spare 8-9-10-11

ABOVE: Figure 9.19
Madderty was one of the principal crossing stations on the Crieff to Perth line and, as such, had a fully signalled passing loop. This diagram shows the signalling after the 1892 resignalling.

Plate 9.17
A view of Madderty signal box from the east in April 1963. This signal box was located at the east end of the Up platform, and was another standard Caledonian Railway design brick-built box. The box, which controlled the main passing loop on the Crieff to Perth section of line and along with Methven Junction, was retained after passenger services were withdrawn in 1951 to handle the continuing goods traffic. It finally closed in 1962, and was therefore already out of use when this photograph was taken.
Author

INNERPEFFRAY

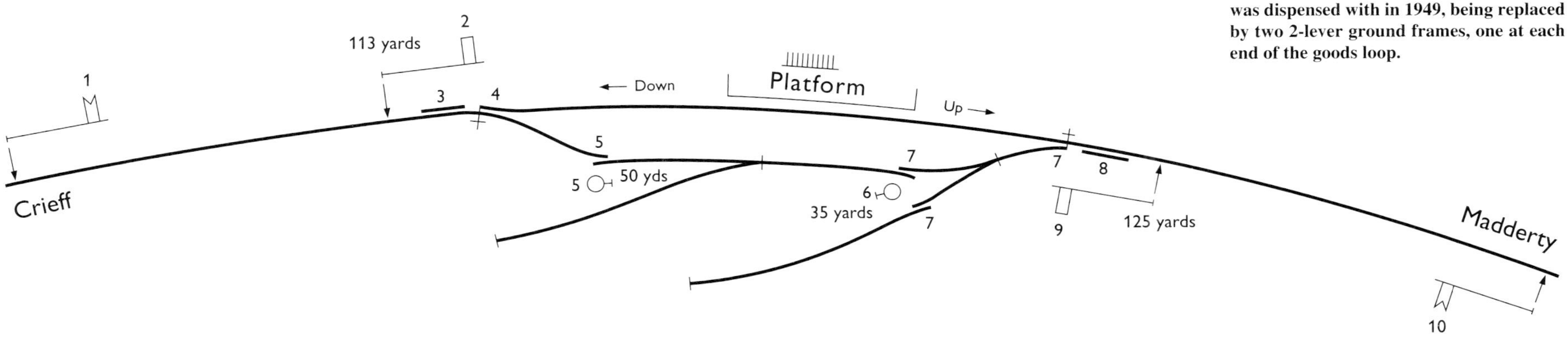

Figure 9.20
The signalling at Innerpeffray as installed in 1892. Although it was a block post until 1917, like Almondbank it had no facility to cross trains. This 10-lever ground frame was dispensed with in 1949, being replaced by two 2-lever ground frames, one at each end of the goods loop.

Diagram date - 1892
10 levers (G.F.)
Tablet post

Note: When opened No. 4 points lay for the main line and the same lever worked the siding traps. No. 5 was the disc only. This arrangement above was adopted very shortly after opening at the suggestion of the Board of Trade.

Plate 9.18
The original signalling installation at Innerpeffray, seen here in LM&SR days. Although classed as a signal box, the lever frame was in fact out in the open on the platform as seen here. The tablet instruments were housed in the booking office, a practice which was not unusual at smaller stations and was also widely used by the Highland Railway. Innerpeffray ceased to be a tablet station on 8th March 1917 and, as with Lochearnhead, was never reinstated. The platform lever frame, however, was retained until 1949 when it was replaced by two 2-lever ground frames, one of which is seen in Plate 9.21.
Lens of Sutton (CRA)

Plate 9.19
One of the 2-lever ground frames which replaced the original lever frame on the platform in 1949. This lever frame was released by the section tablet for Crieff–Madderty. The tablet was inserted in a drawer in the right-hand side of the box-like device seen in the background. When the correct tablet was inserted, the lever on the left was free to be turned. Turning it from left (LOCKED) to right (FREE) released a plunger and allowed the levers controlling the points onto the sidings to be operated.
Author

CRIEFF TO BALQUHIDDER LINE

By the time the Crieff & Comrie Railway finally opened in 1893, and the Lochearnhead, St. Fillans & Comrie Railway opened fully in 1905, railway technology and engineering had advanced considerably, and there were few if any of the accidents and incidents which characterised the earlier lines.

Both these lines were operated from the outset under the electric train tablet system, although not without incident. In early July 1893, only a month after the Crieff & Comrie Railway opened, the telegraph broke down one Monday morning. Tablet working had to be suspended, and 'Pilot Working' instituted until the fault was repaired. The Pilotman who rode on the engine was referred to by the locals as the 'Red Cap Messenger' on account of his distinctive uniform. It was subsequently discovered that at some time on the Sunday some Crieff boys had '*interfered with the wires*'.

Despite the supposedly fool-proof nature of the electric train tablet system there was one very near miss on the Crieff to Perth line at the turn of the century. In mid-August 1900, a head on collision between the 4.25pm Perth to Methven passenger train and a goods train from Crieff was narrowly averted thanks to the alertness and prompt actions of the driver of the Perth train. The train had just left Almondbank station when the driver saw the goods train coming towards him on the single line. He rapidly applied the brake and brought his train to a stand. The newspaper recorded that '*the Goods train had for some unaccountable reason been allowed to pass Methven Junction*'. Assuming that the driver of the Perth train had in his possession the tablet for the section from Almondbank to Methven Junction, one can only speculate as to how the goods train was allowed to leave Methven Junction. It is likely that some breach of the regulations was committed either by the driver of the goods train or the signalman at Methven Junction or by both, but history does not record the outcome of any investigation.

There were still the odd mishaps such as that in April 1896 when the 11.23am train from Crieff Junction hit the buffers, quite literally, at Comrie, then still a terminus station. The buffers were demolished, earth bank pushed back, and the leading wheels of the engine derailed. Fifteen passengers were injured and the guard rendered unconscious in this accident, which apparently occurred after the driver had shut off steam, but the Westinghouse brake had failed. There would have seemed to have been some issue regarding the connecting and testing of the brake system before the train left Crieff, for in addition to the driver and guard being dismissed by the Caledonian Railway, a porter from Crieff was also dismissed as a result of this accident.

It was an unhappy blemish on the career of Driver Mungo Headrick, being the only accident he had had in 35 years in which a passenger had been injured. Although it was the end of his railway career, it was not the end of his association with railways, for by November that year he had set himself up as a coal agent at Crieff.

The only other incident of note in the early years was a derailment at St. Fillans a day or so after the line opened, for a report appeared in the *Strathearn Herald* on 3rd October 1901, the line having only opened on the 1st October. The engine shunting wagons for the 2.30pm goods train to Perth derailed in the goods yard causing considerable damage to the track, which was a rather inauspicious start for St. Fillans.

Sadly, St. Fillans was the scene of a more spectacular derailment involving a livestock train conveying wintering sheep in October 1921. This even made the *Glasgow Herald* which reported that:

'A special train conveying sheep from Oban and intermediate stations to Perth was derailed at St. Fillans on Monday evening and over 300 sheep were killed. While proceeding down the incline at St. Fillans, the train became out of control owing, it was alleged, to insufficient brake power, and on entering a siding over-ran the dead end and collided with the rocky embankment. The engine toppled over on its broadside, the driver and fireman having a miraculous escape. Some 18 or 19 of the trucks were telescoped, killing a large number of sheep, while others were so badly injured that they had to be destroyed. Breakdown gangs were speedily on the scene from Motherwell and Perth, with cranes and other apparatus and the work of rescuing the stock and clearing the line occupied all night. It was not until yesterday afternoon that the permanent way was restored to traffic.'

This was a horrendous accident, but as it did not involve a passenger train and no one was killed it attracted little attention beyond the regional press.

Accidents to staff, passengers and members of the public were mercifully few on the Crieff to Balquhidder section compared with the early lines to Crieff. Unfortunately the same could not be said for the navvies, and there were a number of fatal accidents during the construction of this stretch of line. The first of these occurred in 1891 when an Irish navvy, Patrick O'Donnel, was killed while undermining the side of a cutting at the north-west side of Baird's Monument during the construction of the approaches to the tunnel there.

The following year there was an even more tragic accident at the same site when a young boy of only fourteen years of age, called McInally, was killed. McInally was employed as a 'Nipper' whose task was to operate the points for the horse-drawn ballast trains used during construction work. Unfortunately, in attempting to jump onto a wagon to get a ride he slipped and was run over, dying almost immediately of his injuries. An even sadder aspect of this accident was the fact that McInally's brother was leading the horse which was pulling the wagons.

Just five months later another navvy was killed in Burrell Street tunnel. Two navvies, the worse for drink had lain down in the shelter of the tunnel and gone to sleep. The following morning the contractor's bogie locomotive drove through the tunnel. One navvy was struck a glancing blow and knocked aside, but the other, 60-year-old Archibald Goulder, lost both his legs, and succumbed to his injuries in Perth Infirmary later that day.

Later that same year, another navvy, Peter Ross, aged 55, from Caithness, died in a freak accident during the excavation of Drummwhandie cutting near the same Burrell Street tunnel. During blasting operations a piece of stone rebounded about 40 yards and hit Ross, who died of his injuries the following day.

Seven years later, in 1899, during the construction of the line through to St. Fillans, the body of a navvy was found next to the line near Comrie. It was believed that he had lain down to sleep too close to the line and had been struck by a train, although this was probably conjecture.

As described elsewhere, the opening of the Crieff & Comrie Railway resulted in a complete remodelling of Crieff station and the creation of a new passenger station. This necessitated a completely new signalling layout and two new signal boxes. The larger of these, Crieff East, controlled the approaches from Highlandman and Innerpeffray, the goods yard, locomotive depot and the east end of the station, while the smaller Crieff West controlled only the west end of the station and the line out to Comrie. Both boxes were opened on 1st June 1893, as was Comrie. Crieff West was closed by the LM&SR as an economy measure on 3rd April 1932, from which date Crieff East was renamed plain 'Crieff'. The signalling at Comrie was altered when the line through to St. Fillans was opened and the original signal box was closed and reopened in its new configuration on 1st July 1905. Dalchonzie Platform and St. Fillans signal boxes opened with line on 1st October 1901, although Dalchonzie was never a 'block post'.

The new Lochearnhead signal box opened on 30th June 1904, and for the next ten months Lochearnhead was worked as a terminus until the line to Balquhidder opened on 1st May the following year. The signal box at Lochearnhead had a relatively short life, being closed from 7th March 1917 to 6th January 1919 as a wartime economy measure, it was abolished altogether on 13th July 1921, after an operational life of only fifteen years. The signal box was demolished and replaced by a Ground Frame, and the Up platform line was removed as Lochearnhead was no longer a tablet station where trains could pass.

Balquhidder was not only remodelled but also renamed with the opening of the branch line to Crieff. Previously called Lochearnhead, it was a small and relatively insignificant wayside station on the Callander & Oban line. All that changed in 1905, with the opening of the junction. The station was extensively remodelled and enlarged, and as at Crieff, two new signal boxes were built, Balquhidder East and Balquhidder West. This in itself was confusing as the East box was at the south end of the station and the West box was at the north end. Both were substantial brick structure of Caledonian design, the East box having 36 levers while the West box which controlled the line to Crieff, was the larger of the two with 48 levers. Balquhidder East opened on 18th December 1904 and Balquhidder West on 1st May 1905.

The line from Crieff West to Balquhidder West was operated by Tyer's train tablet instruments from the outset, the sections being:

– Crieff West–Comrie
– Comrie–St. Fillans
– St. Fillans–Lochearnhead
– Lochearnhead–Balquhidder West

The Crieff West tablet instrument was transferred to Crieff East when the former closed in 1932, and the section became Crieff–Comrie. Likewise, when Lochearnhead closed in 1921, the tablet section became Balquhidder West–St. Fillans.

One incident in the later years of the Caledonian Railway era which had the potential to have been a much more serious accident was that which occurred at Methven Junction in March 1917. Here, the 6.10pm Perth to Crieff train was due to cross with the 6.5pm train from Crieff to Perth. For some reason, probably brake failure, the Crieff train overran the signals. Driver James Baxter of the Perth train, on seeing the Crieff train coming towards him on the single line, realised the danger and immediately stopped his train and put his engine into reverse to lessen the impact. Despite this, the resultant head on collision resulted in both locomotives being derailed, and the leading carriage of each train being damaged. Fortunately no passengers or staff were injured, and new engines having been sent out, the passengers were able to resume their journey by simply changing trains to the undamaged coaches of the other train, those of the Crieff train returning to Crieff and similarly those from the Perth train heading back there.

CRIEFF EAST

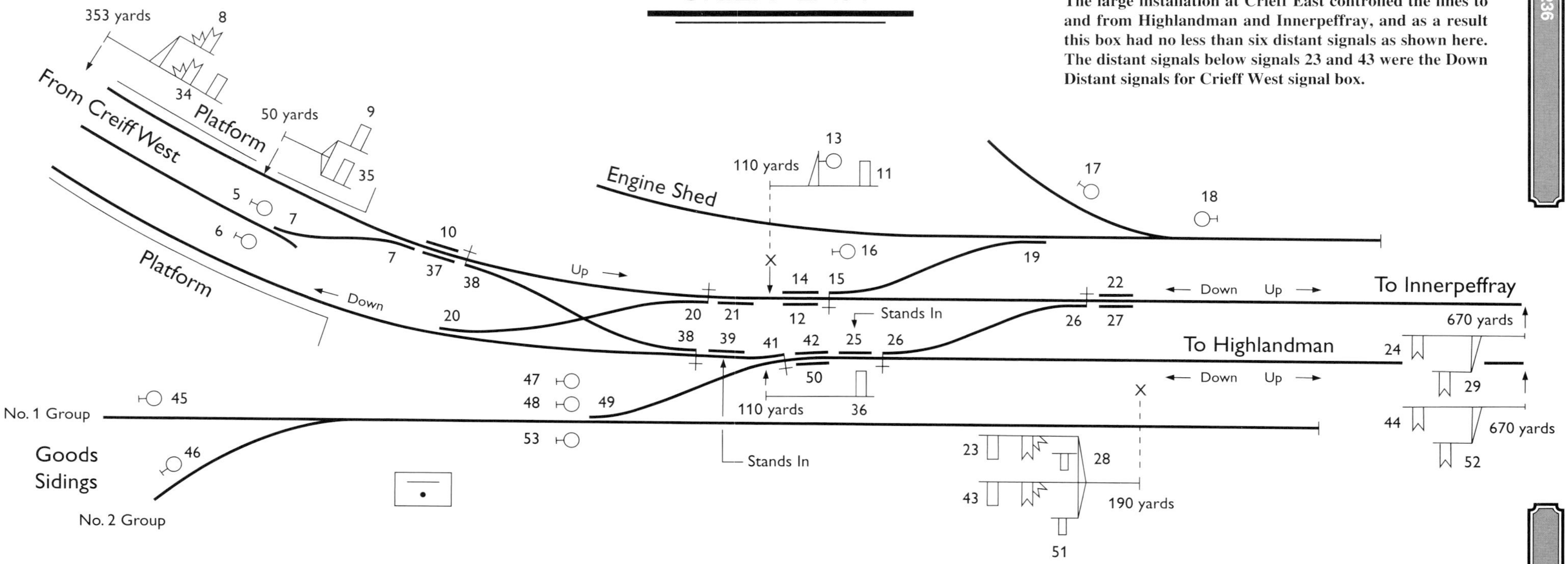

Figure 9.21
The large installation at Crieff East controlled the lines to and from Highlandman and Innerpeffray, and as a result this box had no less than six distant signals as shown here. The distant signals below signals 23 and 43 were the Down Distant signals for Crieff West signal box.

Diagram date - 1893
Opened - 1/6/1893
Closed - 7/5/1965
Stevens O.P. 5¼" frame
54 levers
Spaces - 1-2-54
Spare - 3-4-30-31-32-33-40

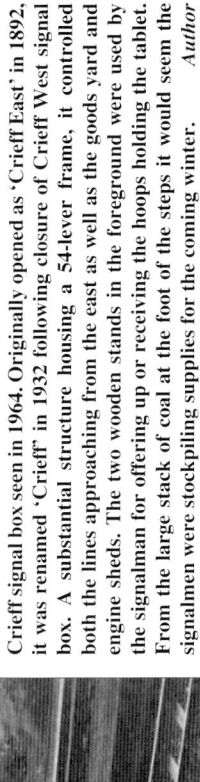

Plate 9.20
Crieff signal box seen in 1964. Originally opened as 'Crieff East' in 1892, it was renamed 'Crieff' in 1932 following closure of Crieff West signal box. A substantial structure housing a 54-lever frame, it controlled both the lines approaching from the east as well as the goods yard and engine sheds. The two wooden stands in the foreground were used by the signalman for offering up or receiving the hoops holding the tablet. From the large stack of coal at the foot of the steps it would seem the signalmen were stockpiling supplies for the coming winter. *Author*

CHAPTER 9: SAFETY AND SIGNALLING

Plate 9.21
Signalman Doig, who had by then transferred from Methven Junction signal box, relaxing between trains in this view of the interior of Crieff signal box. Again, this shows a Caledonian Railway Stevens pattern lever frame, with the characteristic ratchet wire adjusters on the front of the levers for some signals, which were favoured by the Caledonian. The short block shelf would have housed a Tyers block instrument on the left-hand end in the days when Crieff West signal box was still in existence. The remainder of the instruments are a variety of signal and light repeaters. The Tyers No. 7 tablet instrument for the Crieff–Muthill section is on the extreme right of the bench; the space next to it would have housed the instrument for the Crieff–Madderty section which had been dispensed with by the time this photograph was taken. Note the trusty arm chair which was a feature of such signal boxes. *Author*

Plate 9.22
The tablet stand for Up trains at Crieff. Sited opposite the signal box, it was used by the signalman to pick up the tablet for the Comrie–Crieff section and at the same time offer up either the tablet for the Crieff–Muthill section for Gleneagles-bound trains or the tablet for the Crieff–Madderty section for trains heading towards Almond Valley Junction. The stand allowed the signalman to be at an appropriate height to handover or receive a tablet hoop from the footplate crew. The gas lamp provided illumination at night to reduce the risk of a tablet hoop being dropped. Note the gravel crossing in the foreground which led back to the signal box which was behind the photographer. *David Stirling*

CRIEFF WEST

Figure 9.22
The short-lived signal box at Crieff West had a small 14-lever frame, although only ten levers were ever fitted. Closed in 1932, it was replaced by a 2-lever ground frame sited near points No.2 on this diagram, with the remainder of the signals being transferred to Crieff East.

Diagram date - 1893
Opened - 1/6/1893
Closed - 3/4/1932
14 levers
Spaces - 11-12-13-14
Spare - 8

Plate 9.23
A rare shot of Crieff West signal box in about 1922, showing the cramped location of the box on the Up platform. A bespoke wooden structure with a lean-to roof, it backed onto the retaining wall for the station approach road and was accessed by a short set of steps. No tablet stands were necessary here as the tablet hoops were collected at platform level when trains entered the station from Comrie, and were handed to the driver from the Down platform for trains leaving Crieff. Both the Down Starting signal on the platform and the 'Calling On' signal by the King Street bridge have the original Stevens oval spectacle plates rather than the standard Caledonian Railway pattern. Crieff West signal box closed in 1932.
CRA collection

COMRIE

Crieff West — St. Fillans

Date - 1909

Figure 9.23
The diagram of the signalling at Comrie after the line had been extended through to St Fillans with the points and head-shunt added at the west end of the station beyond the new road bridge.

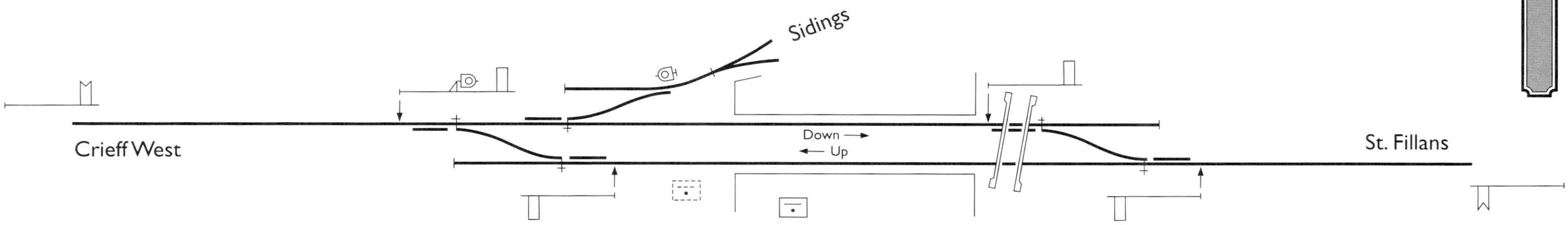

Plate 9.24
A close up view of the original signal box at Comrie. This all-wooden structure was unlike any of the other signal boxes on the line, even though it was opened in 1893 after the widespread resignalling of the other lines to Crieff by the Caledonian Railway. It would appear to have housed a large number of potted plants, some of which are just visible through the window. These were more likely to be part of the Best Kept Stations effort rather than a hobby on the part of the signalman. This box was burned down in 1950, a fate which befell more than a few wooden signal boxes, to be replaced by a very temporary looking structure as shown in Plate 9.27.
Courtesy Bernard Byrom

Plate 9.25
The replacement signal box at Comrie erected after the original was burned down in 1951. Whether it was because the future of the line to Balquhidder was very much in question at that time or simply a post-war economy measure, it was a pretty rudimentary affair which hardly merited the title of a signal box – it was more of an elevated garden shed containing a lever frame akin to some of the structures on the Callander & Oban line at Strathyre and elsewhere. It would seem the enamel sign survived the fire and has been nailed onto the new erection. This replacement signal box lasted until 1961 when all signals at Comrie were abolished and the line worked under 'OES' regulations from Crieff.   *Robert Butterfield/Robert Humm collection*

DALCHONZIE L.C.

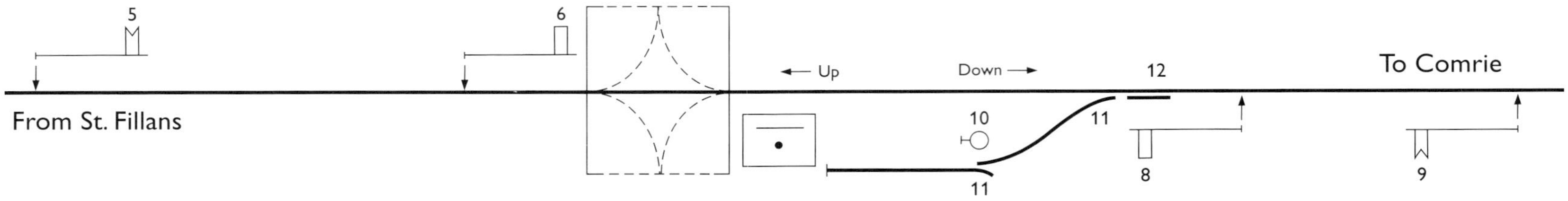

From St. Fillans → ← Up | Down → ← To Comrie

Spaces 1-14
Spares 2-7-13
Gate stops 3
Gate bolt 4
C/O/LMS/1

ABOVE: Figure 9.24
The simple signalling layout at Dalchonzie Platform, protecting the level crossing and working the single siding. The 14-lever frame was probably over generous given the layout, and the large signal box provided to house it even more so.

Plate 9.26
The signal box cum station house at Dalchonzie, photographed a few years after the line closed, clearly shows the design of this building. There were several similar structures on the Callander & Oban line at places such as Glencruitten, but none of these were stations open to the public as was the case at Dalchonzie. By the time this view was taken in 1963, the outside steps and the walkway had been removed, but other than this, the signal box was still recognisable as such. *ADK Young*

ST FILLANS

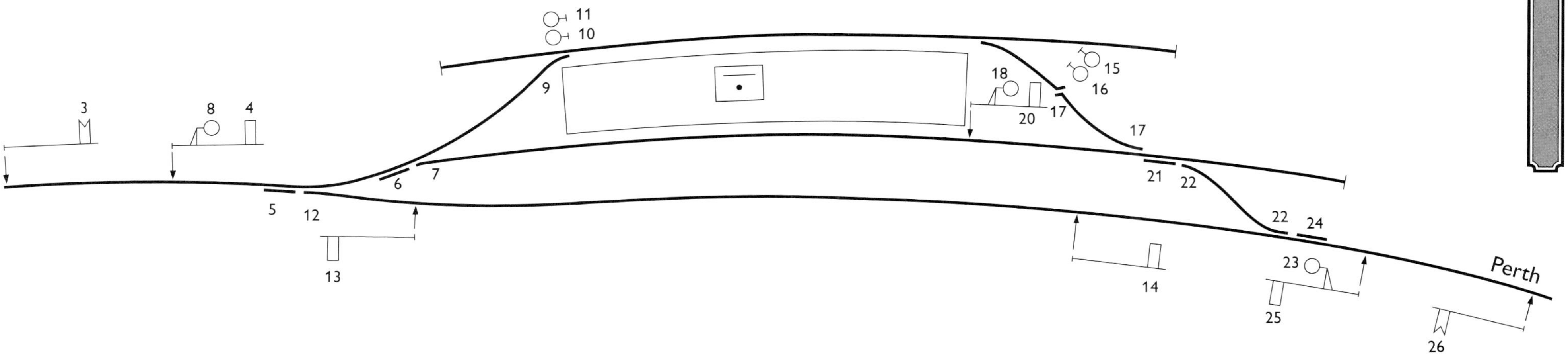

Spaces -1-2-27-28
Spare - 19
Spares (1956) 3-11-15-18-19-21-26

Above: Figure 9.25
St. Fillans was originally fitted with a 28-lever frame which included signalling for the running loop behind the Up platform. This loop was used during the period when St. Fillans was the temporary terminus of the line and in later years to handle the extensive excursion traffic.

Plate 9.27
St. Fillans signal box seen some years after the line closed, but still intact. This was an attractive brick building, whose design followed that of the Southern Division of the Caledonian Railway, which was also adopted later for new works projects on the Northern Division; characteristic of these were the thick mullions and eaves brackets. This signal box was on the Up platform which provided good views in both directions as it was sited on the outside of the gentle curve in the line through St. Fillans station. This signal box survives as part of the caravan park which now occupies the station site.
Author

BALQUHIDDER WEST

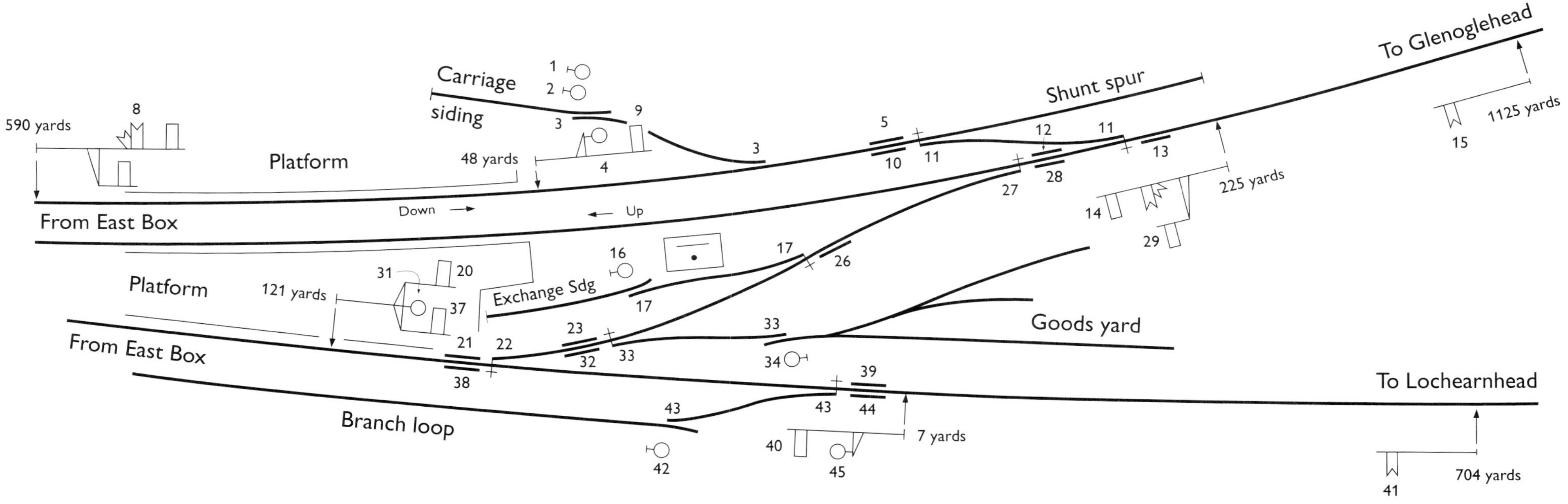

Figure 9.26
The signalling layout at Balquhidder West as installed on the opening of the line to Crieff in 1905. The Callander & Oban line towards Oban curves off to the left. The falling gradient from Glenoglehead required a long braking distance, hence the Up Distant signal is 1,125 yards from the signal box, not far short of three-quarters of a mile.

Diagram date - 1905
Opened - 1/5/1905
Closed - 21/3/1965
48 levers
Spaces - 46-47-48
Spare - 6-7-18-19-24-25-30-36

Electric lock lever to East Box - 35

BALQUHIDDER EAST

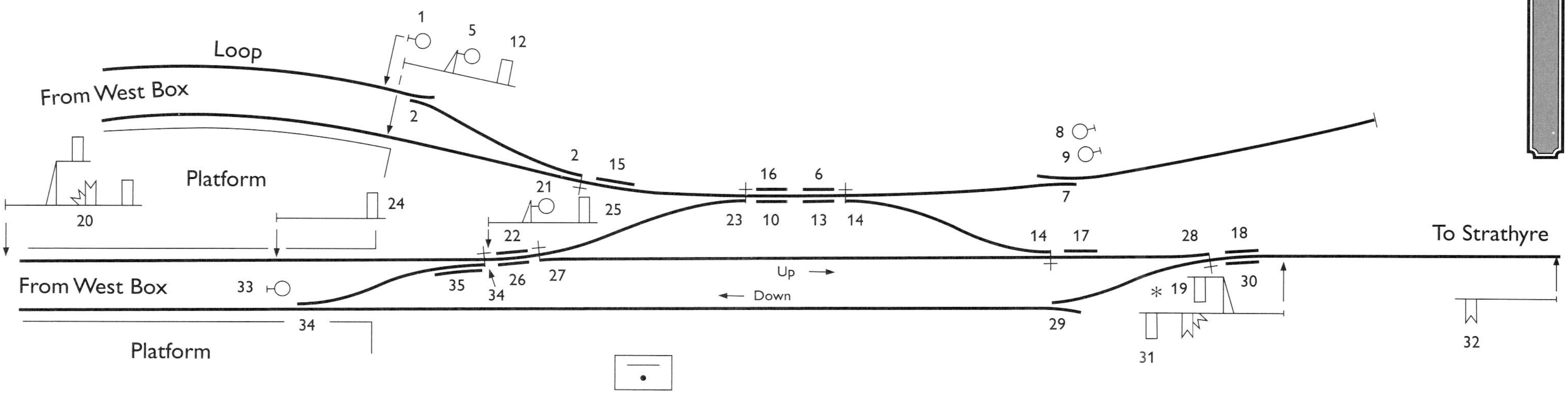

Diagram date - 1907
Opened - 18/12/1904
Closed - 21/3/1965
36 levers
Spare - 3-4-11-36

* Signal 19 electrically released from West Box

ABOVE: Figure 9.27
The signalling at Balquhidder East in 1909 after certain alterations had been made. These included the trap points at No. 29 and the crossover (No. 34) which required the addition of four levers to the original 1905 lever frame, taking the total to thirty-six.

Plate 9.28
Balquhidder West signal box viewed from the end of the Up platform, showing the Callander & Oban line curving away to the left and the loop line running behind the signal box. The line to Crieff ran off to the right behind the rake of wagons visible to the right of the signal box. This was the larger of the two signal boxes at Balquhidder, controlling the small goods yard and engine shed in addition to the branch line to Lochearnhead. Balquhidder still retained its Caledonian Railway signals at this stage, including both elevated and ground-mounted shunting signals.
Courtesy SRS/Kidderminster Railway Museum

The LM&SR Years

The first year of LM&SR ownership saw yet another level crossing incident, when in late August 1923 the 2.28pm Glasgow to Crieff train ran through the gates at Strageath. The crossing keeper, *'an elderly man'* had simply forgotten to open the gates, and fortunately no one was injured.

There were relatively few accidents on the Strathearn branch lines between 1923 and their closure in the 1960s, but a great proportion of them involved level crossings, two accounting for the only two fatalities during this period. One accident which did not was in 1929, when Mr W Miller, a platelayer, was knocked down by a train near Gleneagles – his injuries were such that he was totally incapacitated and, although he survived, he died only three years later at the relatively young age of 48.

In April 1931, two trains were being shunted at Gleneagles when a collision occurred. Coaches were being added to the 8.0pm Glasgow to Dundee train when the movement was misjudged and two carriages were severely damaged. The accident would have been more serious had not a number of passengers already left the train.

Far more serious was the only recorded accident on the Gleneagles Hotel branch line which occurred on 30th May 1932, involving a runaway train. A locomotive was propelling a particularly heavy train of seventeen wagons up the branch line as was required by the regulations. It had crossed over the Crieff to Glendevon road level crossing when it got into trouble. At this point the line curved sharply to the right and climbed through a wooded area in the hotel grounds – the locomotive began to slip, then stalled, and finally began to move backwards. The brakes could not hold the train which ran back, gathering speed. The fireman, John Lynach, leapt from the footplate and ran back to the level crossing to open the gates, but had only managed to half open them when the train ran through them.

The driver, William Lee, then followed his fireman in jumping off the footplate, and the train gathered speed, running over the ungated crossing at Caledonian Crescent at an estimated 45 mph, down the hill and through the run-around loop. Having crashed through the gate at the entrance to the branch line, the train ran tender first into the buffer stop at the end of the head shunt, burying itself in the earth bank. Several wagons telescoped and landed on top of the engine. A breakdown crew were called to sort out the wreckage which fortunately did not foul the Gleneagles–Crieff branch line. The footplate crew were fortunate to escape without serious injury, and it was a blessing that no road traffic was crossing either of the level crossings when the train ran through.

Sadly, this was not the case about three years later on the evening of 25th November 1935, at the level crossing leading to East Third

Plate 9.29
The trailing connection made by the Gleneagles Hotel branch with the Gleneagles to Crieff line on the Auchterarder Common Muir next to the golf course. The points lie in the normal closed position to prevent any wagons from running onto the main line, and would have been in this position when the accident occurred in 1932. The locomotive and wagons would have been diverted into the headshunt to the left and ploughed into the earth bank just behind the second telegraph pole. The dome of the locomotive was still lying in the undergrowth nearly thirty years later!
Author

Plate 9.30
Subsequent to the runaway accident in 1932 illustrated at Plate 9.29, a set of trap points were installed inside the hotel grounds to prevent any future runaways running through the level crossing gates over the Dunfermline to Crieff road, visible at the left of this photograph. This photograph taken in 1963 shows what happened to one of the ancient Caledonian Railway vintage wooden wagons used for shunting at the hotel. It ran away and was derailed and then proceeded to simply break apart. It has been stacked in its component pieces rather like a modeller's kit, except that in this case the scale is 12 inches to the foot! *Author*

CHAPTER 9: SAFETY AND SIGNALLING

Plate 9.31
The user worked level crossing at East Third Farm near Auchterarder on the straight stretch of 1 in 50 falling gradient from Gleneagles to Tullibardine which was the site of a fatal accident in 1935. The folly of leaving a vehicle on the crossing while opening the far gate was amply demonstrated when the train ran into it at speed killing the van man. The profusion of warning signs seen here probably date from that time, but despite this it is evident from the state of the gate that little notice has been taken of these and the gates left permanently open to both road and railway. *Author*

Farm about a mile away, just south of Tullibardine. This was a user worked crossing with hand operated gates which were opened and shut by those using the crossing. The level crossing was part way down a straight stretch of line on a falling gradient of 1 in 50, was not lit or protected by any signals. During daylight hours trains coming from either direction could be observed a good way off, but this accident occurred during the hours of darkness. The engine driver, Mr Alfred White told the Inquiry that on the falling gradient they came down with the minimum of noise and were travelling at about 45 mph when they reached the crossing.

The driver of a butcher's delivery van had unwisely left the van on the crossing while he got out to open the far gate. The van was still there when the Down passenger train hit it, killing the 22-year-old driver. The wreckage of the van was carried, wedged on the locomotive buffer beam, almost to Tullibardine before the train stopped.

The Fatal Accident Inquiry held at Dunblane the following January recommended that a signal be placed at the crossing so that drivers would know when a train was approaching, and that, where practicable, signals be placed at other level crossings. This work was never done, but additional signs were erected, as can be seen from Plate 9.31.

Four years later, in March 1939, the 12.15pm Crieff to Gleneagles service demolished the gates at Pittenzie for the fourth time, although in this case, fortunately, there was no traffic crossing at the time. Sadly, four years later, in almost a repeat of the accident at East Third Farm level crossing, a train hit a van on the Dollerie Farm level crossing, between Innerpeffray and Abercairny, killing the seventeen-year-old van driver.

Perhaps the most serious accident of this period occurred on 20th May 1936 when the 4.53pm St. Fillans to Crieff train derailed just west of Crieff adjacent to Morrison's Academy playing fields. Ex-Caledonian Railway 0-4-4T No. 15216 toppled on its side, although thankfully the two coaches remained upright. The driver, fireman and passengers all had a lucky escape. Initially it was believed that

Plate 9.32
A shot of ex-Caledonian Railway 0-4-4T No. 15216 which came to grief in the accident on 20th May 1936. Although the train derailed, the locomotive did not overturn, coming to rest embedded in the embankment, while the carriages remained more of less upright. Given the location, the results could have been far more severe, and it was fortunate that there were no fatalities. *Author's collection*

the locomotive had hit an obstruction, but there were also rumours that some children had been collecting the wooden keys from the rail chairs for firewood. This was never proved and as the accident did not involve any fatalities or serious injuries it does not seem to have been pursued.

Thankfully that was the last serious accident on the Strathearn lines, and despite the 'black out' and other wartime conditions, there were only a couple of minor incidents during the Second World War. In March 1940, a goods train derailed at Abercairny, the engine and most of the wagons coming off the track; the derailment was sufficiently violent for one of the wagons to be catapulted into a neighbouring field and the breakdown crew from Perth had to work for 5 hours to clear the line. Then in April 1941, a misjudged shunting movement in the carriage sidings at Crieff resulted in one of the carriages crashing through the buffer stops and running up the embankment in the direction of Duchlage Road.

These apart, the only noteworthy incident in late LM&SR days was the failure of the engine on the 8.8am Crieff to Edinburgh and Glasgow service one morning in 1946. The locomotive failed at Tullibardine, and the thirty passengers, including a number of school children had to be sent on their way by bus.

The British Railways Years

The later days of the remaining Strathearn lines were relatively trouble free, with little of note in terms of accidents or incidents. The introduction of the railbus in 1958 was supposed to herald a new era of fast and efficient diesel service, but it was plagued with failures. Whether it was the original AC Cars, or the later Park Royal or Wickham railbuses, they were often breaking down.

One such example was an unusual incident which occurred on 10th September 1959, when Wickham railbus Sc79968 on the 9.53am Crieff to Gleneagles service failed between Muthill and Tullibardine due to problems with the auxiliary drive shaft. Having been towed to Gleneagles by an ex-Caledonian Railway '2F' 0-6-0, probably off one of the morning goods trains shunting there, it was then taken on to Perth by the ex-Great Western 4-4-0 *City of Truro*, which was making its way back 'light engine' from Glasgow, having encountered problems on a special train from Aberdeen. Onlookers were therefore treated to the somewhat bizarre sight of one of British Railways' oldest operational steam locomotives towing a state-of-the-art diesel unit.

These failures were usually caused by minor breakdowns, but the most serious incident occurred in 1961 when a railbus derailed between Tullibardine and Muthill as a result of failure of part of the suspension system. The railbus service continued to limp along for another three years until the line closed to passengers in 1964.

The gradual closure of sections of the Strathearn lines led to a corresponding contraction of the signalling. Even before this happened, however, the original wooden signal box at Comrie was gutted by fire on 7th October 1950, to be replaced by a covered ground frame which had all the appearance of an elevated garden shed.

The complete closure of the Comrie to Balquhidder section on 1st October resulted in the closure of St. Fillans signal box exactly fifty years to the day after it opened. The gate box at Dalchonzie Platform closed on the same day. The remaining signal boxes on the Perth to Crieff line, however, remained after passenger services were withdrawn on the same day, to handle the remaining goods traffic.

The replacement signal box at Comrie only lasted eleven years before being abolished on 15th October 1961, after which date the line from Crieff was worked as a One Engine in Steam section. Tablet working on the Almond Valley Junction to Crieff line was abolished in 1962 and both Methven Junction and Madderty closed on 18th February that year. The surviving signal box at Crieff lasted until 17th May 1965, when it too was closed, and thereafter the line was worked by 'one engine in steam' train staff.

The next round of signalling closures followed the closure of the Gleneagles to Crieff line in 1964. Muthill lingered on for a few months after passenger services were withdrawn on 4th July 1964, closing on 2nd November 1964. Last to go was Gleneagles, which once the branch line closed and goods services had been withdrawn had lost much of its purpose. It was abolished on 14th August 1966, and the main line block section became Blackford to Auchterarder.

Overall, the safety record of the branch lines of Strathearn was pretty good, there having been no accidents due to any failure of the increasingly efficient signalling systems over the years. There were no passengers fatalities, although several members of the public were killed, such as those at level crossings. Only two members of staff, the Perth Almond Valley & Methven worker and the unfortunate Guard James Stanton, died as a result of an accident, although quite a number suffered varying degrees of injury, particularly in the early years. Sadly, the heaviest death toll was among the navvies, particularly during the building of the Crieff & Comrie Railway, although this was probably no greater than the average for such constructions projects in those days.

By and large, railways were a safe, if not the safest, means of travel, and, in this respect, the branch lines of Strathearn were no exception.

Plate 9.33
One of the more serious incidents among the many technical failures which plagued the diesel railbuses during their short lifetime on the Gleneagles to Comrie line occurred when the axle and suspension gave way on a railbus near Tullibardine. This view shows the damage sustained, although thankfully no one was injured and there was minimal damage to the permanent way. The railbus, however, was out of action for some time and yet again a substitute steam hauled service had to be provided.
Author's collection

Chapter 10

British Railways and the Struggle for Survival

Any hope that the brave new world of nationalisation would breathe new life into the branch lines of Strathearn was not to be realised, for life carried on very much as it had before. The post-war years of austerity continued well into the 1950s and, initially at least, there was little new investment in the railways.

Locally, the threat of the complete closure of the Comrie to Balquhidder section had not been annulled by nationalisation, and the 'sword of Damocles' continued to hang over that section of line. Economies, however small, continued to be made. Thus, for example, the signal box at Highlandman was reduced to the status of a 'gate box' on 3rd October 1948, with a consequent saving in staff, and the following year, on 30th November 1949, the lever frame at Innerpeffray was replaced by a ground frame. Staffing at Tullibardine was reduced to a single shift, instructions being issued to the effect that from 20th June 1949 it was to be treated as an 'unstaffed halt' for the early morning 6.0am Stirling to Balquhidder Mail train and the 4.55pm St. Fillans to Gleneagles train in the evening. In addition, the station was closed between 12 noon and 1.25pm.

The passenger services changed little with nationalisation. The new Scottish Region Time Table showed all services for both the former LM&SR and the former L&NER lines in Scotland. The Gleneagles to Balquhidder service became Table 117 and that from Perth to Crieff, Table 118 in the new timetable. The Gleneagles to Crieff service amounted to seven trains each way per day, with an additional Up train on Saturdays, but the service beyond Crieff was less generous. This section had only five trains each way per day, but one of these terminated at Comrie and another at St. Fillans, only three trains per day going through to Balquhidder. This was only marginally better than the latter days of the LM&SR.

Plate 10.1
Ex-LM&SR Fowler '4F' 0-6-0 draws into the Up platform at Crieff in the early 1950s. The station is still resplendent with covered footbridge, flower beds and statues on the Down platform. The poster boards are still headed 'London Midland & Scottish Railway' in this view taken not long after nationalisation. The station appears to be fairly deserted, as, sadly, does the train. *ES Morten*

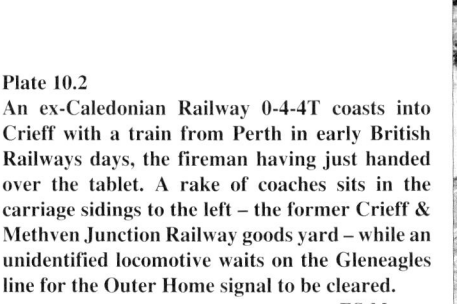

Plate 10.2
An ex-Caledonian Railway 0-4-4T coasts into Crieff with a train from Perth in early British Railways days, the fireman having just handed over the tablet. A rake of coaches sits in the carriage sidings to the left – the former Crieff & Methven Junction Railway goods yard – while an unidentified locomotive waits on the Gleneagles line for the Outer Home signal to be cleared. *ES Morten*

The Perth to Crieff service too was little changed, with three Up and four Down trains on week days and an additional train each way on Saturdays. However, several of these trains only called at Methven Junction, Tibbermuir Siding and Ruthven Road by request, reflecting the low level of passenger traffic from these small wayside halts.

The corresponding Working Time Table for the same period also showed some interesting variations not shown in the Public Time Table. The 6.5pm from Crieff and the 4.17pm and 5.22pm trains from Perth did not call at Ruthven Road, while the 1.52pm from Crieff for some reason did not call at Almondbank. Also, the 5.22pm from Perth was the only train of the day not to call at Tibbermuir. More understandably, the 1.52pm train from Crieff called additionally at Muirton Halt when required to set down passengers. As this halt had been opened by the LM&SR specifically to serve the nearby St. Johnston football ground, this was presumably for the benefit of football supporters going to home games. No special arrangements were shown for their return, which probably was by scheduled services from Perth.

In addition to the local services, the new Scottish Region continued to promote tourist traffic over the Strathearn lines, even while the whole future of these lines was in the balance. The 1948 summer season saw the resumption of the popular Circular Tours from Glasgow and Edinburgh to St. Fillans, both clockwise via Callander and Balquhidder, and anti-clockwise via Gleneagles and Crieff (Figure 10.1).

Excursion traffic continued, with substantial numbers, such as a Sunday school outing from Perth on 5th June 1948. Three churches combined to organise a trip to Crieff with impressive figures totalling 500 passengers, the numbers of adults and children being:

St. Pauls Church	110 + 140
Scone Old Church	50 + 100
Middle Church	40 + 60

Leaving Perth at 1.55pm to arrive at Crieff at 2.23pm, trippers were allowed four hours in Crieff before leaving again at 6.30pm to arrive back at Perth at 7.5pm. The arrival of this eight-coach train with 200 adults and 300 excited children must have been a lively event.

A similar outing arrived at Crieff on 20th July when 4th Kirkcaldy Boys Brigade travelled via Perth from their homes in Fife. Another eight-coach train, weighing 240 tons, this special left Perth at 12.50pm to arrive at Crieff at 1.52pm. This time the boys were allowed a little over six hours before leaving at 7.35pm to arrive at Perth at 8.10pm, although it would have been a while later before they eventually got home to Kirkcaldy.

Another feature of traffic patterns which continued until the Comrie to Balquhidder section closed in 1951 was the annual migration of sheep in the autumn from the Highlands to winter pastures. At the end of September 1948, for example, two substantial specials ran over the Strathearn lines. On 28th September, a '*Special Express Freight Train*' conveyed twenty-one trucks of wintering sheep from Tyndrum to Perth (North).

Tyndrum		7. 0pm
Balquhidder		8.48pm
Crieff	Arr	9.40pm
Crieff	Dep	9.50pm
Almond Valley Jct		10.25pm

The 10 minutes stop at Crieff was to enable the engine to take water. Signal boxes along the route were required to stay open beyond their normal operating hours until the train had passed. However, even after arriving at Perth, the sheep still had a long way to go, for their trucks were then transferred to the 12.15am goods train from Perth (North) to Aviemore.

Two days later, a '*Special Live Stock Train*' was run from Killin Junction to Boat of Garten. What the subtle difference between a '*Special Express Freight Train*' and a '*Special Live Stock Train*' was is not clear, except that in the case of the former, the sheep were listed as '*Spring Sheep*' and the latter were described as the usual '*Wintering Sheep*'. This special consisted of twenty-seven trucks of sheep and was another late night train:

Balquhidder		9.35pm
Crieff	Arr	10.25pm
Crieff	Dep	10.35pm
Almond Valley Jct		11.10pm

Again, water was taken at Crieff, and signal boxes were kept open late. The arrangements for the train engine were interesting, in that it

CIRCULAR ROUTE TICKETS—Continued

To ST. FILLANS
(Strathallan, Strathearn and Strathyre Circle)

From	Return Fares First Class	Return Fares Third Class	Route
	s. d.	s. d.	
Glasgow (Buch. St.)	25 8	17 1	Going by train to St. Fillans via Bridge of Allan, Gleneagles, Crieff and Comrie; returning from St. Fillans via Lochearnhead, Balquhidder, Strathyre, Loch Lubnaig, Pass of Leny and Callander. Or the route may be reversed.
Glasgow (Central)	25 8	17 1	
Edinburgh (Pr. St.)	29 11	19 11	

Figure 10.1
A British Railways brochure published in 1948, the year in which the railways were nationalised, showing that the old LM&SR circular tours of Strathearn had been resurrected by the new Scottish Region and retitled, rather more catchily, 'Strathallan, Strathearn and Strathyre Circle'. St. Fillans remained the focal point, the tour being taken clockwise or anti-clockwise as in LM&SR days. This tour survived for only three more seasons after this.
Author's collection

was attached to the normal 4.17pm Perth to Crieff passenger service and then from Crieff ran as a 'light engine' to Luib on the Callander & Oban line where it collected its train.

Despite the uncertainty over the future of the Crieff to Balquhidder section, the line continued to be maintained to the standard required for passenger traffic as indeed it had to be. In May 1948, the Engineer's weedkilling train ran over the line, this time the full length of the line from Balquhidder through to Almond Valley Junction, but with no side trip to Gleneagles. Yet again the short branch to Methven was excluded. The train sprayed the line for 15½ miles from Balquhidder, another 6 miles from Comrie and, after being replenished with water at Crieff, the final 15½ miles to Almond Valley Junction. The timetable for this run reflected the reduced speed required for the spraying operation:

Balquhidder		4.57pm
Comrie		5.40pm
Crieff	Arr	5.58pm
Crieff	Dep	6.20pm
Almond Valley Jct		7.10pm

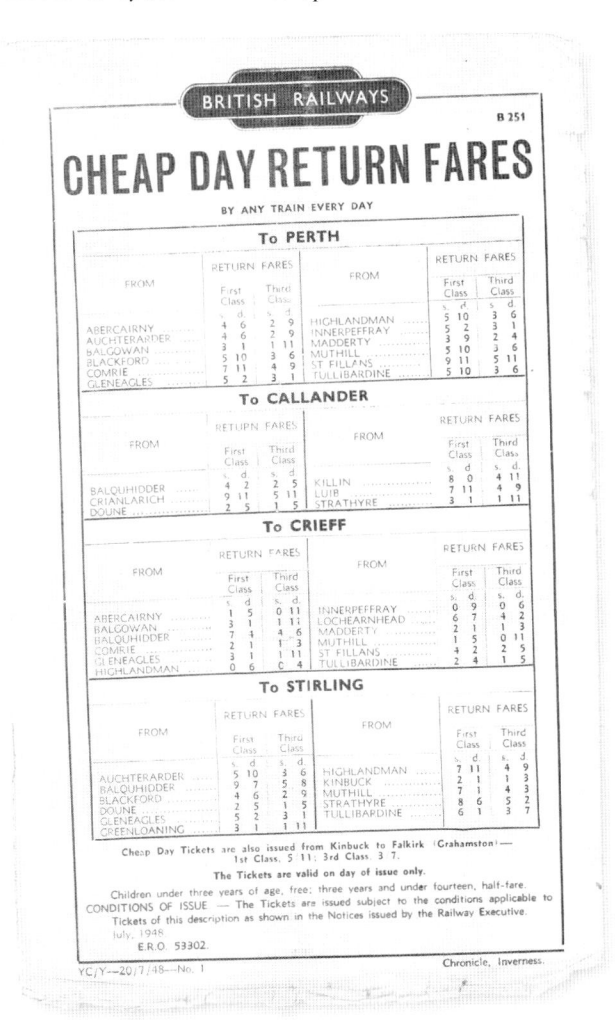

The timing of this weedkilling train was no coincidence, for it was probably in preparation for the Engineer's inspection train which ran over the Perth to Crieff section only a week later on 7th June 1948. Leaving Perth at 10.5am, this train ran to a much extended timetable to allow plenty of time for inspection at various points as shown:

– Almond Valley Jct	10 minutes
– Methven Jct	25 minutes
– Methven Branch	30 minutes
– Balgowan	15 minutes
– Madderty	15 minutes
– Abercairny	15 minutes
– Innerpeffray	15 minutes

The engineers then spent 40 minutes inspecting Crieff station before the train returned to Perth, stopping for 15 minutes at Almondbank to inspect this station on the way. Inspection saloon No. 45036 was used on this train. During this same period, engineering work was also going on further up the line, for the same Weekly Notice showed an engineering train working daily from Perth to St. Fillans during the week 31st May to 7th June.

The engineers returned twice more that year. On 1st September, an Engineer's special ran a rather complicated route from Perth to Ballinluig on the former Highland main line, then back to Burrelton and thence to Crieff, finally returning to Glasgow via Gleneagles. The purpose of this was to include a further inspection of the section between Madderty and Abercairny which included a number of bridges, and Innerpeffray station, where 13 minutes was allowed. This train, which conveyed Inspection saloon No. 45020, then ran at normal speed from Crieff to Gleneagles before returning to Glasgow.

Only a week later, another Engineer's inspection train travelled over the line, this time en route from Oban and Ballachulish to Perth. The schedule allowed for 43 minutes at Balquhidder and an additional 8 minutes were spent between Comrie and Crieff before the train continued on to Perth at normal speed.

1949 saw little change in the routine on the Strathearn lines, and the spring of that year saw the customary procession of specials returning '*Wintering Sheep*' to their Highland homes. Typical of these were two unusually heavy trains from Grantown-on-Spey to Tyndrum which were run on 31st March and 4th April. The first of these special express trains conveyed thirty-eight trucks of what were classed as '*Spring Sheep*'.

Grantown-on-Spey		11.40am
Almond Valley Jct		5.40pm
Crieff	Arr	6.30pm
Crieff	Dep	6.55pm
Balquhidder		7.58pm
Tyndrum		9.20pm

A 21-minute stop was allowed at Crieff for watering and, in addition, the timetable allowed for crossing local Down trains at Madderty and St. Fillans. The second special express freight train was even heavier, conveying no less than forty trucks of sheep. This train ran slightly later, not reaching Crieff until 7.53pm, where a stop of 27 minutes was allowed for watering. In this case signal boxes were required to stay open late as the train did not arrive at Balquhidder until 9.8pm.

Excursion traffic continued that summer, one such being an outing organised by the Perth Society of High Constables on 15th June 1949 to Stronachlacher near Callander. A six-coach train of 120 tons conveyed an estimated 200 passengers on a circular tour from Perth to Callander via Dunblane, returning by Balquhidder and Crieff. Just under eight hours was allowed for the excursion, the timetable being:

Figure 10.2
An early British Railways handbill advertising Cheap Day Return fares from many stations in Strathearn, including a range of fares to Crieff. Interestingly, the only station on the Strathearn branch lines which does not feature here is Almondbank. Methven was already closed, and the three halts, Dalchonzie, Ruthven Road and Tibbermuir did not feature in such leaflets. The printers to the Caledonian Railway and the LM&SR had always been McCorquodale, but British Railways used various printers, including, as seen here, the Chronicle, publishers of a local newspaper in Inverness. *Author's collection*

Perth	Dep	9.15am
Callander	Arr	10.22am
Callander	Dep	6.15pm
Balquhidder		6.53pm
Almond Valley Jct		8. 1pm
Perth	Arr	8. 5pm

That same day, another Engineer's special inspection train visited the line as part of a full day's work, running from Oban to Glasgow via Crieff and Gleneagles. The timings over the Strathearn section being:

Balquhidder	Dep	12.25pm
St. Fillans	Arr	1. 5pm
St. Fillans	Dep	1.55pm
Crieff		2.59pm
Gleneagles		3.26pm
Glasgow	Arr	5.20pm

Unusually, this train conveyed two inspection saloons, No. 45020 and No. 900580, and although the timings allowed for a 50-minute stop at St. Fillans, this may well have been for lunch, as no time was allocated there for inspection purposes. In addition to the inspection times for the Strathearn lines, it is worth noting that the allowed time was no less than 51 minutes for the 3 miles between Bridge of Allan and Stirling on the return journey along the main line to Glasgow. Most of the inspection times allowed were for the Balquhidder to Crieff section of the line:

- Lochearnhead to St. Fillans — 25 minutes
- St. Fillans to Comrie — 20 minutes
- Crieff station — 5 minutes
- Gleneagles station — 5 minutes

Trains for tourists and excursions were not the only specials to run over the Strathearn branch lines that summer, for with the departure of the last German PoWs, the army had found a new role for Cultybraggan as a training camp, not just for the regular army, but also for the TA (Territorial Army) and cadet forces, both the ACFs (Army Cadet Forces) and CCFs (Combined Cadet Forces). Two TA units, one from Aberdeen, the other from Inverness, spent their two-week summer camp at Cultybraggan that year, arriving on 18th June and departing on 2nd July, both moves involved heavy troop trains.

On 2nd July, the Inverness train was first, starting from St. Fillans, where it had been stabled, at 8.0am, as Empty Coaching Stock. It was a twelve-coach train of 350 tons which included two luggage vans and conveyed 396 passengers, 37 in First Class (officers) and 359 Third Class (other ranks). This was followed 40 minutes later by the Aberdeen train which had started from Balquhidder as Empty Coaching Stock at 8.5am, and comprised eleven vehicles at 325 tons, one of which was a baggage train. Again there were fifteen First Class and 350 Third Class passengers, totalling 365 in all. The timetables allowed for crossing Down trains at Crieff, and in the case of the Aberdeen train at Methven Junction was well:

Comrie	Dep	8.50am	9.30am
Crieff	Arr	9. 2am	9.42pm
Crieff	Dep	9.10am	9.47am
Methven Jct	Arr	---	10. 7am
Methven Jct	Dep	---	10.20am
Almond Valley Jct		9.40am	10.30am
Aberdeen	Arr	---	6.14pm
Inverness	Arr	2.15pm	---

These troop trains were to become a regular feature of summer

Plate 10.3
An ex-LM&SR Fowler '4F' 0-6-0 sits at the Down platform at Comrie on 25th August 1955 having just arrived with the solitary through coach off the 4.25pm Edinburgh to Crieff train. The footbridge and Up platform buildings are still intact although the line through to St. Fillans had closed four years previously.
WAC Smith/transporttreasury.co.uk

traffic over the Strathearn branch lines until the closure of the Crieff to Comrie section in July 1964.

Local passenger train services continued much as in previous years, although with traffic ebbing away as competition from road transport increased, it must have become evident that many such country branch lines were living on borrowed time. Life on the branch lines of Strathearn continued at a fairly leisurely pace, and this is reflected in contemporary reports of journeys over the lines by the likes of George Robins, a well-travelled railway enthusiast, writer and photographer.

In May 1949 he travelled on the 4.17pm Perth to Crieff service with ex-Caledonian Railway 0-4-4T 55208 heading a two-coach train. He describes how they '*dawdled along to Almond Valley Junction*', slowing to pick up the tablet before heading off up the branch line. The train did not stop at Ruthven Road, and the only observation about Almondbank was the tidy lawn opposite the station platform. No stop was made at Methven Junction, but at Madderty the train crossed with an ex-Caledonian Railway 'Jumbo' 0-6-0 17449 (still carrying its LM&SR number) heading a solitary coach packed with children on an unadvertised school train. Having changed trains at

Plate 10.4
A good uncluttered view of Gleneagles station in the 1950s. The lower quadrant signal arms on the main line signals have been replaced by upper quadrant arms, but the station has yet to be fitted out with British Railways enamel signage. The sign on the left, 'ALIGHT HERE FOR GLENEAGLES GOLF COURSES', is the original Caledonian Railway sign which was subsequently replaced by the enamel sign shown in Plate 3.1, 'ALIGHT HERE FOR GLENEAGLES HOTEL & GOLF COURSES', when the station received British Railways signs and totems. The author's childhood home can be seen in the woods in the distance, just above the stairs on the island platform.
BRB Residuary

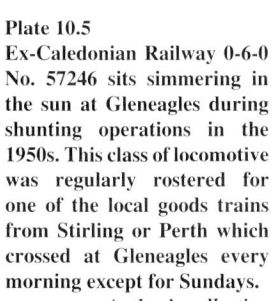

Plate 10.5
Ex-Caledonian Railway 0-6-0 No. 57246 sits simmering in the sun at Gleneagles during shunting operations in the 1950s. This class of locomotive was regularly rostered for one of the local goods trains from Stirling or Perth which crossed at Gleneagles every morning except for Sundays.
Author's collection

Crieff, he took the 5.26pm service to Gleneagles headed by another ex-Caledonian Railway locomotive, 4-4-0 M14476, with two coaches also of Caledonian Railway vintage. Apart from crossing a Down train at Muthill, his only comments were on the state of Tullibardine station, scathingly described as *'What a disgrace, the staff were like tinkers'*, a sad decline from the days when that small station regularly won Best Kept Station awards.

The late Kerr Edgar, a Crieffite and ardent railway enthusiast, wrote about one of his many illicit footplate trips – a run on ex-Caledonian Railway 4-4-0 No. 54476, a Crieff based locomotive for many years, one day in 1950. He described an idyllic scene as 54476 with a light load of only two coaches coasted through the magnificent scenery of Upper Strathearn in the early evening sun, *'the only sound above the musical exhaust is the musical ring of the coupling rods, characteristic of a Scottish 4-4-0'*. He mentioned *'cheery waves from folk out on an early evening stroll'* and *'local folk in their gardens look up and give us a cheery smile'*. He noted that they were two minutes early at Comrie, not difficult, considering the 12 minutes allowed for the 6-mile journey equated to an average of only 30 miles per hour.

Apart from extra stops at Dalchonzie Platform on the way out and on the way back, there is no mention of passengers joining or leaving the train, and the whole impression given is of a backwater of the railway network, with a leisurely pace of life, amid superb scenery, but greatly underused. Another railway enthusiast of the time described a holiday at St. Fillans in 1949, the final leg of the journey starting when ex-Midland Railway '4F' 0-6-0 No. 5251 on the 1.12pm service *'ambled off from Crieff with a sparsely filled train'*.

During the final few years prior to closure of much of the network of Strathearn branch lines, Crieff maintained the air of a busy little country junction, and this is well portrayed by two articles which appeared in a long-defunct local enthusiast's magazine the Scottish Railway Express in 1962 and 1963. Published under the title of 'As I remember it' by '54476', probably a 'nom de plume' used by the late Kerr Edgar, they described *'A day at Crieff Station in 1949'* in detail, and are worth reproducing here in full:

'Suitably prepared for a day out, join me as I make my way to Crieff station to watch the goings on at this fairly busy country junction station, around 6am on a September weekday. From the east end of the Down platform, the two parallel lines beyond the pointwork lead to Perth (left) and Gleneagles (right), while behind us to the west, the line leads to Balquhidder on the Callander & Oban line. To the left of the Perth line are the two loco sheds, outside the larger of which a "Caley Bogie" is taking water. We note that she is No 54447, one of the older McIntosh "Dunalistair IV" super heater type, and is painted black with BR lining, but no sign of ownership on the tender; also the cab lining follows the outside edge of the lower panel only. In the early morning sun, she makes a fine sight, her paintwork gleaming with the attention given her by the regular Crieff men. As she moves off to pick up four corridor coaches which have been stabled at the head shunt, hissing steam heralds the emergence from the small wooden shed of a second "Bogie", this time a Pickersgill M14476, in the earliest BR style of plain black with the title in full on the tender, but like 54447, well groomed. (54476 was always shedded at Crieff up to the closure of the Perth and Balquhidder lines to passenger traffic in 1951, and was only absent for boiler wash out or repairs. The other loco was changed each wash out time.)

A whistle from 54447 produces movement in the signal box to our right, and she moves towards us, the fireman picking up the tablet as he passes the waiting signalman. We note that she carries the Empty Coaching Stock head code on the tender, and is in fact off to St. Fillans to form the 7.35am to Glasgow and Edinburgh. As she disappears in the cutting at the west end of the station, M14476 takes water, then backs on to the two non-corridor coaches ready to form the 8.05am to Perth. About 6.40, the Gleneagles line bell in the signal box gives a single beat followed by 3-1. The morning mail train from Stirling has been offered on. Presently, steam can be seen in the distance as the signals are pulled off for its arrival; the train approaches, and we see that it consists of two non-corridors and a bogie parcels van, headed by Stirling Pickersgill 4-4-0 No 54466, still with "LMS" on her tender, but with new number in place. Some passengers off the overnight train from London alight, and luggage barrows are moved about briskly during the unloading of the day's fish, mail, etc. The loco is uncoupled and draws forward to take water, then backs on to her train again to form the 8.01 am to Balquhidder.

Meanwhile a different bell in the box draws your attention once more, the road is set, and the Perth line to Goods Yard signal drops with a clump. The morning goods is approaching headed by 4F 0-6-0 No 44251. She clatters in to the goods yard, runs around her train and then begins to shunt. Next, M14476 draws her two coaches forward and backs them in to the station to await passengers.

The time is now 7.58, and a whistle heralds the return of 54447 with the train from St. Fillans, which draws in slowly behind the Perth train after receiving the "Calling On" signal. First away is the 8.05 to Perth, followed by the 8.07 to Glasgow and Edinburgh, and the Balquhidder at 8.12. The only activity now is the goods pottering away in the yard. No goods for Comrie today, so 44251 sets off for Perth on completion of her chores, with return traffic; if there is a load for Comrie, the trip is made between 8.15 and 9.15.

At 9.03, 54447 returns, this time with a train of two suburban coaches left at Gleneagles the previous day. A fair number of school children alight and make their way noisily up the road, while 54447 has uncoupled and run around, and waits at the Down platform until the Stirling men return at 10.01 with the 9.17 from Balquhidder to Gleneagles. She then propels her train out into the cutting and draws forward in behind the other train to form the 10.18 to Perth. Both trains having departed, silence returns until at 9.50 signals clear for the 10.00 from Perth behind M14476, which has been turned and coaled there. She shunts her coaches to the Up platform, then runs via the Down line to the Goods Yard to shunt as required until 11.20, when she makes her way to the centre road in the station to await the arrival of the 11.20 from Gleneagles, which once again has the Stirling loco and crew. 54466 is uncoupled and draws forward in to the cutting and backs on to the train to take it forward to Comrie. The Stirling loco now runs through the centre road and backs on to the coaches left by M14476 to form the 12.07 to Gleneagles. M14476 then leaves for Comrie at 11.48, arriving back at 12.22pm; she then takes water, shunts her train out to the siding at the shed, where the van is detached and put in to another siding, and goes "on shed" for fire cleaning, while crews are changed, the early shift men being finished for the day.

As 1.00pm approaches, the Perth line Home signal clatters "off" and 54447 draws in with the 12.30pm Perth – Balquhidder. The back shift crew takes over, and she continues on her way at 1.04. There is now a lull, which gives us time for a bite to eat, before M14476 couples on to her two coaches again and shunts them in to the station to form the 2.25 to Gleneagles. As soon as she reaches Muthill, the "Train out of section" rings out in the box, followed by a lengthy code which means that the afternoon goods from Stirling is on its way. At 2.50, the hoot of a "Caley" whistle produces action in the box, and the goods gets the road in to the station. The loco, "Wee Jumbo" No 57246, runs around her train and then shunts it in to the yard (the run around in the yard only takes about eight wagons), and proceeds to make up her return load. Next, 54447 arrives back at 3.10, shunts her coaches out to the loco shed sidings, and then comes back through the station "wrong line", stopping to take water on the way. Meanwhile, 57246 has gone to the shed to be turned, take water and have the fire cleaned for the return run, then picks up the parcels van left at lunchtime, plus two coaches left by 54447, and draws forward in to the headshunt.

M14476 arrives back at 3.25, this time plus two coaches left by the Stirling men at Gleneagles at 12.27, she runs round via the centre road and shunts the rear two coaches to the other platform, while 54447 couples on to the front two and sets off for St. Fillans at 3.37. M14476 leaves for Gleneagles at 3.40, then 57246 shunts her passenger stock over to the goods yard and picks up the goods part and then moves the lot to the station to form the 4.00pm (SX) "Mixed" to Gleneagles. This train is not advertised in the public timetable and runs during term time only.

After she sets off we have time for tea before the 4.17 from Perth arrives at 4.50. This is a Perth diagram and usually produces an 0-4-4 tank. Today is no exception, and 55208 sails in with four non-corridors behind. Train unloaded, she draws up to the water column for refreshment, and waits there until 54447 arrives back with the 4.05 from St. Fillans, leaving again for Gleneagles at 5.25. After the latter has departed, 55208 shunts her coaches to the Up platform, then goes to the goods yard to make up the evening train for Perth. At 5.35, "Train out of section" rings out from Muthill, followed by "Call attention" then four beats – "Is line clear for express passenger train?" Soon, the unmistakable roar of a "Compound" is heard approaching with the 4.00pm from Glasgow. The loco will be one of four – 41125/6/7 or 8, and sure enough 41126 is "up front". Her three corridors unloaded, she propels them out to the end of the loco shed headshunt ready for the next morning, goes to be turned and then backs into the station to take water and collect her next train, the coaches left by 55208, to form the 6.00pm to Perth and Glasgow.

Next arrival is the 5.30 from Perth behind M14476 (which has run the 4.00pm Gleneagles to Perth since she last left Crieff). The 'Compound' sets off again at 6.00pm, and then M14476 moves off for Balquhidder at 6.04. As soon as the "Compound" clears Madderty, 55208 gets the road with her short goods for Perth, then the 6.03 from Gleneagles comes in, conveying through coaches from Edinburgh next to the loco, the coaches are shunted in to the Up platform, the through coach is detached, drawn forward, then 54447 propels it out to join the Glasgow ones in the headshunt. She then comes back to the station to head the 7.00pm to Gleneagles, returning again at 7.55. Meanwhile, M14476 has arrived back at 7.40 from Balquhidder, shunts her coaches to the sidings and goes for fire cleaning and shed for the night. 54447's train is carrying some passengers for Comrie, so she goes on with them (this only happens if required), returning as ECS. She then shunts her train to the sidings and after fire cleaning retires for the night.

So ends a typical day, and we can make for home.'

This description of Crieff portrayed the swansong of the station as a busy country junction, for barely two years later the line beyond Comrie was to be closed entirely and passenger services withdrawn from the Perth–Crieff line. Even while passenger numbers dwindled, goods traffic on the Perth to Crieff section, however, continued to be an important source of revenue, and as late as 1950 the goods services were still fairly comprehensive, as was reflected in the Working Time Table of the day. The first to go, however, was the goods service between Comrie and Balquhidder, which was withdrawn on 25th September 1950. Although never heavy, the loss of this traffic left the remaining passenger service even more vulnerable.

On the Perth to Crieff line the first goods train of the day was the early morning 5.20am from Perth (North) worked Balgowan and Madderty to arrive at Crieff at 7.50am, while the 6.12am from Perth (North) worked all stations to Methven, arriving there at 7.35am. This train returned to Perth from Methven at 8.35am without any stops. Meanwhile, the 9.10am from Crieff worked all stations except Methven, to arrive back at Perth at 12.10pm. Goods trains, as was not uncommon on rural lines, also had other tasks. The 6.12am from Perth collected empty water cans from Methven Junction, while the 9.10am from Crieff was required to deliver water to Methven Moss level crossing, both these isolated locations being without a mains water supply.

Figure 10.3
Table 86 of the British Railways Scottish Region Time Table for the summer of 1951. This was the penultimate timetable issued before passenger services were withdrawn between Crieff and Perth and the Comrie to Balquhidder line closed completely. By this late date there were just two services per day each way between Crieff and Balquhidder with an additional train or two on Saturdays, and this in the summer tourist season.

Author's collection

In the afternoon, the 2.25pm from Perth (North) to Almondbank worked both the Royal Navy Stores Depot and Bleach Works sidings there. Finally, the 7.15pm from Crieff called at Madderty to collect traffic before heading on to Perth.

The rumours surrounding closure of the line between Comrie and Balquhidder which had first circulated back in 1945 now became a reality. The line survived just a year after the withdrawal of goods traffic, and, significantly, in the final Passenger Time Table for the line from 18th June to 23rd September 1951, all the Strathearn branch lines were merged into one table – No. 86 (Figure 10.3). The Perth to Crieff section was still served by four trains each way per day, while the Gleneagles to Crieff section enjoyed six trains each way per day. Beyond Crieff, however, things were different, with only three Down and two Up trains running the full length of the line between Crieff and Balquhidder, although a few others ran as far as Comrie or St. Fillans.

The 1st October 1951 was a black day for the Strathearn lines. The entire line between Comrie and Balquhidder was closed completely, including St. Fillans and Lochearnhead stations and Dalchonzie Platform. The Lochearnhead, St. Fillans & Comrie Railway which had taken five years to construct at considerable cost had a life of less than fifty years. On the same day, passenger services on the Perth to Crieff line, which faced the most direct competition from buses, were also withdrawn. Huntingtower Siding and Innerpeffray station, two of the least profitable stations, were also closed to goods traffic that day and subsequently closed entirely.

These closures had a significant impact on Crieff, and had other implications. In passenger terms it was no longer a junction, being served only by trains from Gleneagles and a much truncated service to Comrie. The popular Circular Tours, for many years a feature of the summer season, were no longer possible, and with the closure of St. Fillans, the scope for excursions was drastically reduced. Other through traffic such as the bi-annual sheep specials now had to travel by way of Dunblane and the main line to reach Perth. The reduction of the Crieff to Perth section to a goods-only line heralded a gradual but steady decline in maintenance and facilities.

Ironically, the following year, 1952, saw the reintroduction of the camping coaches which had proved so popular before the war. It came too late for Lochearnhead which was now closed, but the Scottish Region deployed twenty-five camping coaches at sites across the country, although initially there were none in Strathearn. This was not rectified until 1959 when a camping coach was sited at Comrie. Again, this came late in the day, and was withdrawn in 1964 when the line closed, having survived only five seasons from 1959 to 1963. The camping coach was located in the disused carriage and horse dock next to the Down platform, and surviving records from 1961 show this to have been Coach No. 25, which had six sleeping berths.

ABOVE: Plate 10.6
A surprise visitor to Gleneagles on an unrecorded date in the early 1950s was ex-L&NER 'Pacific' No. 60535 *Hornet's Beauty* on a diverted 'Heart of Midlothian' express. This train left Aberdeen at 9.45am and usually went by way of Dundee, the Tay Bridge, Fife, and the Forth Bridge to Edinburgh and thence by the East Coast Main Line to London. 60535 was working hard on the climb from Auchterarder and the photographer only just managed to catch it with his 'Box Brownie'. *Author*

ABOVE: Figure 10.4
One of the ubiquitous British Railways totem enamel signs. For some strange reason, Tullibardine was the only branch line station in Strathearn to be re-signed with these standard signs. None were ever erected at Muthill, Highlandman, Crieff or Comrie, which had to make do with wooden painted signs of various sorts. There were only three such totems at Tullibardine, and this rare example from the front wall of the booking office was purchased from British Railways after the station closed.
Author's collection

LEFT: Plate 10.7
Ex-LM&SR Fowler '4F' 0-6-0 No. 44322 heading an Up train on the climb between Muthill and Tullibardine. Theses '4F's were seen regularly on the Strathearn lines in the 1950s, nine of them being allocated to Perth South shed at that time. The overhead telegraph route on the left looks as though it could do with some attention.
WAC Smith/transporttreasury.co.uk

These coaches were equipped with a myriad of domestic items, including crockery, cutlery, bedding and other necessities similar to modern self-catering establishments, the inventory running to five foolscap typed sheets. No item was too small to be included, and there were even such items as a tea pot stand, a tea cosy, three 'Pots de chambre' and in a reflection of the times, four ashtrays.

Camping coaches were rented out on a weekly basis, and, in addition to the rent charged, the other benefit to the railway was that campers usually travelled by rail, often considerable distances, to the site. They then also tended to travel around the area using Holiday Runabout tickets, although in the case of Comrie, these were of limited use due to the rather sparse passenger service.

As was often the case in those days, the track between Comrie and Balquhidder was not lifted immediately and lay derelict for a number of years. The section from Comrie to a point 3 miles west of St. Fillans was the first to be recovered around 1957, but the remainder of the line was retained temporarily to provide rail access for materials being brought in for the North of Scotland Hydro Electric Board project at Breadalbane. This only provided a brief stay in execution for a few more years, with the remaining stretch being dismantled in 1959 as detailed in the Scottish Region Supplementary Operating Instructions dated 21st August 1959:

'Comrie – Balquhidder. The line between Comrie and a point three miles west of St. Fillans is uplifted, and contractors are engaged in uplifting the line from the latter point to a point 65 feet on the Lochearnhead side of the connection from the single line to the loop at Balquhidder. Yard working is in operation between these points.

Wagons must be propelled from Balquhidder to the site of work, and drivers must exercise great care and run their trains at reduced speed to and from the site.'

Meanwhile, St. Fillans station, including the main buildings and the signal box, remained largely intact – although the steel footbridge and all the signals were recovered for scrap – and was eventually bought and converted into a caravan site, which it remains to this day. The island platform and station buildings at Lochearnhead also survived, although the signal box is long gone, having closed back in 1921. This site was eventually acquired by the Hertfordshire Scouts who continue to use it as a base for their outdoor activities in the area.

Although the Gleneagles to Crieff and Comrie section had survived the first round of closure, it was not long before further rumours began to circulate about its future. As early as February 1955, the *Strathearn Herald* reported a comment raised by Councillor Park, a regular rail user, at a meeting of the Crieff Burgh Council to the effect that '*I have heard it on very good authority that the branch line is to be closed*'. The response from the then stationmaster at Crieff, Mr Roger was a curt '*We have no official news*', which is probably all he was allowed to say by senior railway management, but it did little to assuage public concern.

A month later, Crieff Burgh Council itself came under fire when it was criticised by a discussion group which met at the George Hotel who also complained that not enough publicity was being given to the matter of closure of the Gleneagles to Comrie line. The following week, it was reported that the council met with local organisations to discuss the withdrawal of the Gleneagles to Comrie passenger service, although no details were given. Significantly, no mention was made of the goods service. At the same time, Sir George McGlashan, Convenor of the Perth & Kinross County Council, revealed details of the planned closure of fifteen stations in Perthshire and made reference to the proposals to close the Gleneagles to Comrie line. In the event, it was the withdrawal of stopping services on the Stirling to Perth, Strathmore, and Perth to Dundee lines which resulted in the

Plate 10.8
A nicely posed shot of ex-Caledonian Railway Pickersgill 4-4-0 54500 outside the main shed at Crieff on 16th July 1956. No. 54500 was one of the regular locomotives on the Gleneagles to Comrie line at that time, and appears in good condition, which is more than can be said for the doors of the wooden engine shed in the background. That shed was dismantled long before the line closed, although the turntable was retained.

WAC Smith/transporttreasury.co.uk

Plate 10.9
A Glasgow (Buchanan Street) to Perth stopping train hauled by British Railways Standard 2-6-4T No. 80125 in the branch line platform at Gleneagles on 30th April 1956 while a Down Fast train stands in the main line platform. Gleneagles was one of only two stations between Stirling and Perth where local trains could be put into a loop platform to clear the main line for express trains, the other being Dunblane. The signalman's motor cycle stands against the end of the building, having been ridden down the path from the booking office and along the island platform. *GH Robins*

Plate 10.10
The two morning local goods trains shunting at Gleneagles in the late 1950s. The 'Perth bogies', as it was known locally, on the left was headed by ex-Caledonian Railway 0-6-0 No. 57252, a regular visitor to Gleneagles. The 'Stirling bogies' on the right was headed by another regular, ex-LM&SR '4F' 0-6-0 No. 44254. Apart from exchanging traffic at Gleneagles, the Stirling turn was responsible for making the daily trip up to the hotel before it returned to Stirling. *Author*

Plate 10.11
Ex-Caledonian Railway 0-6-0 No. 57232, another regular visitor to Gleneagles, is seen here shunting on a snowy morning in the late 1950s. The locomotive does not look in the best of condition and the cold air exaggerates the steam which appears to be escaping from many more places than just the safety valve. The entrance building and booking office is at the far end of the footbridge to the island platform from which this shot was taken. *Author*

closure of many stations. Local trains on these lines were withdrawn from 1956, resulting in the closure of stations such as Auchterarder, Dunning, Forteviot, Forgandenny and many more. The Gleneagles to Comrie line survived for the time being.

The following year, the railway author and photographer RD Steven described the Gleneagles to Crieff branch as '*a leisurely little line*' and commented that:

'Permission has not yet been granted to withdraw the passenger service between Gleneagles and Crieff. If this were to be done, it is intended to lift the branch beyond the hotel siding at Gleneagles. Freight traffic to Crieff would operate from Almond Valley Junction.'

Although his prediction was somewhat premature, it did indicate that the future of the branch line was under threat. He was correct in forecasting that in the event of passenger services being withdrawn, goods traffic from Crieff would be routed over the Methven Junction line to Almond Valley Junction, but in the event the hotel branch did not survive beyond closure of the line, being closed the same day.

Goods traffic from stations on the Methven Junction line, including Methven, the Royal Naval Stores Depot and Ruthvenfield Bleach Works, continued at moderate levels. Traffic was particularly heavy during the seed potato season when additional trains were run when required. A 1956 Instruction on the Distribution of Sheets, Ropes and Chains, warned stations against over-estimating requirements and understating stocks of these important assets, daily returns were required to be made to the 'Sheet Depot Station' by 10.30am. Helpfully, this reveals which stations were still sending out consignments of such traffic. Almondbank and Methven sent their returns to Perth, but stations required to send their returns to Crieff were:

– Abercairney (*sic*)
– Balgowan
– Madderty
– Highlandman
– Muthill
– Tullibardine
– Comrie

Gleneagles was not mentioned, but it is known that it too sent out considerable quantities of such traffic, for a feature article in the Scottish Region Magazine of January 1957 revealed that in 1955/56 1,000 tons of seed potatoes were sent to stations in the United Kingdom while a further 600 tons were exported to the continent. The article also mentions that 15,000 passengers were booked from Gleneagles that same year.

The Gleneagles to Comrie branch line was not alone in the struggle for survival in the mid-1950s, for throughout the British Railways network, receipts from many rural lines were declining sharply in an era of increasing car ownership. Faced with the dual problems of replacing ageing rolling stock and attempting to make such lines more viable, British Railways embarked on a programme of modernisation. The first Diesel Multiple Units (DMUs) were introduced in the early 1950s; although one of these was trialled on the Gleneagles–Comrie

Plate 10.12
Ex-Caledonian Railway 0-6-0 57396 draws into Muthill with an afternoon Up mixed train in the mid-1950s. This was probably the school train which was not advertised in the Public Time Tables but conveyed school children from Crieff to stations along the line. This view shows the Down platform before it was rebuilt and shortened.
WAC Smith/transporttreasury.co.uk

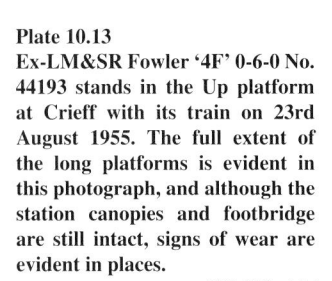

Plate 10.13
Ex-LM&SR Fowler '4F' 0-6-0 No. 44193 stands in the Up platform at Crieff with its train on 23rd August 1955. The full extent of the long platforms is evident in this photograph, and although the station canopies and footbridge are still intact, signs of wear are evident in places.
WAC Smith/ transporttreasury.co.uk

Plate 10.14
Ex-LM&SR '4F' 0-6-0 No. 44253 at Abercairny with the daily goods train from Crieff one day in the 1950s. Traffic that day was sparse, amounting to the solitary van seen here. At this stage Abercairny was still open for parcels and goods traffic, as the notice on the left indicates.
Photograph by Hugh Davies/ Photos from the Fifties

ABOVE: **Plate 10.15**
Ex-LM&SR Class '5' No. 44705 speeding across the viaduct over the River Earn as it approaches Highlandman with the 4.35pm Gleneagles to Crieff train on 10th May 1958. This view shows the upstream side of the viaduct with the protection which was added to the pier on the left to prevent damage to the column by ice. The build-up of debris would be removed periodically.
WAC Smith/transporttreasury.co.uk

BELOW: **Plate 10.16**
On the same day as Photo 10.15, the same locomotive pauses at Highlandman on a return journey to Gleneagles. The low platform and the cant of the track made boarding or alighting from conventional carriages tricky, as seen here, and portable box steps were provided for the convenience of passengers. Class '5's were too large for the turntable at Crieff so half the day was invariably spent running tender first.
WAC Smith/transporttreasury.co.uk

LEFT: Plate 10.17
Ex-L&NER 0-6-0 No. 64625 shunting in the exchange sidings at Almondbank. The overhead wires for Lumsden & MacKenzie's private electric locomotive are clearly visible. Originally there was just one loop line here, but more sidings were added when the Royal Naval Stores Depot was built.
WAC Smith/transporttreasury.co.uk

LEFT: Figure 10.5
A British Railways wagon label for a typical load of agricultural traffic shipped out from Strathearn's stations, in this case a consignment of potatoes from Comrie to Nottingham. This wagon was routed via Perth, Berwick and Doncaster to London Road station on the GN (Great Northern) section. This was to distinguish the destination from the former Midland, L&NWR and Great Central lines which also served the city.
Author's collection

ABOVE RIGHT: Figure 10.6
A British Railways wagon label for a typical load sent to one on the Strathearn stations, in this a case a load of fertilizer from the Boulby potash mine near Skinningrove, Middlesborough to Tullibardine. Originating from a former North Eastern Railway station it was routed over the East Coast Main Line via Berwick and the Forth Bridge. Sir James Denby Roberts was the then owner of Strathallan Estate, of which Hillpark Farm was a part.
Author's collection

line for a period, it was not gauged a success, possibly because the numbers of passengers did not justify a two-car unit. In 1957 it was decided to experiment with 4-wheeled diesel railbuses which had already found favour on the continent, particularly in Germany.

A total of twenty-two railbuses were ordered from no fewer than five different manufacturers. The first BR railbuses were built by AC Cars Ltd of Thames Ditton, and the Gleneagles to Comrie line was one of those chosen to spearhead this new venture.

The AC Cars railbuses were 37 feet long, weighed 11 tons, seated forty-eight passengers, all Second Class, and had a top speed of about 60 mph. They had a driving compartment at each end, and large windows which gave good all-round views and a light and modern feel to the passenger area. On each side they had an air-operated door and a set of extending steps for use where there was no station platform.

Although the Gleneagles to Comrie line was just one of a number of branch lines in Scotland selected for these new railbuses, it was the first to have one and the introduction of the new service was highly publicised. AC Cars railbus No. Sc79979 was the first to arrive in Scotland on 8th August 1958, even posing for an official photograph at the English/Scottish border (Plate 10.20).

The official launch of the new railbus was held at Gleneagles station ten days later on 19th August 1958, when Sir Ian Bolton Bt KBE, Chairman of the Scottish Area Board, and Scottish Region General Manager Mr James Ness, welcomed a selected audience to see the new vehicle. Guests included Sir George McGlashan, Convenor of the Perth & Kinross County Council together with the Provosts of Auchterarder and Crieff, business and press representatives, and, somewhat unusually, the Principal of St. Andrews University. Despite the damp weather, it was an upbeat occasion and guests were treated to a trial trip in the railbus along the main line to Blackford and back.

The railbus entered service on 15th September 1958 (Figure 10.7), with the first run being the 8.50am Gleneagles to Comrie service. The railbus was well filled with local folk eager to experience this new form of travel first hand, and again the press were in attendance. It still being the school holidays, the author also travelled on this inaugural trip as can be seen from Plates 10.24 and 10.25.

The initial service provided nine trains each way per day between Gleneagles and Crieff, but only three between Crieff and Comrie, with an additional train from Crieff on Saturdays. The early morning Mail train from Stirling, which called only at Gleneagles, Muthill

CHAPTER 10: BRITISH RAILWAYS AND THE STRUGGLE FOR SURVIVAL

Plate 10.18
A two-car diesel multiple unit (DMU) on an Up train at Muthill in the late 1950s. These DMUs were used on the Gleneagles to Comrie line for a short period of evaluation, but were not introduced on a permanent basis, the railbus introduced in 1958 probably being judged adequate for the level of traffic carried. By the date of this view the footbridge at Muthill had been removed.
WAC Smith/transporttreasury.co.uk

Plate 10.19
The two-car diesel multiple unit which ran for a trial period on the Gleneagles to Comrie line, sitting in the branch line platform at Gleneagles. The number of the rear unit, E74274, indicating that this DMU is on loan from the Eastern Region of British Railways for the duration of the trial period in Scotland. *BRB Residuary*

Plate 10.20
The first diesel railbus to enter Scotland, AC Cars No. 79979, seen here at the Scottish border. The driver and guard pose here with another member of staff. The line must have been closed while this shot was taken, as the steps are extended into the six foot and the photographer is standing on the Up main line. *Author's collection*

Plate 10.21
AC Cars No. 79979 standing in the branch line platform at Gleneagles on the day of the launch of the new diesel railbus service in September 1958. Apart from the official welcoming party for this preview day, the event attracted quite a number of onlookers and photographers, as can be seen here. *Author's collection*

LEFT: **Plate 10.22**
The day of the official launch was wet and miserable, as can be seen in this view of the railbus in the branch line platform at Gleneagles. It would appear that various guests are being shown round the vehicle as it stood at the platform. Note that the destination blinds have yet to be fitted and, despite the modern technology it represented, the railbus still had to carry a conventional oil tail lamp.
Author's collection

BELOW: **Plate 10.23**
A trial demonstration run from Gleneagles to Blackford afforded a rare view of the railbus out on the main line. The railbus was well filled for this short trip, including the various dignitaries mentioned elsewhere.
Author's collection

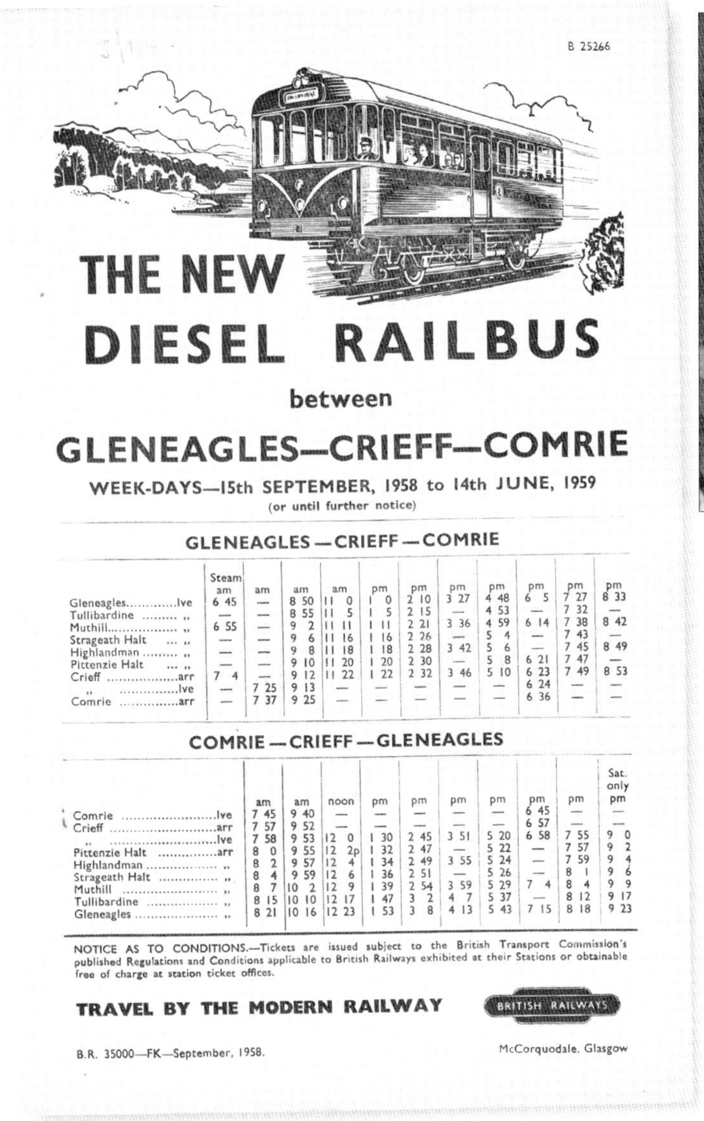

CHAPTER 10: BRITISH RAILWAYS AND THE STRUGGLE FOR SURVIVAL

ABOVE: Plate 10.24
A publicity photograph taken on 15th September 1958, the first day of public service of the new railbus. Guard Tommy Blair is seen here issuing tickets. The railbus was crowded that day with locals keen to experience this new form of transport, but, despite this, the author was able to secure one of the seats at the front next to the driving compartment.
Author's collection

LEFT: Figure 10.7
A British Railways handbill for the new diesel railbus service introduced between Gleneagles, Crieff and Comrie on 15th September 1958. The railbus depicted was an AC Cars vehicle, the type first introduced on this service, although Wickham and Park Royal railbuses were also used. The artwork for subsequent years used the same AC Cars image, although from 1959 onwards the title dropped the word 'new'. Handbills were printed different colours each year to differentiate from the previous years.
Author's collection

ABOVE RIGHT: Figure 10.8
A ticket from the first day of service of the new diesel railbus, issued on 15th September 1958. These Bell Punch type tickets were issued by the guard from a ticket machine similar to those used on buses at the time. This particular ticket was issued to the author for the return trip from Crieff to Gleneagles. Unfortunately, the marks are the result of it having been Sellotaped into a scrap book by an individual who should not be named. No names no pack drill!
Author's collection

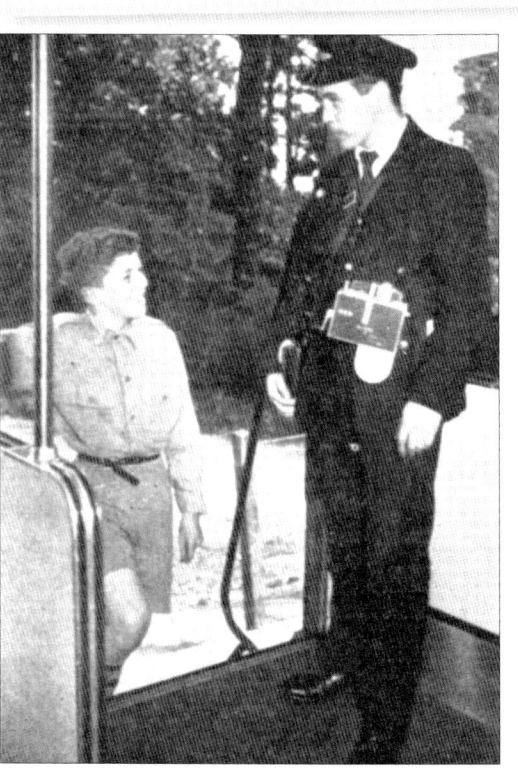

LEFT: Plate 10.25
The caption on this photograph when it appeared in the British Railways (Scottish Region) staff magazine was '*A young passenger joins the train at Strageath*', proving that the camera can indeed lie. The author, who was '*the young passenger*', had joined the railbus at Gleneagles, but in the absence of any real passengers at Strageath was asked to get off and then to pretend to board the railbus. Tommy Blair, never a great fan of railway enthusiasts, did his best to muster a smile for the camera. *Author's collection*

RIGHT: Plate 10.26
A genuine shot of a family joining the railbus at Pittenzie which appeared in the same article as Plate 10.25. Despite the extending steps, passengers still had to be fairly fit and agile to board or leave the railbus, and handling luggage and items such as this push chair was invariably a challenge. *Author's collection*

In goes the important member of the family at Pittenzie Crossing

Plate 10.27
Ex-LM&SR Class '5' No. 44724 on one of the all too frequent replacement steam services deputising for a failed railbus in the early 1960s. Crieff station was by now showing signs of neglect – large sections of the canopy had been dismantled as it was unsafe, and the Down platform had been shortened considerably by removing the platform edge, as can be seen in the foreground. *Author*

and Crieff, continued, however, to be steam hauled. Two new halts were opened at Strageath, between Muthill and Highlandman, and Pittenzie near Crieff. Both these were existing level crossings and facilities provided were somewhat spartan, amounting to no more than cement slabs to form a short platform accessible from the road, but no form of shelter whatsoever.

With the advent of the railbus, two of the intermediate stations, Tullibardine and Highlandman, became unstaffed halts, although railway families continued to occupy both station houses. In the case of Tullibardine, the porter there was transferred to Gleneagles, and at Highlandman, Mr Doig was one of the signalmen at Crieff, while his wife was the crossing keeper.

The railbus had a crew of two – a driver and a guard. In addition to his normal duties, the guard also operated the doors and steps and issued tickets. For stations along the line he issued tickets from a machine similar to those used by bus conductors, and for stations beyond Gleneagles he could issue written tickets.

The original AC Cars railbus was subsequently replaced by a Wickham railbus, and on occasions a Park Royal railbus was also used on the line. The experimental nature of these railbuses was reflected in the fact that they often broke down, and when they did, steam locomotives came to the rescue. On these occasions it was not unusual to see an ex-LM&SR Stanier Class '5' 4-6-0 or a BR Standard Class '5' 4-6-0 hauling a single coach on the replacement service.

Unfortunately these arrangements had several drawbacks. Foremost among these was the fact the timetable was designed for railbus operation where reversing direction at the end of a run was simply a matter of the driver walking to the cab at the other end, while the guard changed the tail lamp from one end to the other. With steam trains, the locomotive had to be uncoupled from the train, run round it in the loop line, reverse onto it, be recoupled and the brakes tested. Achieving all this within the 8-10 minutes allowed, which was ample for the railbus, required some nimble operation. However, if the train was late in leaving, time could usually be made up by these powerful locomotives with such light loads.

The other problem arose when passengers wanted to join or leave the train at Strageath or Pittenzie halts where there was no standard-height platform. The only solution was for the unfortunate passengers to use the emergency ladder from the guard's compartment (Plate 10.28), a hazardous and undignified operation and certainly not a good advertisement for the 'Modern Railway'.

The railbus was shedded at Crieff during the week, but travelled to Perth every Saturday for maintenance before returning to Crieff the following Monday morning. Shown in the Operating Instructions as Set 441, it left Perth Motive Power Depot on a Monday at 3.50am for Perth Up Yard. It then did not leave Perth until 5.50am, travelling along the main line to Gleneagles, arriving at Crieff loco shed at 6.40am. Having been prepared for the day's work, it left the shed at 7.10am, three minutes being allowed for the short journey to Crieff station, ready for the first trip of the day, the 7.25am to Comrie.

On Tuesdays to Saturdays, it simply left Crieff shed where it had been stabled overnight at the usual time of 7.10am. On Mondays to

CHAPTER 10: BRITISH RAILWAYS AND THE STRUGGLE FOR SURVIVAL

Plate 10.28
Replacement steam services, such as that shown at Plate 10.27, presented other problems. Here a member of staff is trying to work out how to provide some form of safe access to a steam-hauled carriage with a set of steps at Strageath Halt. A cyclist, delayed by the closed level crossing gates, takes an interest, while the intending passenger is no doubt offering free advice.
ADK Young

Fridays, the railbus worked the last train of the day which arrived at Crieff at 8.54pm and was back at Crieff loco shed at 9.00pm for the night. On Saturdays, the railbus made the extra trip from Crieff at 8.58pm, arriving at Gleneagles at 9.20pm. It then ran as Empty Coaching Stock (Emcar as it was termed for diesel units) back to Perth, arriving at the MPD at 9.45pm.

Special Operating Instructions were issued for these new railbuses. Because they could not be guaranteed to activate track circuits, special instructions were laid down for railbuses operating on main lines, particularly in areas controlled by colour light signalling. Additionally, whenever a driver left the railbus, he was required to stop the engine, remove the reversing lever, and put the brake hard on. The rules also prohibited any additional vehicles being attached to a railbus. Finally, if the bell communication between the guard and the driver failed, the guard's signal to start was to be two short blasts on his whistle given *inside* the vehicle, which must have been somewhat startling for the passengers!

While the 48-seat railbus was employed on all the timetabled passenger services other than the early morning mail train from Stirling, locomotive hauled trains were still seen on the line from time to time other than for the replacement services mentioned above. There was some excursion traffic, although nothing on the scale seen prior to closure of the Comrie to Balquhidder section in 1951. In the summer of 1953, for example, a special on 30th May conveyed visitors from St. Mungo Parish Church Sunday School in Alloa to Crieff for the afternoon. The visit to the capital of Strathearn was enjoyed by 250 adults and 450 children, Crieff station having to cope with the impressive influx of 700 passengers from a single train. The special travelled via Stirling to Gleneagles and allowed visitors just under four hours in Crieff:

Alloa	Dep	1.15pm
Gleneagles		1.58pm
Crieff	Arr	2.17pm

Crieff	Dep	6. 5pm
Gleneagles		6.27pm
Alloa	Arr	7. 6pm

About a fortnight later, on 16th June 1953, a much smaller excursion was made by a party from Morrison's Academy when three staff and sixty-three pupils went to Edinburgh for the day. On this

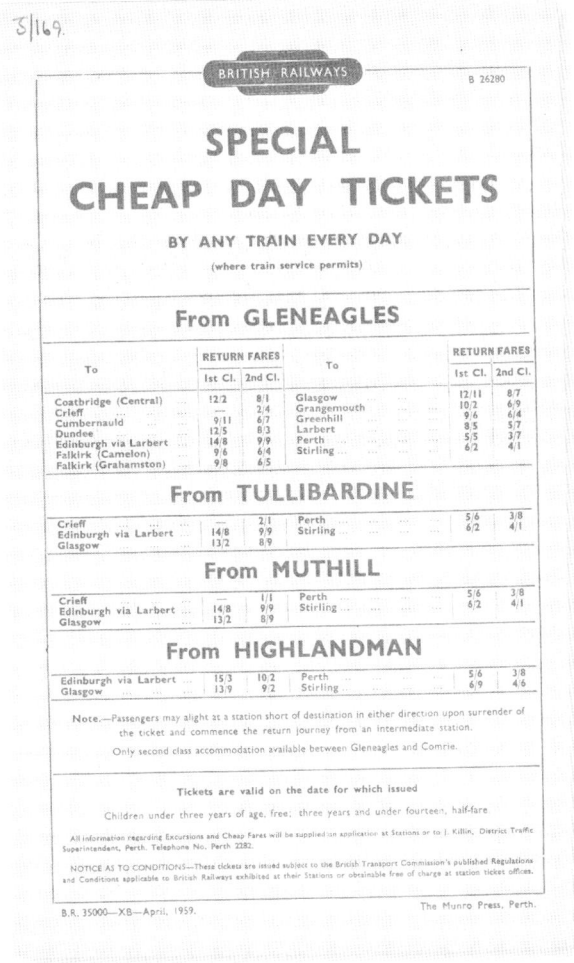

Figure 10.9
A handbill advertising special cheap day tickets from the surviving stations on the Gleneagles to Comrie line the year after the introduction of the railbus. The two new halts at Strageath and Pittenzie are not mentioned here, but note is made that only Second Class accommodation was available on the railbus. This is another example of a locally printed handbill, this one from the Munro Press in nearby Perth.
Author's collection

RIGHT: Figure 10.10
The combined Stephenson Locomotive Society and Railway Correspondence & Travel Society Scottish Railtour of June 1960 included the surviving Strathearn lines. This commemorative booklet was issued to participants after the event and included a narrative and a number of photographs. *Author's collection*

BELOW: Figure 10.11
Two tickets from the rail tours which ran over the surviving Strathearn branch lines during the final decade. The SLS tour was a round trip from Glasgow specifically to travel over the Crieff & Methven Junction line as indicated in the routing shown. The other ticket is for the 1960 rail tour illustrated at Figure 10.10. *Author's collection*

LEFT: Plate 10.29
Caledonian Railway 'Single' No. 123 entering Crieff on 11th October 1958 with an SLS special. The pilotman, distinguishable by his armband, is making the most of the occasion, while the passengers vie for a good view out of the windows. The signal at the extreme right is not a 'Splitting Distant' but carries the Pittenzie level crossing Up Distant for both the Methven Junction line on the left, and the Gleneagles line on the right. *C Lawson Kerr*

RIGHT: Plate 10.30
An interesting contrast of technologies is provided at Muthill by this view of CR No. 123 heading towards Gleneagles with a rail tour, and a Crieff-bound railbus in the other platform. The SLS special had travelled over the Methven Junction line to Crieff, where No. 123 was turned on the turntable before setting off for Gleneagles. As usual, camera-equipped enthusiasts are much in evidence.

WAC Smith/transporttreasury.co.uk

occasion, the 6.10am from Stirling which normally terminated at Crieff was extended through to Comrie in place of the first railbus trip of the day. The train then left Comrie at 7.45am and ran to the same timetable as the railbus would have done, leaving Crieff at 7.58am to arrive at Gleneagles at 8.21am. The railbus then followed as Empty Coaching Stock, to resume normal service as the 8.50am departure from Gleneagles. The 7.45am from Comrie was strengthened by a Brake Second Class coach to accommodate the Morrison's party.

Another feature of many rural lines in the late 1950s and early 1960s, particularly those threatened with closure, was the proliferation of steam hauled railtours for railway enthusiasts. Unsurprisingly, the Perth to Crieff and Gleneagles to Comrie lines featured in these programmes, and even the short branch to Methven was visited on occasions. Run by organisations such as the Stephenson Locomotive Society (SLS) or the Railway Correspondence & Travel Society (RCTS), these tours were usually run in the summer months when the weather and photographic conditions were more likely to be favourable. Line speeds were slow and frequent stops were made at stations, even closed ones, to allow for photography. Safety regulations were much more relaxed in those days, and it was not unusual, as can be seen from some of the photographs taken at the time, for passengers to wander all over the track, or to climb signals and other vantage points to get the photograph they wanted.

The first of these was an SLS tour in 1958 when the venerable Caledonian Railway 4-2-2 No. 123 hauled a short train consisting of a pair of equally venerable restored Caledonian Railway coaches. This train came by way of Almond Valley Junction to Crieff and from there to Gleneagles. Stops were made at Almondbank, Methven Junction, Madderty and Abercairny. The train then changed direction at Crieff, where No. 123 was turned on the turntable and carried on to Gleneagles, stopping only at Muthill where it crossed with a Down railbus service.

In 1960, a more ambitious railtour traversed a number of lines in Scotland over the week 12-17th June, visiting the Strathearn lines on the 15th June. This was a larger excursion of five coaches, again including the two restored Caledonian Railway vehicles, but this time hauled by ex-Caledonian Railway Pickersgill 4-4-0 No. 54485, a Perth engine and a familiar visitor to the lines in earlier years. Again, the train ran from Perth to Crieff via Almond Valley Junction, but this time a visit was made to Methven, where 54485 ran around the train and hauled it tender first back down to Methven Junction, before resuming the journey to Crieff. This train also ran on to Comrie, where again 54485 ran round the train to return to Crieff before setting off for Gleneagles, running tender first all the way. Here the railtour returned via the main line to Perth for an overnight stay before setting off the following day for a tour to Montrose and the Inverbervie branch

Although such railtours passed over the Perth to Crieff line, this was no longer maintained to the standard required for regular passenger services, being used only by goods traffic. The Gleneagles to Comrie section, on the other hand, continued to be inspected and maintained on a regular basis to passenger traffic standards. The two remaining tunnels were both on the Crieff to Comrie section, and they required a specialist inspection train, one of which travelled

ABOVE: Plate 10.31
Ex-Caledonian Railway Pickersgill 4-4-0 54485 on an SLS rail tour at Abercairny in 1960. The first two carriages of the train are the two restored Caledonian Railway vehicles which were often used with the famous Caledonian Railway 'Single' No. 123. Abercairny goods yard is looking abandoned and overgrown, but the vegetable garden and hen-run in the foreground appear to be thriving.
GE Smith

RIGHT: Plate 10.32
Preserved ex-North British Railway 4-4-0 No. 256 *Glen Douglas* heads an SLS special through Madderty in 1962. Although the signal box is extant, signals have been dispensed with and the special is running wrong road through the station which was no longer a passing place.
Author's collection

LEFT: Plate 10.33
Houses platoon of the Edinburgh Academy CCF about to entrain at Waverley station for Comrie to attend the annual camp at Cultybraggan. The special troop train was composed of a mix of rolling stock including the ex-L&NER teak-bodied vehicle on the right. The author is standing second from the right in the centre rank. *Author's collection*

BELOW: Figure 10.12
An extract from the British Railway Weekly Traffic Notice for the last week of July 1960, showing details of some of the troop trains taking ACF and CCF cadets to their annual camp at Cultybraggan near Comrie. The author was one of 200 cadets from the Edinburgh Academy which were part of the load of Train No. 631. *Author's collection*

over the line in 1959. The make-up of the train was task specific, with the central scaffold wagon having a gantry which allowed close inspection of the tunnel walls and roof:

– Saloon 45036
– Mess van
– Low wagon
– Scaffold wagon
– Low wagon
– 'Lowmac' wagon
– Brake van

Starting from Perth at 8.0am, the train arrived at Crieff at 10.0am. Setting off at 10.15am, 15 minutes were allowed for the inspection of the short tunnel at Burrell Street, and a further 25 minutes for the longer Strowan tunnel. Having arrived at Comrie at 11.30am, the train then returned to Crieff at normal speed. Here, however, the brake van and wagons were detached, the Inspection Saloon alone being taken back to Perth via Gleneagles. The remainder of the train left at Crieff was then worked back to Perth by the afternoon goods train.

Some specials did not actually traverse the branch line, but served only Gleneagles bringing visitors to events such as the Dunlop Masters Golf Tournament held at Gleneagles Hotel from 5th to 7th May 1960. On that occasion special fares were available from Aberdeen and Stonehaven, the visitors travelling by two of the most prestigious Aberdeen to Glasgow expresses – 'The Bon Accord' and 'The Saint Mungo'. The first of these left Aberdeen at 6.20am and called at Gleneagles at 9.5am, while the latter left Aberdeen at the more civilised hour of 9.30am to reach Gleneagles at 12.13pm. Visitors could return by the 6.13pm or 6.37pm timetabled departures, or a special leaving Gleneagles at 8.35pm arriving at Stonehaven at 10.32pm and Aberdeen at 10.55pm.

The summer seasons also saw a regular series of troop trains taking TA units and ACF and CCF cadets to training camps at Cultybraggan. These trains from all parts of the country ran up to Comrie where the soldiers or cadets, in military parlance, 'detrained' for the short journey to Cultybraggan, usually by army lorry.

The author had first-hand experience of this two years running in 1959 and 1960 as a member of the Edinburgh Academy CCF. On 26th July 1960 he was part of the contingent from the school which marched in FSMO (Full Service Marching Order) behind the Pipes & Drums from Henderson Row up the hill to George Street and then along Princes Street to Waverley station (Plate 10.33). Here they were joined by Fettes and Merchiston Castle CCFs to board the twelve-coach train which took them via Polmont, Falkirk and Larbert to Gleneagles, and thence up the branch line to Comrie, where they arrived at 12.35pm (Figure 10.12). Having 'detrained', the bulk of

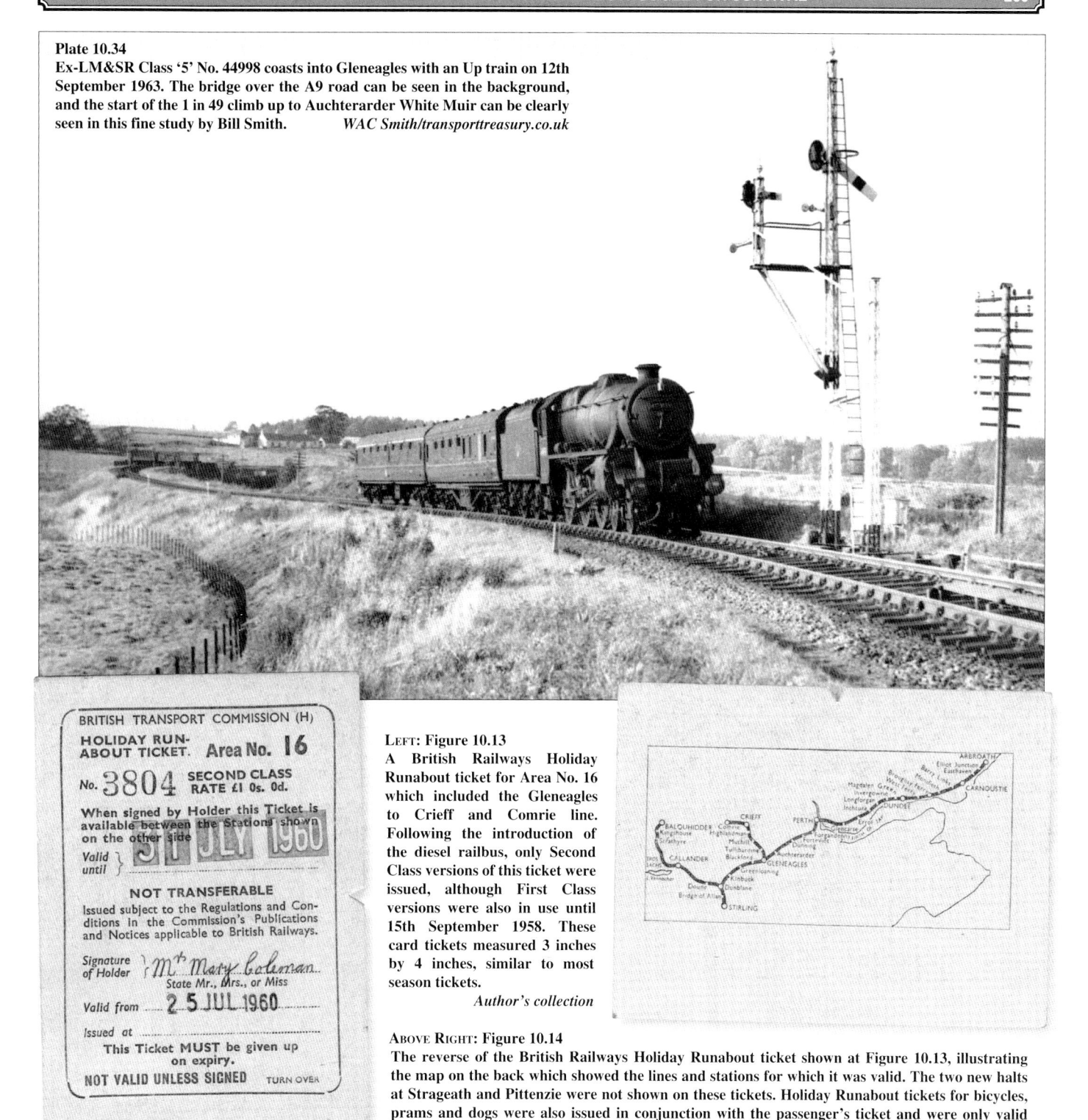

Plate 10.34
Ex-LM&SR Class '5' No. 44998 coasts into Gleneagles with an Up train on 12th September 1963. The bridge over the A9 road can be seen in the background, and the start of the 1 in 49 climb up to Auchterarder White Muir can be clearly seen in this fine study by Bill Smith. *WAC Smith/transporttreasury.co.uk*

LEFT: **Figure 10.13**
A British Railways Holiday Runabout ticket for Area No. 16 which included the Gleneagles to Crieff and Comrie line. Following the introduction of the diesel railbus, only Second Class versions of this ticket were issued, although First Class versions were also in use until 15th September 1958. These card tickets measured 3 inches by 4 inches, similar to most season tickets.
Author's collection

ABOVE RIGHT: **Figure 10.14**
The reverse of the British Railways Holiday Runabout ticket shown at Figure 10.13, illustrating the map on the back which showed the lines and stations for which it was valid. The two new halts at Strageath and Pittenzie were not shown on these tickets. Holiday Runabout tickets for bicycles, prams and dogs were also issued in conjunction with the passenger's ticket and were only valid with it.
Author's collection

the cadets then boarded trucks to take them to Cultybraggan – all, that is, save the Edinburgh Academy CCF. It was decided that they would have the honour of marching behind the Pipes & Drums all the way out to Cultybraggan.

Thankfully, trucks were provided for the return trips on 3rd August when the same contingents returned whence they had come. The London train (No. 600) conveyed twenty-two officers and 450 cadets to St. Pancras in a twelve-coach train. The Edinburgh train (No. 603) had nine officers and 420 cadets in a ten-coach train. Fortunately, the author, being an Auchterarder lad, managed to persuade the military authorities to let him get off at Gleneagles rather than have to go all the way to Edinburgh and back again. The locomotives and rolling stock for both these trains came from Stirling as shown:

		Troop Train No.	
		600	603
Stirling	Dep (ECS)	5.20am	6.45am
Comrie	Arr (ECS)	6.35am	8.15am
Comrie	Dep	7. 5am	8.55am
Gleneagles		7.37am	9.33am
Edinburgh	Arr	------	10.58am

Meanwhile, the railbus service continued to be problematical, with both the Wickham and later the Park Royal railbuses suffering from mechanical problems from time to time. This resulted in the substitute steam operated service being hauled by a variety of locomotives depending on what was available, no doubt to the delight of local railway enthusiasts, if not the passengers. This included both ex-LM&SR Stanier and BR Standard Class '5' 4-6-0 locomotives, BR Standard 2-6-4Ts and ex-L&NER Class 'B1' 4-6-0s – on one occasion *Strang Steel* was spotted. Although most were Perth engines, with 44978, 44979, 44998 and 73008 being noted, a number were from Corkerhill shed in Glasgow, including 44699, 44764 and 73107.

Goods traffic over the Perth to Crieff line continued to be worked by Perth 'Trip' P.17, with an ex-Midland Railway '4F' 0-6-0 rostered, usually 44251 or 44253. The timetable for this train was fairly complex, and varied significantly between the seed potato season and the rest of the year, as shown in Figure 10.16. In later years, the '4F' allocation was replaced by a Class '5' locomotive, while the trip to the Royal Naval Stores Depot at Almondbank was worked by a diesel shunter from Perth North yard.

Goods traffic for the Gleneagles Hotel, however, continued to be worked be a Stirling turn, No. N396, which was allocated one of the smaller '2F' locomotives, usually an ex-Caledonian Railway 0-6-0.

```
           P.22.
       Class 4F Engine.
   DURING SEED POTATO SEASON
     12. 5pm. to 8. 5pm. SX.
     9.40am. to 5.40pm. SO.

        Perth Guard
     12.40pm. to 8.40pm. SX.
     10.10am. to 6.10pm. SO.

                   S.X.    S.X.
                   Arr.    Dep.    Class
                   p.m.    p.m.
    Perth E.S.      ..    12.50    LE.
    Perth North    1.00    1.15    K.
    Methven        2.10    2.40    K.
    Perth North    3.45     ..

     Works to Control Instructions.

    Perth E.S.     7.50     ..

    Works Stations and Sidings between
          Perth and Methven.

                   S.O.    S.O.
                   Arr.    Dep.    Class
                   a.m.    a.m.
    Perth E.S.      ..    10.25    LE.
    Perth North   10.35   10.45    K.
    Bankfoot      11.35   11.55    K.

                   p.m.    p.m.
    Perth North   12.45    1.15    K.
    Methven        2.10    2.40    K.
    Perth North    3.45     ..

     Works to Control Instructions.

    Perth E.S.     5.25

  Works Stations between Perth and
  Bankfoot and Stations and Sidings
     between Perth and Methven.
```

```
            P.17.
      Class 4F Engine (0-6-0)
         Engine Prepared.
       4.40am. to 1.20pm.
       2.35pm. to 10.35pm.

          Perth Guard.
       4.45am. to 1. 5pm.
       2.15pm. to 10.15pm.

                   Arr.    Dep.    Class
                   a.m.    a.m.
    Perth E.S.      ..     4.35    LE.
    Perth North    4.45    5.00    K.
    Crieff         7.20    8.00
    Comrie         8.17     ..

  Returns Comrie to Crieff immediately
  after necessary work has been performed
  but not later than 8.50am. Work as
  required at Crieff and trip to
  Gleneagles Branch as required.

    Crieff          ..    10.00    K.

                   p.m.    p.m.
    Perth South   12.35   12.40    LE.
    Perth E.S.    12.45    2.45    LE.
    Perth South    2.47    2.50    KBV.
    Gleneagles     3.15    3.16    E&V.
    Crieff         3.34     ..

        Work as required.

    Crieff          ..     5.11    C.Pcls.
    Gleneagles     5.26    5.45    C.Pcls.
    Crieff         6.00     ..

   DURING SEED POTATO SEASON
    Crieff          ..     6.45    K.
        via Methven Jct.
    Perth So.     10. 5   10.15
    Perth E.S.    10.20    ..

   OUTWITH SEED POTATO SEASON
    Crieff          ..     6.30    H.
    Gleneagles     6.54    7.00    H.
    Perth South    7.32    ..

        Work as required.

    Perth E.S.     9.45     ..

  Works stations between Perth and
            Crieff.

   DURING SEED POTATO SEASON
  5.45pm. 'C' Parcels, Gleneagles
  to Crieff, to uplift Potato
  Traffic at Muthill and
  Highlandman for working to Perth
  by 6.45pm. 'K' ex Crieff.
```

```
            P.17.
       Class 5MT Engine
        Engine Prepared
   Outwith Seed Potato Season

  Locomen :   8.40am to 4.40pm
  Guard :     8.45am to 4.45pm

                  MWFO    MWFO
                  Arr.    Dep.    Class
                  a.m.    a.m.
    Perth E.S.     ..     8.55    L.E.
    Perth Yard    9. 5    9.15    9

   Works stations to Crieff as
            required.
    Crieff       11.15
                          p.m.
         "                1.45    9

    Works stations en route
         as required.
                  p.m.    p.m.
    Almondbank     ..     3.45    9
    Perth Yard    4.10    4.20    L.E.
    Perth E.S.    4.30

                  T.TH.O  T.TH.O
                  Arr.    Dep.    Class
                          a.m.
    Perth E.S.     ..     8.55

   Works to Control instructions
             until
                          p.m.
    Perth Yard            2.30    9
                  p.m.
    Almondbank    2.55    3.45    9
    Perth Yard    4.10    4.20    L.E.
    Perth E.S.    4.30     ..

    During Seed Potato Season
         Engine Prepared

  Locomen :   8.40am to 4.40pm SX
  Guard :     8.45am to 4.45pm SX

                  S.X.    S.X.
                  Arr.    Dep.    Class
                  a.m.    a.m.
    Perth E.S.     ..     8.55    L.E.
    Perth Yard    9. 5    9.15    9
                          p.m.
    Crieff       11.15    1.45    9
                  p.m.
    Perth Yard    4.10    4.20    L.E.
    Perth E.S.    4.30

  Works stations Perth to Crieff as require

  Uplifts traffic from R.N. Stores,
   Almondbank at 3.45pm SX.
```

ABOVE LEFT: Figure 10.15
An extract from the 1961 instructions, showing Trip P.22 which worked both the stations out as far as Methven and the short Bankfoot branch. The trip to Methven included Ruthven Road, Lumsden & MacKenzie and the Royal Naval Stores Depot at Almondbank, and any traffic for Methven Junction. Allocated a '4F' 0-6-0, this trip was a shorter day than Trip P.17, requiring only a single shift. *Author's collection*

ABOVE CENTRE: Figure 10.16
A similar extract from the Train Trip and Shunting Engine Notice for Perth District in January 1961. This shows Trip P.17 which worked the goods traffic on the remaining Strathearn branch lines except stations between Perth and Methven on the branch line. It was a long day with the Class '4F' 0-6-0 coming off shed at 4.35am, and not returning to Perth shed until 10.35pm. As a result, two crews were rostered for this duty. *Author's collection*

ABOVE RIGHT: Figure 10.17
The Train Trip notice for Trip P.17 in January 1965, following complete closure of the Gleneagles to Crieff and Crieff to Comrie lines. This shows that the workings both during and outwith the important seed potato season were markedly different. The locomotive allocation was now a Class '5MT' which would have been more than adequate for the task. Note that this trip also picked up traffic from the Royal Naval Stores Depot at Almondbank. *Author's collection*

Leaving Stirling at 6.20am, this train, known locally as the 'Stirling bogies', worked all the intermediate stations to arrive at Gleneagles at 8.5am. Here it met with a similar train from Perth – the 'Perth bogies' which had worked all the intermediate stations from there to Gleneagles. The Stirling locomotive then worked the traffic up to the hotel when required, which was almost daily, Mondays to Saturdays, and did not set off from Gleneagles until 11.25am, finally arriving back at Stirling at 1.29pm. Outwith the seed potato season, this train also worked traffic to Auchterarder on Tuesdays, Thursdays and Saturdays, but during the season on Saturdays only.

In the early 1960s, the future of the Gleneagles to Comrie service was once again under threat, and along with scores of other lines, it was examined as part of the study into the 'Reshaping of British Railways' carried out on behalf of the government by Dr Beeching. The publication of this report in the spring of 1963 caused a furore nation-wide, recommending as it did, the whole-scale closure of hundreds of miles of railway and thousands of stations.

Unsurprisingly, the Gleneagles to Comrie service was one of these, but to make matters worse, it was singled out as a classic example of an unremunerative branch line, with details quoted in full at page 97 of the report:

Gleneagles – Crieff – Comrie

This is a rural service of ten trains a day in each direction. There is an element of summer holiday traffic. The service is operated by a diesel rail bus on weekdays only over a distance of 15 miles. Connections are made at Gleneagles with mainline trains to and from Glasgow and Edinburgh. The stations served are:

Gleneagles	*Highlandman*
Tullibardine	*Pittenzie Halt*
Muthill	*Crieff*
Strageath Halt	*Comrie*

All stations except Gleneagles would be closed to passengers.

Some 340,000 passenger miles accrue to this service which accounts for 65,000 train miles per year. On average there are 5 passengers on a train at any one time. Earnings are £1,900 and these represent little more than a quarter of train movement expenses of £7,500. Station terminal expenses bring the total of direct expenses to nearly £11,000, less than a fifth of which is covered by the earnings of the service. When track & signalling expenses are added – £8,200 – the total expenses are ten time the earnings of the service.

Passengers using this service in combination with other services contribute £12,000 to the earnings of other rail services, and it is estimated that withdrawal of the service would result in a loss of £9,000 of this contributory revenue. Because there would be no alternative rail service on this line after withdrawal, none of the earnings of this service would be retained.

Despite the estimated contributory loss, which is probably high, bearing in mind that holiday makers may travel elsewhere, the overall net financial improvement expected from the withdrawal is nearly £8,400, or more than two-fifths of the present level of total direct expenses attributable to the service.

Region	*Scottish*
Service	*Gleneagles – Crieff – Comrie*
Traction	*Diesel rail bus*
Type of service	*Holiday/rural*
Route miles	*15*
Train miles	*65,100*
Earnings total	*£1,900*
Expected to be lost	*£1,900*
Gross contributory revenue	*£12,280*
Expected to be lost	*£9,000*
Expected loss in total gross revenue	*£10,900*
Movement expenses	*£7,500*
Expenses per train mile	*2s 4d*
Net effect on Movement expenses	*-£3,400*
Terminal expenses	*£3,480*
Total Movement & Terminal expenses	*£10,980*
Net effect Total Movement	*+£80*
Direct Track & Signalling expenditure	*£8,280*
Net effect on total Direct expenditure	*+£8,360*

There was some debate about the veracity of these figures, for example that traffic samples had been taken on days when there was only light traffic, fuelled by the usual scepticism that statistics can

Plate 10.35
BR Standard 2-6-4T No. 80063 takes water at the column at Gleneagles. The antiquated brazier with a stovepipe chimney on the right was lit in frosty weather to prevent the water supply from freezing.
Author's collection

be manipulated to mean whatever you want. That said, in the case of the Gleneagles to Comrie line, the magnitude of the losses were such that any errors or bias would have been unlikely to change the final outcome. The formal proposals to withdraw passengers services were published in the press (Figure 10.18), and the dreaded posters appeared at stations along the line.

As was the case with nearly all these proposals, numerous objections were raised and a meeting of the Transport Users Consultative Committee (TUCC) was duly held in Crieff. Even then there were complaints that the meeting, held in the Masonic Hall at 2pm on Tuesday 26th November 1963, had been poorly advertised and timed such that few people would be able to attend. The Crieff Merchants and Hotel Keepers Association and others lodged objections and representatives of the Scottish Railway Development Committee were in attendance to assist and advise.

All this was to no avail, and on 23rd May 1964 the formal notice of closure appeared in the press, announcing that passenger services would be withdrawn with effect from Monday 6th July 1964, which as there was no Sunday service, meant that the last train would run on Saturday 4th July.

The impending closure of the line attracted a good deal of publicity, both locally and among railway enthusiasts nationally, such that the last train to leave Comrie on the last day, the 6.45pm to Gleneagles, was specially strengthened. In place of the usual railbus, Stirling based BR Standard Class '4' 2-6-4T No. 80063 was provided to head a four-coach train. Crowded with locals and enthusiasts, this train heralded the end of the Crieff & Comrie Railway which had eventually opened with such enthusiasm and excitement almost seventy-one years earlier, on 1st June 1893. The 4th July 1964 evoked almost the opposite sentiments, although there was no public display of sadness such as the wreaths and placards which adorned many such last trains.

This was not, however, the last train. That honour fell to the 8.58pm (Saturdays Only) railbus service from Crieff to Gleneagles. On Saturdays this was the extra train run such that the railbus finished its week's work at Gleneagles from whence it could return to Perth for its weekly maintenance. On 4th July 1964, this would be a one-way trip made for the last time.

Deservedly, this sad occasion attracted considerable local interest, and a sizable crowd gathered on the Up platform to see the railbus off. Proceedings were enlivened by a local group, 'Archie Fisher and the Kullions', who gave the 8.58pm departure a rousing send off. The police were present as a precaution, but the crowd were good natured and well behaved, and their services were not required. The closure of the line and the last train made the front page of the *Strathearn Herald* for one last time in an article written by the author under the headline '*Crieff is off the railway map*'.

This, however, was not the end of the story, for the granting of permission to withdraw passenger services had been granted conditionally on the provision of an adequate alternative bus service. This was introduced by W. Alexander & Sons from the following Monday, 6th July 1964 (Figure 10.21). This service, however, was a poor substitute for the rail service it replaced, taking 35 minutes for the journey from Crieff to Gleneagles, 12 minutes longer than the railbus, and on a par with the Crieff Junction Railway of over 100 years earlier. The service attempted to replicate the route of the railbus, so went via Muthill and Tullibardine stations, both now deserted outposts in the middle of nowhere. Not surprisingly,

Figure 10.18
The formal notice placed in a number of local newspapers by British Railways at the end of June 1963 announcing their intention to withdraw passenger services between Gleneagles and Comrie as and from 9th September that year subject to the statutory consultation process. The notice included details of existing bus services which were deemed to provide an adequate alternative to the railway services to be withdrawn. Objectors were given six weeks in which to lodge objections. *Author's collection*

Figure 10.19
Once the Transport Users Consultative Committee had considered any objections to the proposal at Figure 10.18 and an additional alternative bus service had been agreed, the Minister of Transport approved the proposed closure. The British Railways Board published this formal notification in the local newspapers. It was in effect the 'Obituary Notice' for the Gleneagles to Comrie line. *Author's collection*

British Railways Board
WITHDRAWAL OF RAILWAY PASSENGER SERVICES

Reproduced below is a letter from the Ministry of Transport intimating the Minister's consent to the discontinuance of all railway passenger services between Gleneagles, Crieff and Comrie involving the discontinuance of all railway passenger services from the following stations:—

TULLIBARDINE, MUTHILL, STRAGEATH HALT, HIGHLANDMAN, PITTENZIE HALT, CRIEFF, COMRIE

Reference: RB. 3/7/018.

Ministry of Transport,
London, 25th May, 1964.

Sir,—I am directed by the Minister of Transport to refer to the report of the Transport Users Consultative Committee for Scotland upon objections and representations relating to the proposal to discontinue all railway passenger services between Gleneagles, Crieff and Comrie in the County of Perthshire involving the discontinuance of all railway passenger services from the stations at Tullibardine, Muthill, Highlandman, Crieff and Comrie and the halts at Strageath and Pittenzie. This proposed discontinuance is referred to in this letter as "the closure."

2. The Minister has considered the report of the Consultative Committee and all other relevant factors. He accepts the view of the Committee that, having regard to the bus services at present being provided, no case of hardship would arise from closure of the service between Crieff and Comrie. He also accepts their view that, having regard to the bus services at present being provided and subject to the provision of certain additional bus services, no real hardship would arise from closure of the service between Gleneagles and Crieff. He has therefore decided to give his consent to the closure subject to the conditions mentioned below which, inter alia, require the provision of additional bus services.

3. Accordingly the Minister, in exercise of his powers under section 56 of the Transport Act 1962, hereby gives his consent to the closure subject to the following conditions:—
   (i) The closure shall not take place unless and until the provision of the additional bus services set out in Part 2 of the Annex to this letter (hereinafter referred to as "the additional bus services") has been authorised by road service licences granted under the Road Traffic Acts 1960-62 and until all necessary arrangements have been made to ensure that these services are available to the public immediately upon the closure taking place.
   (ii) Whenever the Board become aware:—
      (a) of any proposal for an alteration of any of the bus services at present being provided which are set out in Part 1 of the Annex hereto (whether they are being provided by the persons named in Part 1 or by any other person) or of the additional bus services set out in Part 2 of the Annex by withdrawing or substantially reducing the frequency of any such service, or
      (b) of any such alteration having been made,
      the Board shall forthwith notify the Minister of any such proposal or alteration and give him all such information with respect thereto as he may reasonably require.
   (iii) The Board shall take reasonable steps to keep themselves informed of any such proposal or alteration as is mentioned in the last foregoing condition.
   (iv) The foregoing conditions shall have effect until the Minister notifies the Board that they are no longer to apply or until they are varied under section 56(11) of the Transport Act 1962.

4. I am directed by the Minister to make it clear that in imposing the conditions contained in paragraph 3 of this letter the Minister has been concerned only to discharge his functions under section 56 of the Transport Act 1962, and that these conditions have been framed in the light of the information before him for that purpose. In particular it should be clearly appreciated that the additional bus services can only be provided and the existing bus services maintained in so far as their provision and maintenance is authorised by road service licences issued by the Traffic Commissioners under the Road Traffic Acts and that nothing in this letter affects the powers and duties of the Traffic Commissioners under those Acts in relation to the provision and maintenance of any of these services. Furthermore in the event of any appeal to the Minister from any decision of the Traffic Commissioners the Minister will deal with that appeal in accordance with the provisions of the Road Traffic Acts and in the light of the information properly before him on the appeal. Should the additional services eventually authorised by road service licences differ from those services required by the conditions contained in paragraph 3 of this letter, those conditions would be open to reconsideration and variation by the Minister.

The Secretary,
British Railways Board,
222 Marylebone Road,
London, N.W.1.

I am, Sir,
Your obedient Servant,
J. H. H. BAXTER.

ANNEX
PART 1
Existing bus services provided under road service licences granted under the Road Traffic Acts 1960-62.
SERVICES PROVIDED BY W. ALEXANDER & SONS (MIDLAND) LTD.

Route No. 45A	Crieff, Comrie, St. Fillans and Callander.
Route No. 47	Crieff—Perth, via Kinkell Bridge (Saturday only).
Route No. 46	Crieff—Perth, via Auchterarder and Dunning.
Route No. 51	Dunfermline—Crieff, via Rumbling Bridge and Auchterarder.
Route No. 20A	Glasgow—Crieff, via Muirhead, Cumbernauld, Denny and Stirling.
Route No. 322	Edinburgh—Crieff, via Linlithgow, Falkirk and Stirling.

PART 2
ADDITIONAL BUS SERVICES.
A bus service between Gleneagles station and Crieff of at least six journeys each way Monday to Friday and winter Saturdays, and of at least nine journeys each way daily on summer Saturdays to provide reasonable connections with the main-line trains.

IN ACCORDANCE WITH THE ABOVE DECISION BRITISH RAILWAYS (SCOTTISH REGION) ANNOUNCE THAT THE CLOSURE WILL TAKE EFFECT AS FROM MONDAY, 6th JULY, 1964

Figure 10.20
A copy of the British Railways Board poster announcing the withdrawal of passenger services between Gleneagles and Comrie with effect from Monday 6th July 1964, and the closure of the stations involved. These posters were exhibited at all the stations along the line and elsewhere locally. Similar posters could be seen up and down the country during the mid-1960s as many lines and stations were closed in the wake of the Beeching Report.   *J Paton collection*

Above: Plate 10.36
The last train from Comrie on 4th July 1964. In anticipation of the numbers who would want to travel on the last train, BR Standard 2-6-4T 80063 and a rake of four coaches were provided in place of the usual railbus for this service. The Up platform at Comrie had been out of use for many years, as is evident here, but offered a good viewpoint for Bill Smith who recorded this sad occasion.
WAC Smith/transporttreasury.co.uk

Left: Plate 10.37
The last train from Crieff, the 7.55pm on 4th July 1964 stands ready to leave. A large crowd of well-wishers turned up to see the last rain away, with added musical accompaniment. Even in 1964, the original Caledonian Railway enamel signs adorned the station. *Author's collection*

Plate 10.38
The railbus departs from Crieff for the final time as the 7.55pm sets off for Gleneagles on 4th July 1964. The crowd watch as it disappears under Duchlage Road bridge, no doubt with mixed emotions, as the station staff turn to the task of shutting up the station for one last time. One hundred and eight years of railway history had come to an end. *Author's collection*

the service was not well patronised, and a little over three years later, Alexander's applied for and were granted a variation which effectively meant the end of the route. As was the case in a number of areas, the much vaunted replacement bus service amounted to not much more than a means by which the closure of lines could be pushed through.

The Scottish Railway Preservation Society (SRPS) did at one time express an interest in acquiring part of the line, and there were hopes that it could be rescued, but in the event these discussions came to nought. The SRPS eventually established their base at Falkirk, subsequently moving to Bo'ness.

As predicted by RD Steven some years earlier, once passenger services were withdrawn, the surviving goods service would utilise the Perth to Crieff route. The goods service between Crieff and Comrie had already ceased on 15th June 1964, and barely two months after passenger services were withdrawn, goods services between Gleneagles and Muthill were also withdrawn. Two months later, the remaining goods service between Muthill and Crieff was withdrawn, and on the same day Gleneagles station was closed to goods traffic. Abercairny, which had only handled full wagon loads since 1st April 1959, closed entirely on 7th September 1964. The remaining intermediate stations lasted only a few more months, and, on 25th January 1965, Almondbank, Madderty and Methven closed to goods traffic.

In the meantime, demolition of the line proceeded rapidly. On a wet morning on 14th September, an Engineer's train was propelled along the branch line from Gleneagles to a point just north of Machany cutting not far from Muthill (Plate 10.39). Significantly, this stretch of track was laid on concrete sleepers and was far from life expired, so was recovered in 60-foot panels for re-use elsewhere.

The first break in the rails was made at 10.20am, and thereafter work proceeded rapidly, each panel being lifted bodily by a machine which ran on special temporary rails laid in the cess, and loaded onto bogie wagons.

The track was lifted in this fashion, working back towards Gleneagles, to a point just north of the junction with the hotel branch line. This was not done to allow goods traffic to continue to run up to the hotel, for the last goods wagons had been recovered on 4th

Figure 10.21
The W Alexander & Sons (Midland) Ltd timetable booklet for the new bus service to be introduced from 6th July 1964. This service was one of the measures which stemmed from the many objections raised the previous summer to the original notice shown in Figure 10.18. The service, which took a circuitous route to call at the now abandoned stations at Muthill and Highlandman, was never well patronised and was itself withdrawn a few years later. *Author's collection*

```
                P17
        Class 4 MT Engine
              Engine Prepared
        Outwith Seed Potato Season

        Locomen              08 40 to 16 40 MWFO
                             08 25 to 16 40 TTHO
        Guard                08 45 to 16 45 MWFO
                             08 30 to 16 30 TTHO

                             MWFO     MWFOClass
                             arr      dep
        Perth ES              -       08 55LE
        Perth Yard           09 05    09 15    9

        Works stations to Crieff as required.
        Crieff               11 15
           "                          13 45    9

        Works stations en route as required.
        Almondbank                    15 45    9
        Perth Yard           16 10    16 20 LE
        Perth ES             16 30
                             TTHO     TTHO
                             arr      dep
        Perth ES                      08 40 LE
        Perth Yard           08 50    09 00
        Forteviot            09 25    09 40
        Auchterarder         10 05    10 25
        Blackford            10 50    11 20
        Perth Yard           12 15    12 30
        Burrelton            13 00    13 10
        Coupar Angus         13 18    13 33
        Perth Yard           14 20    14 40
        Almondbank           15 05    15 45
        Perth Yard           16 10    16 20 LE
        Perth ES             16 30
              During Seed Potato Season
                 Engine Prepared
        Locomen              08 40 to 16 40 SX
        Guard                08 45 to 16 45 SX
                             SX       SX
                             arr      dep
        Perth ES                      08 55 LE
        Perth Yard           09 05    09 15
        Crieff               11 15    13 45
        Perth Yard           16 10    16 20LE
        Perth E S            16 30
```

Figure 10.22
The final arrangement of Trip P.17 in June 1966. By now the level of traffic to be worked on the surviving Perth to Crieff line had reduced to such an extent that the duties for this trip were now combined with trips to Blackford and to Coupar Angus. The locomotive power allocation was once again a Class '4'. *Author's collection*

ABOVE: Plate 10.39
The beginning of the end of the Crieff Junction Railway. On a wet morning on 14th September 1964 an Engineer's train was propelled from Gleneagles to a site just north of Machany cutting. Here rails were laid either side of the line for the track lifting rig to run on, and at 10.20am the first panel was lifted out. British Railways only recovered the concrete sleeper section, leaving the remainder of the wood sleeper length for the scrap contractors. *Author*

BELOW: Plate 10.40
The first track panel is run back to be loaded on the bogie flat wagons of the Engineer's train. Fishplates were unbolted and laid on the sleepers as seen here, and the next panel was ready to be lifted. The whole operation took only a matter of minutes for each panel to be recovered, and in a short space of time about a quarter of a mile of track was lifted and the link the line had provided for nearly 110 years was broken for good. *Author*

July as described in Chapter 7, but was to allow a demolition train to work up the hotel siding recovering the track. This being only fit for scrap, it was cut up on site and recovered in wagon loads as shown in Plate 10.41.

The demolition of the goods yard at Gleneagles and Crieff passenger station followed soon afterwards. Again, the track was cut up in situ, signals felled, and any other ferrous scrap recovered by the contractors. What remained was often disposed of on bonfires. In this respect the 1893 economy of constructing Crieff station largely of wood made the task easier, and it was not long before all that remained of these once splendid buildings were the concrete foundations.

The complete closure of the line to Comrie and the short branch to Methven also allowed a full scale rationalisation of track and signalling at Crieff and Methven Junction. At Crieff, all trackwork other than the line running into the goods yard was lifted, signals were dispensed with and on 17th May 1965 the signal box was closed. Similarly, at Methven Junction, all points and loops were removed and the track reduced to plain line, while the same was done at Madderty. The line from Almond Valley Junction to Crieff was now worked by a 'One Engine in Steam' staff.

Even this much simplified layout did not last long. Goods traffic to Crieff lingered on, but shorn of any traffic from the intermediate stations and faced with increasing road competition, goods traffic continued to dwindle. Trains ran only as required rather than daily, their loads often amounted to only a handful of trucks, and the complete closure of the line was not long in coming. On 11th September 1967, a little over three years after passenger traffic ceased, the Crieff line was closed completely, save for a short stretch to Dewar's siding on the outskirts of Perth.

CHAPTER 10: BRITISH RAILWAYS AND THE STRUGGLE FOR SURVIVAL

LEFT: Plate 10.41
The scrap contractor at work at Gleneagles in September 1964. This view, taken from the same point as Plate 10.10, presents a sorry sight. Track has been cut up in situ, point rodding burned through and then piled up, and near the van a mangled heap of wood and metal is all that is left of a Caledonian Railway signal. Parcels traffic was still brisk, however, and at least the delivery lorry driver could now bring his lorry right up to the platform edge. *Author*

BELOW: Plate 10.42
The south end of Gleneagles station during demolition work. The track has been lifted back towards the goods yard, and the remaining track leading to the main line is already heavily rusted. All the wooden Caledonian Railway signal arms have been removed, and the signal posts await their fate, in this depressing view from the footbridge. *Author*

BELOW: Plate 10.43
Demolition work under way at the other end of the line at Crieff, with the contractor's trolley on the line in the cutting between Burrell Street and the King Street bridge, seen in the background. This view would be impossible today as this stretch of the former railway is 15 feet or more beneath a supermarket car park. *Author*

The line was lifted not long afterwards and buildings either demolished or sold off into private ownership. Some of the steel bridges were recovered, but the majority being of masonry construction were left in place. Over the years, nature has gradually reclaimed the trackbed and although in places the line of the former railway can be discerned, in many places no trace exists of the network of branch lines which were once the lifeblood of the district.

For over a century the branch lines of Strathearn played an important role in the development and prosperity of the district. For many local people, who lived through the latter part of the 19th and first half of the 20th centuries, these railways were a part of everyday life. Indeed the term 'Permanent Way' applied to the railway track reflected the assumption that they would always be there.

Now, sadly, these local railways have been swept away by the rise of the motor vehicle in much the same way that they themselves brought about the demise of centuries of horse-drawn transport over 100 years ago.

They leave, however, a lasting legacy, and in some cases – such as Lochearnhead and St. Fillans stations and, above all, Gleneagles Hotel – physical reminders of this once busy network. It is perhaps ironic that the one remaining station at Gleneagles occupies the site of the former Crieff Junction station, the starting point of the first branch line in Strathearn in 1848.

Plate 10.44
A view of a sad looking Crieff passenger station after the track had been lifted and signals removed, taken from the King Street bridge. The extent to which the Down platform had already been shortened can clearly be seen here. *Photograph by David Lawrence/Photos from the Fifties*

Figure 10.23
The British Railways amendments to the Operating Instructions in 1965 reflecting the work already carried out to lift the Gleneagles to Crieff and Crieff to Comrie lines, and the ongoing work to lift the Methven Junction to Methven branch line. Some reusable track, such as the concrete sleeper panels recovered from Machany, was removed by British Railways engineers, but for the remainder a scrap contractor would remove all track, signalling and other ferrous scrap and clear the site. *Author's collection*

> **Between Gleneagles and Muthill:** The item appearing under this heading at page 22 of the S.W. Supplementary Operating Instructions booklet is amended as follows:—
>
> **Gleneagles/Crieff: Until further notice** contractors are engaged in uplifting this branch from Gleneagles to the connection with the Perth lines at Crieff.
> Should it be necessary for trains to work to and from the site of work these must be worked under "Yard" working conditions.
> All connections worked from Gleneagles box have been put out of use.
> (Amended 7/4/65)(RTG.202/63.G)
>
> **Between Gleneagles and Comrie**—The item appearing on page 22 of Supplementary Operating Instructions Booklet is amended to read:—
> **Between Gleneagles and Comrie**—This branch from a point 70 yards on Comrie side of Crieff Up inner home signal to the end of the branch has been removed.
> The Up outer home and distant signals for Crieff have been removed.
> (Amended 19/12/64)(RTG.202/63G)
>
> **Methven Branch—Until further notice**—Contractors are engaged in uplifting this branch from Methven to the connection with the single line at Methven Jn.
> Trains to and from the site of work are worked under "Yard" working conditions.
> (RTG.486/64M)(22/3/65)

Plate 10.45
The site of Muthill station in May 1968, by which time everything other than the platforms had been demolished. Only the notice announcing withdrawal of the passenger service nearly four years earlier survives. Contrast this scene of desolation with the scene in Plate 3.20 taken from the same spot. *Author*

CHAPTER 10: BRITISH RAILWAYS AND THE STRUGGLE FOR SURVIVAL

ABOVE: Plate 10.46
The demolition of Crieff passenger station is well under way in this view from King Street bridge taken in March 1967. The canopies have already gone, with only the stumps of the supporting columns remaining. The scrap contractors have cut down the footbridge and just finished demolishing the steps on the Down platform. Despite this scene of desolation, the goods yard still appears busy, with a number of vans, probably for seed potato traffic, visible in the background.
Keith Fenwick

BELOW: Plate 10.47
A good action shot of the footbridge stairs on the Up platform at Crieff collapsing just moments after having been dealt a hefty blow by the contractor's digger. The mangled remains of the footbridge lie where they fell, while the main timbers from the canopy lie about the platform awaiting removal. The Up platform buildings, now in a sorry state, await their fate.
Keith Fenwick

Plate 10.48
The final train from Crieff was this goods train on 12th September 1967 which recovered all the remaining wagons from the goods yard there. The coal merchants appear to have stocked up for the winter and brought in what coal they could by rail before the line closed. The site of Crieff passenger station on the extreme right shows how little of the station remained once the largely wooden structure had been swept away. By this date the two more recent goods sheds seen in Plate 5.6 had been demolished and, ironically, the one remaining building was the original Crieff Junction Railway terminus of 1856.

Kerr Edgar Courtesy David Ferguson

Appendix 1: Chronology of Main Events

15.04.1853	Royal Assent given for Crieff Junction Railway
12.03.1856	Official opening of the Crieff Junction Railway
14.03.1856	Crieff Junction Railway open for goods traffic
16.03.1856	Crieff Junction Railway open for passenger traffic
29.07.1856	Royal Assent given for the Perth Almond Valley & Methven Railway
24.01.1857	Tullibardine station open for goods and mineral traffic
03.92.1857	Cutting of the first turf for the Perth Almond Valley & Methven Railway
02.05.1857	Passenger trains now booked to stop at Tullibardine
02.11.1857	Perth Almond Valley & Methven Railway open for goods traffic
01.01.1858	Perth Almond Valley & Methven Railway open for passenger traffic
14.07.1864	Royal Assent given for Crieff & Methven Junction Railway
01.08.1865	Scottish Central Railway takes over Crieff Junction Railway
23.03.1865	First turf cut for the Crieff & Methven Junction Railway
01.08.1865	Caledonian Railway takes over Scottish Central Railway
21.05.1866	Crieff & Methven Junction Railway opens
25.07.1890	Royal Assent given for Crieff & Comrie Railway
01.06.1893	Crieff & Comrie Railway opens
09.04.1897	Royal Assent given for the Lochearnhead St. Fillans & Comrie Railway
01.08.1898	Caledonian Railway takes over Crieff & Comrie Railway
01.10.1901	Railway from Comrie to St. Fillans opens
01.08.1902	Caledonian Railway takes over Lochearnhead St. Fillans and Comrie Railway
01.07.1904	Railway opens from St. Fillans to Lochearnhead
01.05.1905	Railway opens from Lochearnhead to Balquhidder
01.10.1912	Crieff Junction station renamed Gleneagles
01.01.1917	Highlandman, Innerpeffray and Lochearnhead stations temporarily closed during the war
01.02.1919	Highlandman and Lochearnhead stations reopened
02.06.1919	Innerpeffray station reopened
01.10.1919	New Gleneagles station opened
05.06.1924	Gleneagles Hotel opened
27.09.1937	Methven Junction to Methven branch line closed to passengers
28.02.1942	Balquhidder engine shed closed
11.04.1947	Gleneagles Hotel returned to the LM&SR after wartime use as a hospital
25.09.1950	Freight service withdrawn between Comrie and Balquhidder
01.10.1951	Comrie to Balquhidder section closed completely
01.10.1951	Almond Valley Junction to Crieff section closed to passengers
01.10.1951	Huntingtower Siding and Innerpeffray closed completely
12.09.1958	Railbus enters service between Gleneagles and Comrie
	Strageath Halt and Pittenzie Halt opened for passengers
	Tullibardine and Highlandman become unstaffed stations
01.04.1959	Abercairny station closed to all goods traffic except full truckloads
02.11.1959	Tullibardine station closed to goods traffic
	Comrie becomes unstaffed station
27.01.1964	Balquhidder and Tibbermuir stations closed to goods traffic.
15.06.1964	Freight traffic withdrawn between Crieff and Comrie
06.07.1964	Gleneagles to Comrie section closed to passenger traffic
01.09.1964	Freight services withdrawn between Gleneagles and Muthill
07.09.1964	Abercairny closed to goods traffic and closed completely
02.11.1964	Freight service withdrawn between Crieff and Muthill
	Gleneagles station closed for goods
25.01.1965	Almondbank, Madderty and Methven stations closed for goods traffic and closed completely
17.05.1965	Crieff signal box closed
	Line from Almond Valley Junction worked by 'One Engine in Steam'
11.09.1967	Line between Dewar's Siding (Perth) and Crieff closed completely

Appendix 2: Station Codes

All Caledonian Railway stations were identified by station codes which were used for management and accounting purposes. These station codes were also printed along the bottom of the Edmondson card tickets issued by the station concerned. Thus tickets issued at Crieff Junction would bear the figures '223' in the centre at the bottom of the ticket.

The numbers issued by the Caledonian were generally sequential for the various lines, as shown below, depending on when a particular line opened. Thus Comrie has a much higher number than Crieff having only opened in 1893, and those for St. Fillans and Lochearnhead are similarly higher. Balquhidder took on the number allocated to the original Lochearnhead station which was part of the numbering sequence for the Callander & Oban line.

Ruthven Road and Tibbermuir were not allocated numbers during Caledonian Railway days, only becoming halts during LM&SR times. Similarly, Methven Junction did not become a station as such until the Methven branch line closed in 1937, when it was allocated the Methven code number.

Dalchonzie Platform also did not have a station code during Caledonian days but was allocated one by the LM&SR. This was the same code as St. Fillans but with the suffix 'D' added, the former being the accounting station for traffic handled by Dalchonzie.

Caledonian Railway Codes	
Crieff Junction	223
Gleneagles	223
Tullibardine	224
Muthill	225
Highlandman	226
Crieff	227
Almondbank	251
Ruthven Road	----
Tibbermuir	----
Methven Junction	----
Methven	252
Balgowan	253
Madderty	254
Abercairny	255
Innerpeffray	256
Comrie	305
Dalchonzie	----
St. Fillans	350
Lochearnhead	376
Balquhidder	207

LM&SR (Northern Division) Codes	
Gleneagles	4279
Tullibardine	4280
Muthill	4281
Highlandman	4282
Crieff	4283
Almondbank	4308
Ruthven Road Halt	4366
Tibbermuir Halt	4367
Methven Junction	4309
Methven	4309
Balgowan	4310
Madderty	4308
Abercairny	4312
Innerpeffray	4313
Comrie	4284
Dalchonzie Platform	4285D
St. Fillans	4285
Lochearnhead	4286
Balquhidder	4255

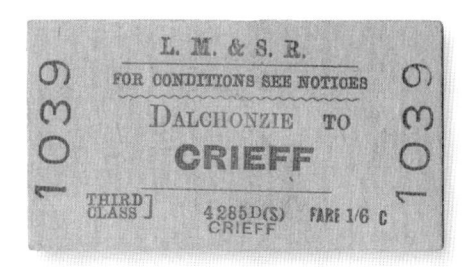

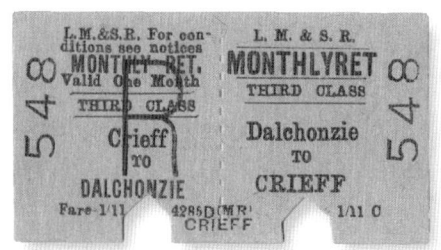

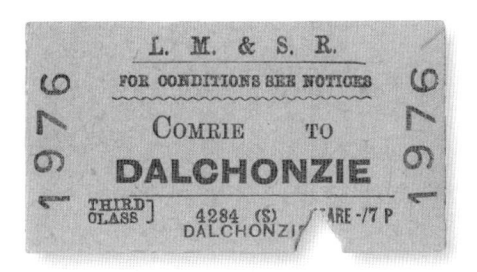

A selection of local tickets from Dalchonzie, the small request halt between Comrie and St. Fillans. Being only a Platform, tickets were issued by the guard and there were very few printed types. One popular destination would have been Crieff, but even this LM&SR Third Class Single was not issued until 29th September 1951, the last day of operation. The Third Class Monthly Return to Crieff is unused, as is the Third Class Single from Comrie, one of the few stations to carry printed tickets to Dalchonzie.

Author's collection

Appendix 3: Telegraph Message Circuits

Extracts from the Caledonian Railway Appendix to the Working Time Table No. 39 effective from 1st May 1915 listing the stations and signal boxes on the Strathearn lines connected to message telegraph and telephone circuits.

Calls	Stations and Signal Boxes	Hours of Attendance Weekdays	Sundays
A.C.	Abercairny Station	8. 0am - 7.30pm	------
A.D.	Almondbank Station	8. 0am - 7.45pm	------
A	Almond Valley Junction Box	Always	Sat 11.0pm - Mon 4.30am
B.G.	Balgowan Station	8. 0am - 8. 0pm	------
B.A.	Balquhidder West Box	6.30am - 7.40pm	------
B.E.	Balquhidder East Box	6.30am - 7.40pm	------
L	Balquhidder Station	8. 0am - 7.40pm	9.40am - 9.25am
Ph	Comrie Station	8. 0am - 7.30pm	------
Ph	Comrie Box	6.10am - 8. 0pm	On duty 5.40am Monday
C.I.	Crieff Station	8. 0am - 8. 0pm	------
B	Crieff East Box	6. 0am - 9. 0pm	On duty 5.0am Monday
C.F.	Crieff West Box	6. 0am - 9. 0pm	On duty 5.0am Monday
Ph	Gleneagles Box	Always	3.0am 1.0am Mon
C.J.	Gleneagles Station	8. 0am - 7.15pm	(Except between 1.0pm & 2.0pm)
Ph	Highlandman Box	6.10am - 8.50pm	------
I.F.	Innerpeffray Station	8. 0am - 8. 0pm	------
Ph	Lochearnhead Station	7.30pm - 7.30pm	------
Ph	Lochearnhead Box	7.30am - 7.30pm	------
Y	Madderty Box	------	------
D.Y.	Madderty Station	8. 0am - 8. 0pm	------
M.E.	Methven Station	8. 0am - 8.20pm	(Except 12.15pm - 1.0pm and 5.0pm - 5.45pm)
M.J.	Methven Junction Box	5.10am - 8.20pm	Sat 10.45pm. On duty Monday 4.30am
Ph	Muthill Box	6. 5am - 8.45pm	------
Ph	St. Fillans Station	8. 0am - 6.30pm	------
Ph	St. Fillans Box	6.30am - 7.30pm	------
Ph	Tullibardine Station	6. 0am - 8.30pm	------

Note: 'Ph' indicates that a telephone had replaced the telegraph instrument at that place, hence no telegraph code was in use.

A LM&SR wagon label for livestock, this one printed 'From PERTH To INNERPEFFRAY', again 'Via LMS Railway'. It is surprising to find pre-printed labels to such a small station as Innerpeffray, but perhaps not so surprising that surplus stocks of unused labels survived. The reverse of the label has been used by someone at Perth North goods yard to record the holdings of wagon stock on 25th June 1941. *Author's collection*

Appendix 4: LM&SR Country Lorry Services

The Caledonian Railway had for many years offered cartage services from its stations, and the LM&SR were not slow in harnessing motor lorries to provide an even more extensive door-to-door service, in particular collection and delivery for farmers' traffic in such rural areas as Strathearn.

Below is an extract from the LM&SR booklet Country Lorry Services for Scottish Farm and Village, published in 1930, showing the towns and villages served by the stations on the branch lines in Strathearn.

LM&SR Country Lorry Services

Town, Village or Hamlet	Station Serving	Distance (miles) from Station	Service at Station	Farmers Cartage Scale
Abercairny	Abercairny	-	X	A
Almondbank	Almondbank	-	X	A
Balgowan	Balgowan	-	X	A
Balquhidder	Balquhidder	-	-	-
Clathey	Balgowan	2	X	A
Comrie	Comrie	-	XC	A
Crieff	Crieff	-	XC	A
Fowlis Wester	Abercairny	2½	X	A
Gilmerton	Crieff	2½	XC	A
Gleneagles	Gleneagles	-	X	A
Highlandman	Highlandman	-	X	A
Innerpeffray	Innerpeffray	-	X	A
Lochearnhead	Lochearnhead	-	-	-
Logiealmond	Methven	4½	X	A
Madderty	Madderty	-	X	A
Methven	Methven	-	X	A
Muthill	Muthill	-	X	A
Pitcairngreen	Almondbank	1¼	X	A
Ruthvenfield	Almondbank	¾	X	A
St. David's	Madderty	¾	X	A
St. Fillans	St. Fillans	-	-	-
Tibbermore	Almondbank	½	X	A
Tullibardine	Tullibardine	-	X	A

Key to symbols:

X   Country Lorry Collection & Delivery Services
XC   Country Lorry Collection & Delivery Services + Ordinary C & D service
A   Minimum weight for Delivery 10 cwts. Delivery undertaken within 5 miles

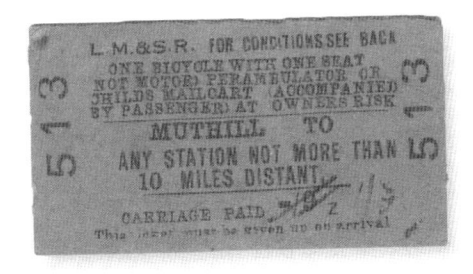

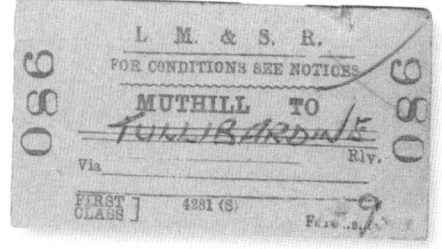

A selection of tickets from Muthill. With an ammunition depot near the station, it is not surprising that Forces Leave tickets were printed, this LM&SR example being issued in late 1945. The LM&SR First Class Single made out to Tullibardine is dated 28th May 1957, nearly ten years after nationalisation, so there would appear to have been little call for such tickets. Similarly the LM&SR Cycle ticket was issued in 1955. *Author's collection*

APPENDIX 5: WHISTLES FOR ENGINES

Engine whistle codes were used at junctions and larger stations to enable drivers to indicate to the signalman which line to set the points and signals for. In Caledonian Railway days, whistle codes were also laid down for Almond Valley Junction and Methven Junction, but by 1931 these had been dispensed with.

The following is an extract from the LM&SR Appendix to the Working Time Table dated 1st January 1931, listing the engine whistle codes in use at certain stations on the branch lines of Strathearn:

CRIEFF EAST SIGNAL BOX	
From Centre Station Road to Gleneagles	1 long and 1 short
From Centre Station Road to Methven Branch	2 long and 2 short
From Centre Station Road to dead-end	4
From Main line or Engine Shed to Methven Sidings or dead-end	3
From Engine Shed Sidings to dead-end	1 long and 1 short
CRIEFF WEST SIGNAL BOX	
From Centre Station Road to Down Line	2
From Centre Station Road to Up Main Line	2 and 1 crow
GLENEAGLES	
Down Main Line to Goods Loop	3 short
Down Main Line to Goods Yard	4 long
To or from Branch Platform and south dead-end	3 short and 1 crow
To or from Goods Loop and south dead end	4 short and 1 crow
To or from Goods Yard and south dead-end	5 short and 1 crow
To or from Goods Yard and Up Main Line	2 long and 3 short
To or from Goods Loop and Up Main Line	3 long and 2 short
To or from Down Main Line and Goods Loop via north connection	3 short and 2 long
To or from Crieff Branch and Goods Loop	4 short
To or from Crieff Branch and Goods Yard	5 short
BALQUHIDDER WEST SIGNAL BOX	
To or from Branch Platform and C&O Line	2
To or from Branch Platform and Branch Line	3
To or from Branch Loop Siding and Branch Line	4
To or from Exchange Sidings and C&O Line	1 crow and 2
To or from Branch Platform and Goods Yard	2 long and 1 short
To or from dead-end and Down Platform	4 short
BALQUHIDDER EAST SIGNAL BOX	
From Up Main Line to dead-end	1 short and 1 long
To or from Down Main Line or Branch Line and dead-end	4
To or from Main Line and Branch Line	2
To or from Main Line and Branch Loop Siding	2 long and 1 short
To or from Branch Loop Siding and dead-end	1 crow and 1

Tickets with the destination station pre-printed were usually only provided where the level of passenger traffic justified this additional expense. This Lancashire & Yorkshire Railway ticket printed from Liverpool (Exchange) to Crieff is therefore particularly interesting, albeit with a low serial number indicating that it is probable few were printed. Crieff is shown as Crieff (Cal) although there was only one station at Crieff - the Caledonian one. The routing was detailed, being via Preston, Carlisle, Carstairs, Coatbridge and Dunblane, ensuring that the passenger travelled by the West Coast route throughout.

Author's collection

Appendix 6: Routes Over Which Engines May Run

Following the Grouping and with the introduction of larger more modern locomotives, the LM&SR found it necessary to issue instructions regarding restrictions of the routes which certain classes of locomotives could run. This could be because of axle weights, load gauges or other reasons. Many non-standard English types were not allowed to run north of Carlisle. Engines were referred to by the code given in the first column of the table, the figure indicating the Motive Power classification which was shown on the cab side. The locomotives listed as being prohibited over certain branch lines in Strathearn were:

Code	Wheels	Locomotive Type
5B	2-6-0	Freight Tender (LM&SR Standard – Parallel Boiler)
5C	2-6-0	Freight Tender (LM&SR Standard – Taper Boiler)
5XA	4-6-0	Passenger Tender (LM&SR Standard – Parallel Boiler)
5XB	4-6-0	Passenger Tender (LM&SR Standard – Taper Boiler)
6A	4-6-0	Passenger Tender (Royal Scot – Parallel Boiler and *British Legion* – No. 6170)
6D	4-6-0	Passenger Tender (Converted Royal Scot and 5X – Taper Boiler)
7A	4-6-2	Passenger Tender
8A	2-8-0	Freight Tender (LM&SR Standard)

The following is an extract from the LM&SR (Northern Division) instruction booklet dated 1st October 1945 specifying routes over which locomotives may run in respect of the branch lines of Strathearn.

Route	Code	Engines Prohibited
Crieff – Gleneagles	6A	LM&SR Royal Scot
	7A	LM&SR 4-6-2
Balquhidder (East) – Crieff	5XA	LM&SR 4-6-0
	5XB	LM&SR 4-6-0
	6A	LM&SR Royal Scot
	6D	LM&SR Royal Scot rebuilt
	7A	LM&SR 4-6-2
Crieff – Almond Valley Junction	5B	LM&SR 2-6-0
	5C	LM&SR 2-6-0
	5XA	LM&SR 4-6-0
	5XB	LM&SR 4-6-0
	6A	LM&SR Royal Scot
	6D	LM&SR Royal Scot rebuilt
	7A	LM&SR 4-6-2
	8A	LM&SR 2-8-0
Methven – Methven Junction	5XA	LM&SR 4-6-0
	5XB	LM&SR 4-6-0
	6A	LM&SR Royal Scot
	6D	LM&SR Royal Scot rebuilt
	7A	LM&SR 4-6-2

A selection of tickets from Balquhidder, the junction station on the Callander & Oban line. Two of these are to Lochearnhead, the first stop on the branch line, one being an LM&SR ticket, the other a British Railways specimen from the 1948-51 period. Neither are dated so may never have been issued. The LM&SR Third Class Single to St. Fillans was issued, although the date may seem confusing – in this case the year of issue (1932) is shown in front of the month and day.
Author's collection

Appendix 7: Caledonian and L&NWR Souvenir Time Table & Guide 1912

An extract from the Souvenir Time Table and Guide issued jointly by the Caledonian and London & North Western railways in 1912. This included much of the information which was usually published in the annual holiday guides, but in this case included a full list of all the fishing resorts in addition to the usual list of golf courses and so forth.

The information relevant to Strathearn is listed below.

List of Fishing Resorts Reached by the Caledonian Railway

Station	River or Loch	Fish	Fishing
Almondbank	River Almond	Trout	Free
Balquhidder	Loch Earn	Trout	Free
Balquhidder	Loch Voil	Trout & Salmon	Preserved
Balquhidder	Loch Doine	Trout	Preserved
Balquhidder	Loch Lubnaig	Trout & Salmon	Free
Comrie	Loch Earn	Trout	Free
Comrie	Loch Boltachan	Trout	Free
Comrie	Loch Monzievaird	Trout	Free
Comrie	River Earn	Trout & Salmon	Free
Comrie	River Ruchil	Trout & Sea Trout	Free
Comrie	River Lednock	Trout	Part free
Comrie	Drummond Water	Salmon	Preserved
Comrie	Hill burns	Trout	Mostly free
Crieff	River Earn	Trout & Salmon	Preserved
Crieff	River Almond	Trout	Free
Crieff Junction	River Devon	Trout	Free
Highlandman	River Earn	Trout & Salmon	Preserved
Highlandman	River Powburn	Trout	Free
Innerpeffray	River Powburn	Trout	Free
Methven	River Almond	Trout & Salmon	Free
Muthill	River Earn	Trout & Salmon	Preserved

List of Golf Courses at Holiday Resorts

Station	Golf Course	Holes
Comrie	Comrie Lawers	9
Crieff	Crieff	9
Lochearnhead	Hotel	9
St. Fillans	St. Fillans	9

Special tickets were sometimes printed for particular events, usually excursions, but this ticket is most unusual in not only being printed for a specific period, but also issued by a different company, in this case the Great Northern Railway (GNR) as indicated along the centre bottom of the ticket. The Royal Horse Guards' Band Party started their tour on 3rd October 1900 and were due to complete it by 10th October. This particular ticket was for the Crieff to Dundee leg of their tour. Thus a ticket headed Cal Ry was printed and issued by the GNR, part of the East Coast route. This ticket was never issued and with the serial number '000' may well have been a printer's proof copy, a number of which have been noted in recent years.

Author's collection

Appendix 8: The Methven Railway Song

This song was sung by Mrs Jas. Sword at the Railway Festival held in Methven on 6th February 1861, and reflects well the immense pride felt by the townsfolk in their new railway. The song was sung to the musical air 'Dainty Davie'. The original manuscript was provided in the mid-1960s by the grand-daughter of the first station master at Methven.

What's this I hear Auld Methven Toon,
You're growin' prood ye upstart loon,
On neebour toons you'd fain look doon,
Because you've got a Railway.
Its no sae lang syne yet ye Brat,
Ye hunkerin dowie tradeless sat,
Wi' wafee face, some say ye grat,
An nae word o' a Railway.
But noo you've brighten'd up 'am tauld,
An' fain would ye forget the Auld,
Afore ye had a Railway.
Wi' Royal Bank, an' Gasworks braw,
An street lamps too, preserve us a',
You're fain tae clap your wings and craw,
In Methven wi' a Railway.

*Chorus: Dumfouner'd like it does me ding,
          Its unco queer it cowes a' thing,
          Nae' wonder who I try tae sing,
          O' Methven wi' a Railway.*

When first a train ran on your line,
Years two or three hae passed sin' syne,
The toon near toom'd for fear they'd tyne,
The first sicht on' the Railway.
A' kinds o' Fouk, baith frien's and foes,
Auld wives in sow backs, bairns in hose,
An' some wi' specks astride their nose,
Ran doon tae see the Railway.
Ere lang it roun' the Millknowe cam,
Loud snortin' past the Auld Mill dam,
An' landed trucks as fou's they'd cram
Wi' guids upon the Railway.
That done, the whistle blew a screech,
Auld Tibbie Smith, lap two 'ell heich,
An' heels ower head 'boon Rab McKeich,
Clean frichted at the Railway.

*Chorus: Dumfouner'd like it does me ding,
          Its unco queer it cowes a' thing,
          Nae' wonder who I try tae sing,
          O' Methven wi' a Railway.*

It was tae Methven fouk a sicht,
The shuntin' puttin' a' thing richt,
An' sair'd them meastly a' the nicht,
Tae crack aboot the Railway.
When aff she gaed some did ajourn,
Tae see her tack the Millknowe turn,
But there she slid doon in the burn,
Clean aff the Methven Railway.
"Rin Tammas rin" cried Mary Dou,
Tis perfect wild at Jacksons Sou.
There'll be a bluddy Waterloo
Between it an' the railway.
Losh guid's us woman but your green,
The Engine's air'n its breath's but steam.
Mair than tae fecht a sou I ween,
Has ta'en her aff the Railway.

*Chorus: Dumfouner'd like it does me ding,
          Its unco queer it cowes a' thing,
          Nae' wonder who I try tae sing,
          O' Methven wi' a Railway.*

The first time aff was nae the last,
As scarcely ere a train got past,
But stuck aye there baith firm an' fast,
At this bit o' the Railway.
But noo a change comes ower my sang,
For years hae pass'd wi' naething wrang,
Bairns a'maun creep afore they gang,
Sae fair'd it wi' our Railway.
Lang may it rin and keep the line,
Its fame o' safety never tyne,
An' nae mair jokes about our swine,
Be pointed at our Railway.
Lang may its servants keep their place,
Wi' honest worth and manly grace,
And unborne age a blessin' trace,
To Methven frae its Railway.

*Chorus: Dumfouner'd like it does me ding,
          Its unco queer it cowes a' thing,
          Nae' wonder who I try tae sing,
          O' Methven wi' a Railway.*

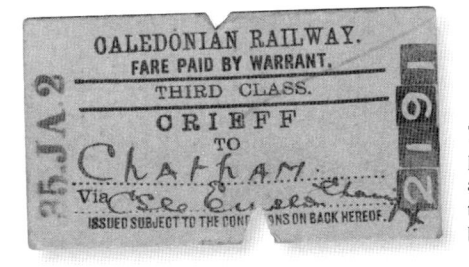

Members of Her (later His) Majesty's Armed Forces often travelled by rail, both on duty or on leave. They would usually be issued with a Warrant which was presented at the booking office in lieu of payment, which would subsequently be recovered by the railway from the Admiralty, War Office or, after 1918, the Air Ministry. This Third Class single from Crieff to Chatham was one such ticket issued to a sailor or Royal Marine in 1902. Again the routing via Carlisle and Euston ensured that he travelled by the West Coast route as far as London.
Author's collection

Appendix 9: The Crieff & Methven Junction Railway Song

Local people were proud of their new railways and in additon to the ceremony of cutting the first turf, songs were often written in celebration of the event. The following song heralded the coming of the Crieff & Methven Junction Railway in 1865, and is reproduced below. It was originally published in *The History of Crieff*, by Alexander Porteous, published by Oliphant, Anderson & Ferrier, Edinburgh and London, 1912. The notes provide a useful historical explanation. Sung to the tune of 'Bonnie Dundee'.

'The Gude Folks o' Crieff'

We hae gotten a start in the richt way at last,
For commerce and railways are multiplyin' fast;
And soon from our home in the North we can ride [1]
To the banks of the Tay, the Forth or the Clyde.

Chorus: The gude folks o' Crieff desrve noo a sang,
For a nice thriving place they'll mak' it ere lang;
Wi' railways, and Bailies, a Provost, and a' - [2]
Us Crieff folks, ye see, are gettin' fu' braw.

The days o' stage-coaches, I fear, are noo ower;
Tho' the *Rapid* coach ran sixteen miles an hour, [3]
And the *Victor* and *Champion* ran mony a tough race, [4]
Wi' the march o' progress they couldn' keep pace.

But railways, my friends, keep pace wi' the age,
And travelling by steam is now all the rage;
From John-o'-Groats House to famed Gretna-Green,
Ye're back, ere folks guess where ye can hae been.

Since the Crieff and Methven line's first turf is cut,
There's gladness in many a hamlet and hut, -
And many an anxious bit wish for the day
When an engine shall puff on the Methven Railway.

The lady we thank here, who opened this line, [5]
And all who joined the procession so fine -
Our Provost, the Masons, and Crieff Volunteers,
Let's gie them, dear friends, three loud ringin' cheers.

Notes

1. The Crieff & Methven line was seen to complete a link from Strathearn to and from the North, whereas the Crieff Junction linked Strathearn to the South.
2. Crieff became a Municipal Burgh on 23rd March 1864 under the General Police and Improvement Act 1862.
3. The *Rapid* stagecoach plied between Perth and Stirling via Crieff, halting at Robertson's Inn, now the Drummond Arms.
4. The *Victor* stagecoach plied between Perth and Stirling via Crieff, halting at Robertson's Inn, now the Drummond Arms. The *Champion* stagecoach was owned by Peter McGlashan and plied between Perth and Stirling via Crieff, halting at McIlvride's Inn, James Square. Going by this coach, arrangements were made for conveying passengers from Stirling to Glasgow by the canal.
5. Lady Lucy Dundas of Dunira was to have cut the first turf, but ill health prevented her, so Mrs Maxtone Graham of Cultoquhey officiated instead.

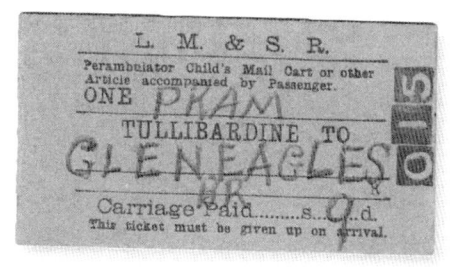

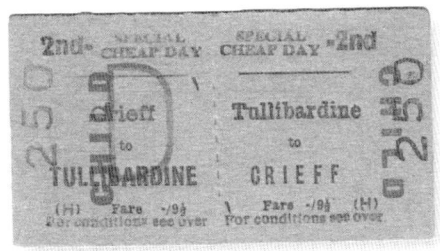

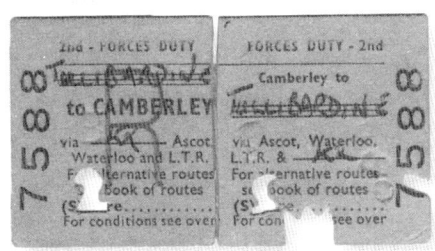

A selection of tickets from Tullibardine prior to it becoming an unstaffed halt with the introduction of the railbus in September 1958. The LM&SR Pram ticket was used until after nationalisation in 1948 as indicated by the reference to 'BR'. The Forces Duty ticket from Camberley was issued to the author on 30th July 1964, nearly a month after the station had closed. The two half tickets were retained and subsequently reunited. *Author's collection*

A lovely action shot of Caledonian Railway 0-6-0 No 757 on an Up train entering Highlandman station. The fireman, who is hanging out of the cab, and the signalman, are about to exchange the hoops for the single line tablet. Meanwhile, a number of passengers wait for the train to come to a stop, and a porter standing by the signal box is ready to load either a large parcel or an item of luggage. This photograph represents an everyday scene typical of the numerous small wayside stations along the branch lines of Strathearn.
CRA collection

Bibliography

F. Alexander and E.S. Nicoll, *The Register of Scottish Signal Boxes*, 1990

Angus Railway Group, *Steam Album Volume 3 Perthshire*, ARG, 1983

Alan W. Brotchie, *Tramways of the Tay Valley*, Dundee Museum & Art Gallery, 1965

J. Bruce-Watt, *The Gleneagles Hotel*, Gleneagles Hotel, 1984

Bernard Byrom, *The Railways of Upper Strathearn*, Oakwood Press, 2004

Ewen W. Cameron OBE, *Strathyre, Balquhidder & Lochearnhead in Old Photographs*, Stirling District Libraries, 1994

H.J. Campbell, *Forty Years of Caledonian Locomotives, 1882-1922*, David & Charles, 1974

Guy Christie, *Crieff Hydro 1868 – 1968*, Crieff Hydro Limited 1967, 1986

C.R. Clinker and J.M. Firth, *Clinker's Register of Closed Passenger Stations and Goods Depots in England, Scotland and Wales*, 1971

Niall Ferguson & David Stirling, *Caledonian in LMS Days*, Pendragon, 2007

Stanley Hall, *The History & Development of Signalling in the British Isles, Volume 1: Broad Survey*, Friends of the NRM, 2000

Chris Hawkins and George Reeve, *LMS Engine Sheds Volume 5, The Caledonian Railway*, Wild Swan Publications Ltd, 1987

Leonard P. Lewis, *Railway Signal Engineering (Mechanical)*, Constable & Son, 1912

London Midland & Scottish Railway, *The Centenary of the Caledonian Railway, 1847-1947*, LM&SR, 1917

Peter Marshall, *The Scottish Central Railway*, Oakwood Press, 1998

R.J. MacLennan, *Golf at Gleneagles*, McCorquodale, 1921

A.J. Mullay, *Through Scotland with the Caledonian Railway*, Stenlake Publishing, 2010

George C. Nash, *The LMS at War*, LM&SR, 1946

Roderick de Norman, *For Fuhrer and Fatherland*, 1996

O.S. Nock, *The Caledonian Railway*, Ian Allan, 1961

Jane Nottage, *The Gleneagles Hotel*, Harper Collins, 1999

P.J.G. Ransom, *Old Almondbank, Methven and Glenalmond*, Stenlake Publishing, 2010

David Ross, *The Caledonian, Scotland's Imperial Railway: A History*, Stenlake Publishing, 2013

Don Rowland, 'Early Days of Gleneagles', *BackTrack*, Special Issue No. 1, 1999

Signalling Study Group, *The Signal Box*, Oxford Publishing Co, 1986

W.A.C. Smith and Paul Anderson, *An illustrated History of Tayside's Railways Dundee and Perth*, Irwell Press, 1997

Stephenson Locomotive Society, *Caledonian Railway Centenary*, SLS, 1947

David Stirling, *The History & Development of Signalling in the British Isles, Volume 2 Part 1, The Telegraph & Absolute Block*, Friends of the NRM, 2002

John Thomas, *The Callander & Oban Railway*, David & Charles, 1966

John Thomas, *Forgotten Railways of Scotland*, David & Charles, 1976

Nelson Twells, '75 Years of the Gleneagles Hotel', *BackTrack*, Special Issue No. 1, 1999

Nigel Welbourn, *Lost Lines: Scotland Revisited*, Ian Allan, 2013

Periodicals

Auchterarder & District Local History Association Magazine
BackTrack
Blastpipe, Journal of the Scottish Railway Preservation Society
Railway Magazine
Railway World
Steam Days
Trains Illustrated
The Courier & Advertiser
The Perthshire Advertiser
Perthshire Courier
The Scotsman
'Scottish Railway Express'
The True Line, Journal of the Caledonian Railway Association
Strathearn Herald
The Times

Official Publications

British Railways, Holiday Guide No. 1: Scotland, various years

British Railways (Scottish Region), Passenger Services, various years

British Railways (Scottish Region), Working Time Table of Goods Trains, various years

British Railways (Scottish Region), Working Time Table of Passenger Trains, various years

Caledonian Railway, Appendix to the Central, Northern and Callander & Oban Sections, Working Time Tables No. 25, 25 August 1889

Caledonian Railway, Appendix to the Working Time Tables No. 39, 1 May 1915.

Caledonian Railway, Audit Office Instructions, 1899

Caledonian Railway, Block Telegraph Train Tablet Regulations, 1 May 1915

Caledonian Railway, Official Tourist Guide, various years

Caledonian Railway, Scottish Holiday Resorts, various years

Caledonian Railway, Supplement to Appendix No. 39, 24 October 1921

Caledonian Railway, Time Tables, various years

Caledonian Railway, Through Scotland by the Caledonian Railway, various years

Caledonian Railway, Train Telegraphing Arrangements, 1 March 1922

Caledonian Railway, Working Time Tables, various years

Caledonian Railway and London & North Western Railway, Scotland for the Holidays, various years

Caledonian Railway and London & North Western Railway, Summer Tours in Scotland & England, various years

Crieff Junction Railway, Rules & Regulations, 1855

London Midland & Scottish Railway, Guide to Scottish Holiday Resorts, various years

London Midland & Scottish Railway, Sectional Appendix to the Working Time Tables Northern Division, 1934

London Midland & Scottish Railway, Sectional Appendix to the Working Time Tables Northern Division, 1937

London Midland & Scottish Railway, Time Tables for Scotland, various years

London Midland & Scottish Railway, Tourist Programme, 1926

London Midland & Scottish Railway (Northern Division), Instructions additional to the Appendix to the Working Time Tables, 14 July 1924

London Midland & Scottish Railway (Northern Division), Loading of Passenger and Freight Trains, 1 October 1945

London Midland & Scottish Railway (Northern Division), No. 1 Guards Running, 1 October 1923

London Midland & Scottish Railway (Northern Division), Programme of Tours & Excursions in Scotland and Tourist Fares to Places in England & Scotland, various years

London Midland & Scottish Railway (Northern Division), Rules & Regulations, 1926

London Midland & Scottish Railway (Northern Division), Working Time Tables for Passenger Trains No. 2 Section, various years

ABOVE: An interior view of Gleneagles station shortly after opening, which appeared in the Caledonian Railway's promotional book Golf at Gleneagles, mentioned in Chapter 7. Taken from the Down platform, it shows the stationmaster at the foot of the stairs leading down to the island platform. The hanging flower baskets are much in evidence, while a lone passenger on the left studiously reads his newspaper. The Post Office letter box set into the wall on the left was removed some years later. *Author's collection*

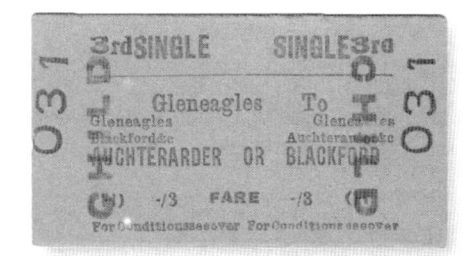

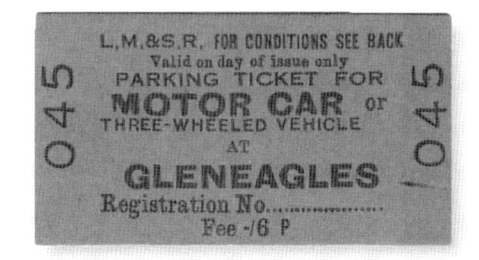

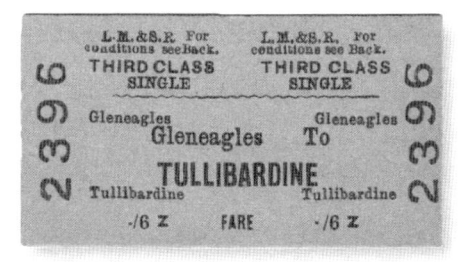

A selection of tickets issued at Gleneagles. The Third Single could be used to travel either north to Auchterarder or south to Blackford, the two adjoining stations to Gleneagles. Such multi-destination tickets were printed where the same fare applied to more than one station. The LM&SR Third Single to Tullibardine was issued on 6th September 1958, only ten days before the introduction of the railbus. *Author's collection*

INDEX

Abbey Bridge   29
Abbey Cut   29
accidents
  animals   213, 35
  collisions   213, 224, 234, 244
  derailments   212, 213, 223, 235,244 245, 246
  level crossings   223,224,244,245
  mechanical   212, 213, 222, 223
  passengers   213, 235
air raids   204
Almond Valley Jct   31, 73, 74, 224
Army movements   191, 250, 268, 269
Auchterarder   19, 63, 117, 130, 144, 153, 161, 192, 193

Beeching Report   128, 271, 272
Best Kept Station competition   141, 188, 194, 210
Black Watch, The   136, 145
Board of Trade   13, 22, 29, 31, 36, 43, 47, 212, 224 et seq
Bouch, Sir Thomas   34, 99
bridges   13, 29, 30, 63, 96, 100, 105
British Railways   247 et seq
bus competition   133, 142, 183, 191, 192, 193, 195, 207
Butter Malcolm, Mr   18

Caird, Mr Edward   24
Camping Coaches   103, 199, 200, 254, 255
circular tour   26, 120, 133, 143, 145, 194, 197, 248, 254
closures   206, 246, 247, 253, 254, 271, 272
coaches   36, 37, 19, 120, 124, 125, 135
Comrie   37
  Laggan Park   41, 46
  Royal Hotel   33, 37, 127, 133
contract tickets   198
Cowdens   29
Craiglea Quarry   121, 123
Crieff   18
  Drummond Arms Hotel   12, 28, 29, 32, 35
  Duchlage Road   42, 96
  Highland Games   117, 121
  Strathearn Hydropathic   115, 117, 119, 120
  town council   120, 131, 133, 206, 255
crime   19, 41, 135
Crouch & Hogg   46, 53
cruise trains   197, 200
Cultybraggan   203, 204, 205, 268, 269

Dalton, Captain   212
demolition   178, 255, 275, 276-79,
Donop, Colonel   47
Doric, SS   195
Drummond Castle   14, 18, 19, 139
Drummond, Mr Moray   32
Dundas, Sir David   10, 26, 38

Donora   123
DMU 134, 257, 261

electric telegraph   20, 32, 117, 122, 283
engine sheds
  Balquhidder   112, 114
  Comrie   42
  Crieff   99, 120, 131, 255, 264
  Methven   84, 85, 116
Engineers   209, 249, 250, 267, 268
excursions   14, 17, 115, 121, 123, 126, 140, 189, 190, 195, 197, 249, 267

farm moves   134, 186
fires   117, 120, 123
football specials   194, 199, 207, 248

General Strike   183, 184
Glasgow Herald   235
Gleneagles
  golf courses   156 et seq
  Hotel   155-78, 179, 180, 181, 200, 202, 206
  hotel branch   63, 148, 219
golf   142, 151, 145, 155-61, 179
Gowans, Mr   33
gradient diagrams   62, 73, 94
Greenwells Farm   61, 63, 176
grouse   117, 122, 129
guide books   115, 124, 125, 126, 135, 137, 143, 146, 183, 197, 198, 201

Haldane, Mr   155
Holiday Runabout tickets   197, 269
hospital train   173
Huntingtower Bleach Works   75, 76
Hutchinson, Major General   43, 224

Inchaffray Abbey   88, 89
Innerpeffray Library   92
Ironside, John   14

Jerviston viaduct   162, 164

Kerr, Mr Edgar   252-53

Laggan Park   41, 46
level crossings
  Auchterarder Road   145, 215, 220
  Balgowan   88
  East Third Farm   245
  Gleneagles Hotel   177
  Huntingtower   76, 227
  Methven Moss   85, 86, 224
  Pittentian   71
  Pittenzie   71, 72, 224, 245, 263
  Ruthven Road   227
  Strageath   69, 218, 244, 265
  Tibbermuir   177
  Tippermallo   224
locomotives   116, 132, 133, 144, 150, 151, 153, 154, 177, 178, 188, 189, 191, 192, 201, 210, 251, 252-53, 254, 256, 257, 258, 259, 271
Lumsden & MacKenzie   76, 77, 142, 143, 250

Machany Cutting   13, 66, 275-76
Mansfield, Lord   23
maps   6, 31, 73, 112, 165, 203
Matheson, Donald   38, 147, 155, 162
Maxton, Mr Graham   26, 28
Menteith, Mr Alexander   18
Methven   32
  branch   116, 201
McGregor, Lady Helen   45
McKay & Sons   42
miners' strike   133, 150, 152
Moncrieffe
  Hill   9
  tunnel   203, 214
Monzie
  castle   145
  Rover Scout Meet   201, 202
Morrisons Academy   17, 35, 265
motor cars   146, 148
motor buses   142, 170, 192, 193, 275
Murray, Sir Patrick   131
Murray, Mr Peter   33

navvies
  accidents   235
  welfare   46, 47
  work   41

Ochtertyre   18

Parkinson's Tours   190, 193, 197
Paton, Mr John   46, 51
Perthshire Advertiser, The   26, 40
Post Office   58, 60-61, 129
potato traffic   17, 18, 25, 32, 78, 83, 131, 210, 260, 276
PoW Camp 21   203, 204, 205
posters   124, 142, 149, 154, 156-59, 192
publicity   165, 167, 180, 193, 194, 197, 249, 263, 265
Pullman Cars   189

railbus   95, 246, 260, 261-63, 266, 270
railtours   266
railways
  Caledonian   36, 45, 115 et seq, 179
  Callander & Oban   17, 35, 44, 45, 189
  Crieff & Comrie   29, 33 et seq, 38, 39, 40, 41, 44, 95, 131
  Crieff Junction   9, 10, 11, 14, 211
  Crieff & Methven Jct   20, 26 et seq
  Glendevon & Crieff Jct   20
  Highland   17
  Lochearnhead, St Fillans & Comrie   44 et seq, 53,

London & North Western   115, 137, 140
London Midland & Scottish   179 et seq
North British   20, 45, 118
Perth Almond Valley & Methven   17, 21 et seq, 25, 83, 116
Scottish Central   9, 19, 20, 21, 212
Scottish Midland Junction   22
Scottish North Eastern   21, 22, 24, 25, 26, 28, 32, 116
Ross, Mr Rae   53
Royal Navy Stores Depot   76, 77, 79, 302, 257, 270
royal visitors   139
Ruthvenfield Bleach Works   257

Scotsman, The   20
Scottish Railway Preservation Society   275
Sentinel steam railcar   186
Shaw, Mr   43
signal boxes
  Almond Valley Junction   74, 225, 226
  Almondbank   78, 226, 228, 229
  Balquhidder East   114, 235, 243
  Balquhidder West   114, 208, 235, 242, 243,
  Comrie   102, 246
  Crieff East   95, 99, 207, 235, 237, 276
  Crieff Junction   13, 215, 216
  Crieff West   99, 195, 235, 238
  Dalchonzie   104, 239, 240
  Gleneagles   217, 218, 246
  Highlandman   207, 218, 222, 223, 247
  Innerpeffray   93, 226, 233, 234
  Lochearnhead   111, 137, 235
  Madderty   232, 246
  Methven Junction   83, 230, 231, 246, 276
  Muthill   67, 215, 221, 246
  St. Fillans   107, 210, 241, 246
  Tullibardine   215, 220

signals   30, 61, 150, 211, 212, 216, 218, 219, 221
slip coaches   140
staff
  Amos, Robert   148, 153, 179
  Blair, Tommy   263
  Crerar, John   126
  Doig, Mr   231, 237, 264
  Durward, Mr   194
  Haggart, Edmund   118
  Headrick, Mungo   234, 235
  Maxwell, George   196
  McArthur, Mr   27, 32
  McPherson, Thomas   181
  Millar, William   142, 148, 187
  Morrison, Mr   30, 187
  Ogilvie, Mrs   141
  Petrie, David   192
  Roberts, William   17
  Smith, James   181
  Stanton, James   225
  Taylor, James   117
  Wishart, William   179
stations
  Abercairny   30, 91, 92, 122, 144, 246, 258, 267
  Almondbank   22, 77, 78, 79, 121, 122, 134, 196, 203
  Balgowan   87, 88, 203
  Balquhidder   7, 54, 113, 114, 136, 144, 192, 193, 282
  Comrie   7, 42, 102-104, 131, 210, 250, 254
  Crieff   16, 42 et seq, 95 et seq, 111, 126, 140, 148, 187-88, 189, 247, 252 et seq, 258, 264, 276, 277, 279
  Crieff Junction   11, 12, 13, 55 et seq, 143
  Dalchonzie Platform   51, 105, 149, 150, 254, 282,

Gleneagles   4, 55-62, 143, 145, 150, 151, 181, 182, 251, 256, 257, 261, 262, 263, 277
Highlandman   31, 70-71, 121, 207, 259
Huntingtower Siding   75, 76, 123, 254
Innerpeffray   30, 93, 254, 282
Lochearnhead (old)   112
Lochearnhead (new)   52, 53, 54, 110, 111, 112, 136, 137, 254
Madderty   29, 89, 90, 121, 257
Methven   23, 83, 84, 116, 186, 267
Methven Junction   81, 82
Muthill   66-67, 258, 261, 266, 277
Pittenzie Halt   71, 264
Ruthven Road Halt   74, 75
St Fillans   7, 47, 48, 50, 106-108, 111, 195, 209, 210, 254
Strageath Halt   6, 69, 254
Tibbermuir   80, 81
Tullibardine   13, 63-65, 130, 247, 252, 254
Stirling, Mr Graham   40
Strathearn Express   131
Strathearn Herald   19, 20, 28, 30, 32, 33, 34, 35, 36, 39, 40, 115, 118, 119, 123, 125, 183, 190, 195, 196, 208, 212, 224, 225, 272
Strathearn Railway Committee   206
Strathallan, Viscount   63
Sunday Schools   119, 185, 186, 190, 201, 248, 265

Times, The   10
timetables
  public   14, 23, 49, 121, 130, 132, 138, 139, 150, 182, 183, 208, 247, 253
  working   28, 130, 199, 270, 276
tours   36, 115, 125, 126, 127, 135
tourism   118, 122, 129, 133, 148

An example of a General Parcels Waybill from one of the Strathearn stations, in this case Almondbank. Made out to Milnathort on the North British Railway via Perth, this was for a box from a Mr Pearson, dispatched by the 5.30pm train on 17th August 1900. Although these Waybills were very common, being used in their thousands every day, this particular one is of interest as yet again the guard was Robert Amos who has duly stamped the document at the top left where the guards' signatures were required. Although paper salvage drives, particularly during the two world wars, meant that the majority of such paperwork did not survive, interesting examples of ephemera still occasionally turn up. *Author's collection*

INDEX

train staff   214, 226, 231
Tyer's train tablet   214, 215, 219, 226, 231, 234, 235
Thompson, Mr William   23
tunnels
  Burrell Street   100, 235, 267
  Strowan   41, 43, 102, 267
  St. Fillans   51, 108
Tyler, Captain   22, 29, 224
traffic
  carriages   127-28
  goods   127-28, 134
  horses   127-28, 147
  livestock   127-28, 129, 147, 186, 193, 194, 199, 208, 248
  milk   127-28, 129, 149
  minerals   127-28, 133
  parcels   127-28, 129
  passenger   51, 127-28

Upper Strathearn Combination Poorhouse   15

viaducts
  Comrie   48, 104
  Dundurn   50
  Edinchip   54, 111, 112
  Glen Ogle   109, 190, 200
  Glen Tarken   51
  Highlandman   68, 70, 121, 259
Villa tickets   16
Volunteers, Army   19, 25, 119, 121, 131, 137

water supply   118, 186, 189
weather   188, 189, 199
weed killing trains   205, 248
White Muir
  fires   117
  land at Gleneagles   55, 176
Williamson, Colonel   26, 34, 38, 41, 43, 47, 126
Williamson, Lady Serena   41
wintering sheep   248
World War
  First   93, 147, 158, 161
  Second   66, 87, 173, 174, 201 et seq, 210
Wynne, Colonel   13

Yolland, Colonel   31
Young
  John, CE   38, 41
  KG   172, 177
  Major TE   142, 145, 162, 165, 169
  William   10

Lochearnhead, Caledonian Railway station and viaduct from East. *Neil Parkhouse collection*

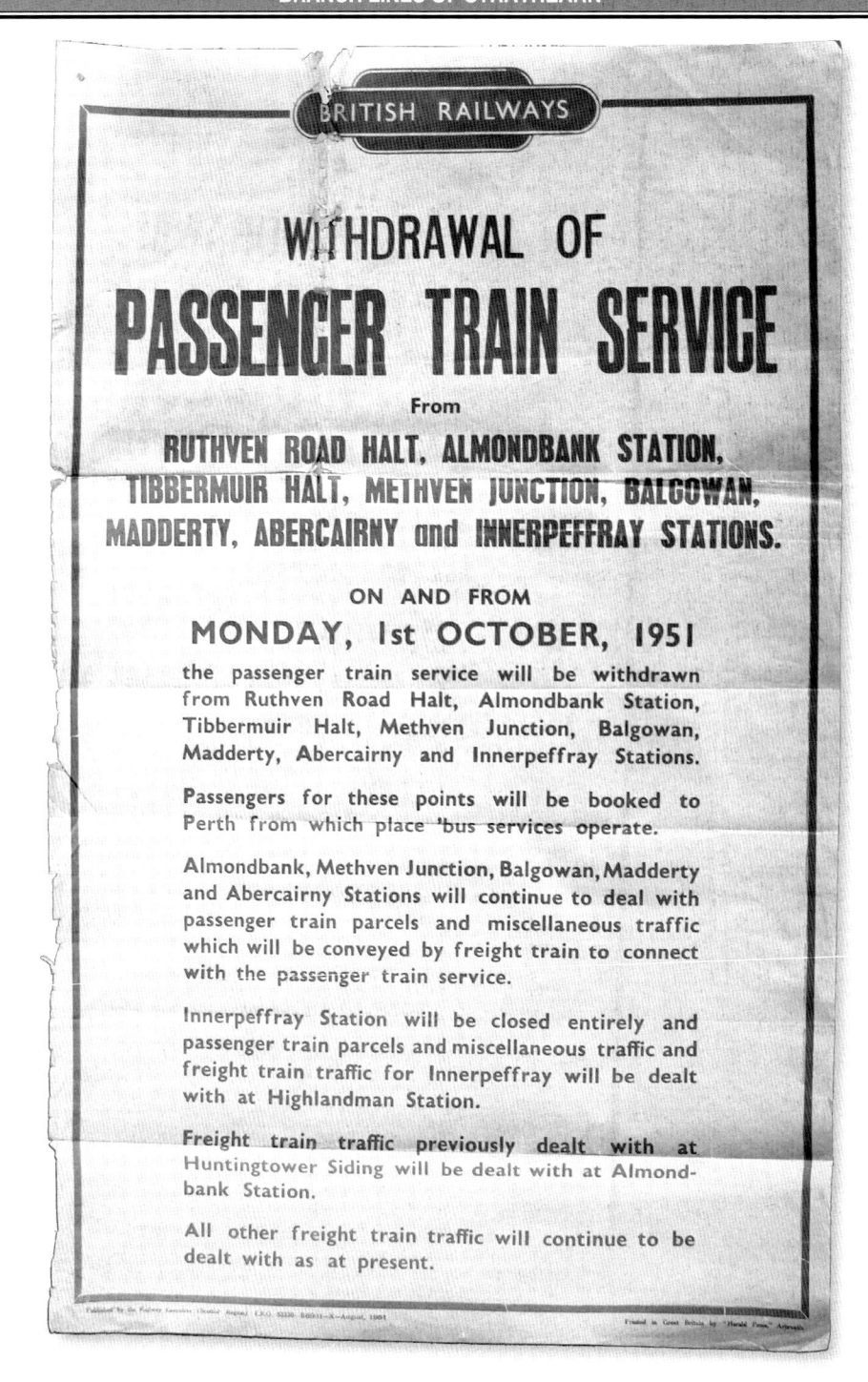

BRITISH RAILWAYS

WITHDRAWAL OF PASSENGER TRAIN SERVICE

From

RUTHVEN ROAD HALT, ALMONDBANK STATION, TIBBERMUIR HALT, METHVEN JUNCTION, BALGOWAN, MADDERTY, ABERCAIRNY and INNERPEFFRAY STATIONS.

ON AND FROM

MONDAY, 1st OCTOBER, 1951

the passenger train service will be withdrawn from Ruthven Road Halt, Almondbank Station, Tibbermuir Halt, Methven Junction, Balgowan, Madderty, Abercairny and Innerpeffray Stations.

Passengers for these points will be booked to Perth from which place 'bus services operate.

Almondbank, Methven Junction, Balgowan, Madderty and Abercairny Stations will continue to deal with passenger train parcels and miscellaneous traffic which will be conveyed by freight train to connect with the passenger train service.

Innerpeffray Station will be closed entirely and passenger train parcels and miscellaneous traffic and freight train traffic for Innerpeffray will be dealt with at Highlandman Station.

Freight train traffic previously dealt with at Huntingtower Siding will be dealt with at Almondbank Station.

All other freight train traffic will continue to be dealt with as at present.

Biography of the Author

John Young was brought up in Auchterarder and went first to Morrison's Academy in Crieff before schooling at Seascale in Cumberland and the Edinburgh Academy. He is the second son of Mr KG Young WS, the fourth generation of prominent Auchterarder lawyers, all of whom had professional connections with the local railways. He developed an interest in railways at an early age, spending much of his childhood at Gleneagles station or in Auchterarder signal box. The family home at the top of the Orchil Road was only fifty yards from the Gleneagles to Crieff branch line.

After graduating from the Royal Military Academy Sandhurst in 1965, John was commissioned into the Royal Corps of Signals. He served for thirty-seven years in the army, much of this time abroad in Germany, Singapore, Australia, Canada and the USA, and at sea with the Royal Navy, culminating with a three year tour as Military & Air Attaché in the British Embassy in The Hague. He maintained his interest in railways during his army career, but research on this book was necessarily interrupted.

Now in active retirement, John is involved, amongst other work, in a number of railway heritage projects, is a judge for the National Railway Heritage Awards and has a consulting role with the National Railway Museum in York. He lives with his wife Sue, in Gilling West near Richmond in North Yorkshire.